The Journalist's Legal Guide

Fifth Edition

Michael G. Crawford, B.B.A., LL.B.

THOMSON ™

CARSWELL

National Library of Canada Cataloguing in Publication

Crawford, Michael G., 1959-
  The journalist's legal guide / Michael G. Crawford — 5th ed.

Includes index.

ISBN 978-0-7798-1731-3

1. Press law — Canada.   2. Mass media — Law and legislation — Canada.
3. Broadcasting — Law and legislation — Canada.   I. Title.

KE2550.C73 2002   343.7109'98   C2002-901862-5

The paper used in this publication meets the mini~~~~~ ~~~~~ ~~rements of the American Nati~~~~~ ~~~~~ ~~ ~~~~~ ~~e of Paper for Printed

On
207
Sca
M1'

Customer Care:
~~~~~ronto 1-416-609-3800
~~U.S. 1-800-387-5164
Fax 1-416-298-5094
~~://www.carswell.com
@thomsonreuters.com

Dedicated to Jeanna,
whose unwavering love, support and humour
inspire me every day.

PREFACE

Since this book was first published in 1986, the laws affecting Canadian journalists and their craft have continued to evolve rapidly and, in some cases, have changed dramatically. In recent years, courts and lawmakers have grown more comfortable with the Charter of Rights and Freedoms and its promises of freedom of the press and freedom of expression. These are exciting times for those who keep a close eye on the evolving scope of press freedoms and rights.

This edition is current to September 2008. Every chapter has been revised and updated with the latest significant cases and revisions to federal and provincial legislation. A new chapter has also been added, which discusses the intersection of law and ethics — an increasingly popular topic in Canada's journalism schools and programs.

The initial objective of this book has never changed. *The Journalist's Legal Guide* is for the working writer, editor and manager who needs quick, yet comprehensive answers to both common and unusual legal dilemmas arising in the reporting and uncovering of news. It has also become a valuable tool and essential text for many journalism students. For each of these audiences, this book aims to provide a detailed, yet practical outline of the rights and obligations of Canadian journalists.

As always, care has been taken to create a reference book that is useful to journalists at all levels of experience. In many topic areas, explanatory footnotes — complete with case law citations — have been provided for those with an intrepid desire to know more about a point of law that's cited.

A final thought on why it's important for every journalist to strive to understand the law affecting the news media. This book isn't just about avoiding expensive lawsuits. The true benefits of knowing your legal rights and limits as a journalist are confidence and improved quality in your stories. Without an understanding of the legal rights and limits, a journalist's work suffers and the public, in turn, suffers.

Sometimes, the fear that comes from a lack of knowledge about the law can kill a story the public should know. On the flip side, ignorance or recklessness in publishing or broadcasting news can end up distorting the truth.

By knowing how the law affects the news media, a journalist can produce a far more valuable story.

Contents

Table of Cases

THE JOURNALIST'S LEGAL QUIZ

Think you have a good handle on the laws affecting journalists in Canada? Before you dive into the following chapters, take this brief quiz and test your knowledge.

		True	False
1.	Under Canada's Charter of Rights and Freedoms, an accused's right to a fair trial is always paramount over other rights, such as freedom of the press.		X
2.	Anything said in open court or Parliament can be published or broadcast, even if it is known to be false and defamatory.	X	
3.	Hurting someone's feelings or offending them is enough to support a successful defamation action.		X
4.	If you didn't mean to defame someone or accidentally published or broadcast defamatory statements, you can't be successfully sued.		X
5.	Under Canada's defamation laws, you can go further in what you say about a public figure than what you can say about a private citizen.	X	
6.	During the preliminary hearing of a criminal proceeding, evidence entered into court of an accused's confession can be published immediately as long as there is no publication ban ordered by the judge.		X
7.	Judges in civil and criminal proceedings have no authority to exclude the public (including the news media) from hearings.		X
8.	Under Canadian copyright law, an "exclusive" news story cannot be reported or used by competing media organizations.		X
9.	Under the law, a journalist does not have to reveal or identify a confidential source.		X
10.	When documents are filed by parties to a court action, a journalist cannot report on their contents until they are submitted as evidence in an open hearing.	X	

For the answers to this quiz, see how you did on the next page...

Answers to the Journalist's Legal Quiz

1. FALSE. *Under Canada's Charter of Rights and Freedoms, an accused's right to a fair trial is not always paramount over other rights, such as freedom of the press.*

For many years, judges did indeed think an accused's right to a fair trial was to be guarded above all other rights. In 1994, the Supreme Court of Canada issued a landmark ruling in the *Dagenais* case that there may be occasions when the freedom of the press is more important and outlined guidelines for judges to follow in considering restrictions on the media. For more information, see Chapter 1 on Freedom of the Press.

2. TRUE. *Anything said in open court or Parliament can be published or broadcast, even if it is known to be false and defamatory.*

As explained in Chapter 2 on Defamation, anything said in official proceedings of a court, Parliament or legislature is protected by the defence of absolute privilege and journalists enjoy the same privilege for fair and accurate reports of any statements that are published without added commentary.

3. FALSE. *Hurting someone's feelings or offending them is not enough to support a successful defamation action.*

If the statement is true and can be proven, the courts in most jurisdictions of Canada will not support a claim of defamation for hurt feelings. In Quebec, the civil code requires that a true statement must also be published in the public interest and without malice. See Chapter 2 on Defamation.

4. FALSE. *If you didn't mean to defame someone or accidentally published or broadcast defamatory statements, you can be successfully sued.*

The lack of an intention to defame someone does not remove the fact that they have suffered damage to their reputation. In most courts, an unintentional defamation may mean lower damages will be awarded, particularly if an apology is issued quickly. See Chapter 2 on Defamation.

5. FALSE. *Under Canada's defamation laws, you cannot go further in what you say about a public figure than what you can say about a private citizen.*

In fact, Canadian courts have ruled that public figures may be owed even more protection from defamation than the average citizen because of the greater potential for damage to their reputation. See Chapter 2 on Defamation.

6. FALSE. *During the preliminary hearing of a criminal proceeding, evidence entered into court of an accused's confession cannot be published.*

Section 542 of the Criminal Code specifically prohibits the publication of a confession entered as evidence in a preliminary hearing, even if no bans on publications have been ordered. See Chapter 7 on Publication Bans and Restraining Orders.

7. FALSE. *Judges in civil and criminal proceedings have full authority to exclude the public (including the news media) from hearings.*

Under their inherent common law powers, the Criminal Code and other legislation, judges may exclude the public (and news media) for a variety of reasons, including "the best interests of the administration of justice." See Chapter 8 on Gaining Access to Public Hearings and Meetings.

8. FALSE. *Under Canadian copyright law, an "exclusive" news story can still be reported or used by competing media organizations.*

As explained in Chapter 13 on Copyright, there is no exclusive right to the "news" or any idea or information. Only the specific expression of an idea or information (words, images, etc.) is protected. A substantial rewrite of the facts in an "exclusive" story will often avoid copyright infringement.

9. FALSE. *Under the law, a journalist may eventually have to reveal or identify a confidential source.*

While the courts will often go the extra distance to ensure the disclosure of a source's identity is absolutely necessary, a judge in a civil or criminal proceeding can and will order it disclosed if it is vital to settling the matter at hand. See Chapter 3 on Confidentiality of News Sources.

10. FALSE. *When documents are filed by the parties in a lawsuit, a journalist can report on their contents.*

Until the 1995 Supreme Court of Canada decision in *Hill v. Church of Scientology of Toronto*, the common law rule was that pre-trial documents, even those filed in court, were not protected by any privilege until they were in evidence in an open hearing. No longer. Take extra care, however, in fairly reporting the contents of any pre-trial documents (noting they contain allegations yet to be proven). See Chapter 7 on Publication Bans and Restraining Orders.

1

FREEDOM OF THE PRESS: DEFINING THE PUBLIC'S RIGHT TO KNOW

Since this book was first published over two decades ago, there have been over 500 reported court rulings and dozens of legislative amendments responding to the promise of "freedom of the press" in the Canadian Charter of Rights and Freedoms.[1] In the five years since the last edition of this book, there have been dozens of notable court decisions on the scope of freedom of the press, including some significant rulings at the Supreme Court of Canada and provincial appeal court levels.

It should surprise no one that it has taken this long for the courts, legislators and journalists to get a feel for what freedom of the press means

---

1 Part I of the Constitution Act, 1982, being Schedule B of the Canada Act 1982 (U.K.), 1982, c. 11 (hereinafter, Charter).

in Canada. When it was first entrenched in the Constitution, many predictions were made about how it would soon change what we reported about public figures, wipe out publication bans, allow cameras in the courts, alter contempt and defamation laws, and throw open new doors to many other rights.

In fact, the first edition of this book optimistically and boldly declared in 1986 that it was a new era for journalists in Canada. By the second edition in 1990, however, the tone was lowered. Yes, there had been victories for press freedoms, but the more liberal expansion of media rights predicted earlier had failed to materialize. As the third and fourth editions of this book came along, the new era of press freedom had finally begun to arrive. With this fifth edition, it is fair to suggest the courts and legislators are finally coming to terms with the Charter's fundamental principles and the parameters of freedom of the press. Now, we are entering yet another phase in the development of this area of law — one that is laying concrete ground rules and guidelines for all judges to follow when weighing the Charter's guarantees of a free press and freedom of expression.

Today, courts and lawmakers routinely acknowledge the importance of the Charter's guarantee of freedom of the press relative to other guarantees, such as an accused's right to a fair trial. Thanks to the Supreme Court and some provincial courts of appeal, judges across Canada have several landmark and precedent-setting cases setting out tests and rules to apply when balancing the media's rights against those of competing interests. Courts have carved relatively huge swaths into decades of outmoded and unnecessary press restrictions. Legislators, by and large, have also now seen the writing on the wall and know the Charter's guarantee is not to be taken lightly.

One reason why we can say a new era of press freedoms has begun is that the Supreme Court itself has said so. In 1994, the highest court handed down a ruling saying that the traditional rule judges have lived by for years which emphasized the paramountcy of a person's right to a fair trial, in the context of "post-Charter Canadian society," does not provide sufficient protection for freedom of expression.[2] In that one decision and others to follow, reviewed in detail below, the Supreme Court has urged the judiciary to adopt a fresh approach to determining the rights and responsibilities of the news media in post-Charter Canadian society.

Still, the news media do not win all their battles. Many of the cases the news media do win, though, are important victories that will measurably enhance the Canadian public's right to know in years to come. As an example, here are just some of the notable court decisions affecting the news media in the past decade:

---

2 *Dagenais v. Canadian Broadcasting Corp.*, [1994] 3 S.C.R. 835.

Defamation

Qualified privilege: In 2007, the Ontario Court of Appeal adopted a new "public interest responsible journalism" defence that broadens a reporter's ability to claim qualified privilege in defamation cases. Already accepted by leading courts in the U.K. and U.S., the defence protects properly researched stories on matters "the public has a legitimate interest in hearing," and that journalists have "every reason to believe" are true and meet the standards of responsible journalism.[3]

Fair comment: In 2008, the Supreme Court of Canada overturned a B.C. appeal court decision that attempted to narrow the fair comment defence. The Supreme Court upheld and modified the "cardinal test" for defamatory opinions on matters of public interest — so long as someone could honestly hold or believe the opinion stated, it is clearly opinion, it is drawn from known or provable facts, and there is no evidence of express malice, the defence will succeed. The B.C. appeal court took the unusual stance that, if a judge rules a comment has a reasonable meaning to others that the defendant does not honestly believe or intend, then the defence of fair comment fails.[4] The Supreme Court used this case to emphasize the importance of allowing unfettered commentary as a mode of free expression.

Governments suing in defamation: Contrary to case law pre-dating the Charter, the list of entities that may sue in defamation no longer includes governments. Two 2006 Ontario court rulings made it clear that, while governments have a reputation and, in some cases, even a business reputation, the Charter's guarantee of freedom of expression ensures that "everyone should be free to criticize democratically elected governments."[5]

Common law and the Charter: In 2000, an Alberta provincial politician failed to convince a court the common law of defamation is inconsistent with his freedom of expression. The court ruled "the common law of defamation did not infringe an individual's right to free speech. Freedom of

---

3 *Cusson v. Quan,* 2007 ONCA 771 (C.A.), leave to appeal to the Supreme Court of Canada granted (April 3, 2008), (S.C.C.).

4 *Simpson v. Mair* (2006), 55 B.C.L.R. (4th) 30 (C.A.), overturned by the Supreme Court of Canada in *WIC Radio Ltd. and Rafe Mair v. Kari Simpson,* 2008 SCC 40.

5 See *Halton Hills (Town) v. Kerouac,* 2006 CarswellOnt 2444, [2006] O.J. No. 1473 (S.C.J.) and *Montague (Township) v. Page* (2006), 79 O.R. (3d) 515 (S.C.J.). While other provinces may not have ruled on the issue of governments suing in defamation, these rulings will be persuasive.

speech was not an unfettered right, and could not be interpreted in a manner that departed from the recognition of a free and democratic society."[6]

A B.C. broadcaster was also unsuccessful in convincing a court that defamation law is incompatible with the Charter, specifically that there is a "reverse onus" on the media defendant to prove the truth of allegedly defamatory matter or offer some other defence. The judge ruled that "while freedom of public debate was very important, so also was reputation, and statements of fact did not contribute usefully to public debate unless they were true."[7]

Criminal libel: The Supreme Court of Canada upheld key criminal libel laws, ruling the Criminal Code sections are a reasonable limit on freedom of expression because they are very specific as to the types of conduct that is punishable. The existence of a civil remedy in defamation "does not render the defamatory libel provisions in the Criminal Code overbroad" because the Criminal Code sections are for offences "so grave and serious that the imposition of a criminal sanction is not excessive."[8]

Criminal Law

Media and police searches: In a landmark 2006 case,[9] RCMP officers were found to have improperly obtained search warrants by alleging a journalist had violated sections of the Security of Information Act, dealing with official secrets and national security. An Ontario judge concluded the RCMP had engaged in abuse of process. The court found it was reasonable to infer the warrant and allegations of criminality "were used to gain access to [the reporter] for the purpose of intimidating her into compromising her constitutional right of freedom of the press; namely, to reveal her confidential source or sources of the prohibited information."

Meanwhile, allowing a CBC TV crew to accompany police executing a search warrant violated an accused's Charter right to protection from unreasonable search. As agents of the state, the police should not have been assisting the media to film inside a private residence where they had no right to be, said the court.[10]

Subpoenas of journalists: Whether journalists are "likely to give material evidence" in a criminal case as third parties was put to the test in 2007 in a

---

6 *Goddard v. Day* (2000), 194 D.L.R. (4th) 559 (Alta Q.B.).
7 *Pressler v. Lethbridge* (1997), 153 D.L.R. (4th) 537 (B.C. S.C.).
8 *R. v. Lucas* (1998), 157 D.L.R. (4th) 423 (S.C.C.).
9 *O'Neill v. Canada (Attorney General)* (2006), 272 D.L.R. (4th) 193 (Ont. S.C.J.).
10 *R. v. West* (1997), 122 C.C.C. (3d) 218 (B.C. C.A.).

high-profile challenge of a subpoena issued to an Ontario writer.[11] The Crown sought to make author Derek Finkle a "witness for the prosecution," as a judge later put it, and issued subpoenas for production of evidence, such as notes and printed material related to the case. The court ruled the Crown blatantly failed to prove Finkle was "likely to give material evidence" — that is, prove there was a distinct probability that material evidence would be given, not merely a possibility. Citing Supreme Court rulings on court orders involving the news media, the court noted alternate sources for the information should be pursued first before resorting to calling journalists as witnesses.

Publication bans: A citizen who acted on a belief that his right to freedom of expression was trampled by a judge's temporary publication ban on evidence in a trial was convicted by an appeal court that said "even orders that are constitutionally unsound must be complied with unless set aside in a proceeding taken for that purpose."[12]

Excluding the public: The Supreme Court of Canada upheld the constitutionality of the Criminal Code section allowing judges to exclude the public from a hearing, but said a judge must not do it unless:

    i) there are no reasonable and effective alternatives to excluding the public;
    ii) the order is as limited as possible; and
    iii) its salutary effects are proportionate to its deleterious effects.[13]

In another case, the families of two girls brutally murdered by Paul Bernardo and Karla Homolka failed to convince an Ontario appeal court that the public should be excluded from courtrooms when videotapes of their daughters are shown. The court ruled the families' right to freedom of religion and to be protected against cruel and unusual treatment or punishment were not violated. The court said openness is the rule and exclusion of the public is the exception.[14]

Access to the media: The Federal Court of Appeal ruled that serial child killer Clifford Olson's freedom of expression was not violated when his access to the media was restricted. The court noted prison inmates are

---

11 *R. v. Baltovich*, (unreported ruling on motion to quash subpoena, *R. v. Finkle*, 2007 CarswellOnt 7365 (S.C.J.)).
12 *R. v. Domm* (1996), 111 C.C.C. (3d) 449 (Ont. C.A.).
13 *Canadian Broadcasting Corp. v. New Brunswick (Attorney General)* (1996), 139 D.L.R. (4th) 385 (S.C.C.).
14 *French Estate v. Ontario (Attorney General)* (1998), 157 D.L.R. (4th) 144 (Ont. C.A.).

restricted in many ways and reducing Olson's public notoriety was justifiable as part of his rehabilitation process.[15]

Access to Courts and Other Hearings

Cameras in the courts: A B.C. judge said "the time has now arrived to permit" cameras and other electronic reporting devices in the courts so long as the news media uses modern equipment that is not disruptive, that concerns are addressed about specific witnesses on a case-by-case basis, and that no party objects. There were objections in this case, but the judge did allow cameras to record lawyers' closing arguments and the judge's instructions to the jury.[16]

In Québec, however, new court rules in 2004 and 2005 restricted media interviews and the use of cameras to very specific marked areas around and in courthouses. Reporters could no longer "hinder or disturb the free circulation of users in public areas," "pursue persons with cameras or microphones inside the courthouses," or conduct interviews at courtroom exits or in areas adjacent to courtrooms. In 2006, the court hearing a media petition dismissed their complaints, and held the impairment of freedom of expression and freedom of the press is "very minimal" and justifiable in the proper administration of justice.

Public hearings: A P.E.I. court struck down police department rules that "all [police] discipline hearings will be closed to the public," ruling it violated the Charter because it was an absolute prohibition allowing for no use of discretion.[17]

A media application for access to a RCMP disciplinary hearing was granted after a court found a section of the force's governing legislation that stated disciplinary hearings "shall be" held in private was inconsistent with the Charter since it also was an absolute prohibition.[18]

---

15 *Olson v. R.*, [1996] 2 F.C. 168 (Fed. T.D.), affirmed 1997 CarswellNat 2734 (Fed. C.A.).
16 *R. v. Cho* (2000), 189 D.L.R. (4th) 180 (B.C. S.C.).
17 *Canadian Broadcasting Corp. v. Summerside (City)* (1999), 170 D.L.R. (4th) 731 (P.E.I. T.D.).
18 *Southam Inc. v. Canada (Attorney General)* (1997), 154 D.L.R. (4th) 370 (Ont. Gen. Div.).

Generally

Election results and opinion polls: A section of the Canada Elections Act, prohibiting the publication of opinion survey results during the final three days of a federal election campaign, was declared to be an unjustified infringement of Charter rights, according to a majority of the Supreme Court of Canada.[19]

In 2007, however, the Supreme Court decided the legislated restriction on reporting voting results before polling stations close on voting day is justified.[20] During a federal election, a B.C. citizen posted results on his website for 32 ridings in Atlantic Canada while polls remained open in other provinces. A majority of the Court upheld his conviction under the Canada Elections Act and ruled that, while it did infringe freedom of expression, it was justified.

Reporters' sources: This area of law continues to be fought on a case-by-case basis in the trenches. In 2008, the Ontario Court of Appeal overturned a lower court's attempt to set the bar high for law enforcement authorities seeking to force a journalist to reveal sources in a criminal investigation.[21] The critical issue for the appeal court was whether the reporter and his source had a privileged relationship such that the actual documents and the source's name were confidential and beyond the reach of law enforcement. While the appeal judges accepted "the gathering and dissemination of news and information without undue state interference is an integral component of [journalists'] constitutional right of freedom of the press under s. 2(b) of the Charter. . . this does not mean that press organizations or journalists are immune from valid searches under s. 8 of the Charter. And s. 2(b) does not guarantee that journalists have an automatic right to protect the confidentiality of their sources."

In contrast, the same appeal court in 2008 overturned a trial judge's 2004 ruling that a reporter was in contempt of court for refusing to reveal his source.[22] A majority of appeal judges ruled the judge was too quick to use his contempt power. A judge should first explore other means of proceeding that are "less intrusive to the journalist-informant relationship of confidentiality." Another key factor was the judge had failed to consider that "[f]reedom of expression and freedom of the media, protected by s.

---

19 *Thomson Newspapers Co. v. Canada (Attorney General)*, [1998] 1 S.C.R. 877.
20 *R. v. Bryan*, 2007 CarswellBC 533, [2007] S.C.J. No. 12 (S.C.C.).
21 *R. v. National Post* (2004), 69 O.R. (3d) 427 (S.C.J.).
22 *St. Elizabeth Home Society v. Hamilton (City)*, 2004 CarswellOnt 9835, [2004] O.J. No. 5015 (S.C.J.), reversed 2008 ONCA 182 (C.A.).

2(b) of the Charter, have a direct bearing on a journalist's claim to confidentiality."

Reporters' notes: A B.C. court was not convinced that ordering the production of a reporter's notes in a criminal trial violated his right to freedom of expression and freedom of the press. The accused requesting the notes had a right to a full defence, much of the information was already in the public domain and any infringement of the right to freedom of the press was not substantial.[23]

Meanwhile, in a civil defamation case, an Alberta judge refused to force the CBC to disclose its documents identifying confidential sources during pre-trial proceedings. This 2005 ruling was the first to rule on a strict application of the "Newspaper Rule" where evidence showed a confidential relationship (confidential information from a source and communications between solicitor and client) and where the Charter's right to freedom of the press was raised.[24] While the judge stated a journalist-source privilege can only be applied on a case-by-case basis, he ruled he must consider the "public policy rationale underlying the Newspaper Rule" and apply the test for qualified privilege "in accordance with the constitutional guarantee provided under s. 2(b) of the Charter."

By no means are these the only significant decisions in recent years on the Charter's guarantee of freedom of the press. Specifically, a trilogy of Supreme Court decisions (*Dagenais*, *Mentuck* and *Toronto Star*) that significantly strengthen the news media's entitlement to fair treatment under the law will be discussed in greater detail below.

Freedom of the press can no longer be regarded as a second-class right within the Charter. There will still be times when the rights of the press will have to give way to the greater good of another right, but those occasions may be fewer and tougher to prove. It has become clear in recent years that many lower courts are paying heed to the Supreme Court's 1994, 2001 and 2005 directives to give freedom of the press greater weight. Regardless, for journalists, the legal ammunition is now readily at hand for continuing rounds of challenges to any unjust new and remaining press restrictions.

---

23 *R. v. Hughes* (1998), [1998] B.C.J. No. 1694 (S.C.).
24 *Wasylyshen v. Canadian Broadcasting Corp.* (2005), 2005 CarswellAlta 1820, [2005]A.J. No. 1685 (Q.B.).

FREEDOM OF THE PRESS BEFORE THE CHARTER

The entrenchment of "freedom of the press" in the Charter in 1982 formally acknowledged the special role of the news media in society. Section 2(b) of the Charter states that everyone has the fundamental freedom:

> . . . of thought, belief, opinion and expression, including freedom of the press and other media of communication.

Courts and legislators have always recognized that the media are an integral part of society, but freedom of the press had never before been formally noted in a Canadian constitutional document. The Charter's classification of "freedom of the press" as a fundamental freedom gave courts more authority to define closely the limits of media rights. In fact, soon after it came into force, the constitutional guarantee was having an effect on media-related law, invalidating some long-standing statutory provisions that limited the media's news gathering opportunities.

To understand why entrenching freedom of the press in the Constitution is important, it helps to know from whence we came.

Historically, the news media in Canada, as in most democracies, have always fought for the right to express opinion and report news freely. In one of the most famous court cases in Canada's early history, Nova Scotia newspaper editor Joseph Howe was tried in 1835 on a charge of criminal libel after he criticized local government officials in his publication. Although he was technically guilty of the offence, the jury acquitted him after his emotional plea for a free press.

In the United States, the Fathers of the American Revolution had already seen the need for a constitutional recognition of press freedoms after suffering under the oppressive and restrictive rule of the English monarchy. The First Amendment of the U.S. Constitution promised in 1791 that no law of Congress shall abridge the freedom of speech or the press. The early presence of this constitutionally-entrenched guarantee helped shape an approach to defining the role of the news media in American society, which is somewhat more liberal in many areas of the law than the rights accorded to the press in Canada. For example, the First Amendment has helped American reporters win the right to televise court proceedings in most states and allowed for broader criticism of public figures.

A "Freedom of the Press" Myth

The danger in the term "freedom of the press" is that it implies a special right has been imparted upon the news media that is above the rights of the general public. That is not the case. The issue of whether the press enjoy some sort of special privilege has been dealt with by the courts on many occasions over the years, as can be seen in the 1914 British case of *Arnold v. The King-Emperor*, which dealt with a charge of criminal libel brought against a journalist who had accused a magistrate of improper conduct:[25]

> Their lordships regret to find that there appeared on the one side in this case the time-worn fallacy that some kind of privilege attaches to the profession of the Press as distinguished from the members of the public . . . but, apart from statute law, his privilege is no other and no higher.

While the news media are not considered to have any greater privileges than the average citizen, an important corollary is that the courts have recognized that the news media are members and representatives of the public.

This is not to say that Parliament has not recognized the role of the news media. In 1961, Parliament enacted the Canadian Bill of Rights which listed, among other rights, freedom of the press.[26] Unfortunately, the Bill of Rights is not a part of our Constitution, it applies only to federal statutes and has been narrowly interpreted by the courts as simply being an instrument for statutory interpretation. However, on occasion, the principle behind the Bill has not been ignored by the courts.

In 1977, a British Columbia court quashed a search warrant that gave the federal Department of Consumer and Corporate Affairs permission to search the offices of a newspaper for information about picketers who had interfered with an inquiry.[27] The newspaper's only involvement in the picketing was in covering it as a news event. As it turned out, the only reason why the search warrant was directed at the newspaper was because its reporters had been seen speaking with the demonstrators and the investigators wanted the reporters' notes to find who the demonstrators were and what they said.

---

25 (1914), 30 T.L.R. 462 at 468 (P.C.).

26 R.S.C. 1985, App. III, s. 1(f).

27 *Pacific Press Ltd. v. R.*, [1977] 5 W.W.R. 507 (B.C. S.C.). Unfortunately, as the chapter on search warrants outlines, there has been a recent swing of the pendulum in several courts, including the Supreme Court of Canada, allowing police to search and seize news media materials in the course of an investigation. That said, in light of the Charter, the courts are still cautious about granting such searches.

The court, noting the Bill of Rights' promise of freedom of the press, nullified the warrant after determining that the government investigators had failed to prove that all other reasonable channels to get the information had been exhausted. In other words, the court was saying that freedom of the press should only be infringed upon as a last resort.

How Courts Have Viewed Press Rights

Over the years preceding the Charter, the onus to protect and develop the legal rights of the news media in Canada largely fell on the courts. The courts have used many diverse sources to develop media rights, with some-times cumbersome and conflicting results. Our media law is actually a mish-mash of law imported from Great Britain and the United States, with some of our own creations thrown in. In addition, the peculiarities of our own history have resulted in some rights of the press evolving differently in various parts of the country. For example, the law of defamation in Québec, which is largely drawn from its European-based Civil Code, can be sub-stantially different in some respects from the law of defamation in the English-based common law provinces. The socialist background of Alberta had early ramifications for the press in that province and most provinces to this day place their own peculiar restrictions on the news media in certain areas.

The result is that equal treatment of the media throughout Canada in many areas of the law has been sporadic, depending on the political and social characteristics of each province. Fortunately, though, Canadian courts have held a generally consistent view of the basic right and value of "freedom of the press."

One of the first major assaults on freedom of the press was attempted by the Social Credit government of Alberta in 1938. The provincial legislature enacted a law that sought to control any statement in newspapers relating to any policy or activity of the government. Bill No. 9 was entitled "An Act to ensure the Publication of Accurate News and Information."[28] The preamble of the law stated that it was

> . . . expedient and in the public interest that the newspapers published in the Province should furnish to the people of the Province statements made by the authority of the Government of the Province as to the true and exact objects of the policy of the Government and as to the hindrances to or difficulties in achieving such objects to the end that the people may be informed with respect thereto.

---

28 See *Ref. re Alberta Legislation*, [1938] 2 D.L.R. 81 (S.C.C.).

The so-called "Press Bill" gave a designated official of the provincial government the right to demand that newspapers publish official rebuttals to any criticisms or misleading statements in the news media about the government's social credit system. The Act also gave the official the authority to demand to know the identity of the author and sources of a story. The official could also levy penalties prohibiting the publication of the newspaper and gag specific reporters by prohibiting any further publication of their stories.

The nation's press vehemently opposed the law. As a result of the adverse press reaction, the "gag law," as it was called by journalists, and two other related bills were referred to the Supreme Court of Canada for an opinion as to whether they were within the provincial government's constitutional powers.[29] Not surprisingly, the court found the proposed Press Bill to be beyond the legislature's powers.

In its landmark decision, the high court reiterated the public's right of expression, particularly in the news media:[30]

> Freedom of discussion is essential to enlighten public opinion in a democratic State; it cannot be curtailed without affecting the right of the people to be informed through sources independent of the Government concerning matters of public interest. There must be an untrammeled publication of the news and political opinions of the political parties contending for ascendancy.

The Supreme Court spoke on several occasions after that on the question of freedom of expression and, consequently, freedom of the press. For example, the court indirectly dealt with the limits of freedom of expression in the 1979 case of *Gay Alliance Toward Equality v. Vancouver Sun*, which involved the right of a newspaper to refuse advertising.[31] In this case, a homosexual group wanted to run an advertisement for its newspaper, "Gay Tide," in the *Vancouver Sun*. But the ad was refused. The gay organization then alleged the newspaper had infringed the Human Rights Code of British Columbia by denying a class of persons, without reasonable cause, "a service customarily available to the public," as guaranteed by the Code.

A majority of the Supreme Court justices felt the *Sun* had not violated the Code. They found that, while newspaper advertising is a service available to each member of the public, the nature and scope of that service is determined by the newspaper itself:[32]

---

29 *Ibid.*
30 *Ibid.*, at 119.
31 (1979), 97 D.L.R. (3d) 577 (S.C.C.).
32 *Ibid.*, at 591.

The law has recognized the freedom of the press to propagate its views and ideas on any issue and to select the material that it publishes. As a corollary to that, a newspaper also has the right to refuse to publish material that runs contrary to the views it expresses.

Although the decision wasn't directly on point in dealing with journalists' rights, it once again reiterated the view that the news media are an important instrument for disseminating public opinion — even opinions others do not agree with.

The Limits of a Free Press

For much of our history, the courts have recognized the value of freedom of expression and freedom of the press, but have not allowed the media complete freedom to report news where other important interests are at stake. For example, the courts and legislators have traditionally been very careful to balance the freedom of the press against the rights of individuals to a fair trial (for example, the Criminal Code[33] allows the court to ban publication of evidence given at a preliminary hearing).

Fortunately, attempts to make the news media's rights less than those enjoyed by the general public have failed. In *Re F.P. Publications (Western) Ltd. and R.*, a trial judge barred a reporter, but not the rest of the public, from attending a trial where charges of keeping a common bawdy house were being heard. The reporter had earlier refused to agree not to publish the names of witnesses. The exclusion order was clearly directed at preventing publication of the names. The Manitoba Court of Appeal held that the presiding judge cannot use s. 486(1) of the Criminal Code to exclude members of the public and to create a select audience or censor the news. The appeal court said the reporter was only doing his job and his presence in the courtroom was not causing any disturbance in the proceedings. The court held that the lower court order was an unjust infringement on the freedom of the press and ran against the principle of an open court.[34]

THE CHARTER AND FREEDOM OF THE PRESS

While it may seem that judges were doing a fairly good job of defending the rights of the press before the Charter came along, freedom of the press was not an easy issue for them. The rights of parties to a court action and the existence of express statutory provisions restricting the news media's

---

33 R.S.C. 1985, c. C-46.
34 (1979), 51 C.C.C. (2d) 110 at 125-126 (Man. C.A.).

reports, all served to act as an imposing barrier to the rights of the press in the eyes of many judges. The main problem was that there were few grounds beyond the common law to justify the courts making radical changes to media-related laws.

However, that changed with the Charter, which carries the full authority of being part of the Constitution, the supreme law of the land. When it came into effect, many people accurately predicted that the Charter would give judges new powers and authority to strike down inconsistent laws and practices. The Charter had special significance for those who followed media law since it appeared that it would finally deliver the necessary authority for judges to quash restrictive legislation and outmoded case precedents.

For the most part, the constitutional entrenchment of freedom of the press has proved to be a valuable tool for the news media in expanding their rights. But, as numerous unsuccessful court cases have illustrated since 1982, freedom of the press is not an absolute right and it must still compete with other rights and freedoms, such as the right to a fair trial.

The "great equalizer" in determining the extent and limits of freedom of the press is s. 1 of the Charter, which says that constitutional rights and freedoms are:

> subject only to such reasonable limits prescribed by law as can be demonstrably justified in a free and democratic society.

This is the test against which all laws and practices that infringe upon rights and freedoms are subjected to. If a law restricts a fundamental right, such as freedom of the press, and it cannot be "demonstrably justified" by the individual seeking to uphold the restrictive law, then it will be declared unconstitutional. This provides the authority courts have needed to help extend the boundaries of freedom of the press. But it's also a two-edged sword that can work against the press.

How Courts Apply the Test

One of the first laws to be successfully challenged by the news media under the Charter was a section of the now-repealed Juvenile Delinquents Act[35] that barred the public from attending any juvenile trial. The Ontario Court of Appeal held the absolute ban on the news media's right to attend trials (and conversely, the juvenile accused's right to a public trial) without

---

35 S. 12.

any use of judicial discretion, was a violation of the Charter's guarantee of freedom of the press.[36]

The court said that an absolute ban on public access is rarely a reasonable limit in all circumstances. The judges felt the absolute ban cast too wide a net for its intended purposes and society lost more than it gained because of it. While the court struck down this provision, it also noted that the guarantee of freedom of the press is not absolute. The judges said the invalid section would have withstood the Charter's scrutiny if it had provided for a discretionary use of judicial power.

That rationale has been carried on to other cases. The Ontario Court of Appeal again dealt with the meaning of freedom of the press in *Canadian Newspapers Co. v. A.G. Canada*.[37] This 1985 case involved a challenge of a Criminal Code provision that allows a complainant (that is, victim) in a sexual assault case to ask for a court order banning publication of the complainant's identity. According to the Code, once the request is made, the judge has no choice in issuing the ban. At the time, s. 442(3) stated:

> Where an accused is charged with an offence mentioned in section 246.4, the presiding judge, magistrate, or justice may, or if the application is made by the complainant or prosecutor, shall, make an order directing that the identity of the complainant and any information that could disclose the identity of the complainant shall not be published in any newspaper or broadcast.

The newspaper challenged the section not because it wanted to reveal the identity of sexual assault victims, but because of an unusual problem the story presented for journalists. The victim had brought the assault charge against her own husband. If the newspapers followed the letter of the law and did not report the victim's name, but did report the accused's identity, it would not be able to report the unusual nature of the case because it would reveal the victim's identity. In court, the newspaper objected to the fact that the Code imposed an absolute ban on the publication of the victim's identity if the complainant or prosecutor requested it.

The provincial appeal court used the s. 1 test to determine whether the infringement on freedom of the press was in violation of the Charter. As in any Charter case, the onus was on the party upholding the present law to prove it's a reasonable limit that can be justified in a free and democratic society. The Crown, in this case, had to prove it was reasonable to allow an absolute publication ban in all sexual assault trials. The Crown called a witness who testified that many victims worry that their identity will come

---

36 *Re Southam Inc. and R. (No. 1)* (1983), 41 O.R. (2d) 113 (C.A.).
37 (1985), 49 O.R. (2d) 557 (C.A.).

out at trial and one concern was that women might not bring charges against sexual offenders if names could possibly be released.

The Ontario court noted that the concern of a sexual assault victim is a social value that should be protected and that a publication ban is a reasonable limit. But the court then went on to question whether it is a limit that must be applied in all cases. The judges suggested there may be occasions when it may be necessary to publish a victim's name — perhaps to bring forward more witnesses or where someone has previously accused other people of sexual assault without justification.

In the end, the provincial appeal court held that an absolute ban is not reasonable because it does not allow a judge to exercise any discretion once the complainant has asked for the ban.

While this was a significant victory for advocates of a free press, the case went on to the Supreme Court of Canada. There, the lower court decision was overturned.[38] The Supreme Court justices agreed that the mandatory publication ban was a *prima facie* infringement of freedom of the press. However, applying the same s. 1 test, they held that the mandatory ban was required to achieve Parliament's objective of facilitating complaints by victims of sexual assaults. Thus, the two-edged sword of s. 1 swung back against the press, in favour of a greater public end. That said, Parliament has amended this Criminal Code section, now s. 486.4, giving judges some discretion in issuing a publication ban.

The *Dagenais, Mentuck* and *Toronto Star* Cases

Once in a while, cases come along that allow the Supreme Court of Canada to not only rule on the immediate dispute at hand, but to also take a moment to set out new judicial policy in an area of law that has changed significantly or is spawning conflicting lower court rulings. In 1994, *Dagenais v. Canadian Broadcasting Corp.*[39] was the first of a trilogy of such cases.

Dagenais

Though the Charter had made it clear that freedom of the press is a fundamental right, judges were all over the map in determining how far the right extended when there were competing Charter interests, such as a fair trial. In fact, it seemed court-ordered publication bans and restrictions were actually on the rise in the years leading up to *Dagenais*. While the media

---

38 (1988), 43 C.C.C. (3d) 24 (S.C.C.).
39 [1994] 3 S.C.R. 835.

were quite often successful in quashing overly-restrictive bans, the time was right for a guiding hand from above.

In 1994, *Dagenais* quickly rose to the Supreme Court of Canada level. It involved a 1992 cross-Canada publication ban against the broadcast of a fictional TV drama, "The Boys of St. Vincent," which dealt with child sexual and physical abuse in a Catholic orphanage. The ban was issued by a lower court judge after hearing an application by lawyers for four members of a Catholic order who were charged with physical and sexual abuse of young boys in Catholic training schools.

Since they would soon be facing trial in Ontario, the judge agreed the television program might influence potential jurors and a ban was necessary to ensure the proceedings were fair. Since no legislation expressly outlined what a court should do in these circumstances, the judge relied on the judiciary's inherent discretionary authority to do what is necessary to preserve the proper administration of justice. The judge issued an extremely expansive ban, far beyond what was needed.

The ban against broadcasting the TV mini-series would last until the end of all four trials and the judge also granted an order prohibiting publication of the fact of the ban application, or any material relating to it. The CBC challenged the order, but the appeal court said the ban was needed to ensure a fair trial — a right it and other courts have long considered sacrosanct. It did, however, limit the ban's scope to Ontario and Montreal and reversed the order banning publicity about the broadcast and the proceedings that gave rise to the ban.

In a 6-3 decision, the Supreme Court of Canada ruled that while the constitutionally guaranteed right to a fair trial is important, freedom of the press is of equal and sometimes greater importance. Traditionally, the high court noted, judges have issued a discretionary ban after determining there is a real and substantial risk of interference with the right to a fair trial. The Supreme Court said, however, the discretionary power conferred on a judge by the common law must be exercised within the boundaries of the Charter.

The Supreme Court said the common law rule that a fair trial is paramount can no longer be applied in the context of post-Charter Canadian society and does not provide sufficient protection for freedom of expression. Since the old rule wasn't working, a new approach was needed. It set out a modified rule, telling judges these factors must be considered before issuing a publication ban:[40]

> (a) Such a ban is *necessary* in order to prevent a real and substantial risk to the fairness of the trial, because reasonably available alternative measures will not prevent the risk; and

---

40 *Ibid.*, at 878.

(b) The salutary effects of the publication ban outweigh the deleterious effects to the free expression of those affected by the ban.

The Court said, in some cases, there may be evidence of a real and substantial risk to a fair trial. The Court noted, however, the party, Crown or accused, wanting a publication ban bears the burden of justifying the limitation on freedom of expression. The Supreme Court also said the ban should be as limited as possible. For example, in this case, the initial ban was too broad in prohibiting broadcast throughout Canada and even reporting on the ban itself.

There were several nuggets of judicial commentary in the judgment that fueled Charter challenges in the years to follow. For instance, the Supreme Court was clear that judges shouldn't use their discretionary authority to issue bans in an attempt to wipe out all potential risks to a fair trial:[41]

> It must be noted, however, that while the Charter provides safeguards both against actual instances of bias and against situations that give rise to a serious risk of a jury's impartiality being tainted, it does not require that all conceivable steps be taken to remove even the most speculative risks . . . the Constitution does not always guarantee 'the ideal'. . . . As the rule itself states, the objective of a publication ban authorized under the rule is to prevent real and substantial risks of trial unfairness — publication bans are not available as protection against remote and speculative dangers.

Also, note that in the Supreme Court's modified rule, the majority said that judges need to consider first whether reasonably available alternative measures would be preferable to a rights-infringing publication ban:[42]

> Possibilities that readily come to mind, however, include adjourning trials, changing venues, sequestering jurors, allowing challenges for cause and *voir dires* during jury selection, and providing strong judicial direction to the jury. Sequestration and judicial direction were available for the Dagenais jury. Apart from sequestration, all of the other effective alternatives to bans were available for the other three accused. For this reason, the publication ban imposed in the case at bar cannot be supported under the common law.

Suggesting that judges should consider such alternatives sent a strong message that restricting the press is a last resort rather than an easy option. Finally, the Court also outlined some reasons why a publication ban is not a healthy thing for the justice system:[43]

---

41 *Ibid.*, at 879-880.
42 *Ibid.*, at 881.
43 *Ibid.*, at 883.

It should also be recognized that *not* ordering bans may:
— maximize the chances of individuals with relevant information hearing about a case and coming forward with new information;
— prevent perjury by placing witnesses under public scrutiny;
— prevent state and/or court wrongdoing by placing the criminal justice process under public scrutiny;
— reduce crime through the public expression of disapproval for crime; and
— promote the public discussion of important issues.

Mentuck

In 2001, the Supreme Court decided that the rule in *Dagenais* needed refinement. In *R. v. Mentuck*,[44] the accused was charged with second-degree murder, but had to be re-tried after key evidence was ruled inadmissible. The RCMP gathered better evidence in an undercover operation and a second trial began. The Crown asked for a publication ban to protect the identity of the officers and operational methods used in the investigation. The media and accused opposed the motion for a ban. The trial judge, however, granted a one-year ban as to the identity of undercover police officers while refusing a ban as to operational methods used.

After hearing the case, the Supreme Court of Canada dismissed the media's appeal of the ban and allowed the one-year ban as to the identity of the undercover police officers. While it was not a victory for the news media, the Court decided to reformulate or modify its test for issuing court orders restricting access and publication by requiring that judges consider the following factors:

1) such an order is necessary in order to prevent a serious risk to the proper administration of justice because reasonable alternative measures will not prevent the risk; and

2) the salutary effects of the publication ban outweigh the deleterious effects on the rights and interests of the parties and the public, including the effects on the right to free expression, the right of the accused to a fair and public trial, and the efficacy of the administration of justice.

This has now become known as the "*Dagenais/Mentuck* test" and many courts are applying it to cases involving the news media today. In *Mentuck*, the Court sought to broaden the original test to allow judges to not only consider the impact of a ban on the case itself, but also to consider other rights or outside factors — particularly, the overall administration of justice.

---

44 [2001] 3 S.C.R. 442.

The first part of the test remains essentially the same. The risk to the fairness of the trial must be serious or, as originally stated, "real and substantial." Any risk must be based on reality and be well-grounded in evidence offered to the court considering the ban. The Court said it must also be a risk that poses a serious threat to the proper administration of justice.

Consideration of the impact on the justice system as a whole also comes into play in the second part of the test. In weighing the salutary and deleterious effects of a ban, judges were cautioned by the Supreme Court to use discretion in protecting the "administration of justice." For example, while police informers or witness protection programs are part of the administration of justice, "courts should not interpret that term so widely as to keep secret a vast amount of enforcement information the disclosure of which would be compatible with the public interest."

The Court also stressed that judges should consider reasonable alternatives to a ban and, if a ban is still necessary, restrict its scope as much as possible to minimize its impact on the news media.

Toronto Star

Again, in a 2005 case involving the *Toronto Star*,[45] the Supreme Court continued to explain its line of thinking in *Dagenais/Mentuck*. The *Toronto Star* case was designed to send a message to lower courts and legislators by stressing that the *Dagenais/Mentuck* test and its presumptions in favour of access apply to "all discretionary court orders that limit freedom of expression and freedom of the press in relation to legal proceedings."

This case dealt with search warrants issued in the investigation of alleged violations of provincial laws. The Crown wanted a court order sealing the search warrants, the informations used to obtain the warrants and related documents. It claimed that public disclosure of the material could identify a confidential informant and interfere with a criminal investigation. The news media successfully challenged the court order and the documents were to be made public, except to the extent that they disclosed the identity of a confidential informant. On further appeal, the province's high court applied the *Dagenais/Mentuck* test and agreed the sealing order should be quashed, but edited the materials more fully to protect informant's identity.

The Supreme Court dismissed the Crown's appeal of the lower court decisions. The Crown had argued the *Dagenais/Mentuck* test only applied to certain types of court orders and that it was not applicable at pre-charge or the "investigative stage" of criminal proceedings. The Supreme Court

---

45 *Toronto Star Newspapers Ltd. v. Ontario*, [2005] 2 S.C.R. 188.

declared that the *Dagenais/Mentuck* test must be applied to all discretionary court orders that limit freedom of expression and freedom of the press in relation to legal proceedings, including orders to seal search warrant materials made upon application by the Crown.

The Court said there is, first and foremost, a presumption that all court proceedings are "open" in Canada and that public or media access should only be barred when a court, in its discretion, "concludes that disclosure would subvert the ends of justice or unduly impair its proper administration."

If anyone in a legal proceeding believes access should be limited, that party must prove to the court's satisfaction the order is necessary because there is a "serious risk" to the proper administration of justice with no reasonable alternatives available. That party also needs to demonstrate that the need for the restriction or ban outweighs the harmful effects it will have on the press, the accused and the justice system.

In this specific case, the Court said the Crown's evidence supporting its application to delay media access "amounted to a generalized assertion of possible disadvantage to an ongoing investigation. . . The party must, at the very least, allege a serious and specific risk to the integrity of the criminal investigation. The Crown has not discharged its burden in this case."

Together, the *Dagenais*, *Mentuck* and *Toronto Star* rulings have set down a significant body of law favouring freedom of the press and heralding a new phase in the maturation of this area of the law.

That said, there will be uncertainty in applying aspects of these rulings in the coming years. Some judges will no doubt believe they are properly weighing all the factors when they decide to issue bans or other court orders. It may take years of subsequent appeals in other matters to develop the fine points of these rulings. That said, a new benchmark has been set for courts and legislators to meet.

Of course, these decisions do not spell the end of news media court challenges of limits on the press. It's important to note that "freedom of the press" is such an all-encompassing concept covering so many different aspects of the public's interests that no single ruling or trilogy of cases can be expected to set the tone for interpreting the Charter's free press guarantee.

As almost every chapter in this book illustrates, the courts have had to consider the effect of the Charter's guarantee in a multitude of different areas of the law and reconsider long-standing rules on an on-going basis. There will continue to be both wins and losses. Still, the Charter is doing an admirable job of furthering the position of the news media in challenging restrictions and barriers on their activities.

CHALLENGING INFRINGEMENTS ON THE PRESS

What many journalists may not know is that the Charter has given them more authority than ever before to challenge infringements on their "right" to gather and disseminate news. Commonly, the most imposing restrictions or barriers are set out by courts or statutes. What is important to note these days is that judges are now more open than ever to hearing legal arguments as to why a court order or statute is unjust.

In almost every case, the challenge of a court order or law will involve legal counsel. But if a journalist is at a proceeding where an application is made to exclude the public or ban the publication of information, and he or she feels the order is unjust, the reporter should respectfully request that the proceeding be adjourned to allow the reporter to contact his or her lawyer. The judge may refuse the request, but it is worth trying.

In the *Dagenais/Mentuck* cases, the Supreme Court outlined the proper procedures and rules to follow in deciding or challenging a court order. For a discretionary ban to be issued, the Crown and/or the accused must prove the need for it in a motion before the trial judge appointed for the case or before a judge in the court at the level where the case will be heard. At the very least, the motion should be made before a superior court judge.

The Court said a judge hearing a motion for a ban should consider whether notice of the application should be given to third parties, such as the media. It is within the discretion of the individual judge, said the Supreme Court, as is the decision to grant the media and others any standing to argue their points at the hearing. If third parties want to oppose the motion and don't receive notice, the Supreme Court said they should attend the hearing anyway, argue for status, and if given it, make their case. The Supreme Court then laid out a road map for appeals of lower court decisions, potentially leading to the high court itself.

The underlying point to remember is that the Supreme Court of Canada and many other courts are highly supportive of the media's right to challenge restrictions.

SOME FINAL THOUGHTS

While the rights of the news media will continue to expand, as stated in this book's first edition, the Charter is unlikely to change the principle that the news media have no greater rights than the average citizen.

However, we are still witnessing the development of a Canadian version of what Americans refer to as "the public's right to know," using the Charter's guarantee of freedom of the press.[46] The Charter still holds great

---

46   In fact, in the case of *R. v. Harrison* (1984), 14 C.C.C. (3d) 549 at 552 (C.S.P.), the court

potential to expand the rights of the news media and, at the same time, the public's rights, and it can be safely predicted the constitutional entrenchment of the fundamental freedom of the press will continue to play an ever-increasing role in activities of the news media.

said in light of the Charter "the media are now the custodians of the public's right to know." The phrase was first used by American journalist Kent Cooper in the 1940's.

In Eugenia Zerbinos, "The Right to Know: Whose Right and Whose Duty?," (1982) V. 4, No. 1, "Communications and the Law", at 33, the author discusses the lack of an all-encompassing definition of the "right to know" in the United States. There is no "right to know" mentioned in the U.S. Constitution, but it is argued that the public's right to know is inherent in a democratic system of government. The author suggests the right to know is actually an umbrella term for several specific rights accorded to the public (of which, the press is the self-declared agent).

2

DEFAMATION

Generally, defamation is the publication of a statement that harms another individual's reputation in the eyes of others. For most journalists, defamation is one of the primary areas of concern. And rightly so. In the past few decades, the news media have increasingly found themselves under attack in the courts, embroiled in lengthy and very expensive defamation actions.

Encouragingly, while Canada's defamation statutes remain largely unchanged from the mid-20th century when broadcasting was young and the Internet non-existent, the courts in several provinces have recently begun to dramatically reshape the law of defamation as it applies to all forms of news gathering and, particularly, reporting on matters of public interest. As will be discussed in more detail below in the section on qualified privilege, the most significant development is the adoption by Ontario's Court of Appeal in 2007 of a new and broader "public interest responsible journalism" defence, similar to that accepted by leading courts in other common law countries, including the U.K. and U.S. As one legal observer cleverly suggested, the "chill" is now gone from Canada's common law of defamation, replaced by the "thrill" of publishing properly researched stories on matters "the public has a legitimate interest in hearing," and that journalists have "every reason to believe" are true and meet the standards of responsible journalism.

While the defence of qualified privilege undergoes positive change, some courts have shown a willingness to undermine recent advances with increasingly restrictive interpretations of other aspects of modern defamation law. Prominent in this category is a recent B.C. appeal court decision that attempted to narrow the use of the fair comment defence by news media. As will be explained in more detail below, that restrictive view of the B.C. court was eventually overturned the Supreme Court of Canada in 2008.

Along with the shifting views of defamation, there have also been some spectacularly large damage awards sought by aggrieved plaintiffs in recent years, particularly those in the public eye who believe they have more to lose when their reputation is sullied. If there was apathy towards the threat of defamation lawsuits among Canadian journalists, much of it was probably shaken off starting with the billionaire Reichmann family's $102-million lawsuit against *Toronto Life* magazine, which settled out of court in 1991 after four years readying for trial.

In the end, bloody and bowed, *Toronto Life* publicly apologized and admitted it made "serious mistakes in the writing, editing and presentation" of an article about the family's history. Since then, many other news organizations have also been threatened with and hit by increasingly large damage awards, often ranging between six and seven figures.

One of the largest defamation awards in Canadian history, $1.6 million against a lawyer and his client who defamed a Crown attorney, was upheld as a fair amount by the Supreme Court of Canada in 1995. Since then, a Québec court has awarded a $2 million judgment against the French division of CBC and a professional association for lawyers. And, in 2008, a jury awarded a commercial pilot $3 million after his employer unfairly defamed him by alleging he had been seen drinking alcohol shortly before a flight. While some courts have publicly stated that such awards are getting too high, a six-figure award is quite common these days.

New threats to Canadian journalists continue to lie on the horizon. First, in most provinces, class action lawsuits can be launched by hundreds or thousands of similarly aggrieved plaintiffs under the umbrella of one lawsuit. In theory, a defamatory statement alleging all members of a certain profession or an ethnic group exhibit criminal or immoral traits may one day bring a journalist to court to answer to thousands of aggrieved class members. As will be discussed below in the section on defamation of a group, attempts so far to sue on behalf of classes of people have been unsuccessful. Class action laws, however, provide an easier mechanism for one or two people to sue on behalf of many and, even if a defamation action eventually fails, a media outlet may have to defend itself against this new type of lawsuit in the future.

Another area of ongoing concern is the Internet. Some dangers are obvious, such as the risk in using unverifiable or anonymous online infor- mation. Other risks won't surface right away. For example, many news outlets, big and small, are providing copies of their latest stories online. In the past, damage awards to plaintiffs often reflected the size of the audience or readership. How will awards be calculated when the whole world has an opportunity to read about a small town politician accused of bilking tax- payers? The distribution of news and stories to other countries via online services also increases the risk that publishers will have to answer to a lawsuit in another country with different defamation laws.[1]

---

1   It appears that our courts will not enforce defamation judgments from foreign courts if they fail to meet Canadian standards of proof or merit. In *Braintech, Inc. v. Kostiuk* (1999), 171 D.L.R. (4th) 46 (B.C. C.A.), the plaintiff was a technology company incorporated in Nevada, domiciled in B.C., and doing business in various U.S. jurisdictions. It sued in Texas against a B.C. resident alleging the defendant put defamatory information on an Internet bulletin board. The defendant had no other connection with Texas other than that his comments could be read by Internet users there. The Texas Civil Practice and Remedies Code deems a non-resident to be doing business in the jurisdiction if it commits a tort or wrong there. The plaintiff got a default judgment in Texas and tried to have it enforced in B.C. The B.C. appeal court overturned the Texas court's judgment, ruling that a wrongdoer must have a "real and substantial connection" to a foreign jurisdiction. In this case, the defendant's only connection to Texas was "passive posting on an Internet bulletin board." Since there was no proof anyone in Texas saw the alleged defamatory material, the court said it could not simply presume damages occurred in jurisdictions where the defamatory

With large court awards, increasing legal costs and a scarcity of libel insurers, the spectre of "libel chill" is often raised in debates about defamation laws. While it is quite true the threat of a lawsuit could make a publisher or broadcaster think twice about running an aggressive story, there is really nothing wrong with encouraging responsible journalism. In fact, few news outlets will back away from a story when they firmly believe they can mount a defence in court, if need be.

That is really the crux of this chapter. Understanding how the courts interpret defamation can actually improve how you tell a story. While defamation laws tell you your limits, they also give you a guide to how far you can go.

WHAT IS DEFAMATORY?

Over the years, the courts have developed several definitions of what is defamatory. A defamatory statement tends to discredit or lower an individual "in the estimation of right-thinking members of society generally."[2] It may also expose an individual to other's hatred, contempt, ridicule or injure his or her reputation in an office, trade or profession.[3]

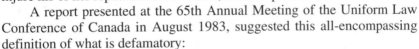

A report presented at the 65th Annual Meeting of the Uniform Law Conference of Canada in August 1983, suggested this all-encompassing definition of what is defamatory:

"Defamatory matter" is published matter concerning a person that tends to:

(a) affect adversely the reputation of that person in the estimation of ordinary persons; or
(b) deter ordinary persons from associating or dealing with that person; or
(c) injure that person in his occupation, trade, office or financial credit.

A defamatory statement can harm the reputation not only of a person,

---

statements are accessible, and likely to have been read. An application for leave to appeal to the Supreme Court of Canada was dismissed.

2 *Sim v. Stretch* (1936), 52 T.L.R. 669 at 669-670 (H.L.). It is important that society generally, and not just a few select individuals, find the statement defamatory. For instance, in *Burnett v. C.B.C. (No. 1)* (1981), 48 N.S.R. (2d) 1 (T.D.), the court said it could not find a statement defamatory if a person's reputation is only lowered within a particular class or section of the community which has a "standard of opinion" the courts cannot identify or approve.

3 For example, see *Thomas v. C.B.C.*, [1981] 4 W.W.R. 289 at 302 (N.W.T. S.C.), where an engineer was defamed by allegations that he had acted negligently in his job.

but also corporations,[4] unions[5] or almost any legal entity since they, too, have reputations.

After a fatal house fire, a citizen publicly criticizes the local municipality and its fire department. Based on his observations of the fire service's conduct, the citizen wrote a highly critical letter to the Chief Coroner, with copies to the Ontario Fire Marshal and municipality. Representatives of the municipality responded with outrage to the citizen's criticisms, as well as to the fact they were circulated to third parties. The municipality demanded an apology and retraction, and eventually proceeded to litigation. Can a municipality sue for defamation?

No. Contrary to the Canadian case law pre-dating the Charter of Rights and Freedoms, the list of entities that may sue in defamation no longer includes governments. Two recent Ontario court rulings have made it clear that, while governments have a reputation and, in some cases, even a business reputation, the Charter's guarantee of freedom of expression makes it clear "everyone should be free to criticize democratically elected governments."[6] As in the example above, one case involved a citizen criticizing local government and its methods, while the other concerned a local Internet-based news purveyor's allegations of corruption against a specific municipal official. In the latter case, while the government

---

4 The defamatory matter must injure the company in the way in which it does business or functions. In *Price v. Chicoutimi Pulp Co.* (1915), 51 S.C.R. 179 at 188-189, the Supreme Court of Canada said the defamatory words must be directed at the corporation as apart from its employees or owners and attack the corporation in the method of conducting its affairs (for example, accusing it of fraud or mismanagement). The case of *Georgian Bay Ship Canal Co. v. World Newspaper Co.* (1894), 16 P.R. 320 at 322, states a company could also be defamed if a defamatory statement wrongly alleges that officers or employees, while acting in the best interests of the company or in the regular conduct of business, have committed a criminal act.

The defamation action may fail if the corporation is not capable of the alleged act. Corporations cannot themselves commit murder, rape or actually perform an act. For example, the court in *Church of Scientology of Toronto v. Globe & Mail* (1978), 84 D.L.R. (3d) 239 at 242 (Ont. H.C.), held that while a non-profit corporation could be defamed, the one in this case could not sue for a statement alleging that its members were practising medicine without a licence. The court said the statements were in reference to the members only and a corporate entity itself could not practise medicine.

5 *P.P.F., Loc. 488 v. Canadian Broadcasting Corp.* (1979), 97 D.L.R. (3d) 56 (Alta. T.D.). Also see, *Pulp and Paper Workers of Canada v. International Brotherhood of Pulp, etc.* (1973), 37 D.L.R. (3d) 687 (B.C. S.C.), where one union sued another for libel.

6 See *Halton Hills (Town) v. Kerouac*, 2006 CarswellOnt 2444, [2006] O.J. No. 1473 (S.C.) and *Montague (Township) v. Page* (2006), 79 O.R. (3d) 515 (S.C.). While other provinces may not have ruled on the issue of governments suing in defamation, these rulings will be persuasive.

entity itself could not sue, the court noted the government employee who had been accused of corruption was free to launch his own personal defamation action since he had a professional reputation to maintain.

The courts in Canada have been reluctant to allow defamation actions by groups that do not enjoy a legal status (for example, *ad hoc* citizen's committees or war veterans).[7] But, a member of an identifiable class or group may be able to successfully sue if a defamatory statement directed at the class or group can be proven to be reasonably understood to refer to that person as a member.[8]

The responsibility for publication of a defamatory statement does not stop with the journalist — it continues throughout the chain of command, so that editors, news directors, producers, owners, publishers, announcers and even those delivering a publication to the street can be held responsible. Anyone who has knowledge, or should have knowledge, of the defamatory

7   Most recently, veteran Canadian bomber airmen failed in an attempt to sue the CBC under a class action law for alleged defamation in *Elliot v. Canadian Broadcasting Corp.* (1995), 125 D.L.R. (4th) 534 (Ont. C.A.), affirming (1993), 108 D.L.R. (4th) 385 (Ont. Gen. Div.). In this case, the plaintiff sued on behalf of 25,000 other aviators, alleging that a CBC documentary injured their reputation. The court said a group of 25,000 cannot be defamed and no individual aviator in the group was singled out. The court also found the documentary was not disparaging of all Canadian airmen in the war, even if the group action had been allowed.

Also see *McCann v. Ottawa Sun (The)* (1993), 16 O.R. (3d) 672 (Gen. Div.), in which the mayor of a town of 13,500 sued on behalf of residents after a columnist made allegedly defamatory comments about spectators at a hockey game, suggesting they were probably from the mayor's town and other named areas. The court ruled the action had no basis and said that an action for defamation is "uniquely personal" and each plaintiff would have to show he or she was clearly identified by the column. The court said this is only likely to happen in cases where the group is very small and easily identified. As for the mayor's own claim, the court said there was nothing in the columnist's comments to indicate he was referring to the mayor himself.

Manitoba is the only province that protects against libel of a race or creed in its defamation statute. The Uniform Law Conference's report mentioned at the beginning of this chapter suggests "group defamation" is a difficult issue because the group and its membership often cannot be defined. The report says supplying a civil remedy for defaming such a group might also stifle public debate on important issues.

8   *Knupffer v. London Express Newspapers Ltd.*, [1944] A.C. 116 (H.L.). The defamation must clearly point to the plaintiff as a member of the group. For example, in *Booth v. BCTV Broadcasting System* (1982), 139 D.L.R. (3d) 88 (B.C. C.A.), a news report quoted a hooker saying two members of the narcotics squad "that are high up — right up on top — take payoffs." The court held that only the two senior officers in the squad could sue and dismissed lawsuits brought by nine other members of the squad who felt they were implicated.

statement and subsequent control over its publication, is potentially responsible.[9]

Important *Editors chose to run the article*

A common concern of freelance journalists is whether they can be held
wholly responsible for a defamatory article since a publication is only
purchasing the story and it has no vicarious liability for the actions of non-
employees. As a link in the publishing chain, however, it exercises control
over the article and is held as liable for it as the original author. That said,
if a freelancer hands in a story that is recklessly written or knowingly false,
there is nothing stopping a publication from suing him or her to recover any
damages it may have to pay.

THE PECULIARITIES OF DEFAMATION

One aspect of a defamation lawsuit that makes it different from any
other civil action is that the plaintiff (the offended individual) does not have
to prove the defamatory matter is false. Under the common law, the courts
immediately presume that any statement that adversely affects someone's
reputation is false.[10]

Indeed, even a true statement can, technically speaking, be defamatory
in accordance with the definition that it subjects someone to ridicule or
contempt. As the saying goes, the truth hurts. But, in all provinces except
one, proving the truth of a statement acts as a complete defence to a defamation action.

This leads to an important point to remember. A statement may be
defamatory, but may not be actionable (in other words, successful) in court.
As will be discussed later, a statement may be proven true, or there may be

---

9 *Popovich v. Lobay*, [1937] 3 D.L.R. 715 (Man. C.A.). In the English case of *Emmens v.
   Pottle* (1885), 16 Q.B.D. 354 (C.A.), the court stated that, to be found not liable or
   responsible, there must be no knowledge of the libel, no negligence in not knowing of it
   and that the defendant did not know, nor should have known, the publication was of a
   bad character. This is what often relieves newsstand distributors and other secondary
   players from any liability.

10 *Belt v. Lawes* (1882), 51 L.J.Q.B. 359 at 361 (D.C.). The Uniform Law Conference report
   argued against including a requirement for "falsity" in any definition of defamation
   because it would mean that the plaintiff would first have to prove an offending statement
   is false before claiming it was defamatory. The report reasoned that because a person's
   reputation is at stake, the onus should always be on the defendant to prove the truth of
   defamatory statements or call some other defence. More recently, in *Pressler v. Lethbridge*
   (1997), 153 D.L.R. (4th) 537 (B.C. S.C.), a TV broadcaster was unsuccessful in seeking
   a declaration that the common law of defamation is incompatible with the Charter of
   Rights, specifically that the onus of proof in justification (the truth defence) should be on
   the plaintiff. The judge ruled that "while freedom of public debate was very important,
   so also was reputation, and statements of fact did not contribute usefully to public debate
   unless they were true."

a special defence available that can permit even a completely false statement to be published in unique circumstances (for example, qualified privilege). It is for this reason that journalists can still write controversial or critical stories.

A word of warning, though. A true, yet defamatory, statement may still be successfully pursued in the courts in certain circumstances. As mentioned above, the truth is a complete defence in all provinces, but one. The exception is Québec, where the true defamatory statement must also be in the public interest and made without malice. Also, the rare charge of defamatory libel under the Criminal Code[11] has a "truth" defence that requires that the defamatory statement must have an element of public benefit at the time of publication. At least one trial judge has declared this unconstitutional. A final warning about publishing true defamatory statements is that in some provinces, a civil action may be successfully pursued under provincial Privacy Acts if the offending statement is not made in the public interest.[12]

WHAT'S THE DIFFERENCE BETWEEN LIBEL AND SLANDER?

Historically, defamation has fallen into two categories. *Libel* is defamation through a permanent form, such as writing.[13] *Slander* is defamation by the spoken word or gesture.[14] There is a reason for the distinction. In a case of libel, the plaintiff does not have to offer proof that the defamation caused any actual damage to his or her reputation. In a case of slander, the plaintiff must show that actual damage (for example, loss of credit) resulted from the defamatory words.[16] The distinctions are less important today.

For instance, a court action against a broadcast journalist will be in libel because alleged defamations in broadcasting are usually preserved in

---

11 R.S.C. 1985, c. C-46.

12 See the chapter on "Invasion of Privacy."

13 *Osborn's Concise Law Dictionary*, 6th ed. (London: Sweet & Maxwell, 1976), at 203.

14 *Ibid.*, at 307. But, in *Stopforth v. Goyer* (1978), 87 D.L.R. (3d) 373 at 375 (Ont. C.A.), the court said it is settled law that when a person speaks defamatory words to the press with the intention or knowledge that they will be republished, the speaker is responsible in libel instead of slander.

15 This was recognized in *Thorley v. Lord Kerry* (1812), 128 E.R. 367 at 371.

16 There are occasions when the common law will allow a slander action without proof of damage. *Gatley on Libel and Slander*, 8th ed. (London: Sweet & Maxwell, 1981), at 73, states that slander is actionable without proof of actual harm where a crime has been imputed, an infectious or contagious disease has been suggested, a business reputation has been hurt or the chastity of a woman or girl is questioned.

a permanent form, such as audio or video tape[17] and most provinces have legislation that states that a defamation in broadcasting is libel.[18]

DEFAMATION CAN EVEN BE A CRIMINAL OFFENCE

Defamation can be the subject of either civil or criminal proceedings. The law applying to criminal defamation is, for the most part, substantially different from civil defamation laws. The standard of proof called for in a criminal case is much more demanding than that found in civil cases. Also, because of different historical backgrounds, criminal and civil offences and defences in defamation actions are sometimes a world apart.

Most court actions against the news media are civil, with the plaintiff seeking compensation for his damaged reputation. Criminal actions are rare and involve serious and malicious defamations likely to incite public hatred, contempt or ridicule against the individual.[19] The criminal charge of defamatory libel punishes the offence against society, not just the offence against the individual. While a criminal charge of defamatory libel is rare, a journalist should realize that a seriously defamatory statement could be the subject of criminal proceedings.[20]

THE CIVIL LAW OF DEFAMATION

Assessing the Risk of Defamation

Journalists can best avoid losing a defamation lawsuit by understanding how the law examines a story. There are essentially three key questions:

---

17 A 1981 report by the Law Reform Commission of British Columbia, L.R.C. 50, "Report on Cable Television and Defamation," suggests a broadcast delivered from a script or played back from a recording is libel. But it suggests a "live" broadcast remark is slander.

18 British Columbia, Ontario, and Nova Scotia expressly state that defamations in broadcasting are libel. Alberta, Manitoba, New Brunswick, Newfoundland, Prince Edward Island, the Northwest Territories, Nunavut and the Yukon have eliminated the distinction between libel and slander altogether, making all defamations actionable without proof of damage. Saskatchewan's legislation provides only for "newspaper libel," leaving broadcasters to the common law distinctions between slander and libel. Québec's Civil Code does not recognize a distinction between slander and libel. Québec's Press Act allows anyone who "deems himself injured" to initiate an action against a newspaper.

19 *R. v. Cameron* (1898), 7 Qué. Q.B. 162 at 163.

20 The Canadian Centre for Justice Statistics recorded 36 people charged with criminal libel offences between 1963 and, the last year recorded, 1973.

The Law Reform Commission of Canada has recommended that criminal defamatory libel be repealed.

Is There Defamatory Matter?

Based on plain meaning of the words. To succeed in court, one of the first things the plaintiff must prove is that the words are defamatory. But it is not good enough that the plaintiff feels the words are objectionable. The court (the jury or judge sitting alone) must also be convinced the words will lower an individual's reputation in society. Mere insults or affronts to a person's dignity, for example, have not usually been considered defamatory. If there is a dispute about whether the words are defamatory, the judge will use the clear and obvious meanings of the words, such as set out in a dictionary, to decide what they could mean.

If not clearly defamatory, is there an innuendo? Sometimes, a plaintiff may allege that the words, while not defamatory by definition, may carry a defamatory innuendo to the public or people with knowledge of special facts.[21] The essence of defamation is the transmission of ideas that adversely affect a person's reputation despite whether it is express or by implication. While the plaintiff can always allege that a statement carries an innuendo, he has the burden of proving that there is an innuendo.[22]

> A newspaper reported, among other things, that a training consultant working on equity issues for government organizations told a group of Crown Attorneys in a racism training seminar the Holocaust was not a racist act. The consultant, who served as a police board commissioner, sued the newspaper and its reporters over the 28 articles, cartoons and editorials focusing on his statements. At trial and on appeal, the consultant argued the newspaper raised the innuendo he practised "anti-Semitic teachings" and the onus was on

---

21 In *Mark v. Deustch* (1973), 39 D.L.R. (3d) 568 at 571 (Alta. T.D.), the court stated the plaintiff does not have to prove that everyone derived a defamatory innuendo from a statement, only that it could be understood that way and that such people exist. Another interesting example of innuendo arose in *Bordeleau v. Bonnyville Nouvelle Ltd.* (1992), 6 Alta. L.R. (3d) 128 (Q.B.), in which a single, 18-year-old woman sued a newspaper for publishing a notice headed "Surprise! Congratulations" and announcing her pregnancy. The woman wanted the information kept private. The court dismissed the action on other grounds, but did comment that "there was an element of taunting" used in the headline which was defamatory by innuendo.

22 In the case of *Pherrill v. Sewell* (1908), 12 O.W.R. 63 (Div. Ct.) the court said the innuendo must be clear to the "reasonable man." The appeal court judge borrowed (at 65) this clever quote from a Scottish judge: "I am unwilling to torture innuendoes out of words that do not in a reasonable manner bear the interpretation sought to be put upon them."

> **the publication to prove it. Was the consultant's legal argument correct?**
>
> **No.** At trial, the judge found the articles correctly stated the facts on his statements and were fair comment. The trial judge rejected the innuendo argument and the appeal court agreed, saying the newspaper cannot be held responsible for any inference a reader might draw from an accurately reported fact. Application for leave to appeal to the Supreme Court of Canada was dismissed.[23]

Unfortunately for well-meaning journalists, innuendoes can happen quite innocently. For instance, the use of file footage or stock photographs that single out an identifiable person can be dangerous when coupled with a controversial story. In one case, stock footage of a hospital worker preparing an operating room was used in connection with a story on abortion. The hospital worker was a devout Roman Catholic and felt that people who knew him would think he condoned abortion. Another example would be pictures showing two people talking on a street in the context of a story on illegal drug trafficking, insinuating that either person deals in narcotics. If either person proves he could be identified, he could sue, putting the onus on the journalist to prove the truth of the innuendo.

Is it defamatory in the context of the entire story? Since words can be defamatory on their own, but perhaps not when considered in the context they were used, a judge may also consider the tenor of the whole story or, at least, relevant segments. For example, in a case involving Soviet defector Ivan Gouzenko in 1976, the court stated that although isolated words in a story may be defamatory, the entire article must be considered. Although the journalist used some strong language to describe Gouzenko, the judge said words like "traitor" and "defector" were accurate descriptions of the plaintiff.[24]

A recent example of a court using the context of a story to find defamation as opposed to one segment resulted in one of Canada's highest damage awards in this area of law.[25] A trial judge awarded Dr. Frans H.H. Leenen general, aggravated and punitive damages of $950,000, together

---

23 *Minors v. Toronto Sun Publishing Corp.*, 1999 CarswellOnt 1993, [1999] O.J. No. 2421, Docket No. C26963 (C.A.).

24 *Gouzenko v. Harris* (1976), 13 O.R. (2d) 730 (H.C.). Also, see *McCrea v. Canada Newspapers Co.* (1993), 126 N.S.R. (2d) 212 (C.A.), affirming (1993), 122 N.S.R. (2d) 411 (S.C.), in which the court said an entire series of six articles was relevant even though the plaintiff complained about only one in the series.

25 *Leenen v. Canadian Broadcasting Corp.*, [2001] O.J. No. 2229, Docket No. C34272 (Ont. C.A.), leave to appeal dismissed [2001] S.C.C.A. No. 432 (S.C.C.).

with court costs, for a CBC fifth estate program called "The Heart of The Matter." The news program focused on questions in the medical science community about the safety of heart medications known as calcium channel blockers and, specifically, one called nifedipine.

The theme of the program was that nifedipine, which was approved by Health Canada for angina but was also being prescribed for hypertension, was dangerous. The program alleged the government was not moving quickly enough to investigate the use of nifedipine. After viewing the story and hearing evidence, the trial judge concluded that the juxtaposition of interview guests, including Dr. Leenen, followed a "good guy/bad guy" scenario.

In the editing process, said the judge, Leenen's own statements were used to unfairly portray him as one of the "bad guys." While his words and statements were true, the innuendoes raised implied he supported the prescribing of killer drugs, was in a conflict of interest, received a kickback from a drug company, and acted negligently or dishonestly as the chairman of an *ad hoc* government advisory committee. The province's appeal court upheld the $950,000 damages. Leave to appeal to the Supreme Court of Canada was denied in 2002.

Once it is decided that the words or the context of the story are capable of being defamatory, the jury or judge sitting alone must decide if they are truly defamatory in this case. As mentioned, the statement must be defamatory in the estimation of "right-thinking members of society" as represented by the jury or the judge in non-jury trials.

Does the Defamatory Matter Refer to the Plaintiff?

Is it a direct or indirect reference? It is important to the plaintiff's case to prove that the offending statement refers to him or her, even if he or she is not expressly identified.[26] As an example, if a story made defamatory references to an unnamed "senior city hall official," a highly placed city official might successfully sue if he could prove that society in general would understand the defamatory statement to be referring to him.

---

26 In the English case of *Le Fanu v. Malcolmson* (1848), 9 E.R. 910 (H.L.), the House of Lords said in cases of alleged innuendo, the plaintiff must prove that at least one person would think it refers to the plaintiff. More recently, in *Aiken v. Ontario (Premier)* (1999), 177 D.L.R. (4th) 489 (Ont. S.C.), teachers were unsuccessful in suing the Premier for comments he made about their protests over proposed changes to the educational system. Premier Mike Harris issued broadcast advertisements attacking the teachers' position. Over 100 teachers sued for libel, alleging the Premier had depicted them as "lawbreakers" and damaged their reputations. None of the plaintiffs was mentioned by name in the broadcasts. The court dismissed the action because the broadcasts could not be regarded as capable of referring to one or more of the plaintiffs as individuals.

What if there was no intention to defame the plaintiff? It is irrelevant that there was no intention to defame someone.[27] For example, a fictitious story that unintentionally uses the name of a real person can be the subject of a successful defamation action.[28] The test is whether a reasonable person receiving the defamatory statement would be likely to think it refers to the individual.[29]

Was the Defamatory Matter Published?

Why it's important to know about publication. Journalism being what it is, this is somewhat of a moot question. Still, there can be no defamation unless the words are published.[30] Publication happens when the defamatory statement is received by someone other than the allegedly defamed victim.[31] A person can even be held responsible for an unintentional publication if it was foreseeable or likely in the circumstance.[32]

---

27 *Planned Parenthood Nfld./Labrador v. Fedorik* (1982), 135 D.L.R. (3d) 714 at 719 (Nfld. T.D.). In *Loos v. The Leader Post Ltd. and Williams*, [1982] 2 W.W.R. 459 at 468 (Sask. C.A.), this appeal court held it does not matter what the defendant intended his words to mean or even what they were understood to mean by the audience. They need only have the potential to be understood in a defamatory manner.

28 *Jones v. E. Hulton & Co.*, [1909] 2 K.B. 444 (C.A.).

29 *Sheppard v. Bulletin Co.* (1917), 55 S.C.R. 454 at 461.

30 In *Jenner v. Sun Oil Co.*, [1952] O.R. 240 at 251 (H.C.), the court held the essential element of the defamation was not the statement itself, but its publication.

31 In *Gallant v. Calder* (1883), 23 N.B.R. 73 (C.A.), referring to the Supreme Court of Canada decision in *Dewe v. Waterbury* (1881), 6 S.C.R. 143, the New Brunswick court held that the defamatory words were spoken only to the plaintiff and the judge properly dismissed the case. But in the Québec cases of *Peters v. Tardivel* (1899), 15 C.S. 401 and *Beaudoin v. Vaillancourt* (1926), 42 K.B. 42, the offending words were published only to the plaintiffs and they won nominal damages under Québec's Civil Code. None of the common law provinces have followed this line of thought.

32 *McNichol v. Grandy*, [1931] S.C.R. 696. For a contrary view, see *Hills v. O'Bryan*, [1949] 1 W.W.R. 985 (B.C. S.C.), where the plaintiff showed a defamatory letter, written by the defendant and addressed only to the plaintiff, to others. The court said the defendant could not foresee that this would happen. More recently, in *Parizeau v. Lafferty, Harwood & Partners Ltd.*, [2000] J.Q. no 682 (Qué. S.C.), Jacques Parizeau, president of the Parti Québécois, and Lucien Bouchard, a Member of Parliament, were awarded damages totalling $40,000 over a defamatory story in the 1993 *Lafferty Canadian Report*. The publication had a very small circulation and was explicitly intended only for 275 subscribers. Despite that fact, it was leaked to a major French daily newspaper, which published a critical story about comments comparing the political actions of both men to those of Hitler. The court ruled the statements were defamatory and that the newsletter publishers were responsible for the subsequent republication of the defamation in the newspaper. In 2003, the Québec Court of Appeal upheld the lower court's findings but also increased the total damages awarded to $200,000, plus interest (see *Lafferty, Harwood & Partners v. Parizeau*, 2003 CanLII 32941 (QC C.A.)).

What if someone else published it too? Unless there is a special privilege or defence, it is irrelevant that a journalist is only repeating what was said or published by another person.[33] In addition, there is no protection offered to a journalist who uses defamatory material, even though another news agency, such as a wire service, originally published it.[34]

WHAT ARE THE DEFENCES?

Co-existing with hundreds of years of case law on defamation, is legislation in each province and territory that sometimes modifies the common law and, in other instances, codifies it. In general, the legislation supersedes any areas of direct conflict with the common law. But, for the most part, the common law rules have been adopted. In qualified privilege, for instance, defamation statutes specifically allow the use of the common law to supplement the legislative provisions.

While all jurisdictions have defamation legislation, individual provincial statutes vary widely in some respects. The most prominent differences are between the common law provinces and Québec. Even the common law provinces have developed their own particular defamation statutes.[35] For instance, Saskatchewan's legislation only addresses defamation actions against newspapers while all others include both print and broadcasting. Some provinces have incorporated more of the common law into their legislation than others. The cumulative effect of all these variations is confusion for journalists and plaintiffs alike. There has been an attempt to get provinces to adopt a Uniform Defamation Act, but differences still exist even in the provinces that have the uniform Acts. The following section will outline the common law and statutory defences in Canada. Variations among provinces will be highlighted and the civil law in Québec will be discussed separately.

---

33 *MacDonald v. Mail Printing Co.* (1900), 32 O.R. 163 at 170 (H.C.). Also see, *Thomas v. Canadian Broadcasting Corp.*, [1981] 4 W.W.R. 289 at 298 (N.W.T. S.C.), where the court said a reporter is responsible for proving the truth of any hearsay statement or quote he uses in his story. A hearsay statement is one in which the person speaking does not have direct knowledge of the truth and is only repeating what he heard from someone else, who is not available to testify.

34 See *Allan v. Bushnell T.V. Co.* (1968), [1969] 1 O.R. 107 (H.C.) and *Chinese Cultural Centre of Vancouver v. Holt* (1978), 7 B.C.L.R. 81 (S.C.), for cases where defamatory news reports in one publication were repeated in another news medium.

35 Defamation Acts, R.S.A. 2000, c. D-7; R.S.M. 1987, c. D20; R.S.N.B. 1973, c. D-5; R.S.N.S. 1989, c. 122; R.S.P.E.I. 1988, c. D-5; R.S.Y. 1986, c. 41; Libel and Slander Acts, R.S.B.C. 1996, c. 263, as amended; R.S.O. 1990, c. L.12; Press Act, R.S.Q. 1977, c. P-19, as amended; R.S.S. 1978, c. L-14, as amended.

The Defence of Truth or Justification

Most responsible journalists believe that everything they write is true and based on facts. Justification is the defence of truth and it is the one defence that most journalists think they can rely on. But, it can be a problematic and difficult defence.

As mentioned at the beginning of this chapter, the law places a heavy onus on the publisher of a defamatory statement to "justify" it or call some other defence.

Proving It

Proving the truth of a statement is not as easy as it sounds. For example, the defence of truth does not simply involve proving that a quoted source did really say the defamatory statement that was published. A journalist and his lawyers will have to present actual proof to the judge and jury of the truth of any source's statements, as well as the journalist's own statements. The evidence, as in any other trial, will have to be admissible and relevant. The court is unlikely to accept hearsay evidence, which is any proof based on the word of a person who is not at the hearing to testify to the truth of the statement. In other words, it is second-hand information. It also does not help to be partly correct. In one extreme case, a publication said the plaintiff owed $59.35 (a large amount of money in 1892). In reality, the plaintiff only owed $24.33 and the court held the plea of justification was not established through partial proof.[36]

To succeed with the defence of justification, a journalist must be able to prove that the alleged facts are true in both fact and substance.[37] That means the plain meaning of the published words must be true, including any alleged innuendo. In the common law, it is unnecessary to prove the truth of every single word, but there must be justification for the gist of the

---

36 *Green v. Minnes* (1892), 22 O.R. 177 (C.A.).

37 In the English case of *Walker & Son, Ltd. v. Hodgson*, [1909] 1 K.B. 239 at 253 (C.A.), the court said: ". . . . the defendant must prove not only that the facts were truly stated, but also that the innuendo is true. He must justify every injurious imputation." This doesn't mean that journalists must prove allegations or charges of impropriety when they are clearly reported as such. For a recent example, see *Bhaduria v. City-TV*, [1998] O.J. No. 5118 (Ont. C.A.). A TV station reported there were allegations against the plaintiff that he had misstated his professional credentials. He sued for defamation, but the court tossed his case out because he admitted during cross-examination that it was true there such allegations and that was what had been reported. Application for leave to appeal to the Supreme Court of Canada dismissed with costs ([1999] S.C.C.A. No. 34).

statement.[38] Ontario and Nova Scotia have adopted a statutory equivalent of the common law requirements for the "truth" defence. The provision in both provinces states that:[39]

> a defence of justification shall not fail by reason only that the truth of every charge is not proved if the words not proved to be true do not materially injure the plaintiff's reputation having regard to the truth of the remaining charges.

The Standard of Proof Required

With one exception, the standard of proof needed to prove the truth of a statement is the same as in any other civil trial. The statement must be proven to be true "on a balance of probabilities based on the preponderance of evidence." This means that the jury or judge will have to be convinced that the statements of fact are in all probability true, based on the evidence.

The exception to the standard of proof is when a criminal or corrupt act is alleged. The standard of proof required of the defendant in such instances is automatically raised to a higher level. While the criminal act does not have to be proven "beyond a reasonable doubt" as in criminal law, the courts have determined that a higher degree of probability than normal is necessary.[40]

Proving the commission of a criminal offence may be extremely difficult. Someone charged with murder and awaiting trial cannot be called a

---

38 First stated in *Edwards v. Bell* (1824), 1 Bing 403 at 408. In the 1994 case of *Sidorsky v. CFCN Communications Ltd.* (1994), 23 Alta. L.R. (3d) 116 (Q.B.), the TV station did a series of 14 stories on a mobile home park sales promotion that the reporter repeatedly called a "swindle," "scam," and "rip-off." The court ruled that only the substance of the allegations needed to be proved and not the truth of each word. As well, the judge stated the words used were apt descriptions. In another case, an Ontario court made it clear that defamation defendants do not necessarily have to answer to the innuendo raised by the plaintiff if a "lesser meaning" can be proved. See *Pizza Pizza Ltd. v. Toronto Star Newspapers Ltd.* (1998), 167 D.L.R. (4th) 748 (Ont. Gen. Div.), affirmed by the Court of Appeal in (2000), 187 D.L.R. (4th) 761. A pizza company sued a newspaper over a headline — *Pizza franchisees form group to get a fairer deal from firm* — that it claimed raised a false innuendo suggesting it cheated a particular franchisee. The newspaper said the meaning of the headline was not as severe as the company alleged and, in its lesser meaning, was actually true. An appeal court ruled the traditional legal rule that prevents libel defendants from arguing a lesser meaning "constituted an unacceptable limit on freedom of expression and the press. A newspaper must be allowed to defend itself by saying 'this is what we meant and what we meant is true.' "

39 Libel and Slander Act, R.S.O. 1990, c. L.12, s. 22; Defamation Act, R.S.N.S. 1989, c. 122, s. 9.

40 This was stated in *York v. Okanagan Broadcasters Ltd.*, [1976] 6 W.W.R. 40 (B.C. S.C.). The court went on to say that even though there was no direct evidence of the alleged criminal acts in this case, the judge could find that it was "reasonably probable" that the plaintiff had committed the acts based on indirect evidence.

murderer. Even evidence of a conviction itself may not be enough, sometimes, to support an allegation that a crime has been committed. For example, if a person has been convicted of possession of stolen property, a
journalist could not say that the plaintiff is a thief. If the plaintiff had been
convicted of theft, the record of conviction would strengthen the defendant's
case, but evidence might still have to be offered to prove that an offence
had been committed by the plaintiff.

Therefore, to rely on the defence of truth, a journalist must keep in
mind who can be called as a witness to offer direct evidence as to the
veracity of a statement. As well, it is important to retain all notes, documents
and recordings used while gathering the information for the story.

The Defence of Consent

It is rare that anyone would consent to be defamed, but it can happen.
The defence of consent is rooted in the legal principle of *volenti non fit
injuria* (that to which a person consents cannot be considered an injury).
The principle is that anyone who knowingly and voluntarily exposes himself
to a danger, should be thought to have assumed the potential consequences.
For this defence to succeed, the defendant must be able to prove that
the plaintiff caused the defamatory statements himself or that the plaintiff
knew what defamatory statements were to be published and gave a full and
knowledgeable consent to the defamation.[41] For example, in one Western
case, a person agreed to appear on a radio program to refute a defamatory
rumour in the community. However, the person made it clear that he only
wanted to make a statement that the rumour was not true and did not want
to be challenged or subjected to questioning by listeners resulting in further
spreading of the rumour. Unfortunately, a caller did just that and the plaintiff
successfully sued the radio station for allowing the caller's defamatory
remarks to go out over the airwaves.[42]

> **In a defamation action involving an investigative story, the defendant
> broadcaster argued that since the plaintiff had declined to partici-
> pate he therefore did not object to a story being done about him and
> had consented to any defamatory comments made by other people
> in interviews. Was the broadcaster correct?**

---

41 In *Jones v. Brooks* (1974), 45 D.L.R. (3d) 413 (Sask. Q.B.), the plaintiff secretly hired
    two investigators to ask the defendant about the plaintiff's reputation. The court found
    the resulting defamatory statements were caused by the plaintiff's own actions and he
    was thus consenting to their publication.
42 *Syms v. Warren* (1976), 71 D.L.R. (3d) 558 (Man. Q.B.).

> **No.** While the plaintiff may have refused an opportunity to participate, the court ruled it was not consent. The plaintiff had a right to expect subsequent comments to be within the confines of the law of defamation.[43]

The Defence of Absolute Privilege

While the law seeks to protect the reputation of individuals, it also must consider the right of society as a whole to public debate in certain forums, such as Parliament or the courts. If the laws of defamation applied to comments in these forums, no one would be willing to bring up controversial issues. Therefore, the law has developed an exception for defamatory statements arising from certain public forums. The special defence of absolute privilege allows the publication of a defamatory statement even if it is made with malicious intent. This defence is usually only available to certain public representatives in government or judicial proceedings. But the privilege is extended to journalists in two situations that will be discussed.

Government Proceedings — When privilege works

Traditionally, elected members of legislative forums enjoy an absolute privilege while performing their legislative duties. However, an absolute privilege does not exist in everything an elected official says or does. Members of Parliament, the Senate or a provincial legislature enjoy this privilege only during votes, in reports and papers presented during proceedings and during the actual proceedings of the House, a provincial legislative assembly or committee meetings.[44] Their absolute privilege exists only in connection with the formal transaction of business in the House, assembly or committee.[45] For example, comments made outside of the proceedings (even on the steps of a legislature) would not enjoy absolute privilege even though the words may be a repetition of statements made in the proceedings.[46]

---

43 *Burnett v. Canadian Broadcasting Corp. (No. 2)* (1981), 48 N.S.R. (2d) 181 (T.D.).

44 Parliament of Canada Act, R.S.C. 1985, c. P-1, ss. 7-8. The common law offers similar protection as seen in the case of *Vezina v. Lacroix* (1936), 40 Qué. P.R. 1.

45 See Maingot, *Law of Parliamentary Privilege In Canada*, (Toronto: Butterworth & Co., 1982), at 69-72.

46 *Stopforth v. Goyer* (1978), 20 O.R. (2d) 262 (H.C.). But, there may be a qualified privilege available.

Judicial Proceedings

Judges, lawyers and witnesses also enjoy absolute privilege during judicial proceedings, except in Québec.[47] In Québec, all words spoken in a judicial proceeding are not absolutely privileged. The absolute privilege only extends to words that are relevant and reasonably necessary to the purpose of the case and spoken without malice.[48]

An absolute privilege can also be extended to bodies that are not formal courts, but do exhibit judicial or quasi-judicial qualities.[49] This can include coroners' inquests, public inquiries and compensation board hearings. But there is a restriction as to how far the absolute privileges of these bodies go. Most of these public bodies, such as coroners' inquests, are not considered "courts of record" (that is, with a formal record of their proceedings and the ability to fine or imprison). Bodies that are not courts of record lose their absolute privilege if the defamatory statements are made outside the authority or purpose of the hearing.[50] As long as the statements are within the purpose of the proceedings defamatory statements can be made, even with malicious intent.

---

47 First stated in the English case of *Munster v. Lamb* (1883), 11 Q.B.D. 588 (C.A.). In *Henderson v. Scott* (1892), 24 N.S.R. 232 at 238 (C.A.), the court said the privilege applies even when the defamatory words have nothing to do with the issues in the case. This rationale was echoed in *Electra Sign Ltd. v. Gallagher* (1995), 38 C.P.C. (3d) 141 (Man. Master), in which the judge found that extraneous comments made during a small claims hearing were absolutely privileged. The case of *Hall v. Baxter* (1922), 22 O.W.N. 207 at 209 (S.C.), states the absolute privilege for participants extends to statements made in their writs, pleadings and affidavits. That rule, however, has been modified substantially by the Supreme Court's 1995 ruling in *Hill v. Church of Scientology*, cited below at note 78, in which the court said publication of information in pleadings is now protected by a qualified privilege so long as a reporter has a right of access to the court documents under legislation or the Charter's freedom of the press guarantee, and there is no evidence of actual malice in the reporting.

48 *Langlois v. Drapeau*, [1962] B.R. 277 at 280-281.

49 *Stark v. Auerbach*, [1979] 3 W.W.R. 563 at 567 (B.C. S.C.), dealt with whether absolute privilege could be extended to bodies other than courts. The court said it can be extended if the public body exercises a judicial function (i.e., weighs evidence, gives reasons for its decision and acts judicially). In the English case of *Royal Aquarium and Summer and Winter Garden Society, Ltd. v. Parkinson*, [1892] 1 Q.B. 431 (C.A.) the court also agreed that the absolute privilege at common law extends only to inquiries of a judicial or quasi-judicial nature. For example, see the Canadian case of *Halls v. Mitchell*, [1926] 4 D.L.R. 202 (Ont. S.C.), where a workers' compensation board was found to have absolute privilege.

50 For example, in *MacKenzie v. McArthur*, [1981] 4 W.W.R. 692 (B.C. S.C.), a coroner was held liable for directing a jury to find that a doctor had carelessly treated someone and caused their death. That type of verdict was outside the authority of the coroner in that province.

A Limited Privilege for Journalists

Journalists enjoy absolute privilege in two cases. The first occasion involves reports of government proceedings. If tabled reports, papers, votes or proceedings of Parliament or a legislature are published by the news media in their entirety they will enjoy absolute privilege.[51] However, it is rare that such matters would be published in their entirety and the more common journalistic practice of publishing extracts of reports, papers, votes or proceedings only enjoys a qualified privilege (that is, typically, requiring an element of legitimate public interest and an absence of malice on the part of the journalist).[52]

Most provinces also extend a limited form of absolute privilege in their legislation to fair and accurate reports of public judicial proceedings. It is actually an absolute privilege in name only because of its restrictions. British Columbia and Nova Scotia simply extend a "privilege" to court reports, with no mention of an absolute privilege. In addition, Saskatchewan's Act only applies to newspapers, leaving broadcasters to the common law principles. This is representative of many of the enacted provisions:

> A fair and accurate report published in a newspaper or by broadcasting, of proceedings publicly heard before any court is absolutely privileged if,
>
> (a) the report contains no comment;
> (b) the report is published contemporaneously with the proceedings that are the subject-matter of the report, or within thirty days thereafter; and
> (c) the report contains nothing of a seditious, blasphemous or indecent nature.

As the provision states, protection from a defamatory statement will only be offered to reports of judicial proceedings held in public. Therefore, a report of details of in camera or closed door proceedings will not be privileged. There is also a requirement for a "fair and accurate" report. That means it must be properly balanced and not one-sided. But, it does not have

---

51 Parliament of Canada Act, R.S.C. 1985, c. P-1, ss. 7-8. The common law principle was first set out in the English case of *Wason v. Walter* (1868), L.R. 4 Q.B. 73, where the court said the advantage to the public far outweighs the private injury that results. In *Lake v. King* (1670), 1 Saund. 131 (K.B.), the court recognized the need to protect the publication of Parliamentary petitions and papers.

52 Parliament of Canada Act, note 51, above, s. 9. See also Maingot, *Law of Parliamentary Privilege in Canada*, note 45, above, at 46.

to be word-for-word. The report must be substantially correct and carry the same meaning as a word-for-word account.[53]

The report must also contain no comment on the proceedings. This provision is intended to prevent journalists from speculating on such things as the quality of the evidence or the possible outcome of the proceedings. This does not mean that a journalist cannot report what he sees in court. But, it is fair to say there are limits to what is observation and what is comment. For instance, a journalist should not make a subjective comment, such as "The accused looked worried about his case."

According to the statutes, the report must also be published contemporaneously or within a reasonable period after the proceedings, usually no more than 30 days. In the common law, fair and accurate reports of any judicial proceedings, regardless of the time frame, are entitled to a qualified privilege.

The law also adds these two qualifications. First, there must be an opportunity for the right of reply:

> No privilege will apply where the newspaper or broadcasting outlet refuses to publish a reasonable statement of explanation or contradiction.

Second, headlines and captions are considered a part of the story. Only British Columbia's legislation makes no reference to the right of reply. As well, British Columbia and Ontario statutes do not make reference to headlines or captions. But the common law clearly states that the headline is part of the story.[54]

---

53 *Nowlan v. Moncton Publishing Co.*, [1952] 4 D.L.R. 808 at 812 (N.B. C.A.). In *Geary v. Alger*, [1925] 4 D.L.R. 1005 (Ont. C.A.), the defence was lost because the journalist added to his report the name of a person who the Crown had not expressly identified in open court. In *Mitchell v. Times Printing and Publishing Co. (No. 2)*, [1944] 1 W.W.R. 400 (B.C. S.C.), the court stated that adding extra comment which imputes guilt will destroy the defence of absolute privilege. The report in question said that a "long-sought killer" had "finally been caught." The accused was later found not guilty. But the court in *Wesolowski v. Armadale Publishers Ltd.* (1980), 3 Sask. R. 330 (Q.B.), said if a journalist correctly describes the situation in court without malice, despite an error in describing the charge, the report is still fair and accurate. In this case, a person was named in the indictment with the accused, but was not charged. The court said the newspaper's reference to the person as "an unindicted co-conspirator" was fair and accurate because it adequately described that part of the judicial proceedings.

54 *Bennett v. Sun Publishing Co.* (1972), 29 D.L.R. (3d) 423 at 436 (B.C. S.C.). Also see *Tedlie v. Southam Co.*, [1950] 4 D.L.R. 415 (Man. Q.B.), where a headline wrongly suggested that negligence in the operation of a train had caused deaths.

The Defence of Qualified Privilege

As noted, the defence of absolute privilege is necessary to allow certain public representatives to speak freely on important matters in the public interest even if there is an underlying malicious motive. The courts have also recognized there may be important occasions in which general members of the public will have a duty to publish statements that could turn out to be defamatory or even untrue.

Thus evolved the defence of qualified privilege, which can be used to defend statements published in the public interest while carrying out a recognized duty, protecting an important interest or reporting on public proceedings.[55] One of the major differences between this defence and absolute privilege is that there must be an absence of malice in the publication of the defamatory statements.

It is important to state at this point, as mentioned at the start of this chapter, that the defence of qualified privilege has undergone a significant change in Canada recently. In 2007, Ontario's Court of Appeal accepted a new defence of "public interest responsible journalism," which may protect journalists who publish properly researched stories on matters "the public has a legitimate interest in hearing" and that journalists have "every reason to believe" are true and meet the standards of responsible journalism. The Ontario ruling and the U.K. decisions that inspired it are discussed in full below. The lines of thinking in these decisions are destined to have a significant impact on journalism in Canada for years to come.

The Statutory Defence

Journalists regularly take advantage of this privilege when publishing extracts of government proceedings and accounts of public meetings, public hearings or other matters of public interest or concern. In some provinces, the legislation also includes private societies, clubs and agencies in the list of bodies offering opportunities of qualified privilege.

As will be seen, this is a complex defence and the statutes do not try to spell out all occasions of qualified privilege. In fact, all the statutes expressly state that any privilege existing by law is not limited or abridged by the legislation, thereby allowing the common law cases to supplement the statutes.

---

55 The principle of qualified privilege was first stated in the English case of *Toogood v. Spyring* (1834), 1 Cr. M. & R. 181, where the court said, "If fairly warranted by any reasonable occasion or exigency, and honestly made, such communications are protected for the common convenience and welfare of society; and the law has not restricted the right to make them within any narrow limits."

All provinces and territories offer a qualified privilege in their defamation legislation for reports of government and other public proceedings. This is representative of the provision in most Acts:

A fair and accurate report, published in a newspaper or by broadcasting of a public meeting or, except where neither the public nor any reporter is admitted, of proceedings in

(a) the Senate or House of Commons of Canada;
(b) the Legislative Assembly of any province;
(c) a committee of any of such bodies;
(d) a meeting of commissioners authorized to act by or pursuant to statute or under lawful warrant or authority; or
(e) any meeting of
   (i)   a municipal council;
   (ii) a school board;
   (iii) a board of education;
   (iv) a board of health; or
   (v)   any other board or local authority formed or constituted under any public Act of the Parliament of Canada or the Legislature of any province, or a committee appointed by any such board or local authority;

is privileged, unless it is proven that the publication was made maliciously.

Notice that the report must be "fair and accurate." This means it must be balanced, but it does not have to be verbatim. The report must be substantially correct and carry the same meaning as a word-for-word account.

The legislation also provides for claims of qualified privilege for reports of public meetings. But, not all public gatherings or meetings will be occasions to claim a qualified privilege under the statute. A "public meeting" is defined elsewhere in the legislation as "a meeting bona fide and lawfully held for a lawful purpose and for the furtherance or discussion of any matter of public concern, whether admission is general or restricted." A closed door meeting is not a public meeting according to the statutory defence which states that it will not apply where "neither the public nor any reporter is admitted." A public meeting has been further defined by the courts as one that has some element of public control[56] — it does not include a lecture, a church sermon or a partisan political rally.

---

56 *Hefferman v. Regina Daily Star*, [1930] 3 W.W.R. 656 (Sask. K.B.). The court also stated the statutory privilege extends only to reports of matters relevant to the discussion at the public meeting. Therefore, a journalist should not publish a defamatory statement merely because it was made at a public meeting. In *Cardwell v. Hutchinson* (June 9, 1995), Doc. Vancouver C933901 (B.C. S.C.), a reporter's "fair and accurate" report of a municipal committee meeting was protected under qualified privilege.

A newspaper published a series on public housing revealing financial and other problems at one building. The articles questioned the business activities of the building owner's president. Some dissident tenants, many of whom spoke little English, asked reporters to attend a "news conference" that was not broadly advertised. After the meeting, the newspaper reported on tenant allegations that a certain building manager took gifts from tenants in return for favourable treatment. The building manager sued for defamation and the newspaper pleaded qualified privilege in reporting about a meeting held for the "furtherance of discussion of any matter of public concern." Was this a "public meeting" within the statute's meaning?

No. The court ruled the newspaper could not claim qualified privilege under the statute because the news conference was not an "organized forum in which public debate would take place." Instead, it was called for the purpose of expressing the views of one dissident group of tenants. That said, the court ruled the newspaper could use the common law defence of qualified privilege. The living conditions in the building were horrible and the article gave the elderly tenants a forum to speak out against the building management. The court found the newspaper had "a moral duty to report their allegations," honestly believed what they wrote, and did it without malice. The lawsuit was dismissed.[57]

The statutory defence will be lost if there is any evidence of malice underlying the publication of the defamatory statements. This will be discussed more fully below, but an example of such malice would be any sensationalized statements.

The legislation also provides for a qualified privilege for some public documents:

> The publication in a newspaper or by broadcasting, at the request of any government department, bureau, office or public officer, of any report, bulletin, or other document issued for the information of the public is privileged, unless it is proved that the publication was made maliciously.

For example, a B.C. case held that reports on documents obtained under freedom of information laws are privileged since they are public documents.[58] Ontario extends a statutory qualified privilege to reports of publicity releases arising out of public meetings.

---

57 *Silva v. Toronto Star Newspapers Ltd.* (1998), 167 D.L.R. (4th) 554 (Ont. Gen. Div.).
58 *Fletcher-Gordon v. Southam Inc.* (1997), 143 D.L.R. (4th) 560 (B.C. S.C.).

The statutory privilege in most provinces is accompanied by three requirements. The first stresses that some matters should never be published under the guise of a privilege:

> No privilege will apply in any of the above situations if there is publication of seditious, blasphemous or indecent matter.

Another important requirement is that the defamed party must be allowed to present his or her side of the story in order for a journalist or news organization to rely on the statutory defence:

> No privilege will apply where the plaintiff shows that the newspaper or broadcasting outlet refused to publish a reasonable statement of explanation or contradiction.

Also, for the statutory defence to succeed, the defamatory statement must involve the element of public interest:

> No privilege will apply where the publication is not of public concern or for public benefit.

At least two provinces have added further explanation to what kinds of occasions offer a qualified privilege. The legislation in Ontario and Nova Scotia expressly extends a qualified privilege to reports of the findings or decisions relating to a person who is a member of, or subject to the control of, certain associations. The legislation includes the following associations:

(i)   Those formed for the purpose of promoting or encouraging interest in art, science, religion or learning, or

(ii) formed for the purpose of promoting or safeguarding the interests of trade, business, industry or professions, or

(iii) formed for the purpose of safeguarding the interests of any game, sport or pastime to the playing or exercising of which members of the public are invited or admitted.

For a short time in 2001, residents of British Columbia had a new statutory defence in qualified privilege available in cases where "strategic" lawsuits had been launched to silence public debate or opposition.[59] The Protection of Public Participation Act was enacted in mid-2001 to combat a growing trend in non-meritorious civil lawsuits against individuals, community groups, public interest groups, and even government officials ex-

---

59 S.B.C. 2001, c. 19. Repealed by S.B.C. 2001, c. 32, s. 28, effective August 16, 2001 (R.A.).

ercising their free speech and protesting on issues of public concern. The lawsuits are known as SLAPPs (Strategic Lawsuits Against Public Participation) and frequently arise in environmental or real estate development disputes. SLAPP plaintiffs frequently launch actions claiming defamation, inducement to breach contract, conspiracy and interference with economic relations.

The lawsuits can be very effective in stopping citizens from writing letters to newspapers or government, circulating petitions, making submissions to government, organizing meetings or boycotts, picketing, or making comments to the news media. The law was designed to ensure early identification and dismissal of SLAPPs, reduce the economic burden of defending them, and create penalties for SLAPPs.

The B.C. Act defined public participation as "communication or conduct aimed at influencing public opinion, or promoting or furthering lawful action by the public or by any government body, in relation to an issue of public interest." Some activities were exempt, such as breaches of the Human Rights Code, damage to or destruction of property and any other typical unlawful behaviour. Section 3 declared that any public participation "constitutes an occasion of qualified privilege" and "is deemed to be of interest to all persons who, directly or indirectly" receive the communication or witness the conduct. A first of its kind in Canada, the SLAPP law was repealed by a new provincial government within mere months of its enactment.

The Common Law Defence

The common law has identified several other occasions in which a qualified privilege can be claimed. Keep in mind that the recent Ontario decision on the "public interest responsible journalism" defence may create special common law exemptions for journalists now. This will be discussed in full below.

Essentially, in most circumstances where the common law is relied upon, the courts look to see if the defamatory communication between the maker of the statement and those receiving it is important and necessary. For this reason and others outlined below, the news media, which publish statements to the world at large, rarely had occasion in the past, other than those listed in the legislation, to claim a common law qualified privilege. As noted above, that has now changed.

That said, there are several requirements to the common law defence:

1.   the defamatory statement must be fair and accurate;

2. the defamatory statement must involve an important matter of public interest;

3. there must be a legal, social or moral duty to publish the defamatory information and any person receiving the information must have a valid interest in receiving it; and

4. there must be no actual malice in publishing the statement or knowledge that the statement is untrue.[60]

The defamatory statement must involve an important matter of public interest. The fact that a statement would be "interesting" to other members of the public is not good enough to prove that the matter is one of "public interest." There must be "valid, social reasons" to report the statement.[61] It is irrelevant that the journalist thinks it is a matter of public interest.[62] The "reasonable person," represented by the jury or the judge, must feel it is of important general or public interest.[63] Some examples of matters of public interest are: state matters, the public conduct of those involved in public affairs, legal matters, church matters and literary and artistic works. And even if you do prove that the statement did concern a matter of public interest, it will not be enough to sustain this defence.[64]

The crucial element to the common law defence of qualified privilege in most cases relying on the common law is this next requirement, which can be the most complex and difficult element to prove. The person making or publishing the defamatory statement must have a legal, social or moral

---

60 There are rare instances in which someone may be protected by qualified privilege even though the statement is known to be false. *Gatley on Libel and Slander*, 8th ed. (London: Sweet & Maxwell, 1981), at 333, states the privilege will exist when someone has a legal, moral or social duty to report another person's statement even if he does not believe it. The English case of *Horrocks v. Lowe* (1974), [1975] A.C. 135 at 150 (H.L.), stated that sometimes there may be a duty to pass on a defamatory statement without endorsement. An example is given by *Gatley*, at 242, where an accountant may be bound to report that evidence surrounding a suspected theft leads to one employee, even though the accountant does not believe the employee did it.

61 As stated in *Littleton v. Hamilton* (1974), 4 O.R. (2d) 283 at 285 (C.A.).

62 *Hare v. Better Business Bureau of Vancouver*, [1946] 2 W.W.R. 630 at 633 (B.C. S.C.).

63 *Halls v. Mitchell*, [1928] S.C.R. 125 at 133.

64 In *Brown v. Elder* (1888), 27 N.B.R. 465 (C.A.), the court said the mere fact a matter is of public interest is not enough. There must be an "exceptional" duty imposed upon someone to publish the statement. Also see *Parks v. C.A.I.M.A.W.* (1981), 122 D.L.R. (3d) 366 (B.C. S.C.), where the court found defamatory remarks broadcast over the radio about a lawyer were not of interest to the public generally and not protected by a qualified privilege. The remarks stemmed from a dispute between the lawyer and a union leader who made the comment. Both of these cases are likely to hold less weight today in light of the *Cusson*, note 70, cited below (leave to appeal to the Supreme Court of Canada granted for *Cusson* on April 3, 2008 (2008 CanLII 18972 (S.C.C.))).

duty to convey the information and any other person hearing or reading it must have a reciprocal duty or interest to receive the information.[65] The duty must be clear and it is irrelevant that a person simply believes there is a duty to convey or receive defamatory information.[66]

The New "Public Interest Responsible Journalism" Defence

Since the cornerstone of qualified privilege is that the maker of the statement has a duty to publish it and the receiver of the statement has a legitimate interest in hearing it, the common law privilege will typically be lost if the information is published to anyone who does not have an interest in receiving it.[67]

Until recently, it was this element of the common law defence that most often defeated the use of it by the news media. The Supreme Court of Canada itself even said in 1960 that the news media will rarely be in a position of qualified privilege when publishing to the general public.[68] The Supreme Court said then the *duty* to report on a matter of public concern must not be confused with the *right* to comment fairly on issues. In other words, the defence of qualified privilege must not be confused with the defence of fair comment. The duty must be one that would be recognized by the "reasonable man."[69]

---

65 See, for example, *Planned Parenthood Nfld./Labrador v. Fedorik* (1982), 135 D.L.R. (3d) 714 at 721 (Nfld. T.D.), where the court found there was no social or moral duty for the defendant to allege through a radio interview that the plaintiff's sex education program was responsible for an increase in teenage abortions and illegitimate births.

66 As stated in *Wing Lee v. Jones*, [1954] 1 D.L.R. 520 at 528 (Man. Q.B.). In *Arnott v. College of Physicians and Surgeons of Sask.*, [1954] S.C.R. 538 at 541, the Supreme Court of Canada said the duty must be recognized by "people of ordinary intelligence and moral principles." In *Bennett v. Stupich* (1981), 30 B.C.L.R. 57 (S.C.), the court found there was no public duty on the part of a columnist to suggest that the Premier of the province was drunk in the legislature.

67 In *Jones v. Bennett* (1968), [1969] S.C.R. 277, a politician was defending himself at a party meeting and issued some defamatory remarks. The Supreme Court of Canada said at 284 that the occasion of qualified privilege was lost by the politician because he knew the news media was present and whatever he said would be published to the general public.

68 As stated in *Globe and Mail Ltd. v. Boland*, [1960] S.C.R. 203.

69 *Ibid.*, at 207. In *Littleton v. Hamilton* (1974), 4 O.R. (2d) 283 (C.A.), the court dealt with a book that made defamatory statements in connection with the history of an organization which was established with public funds and had received substantial publicity. Though the topic was one of public interest, the court found there was no "special duty" of the author to tell all Canadians the defamatory statements. More recently, the difference between qualified privilege and fair comment defences was explored in *B.S.O.I.W., Local 97 v. Campbell* (1997), 152 D.L.R. (4th) 547 (B.C. S.C.). A defamatory news release was issued to the legislative press gallery. In it, the Opposition party suggested the government

That has changed now with the Ontario Court of Appeal's 2007 decision in *Cusson v. Quan*.[70] In this case, an Ontario Provincial Police (OPP) constable, on his own initiative, went to New York City to help with the search and rescue operations immediately after the September 11, 2001 attack on the World Trade Center. The OPP, however, quickly recalled the constable to his duties in Ottawa amid much controversy. Most news stories portrayed him as a hero, but the *Ottawa Citizen*, among others, published articles questioning whether the officer had misrepresented himself to the New York police by allegedly posing as a member of the RCMP, and suggesting he may even have compromised rescue operations at Ground Zero. Among the sources in the story was a senior OPP officer.

At trial, the newspaper attempted to prove the truth of some statements, relied on the fair comment defence for others, and argued the articles were published on occasions of qualified privilege — that is, the articles were matters of public interest and there was a public duty to publish the information. Unless the defendants were guilty of some malice, argued the newspaper, the privilege should protect it from any liability.

While the trial judge agreed the articles were of public interest, there was no "compelling, moral or social duty" to publish them and they did not attract the defence of qualified privilege. While some of the other defences succeeded and there was no evidence of malice, the jury found some statements were defamatory and awarded the plaintiff $120,000 in general damages.

On appeal, the basic issue before the Ontario Court of Appeal was among the most commonly disputed questions at the intersection of defamation law and journalism — where to strike the balance between protecting a person's reputation, and respecting the media's right to freedom of expression? Unless the news media acts maliciously or is knowingly or reck-

---

was involved in a kickback scheme with trade unions. A columnist based a commentary on the press release and a union sued both the news organization and the political party for defamation. The court held that the party could take refuge in the defence of qualified privilege, since the Opposition has a duty to expose government impropriety and the electorate has a corresponding interest in receiving that information. There was no evidence of malice against the trade union itself. The fact the Opposition wanted to unseat the government was also not evidence of malice. The columnist, however, was not entitled to rely on qualified privilege but rather fair comment. The qualified privilege defence failed here, said the court, because the column "went well beyond a recital of the facts in the press release." The fair comment defence was successful, though, because the column was identified as commentary, it was of public interest, and the column was an honest representation of the columnist's views. Each of these cases is likely to hold less weight today in light of *Cusson*, note 70, below. Leave to appeal to the Supreme Court of Canada granted on April 3, 2008 (2008 CanLII 18972 (S.C.C.)).

70 2007 ONCA 771 (CanLII). Leave to appeal to the Supreme Court of Canada granted on April 3, 2008 (2008 CanLII 18972 (S.C.C.)).

lessly misstating the facts, asked the appeal court, should journalists be allowed to rely on a defence of qualified privilege when reporting on all matters of public interest?

Guiding the Ontario appeal court's hand, to some degree, were two recent decisions of the English courts[71] and other foreign jurisdictions that protected a news media defendant that proved it followed standards of "responsible journalism" when it reported on a matter of public importance. The appeal court was urged to adopt this broader defence of qualified privilege for reports on matters of public interest — so-called "public interest responsible journalism." Not only does our Charter of Rights support this, it was argued, courts in the United Kingdom, Australia, New Zealand, South Africa, and the United States have all ruled "the traditional law of defamation unjustifiably limits freedom of expression and freedom of the media."

For more than half a century, Canadian courts have treated the news media the same as any other defendant and have generally ruled that qualified privilege does not apply to statements published to the world at large. As the Ontario appeal court put it, "should the law of qualified privilege remain frozen in its 1950s, 60s and 70s state, or should it evolve to afford the media greater latitude when reporting on matters of public interest?"

Fortunately for journalism, Ontario's highest court seized the opportunity to bring the Canadian law of defamation into the 21st century. As the appeal court noted, the law of defamation was originally designed to have a "chilling effect" on free expression such that individuals would take care in making statements affecting another's reputation. The problem, stated the court, is that defamation law sets a very high standard for the news media.

"There is a very real difference between what a speaker honestly and reasonably believes to be true and what can be proved to be true in a court of law," the court stated, adding: "The threat of litigation under a legal regime that leaves no margin for error, even where the speaker took all reasonable steps to verify the facts, discourages free and open debate on matters of public importance."

As a result, the Ontario court believed it was time to adopt a made-in-Canada form of the "public interest responsible journalism" defence similar to that found in other common law countries. The U.K.-based *Reynolds-Jameel* defence, noted the court, "rests upon the broad principle that where a media defendant can show that it acted in accordance with the standards of responsible journalism in publishing a story that the public was entitled to hear, it has a defence even if it got some of its facts wrong."

---

71 See *Reynolds v. Times Newspapers Ltd.*, [2001] 2 A.C. 127 and *Jameel v. Wall Street Journal Europe Sprl*, [2007] 1 A.C. 359 (Eng. H.L.).

The standard for "responsible journalism" would have to be "objective and legal," as determined by a court and not journalists. To use the defence, the court stated that the news media must show *it took reasonable steps in the circumstances to ensure that the story was fair and its contents were true and accurate."* The court also favoured a list of 10 factors for determining standards of responsible journalism that the English courts considered non-exhaustive but instructive:

1. The seriousness of the allegation. The more serious the charge, the more the public is misinformed and the individual harmed, if the allegation is not true.
2. The nature of the information, and the extent to which the subject-matter is a matter of public concern.
3. The source of the information. Some informants have no direct knowledge of the events. Some have their own axes to grind, or are being paid for their stories.
4. The steps taken to verify the information.
5. The status of the information. The allegation may have already been the subject of an investigation which commands respect.
6. The urgency of the matter. News is often a perishable commodity.
7. Whether comment was sought from the plaintiff. He may have information others do not possess or have not disclosed. An approach to the plaintiff will not always be necessary.
8. Whether the article contained the gist of the plaintiff's side of the story.
9. The tone of the article. A newspaper can raise queries or call for an investigation. It need not adopt allegations as statements of fact.
10. The circumstances of the publication, including the timing.

The end result of this approach for future defamation cases involving the news media, particularly those pleading the defence of qualified privilege, is that Ontario courts will now be required to shift their focus away from deciding whether there is truth or some other defence available to whether the conduct of the media defendant met the standards for responsible journalism. In the view of Ontario's appeal court, "this is an acceptable price to pay for free and open discussion."

While courts in other provinces do not have to follow the Ontario appeal court ruling, judges in other provinces will, at the very least, find the ruling compelling. Indeed, the Ontario appeal court openly suggested that Canadian courts should not adopt the *Reynolds-Jameel* defence in a "slavish or literal fashion," but interpret it in a fashion that "best reflects Canada's legal values and culture."

Ironically, it should be noted, the media defendants in this case were not allowed to take advantage of the new defence because an expanded view of qualified privilege based on the emerging English law was not argued at trial. As a result, the Ontario Court of Appeal dismissed the appeal in favour of the plaintiff.

The two English cases that influenced the Ontario Court of Appeal in the 2007 *Cusson* case are likely to have a long-term impact on Canada's defamation law.

Reynolds v. Times Newspapers Ltd.

In *Reynolds*, the former Prime Minister of the Irish Republic had sued *The Sunday Times* for libel after an article suggested he had deliberately misled his Parliament and cabinet. At trial, the jury found the allegations defamatory, but awarded the plaintiff "zero damages," which the judge increased to one pence. When the case reached the House of Lords, Britain's top court affirmed the lower court decision but also ruled a new form of qualified privilege should be available to the news media that follows the standards of responsible journalism when reporting on a matter of public interest.

In the lead ruling, the House of Lords stated "people must be able to speak and write freely, uninhibited by the prospect of being sued for damages should they be mistaken or misinformed. In the wider public interest, protection of reputation must then give way to a higher priority."

This includes publication to the world-at-large because, without freedom of expression by the media, "freedom of expression would be a hollow concept." The defence can still be defeated by evidence of malice, but the top court realized the news media needed a "flexible and malleable standard of responsible journalism."

In addition to setting out the 10 factors that a court might consider, the lead judgment noted: "The court should be slow to conclude that a publication was not in the public interest, and, therefore, the public had no right to know, especially when the information is in the field of political discussion. Any lingering doubts should be resolved in favour of publication."

Jameel v. Wall Street Journal Europe Sprl

In 2002, *The Wall Street Journal Europe* published an article that asserted, at the request of U.S. law enforcement agencies, that the Saudi Arabian Monetary Authority was monitoring bank accounts of prominent businessmen to ensure they would not be used to transmit funds to terrorist organizations. The article listed companies and individuals, including Jameel, and stated they could not be reached for comment on the allegations.

The article was found to be defamatory at trial. The Court of Appeal agreed the trial judge was right to deny a *Reynolds* privilege since the newspaper had not waited long enough before running its story without comment.

The House of Lords disagreed with the trial judge and Court of Appeal. Their view of the *Reynolds* defence was too restrictive. The House of Lords declared that a publisher need not establish it acted as a responsible journalist in relation to each defamatory statement if it can establish that it acted responsibly in relation to the story as a whole – that "the thrust of the article is true, and the public interest condition is satisfied."

The House of Lords also stated that "in matters of public interest, there can be said to be a professional duty on the part of journalists to impart the information and an interest in the public in receiving it." If the article as a whole is in the public interest, the focus of a court must shift to determining if the defamatory statements were "part of the story." The courts, it said, must respect "editorial judgment" in determining public interest.

While the *Cusson* case is very significant, Canadian courts have shown in the past that they were ready for this approach. There have been rare occasions in which the law has recognized a right of the press to report defamatory matter and claim the defence of qualified privilege. It appears that this usually only happens when someone has a duty to make the comment through the news media and the subject-matter is of important public interest. One of the most prominent examples of this involved defamatory statements made by a federal minister outside Parliament. The minister claimed in the House that a particular senior civil servant was grossly negligent and had misled him and then when the minister was outside the proceedings, he repeated the same allegations to the waiting press. The Ontario Court of Appeal held that this was an occasion of qualified privilege because the public has a real and *bona fide* interest in the issue and the person making the statement has a corresponding public duty or interest to make the statement. The court said the public had an interest in knowing whether the comments in the House were justified and the minister had a duty to "satisfy that interest" as long as the comment was made without malice.[72] Other than in reporting remarks of other people, this exception to

---

72 See *Stopforth v. Goyer* (1978), 20 O.R. (2d) 262 at 271 (H.C.). In *Mallett v. Clarke* (1968),

the general rule does not seem to apply to comments by journalists themselves.

The Dangers of Malice

The issue of malice continues to be important in this defence and laced with potential pitfalls for reporters. The fact that a qualified privilege exists does not allow a reporter to knowingly publish false and defamatory statements.[73] If the publication is out of spite, ill will, to sensationalize or gain audience ratings at the risk of injuring someone, the court will find there was malice. The courts have even found malice where the reporter used stronger language than the circumstances warranted.[74] The plaintiff must be able to prove there was malice and offer actual proof of it.[75]

As stated before, this is sometimes a confusing and complicated defence. In *Cusson*, the Ontario appeal court showed it was willing to accept that the guarantee of freedom of the press in the Canadian Charter of Rights and Freedoms[76] should loosen the restrictions in this defence and allow journalists to claim qualified privilege on more occasions. Courts, however, have so far rejected the idea that present defamation laws violate the

---

70 D.L.R. (2d) 67 at 72 (B.C. S.C.), the principal of a hairdressing school made some defamatory remarks about the plaintiff in the media after the plaintiff made some serious allegations about the school. The court found the principal was under a "duty" to respond in the media to the allegations because the school's reputation had been called into question. In the case of *McGugan v. Davidson* (1984), 58 N.B.R. (2d) 103 (Q.B.), a trial court held that a qualified privilege applied to defamatory remarks made by a union leader on television. The court accepted the argument that during a strike, as was the case here, the union could only communicate with its province-wide membership through the media and the remarks were thus made to a group which had a rightful "interest" in receiving the comment. The remarks were in response to an unjustified attack on the union.

73 In *Hefferman v. Regina Daily Star*, [1930] 3 W.W.R. 656 at 665 (Sask. K.B.), the court held that simply because a false and defamatory statement was made at a public meeting it was not automatically privileged. In *Vogel v. Canadian Broadcasting Corp.*, [1982] 3 W.W.R. 97 (B.C. S.C.), the court said a lack of belief in a defamatory statement can be proof of malice.

74 *Burnett v. Canadian Broadcasting Corp. (No. 2)* (1981), 48 N.S.R. (2d) 181 at 223 (T.D.). Other examples of proof of malice are failing to check the accuracy of information (*Robinson v. Dun* (1897), 24 O.A.R. 287), careless exaggeration of information (*Brown v. McCurdy* (1888), 21 N.S.R. 201 (S.C.)) and omission of key information (*Color Your World Corp. v. Canadian Broadcasting Corp.* (1994), 17 O.R. (3d) 308 (Gen. Div.)).

75 In *Silbernagel v. Empire Stevedoring Co.* (1979), 18 B.C.L.R. 384 (S.C.), the court said there must be more than a "mere possibility" of malice and if there is not enough proof of malice the benefit of the doubt must go to the defendant.

76 Part I of the Constitution Act, 1982, being Schedule B of the Canada Act 1982 (U.K.), 1982, c. 11 (hereinafter, Charter).

Charter's guarantees, particularly when public officials are involved.[77] In fact, in 1995, the Supreme Court of Canada affirmed an Ontario Court of Appeal ruling that public officials are entitled to the same protection against defamation as other citizens and rejected the idea that a public official should have to prove there was malice before collecting damages, as in the U.S.[78]

---

77 Interestingly, at least one public official has tried to argue that the common law on qualified privilege restricts his freedom of expression. In *Goddard v. Day* (2000), 194 D.L.R. (4th) 559 (Alta. Q.B.), an Alberta provincial politician published a letter in a newspaper criticizing a lawyer, who was also a school trustee, for challenging the constitutionality of the criminal offence of possession of child pornography. In the ensuing defamation action, Stockwell Day raised several defences, including that qualified privilege applied to political comments made in the absence of malice, that the common law of defamation was inconsistent with his Charter rights, and was also inconsistent with the Alberta Bill of Rights, which protects the right of freedom of speech. The court refused to create a new category of qualified privilege based on political discussion. "Such a defence did not exist in Canada, and should not be created. To do otherwise would allow individuals who had attained public office to be subjected to defamatory and false remarks, which would constitute an undue discouragement to those seeking political office," noted the judge. As for the Charter and Alberta Bill of Rights, the court noted this lawsuit involved purely private litigation, not government action. "The common law of defamation did not infringe an individual's right to free speech. Freedom of speech was not an unfettered right, and could not be interpreted in a manner that departed from the recognition of a free and democratic society."

78 *Hill v. Church of Scientology of Toronto*, [1995] 2 S.C.R. 1130, affirming (1994), 114 D.L.R. (4th) 1 (Ont. C.A.). In this case, the courts awarded $1.6 million to the plaintiff, a Crown Attorney who was defamed during a news conference by a lawyer acting for the Church. The defendants argued that the court should require public officials to prove knowledge of falsehood or a reckless disregard for the truth. The Court of Appeal said the defendants failed to raise enough evidence to establish a constitutional challenge of defamation laws and said the protection of the reputation of public officials is of "paramount importance."

In Doody, "Freedom of the Press, The Canadian Charter of Rights and Freedoms and a New Category of Qualified Privilege," (1983), 61 Can. Bar Rev., at 124-150, the author argues that the guarantee of freedom of the press gives courts the opportunity to broaden the defence of qualified privilege to allow more criticism of public officials. In the U.S., the landmark American case of *New York Times Co. v. Sullivan*, 376 U.S. 254 (1964) allowed unlimited criticism of a public official except where there is proof of malice, such as a reckless disregard for the truth.

The author notes that subsequent American decisions have toned down the effect of this case by narrowly defining what is a "public official." As it now stands, a public official in the U.S. is someone who has the opportunity to counter the views expressed in the press and is in a legitimate public controversy, not just someone who is a topic of public interest. American law has also created the "limited purpose" public official who represents a particular cause or issue, but is not constantly in the public eye.

The Defence of Fair Comment

Journalism not only involves the reporting of the news, but also the interpretation and analysis of the news. Journalists also express their own opinions in stories or repeat someone else's opinion. On occasion, these opinions and interpretations may be severely critical of other individuals and, in keeping with the definition of defamation, can be defamatory. The defence of fair comment is specifically designed to allow people to express their own opinions on important public matters even if the opinion is technically defamatory.

In 2008, the Supreme Court of Canada revisited the defence of fair comment and modified the common law defence in favour of the news media and others expressing opinions.

The Common Law Defence

In the common law, there are several elements to the defence:

1. the comment must be on a matter of public interest;
2. the comment must be a based on fact;
3. the comment, though it can include inferences of fact, must be recognizable as comment;
4. the comment must satisfy the objective test: could any one honestly express that opinion on the proved facts?; and
5. there must be no actual or express malice underlying the comment.

The first important factor is that the subject-matter of the comment be of public interest. It should be a genuine interest and not just mere gossip.[79] It does not appear though, that the courts call for as stringent a test for the public interest requirement in fair comment, as they do in the defence of qualified privilege. It is irrelevant that the author of the statement felt it was a matter of public interest. It will be up to the judge or jury as representatives of the "reasonable person" to determine whether it was an important matter of public interest.[80]

It must be obvious to the reader, viewer or listener that the defamatory statement is simply an opinion. It is not even necessary for the opinion to be one that everyone would hold. Although the defence is called "fair comment," the courts have held that the opinion does not really have to be

---

79 *Cook v. Alexander*, [1973] 3 All E.R. 1037 (C.A.).
80 *England v. Canadian Broadcasting Corp.*, [1979] 3 W.W.R. 193 at 214 (N.W.T. S.C.).

"fair" as most people understand the word (for example, reasonable or moderate). It does not even have to be a sensible perspective on the facts.[81]

It is also essential that the defamatory comment must be seen to be an opinion someone could honestly hold based on the provable facts, and that the opinion itself must not appear to be an assertion or statement of known fact.[82] For example, in one case it was reported an expert witness testifying at a trial was being paid $1000 a day plus expenses. The journalist then commented that the witness is an example of an expert hired to give favourable testimony for his client. That was an "opinion" which was not based on any of the stated facts in the story. Moreover, to the average person, it would have been considered a statement of fact instead of opinion or inference.[83]

The Test

The "cardinal test" for succeeding in this defence is whether one could honestly believe, express or hold such an opinion, and whether it could be drawn from the known facts.[84] In 2008, the Supreme Court of Canada upheld this test and adjusted it in favour of the news media or anyone else expressing

---

81   In *Vander Zalm v. Times Publishers*, [1980] 4 W.W.R. 259 (B.C. C.A.), a political cartoon showed the plaintiff pulling the wings off a fly in apparent glee. The court said at 265 it was fair comment so long as the author has an honest belief in what he says and it is unnecessary for the comment to be a reasonable perspective on the facts. The court said the opinion may even be exaggerated or prejudiced, as long as it is an honest view that could be held by someone. In *Pearlman v. Canadian Broadcasting Corp.* (1981), 13 Man. R. (2d) 1 (Q.B.), the plaintiff was referred to as a "slum landlord" with "no morals, principles or conscience." Based on the facts as stated in the story, the court said at p. 8, it was a fair comment made without malice. And in *Gouzenko v. Harris*, note 24 above, the court held that the words "traitor" and "defector," used to describe a Soviet turncoat, were fair and true descriptions of the plaintiff. Recently, the New Brunswick Court of Appeal reaffirmed the law as it applies to political cartoons. In *Beutel v. Ross* (2001), 201 D.L.R. (4th) 75 (N.B. C.A.), the appeal court overturned a trial judgment awarding damages to an anti-Semite teacher, Malcolm Ross, after a cartoon compared him to Joseph Goebbels, Hitler's propaganda minister. The appeal judges said "cartoons are not to be literally construed but are to be considered as rhetorically making a point by symbolism, allegory, satire and exaggeration." Since the opinion expressed was an honest belief of the cartoonist based on provable facts, he could rely on the defence of fair comment and did not have to prove Ross was a Nazi or actually advocated extermination of Jews.

82   *Sheppard*, note 29, above, at 466.

83   *Barltrop v. Canadian Broadcasting Corp.* (1978), 86 D.L.R. (3d) 61 (N.S. C.A.).

84   *Chernesky v. Armadale Publishers and King*, [1978] 6 W.W.R. 618 (S.C.C.). In England, see *Slim v. Daily Telegraph Ltd.*, [1968] 1 All E.R. 497 at 503 (C.A.). More recently, see *Sara's Pyrohy Hut v. Brooker* (1991), 83 Alta. L.R. (2d) 131 (Q.B.), affirmed (1993), 8 Alta. L.R. (3d) 113 (C.A.). In this case, a restaurant reviewer for a radio station described a meal as bland, overpriced and inferior. The court dismissed the action, stating that while

opinions. Previously, Canadian case law had required that the author must honestly believe his or her opinion. If the commentator did not believe what was said, courts would not permit the defence. The Supreme Court decided unanimously (9-0) to modify the "honest belief" element such that a comment must only satisfy this new objective test: Could any person honestly express that opinion on the proved facts?

In this case, *Simpson* v. *Mair*,[85] the well-known Vancouver radio talk show host Rafe Mair criticized Simpson, who publicly opposed hiring homosexuals as teachers. In Mair's commentary, he suggested Simpson was a bigot and compared the family rights activist to Hitler, among others. Simpson sued, alleging Mair's comments implied the plaintiff condoned violence against homosexuals. Even though Simpson's public speeches often made reference to a "war" being fought over gay rights and "militant homosexuals," Mair said he did not personally believe she condoned violence. The trial judge, sitting alone, agreed with Simpson's interpretation that the commentary suggested she condoned violence, but held Mair was still entitled to the defence of fair comment, even though his comments exaggerated his own personal beliefs. On appeal, the B.C. high court disallowed the fair comment defence, in large part because of Mair's testimony that, while he thought Simpson was a bigot, he didn't personally believe she condoned violence, and the judge's finding as to how the comment might be interpreted by others (that, like Hitler, Simpson condoned violence).

The B.C. appeal court took the stance that, if a trier of fact (judge) rules a comment has a reasonable meaning to others that the defendant does not honestly believe or intend, then the defence of fair comment fails, regardless of the intent and honest belief of the speaker. If the B.C. decision had been allowed to stand unchallenged, this defence would have been seriously undermined since some plaintiffs would likely have done their utmost to twist unintended meanings out of fair comments, such as suggesting criminal or immoral behaviour was alleged.

The Supreme Court used this case as an opportunity to emphasize the importance of allowing unfettered commentary as a mode of free expression. Notably, the court stated that, while "this is a private law case that is not governed directly by the Canadian Charter of Rights and Freedoms, the evolution of the common law is to be informed and guided by Charter values. . . The traditional elements of the tort of defamation may require

---

the words were defamatory, the comments were the reviewer's own opinions on a matter of public interest and were not conveyed as statements of fact.

85 *Simpson v. Mair and WIC Radio Ltd.* (2006), 55 B.C.L.R. (4th) 30 (C.A.), recently overturned in the Supreme Court at *WIC Radio Ltd. and Rafe Mair v. Simpson*, 2008 SCC 40.

modification to provide broader accommodation to the value of freedom of expression."

Writing separately from the majority, one Supreme Court judge added that courts should not be "too quick to find defamatory meaning" in cases involving expressions of opinion. Justice Louis LeBel wrote that judges must be mindful of ensuring the plaintiff's reputation is "actually threatened by the impugned statements before turning to the available defences." He suggested that relevant factors to be considered in assessing whether a statement is defamatory include: whether the impugned speech is a statement of opinion rather than of fact; how much is publicly known about the plaintiff; the nature of the audience; and the context of the comment. In this case, LeBel said Mair's listeners were aware of his "well-known style, which involves strong opinions sometimes conveyed with colourful and provocative language," and his comments posed no realistic threat to Simpson's reputation. It will be interesting to see if lower courts, in the future, follow LeBel's advice of setting a high threshold for finding statements to be defamatory in matters involving expressions of opinion.

As noted above, the courts have long held that an opinion does not have to be "fair" or a reasonable perspective on the facts. That said, there are limits. The courts have traditionally held that a comment that accuses an individual of illegal, corrupt, criminal or morally reprehensible conduct is beyond the limits of fair comment.[86] For instance, it would not be a fair comment to say a politician is using his public office for private gain without specific evidence supporting the accusation and it would not matter that the commentator believed what he was saying.

This brings up an important point. The facts stated in the story must be true and provable. It is not enough to say that it is reasonable to believe the facts to be true or that everyone knows the story is true.[87] In court, a journalist using the defence of fair comment will have to prove that each of

---

86   The English case most commonly referred to is *Campbell v. Spottiswoode* (1863), 3 B & S 769. In Canada, see the 1993 case of *Mapes v. Hub Publications Ltd.*, [1993] N.W.T.R. 174 (S.C.) in which a cartoon suggested a well-known businessman had committed the crime of illegally operating a commercial fishing camp on Crown land. The cartoon showed the plaintiff holding a gun, standing over a cash register full of money and with a "donations" label near a sign declaring "The Non-Licensed, No-Name, Not-Really-Here, Fishing Camp." The court found the imputation untrue and defamatory. Cartoonists have also gotten into trouble by suggesting the crime of misuse of public office. In *Mitchell v. Nanaimo District Teachers' Assn.* (1994), 94 B.C.L.R. (2d) 81 (C.A.), the appeal court affirmed a trial ruling that the association had defamed a school principal in an advertisement's cartoon. It showed the principal sitting at a desk in an open field, along with text claiming the school board had hired a principal for a school that had yet to be built. The court found the cartoon suggested the principal was greedy and would willingly be on the public payroll doing nothing for a year.

87   *Man. Free Press Co. v. Martin* (1892), 21 S.C.R. 518 at 529.

the facts that formed the basis of the opinion is true. There is a special allowance made for comments based on information originating in a public forum that carries absolute privilege (such as Parliament). For example, if a Member of Parliament alleges that an industrial plant is polluting the atmosphere, it is only fair that journalists and other members of the public should be able to comment on the remark as well as report it. As a rule of public policy, "facts" raised in such public forums are deemed to be true for the purposes of comment.[88]

The Statutory Defence

Six provinces and both territories have enacted statutory versions of the fair comment defence. These statutory provisions may have to be amended in the future, in light of the 2008 Supreme Court decision. Ontario and Nova Scotia have legislated a general provision that saves a defendant from having to prove all the facts stated in a defamatory comment:[89]

> In an action for libel or slander for words consisting partly of allegations of fact and partly of expression of opinion, a defence of fair comment shall not fail by reason only that the truth of every allegation of fact is not proved if the expression of opinion is fair comment having regard to such of the facts alleged or referred to in the words complained of as are proved.

Ontario, Alberta, Manitoba, New Brunswick, Newfoundland and the two territories also have a special form of a fair comment defence, which was designed to protect newspapers publishing letters to the editor. However, the provision could be used to support fair comments by a journalist sometimes. For example, Manitoba has enacted this provision:[90]

> Where the defendant published alleged defamatory matter that is an opinion expressed by another person, a defence of fair comment shall not fail for the reason only that the defendant did not hold the opinion if
>
> (a) the defendant did not know that the person expressing the opinion did not hold the opinion; and
> (b) a person could honestly hold the opinion.

Alberta, Newfoundland and both territories have a provision similar to Manitoba's. In Alberta, the defence is only available to defendants (such

---

88 *Mangena v. Wright*, [1909] 2 K.B. 958 at 976-977.
89 Libel and Slander Act, R.S.O. 1990, c. L.12, s. 23; Defamation Act, R.S.N.S. 1989, c. 122, s. 10.
90 Defamation Act, R.S.M. 1987, c. D20, s. 9(1).

as journalists) if the opinion published is one of non-employees and non-agents of the publishing outlet.

There are some other distinctions in the other jurisdictions. In the territories, there is no obligation on the part of the defendant to inquire whether the person expressing the opinion holds that opinion. In New Brunswick, there is an additional requirement that the person expressing the opinion must be identified in the publication. In Ontario, the statutory defence is very broad. In that province, the statutory defence will not fail even if neither the publisher nor the author of the comment holds the opinion, as long as someone honestly could hold the opinion. This is generally in line with the 2008 Supreme Court decision.

The statutory fair comment provisions were originally in reaction to the Supreme Court of Canada's 1978 decision in *Chernesky v. Armadale Publications Ltd.*, which involved the publication of defamatory opinions in a letter to the editor in a newspaper.[91] The court ruled the defence of fair comment was not available to a newspaper or its editors because they did not hold the same opinion as the authors of the published letter nor did the newspaper know if the authors themselves honestly held the opinion expressed (the authors had left the province). At that time, the court said that what its decision meant was that a newspaper could not publish a defamatory letter or comment and then automatically claim the defence of fair comment without knowing if it is an honest opinion. The legislation enacted in the provinces now either requires the publisher to identify the author of an opinion or absolves the publisher of having to ask about the beliefs of the author. Again, however, these statutory defences will likely have to be amended now, in light of the 2008 Supreme Court decision in *WIC Radio*.

How to Avoid Losing this Defence

When writing a story that expresses an opinion, it is important to include all of the necessary facts. Every known background fact does not have to be stated, but enough facts must be published to support the opinion.[92] In addition, the way in which the facts are stated must be fair and they cannot be twisted or taken out of context. There must not be any large difference between the facts as stated and the known truth.[93]

---

91 [1978] 6 W.W.R. 618 (S.C.C.).
92 *Holt v. Sun Publishing Co.* (1979), 100 D.L.R. (3d) 447 at 450 (B.C. C.A.).
93 *Ibid.*

The Special Case of Québec

The Civil Law

A civil defamation lawsuit in Québec is subject to a substantially different system of law than that in the rest of Canada. Québec relies on its Civil Code, which was recently overhauled. The particular provision that is applicable to defamation is Article 1457:

> Every person has a duty to abide by the rules of conduct which lie upon him, according to the circumstances, usage or law, so as not to cause injury to another. Where he is endowed with reason and fails in this duty, he is responsible for any injury he causes to another person and is liable to reparation for the injury, whether it be bodily, moral or material in nature. He is also liable in certain cases, to reparation for injury caused to another by the act or fault of another person or by the act of things in his custody.

Among the few "exemptions" or defences is that "superior force" caused the injury through "an unforeseeable and irresistible event." The Code also contemplates situations where information may have to be published in the interests of public safety. The Code will not permit exemptions if there is evidence of "gross fault," recklessness, carelessness or negligence.

Québec law requires that the plaintiff prove three elements. Each element must be proven on the balance of probabilities.[94] The plaintiff must first prove there is *fault* on the part of the defendant.[95] The plaintiff must also prove that he has suffered damage[96] and there is a causal relationship between the fault of the defendant and the damage.[97]

The standard of care expected is that of the reasonable journalist (the generically-applied Civil Code standard of *bon pere de famille*) acting in

---

94 *Thibeault v. Porlier Transport*, [1971] C.A. 518.

95 The courts presume fault once the plaintiff proves the circumstances existed for it. It is unnecessary to prove the defendant intended his act or omission. Fault is defined as a mode of behaviour of a person, who is capable of realizing the nature and consequences of an act or omission, and does something contrary to law or fails to meet a standard of care set out by the courts. It can be proven with evidence of malice, imprudence, neglect or want of skill. See Nicholls, *Offences and Quasi-Offences in Québec* (Toronto: Carswell, 1938), at 22, 38-39.

96 *Ibid.*, at 39, where the author points out "damage" can even include hurt feelings or sensibilities. Also, in *Cass, April 26, 1810; Pandictes Francaises, vo. Diffamation; Injure No. 25*: "Anything which, with intention or malice, gives offence or affronts another is injurious."

97 Nicholls, note 95 above, at 21. Even if fault is proven, the plaintiff will not succeed unless he can prove the causal link between the fault and damage.

the same circumstances.[98] This is determined from an objective point of view and it does not matter that the journalist thought he was acting with the proper standard of care (if other journalists in the same circumstance would act differently).

Québec is the only province where publication of the defamation is unnecessary. Sometimes, the objectionable statements were made only to the plaintiff and no third parties.[99] Québec also allows living descendants to sue for defamations of their ancestors, where the defamation injures the descendant's reputation.[100]

In Québec, one of the most important issues in a defamation action is whether the publication of the words was in the public interest. The presence of public interest can serve as a complete defence provided there is no proof of malice.[101]

Even truth is not a complete defence. A failure to prove that the defamation was in the public interest, or that the publication's only purpose was to injure the person, can destroy the defence of justification.[102]

The defences of absolute and qualified privilege are not recognized in Québec[103] (except for statutory privileges set out below). While the privilege defences are somewhat different, the defence of fair comment is relatively unchanged in comparison.[104]

---

98 *Ibid.*

99 *Ibid.*, at 39.

100 In *Chiniquy v. Begin* (1915), 24 D.L.R. 687 (Qué. C.A.), a publication questioned the marriage of the plaintiff's parents. The court allowed an action by the daughter because the publication suggested she was illegitimate. The court said, at 693, the action allowed her to "vindicate" her parents' memory.

101 Nicholls, note 95 above, at 40, where the author suggests even a private affair of a public official can be published if it is indicative of public performance (citing *Belleau v. Mercier* (1882), 8 Q.L.R. 312 (S.C.) and other cases).

102 Nicholls, note 95 above, at 41. The defence of truth may be established if the defendant can prove there was reasonable and probable cause to believe in the truth and public interest of his statements. If a statement is not in the public interest, but is true, it may help reduce the damages. The courts have also adopted this rule stated in *Cass, April 26, 1810; Pandictes Francaises, vo. Diffamation; Injure No. 39*: "Any truth causing injury, made other than in the course of justice, is punishable even if it brings a crime to light which it would have been well to punish in the public interest."

103 Nicholls, note 95 above, at 38. For example, defamatory comments made during a judicial proceeding are actionable if the words are beyond the subject-matter of the proceedings. See note 45.

104 In *SRJ Consultants Inc. v. Fortin* (1982), 20 C.C.L.T. 221 (C.S. Qué.), the court said the defendant municipal councillor had a right to question and comment on the viability of a proposed ski hill development. The court said a statement is untrue when it is based on a lie and a lie is an assertion which is *knowingly* against the truth. This is similar to the common law requirements of honest opinion based on facts.

One case involving high damages illustrates the sharp differences in a defamation action under Québec's civil law.[105] Damages of $2 million were awarded to a communications advisor and his company for a 1995 CBC broadcast and a news release by a former client that violated fundamental rights of reputation, privacy and security. The Société Radio-Canada was held liable for broadcasting the contents of a private letter, written by Gilles Néron on behalf of the Chambre des notaires du Québec, about delays in processing complaints against lawyers. The TV show, Le Point, asked him to respond to what it said were errors in the private letter, but broadcast the letter before he had a chance to answer. In the controversy, the notary body ended its contract with Néron, announcing the decision in a news release sent to 3,500 lawyers, other professional associations and the media. He sued his former client as well, claiming severe financial losses.

The judge concluded the CBC failed to hold this "private correspondence" confidential, which limited Néron's fundamental rights of thought and expression and exposed the author to violations of reputation and private life. The broadcaster committed several civil faults, including treating the letter as an official document even though it was of a private nature, broadcasting information they knew to be false and broadcasting a letter without the authorization of its author. The Chambre was also held liable for its actions. This judgment stands as one of the largest defamation awards in Canadian history.

The Legislation

The Press Act,[106] the only Québec legislation dealing with defamation, refers only to newspapers. Broadcasters must rely largely on the case law in Québec. This Act provides limited protection for journalists.

Privilege, similar to that offered in the common law provinces, is granted for accurate reports, published in good faith, of:

1. proceedings of the Senate, House of Commons, the Assemblée nationale du Québec, and committees from which the public are not excluded;

2. reports of the Public Protector laid before the Assemblée nationale;

3. any notices, bulletins or recommendations from a government or municipal health service;[107]

---

105 *Gilles E. Néron Communication Marketing Inc. c. Chambre des notaires du Québec*, [2000] J.Q. 2011 (Qué. S.C.). This ruling was upheld in the Court of Appeal (2002 CarswellQue 2092) and at the Supreme Court of Canada ([2004] 3 S.C.R. 95).
106 R.S.Q. 1977, c. P-19.
107 In *La Tribune Ltee v. Restaurant Chez Toni Sherbrooke Inc.*, Qué. C.A., July 11, 1983,

4. public notices given by the government or a person authorized by it respecting the solvency of corporations and the value of security issues; and

5. judicial proceedings held in public.

As in the common law provinces, the privilege will not apply to reports of *in camera* proceedings of courts. As well, the Act states that it does not "affect or diminish the rights of the press under common law."

However, the Act does expressly state no newspaper may avail itself of the provisions of this legislation in either of the following cases:

1. when the offended party is accused by the newspaper of a criminal offence; or

2. when the offending article refers to a candidate in a parliamentary or municipal election and was published within the three days prior to nomination day and up to the polling day.

FACTORS THAT CAN MITIGATE A LOSS

haute lessen damages

The defences outlined above are all that journalists have to call on. In the unfortunate event that none of the defences can be established and the plaintiff wins, it is worth mentioning there are several factors that can help to mitigate the damages or lessen the blow. Some of these mitigating factors must be present before the case goes to trial and so it is wise to keep them in mind.

It should also be noted that certain types of high-handed or reckless behaviour on the part of a news media outlet or journalist alleged to have defamed an individual can aggravate the situation and result in higher than normal damages. For example, repeating the defamation after being told it is untrue, exhibiting false bravado in an attempt to discourage a plaintiff from suing, or piling new defamatory statements on top of an already disputed matter. Recently, one case amply illustrated the financial consequences of this dangerous approach.[108]

---

a newspaper published false information from a health officer regarding the seizure of meat from a restaurant. It was found not to be privileged within s. 10 of the Press Act because the health officer was not warning the public. The information was false, not issued in good faith or in the public interest. The health officer did not confirm the information and was not acting as the "bon père de famille."

108 *Southam Inc. v. Chelekis*, [1998] B.C.J. No. 848, Vancouver Registry No. C952513, (S.C.), affirmed (2000), 73 B.C.L.R. (3d) 161 (C.A.). Application for leave to appeal to

David Baines, a well-known B.C. business reporter and newspaper columnist, was interviewed by George Chelekis, a Florida-based journalist writing for investment newsletters published over the Internet. After a telephone interview that left the columnist unsettled, Baines decided he didn't want his name published or quotes used and sent a fax saying so to Chelekis.

Chelekis went ahead and wrote an article saying the columnist threatened him and was to be the subject of an criminal investigation. The article attacked the reputation of Baines and another person, characterizing them as "muckrakers, snitches and pipelines of information." A second article in the newsletter, which had a circulation of 30,000 copies, implied the two individuals were involved in criminal offences relating to a conspiracy to receive illegal payments.

Other publishers picked up the story, but a major newspaper eventually reported the allegations were false. Undaunted, Chelekis issued a news release repeating what he wrote and again saying the columnist received illicit payments. That release was sent to all media through a news service, which later issued an apology. Chelekis also falsely told a group of business people and journalists that the columnist was HIV positive.

No surprise, the business columnist successfully sued Chelekis. The court ruled the first set of allegations were untrue, he knew they were false and "his publisher was indifferent to their truth." The subsequent statements were even more damaging and malicious. Damages were awarded against the defendant and his publisher for $75,000 for the first article and $200,000 for the second article. Further damages of $250,000 were awarded against Chelekis and a publisher who republished the story. Chelekis was also liable for $100,000 for the press release and $50,000 for the slander. Aggravated damages of $100,000 were awarded against Chelekis for his conduct, which the court called arrogant, vindictive and continuous. Punitive damages were also ordered for $150,000 because Chelekis' intention was to inflict maximum damage. The Supreme Court of Canada rejected an application for leave to appeal based, in part, on the size of the damages.

Apology or Retraction

Many defamed individuals will be quite happy simply to get a written apology or a formal retraction of the defamatory story. Unfortunately, such apologies are not a complete defence. The damage to a person's reputation can still exist despite an apology — even an apology immediately after the defamation.

the Supreme Court of Canada dismissed with costs (without reasons), [2000] S.C.C.A. No. 177.

But an apology can go a long way in reducing the damage award to a plaintiff. The important factor is that the publisher of the derogatory statement must show regret for his mistake and the apology must be full and fair.

Recently, there have been several important court rulings on how apologies should be made and what level of prominence they should receive in a publication or broadcast. Statutes in all the provinces and territories state that a formal "retraction" can completely preclude the awarding of any "general" or non-specific damages. If the proper circumstances are met, the courts will confine the award to what are called "special damages." These are damages that are a foreseeable result of the defamation, such as the loss of financial credit. These special damages must be specifically pleaded and proven. The circumstances for mitigation of special damages are quite particular:[109]

> The plaintiff shall recover only special damage if it appears on the trial,
>
> (a) that the alleged defamatory matter was published in good faith; and
> (b) that there was reasonable ground to believe that the publication thereof was for the public benefit; and
> (c) that it did not impute to the plaintiff the commission of a criminal offence; and
> (d) that the publication took place in mistake or misapprehension of the facts; and
> (e) [that there was] a full and fair retraction . . . and . . . apology [as required by the legislation] . . . before the commencement of the action.

One of the leading cases concerns what constitutes "good faith" in the unintentional publication of a defamatory statement and what is a "full and fair" apology or retraction. In 1989, the Ontario Court of Appeal dismissed an appeal from a weekly newspaper over a defamatory advertisement that was carelessly published by staff when the publisher was away from the office.[110]

An advertisement had been submitted to the newspaper that contained defamatory statements about a local law firm. The editor of the community

---

109 See, for example, s. 17(1) of the Defamation Act, R.S.N.B. 1973, c. D-5; *LeBlanc v. L'Imprimierie Acadienne Ltée*, [1955] 5 D.L.R. 91 (N.B. Q.B.) invoked a similar predecessor provision. The wrong person was named in a story as being charged with theft. An apology was made within three weeks. The court restricted an award to special damages in accordance with the legislation, for the public benefit and because there was an apology.

110 *Teskey v. Canadian Newspapers Co.* (1989), 59 D.L.R. (4th) 709 (Ont. C.A.), leave to appeal to S.C.C. refused (1990), 37 O.A.C. 396 (note) (S.C.C.).

newspaper knew the advertiser had unfairly attacked the law firm on pre-vious occasions, but the manager of the paper's advertising was not aware. The editor did not have authority to overrule the advertising manager, but suggested the word "advertisement" be placed above the item. Both saw the headline, "The Betrayal of Tiny Township," but said they didn't read the ad itself.

As soon as the law firm delivered a notice announcing its intention to sue, the newspaper ran an apology saying: "We are not aware of any evi-dence which would support such allegations. We believe that [the plaintiffs] have at all times acted in accordance with the highest ethical standards of the legal profession." At trial and on appeal, the courts found the apology was not "full and fair" and that an honest belief in the truth of published material was not enough to constitute good faith, unless the belief was based on reasonable grounds. Here, the ad manager knew the editor had concerns. The appeal court said the editor's lack of authority to overrule advertising in a small newspaper "was not appropriate."

Another important issue lately has been the prominence in a publication or broadcast of an apology, correction or retraction. Most plaintiffs would likely prefer to see every correction or apology on the front page or as the lead story. News outlets, though, don't usually agree. Many newspapers, for example, have a standard spot for publishing corrections on an inside page, which they argue is known to readers. The legislation on this topic only suggests the retraction must be as conspicuous or prominent as the original defamation, but does not require any particular positioning.

In a 1995 Ontario case, a newspaper published an uncomplimentary paragraph about an orchestra's public performance, which it said drove some patrons out the door.[111] The talent company for the orchestra sued and the newspaper published two retractions in the same section of the news-paper where the article appeared. The second retraction appeared in a box headed "Correction" and the text was the same size type as the alleged defamation. A trial judge thought it was not prominent enough, but an appeal court ruled the retraction complied with the requirements of Ontario legis-lation. The court said the retraction had to be as conspicuous as the libel itself, but not as conspicuous as the entire original article. Also, the retraction was set off from other items on the page and attracted attention. Since the talent company could prove no actual damages, it was awarded nothing.

A ruling in another case underlines the importance of carefully choos-ing the words used in retractions and apologies.[112] An award-winning re-porter wrote a feature story on the sex trade that briefly mentioned a lawyer.

---

111   *Murray Alter's Talent Associates Ltd. v. Toronto Star Newspapers Ltd.* (1995), 124 D.L.R. (4th) 105 (Ont. Div. Ct.).

112   *Ungaro v. Toronto Star Newspapers Ltd.* (1997), 144 D.L.R. (4th) 84 (Ont. Gen. Div.).

The writer mistakenly reported there had been a successful action against the lawyer for negligence, poor courtroom performance and inept defence of a client. In fact, the action had been only for failure to appear in court and was dismissed.

The reporter failed to confirm her information and relied on others' articles that mentioned the case. Told of the mistake, the newspaper published a correction, but did not speak with the lawyer before publishing it. Despite the correction, the lawyer sued and won a judgment for $25,000. At trial, the newspaper and reporter agreed the article was defamatory, but argued the lawyer was only entitled to actual or provable damages since a correction was published.

The court ruled a "full and fair retraction" was not published. The correction stated the lawyer had been the subject of an action citing poor courtroom performance, but that it was not successful. The court said this implied there was some measure of poor performance. The court criticized the newspaper's policy of quickly publishing brief corrections that resulted in an "indifferent effort to comply with the statutory requirement of a full and fair retraction."

Another Ontario decision in a related area could have an impact on newspaper and magazine publishers relying on libel legislation to limit their exposure and is mentioned here to also highlight the need for careful compliance with defamation laws. In Ontario, s. 8(1) of the legislation requires that the name and address of the proprietor and publisher be printed at the head of editorials or on the front page of the periodical. In this case,[113] the name and address was at the bottom of the editorial page, as it is in many newspapers. The court ruled that this simple difference meant the newspaper could not rely upon the fact that the plaintiff did not launch an action within the three-month limitation period for defamation by a newspaper or broadcast, as required under Ontario's *Libel and Slander Act*.

Limitation Periods

One defence, of sorts, that can be claimed by journalists in newspapers and broadcast media is that the plaintiff did not launch his or her legal action within the limitation period set out by legislation. Each province has laws regarding the time limits for launching lawsuits and most have special rules for defamation actions involving the news media.

In Ontario, for example, the *Libel and Slander Act* requires a notice be served upon a newspaper or broadcaster within six weeks after the alleged libel has come to the plaintiff's knowledge. The notice must be delivered

---

113 *Hermiston v. Robert Axford Holdings Inc.* (1994), 21 O.R. (3d) 211 (Div. Ct.).

to the defendant in writing, specifying the matter complained of, using the same format as a formal statement of claim. Then, the lawsuit or action itself must be commenced within three months after the alleged libel has come to the plaintiff's knowledge. For other individuals and news media other than newspapers and broadcasters, such as book publishers, the limitation period is two years for launching an action.

Other provinces may have longer or much shorter notice periods for actions against the news media. In Saskatchewan, the notice period is five days for a daily newspaper and 14 days for a weekly (no mention of electronic media). In Alberta, Manitoba, Newfoundland and Labrador, New Brunswick, Nova Scotia and Prince Edward Island, a plaintiff has seven days to serve notice upon a daily newspaper and 14 days for any other type of newspaper or broadcaster. In the Northwest Territories, Nunavut and Yukon, a newspaper publisher or broadcaster must receive notice within 14 days and the action must begin within six months. Québec's *Press Act* requires three days' notice, not including holidays, for newspapers (no mention of broadcasters) and three months to launch an action. Most unique of all is British Columbia, where the *Libel and Slander Act*'s s. 5 states: "one clear day must be allowed to elapse between the cause of action complained of and the issue of the writ on the libel."

The time limit for the publication of the retraction varies from province to province and depends on whether a newspaper or broadcasting outlet makes the apology. Usually the retraction has to be made after the notice of the defamation action is received or soon after. As noted above, the retraction must also be complete. To say, "I apologize for calling you a thief," is not good enough. The apology must clearly establish the truth of the matter and also should not be half-hearted.[114]

The legislation also attaches special importance to defamations that happen during election campaigns because of the potential for far-reaching damage. Retractions involving candidates for public office must be made within the time period set out in the legislation, which is usually at least five days before the election.

---

114   In *Thompson v. NL Broadcasting Ltd.* (1976), 1 C.C.L.T. 278 (B.C. S.C.), the court said the news outlet's apology should have said the editorial was unfounded, published without knowledge of the facts and that the incident was regretted. In *Kerr v. Conlogue* (1992), 65 B.C.L.R. (2d) 70 (S.C.), the newspaper published a defamatory article on the front page of its arts section about a theatre company director whose direction was "so bad . . . he was asked not to return." The apology published a few days later was on the second page of another section and simply said the plaintiff's decision to leave the company was his own.

In Québec, under the Press Act, which as stated, governs only newspapers, a newspaper may escape "prosecution" by publishing a full retraction in good faith in the next issue published after the notice of the defamation lawsuit was received and allowing the plaintiff to publish in the newspaper a reasonable reply to the defamatory statements. If the retraction and reply are published without comment, the plaintiff will not be able to sue at all. If a newspaper only publishes the retraction and the plaintiff does not exercise his right to reply, the court will only award actual (special) damages. The Press Act does not offer any protection to newspapers where an article defaming a candidate in an election is published within three days before nomination day and up to polling day.

Offer of Settlement

Another way to mitigate damages is to settle out of court. In one province, an offer to settle before the matter reaches trial can also have an effect on damages awarded if the plaintiff still wants to go to court.

Nova Scotia's law has a provision allowing an "innocent defamer" to offer to make amends. The "innocent defamer" is someone who did not intend to defame the plaintiff and did not know of any circumstances that might allow the defamatory words to be understood to refer to the plaintiff.

An innocent defamer can also be someone who publishes words that are not defamatory on their face and is not aware of the circumstances by which they might be taken in a defamatory manner. The latter requirement is not available to a publisher who is not the author, unless he or she can prove the author wrote without malice. If the offer to settle is refused, the Nova Scotia court will consider the refusal a valid defence to the innocent defamation.

Distribution

The distribution area of the newspaper or broadcasting signal can also affect the size of the award. For example, in a case against a network such as the Canadian Broadcasting Corporation, an award may reflect the fact that the defamation was national in scope. A small town newspaper is unlikely to be saddled with as large an award.[115] The distribution of defam-

---

115 For example, see *Stieb v. Vernon News*, [1947] 4 D.L.R. 397 (B.C. S.C.), where the court considered that the small newspaper had apologized and that most of its readers were paid subscribers. That said, also see *Parizeau*, note 31 above, where a court held a publisher of a small circulation newsletter responsible for defamation to a larger population after a major newspaper brought attention to its defamatory comments.

atory material via the Internet may significantly increase the risk to publishers, but so far Canadian courts have not allowed plaintiffs to take advantage of the Internet's widely spread audience without adequate proof of damage to reputation in other jurisdictions.[116]

Reputation of the Plaintiff

Since the law of defamation aims to compensate someone for lost reputation, it only stands to reason that a person with a bad reputation will have little to preserve. Although it should never be a consideration in deciding whether to use a defamatory comment, the courts have kept damages to a nominal level when the plaintiff has a bad reputation. In one case, a newspaper published a story which said the plaintiff was involved in drug trafficking. In the defamation trial, evidence showed the plaintiff associated with known criminals, that he did indeed have a criminal record and that earlier news reports had also connected him with drug trafficking and he did not sue them. The court held the plaintiff had been defamed and awarded him one dollar while saying the plaintiff had no reputation capable of being injured.[117]

THE CRIMINAL LAW OF DEFAMATION

The Criminal Code creates offences for the publication of defamatory statements and certain other objectionable remarks. The potential punishment is harsh. For example, a defamatory libel under the Criminal Code carries a maximum sentence of two years or a maximum of five years if the statement is known to be false when it is published. Unlike the mixed bag of legislation in civil defamation actions, the criminal law is the same in all provinces without exception. Until recently, some predicted the Criminal Code provisions dealing with defamation would be struck down eventually under the Charter or simply wiped off the books by Parliament.[118] Recently, however, the Supreme Court of Canada ruled some of the criminal provisions still have a life in a post-Charter world.

---

116 See *Braintech*, note 1, above.

117 *Leonhard v. Sun Publishing Co.* (1956), 4 D.L.R. (2d) 514 (B.C. S.C.).

118 The Law Reform Commission of Canada in *Defamatory Libel* (Working Paper 35, 1984) proposed that the Criminal Code offence of defamatory libel be struck from the books because there are enough civil remedies available. The L.R.C. said (at 33-44) that the defamatory libel section infringes on the guarantees of freedom of expression, it is poorly worded, confusing and inconsistent with the civil law tort of defamation.

Defamatory Libel

As mentioned at the beginning of the chapter, prosecutions for criminal libel are rare. The Supreme Court of Canada, though, recently had an opportunity to consider a case of criminal libel and state its position on the Charter's effect.[119] A police officer was investigating allegations by three children of sexual abuse. Criminal charges were laid against 16 people, but later some charges were stayed. Afterwards, some of the accused individuals contacted a Mr. Lucas and his wife, who were involved in a prisoners' rights group. They were told by some of the accused that one of the children was sexually abusing the other two.

Lucas concluded the police officer must have known what was happening and should do something about it. He complained to the police but didn't get the response he expected. Lucas and others picketed outside the provincial court and police headquarters with signs accusing the officer of actually assaulting a child and suggesting he had a "touching problem."

The accused were convicted of criminal libel and eventually appealed to the Supreme Court of Canada. In dismissing the appeal, the judges ruled that the Criminal Code sections are a reasonable limit on the freedom of expression under the Charter because they are very specific as to the types of conduct that is punishable. For example, s. 299 (discussed below) requires the defamatory matter be published in one of three specific ways and the Crown must prove it was objectively defamatory, that the accused knew the libel was false and there was an intention to defame.

The Supreme Court said that existence of a civil remedy in defamation "does not render the defamatory libel provisions in the Criminal Code overbroad" because the Code sections are for offences "so grave and serious that the imposition of a criminal sanction is not excessive."

As the Supreme Court said, criminal prosecutions are reserved for serious and malicious defamations likely to incite hatred, contempt or ridicule against the individual.[120] But, the definition of defamation in the Code is very similar to the definition in civil law and therefore the potential is there for a criminal charge to be laid for almost any defamation. Section 298(1) states:

> A "defamatory libel" is matter published, without lawful justification or excuse, that is likely to injure the reputation of any person by exposing him to hatred, contempt or ridicule, or that is designed to insult the person of or concerning whom it is published.

---

119 *R. v. Lucas* (1998), 157 D.L.R. (4th) 423 (S.C.C.).
120 *R. v. Cameron* (1898), 7 Qué. Q.B. 162.

Section 298 then goes on to state defamatory libels can be expressed through express words "legibly marked upon any substance" or "by any object" and by innuendo:

> (2) A defamatory libel may be expressed directly or by insinuation or irony
>   (a) in words legibly marked upon any substance, or
>   (b) by any object signifying a defamatory libel otherwise than by words.

The wording in this part of s. 298 is cumbersome and vague. It seems to expressly rule out defamations by slander and it may be difficult to prove that broadcasters who speak without a script have expressed a defamatory libel because the words are not "legibly marked upon any substance." There may be some argument that a video or audio tape of the defamatory broadcast could be considered "any object," but the answer is unclear.

Section 299 defines the "publication" of a defamatory libel. With the usual definitions of publication found in civil law, the section also states that a criminal libel will be published even if it is only seen by the person whom it defames. In the *Lucas* case above, the Supreme Court struck this part, s. 299(c), down, saying: "[T]he fundamental element of libel is publication to a person other than the one defamed. Section 299(c) of the Criminal Code is so contrary to this principle that it cannot be justified."

It appears that, contrary to most other criminal offences, there does not have to be an intention to injure the reputation of the victim. Certainly, in one British Columbia case the lack of an intention in the publisher to defame his subject did not matter. The newspaper published an article awarding a local judge a satirical "honour" that was quite derogatory (a Pontius Pilate Award). The court said it did not matter that the libel was intended as a joke and found the newspaper guilty.[121]

Seditious Libel

One of the grander aims of the Criminal Code is to protect the government from acts of sedition. Sedition is anything that incites people to commit treason or anything that advocates the use of violence in overthrowing or reforming the government. Section 59 says a "seditious libel" is one that expresses a seditious intention and a "seditious intention" is as follows:

> (4) Without limiting the generality of the meaning of the expression "seditious intention," every one shall be presumed to have a seditious intention who
>   (a) teaches or advocates, or

---

121 *R. v. Georgia Straight Publishing Ltd.* (1969), [1970] 1 C.C.C. 94 (B.C. Co. Ct.).

(b) publishes or circulates any writing that advocates, the use, without the authority of law, of force as a means of accomplishing a governmental change within Canada.

Section 60 provides this defence:

. . . no person shall be deemed to have a seditious intention by reason only that he intends, in good faith,

(a) to show that Her Majesty has been misled or mistaken in her measures;
(b) to point out errors or defects in
(i)   the government or constitution of Canada or a province,
(ii) Parliament or the legislature of a province, or
(iii) the administration of justice in Canada;
(c) to procure, by lawful means, the alteration of any matter of government in Canada; or
(d) to point out, for the purpose of removal, matters that produce or tend to produce feelings of hostility and ill-will between different classes of persons in Canada.

Section 59 was the focus of a 1951 Supreme Court of Canada case.[122] It involved a Jehovah's Witness who was convicted at trial of seditious libel after he published pamphlets that severely criticized the Québec government and the Québec courts. A majority of the court ordered a new trial on the basis that the trial judge did not properly explain to the jury the defence in s. 60. The court took the opportunity to discuss the scope of the crime of seditious libel. The court said a seditious intention is one that intends to incite violence or create a public disorder or disturbance against the Crown or any institution of government. They said it can also include any act with a view to inciting the public such that it defeats the functioning of the courts.

Blasphemous Libel

This is a rather outdated offence that involves the publication of inflammatory or outrageous statements about a religion. The penalty for the offence is set out in s. 296, but it offers no express definition of what is blasphemous libel. It does say that it is a question of fact whether any matter that is published is a blasphemous libel. In other words, a judge or a jury will decide in each particular case if a statement is blasphemous. The offence carries a maximum sentence of two years in prison, but no convictions or charges have resulted from this section in recent years.

---

122 *Boucher v. R.* (1950), 99 C.C.C. 1 (S.C.C.).

The courts have been left to properly define blasphemy. The case law says a blasphemous libel is an attack on the Deity or expressions grossly repugnant to religious sentiments, exceeding the limits of decent controversy and having as their sole object the outraging of the feelings of every believer in religion.[123] An attack on the clergy or on a doctrine of the church is not a blasphemous libel.[124]

Section 296(3) does offer this defence which allows fair discussion and comment on religious matters:

> No person shall be convicted of an offence under this section for expressing in good faith and in decent language, or attempting to establish by argument used in good faith and conveyed in decent language, an opinion on a religious subject.

The Criminal Code Defences

The Criminal Code lists many defences to the offence of defamatory libel. Generally, the defences fall into the same categories as the common law defences (such as absolute privilege, fair comment). But the list is not exhaustive. Section 8(3) preserves any defence that exists in the common law, except where it is inconsistent with the provisions of the Code. For example, the common law defence of absolute privilege enjoyed by Members of Parliament, which is not listed in the Code, can be used to defeat a criminal charge.

In many respects, the specific Code defences vary greatly from the common law. Some Code defences are broader in scope than civil defamation law defences, others are narrower and at least one is non-existent in the civil law of common law provinces (the defence of public benefit). As with the libel offences listed in the Code, many defences are obsolete and could be challenged in the future or wiped off the books.

Judicial Proceedings and Inquiries

Section 305 states that no person shall be deemed to have published a defamatory libel for publishing defamatory matter:

> (a) in a proceeding held before or under the authority of a court exercising judicial authority; or

---

123 *R. v. St. Martin* (1933), 40 R. de Jur. 411 (Qué.). In *Bowman v. Secular Society Ltd.*, [1917] A.C. 406 (H.L.), the court said a corporation promoting anti-Christian beliefs could not be charged with a criminal offence simply because it denied Christianity.

124 *R. v. Kinler* (1925), 63 Qué. S.C. 483.

(b) in an inquiry made under the authority of an Act or by order of Her Majesty, or under the authority of a public department or a department of the government of a province.

This section protects individuals (such as witnesses, lawyers, judges) participating in judicial proceedings or inquiries from prosecution for defamatory libels.[125] A strict reading of this section suggests that this does not apply to journalists who publish reports of judicial proceedings or inquiries and do not make defamatory statements "in" these proceedings. This is strengthened by the fact that the defence of qualified privilege for reports or extracts is in a later section.

Parliamentary Papers

Section 306 states that no person shall be deemed to have published a defamatory libel for publishing defamatory matter contained in petitions presented to the House of Commons, the Senate or a legislature and in papers published by order or under the authority of one of those bodies. Journalists may publish extracts of these petitions and papers without prosecution providing the publication is in good faith and without ill-will to the person defamed.

Fair Reports of Government or Judicial Proceedings

Section 307(1) states that no person shall be deemed to have published a defamatory libel by reason that he:

> . . . publishes in good faith, for the information of the public, a fair report of the proceedings of the Senate or House of Commons or the legislature of a province, or a committee thereof, or of the public proceedings before a court exercising judicial authority, or publishes, in good faith, any fair comment on any such proceedings.

This is very similar to the common law defence.[126] Note that it includes the common law principle that fair comments on matters brought up in absolute privilege forums are privileged when published in good faith.

---

125 The Law Reform Commission of Canada, above, note 118, suggests at 22 that this is a wider defence than that offered in the common law because it includes all inquiries, including those which are not judicial or quasi-judicial.

126 The defence failed in *R. v. Buller* (1954), 108 C.C.C. 352 at 354-355 (Qué. S.C.), because the newspaper article suggested in extra comment that the accused's guilt was known or established.

Fair Reports of Public Meetings

Section 308 protects anyone who publishes in good faith a fair report of the proceedings of any public meeting, if the meeting is lawfully convened for a lawful purpose and is open to the public. This only applies to newspapers and the report must be fair and accurate. There also must be no refusal to publish a reasonable explanation or contradiction offered by the person defamed.

Public Benefit

Section 309 is a defence that is unavailable in the common law.[127] It makes a publication for the public benefit a complete defence. It says no person shall be deemed to have published a defamatory libel who:

> . . . publishes defamatory matter that, on reasonable grounds, he believes is true, and that is relevant to any subject of public interest, the public discussion of which is for the public benefit.

Fair Comment on a Public Person or Art

Section 310 protects anyone who publishes a fair comment on:

the public conduct of a person who takes part in public affairs

or fair comment on a book, artwork, performance

or on any other communication made to the public on any subject, if the comments are confined to criticism thereof.

Truth

Section 311 is the defence of justification and it protects anyone who proves that the publication of defamatory matter was

for the public benefit at the time when it was published and that the matter itself was true.

---

127 For instance, in *Banks v. Globe and Mail Ltd.* (1961), 28 D.L.R. (2d) 343 at 350-351 (S.C.C.), a defamatory editorial supposedly published for the public's benefit was held not to be protected by any privilege in civil law.

This is a narrower version of the "truth" defence than that found in civil defamation law which only requires the allegation to be true. The Code defence requires that a statement not only be true, but also published for the public benefit at the time of publication.

Publication Invited or Necessary

Section 312 says no person shall be deemed to have published a defamatory libel if the defamatory matter arises on the invitation or challenge of the defamed person. It also protects a person who finds it necessary to answer to defamatory matter published by another person.

The accused person seeking to rely on this defence must believe that his statement is true and the statements must be relevant to the invitation, challenge or necessary refutation without exceeding what is reasonably sufficient to say in the circumstances.

Answer to Inquiries

Section 313 says no person shall be deemed to have published a defamatory libel if the defamatory matter is in answer to an inquiry made by a person who the publisher believes, on reasonable grounds, has an interest in knowing the truth.

The person seeking to rely on this defence must publish the information in good faith for the sole purpose of answering the inquiry, he must believe the defamatory material is true, it must be relevant to the inquiry and cannot exceed what is reasonably sufficient to say in the circumstances.

Giving Information to an Interested Person

Section 314 says no person shall be deemed to have published a defamatory libel if the defamatory information is given to someone who, he believes on reasonable grounds, has an interest in hearing the truth about a certain subject.

This is different from s. 313 since no one has made an inquiry that has prompted the defamatory libel. The accused is making the defamatory statement of his own volition. The conduct of the person giving the information must be reasonable in the circumstances, the defamatory information must be relevant to the subject-matter and it must be true, or if not, it must be given out with no malice to the person defamed and with the belief it is true.

To Redress a Wrong

Section 315 says no person shall be deemed to have published a defamatory libel if the defamatory information is published in good faith:

> for the purpose of seeking remedy or redress for a private or public wrong or grievance from a person who has, or who on reasonable grounds he believes has, the right or is under the obligation to remedy or redress the wrong or grievance.

The accused must believe the defamatory matter in question is true and that the defamatory matter is relevant to the remedy in question and the statements do not exceed what is reasonably sufficient in the circumstances.

GENERAL PROBLEMS IN DEFAMATION

Many questions reporters commonly ask have been addressed by case law and legislation. While any specific problems should always be referred to legal counsel, the following list highlights the danger zones plus a brief discussion of the related law.

Consumer Reports

Although most consumer organizations are reliable, journalists must be on guard for possible untruths in consumer reports that could unjustly damage the reputation of a product or a company. In situations where the public's health or safety is in immediate danger, a qualified privilege can likely be claimed in theory by a consumer report, consumer organization or consumer journalist if the defamatory statement is honestly believed. In one case, the defendant was told by a seemingly reliable source that a certain product was dangerous. Motivated by a concern for the public welfare, the consumer journalist published a story identifying the dangerous product. While the information from the source was wrong, the court held there was a qualified privilege because the report was honestly believed (that is, no malice), it was an important matter of public interest, it was done out of a sense of public duty and the general public had a valid interest to hear the information.[128]

---

128 *Camporese v. Parton* (1983), 150 D.L.R. (3d) 208 (B.C. S.C.). Also, see *Upton v. Better Business Bureau of the Mainland of B.C. Ltd.* (1980), 114 D.L.R. (3d) 750 (B.C. S.C.), where defamatory credit information about the plaintiff was found to have a qualified privilege because the information was distributed only to B.B.B. members and not the general public.

Contagious Diseases

Many provinces have legislation that prohibits the publication of any information identifying a person who has a venereal disease. Caution should be exercised whenever it is suggested that a person has a contagious disease. The common law does not require any proof of actual damage for a defamation action to succeed if a contagious disease has been imputed. The damage to a person's reputation can be significant and it may be difficult to prove at trial (for example, a doctor may refuse to reveal test results).

Corporations

It is possible to defame a corporation. The defamatory matter must attack the corporation in its method of conducting its affairs, accuse it of fraud or mismanagement or harm its financial position. To be successfully pursued in court, the defamatory matter must damage the reputation of the corporation as distinct from defaming the individuals who run it.[129] The defamation of a corporate official, such as the chief executive officer, is usually not enough to sustain an additional action by the company. But it may be defamatory of the corporation to accuse its employees, officers or agents of criminal or corrupt conduct while doing their regular duties or while acting in the best interests of the corporation such that it appears to be an action of the company.[130]

While a corporation is considered a legal entity on its own, it can only sue for defamation if it is capable of doing the act that is alleged. For instance, a corporation cannot commit murder or bribe a city official. Its officers can, but the corporation itself cannot. In one case, a journalist accused the members of a non-profit corporation of practising medicine without a licence. The court said it may be defamatory of the members of the corporation, but not the corporation itself, since it is not capable of practising medicine.[131]

---

129 *Price v. Chicoutimi Pulp Co.* (1915), 51 S.C.R. 179.
130 *Georgian Bay Ship Canal Co. v. World Newspaper Co.* (1897), 16 P.R. 320.
131 *Church of Scientology of Toronto v. Globe & Mail Ltd.* (1978), 84 D.L.R. (3d) 239 (Ont. H.C.).

Criminal Charges

When criminal charges have been laid and the accused is awaiting trial, a journalist must be careful not to suggest that a person or business is guilty of the crime.[132] This could happen if you speak of the charge as being a fact. For example, saying the accused "stole the money last month and is now awaiting trial" is both defamatory and a contempt of court.

The exact wording of the charge should be used as much as possible in the story. It is dangerous to paraphrase some criminal charges or state them incorrectly. For example, there is a great difference in penalty between theft and possession of stolen goods.[133]

As will sometimes happen, an accused can have the same name as another person in a community. Whenever possible, street addresses and full names should be used to identify people accused of a crime in order to avoid confusion.

Criminal Records

A criminal record is public information and not in itself defamatory. Section 6(2) of the Criminal Records Act[134] does prohibit the disclosure of information concerning any conviction for which a pardon was obtained; however, this applies only to those officials who control such information and does not apply to the news media or the general public. Therefore, you can publish the fact that someone has a criminal record if it is important to the story except, of course, when criminal charges are pending. If someone is charged with a new offence, it is highly likely to be a contempt of court to report his or her criminal record before a matter is adjudicated or the record is brought out in court.

---

132 *Lumsden v. Spectator Printing Co.* (1913), 14 D.L.R. 470 (C.A.).

133 In *Desmarais v. La Presse Ltee*, [1977] C.A. 224, the "accused" was charged with possession of stolen goods, not theft, as was reported (a more serious charge), and was served with a summons, not arrested, as was reported. The court felt this story gave an impression of a much more serious crime having been committed. The plaintiff offered proof that his business as a notary had suffered since the news report.

134 R.S.C. 1985, c. C-47. See *Desrosiers v. Groupe Québécor Inc.*, [1994] R.R.A. 111 (C.S. Qué.), where a newspaper reported that a candidate for election had been convicted for armed robbery in 1958. The plaintiff had been pardoned, but was forced by his party to give up his candidacy. The court rejected the defamation lawsuit based on the Criminal Records Act, saying the media had no duty under this law.

Deceased Persons

It is not possible to defame the dead because they can no longer enjoy a reputation or suffer any sort of further injury.[135] It may be possible though to defame a family name such that a defamatory image is cast on certain members of the deceased's living family.[136]

Editing

Reports and quotes of speeches or other people's comments or statements must reflect the material meaning of their message. Any paraphrasing or editing cannot expand on the meaning of the actual statement. In one case, a story reported that a politician had imputed that a nearby village was guilty of gross immorality. He said nothing of the kind and the error was due to paraphrasing by the journalist.[137]

Journalists must also be careful in editing material received on newswires or from other sources. The meaning of the words or the effect of the actual story should not be changed or generalized to the point of defaming someone. In one instance, a criminal charge was generalized to the point where it was a different and more onerous one.[138] In a more recent case, edits made to a letter-to-the-editor were defamatory because they made the writer appear to be irrational and threatening.[139]

---

135 This ruling can be found in *Small v. Globe Printing Co.*, [1940] 2 D.L.R. 670 (Ont. H.C.). In England, see *R. v. Labouchere*, 12 Q.B.D. 320 at 324, where a defamation action by a representative of the deceased's estate was rejected.

136 In *R. v. Ensor* (1887), 3 T.L.R. 366, an English court said defamation of the dead was not actionable unless it caused injury or annoyance to the living. It has been suggested that it is possible to defame the dead in Québec. The decision in *Chiniquy v. Begin* (1915), 24 D.L.R. 687 (Qué. K.B.) ambiguously suggested the memory of the dead could be defamed, but dealt more with the fact that living family members had been defamed. In this case, the gist of the defamatory statement was that the deceased man had never formally married the mother of the plaintiff thereby suggesting the daughter was illegitimate.

137 *Pottle v. The Evening Telegram Ltd.* (1954), 34 M.P.R. 101 at 102 (Nfld. S.C.).

138 See *Allan*, note 34 above, where sloppy editing and use of sources distorted the facts.

139 In *Carter v. Gair* (1999), 170 D.L.R. (4th) 204 (B.C. C.A.), a citizen sent a humourous letter into a local newspaper and requested that it be published unedited. The newspaper agreed, but still altered the letter, making the writer appear to be threatening and irrational. The newspaper later offered to republish the letter unedited and also apologize in print. The plaintiff refused the offer and the newspaper never published its apology. The court held the altered letter was defamatory of its author and the failure to publish an apology, despite the plaintiff's refusal of the offer, limited any reduction in damages for mitigation. The court also noted that the plaintiff could have successfully sued for breach of contract for the newspaper's failure to keep its end of the deal.

Evidence and Exhibits

Any document or evidence that is entered into evidence in open court can be included as a part of a privileged report on judicial proceedings.[140] There is some disagreement about whether all documents filed in a court proceeding can be published under a privilege if they are not referred to or read out in open court. One case has taken the view that all documents filed become a part of the judicial proceedings.[141]

Headlines and Captions

A headline or caption is part of a fair and accurate report. Most provinces have stated expressly in defamation legislation that headlines are considered a part of reports of judicial proceedings and the common law applies the same principle to any news stories. The headline cannot make a comment on the story that is unsupported by fair and accurately presented facts.[142]

Inquests

Inquests are not courts. Reports of defamatory statements made in coroners' proceedings are privileged, but an inquest is not a trial and blame or fault (that is, criminal guilt or civil negligence) is not within the jurisdiction of a coroner or a coroner's jury. An inquest delivers a finding as to how a person died or was injured, without attributing blame to anyone in particular.

Members of a Class or Group

Members of a class or a group can be defamed if the objectionable statement points directly at identifiable individuals. The plaintiff has to be able to prove that the defamatory words clearly identify him in the minds of the reasonable person.[143] For example, to say that "the lawyers in this

---

140 *Hansen v. Nugget Publishers Ltd.*, [1927] 4 D.L.R. 791 (Ont. C.A.).
141 *Butler v. Saskatoon Star-Phoenix Ltd.* (1929), [1930] 1 D.L.R. 1009 (Sask. K.B.).
142 *Tedlie v. Southam Co.*, [1950] 4 D.L.R. 415 (Man. K.B.).
143 In *Booth v. BCTV Broadcasting System* (1982), 139 D.L.R. (3d) 88 (B.C. C.A.), two police officers successfully sued for a story saying two highly placed members of the narcotics squad were taking bribes. Even though names were not mentioned, the court held it would have been clear to the average citizen that the two officers in charge of the unit were the ones being accused of taking the bribes. It should be noted that actions

country are crooks" encompasses such a large group, that no one lawyer could reasonably claim to be identified. But, to say that "the lawyers in this village are crooks" points to a smaller or more identifiable group. It does not matter that there was no intention to defame the plaintiff.

It should be noted that Manitoba's Defamation Act protects against libel of a race or creed that causes unrest or disorder and exposes members of the race or religious creed to hatred, contempt or ridicule. The only remedy though, is an injunction against further publication of the libel.

The Toronto Star published a special series based on an analysis of information in a Toronto police database, relating to criminal and certain non-criminal charges laid since 1996, which concluded, among other things, there was widespread and systemic racism within the Toronto Police Service (TPS). A lawsuit was commenced under Ontario's Class Proceedings Act on behalf of all police officers and civilian TPS personnel, alleging they were defamed by the articles. Were members of this class defamed?

No. At trial and on appeal,[144] the courts held the action could not succeed because the allegedly defamatory statements in the articles were not capable of being understood to refer to the plaintiffs as individuals or to any particular member of the class. The plaintiffs had alleged their reputations were "severely injured by publication of the articles and that they have been brought into public scandal, odium and contempt." The articles cannot, said the court, "reasonably be understood to state or

---

brought by nine other members of the narcotics squad were rejected by the court because they could not be considered as highly placed as the two senior officers.

A group of veteran Canadian bomber airmen failed in an attempt to sue the CBC under class action legislation for alleged defamation in *Elliot*, note 7, above. In this case, the plaintiff sued on behalf of 25,000 other airmen, alleging that a CBC documentary injured their reputation. The court said a group of 25,000 cannot be defamed and no individual airman in the group was singled out. The court also found the documentary was not disparaging of all Canadian airmen in the war, even if the group action had been allowed. Also see *McCann*, note 7, above, in which the mayor of a town of 13,500 sued on behalf of residents after a columnist made allegedly defamatory comments about spectators at a hockey game, suggesting they were probably from the mayor's town and other named areas. The court ruled the action had no basis and said that an action for defamation is "uniquely personal" and each plaintiff would have to show he or she was clearly identified by the column. The court said this is only likely to happen in cases where the group is very small and easily identified. Finally, see *Aiken*, note 26, above, where 100 teachers failed in their attempt to sue the province's Premier for his alleged group libel in saying educators involved in protests were "lawbreakers."

144   *Gauthier v. Toronto Star Daily Newspapers Ltd.* (2003), 228 D.L.R. (4th) 748 (Ont. S.C.), affirmed on appeal at (2004), 245 D.L.R. (4th) 169 (Ont. C.A.).

suggest that every, or any particular, member of the service has partici- pated in the impugned practices or has exhibited racist attitudes." The articles were directed at the police force as an organization and not at specific officers or personnel.

Open-Line Talk Shows

A broadcaster is responsible for the statements made by participants in a live program. In one case, the radio host did not take advantage of his ability to censor, stop or delay calls on his phone-in show. As a result, the radio station was held responsible for a defamatory telephone call that was broadcast.[145]

Pleadings, Affidavits and Other Pre-Trial Documents

Reports of documents such as pleadings and affidavits have tradition- ally not been privileged until entered as evidence or read into open court. That rule has been modified by a 1995 Supreme Court ruling that the publication of information in pleadings is protected by a qualified privilege so long as a reporter has a right of access to documents under legislation or the Charter's freedom of the press guarantee, and there is no malice in the reporting.[146]

Note that Alberta has now repealed a section of its Judicature Act that partly restricted the publication of civil pleadings, affidavits, discovery transcripts or other documents before the beginning of a trial in the province

---

145 In *Syms v. Warren* (1976), 71 D.L.R. (3d) 558 (Man. Q.B.), a public official who had been the subject of local rumours agreed to speak on a radio show to explain the truth. But, he made it clear that he did not want to further debate the allegations on the air. Unfortunately, a caller took the opportunity to accuse the official of lying and further defamed him. The court criticized the radio station for not making use of its ability to censor calls.

146 *Hill v. Church of Scientology of Toronto*, [1995] 2 S.C.R. 1130 (S.C.C.). Since that decision, at least one provincial court of appeal has warned that the news media must be extra careful in reporting on pre-trial information. In *Taylor-Wright v. CHBC-TV*, [2000] BCCA 629 (B.C. C.A.), a reporter used affidavits alleging serious offences to paint a one-sided story that failed to note that opposing affidavits denied the allegations. The court found the broadcaster lost the qualified privilege defence because he did not invest the time and effort needed to produce a balanced report.

or, if no trial, the proper determination of any other type of action started in Alberta.[147]

Police Information and Investigations

A reporter enjoys no privilege in publishing police comments or police information. The police are no different from any other person and their comments can be defamatory.[148] All provinces have legislation that extends a qualified privilege to publications of official reports, bulletins, notices or other documents issued by a public officer for the information of the public.[149] For example, this would include a police bulletin issued for the safety of the public. But other than reporting details of official documents released to the public, stories containing general police comments to the press are not privileged.

Journalists should also be cautious when publishing reports of an ongoing police investigation. It could be defamatory to accuse a person or a business of a crime simply because there is a police investigation involving them.[150] For example, a person may be suspected of a crime but the investigation may turn up nothing and charges may not be laid.

Public Figures

A journalist can comment on the public acts of people, but the private life or moral character of a public figure is regarded in the same manner as a private individual.[151] In fact, the courts have awarded higher damages to defamed public officials because they are more "sensitive to attack than the ordinary man."[152] It has been suggested that the Charter may change this rule and allow Canadian journalists, like their American counterparts, to

---

147 R.S.A. 1980, c. J-1, s. 30(2) is repealed, S.A. 1991, c. 21, s. 15. A journalist was previously only permitted to publish the names and addresses of the parties and their solicitors, and the general nature of the claim.

148 *Farrell v. St. John's Publishing Co.* (1982), 35 Nfld. & P.E.I.R. 181 (Nfld. T.D.).

149 See above, "The Civil Law Defences," particularly the section on "Qualified Privilege."

150 An analogy may be found in *McDonald v. Sydney Post Publishing Co.* (1906), 39 N.S.R. 81 (C.A.), where a liquor inspector successfully sued a newspaper for reporting that he was accused of attempted bribery by a local citizen. No criminal charges had been laid at the time of the report and the citizen's accusation was only made with the aim of getting the inspector fired by the city council. Because the accusation was not actually made at a public council meeting nor in any judicial proceeding, the court held that the newspaper was confined to comment on, or criticism of, the accusation and could not print unsubstantiated "facts" unless it was willing to prove them.

151 *Sheppard*, note 29, above.

152 *Farrell*, note 148, above.

comment more freely on the public and private activities of public figures. Canadian courts, so far, have not taken to this idea and several have rejected it outright, saying public officials, even those acting in their official capacity, are entitled to the same protection as the rest of us.[153]

Public Performances, Restaurant and Other Reviews

Similar rules apply to reviews of public performances and restaurant reviews. A person who enters the public arena, whether it be theatre or food, invites public comment. But the comment must be fair and honestly held. The public acts of a person can be criticized, but the comment cannot extend to the private life of any individual.[154]

---

153 In *Hill*, note 78, above, the Supreme Court of Canada affirmed an Ontario Court of Appeal ruling that awarded $1.6 million to the plaintiff, a Crown Attorney who was defamed during a news conference by a lawyer acting for the Church. The defendants argued that the court should require public officials to prove knowledge of falsehood or a reckless disregard for the truth, as in the U.S. The Court of Appeal said the protection of the reputation of public officials is of "paramount importance" and that the defendants had failed to raise enough evidence to mount a Charter challenge.

    An Alberta judge has also rejected the notion that the Charter supersedes defamation laws. In *Getty v. Calgary Herald* (1990), 104 A.R. 308 (Master), the defendants admitted their newspaper column defamed the plaintiff, but claimed a right to publish it under the Charter. The Master rejected the application to add a Charter argument into the pleadings, ruling that where private parties litigated on the common law and no government action infringed on a guaranteed right, then the Charter did not apply.

    Also, see Doody, note 78, above, where the author outlines the case for using the Charter to broaden the defence of qualified privilege to allow more criticism of public officials, as in the United States. The landmark American case of *New York Times Co. v. Sullivan*, 376 U.S. 254 (1964) allowed unlimited criticism of a public official except where there is evidence of malice, such as a reckless disregard for the truth. The author notes that subsequent American decisions have toned down the effect of this case by narrowly defining what is a "public official." As it now stands, a public official in the U.S. is someone who has the opportunity to counter the views expressed in the press and is in a legitimate public controversy, not just someone who is a topic of public interest. American law has also created the "limited purpose" public official who represents a particular cause or issue, but is not constantly in the public eye.

154 *Sheppard*, note 29, above. More recently, see *Sara's Pyrohy Hut*, note 84, above. In this case, a restaurant reviewer for a radio station described a meal as bland, overpriced and inferior. The court dismissed the action, stating that while the words were defamatory, the comments were the reviewer's own opinions on a matter of public interest and were not conveyed as statements of fact.

Quotation Marks, "Alleged," Attributions

Generally, the use of quotation marks or words like "alleged," "it is claimed" or "reportedly" offer no protection in a defamation action.[155] Similarly, attributing a defamatory statement to another person won't protect you from being sued. A journalist is as responsible for the comments of those he quotes as he is for his own comments (unless the statements are made on an occasion of absolute or qualified privileged).

An exception is in the reporting of a criminal charge. In that case, a journalist should avoid any suggestion of guilt before the verdict is rendered and should note the accused is "alleged" to have committed the crime.

Satire and Humour

Any story or commentary attempting to take a humorous or satirical bent should be examined closely before publication. The courts have generally allowed the defence of fair comment to be used by journalists for satirical or humorous stories or illustrations. The courts have held that a fair comment does not even have to be "fair" in that the comment does not have to have any sort of reasonable perspective on the facts, so long as it was a comment that could reasonably be held by anyone.[156]

But there are limits to humour and the defence of fair comment. The courts have taken the stand that any comment or opinion that accuses someone of criminal, illegal or morally reprehensible conduct is beyond the limits of fair comment.[157] For example, in 1985, a popular magazine columnist wrote a satirical article in which it was noted that two lawyers were rising quickly through their Vancouver law firm. The columnist then said the lawyers had been "cementing their connections through the lawn tennis circuits and wife-swapping brigades." Despite a printed apology later, the

---

155 *Steiner v. Toronto Star Ltd.* (1955), 1 D.L.R. (2d) 297 at 300 (Ont. H.C.).

156 *Vander Zalm v. Times Publishers*, [1980] 4 W.W.R. 259 (B.C. C.A.). Also see *Beutel*, note 81, above.

157 See the English case of *Campbell v. Spottiswoode* (1863), 3 B & S 769. In Canada, see the 1993 case of *Mapes*, note 86, above, in which a cartoon suggested a well-known businessman had committed the crime of illegally operating a commercial fishing camp on Crown land. The cartoon showed the plaintiff holding a gun, standing over a cash register full of money and with a "donations" label near a sign declaring "The Non-Licensed, No-Name, Not-Really-Here, Fishing Camp." Also, see *Mitchell*, note 86, above, in which a teachers' association defamed a school principal in an advertisement's cartoon. It showed the principal sitting at a desk in an open field, along with text claiming the school board had hired a principal for a school that had yet to be built. The court found the cartoon suggested the principal was greedy and would willingly be on the public payroll doing nothing for a year.

trial judge found that the comment went too far in insinuating that the lawyers and their wives "were capable of such immorality" and ordered damages of $10,000 to each lawyer.[158]

Another occasion to note is the after-dinner speech where a person jokes about himself or tells a personally embarrassing story; the journalist must keep the remark within the context in which it was made. The reader or listener must not be led to believe the remark was made as a serious comment or admission.

Sensationalism

Facts that are innocent and not defamatory on their own can carry a defamatory meaning when presented in a sensationalized manner. For example, one story reported that police had seized documents from a lawyer's office, that he was unavailable for comment and went on to suggest that the police investigation was the reason he had resigned from his public office several weeks earlier. In reality, the police were searching the lawyer's office to find documents belonging to a company that he happened to represent, the lawyer was not involved in any crime, he truly was unavailable for comment and he had resigned from his public position for unrelated reasons.[159]

A journalist should also carefully weigh his or her choice of words. For example, to say that someone was "ousted" from an office, when in fact the person resigned or was not reappointed for other reasons, is defamatory because it implies that the person was removed for wrongdoing.[160] Recently, some courts have taken the view that sensationalism by major media outlets can be even more destructive than other media and deserve to be punished with higher damages.[161]

---

158 *Hunter and Swift v. Fotheringham*, summarized (1986), 35 A.C.W.S. (2d) 360 (B.C. S.C.).

159 See *Wells v. Daily News Ltd.* (1976), 13 Nfld. & P.E.I.R. 80 (Nfld. T.D.).

160 *Roberge v. Tribune Publishers Ltd.* (1977), 20 N.B.R. (2d) 381 (Q.B.). Also see *Kerr*, note 114, above, in which a newspaper article about a theatre company director said his direction was "so bad . . . he was asked not to return." The reporter used sources known to be unreliable and the allegation was not provable.

161 In *Leenen*, note 25, above, the trial judge said: "Programs such as the [CBC's] fifth estate have remarkable potential and capacity to cause damage. A program such as this one, by the sensationalized manner in which it was produced, is far more likely to cause damage than other less respected publications or broadcasts. Thus, there is a greater responsibility upon those who produce such programs to ensure that the content is factually correct."

Sloppy Journalism

Failure to corroborate facts or to check the accuracy of documents or sources can contribute to the amount of damages awarded to the plaintiff. When serious accusations are being levelled, at least one court has punished journalists who did not confront the plaintiff before publication.[162] Gross negligence, such as running a story based on an unconfirmed "tip," will only add to the size of court awards.[163]

> **Shortly after the 9/11 attack on New York City, newscasts showed video of two men being taken into custody at gunpoint by RCMP. The announcer stated: "With all the attention focused on investigating the terrorist attack in New York and Washington, a dramatic arrest at gunpoint this afternoon by R.C.M.P. in Cape Breton." The story goes on to say: "[s]ources tell ATV news the pair were being watched by police because of the terrorist attack in New York, Tuesday, but the R.C.M.P.'s Wayne Noonan said that is not true. Noonan admits the men are suspicious but in no way connected to the incidents in New York or Washington." Unreported was that the individuals were released by police shortly after the incident and no charges laid. Can they sue in defamation?**
>
> **Yes.** Even though the broadcast story stated the RCMP did not believe the men were involved in any terrorist attacks, the sensationalistic treatment of other facts and the failure to follow-up with police to determine what happened after the arrests proved fatal to CTV's defence in this case.[164] The court zeroed in on the statements that "[s]ources tell ATV news the pair were being watched by police" and that "Noonan admits the men are suspicious." The "sources" in this matter was a single telephone call from an unidentified person who wrongly claimed "inside information." A compelling factor for the reporter, the court heard, was that the unidentified caller "had a credible voice." The court also noted

---

162 *Munro v. Toronto Sun Publishing Co.* (1982), 39 O.R. (2d) 100 (H.C.).

163 *Tait v. New Westminster Radio Ltd.* (1984), 58 B.C.L.R. 194 (C.A.). Despite a prompt apology, which was taken into account by the court, damages were set at $17,500. That said, it appears the courts will not allow poor research alone to be the determining factor in a plaintiff's claim for damages. In a defamation claim against a newspaper, *Fulton v. Globe and Mail* (1997), 152 D.L.R. (4th) 377 (Alta Q.B.), the plaintiff requested additional damages for negligence arising from "shoddy and incomplete research." The court held defamation and negligence are two, distinct legal actions and "negligent research was not in itself actionable."

164 *Bevis and Karela v. CTV Inc., Burns and Kelly* (2004), 228 N.S.R. (2d) 24 (S.C.).

that if the reporter had bothered to follow-up on the matter, CTV would have known the police released the men within minutes of the arrest with an apology — well before the first broadcast of the story. A jury awarded the one man identified in the story $15,000 in general and aggravated damages, and $27,000 toward court costs. The jury determined the other man was not defamed since the news report did not identify or refer to him specifically.

Defamation of Title or Property

A journalist must be careful of defaming the marketability of property or the title to tangible or intangible property. The plaintiff must prove that there was malice, that actual damage has been suffered and that the statements were untrue.[165]

For example, falsely stating that a product infringes on a patent is a slander of title.[166] To say that a house is haunted and uninhabitable is an example of defaming a property.[167]

Visuals

The careless use of visuals (that is, video, graphics or photographs) can be hazardous. There are a number of different areas to beware of. Television journalists must be careful when matching script with pictures. Watch for references to improper or illegal acts when showing identifiable individuals (for example, protesters or crowd shots).

It is defamatory, for instance, to comment on how some business people use bankruptcy proceedings to escape debts, while at the same time showing an identifiable person or place of business on the screen.[168] The innuendo is that the person or business being shown practises these techniques. It is irrelevant that the comment was not directed at the person or business and the plaintiff would only have to prove that the defamatory comment could be understood to be referring to him.

---

165 *Cross v. Bain, Pooler & Co.*, [1937] O.W.N. 220 (H.C.).
166 *Cousins v. Merrill* (1865), 16 U.C.C.P. 114 (C.A.).
167 *Manitoba Free Press Co. v. Nagy* (1907), 39 S.C.R. 340.
168 *Burnett v. CBC (No. 1)* (1981), 48 N.S.R. (2d) 1 (T.D.).

> **A newspaper published an article on the Middle Eastern terrorist group, Hezbollah, and included a photo of a man referenced in the story. Unfortunately, the photo showed the wrong person. It was an image of a respected Vancouver criminal lawyer, who had represented the other man. The unintentional error was acknowledged immediately by the newspaper and it issued an apology. Does the lawyer shown in the photo have a cause of action?**
>
> **Yes.** Despite the apology and unintentional mix-up, a B.C. court ruled this was "a libel of enormously destructive potential." While he was grateful for the apology, the lawyer continued to suffer humiliation in the community and his distress justified an award of $35,000 for general damages, the court determined. "The [*Vancouver*] *Sun* must accept the risks that go with its drive to get its stories out," said the judge.[169]

Visuals are considered a part of a story and must reflect the facts as reported. This is important when considering the use of stock footage or photographs. A picture is a "freeze-frame" in a person's lifetime and what was true once may not be true now. For example, to use a photo of a child who once received social assistance, but is no longer in need, in connection with a story about poor children, could be defamatory of the child and her family if they are no longer on welfare and the present situation has not been made clear to the audience.[170]

Another problem can arise when stock footage or photos are used that show identifiable individuals in situations different from what is being portrayed. In one instance, a story about abortion showed stock footage of a young hospital worker setting up an operating table. When the visuals were shot the worker was setting up the table for a different type of operation. It turned out that he was a devout Roman Catholic and took offence to being shown setting up the table for an abortion.

Even if you have obtained a formal release or consent from someone to use their picture, you must be careful. A person's consent must be informed and if you use their picture in a context that they could not have been expected to foresee, they could sue. For example, a model who signed a general release form may not expect to see her picture accompanying a story about prostitution.

Journalists must also be careful in choosing graphics or illustrations that may suggest a defamatory message. The graphics and pictures used in connection with a story must reflect true and provable facts. For example,

---

169 *St. Pierre v. Pacific Newspaper Group Inc. and Skulsky*, 2006 BCSC 241 (S.C.).
170 *Dennis v. Southam Inc.* (1954), 12 W.W.R. (N.S.) 379 (Man. Q.B.).

it was held in one defamation case that it added to the defamatory effect of the story to use a graphic of tipped "scales of justice" in a story alleging that a public official interfered with the justice system.[171]

CONCLUSION

There is pressure on several fronts to alter the law of defamation in Canada. As noted above, the Law Reform Commission of Canada has recommended that sweeping changes be made to the criminal libel legislation. The Uniform Law Conference has recommended that the provinces adopt uniform statutes to do away with the inconsistencies between jurisdictions. And there may be even more significant changes coming based on challenges under the Charter.

The concluding point comes from the former ombudsman for a major Toronto newspaper. That newspaper's editors have found that many of the legal and ethical problems in news stories could be avoided by including comments from both sides in a contentious issue in the same story:[172]

> If the target of an attack cannot be reached for comment, the reporter should consider the possibility of withholding the story until he can get the needed comment, rather than slap on an "unavailable-for-comment" ending.

This fundamental principle of fairness could go a long way in defusing a possible defamation court action.

A DEFAMATION CHECKLIST

The following areas should be considered before a story is published or broadcast:

1. Is there "defamatory matter"? Expressly or by implication, does this story contain any of the following (in a written or visual form):
    *   statements or suggestions of criminal, illegal, immoral or improper behaviour or practices?
    *   statements about someone's financial status?
    *   insults or slurs?
    *   statements about someone's health?

---

171 *Vogel v. Canadian Broadcasting Corp.*, [1982] 3 W.W.R. 97 (B.C. S.C.).
172 Rod Goodman, the *Toronto Star's* ombudsman, in a letter to the author, dated August 17, 1984.

- critical statements relating to a person's profession, business, product or trade?
- statements that might adversely affect the reputation of a person or entity in the eyes of ordinary people?
- statements that would deter ordinary people from associating or dealing with that individual or entity?

If so, chances are there is defamatory material in the story. But this doesn't mean it can't be published. Please continue through the checklist.

 2. Does the defamatory matter refer to someone directly or indirectly? Regardless as to whether an individual or entity (group, association or corporation) is named, is it possible that even one person might think the defamatory matter refers to a specific person, entity or its members? If so, this story probably has the basic elements to attract a defamation action (that is, defamatory matter referring to a prospective plaintiff). This doesn't mean the story must be dropped or changed. Chances are there's either a defence or a way to re-write the story to avoid defaming an individual. A lawyer should be called.

 3. Is a defence available?

(a) Is there proof of the defamatory statements, such as:
- documents?
- a witness with first-hand knowledge who is willing to appear in court on your behalf?
- one or two extra sources of corroboration?
- detailed notes from key interviews?
- tape recordings of key statements?

The more of the above you have, the better your chances of relying on the "truth" defence (justification). Please re-read that section.

(b) Was the defamatory matter derived from:
    (i)   open proceedings of Parliament, a legislature, a government committee, a municipal council meeting, a public meeting or a judicial or quasi-judicial hearing?
    (ii) an official report or news release of a government or judicial/quasi-judicial body?

If so, a defence of qualified or absolute privilege may exist. Please re-read that section.

(c) Is this matter "the public has a legitimate interest in hearing," and that you have investigated, have "every reason to believe" are true and meets standards of responsible journalism. Specifically, have you considered:

- The seriousness of the allegation. The more serious the charge, the more the public is misinformed and the individual harmed, if the allegation is not true.
- The nature of the information, and the extent to which the subject-matter is a matter of public concern.
- The source of the information. Some informants have no direct knowledge of the events. Some have their own axes to grind, or are being paid for their stories.
- The steps taken to verify the information.
- The status of the information. The allegation may have already been the subject of an investigation which commands respect.
- The urgency of the matter. News is often a perishable commodity.
- Whether comment was sought from the plaintiff. He may have information others do not possess or have not disclosed. An approach to the plaintiff will not always be necessary.
- Whether the article contained the gist of the plaintiff's side of the story.
- The tone of the article. A newspaper can raise queries or call for an investigation. It need not adopt allegations as statements of fact.
- The circumstances of the publication, including the timing.

If so, the defence of "public interest responsible journalism" may apply. Please re-read the section on qualified privilege.

(d) Is the defamatory matter an honest, non-malicious expression of someone's "opinion" and is it based on provable facts concerning a matter of public interest?

If so, there may be a defence of fair comment. Please re-read that section.

4. Common areas of legal concern include:
- pre-trial court documents or exhibits not dealt with in open court
- wording of criminal charges
- sensationalism distorting the true situation
- headlines, cut lines and captions
- visuals juxtaposed with other stories, casting a defamatory light on an individual
- innuendos in visuals

- generic visuals using recognizable people or businesses in connection with a defamatory subject-matter
- satire or humour that goes too far, perhaps suggesting immoral or illegal behaviour
- presence of malice (for example, reckless or careless reporting)
- subjective comments in court reports
- refusing to allow the subject of defamatory matter the opportunity to reply to the statements

3

CONFIDENTIALITY
OF NEWS SOURCES

It's a fact of life these days that many news stories, particularly controversial ones, involve confidential sources of information. While it's always best to have information attributed and on the record, it's not always possible. Indeed, many worthwhile stories would go unreported if journalists had to insist that sources be identified.

Recently, there have been some important and largely supportive court rulings on the media's need to protect sources. Also, in 2007, a private bill was proposed by a Member of Parliament that would amend the Canada Evidence Act to restrict when a court can order a journalist to name sources. At the time of this publication, the Private Member's bill, like many of its kind, has little chance of becoming law but is illustrative of the journalist "shield" laws found in parts of the United States.

The offer of confidentiality is a powerful weapon in a journalist's arsenal and it shouldn't be used indiscriminately. Most journalists only use confidential sources to help in the search for corroboration from other attributable sources. That said, it is becoming more common for reporters to rely on anonymous sources for controversial stories.

Certainly, there are circumstances when it's obvious that a source will suffer if named and anonymity will be a requirement. In these cases, a source may fear for his or her job or even personal safety. And then there are the more difficult judgment calls where the source is seeking confidentiality merely for convenience's sake or to avoid minor social embarrassment or perhaps the source isn't confident of the truth of his or her comments.

Whatever the circumstances, there is no law governing when a news source can or should be offered a cloak of secrecy. That's up to the individual journalist. However, the law does have something to say about when and if a confidential source must be revealed.

WHEN MUST A SOURCE BE REVEALED?

The general rule is that courts will be unlikely to offer a journalist absolute protection against disclosing the identity of a source if it is considered relevant and necessary to the proper adjudication of a matter.

Disclosure in Criminal Proceedings and Investigations

In a criminal proceeding or police investigation, courts can turn to the Criminal Code[1] to compel a journalist to reveal a source. For example, s. 545 allows a justice conducting a preliminary hearing to send a witness who refuses to testify to jail for periods of up to eight days. If, at the end of the eight days, the witness still refuses to testify, the judge can continue to issue eight-day internments.

If a witness refuses to testify when a criminal matter reaches the trial stage, the judge can cite the offender for contempt of court and order a jail term and/or a fine.

In a 1998 case, there was an unsuccessful attempt to use the Charter of Rights to prevent a reporter from testifying in court and keep his interview notes confidential. The case arose in British Columbia during a high-profile sexual assault case involving an actor.[2] While the trial on six counts of sexual assault was in progress, a newspaper journalist interviewed four complainants. The accused in the trial sought a court order requiring the reporter to testify and produce his interview notes. The accused believed

---

1 R.S.C. 1985, c. C-46.
2 *R. v. Hughes*, [1998] B.C.J. No. 1694 (S.C.).

there were discrepancies in the statements relevant to the credibility of the complainants.

The reporter and his employer argued the court order violated the journalist's right to freedom of expression and freedom of the press. They also argued there is a qualified privilege protecting notes and he could not be compelled to testify. The B.C. court disagreed, ordering the reporter to produce the notes. The court said the notes "constituted a compellable record," adding the complainants did not have a reasonable expectation of privacy since they expected the interviews to be reported. The judge in this case set out seven criteria for deciding whether to compel a journalist to testify:

1.   Relevance and materiality of the evidence to the issues at trial;
2.   Necessity of the evidence to the accused's case and his ability to make full answer and defence;
3.   Probative value of the evidence;
4.   Whether the evidence was available through other means and, if so, whether reasonable efforts had been made on the part of the accused to obtain evidence from that other source;
5.   If the media's ability to gather and report the news will be impaired by being called to give evidence and, if so, the degree to which it is impaired;
6.   Whether the necessity of the evidence in the case at hand outweighs the impairment, if any, of the role of the media; and
7.   Whether the impairment of the media's function can be minimized by confining the evidence adduced to only that which is necessary to the accused's case and his right to make full answer and defence.

As for the Charter claims, the B.C. court ruled the reporter did not have legal standing to claim a Charter violation since the accused was a private person and his right to make full answer and defence in his trial had to be balanced with the right to freedom of expression and the press. An application for leave to appeal to the Supreme Court of Canada resulted in the court order being stayed until the application was heard. Unfortunately, the application was abandoned and the issues were not dealt with by the high court.[3]

More recently, however, an Ontario court attempted to set the bar high for any law enforcement authority seeking to force a journalist to reveal sources, even during a criminal investigation.[4] While the Ontario Court of

---

3   [1998] S.C.C.A. No. 364 (S.C.C.).
4   *R. v. National Post* (2004), 69 O.R. (3d) 427 (S.C.J.).

Appeal overturned the lower court's decision in 2008,[5] the case itself provides an interesting example of the issues involved in balancing the journalist's desire to maintain confidentiality of sources against the purported needs of law enforcement.

In 2004, the lower court ruling quashed search warrants against the *National Post* that sought information that might have identified the source of a "brown paper envelope" and its contents, which were sent anonymously to the newspaper. The journalist who received the information was working on a story about the then-Prime Minister's business dealings in his riding. A document in the envelope purported to place the Prime Minister in a conflict of interest regarding a bank loan.

The RCMP was called in to investigate the document's authenticity and its source. The search warrants were to seize the original document and envelope to check for fingerprints and the DNA of its source. The lower court reviewing the decision of the issuing justice ruled the warrants were authorized without proper jurisdiction since the justice had not given the *Post* notice of the warrant application. The lower court also issued several important statements about the confidentiality of sources.

"Sources want confidentiality for a variety of reasons. They may, themselves, be breaching a duty of confidentiality. They may have stolen the information. They may fear economic reprisals. They may lose their jobs. They may fear for their safety. They may fear for the safety of their families. . . If employee confidentiality were to trump conscience, there would be a licence for corporations, governments and other employers to operate without accountability."

The judge also wrote: "If the journalist-informant relationship is undermined, society as a whole is affected. It is through confidential sources that matters of great public importance are made known."

The court heard extensive evidence on the value of sources, including sworn affidavits from 15 "well-respected journalists" testifying that the use of confidential sources is essential to the uncovering and reporting of matters of public interest. The judge also took the time to list 10 examples of stories that owe their origins to confidential sources:

1. The Watergate story which led to the resignation of President Richard Nixon. (*Washington Post* reporters Carl Bernstein and Bob Woodward relied extensively on anonymous sources, the most famous of whom became known as "Deep Throat.")
2. The tainted tuna scandal that led to the resignation of the Minister of Fisheries in Canada.

---

5 *R. v. The National Post*, 2008 CarswellOnt 1104, [2008] ONCA 139 (C.A.).

3. The story that Airbus Industrie paid secret commissions in the sale of Airbus aircraft.
4. The book *For Services Rendered* about the search for a suspected KGB mole in the RCMP Security Service, and CBC's *The Fifth Estate* program on that mole, code-named "Long Knife."
5. Stories dealing with the City of Toronto's health inspection system for restaurants.
6. A story describing the operation of an illegal slaughterhouse in Vaughan.
7. Stories about the fall of Nortel Networks that contrasted optimistic public forecasts by Nortel executives with internal Nortel discussions warning of a potential devastating market downturn.
8. Stories about wrongdoing by members of the RCMP security service in early 1977, including a break-in to obtain documents from a left-wing news agency in Montréal, *Agence Presse Libre du Québec*, illegal wiretaps in Vancouver, and the use of pin-registers.
9. A story about a briefcase containing highly classified material that was stolen from the car of a CSIS intelligence agent.
10. The uncovering of U.S. companies dumping hazardous waste in Canada because of lax environmental laws.

Finally, the judge stated: "To compel a journalist to break a promise of confidentiality would do serious harm to the constitutionally entrenched right of the media to gather and disseminate information. . . A Justice of the Peace considering a search warrant application must undertake a careful weighing of the privacy interests of individuals in a democratic society against the interest of the state investigating and prosecuting crimes. This weighing and balancing will vary with each case. The media are entitled to this 'special consideration because of the importance of its role in a democratic society.'"

Unfortunately, the Ontario Court of Appeal did not share this generous view of the need for "special consideration" for journalists. In overturning the reviewing judge's decision, the appeal court ruled in 2008 that the newspaper was not entitled to advance notice of the application for the search warrant. In fact, the issuing judge specifically stated in the warrant that, if requested by the *Post*, any items sought by police would be sealed and not disclosed to authorities until the validity of the warrant could be determined in a judicial review or court hearing.

The critical issue for the appeal court was whether the reporter and his source had a privileged relationship such that the actual documents and the source's name were confidential and beyond the reach of law enforcement. The lower court judge had held that the relationship was privileged and that the search warrant violated s. 2(b) of the Charter of Rights. The appeal court disagreed. While the appeal judges accepted "the gathering and dissemination of news and information without undue state interference is an integral component of [journalists'] constitutional right of freedom of the press under s. 2(b) of the Charter. . . this does not mean that press organizations or journalists are immune from valid searches under s. 8 of the Charter. And s. 2(b) does not guarantee that journalists have an automatic right to protect the confidentiality of their sources."

While the appeal court said courts must ensure the privacy interests of the news media are "limited as little as possible," courts must "also balance against the privacy interest of the press the state or other societal interests in getting at the truth."

Though a disappointing turn of events for journalists generally, the appeal court refused the Crown's argument that law enforcement's interest in requiring disclosure "will always trump the media's claim to a journalist-confidential source privilege." The Court of Appeal stated that issues of privilege and confidentiality must always be decided on a case-by-case basis.

Disclosure in Civil Actions

Journalists more commonly are asked to reveal their sources in civil matters, particularly defamation actions. Unlike a criminal proceeding, a civil action permits the parties to examine each other under oath before the trial begins (known as an examination for discovery). The courts are split in this country on whether a source must be revealed at this stage.

In some provinces, such as Ontario and Québec, the courts recognize the special role of the news media and follow what is called the "newspaper rule." Under this common law rule, a court will avoid ordering a journalist to disclose a source until the matter reaches trial.[6]

---

6 In *Hatfield v. Globe & Mail Div. of Can. Newspapers* (1983), 41 O.R. (2d) 218 (Master), it was held that a newspaper may refuse to disclose its sources of information prior to the trial. In the Ontario High Court decision of *Reid v. Telegram Publishing Co. Ltd.* (1961), 28 D.L.R. (2d) 6 (Ont. H.C.), the court said that in a libel action invoking truth and fair comment defences, unless exceptional circumstances exist, the judge should refuse a request to order source disclosure because witnesses would have to be called anyway. In *Drabinsky v. MacLean-Hunter Ltd.* (1980), 108 D.L.R. (3d) 391 (Ont. H.C.), where *Reid* and the English case of *Lyle-Samuel v. Odhams Ltd.*, [1920] 1 K.B. 135 (C.A.), were followed, the court said it is not necessary to disclose sources even if malice is claimed by a plaintiff because the source would likely have to be called by the defendant to prove his defence.

In the case of *McInnis v. University Students' Council of University of Western Ontario* (1984), 14 D.L.R. (4th) 126 (Ont. H.C.), the decision in *Reid* was reaffirmed with the court only allowing the reporter's notes to be produced at discovery with the source's name

The newspaper rule is imported from England, where disclosure is also generally delayed until trial. The United States has taken a statutory approach and some states have passed "shield" laws that limit the situations in which journalists can be ordered to disclose their sources. But even in the U.S., the common law and federal laws recognize no special privilege for news media sources. A few Canadian provinces have toyed with the idea of enacting their own shield laws (for example, Québec), but no such law has been enacted to date (see below for more discussion on a recently proposed federal law).

A few provinces, notably British Columbia and Saskatchewan, have largely rejected the idea that news media enjoy any special privileges and believe the examination for discovery should be full and revealing.[7]

---

blacked-out. The court said the protection of sources at the discovery stage is a matter of public policy. Also see *Hays v. Weiland* (1918), 42 O.L.R. 637 at 642-643 (C.A.), where the court suggested news gathering can only fulfil its proper service to the public by keeping its sources secret where possible.

7   The B.C. courts have ordered disclosure of sources in the discovery process in several cases whenever it is relevant. In *McConachy v. Times Publishers Ltd.* (1964), 49 D.L.R. (2d) 349 (B.C. C.A.), the court said discovery, by its nature, demands broad and searching questions. In this case, the court held that the questions concerning the source of the story's information were proper. In *Wismer v. MacLean-Hunter Publishing Co. and Fraser (No. 2)*, [1954] 1 D.L.R. 501 (B.C. C.A.), the court made a political commentator disclose his source because the defences of fair comment and qualified privilege were being relied upon and the plaintiff was trying to prove that there was malice on the part of the source.

In *Price v. Richmond Review* (1965), 54 W.W.R. 378 (B.C. S.C.), the court held the source had to be revealed at discovery even though the defence was one of justification (that is, truth) and did not involve the issue of malice. The court said the rightful purpose of the demand for the source's name was to ascertain whether the article was pure invention, mere gossip or rumour.

B.C. courts aren't without mercy, however. In the recent case of *Charman v. Canadian Newspapers Co.* (1991), 59 B.C.L.R. (2d) 177 (Master), a reporter published an allegedly defamatory story after an unidentified third-party provided him with a written copy of a court judgment. The court held that while no "newspaper privilege" existed, the disclosure of the source of the document was unnecessary since the story had been based on a public document. Also see the recent case of *Bouaziz v. Ouston*, 2002 CarswellBC 2041, [2002] B.C.J. No. 2014 (S.C.), in which a court declined to apply the newspaper rule during the discovery stage of a civil trial but was willing to accept that a reporter's promise of anonymity to sources can be privileged communications. The B.C. judge agreed the relationship between journalists and sources must be "sedulously fostered" and that the sources had a legitimate concern of job loss if their names were made public. The judge directed the identities be revealed only to opposing counsel and the plaintiff, and prohibited any other public disclosure of the information.

In the New Brunswick case of *Culligan v. Graphic Ltd.* (1917), 44 N.B.R. 481 (C.A.), the defendants were forced to disclose their source of information because the defence of fair comment was being pleaded. The court said the sources would reveal whether the comments were made on "obviously insufficient information."

In the Saskatchewan case of *Wasylyshyn v. Canadian Broadcasting Corp.* (1989), 48

"Who is B?" was the question put to a reporter called as a non-party witness in a civil case. The court sought to identify the confidential source of documents that were critical to the trial. The journalist refused, citing his promise to the source that the identity would not be revealed. The newspaper he worked for supported his decision. Would the journalist be allowed to maintain confidentiality without penalty?

Yes. Despite a trial judge's initial ruling to the contrary in 2004 that *Hamilton Spectator* reporter Ken Peters was in contempt of court for refusing to reveal his source, the Ontario Court of Appeal overturned that decision in 2008.[8] At trial, the judge had found the journalist was the only witness to a central issue at the trial and his refusal to answer, effectively, ended the proceedings. The court was offered evidence that any journalist who revealed a source would never be employed again, but it was to no avail. The judge, while sympathetic to the media's ethical dilemma, imposed an order for costs against the reporter of $31,600. At the Court of Appeal, however, a majority ruled the trial judge was too quick to use his contempt power, noting "it is a mistake to cite the journalist for contempt immediately. The court should first explore other means of proceeding that would be less intrusive to the journalist-informant relationship of confidentiality." Another key factor was that the judge had failed to consider that "[f]reedom of expression and freedom of the media, protected by s. 2(b) of the Charter, have a direct bearing on a journalist's claim to confidentiality." Specifically, the appeal court stated the judge should have considered the Supreme Court's *Dagenais/Mentuck* test, which requires that a judge minimize the impact of discretionary court orders upon the rights and values of the media and that this test could be applied to cases of journalist-informant confidentiality. Finally, even if the finding of contempt was appropriate, the appeal court ruled the penalty imposed was excessive.

C.C.L.T. 1 (Sask. C.A.), the court pointed out that the newspaper rule has not been elevated to a category of special privilege for journalists and is merely an exercise in judicial discretion (in other words, it's up to each judge). While the court said the newspaper rule was still valid in Saskatchewan, it affirmed the trial judge's decision not to follow the "rule." The court also noted that, in this case, there was no evidence of the sources requesting or even needing confidentiality. It suggested the journalist simply preferred not to mention the names of sources in such stories.

8   *St. Elizabeth Home Society v. Hamilton (City)*, 2004 CarswellOnt 9835, [2004] O.J. No. 5015 (S.C.), overturned in *St. Elizabeth Home Society v. Hamilton (City) (in the matter of the citation of Ken Peters for contempt)*, 2008 CarswellOnt 1381, 2008 ONCA 182 (C.A.).

Sometimes it may not be necessary to reveal the name of a source. In the New Brunswick case of *Baxter v. Canadian Broadcasting Corp.*,[9] the court refused to order the network to disclose the name of a person who gave a journalist a confidential document. Although the court noted it wasn't recognizing any special privilege for a journalist's sources, it decided the document itself was more relevant to the trial. If the information in the document had been relayed to the journalist orally, the court said only then would it have ordered the disclosure of the source's identity.

It also may not be necessary to reveal all the confidential sources involved in a news story. The Nova Scotia Court of Appeal illustrated this in the defamation action involving the *Ottawa Citizen* and Robert Coates, the one-time Conservative defence minister who resigned after the newspaper alleged he had compromised security by visiting a West German nightclub.[10] In the discovery stage, a demand was made for the names of five people alleged to be sources for the story.

A chambers judge ruled there was no special privilege for the press and ordered all the names to be revealed. But on appeal, two of the three judges held that while there was no general privilege immunizing the press, the Canadian Charter of Rights and Freedoms' guarantee of freedom of the press[11] must be weighed against the plaintiff's right to disclosure. While the public has an interest in seeing justice done, the judges felt the public also has an interest in seeing that special confidential relationships are respected.

The court then looked at the relevancy of each confidential source in light of what they contributed to the story. There was no evidence of a special confidential relationship for two of the sources and their role was relevant. But the other three sources did not have to be named. One had not given any information used in the story and the other two had merely passed on "gossip and rumours" that had nothing to do with the alleged defamatory statements.

Finally, one recent civil court ruling underlined the importance of offering evidence of a promise of confidentiality. In a 2004 Saskatchewan defamation case[12] involving political and business dealings, a reporter refused during the pre-trial discovery stage to reveal the identity of a source within the Executive Council of the provincial government. The judge determined the identity of the source was important and relevant to the case. However, because there was also evidence the source had requested and was extended undertakings of confidentiality, the judge ruled the identity

---

9   (1978), 22 N.B.R. (2d) 307 at 315 (Q.B.).
10 *The Citizen v. Coates* (1986), 29 D.L.R. (4th) 523 (N.S. C.A.).
11 Canadian Charter of Rights and Freedoms, Part I of the Constitution Act, 1982, being Schedule B of the Canada Act 1982 (U.K.), 1982, c. 11 (hereinafter, Charter).
12 *Reidy v. Leader Star News Services*, [2004] 4 W.W.R. 759 (Sask. Q.B.).

of the source should be revealed solely to the plaintiff and his counsel for the purposes of this litigation only.

Disclosure in Inquiries or Tribunal Hearings

For public inquiries or bodies like coroners' inquests, the legislation creating and governing the particular body may give it the power to sub-poena witnesses. If so, the tribunal may have an inherent common law power to fine or jail tight-lipped witnesses for contempt or the right to ask a superior court to order the witness to comply with requests for information.

HOW COURTS LOOK AT THE ISSUE OF CONFIDENTIALITY

Until recently, the issue of source disclosure by journalists had not been specifically and fully dealt with other than in motions at the trial level. However, in 1989, just such a case was considered by the Supreme Court of Canada. While the court's decision was somewhat disappointing and circuitous on constitutional questions of freedom of the press, it did give some indication of the court's thinking on source confidentiality.

In *Moysa v. Alberta (Labour Relations Board)*, a reporter for the *Edmonton Journal* wrote a story about a union's organizing activities.[13] One of the companies targeted for the union's efforts was the Hudson Bay Company and one week after the story was published several employees were fired, allegedly for trying to organize a union.

Moysa, the reporter, was called before a labour relations board as a witness and the union indicated it wanted to ask her whether she had spoken with anyone at the company before writing her story and what the details of the conversation were. Moysa refused to testify and disclose her sources of information, claiming that communications between a reporter and sources are protected under common law and the Charter. The board disa-greed and ordered her to testify under oath.

The newspaper went to court to get the order quashed. The trial court dealt with the issue in two parts: (i) whether there is a common law privilege; and (ii) whether the Charter offers any protection to journalists as a special class in society.

The newspaper argued that while there was no special category of privilege for journalists under the common law, a general principle of privilege could be applied since freedom of the press is essential to society.

---

13 *Moysa v. Alberta (Labour Relations Board)* (1986), 45 Alta. L.R. (2d) 37 (Q.B.).

The newspaper's lawyer said sources would dry up if the promise of confidentiality couldn't be protected.

But the trial judge refused to stretch the common law that far, noting that if a question is relevant to an inquiry, it is in the public interest to ask about sources of information. The information may have been concocted or sources may have had ulterior motives. The court also rejected the idea that a journalist should only be called as a witness after all other avenues of seeking the information were pursued.

The argument that the Charter's guarantee of "freedom of the press" protects journalists' sources was also rejected. The judge said this "freedom" refers to a "species of intellectual freedom" extended to everyone, and does not impart a separable right to the press as an entity or class. According to the trial judge, compelling a journalist to testify as to his or her sources does not infringe upon the right to use the press. He refused to quash the labour board's order.

The newspaper appealed, but the provincial appeal court agreed with the trial judge that journalists have no special privilege in common law or in the Charter.[14] One appeal judge added that it's up to the legislators to create a journalist's category of privilege.

The Supreme Court of Canada Decision

Unfortunately, the Supreme Court of Canada agreed with the two lower courts.[15] The judges held that the reporter in this case had no special privilege to refuse to testify before the labour board. While the court declined to answer the constitutional questions, it did express some doubt that sources would dry up if journalists had to reveal who they spoke with. The judges suggested that clear evidence of that danger would have to be presented to a court in the future to justify the granting of any privilege based on the Charter's guarantee of freedom of the press.[16]

First, though, the court noted that even if a qualified form of testimonial privilege exists in Canada, in this case, it would not apply, since the union was more interested in the information the journalist gave to Hudson Bay officials concerning the organizing campaign than it was in the identities of

---

14 (1987), 52 Alta. L.R. (2d) 193 (C.A.).

15 [1989] 1 S.C.R. 1572.

16 Subsequently, the Supreme Court of Canada's ruling *R. v. McClure*, [2001] 1 S.C.R. 445, reiterated that while the "journalist-informant" confidential relationship is not protected by a class privilege, it "may be protected on a case-by-case basis" in the same way as doctor-patient, psychologist-patient and religious communications relationships. Again, the court was stressing the need for clear evidence to be presented each time that protection of sources is requested.

the people the journalist spoke to. The judges said the claim of privilege couldn't be applied to disclosure of information.

The court also referred to the leading United States Supreme Court case which held that the U.S. Constitution's First Amendment accords a reporter no privilege against appearing before a grand jury and answering questions as to either the identity of his or her news sources, or information which he or she has received in confidence.[17]

In that case, one judge said that each claim of privilege should be judged on its particular facts by striking a balance between the freedom of the press and the obligation of all citizens to give relevant testimony. The Supreme Court of Canada appears to agree with that and with the idea that the evidence must be crucial to whomever seeks it and also must be relevant. On the facts presented to the labour board, it was held that the evidence sought from the journalist was crucial to the union's allegation of unfair labour practices, and relevant.

The court also referred to one of its earlier judgments on the general question of when a special privilege against disclosure of confidential communications should be established. This case set out a test that may be applied.

Slavutych v. Baker involved an action for wrongful dismissal and the admissibility in court of confidential appraisals of a university professor's work.[18] The confidential information was intended for use only by a tenure committee, but the university used the report as grounds to fire the professor and wanted to introduce the document into court. In deciding whether the communication should be declared privileged, and thus inadmissible, the court acknowledged the theory of an American author on the subject.

J. Wigmore suggests a privilege should be granted to any communication which fulfills the following conditions:[19]

1. The communications must originate in a confidence that they will not be disclosed.
2. This element of confidentiality must be essential to the full and satisfactory maintenance of the relation between the parties.
3. The relation must be one which in the opinion of the community ought to be sedulously fostered.
4. The injury that would inure to the relation by the disclosure of the communications must be greater than the benefit thereby gained for the correct disposal of litigation.

17 *Branzburg v. Hayes*, 408 U.S. 665 (1972).
18 (1975), 55 D.L.R. (3d) 224 at 228 (S.C.C.).
19 *Wigmore: On Evidence*, 3rd ed. (McNaughton Revision, 1961), para. 2285.

Each condition must be fully met in order for a communication to enjoy a privilege from disclosure. The first requirement means that it must be apparent the information is being given only on the condition that it will remain confidential. The second requirement is that the court must be able to recognize there are important reasons for confidentiality. For example, the source could lose his or her job. The third requirement is that the public must agree that the confidential nature of the relationship between the source and recipient of the communication should be protected. The final requirement is that the injury to this confidential relationship resulting from the disclosure of the communications must be greater than the benefit of resolving the court action.

As noted, the Supreme Court avoided the constitutional questions in *Moysa*, but it appears that the Wigmore test will play an important role when the right case does go to the high court. Wigmore's test was also applied in an Ontario case that has some interesting analogies to situations faced by journalists.

That case involved a member of the legislature who refused, during a criminal proceeding, to divulge the name of an informant.[20] Elected members of legislatures and Parliament enjoy many privileges which protect them for such things as defamation actions and arrest arising from civil proceedings.

The question which was directed to the Ontario Court of Appeal was whether the member also enjoyed protection from disclosing his sources while performing his duties in government. The member argued that law enforcement officials, who also work for the Crown, are not required to divulge the names of their informants unless the name would help the accused prove his innocence. The member suggested the same rule should apply here to himself as a servant of the Crown.

It was a difficult issue for the courts. Two of the five judges said there is such a privilege based on public policy grounds. But a majority of the court held the opposite view. Using the Wigmore test, they found the legislative member did not meet the third and fourth requirements. Looking at the third requirement, the court held that the function of the member is in the field of legislation, and not law enforcement. Similarly, journalists report news, they do not enforce the law.

Continuing with a consideration of the third requirement, the court also found that the relationship between the member and the informant is not one which should be "sedulously fostered." The court made the point that informers should go to the police if they have evidence of crimes. The fourth requirement also failed because the injury created by naming the

---

20 *Reference Re Legislative Privilege* (1978), 39 C.C.C. (2d) 226 (Ont. C.A.).

source was felt not to be greater than the benefit of having the case properly determined.

Over the long term, it's difficult to predict how the Supreme Court's decision in *Moysa* will affect the application of the "newspaper rule" but it appears at this time that it is reasonable to expect that courts will continue to offer journalists limited protection until a matter reaches trial.

A former police chief alleged the CBC stated or implied in a documentary program that while he was a member of the Edmonton Police Service, he frequently had sexual relations with prostitutes, had sexually assaulted, robbed and unlawfully confined prostitutes, and participated in an illegal cover-up to ensure no investigation was undertaken. During the pre-trial discovery in a defamation case, he requested the CBC produce all relevant documents in its possession, some of which the CBC claimed revealed confidential sources. Would the CBC be required to produce the documents during the discovery stage?

No. An Alberta judge refused to force the CBC to disclose its documents identifying confidential sources. This 2005 ruling is the first case in Canada to rule on a strict application of the "Newspaper Rule" where evidence showed a confidential relationship (confidential source information and communications between solicitor and client) and where the Charter's right to freedom of the press was raised.[21] While the judge stated a journalist-source privilege can only be applied on a case-by-case basis, he ruled he must consider the "public policy rationale underlying the Newspaper Rule" and apply the Wigmore test for qualified privilege "in accordance with the constitutional guarantee provided under s. 2(b) of the Charter." The judge noted the Supreme Court of Canada has said freedom of the press, "which can include the protection of the journalist-source relationship," is "fundamental" and should not be set aside "except in exceptional circumstances." While the information did not have to be revealed in the discovery stage, the motions judge left it open to the assigned trial judge to reconsider the request before the trial, saying "it would not be fair for Wasylyshyn to have to wait until the beginning of trial to have the disclosure question decided, as this could ultimately lead to a trial by ambush and/or an unwanted adjournment."

---

21 *Wasylyshen v. Canadian Broadcasting Corp.*, [2005] A.J. No. 1685 (Q.B.).

PROPOSED FEDERAL LAW TO PROTECT JOURNALISTS' SOURCES

Bill C-426, a Private Member's Bill, was introduced in the Parliament of Canada on April 17, 2007. At the time of this publication, this proposed law would amend the Canada Evidence Act to restrict when and how a court might order a journalist to name sources.

An individual applying to a court to have a source revealed would have to prove it is in the public interest and show all reasonable steps have been taken to identify the source through alternative means. Judges would also be required to consider the impact on the source before requiring a journalist to name the individual in question. The proposed amendment would also require judges to impose strict conditions on search warrants issued to seize journalists' notes or other documents.

The bill received first reading but is unlikely to become law since the government has other higher priority matters to consider. That said, it is well worth noting the proposed provisions:

39.1 (1) The following definitions apply in this section.

"journalist" means a person who contributes regularly and directly to the gathering, writing, production or dissemination of information for the public through any media, or anyone who assists such a person.

"record" has the meaning assigned to that word by section 3 of the Access to Information Act.

Application

(2) This section applies despite any other Act of Parliament and any other provision of this Act.

Disclosure of the source

(3) Subject to subsection (5), no journalist shall be compelled to disclose the source of any information that the journalist has gathered, written, produced or disseminated for the public through any media or to disclose any information or record that could identify the source.

Power of the judge

(4) A judge may, on his or her own initiative, raise the potential application of subsection (3) and ask the prosecution, the defence and any other party to present an opinion on the matter.

Order

(5) A judge may not order a journalist to disclose to a person the source of any information that the journalist has gathered, written, produced or disseminated for the public through any media, unless the judge considers that

    (a) the person has done everything in the person's power to discover the source of the information; and

    (b) the disclosure is in the public interest, having regard to

        (i)   the outcome of the litigation,

        (ii)   the freedom of information, and

        (iii) the impact of the journalist's testimony on the source.

Burden of proof

(6) A person who requests a judge to order the disclosure of a source has the burden of proving the matters referred to in paragraphs (5)(a) and (b).

Disclosure of unpublished information

(7) A journalist is required to disclose information or a record that has not been published only if the information or record is of vital importance and cannot be produced in evidence by any other means.

Search warrant

(8) A judge may not issue a search warrant, with or without conditions, in order to obtain information or a record that is in the possession of a journalist and have it produced in evidence if, having considered all the circumstances unless, the judge is satisfied that

    (a) all the conditions set out in section 487 of the Criminal Code are met;

    (b) in the circumstances, Her Majesty's interest in the investigation and prosecution of an offence takes precedence over the journalist's right to privacy in gathering and disseminating information;

    (c) the affidavit submitted in support of the application

        (i)   contains sufficient detail to allow the judge to properly consider all the circumstances and determine whether all the conditions referred to in this subsection are met, and

        (ii)   sets out all the alternative sources of information and affirms that they have been consulted and that every reasonable effort has been made to obtain the information from those sources;

    (d) any conditions imposed by the judge will ensure that the journalist and the media will not be unduly impeded from publishing the information; and

    (e) the search will not be unreasonably conducted.

Record seized

(9) Any record seized under subsection (8) shall immediately be placed in an envelope, and the envelope shall be sealed right away and opened only

before a judge who shall determine the manner in which the record is to be kept and disclosed.

Participant in seizure

(10) A person who participates in the seizure of a record under subsection (8) shall keep the content of the record confidential, unless the judge directs otherwise.

Information or record deemed published

(11) For the purposes of this Act, information or a record is deemed to have been published if the publication that contains the information or record or its medium is produced in evidence.

OTHER ISSUES INVOLVING NEWS SOURCES

Although the practice is frowned upon, sometimes a journalist will strike a deal with a source regarding the use of his or her comments and information. Handling these agreements with sources properly involves more than questions of journalistic ethics.

Breach of Contract

If a journalist expressly agrees to allow a source to "veto" or even review a story before it is published, a court may hold the reporter to his or her word.[22] A court could find that the reporter and the source have made an enforceable contract. If a journalist disregards the promise, a source may be able to get an injunction stopping the publication of the comments or he could theoretically sue for breach of contract and claim damages.

---

22 An analogy can be found in the case of *Paddington Press Ltd. v. Champ* (1979), 43 C.P.R. (2d) 175 (Ont. H.C.). An injunction was successfully brought against a television network that planned to broadcast an interview with a prominent personality and author. The book publisher alleged that there was an agreement with the reporter not to broadcast the interview until a certain date. But the reporter claimed he made no such deal. Due to the conflicting claims of each side, the judge granted the injunction until the matter could be dealt with in a trial. In *Peat Marwick Thorne v. Canadian Broadcasting Corp.* (1991), 84 D.L.R. (4th) 656 (Ont. Gen. Div.), the accounting firm succeeded in getting an interim injunction halting the broadcast of an investigative TV report about Romania's former dictator. The accountants said they gave the interview on the condition that no information would be used without the firm's consent. The court granted the temporary injunction saying the alleged agreement was a serious matter and the accounting firm would suffer greater damage to its reputation than the media would incur in having the broadcast delayed.

In 1986, an injunction was granted by an Alberta court barring the national broadcast of a CBC interview with a convicted serial killer. The accused was appealing some of his convictions and, while the program may also have been contemptuous, the judge focused on the fact that the CBC journalist who dealt with the inmate had agreed before a series of interviews to allow him to see the finished program before it aired. The judge held that the CBC had broken its agreement with the interview subject and could not broadcast the story.

If possible, a journalist should not make any deals with sources about the end use of their information. In most cases, giving a source or interview subject the right to have a say in how a story is told can spell legal trouble or, at the very least, editorial disputes between the journalist and his source.

Breach of Confidence or Trust

Another factor to consider is that there is a common law action called *breach of confidence* which involves the unauthorized publication of confidential information.[23] This action can be invoked whenever a third party (that is, a journalist) becomes privy to private information arising from relationships between others that call for confidentiality.

For example, anyone in a master-servant or employer-employee relationship has a common law duty to keep corporate secrets confidential. If a journalist were to be told something confidential by an employee, the employer could claim there was a breach of confidence and ask for an injunction to prevent further publication of the information. In some cases, the employer may also be able to sue for damages up to the value of the information. Other relationships involving a "confidence" are husband-wife, doctor-patient and solicitor-client.

In addition, if an off-the-record comment is used and traced back to the employee, he or she could be fired. That employee could possibly have grounds to sue you for causing his or her dismissal if the information was supposed to be secret.

Problems can also arise when information is provided to a third-party on a confidential basis and a journalist becomes involved. In one case, a company producing a "confidential report" distributed to brokerages applied for an injunction to prevent a newspaper from publishing details in the document.[24] The judge ruled there was no issue to be tried since the newspaper had not received the information on a confidential basis (it came from

---

23 For a good discussion of the tort of "breach of confidence" see Williams, *The Law of Defamation in Canada* (Toronto: Butterworths, 1976), at 41-48.

24 *B.W. International Inc. v. Thomson Canada Ltd.* (1996), 137 D.L.R. (4th) 398 (Ont. Ct. (Gen. Div.).

an undisclosed third-party) and the information was "so widely disseminated it did not have the necessary quality of confidentiality." The court also cited the importance of freedom of the press in denying the request for an injunction. As always, a lawyer is the best individual to assess whether any information received is actually confidential.

There may also be statutory provisions which prohibit some government employees from disclosing confidential information. For example, members of the Canadian Security Intelligence Service are prohibited by law from disclosing the names of sources of information or employees involved in covert activities, as well as any information gained during the performance of their duties.[25] Most governments also require civil servants to take an oath of secrecy.

On or Off the Record?

A common problem arises when a source makes a demand after an interview that all or part of the interview not be used. In that case, the source has no right to make such a demand if there was no mention beforehand that all comments are not for publication. The courts may suggest, in the absence of any agreement, that it should be presumed that all comments to a journalist are on-the-record.[26]

A SOURCES CHECKLIST

1. The general rule is that courts are unlikely to offer absolute protection to a journalist who does not want to disclose the identity of a source, if it is considered relevant or necessary to the proper adjudication of a matter.

2. In a criminal proceeding, courts may use the Criminal Code to compel a journalist to reveal a source. Section 545 allows a justice conducting a preliminary hearing to send a witness who refuses to testify to jail for periods of up to eight days. At trial, a judge can cite a journalist for contempt and order a jail term and/or a fine.

3. In many provinces, civil courts recognize the special role of the news media and follow what is called the "newspaper rule." Under this common law rule, a court will try to avoid ordering a journalist to

---

25 Canadian Security Intelligence Service Act, R.S.C. 1985, c. C-23, ss. 18(1) and 19.

26 For instance, in defamation actions the courts have held that anyone who knows the press are present must expect that their comments could be published.

disclose a source until the matter reaches trial. However, courts in a few provinces don't follow the rule and may order disclosure in the early stages of a court action.

4. Some courts have found that there is no special privilege for journalists in the common law or under the Charter against disclosing a confidential source's name, however, other courts have been willing to give special consideration to the Charter's promise of freedom of the press during pre-trial stages.

5. A journalist should not make promises to sources that he or she doesn't intend to keep (for example, to let the source see the story before it's published). A court may hold the journalist to his or her word and issue an injunction for breach of contract.

6. Some relationships impose an obligation of confidence on the parties (for example, employer-employee, solicitor-client or doctor-patient). If that confidence is breached by one of the parties passing on confidential information to a third party (such as a journalist), the other party may be able to seek an injunction restraining publication.

4

AVOIDING LEGAL RISKS
IN INVESTIGATIVE REPORTING

It is said that every reporter is an "investigative reporter." However, the news gathering industry does recognize a special breed of journalist. As one broadcasting executive once testified in court, "an investigative reporter is simply a reporter who gets stories that nobody wants you to have."[1]

Investigative reporting calls for extensive research and, sometimes, the use of exotic or clandestine techniques. When published or broadcast, an investigative story often attracts great attention and someone's reputation may even be ruined or sullied by it.

No judge has ever said that journalists shouldn't engage in investigative reporting (as long as it doesn't interfere with a police investigation or a judicial process). In fact, the courts have generally supported and encouraged the news media's endeavours to inquire into alleged wrongs against society and other individuals.

By its very nature, though, an investigative story carries more weight than so-called "spot news." As a result, the courts may look for a higher

---

1 *Vogel v. Canadian Broadcasting Corp.*, [1982] 3 W.W.R. 97 at 122 (B.C. S.C.).

standard of care and skill from an investigative reporter. The courts most certainly will not tolerate anything less than the reasonable standard of care expected of all journalists.

In the following case, a judge examined step-by-step how one particularly defamatory investigative story was put together and, in the process, set forth some worthwhile opinions on the potential for abuse that exists in all stories.

THE CASE OF *VOGEL v. CANADIAN BROADCASTING CORPORATION*

In March of 1980, the CBC broadcast three television news stories about Richard Vogel, the then-Deputy Attorney General of British Columbia. The programs said that Vogel had used his position to influence, or try to influence, the course of justice in three criminal cases for the purpose of protecting his friends. The programs were the culmination of a long investigation by a CBC Vancouver journalist. The reporter had had about ten years' experience as a print journalist before joining the CBC in 1979 as an investigative reporter and was considered more than competent.

The first broadcast was a 14-minute special production on the six o'clock news for the British Columbia region. A condensed version ran that night on the late-night news program that followed the national news. The third broadcast was a short story which ran the next night on CBC's *The National* and was seen across the country.

Richard Vogel and his family immediately suffered the effects of the story. He was suspended without pay immediately after the story was aired and there was a flood of demands for his resignation. Two weeks later, the Attorney General announced that an investigation had cleared Vogel of any wrongdoing. But the CBC refused to retract the story, publicly announcing that it would stand by it and defend any court actions.

In the defamation lawsuit that followed, the British Columbia Supreme Court awarded Vogel a total of $125,000. It is among the highest awards granted to a victim of defamation in Canada. The court assessed joint damages against the CBC and the journalist for $100,000. Another $25,000 was levied against the CBC as punitive damages to show the court's disapproval of the corporation's behaviour.

The Use of Sources

As it turned out, the journalist's only source for his story was a senior Crown prosecutor in the province's criminal justice branch. Although the reporter went to great lengths to confirm the source's allegations of wrong-doing, his efforts were fruitless. Nevertheless, the reporter chose to interpret certain events as proof of improper and scandalous behaviour by the Deputy Attorney General and ignore the dead ends in his investigation.

As good journalistic policy dictates, the story was reviewed by CBC executives and lawyers before airing. But the court noted it was still aired even though the executive producer of the program knew there was some doubt about evidence supporting the allegations.

The court had a great deal to say about the use of sources, particularly ones who give out information on a confidential basis. The idea for the story began with a lunch meeting between the journalist and a senior Crown prosecutor in Vancouver. The journalist was hoping to get an investigative piece out of a court case which, at that time, linked the then-Chief Justice of British Columbia to a prostitute. The hooker's story was later found to be a complete falsehood.

The prosecutor hinted that a better story might be found in the actions of Deputy Attorney General Vogel in that case and others. He promised more information. A series of clandestine meetings between the two men were then held over the next several weeks in deserted areas of Stanley Park or while driving in areas of the city where they wouldn't be recognized.

As was his job, the journalist demanded proof of the prosecutor's allegation that Vogel had interfered in the Chief Justice's case and two others. The prosecutor produced a confidential file which outlined some of the office correspondence on the cases, but there wasn't much to substantiate the allegations. The journalist pressed for more information, particularly a letter which was said to have been sent to the Attorney General outlining in detail the complaints against Vogel.

The Crown prosecutor agreed to supply the document secretly. The judge in this case recounted this event:

> [The Crown prosecutor], by that time, was showing some aptitude for playing his role of "Deep Throat." The operation involved [the prosecutor], on a Saturday morning, leaving a copy of the letter in a plain brown envelope in a locker in the Vancouver Bus Depot, hiding the locker key in the angle of a Y-shaped beam in an unfinished building and then informing [the reporter] that he might find something of interest were he to look in that place. The smooth progress of the operation was interrupted because [the reporter] looked in the wrong beam and found an old furniture store invoice. After puzzling for some time as to the hidden message intended to be conveyed by

that piece of paper, he telephoned [the prosecutor], got further directions, and was thus enabled to find the key, find the locker and thus come into possession of the copy of the letter.[2]

The letter, which was produced in court, didn't substantiate the claims of the prosecutor. In fact, the letter actually dispelled the idea that there had been any wrongdoing. But it didn't seem to matter to the reporter at this stage. The judge noted, "[The reporter], by that time, was convinced that he was on the trail of a major scandal, and found it easy to reject any evidence inconsistent with that view."[3]

After getting all the documents he could from his source, the journalist could still find no corroboration for the allegations. Yet, he was urged on by the source. As it later turned out, the prosecutor had a grudge against the Deputy Attorney General. But the journalist chose to accept the word of this single source as the truth, even though his initial investigation found nothing. The judge here felt he knew why:

> [The reporter] prides himself on being a sceptic, but in his dealings with [the prosecutor] he showed himself incapable of scepticism. That inability may result from his romantic view of the investigative reporter as society's bulwark against corruption — fighting a guerrilla war against the "establishment." What he calls "scepticism" is a sourly cynical assumption that corruption is rampant in the establishment and that all attempts by it to maintain privacy or confidentiality are part of a conspiracy to suppress the truth. He is consequently inclined to regard as something of a hero any member of the establishment who is willing to be a "leak." He is not inclined to accept, even as a possibility, that information provided to him in that way may not be reliable.[4]

The reporter's assigning editors were no less guilty. They blindly accepted the reporter's word that the sole source was reliable. Sometimes, the reporter would even get angry if his source's credibility was questioned. Court testimony showed that it got to the point where editors avoided any questioning of the journalist for fear that he would become further agitated by their doubt.

The moral in this is that even high-level sources can have hidden motives. The word of any source, secret or not, must be thoroughly corroborated in the case of serious allegations. Many top journalists adopt a rule that a source's allegations must be corroborated by two or more independent sources of information.

---

2 *Ibid.*, at 123-124.
3 *Ibid.*, at 124.
4 *Ibid.*, at 128.

Ambush Interviews and Deceptive Techniques

The court took a dim view of "ambush interviews" which catch an interview subject off-guard and tend to place the person in a bad light. Invariably, little information of value is added to the story. Similar analogies can be drawn to other "stunts" that appear to be more flash than substance. For example, one might suggest that a television clip showing a reporter beating on a door that no one answers, or shouting for a comment, over-dramatizes the point. The question to be asked is whether the investigative technique justifies the information gained.

While an ambush isn't illegal or even defamatory in and of itself, the court considered its use in Vogel's case as further proof of the reporter's careless and malicious attitude. At one point in the story, a Crown Attorney was shown being interviewed in the ambush interview style. The transcript of the story read as follows:

> Nils Jensen's boss is this man: Brian Weddell, the chief prosecutor for the Kootenays area — the man who's complained to his colleagues about Vogel's interference in this case. But he didn't seem to want to shed much light on it.
>
> [REPORTER]: There are several people that say Vogel phoned one of your prosecutors directly and told him to lay the dangerous driving charge and that the guy checked with you and you said it was O.K. Is that not true?
>
> [BRIAN WEDDELL]: Not that I can recall. I don't recall having any contact with Mr. Vogel at all about this case.
>
> [REPORTER]: No, you weren't supposed to have had contact directly with him — but one of your prosecutors did, and you knew about it. Is that true?
>
> [BRIAN WEDDELL]: Not that I recall.
>
> [REPORTER]: Well, you wouldn't forget something like that, would you?
>
> [BRIAN WEDDELL]: I don't know.[5]

The judge saw this as the point in the story in which the theme of the "good guys" and "bad guys" develops. He described how the interview that appeared on camera differed from what had actually happened:

> Weddell was subjected to an "ambush." The first view, which was taken with a hidden camera at some distance, shows him walking across a parking lot. His hat is pulled down over his eyes, his shoulders are hunched into his coat, his hands are in his pockets and a cigarette dangles from his lips. The impression given is one of shiftiness. The fact apparently is that he was on his

---

5 *Ibid.*, at 138.

way to his office on a cold morning, unaware that he was being watched. In those circumstances, few would come off better, either in appearance or in reacting to the series of questions put sternly by the reporter while a camera is pointed from over his shoulder.[6]

The judge went on to note that the telephone call in question had happened more than a year earlier. The viewers were not told that and the innuendo was that there was a cover-up. The result was that the person came off looking badly in the interview and in this case the "ambush" technique hardly seemed necessary.

The court also mentioned, without comment, two other techniques of investigative reporters. The first technique involved the use of "bogus scripts." The journalist claimed they were the prime tool of the investigative reporter. The scripts were supposedly copies of the story that was ready to go to air. The purpose of the bogus scripts was to lead an interview subject to think that the CBC had solid evidence of the allegations outlined. The script would then be used to persuade the subject to "confirm" the allegations.

A second technique involved the use of hidden microphones and "body packs" to record conversations without the interview subject knowing.

In both cases, the techniques did not turn up any new or corroborating evidence. The interview subjects refused to confirm the allegations and the journalist eventually chose to ignore the results of these investigative methods.

What's important to note here is that the court interpreted the reporter's decision to ignore these investigative results as further proof of malice and an intent to distort the facts.

Manipulation of Facts and Interviews

The Vogel story contained other interviews which the court found slanted or taken out of context in order to produce the story the reporter wanted to portray. One such interview involved another Crown prosecutor in Victoria. The story transcript read as follows:

> The story of Vogel's interference — the phone call to the prosecutor — is common knowledge among some B.C. prosecutors, but no one seems to want to talk about it.
>
> [REPORTER]: You say you don't have any direct knowledge about the phone call, but the story is commonly discussed in Crown counsel circles. How widely is it known?

---

6 *Ibid.*, at 147.

[NILS JENSEN]: I have no idea — I can't comment on that.

[REPORTER]: How long have the stories been circulating?

[NILS JENSEN]: Again — I can't comment on that.

[REPORTER]: But you have heard the story?

[NILS JENSEN]: I prefer not to comment on that.[7]

This may appear to be a typical "no comment" interview. However, the judge explained the unusual manner in which it came about. At the beginning of the interview, Mr. Jensen had initially said "on-camera" that he had heard "something" about alleged interference and about the alleged telephone call. But, in fact, he had no personal knowledge of the call. Realizing that he had gone too far, Jensen asked that the interview not be used.

The journalist agreed not to use the interview if Jensen would consent to start the interview again and state simply "no comment." Jensen agreed and the court noted how the interview was eventually used:

> The interview on screen clearly conveys the impression that Jensen was confirming the truth of what was asserted by [the reporter] in the questions — and [the reporter] agreed that that was the intent. . . . [Jensen's] expression is that of a man anxious to tell the truth and troubled that it is not open to him to do so. Each of his refusals to comment comes after a period of cogitation — the pause, punctuated only by "ah's" of indecision, before he finally says that he would prefer not to comment as to whether he heard the story, is about 15 seconds — a long time, on television.[8]

What was actually an interview with a person who knew nothing of the allegations became a suggestion of a cover-up.

A second interview for the Vogel story was actually rehearsed and then staged to produce a desired effect. The interview was with a friend of a young man who had been caught driving while intoxicated and was charged by police. The accused, a Mr. Rigg, was not convicted and the journalist wanted to portray Vogel as a friend of the family who had helped Rigg out. The reporter set out to ask Rigg's friend what he knew of Vogel's involvement. The judge described the interview that appeared in the story:

> The impression is that [the friend], taken by surprise, gave one responsive answer and clammed up, presumably to protect his friend, Rigg, when the questions turned to the delicate subject of "how he got off." The interview

---

7 *Ibid.*, at 138.
8 *Ibid.*, at 146.

ends with [the friend], looking apprehensive and yet knowing, apparently trying to escape from the interviewer.[9]

In fact, Rigg's "friend" had had a falling out with Rigg soon after the arrest and was more than willing to co-operate with the journalist if it could be done in such a manner that he would appear to be an unwilling participant. The night before the interview, two of the reporters working on the story rehearsed him in the performance he gave.

There was one other staged interview. It was with the Crown prosecutor who was the reporter's source. The interview consisted of the prosecutor refusing to comment on the allegations of wrongdoing. Testimony at court indicated that the object of the interview was to ensure that no one would think the Crown prosecutor was the source of the information.

Sensationalized Packaging

The judge noted that seemingly innocent words on paper can become damning when combined with the right pictures. Both print and broadcast journalists should note this. Throughout his ruling, the judge commented on the influence the visual package had on the story. For example, the news began with these headlines:

> This is the CBC Evening News, with Bill Good, Junior.
>
> British Columbia's Deputy Attorney General has interfered with the judicial system. Tonight, a detailed report.[10]

Of that brief beginning, the judge said:

> The backdrop at this point is a photograph of the plaintiff with a worried, harassed look. That was taken from some film footage obtained by [another reporter] several weeks earlier in preparation for the program, but without the plaintiff's knowledge of the purpose.
>
> This segment, though brief, was of the most attention-getting kind. Its impact, in its context as the lead item, was far greater than can be visualized from reading the words on paper.[11]

Also, the judge noted the graphic used to introduce the item after the headlines was the scales of justice. But the scales were tilted about 30

---

9   *Ibid.*, at 150.
10 *Ibid.*, at 136.
11 *Ibid.*, at 143.

percent, which a CBC executive said was considered "just right" for the story. It appeared several times in the story as a type of logo.

The judge felt the combination of these dramatic visual effects helped make the allegations appear to be even more serious and controversial.

Balance and the Right of Reply

As every journalist knows, it's important in any story to accurately portray both sides and, if possible, allow the subject of the story to answer comments about the issues. This story gave the impression, on at least two occasions, that key people who could have offered the "other side" refused to speak with the CBC.

One segment of the story involved attempts to contact Vogel himself. The script reads as follows:

> We offered Dick Vogel an opportunity to answer questions about his actions, but an associate of the Attorney General's Department declined the offer on Mr. Vogel's behalf.[12]

The truth of the matter was that a public relations representative was contacted by the journalist about a possible interview. The spokesman was told only that the interview would involve allegations about three court cases. Vogel's spokesman wasn't told what the allegations were about and he saw no urgency in arranging an interview. The court said the request was, at best, a deceptive half-truth.

At another point in the script, it was suggested that a lawyer involved in the incidents was faking an illness to avoid comment. "We tried to contact Mickey Moran," the reporter noted, "but were told he was ill and couldn't talk to us."[13]

· In fact, the CBC avoided contact with the lawyer until the story was almost finished. Only one attempt was made to speak to the lawyer — at his house. They were told they couldn't see him and there were no further attempts to get a comment.

---

12 *Ibid.*
13 *Ibid.*, at 144.

Sensationalized Writing

The judge was very critical of the writing technique in the Vogel story. The script was riddled with innuendos and the reporter suggested throughout that there was a cover-up. The truth was there were no facts to back up the allegations.

Even the CBC national news was criticized for its writing. The national reporter in Vancouver at the time reported on the story and the judge was critical of the vague, yet defamatory, style of writing and intonation used by the reporter. For instance, the judge zeroed in on one line in *The National* report that said: "Dick Vogel *had* used his powerful position . . ."[14] [emphasis added].

The judge found that the emphasis on the word "had" gave the impression that it had long been suspected that Vogel was acting improperly. The court found a more serious aggravation of the libel in this closing passage:

> While no cabinet ministers have been implicated in the allegations so far, the whole business is obviously embarrassing to the Social Credit government.[15]

The suggestion was that Vogel wasn't alone and that even cabinet ministers might be involved. There was no proof offered at the trial to justify the statement. The court concluded that it was puffery designed to give the story a more serious tone for the national audience.

The judge had this to say about standards of journalism in this case:

> It is an accepted tenet of our democratic society that the press serves the public interest by exposing corruption and misconduct by those in public life, and that it is essential that it perform that role. It is, however, sometimes hard to see that any public interest is served other than the interest in being entertained. In this case, that was the interest intended to be served. The program was conceived and executed as a form of entertainment presented in the guise of news. . . .
>
> What was considered was, in essence, the question: "Can we get away with it?" That having been answered in the affirmative, the next question was: "How can we produce the greatest effect?"[16]

---

14 *Ibid.*, at 172.
15 *Ibid.*, at 190.
16 *Ibid.*, at 180.

Some Final Thoughts

There is much to be learned from the mistakes of others. It's sad to note that soon after the Vogel story aired, the reporter burned all his notes, the dummy scripts and other documents related to the story. It appeared to have been done to prevent them from being available in a court action.

While the *Vogel* case clearly illustrated the pitfalls of shoddy investigative reporting techniques, it also pointed out how lazy and gullible other journalists can be when such a story breaks. The judge in Vogel's case had some sharp criticisms for the reporting done after the CBC's story broke and the reports on the defamation trial itself. The reporting on the trial sometimes seemed to focus on any hints of incriminating information which might confirm the investigative story ? some reporters refused to believe the story was wrong.

The judge felt the "pack mentality" of journalists can lead to further aggravation of a defamation:

> When one media outlet suggests scandalous conduct on the part of a public figure, it can be expected that its competitors will, if the story is one of widespread interest, assign reporters, commentators and support staff to get their own story and join in the controversy. It can also be expected that there will be a tendency by some to outdo the others by getting a more interesting angle, which is likely to be one which will put the subject in an even worse light.[17]

Perhaps, one final lesson is found in this sentence which the judge quotes from another judgment:

> To only give the public a look at the side of the coin supportive of their comments and opinions and not to show the facts to the contrary on the other side of the coin is to deal in half-truths, and comments made in this way are neither fair nor made in good faith.[18]

AN INVESTIGATIVE STORY CHECKLIST

As noted at the beginning, investigative reporting often involves more care and effort than the average story. Here are some points to keep in mind when researching such a story.

---

17 *Ibid.*
18 *Thomas v. Canadian Broadcasting Corp.*, [1981] 4 W.W.R. 289 at 337-338 (N.W.T. S.C.), quoted in *Vogel* at 187.

1. *Keep notes and outs:* It's a mistake to neglect to make or keep notes during interviews or when doing research. This becomes most apparent when a lawsuit has been launched and you're looking back to justify the story. Admittedly, there are both good and bad points in keeping detailed notes. A journalist's notes can be used by either side in a court proceeding to prove/disprove malice, identify sources or validate quotes.

   Chances are notes will be more valuable than dangerous. For instance, defamation actions often take two years to get to trial and a journalist may need notes to refresh his or her memory. Even if a journalist is taping a conversation, notes should be taken in case the recording fails. Still, one should be careful when taking notes since they can indicate a reporter's attitude at the time. For example, malice could be found in a reporter's jottings that the interview subject "looks shifty" or "is a jerk." One final point. Many journalists now write their notes on computer terminals. Whenever possible, keep these notes in a separate computer file rather than write and edit the story directly from the master file.

   The same guidelines apply to broadcast journalists regarding keeping outtakes or unused video, film or audio clips.

2. *Tape conversations:* It's bothersome and not always possible, but a journalist should record all conversations with key people in a story. Tapes are obviously better than notes for proving that someone said what they said. Remember, however, that simply having a tape of someone saying something isn't good enough to prove the truth of a statement.

3. *Corroborate:* It's essential that all key points or "facts" be backed up by at least one other source. Some journalists insist on corroboration from two to three other sources. In another British Columbia case, a radio station wrongly reported that a local lawyer had been fined for fraud. The story was based solely on an unconfirmed telephone tip. The judge in *Tait v. New Westminster Radio Ltd.* found the reporting to be grossly negligent.[19]

---

19 (1984), 58 B.C.L.R. 194 (C.A.). Also, see *Kerr v. Conlogue* (1992), 65 B.C.L.R. (2d) 70 (S.C.), in which a B.C. newspaper had to pay aggravated damages for using sources known to be unreliable or blatantly subjective in a story about a theatre company's split with an artistic director.

4. *Use an internal checking system:* It would seem obvious, but too many news organizations and editors fail to check and question the reporter's work. The case of *Munro v. Toronto Sun Publishing Corp.* points out the perils.[20] In that case, Munro, a prominent federal cabinet minister was accused of making stock market trades using insider information obtained through his cabinet position. The story was based on "evidence" on a microfiche that a reporter frequently held up before his editors, but never showed them. In fact, no one other than the reporter had looked at the microfiche.

When a second reporter was put on the story to help flesh it out, he didn't look at the microfiche either. After the story was published, Munro promptly denied the allegations of wrongdoing and demanded proof. At that point, the newspaper found it had no proof of its accusations. The key reporter claimed the microfiche was lost or possibly stolen.

As it turned out, the court heard testimony to the effect that this journalist was more determined "to get" the minister than actually find evidence to support the story. The court also determined that the second journalist assigned to develop the story was so driven by a desire to destroy and gain notoriety that he didn't even take the time to look at the documentation alleged to have been available.[21] In the end, the court awarded damages of $100,000 to Munro. The judge said that editors are just as responsible as reporters for the accuracy of a story.

5. *Offer an opportunity for reply:* It's not always possible or desirable, but consideration should be given to allowing the subject of an investigative report the opportunity to respond to allegations. In *Munro*, the supervising editors were chastised by the court for not asking the minister for his comments before the story was published. The judge stated that a journalist should always confront a subject before publishing serious allegations.

However, there are times when it would be imprudent to confront the story subject. For example, the subject may seek an injunction or, in cases involving crime, someone may flee or destroy evidence. A lawyer can help decide whether the subject should be given the opportunity to make a comment before a story comes out.

6. *Review documents carefully:* Documents are nice to have, but they aren't infallible. Affidavits and signed statements, for instance, are only as credible as the person giving the information. Hearsay information

---

20 (1982), 39 O.R. (2d) 100 (H.C.).
21 *Ibid.*, at 123.

sworn under oath is often useless because the person doesn't have personal knowledge of events. Also, someone who gives an affidavit may still have to appear in court and be subjected to cross-examination.

Even court documents and "official" government documents aren't without problems. Pleadings, for example, can be exaggerated or wrong. Finally, don't rely on books, magazine articles or newspaper clippings to back up claims. They carry no authority (even if they make the same allegations and no one sued) unless a journalist can convince the authors to hand over their evidence.

7. *Watch internal documents:* A news organization's own internal documents (story drafts, memos, letters, etc.) are also likely to be a part of a court proceeding. Journalists and their editors should be careful to avoid embarrassing or incriminating comments in such documents. In one case, a radio station reported on the dismissal of a town administrator and suggested it had something to do with an unrelated criminal investigation into missing municipal money.[22] The "slug" on the top of the news script was "Town Caper," indicating the attitude of the reporter at the time.

8. *Don't sacrifice truth for drama:* Whether it is to get the front page or lead the evening news, journalists are too often tempted to tell only half the story because it is more sensational or dramatic than the full story. Courts may interpret this as evidence of malice. Also, remember that sensationalized phrases or words can pack much more defamatory meaning than can be proven, such as reporting a property developer was allegedly "shaken down" for a political contribution.[23]

---

22 *Crawford v. CFBC* (1987), Saint John (N.B. Q.B.).
23 In *Thomas v. McMullan*, 2002 CarswellBC 146, [2002] B.C.J. No. 230 (S.C.), newspaper and radio outlets were held partly liable for a $70,000 damage award after reporting an alleged "shakedown" of a developer. Since no proof of a shakedown was offered at trial, the media outlets suffered for airing the allegation.

5

JOURNALISTS AND INVASION OF PRIVACY

In recent years, Canada has made great strides in developing legislation
that speaks to an individual's right to privacy or, at the very least, the right
to control the collection, use and disclosure of certain personal information
in the course of commercial and government activities. In most jurisdictions
across the country, various statutes and regulations make specific or passing
references to an individual's privacy or the need to be protected against
unreasonable invasion of privacy. A decade or more ago, these references
were few and far between.

It is a different matter when the question turns to whether there is a
common law right to privacy or to be protected from an invasion of privacy?
Across Canada as a whole, there is no general common law tort for breach
of privacy or the right to be protected against invasion of privacy.[1] This,
however, is an area of law in constant flux. For example, some Canadian
courts have refused to say there is no such common law tort, while others
do. Slowly but surely, a body of case law is building in the area, which
some journalists and media lawyers suggest is a Trojan Horse of sorts that
may impede news gathering if unbridled.

Meanwhile, in the absence of clear judge-made law on this issue, five
provinces have enacted legislation to allow a person to seek a civil remedy
for unjust invasion of privacy. While these laws are largely unused, there
have been cases involving the news media. That said, none of the other
provinces have followed suit with similar laws dealing with invasion of
privacy.

Recently, the Supreme Court of Canada has also touched on very
narrow aspects of the right to privacy, such as whether a photo can be
published without an individual's permission (which is discussed further

---

1 Canadian courts have been reluctant to create a separate civil tort of invasion of privacy.
But in the case of *Motherwell v. Motherwell* (1976), 73 D.L.R. (3d) 62 (Alta. C.A.), the
tort of *nuisance* was broadened to remedy a violation of privacy. The court issued an
injunction to stop a woman from making frequent and abusive telephone calls to her father,
brother and sister-in-law, that amounted to undue interference with the enjoyment of their
premises. Courts in some other provinces have expressly disagreed with this decision. But
courts in New Brunswick and British Columbia have gone even further and said there is a
common law tort of invasion of privacy. See *Re K.C. Irving Ltd. and R.* (1971), 4 C.P.R.
(2d) 120 (N.B. Q.B.) and *Re MacIsaac and Beretanos* (1971), 25 D.L.R. (3d) 610 (B.C.
Prov. Ct.). In the Supreme Court of Canada's 1998 ruling in *Aubry*, cited in note 53, below,
a dissenting judge noted the Canadian Charter of Rights and Freedoms doesn't create a
right to privacy. The closest it comes is s. 8, which protects against unreasonable search
and seizure. Even then, it was noted, there is no absolute right to privacy or protection
from searches.

below in *Visual Invasions of Privacy*). There are also provincial and federal laws protecting access to confidential personal or business information that is held by governments. These laws, however, are discussed in the chapter dealing with access to public information.

Naturally, journalists should be concerned with the parameters of privacy laws. Questions about the "right to privacy" arise quite commonly, such as when a reporter secretly records conversations, digs through garbage cans for information or jumps over a fence to check out a story. This chapter sets out those areas where news gathering and "rights" to privacy often converge.

WHAT IS INVASION OF PRIVACY?

Privacy has been described as the right to be left alone, to be secure in one's home, and to be free from unwanted interference or publicity. While Canadians have laws protecting us from trespass, harassment, nuisance, defamation and other interferences, the tort of invasion of privacy is still developing.

A 2006 Ontario court decision is illustrative of the issues courts consider in determining whether there has been a breach of privacy. In *Somwar v. McDonald's Restaurants of Canada Ltd.*[2] the question was whether the plaintiff's claim of "invasion of privacy" was a reasonable cause of action or whether the pleading should be struck. The lawsuit was launched after the plaintiff's employer conducted a credit bureau check without the employee's permission.

The judge refused to dismiss the claim against McDonald's. After reviewing numerous court rulings, the judge concluded "it is not settled law in Ontario that there is no tort of invasion of privacy." While considering the issue, the judge highlighted some useful principles in determining when privacy has been unreasonably invaded. In 1960, the judge noted, a U.S. tort scholar identified four types of invasion of privacy interests:[3]

- intrusion upon the plaintiff's seclusion or solitude, or into his private affairs
- public disclosure of embarrassing private facts about the plaintiff
- publicity which places the plaintiff in a false light in the public eye
- appropriation, for the defendant's advantage, of the plaintiff's name or likeness

---

2 (2006), 79 O.R. (3d) 172 (S.C.).
3 William L. Prosser, "Privacy" (1960) 48 Cal. L. Rev. 383 at p. 389.

In considering whether the plaintiff in this case, a restaurant manager, had experienced an intentional tort arising from the intrusion into his private affairs and credit records, the court noted the scholar describes this type of intrusion as follows:

*   there must be something in the nature of prying or intrusion
*   the intrusion must be something which would be offensive or objectionable to a reasonable person
*   the thing into which there is prying or intrusion must be, and be entitled to be, private, and
*   the interest protected by this branch of the tort is primarily a mental one (that is, the interest is not protected by other torts or remedies, such as trespass, nuisance, etc.)

In this case, for the purposes of the motion to strike the pleading, the judge concluded "the plaintiff's complaint concerning the invasion of his privacy could be categorized as an intentional tort."

Other courts have also considered arguments of invasion of privacy in different settings, with mixed results. Here are some examples:

Defamation vs. Breach of Privacy: In a British Columbia case, a lawyer's photo was incorrectly used in a newspaper story about a terrorist group.[4] The newspaper apologized promptly, but was held responsible for defamation arising from the mistake. The court, however, did not hold the newspaper responsible for a claimed breach of privacy since use of the photo would have been legitimate if there had not been an error. On the question of whether damages for defamation and breach of privacy can be awarded in the same lawsuit, the judge noted a Supreme Court of Canada ruling that the law of defamation is itself intended, in part, to guard people's privacy and damages for a privacy breach would only be possible if defamation was not found.

Privacy Rights of Innocent Parties: In the sentencing stage of a high-profile criminal case,[5] CTV wanted to broadcast the Crown's video showing the unearthing of a two-year-old from a hole where she had been buried for a month. CTV promised it would not show the child's body, but it was argued the victim, her family and the Aboriginal community have a right to privacy as "innocent persons" or third parties. The provincial court judge refused to allow use of the video. "One has to question the motives of CTV

---

4 *St. Pierre v. Pacific Newspaper Group Inc. and Skulsky*, 2006 BCSC 241 (S.C.).
5 *R. v. Mackinaw*, 2004 BCPC 299 (Prov. Ct.).

in seeking to broadcast the inside of the grave," wrote the judge. "Whatever the motive is, it cannot outweigh the interests of innocent people."

In another case[6] involving alleged privacy rights of an "innocent party," there was a different result. A detective constable suspected of a breach of trust was the subject of a search warrant executed at the police station. Later, when the news media tried to access the warrant and other information, the officer argued that, since he was never charged with an offence, his privacy interests were of superordinate importance and a Criminal Code's search warrant provision (s. 487.3(2)(a)(iv)) allowed for an order preventing disclosure of information that would "prejudice the interests of an innocent person." An appeal court disagreed, ruling this was not a search delving into the officer's private affairs, but rather the performance of his public duty. The prejudice to him as an innocent person did not outweigh the public interest in having access to the edited warrant materials.

Prisoner's Right to Privacy: After an appeal of a controversial aggravated assault case, CTV sought permission to broadcast the defendant's videotaped statement to police, filed as an exhibit during his preliminary hearing.[7] The provincial court judge noted that while a person convicted of a criminal offence does not lose all of his or her privacy rights, those rights must be balanced against the media's right to broadcast matters of interest to the public. Since the accused had pleaded guilty, the judge found no privacy interest in the video. The judge, however, said the decision might have been different if his trial was not complete or he had been acquitted.

Privacy of Criminal Records: In a defamation action that alleged, among other things, that the plaintiff had a "criminal record," the plaintiff claimed the Federal Criminal Records Act, which allows for pardons and discharges, he had a right of privacy in refusing to disclose any information on an alleged conditional discharge.[8] The court held the Act's provisions respecting records and their disclosure "do not constitute a hermetic system shielding the fact of a finding of guilt and discharge from the world at large for all purposes."

Increasingly, it is also becoming common to find references to "invasion of privacy" in federal and provincial legislation, such as laws dealing with family and health matters. The Access to Information and Protection

---

6 *Phillips v. Vancouver Sun* (2004), 238 D.L.R. (4th) 167 (B.C. C.A.).

7 *CTV Television Inc. v. R.*, [2005] 10 W.W.R. 167 (Man. Q.B.), reversed [2006] 12 W.W.R. 200 (Man. C.A.). Ironically, the judge still refused CTV access to the video, citing a concern that it would damage the administration of justice if police or future accused knew the news media might later be able to broadcast videotaped statements.

8 *Jay v. Hollinger Canadian Newspapers* (2002), 97 B.C.L.R. (3d) 130 (S.C.).

of Privacy Act[9] for the Northwest Territories, for example, provides a lengthy listing of what does and does not constitute "unreasonable invasion of a third party's personal privacy."[10] In that statute, there is a presumption of unreasonable invasion of privacy involving disclosure of a third party's personal information if it:

- relates to a medical, psychiatric or psychological history, diagnosis, condition, treatment or evaluation
- is compiled and identified as part of an investigation into a possible contravention of law, except to the extent that disclosure is necessary to prosecute the contravention or continue the investigation
- relates to eligibility for government assistance
- relates to employment, occupational or educational history
- is obtained on a tax return or gathered for the purpose of collecting a tax
- describes an individual's finances or credit worthiness
- consists of personal recommendations or evaluations about the individual
- indicates an individual's race, religious beliefs, colour, gender, age, ancestry or place of origin

In determining whether to allow the disclosure of such information, the government must consider if it is desirable in subjecting activities of the government or a public body to public scrutiny; is likely to promote public health and safety or protection of the environment; was supplied in confidence; is likely to be inaccurate or unreliable; or may unfairly damage the reputation of any person.

Clearly, in both case law and legislation, the concept of unreasonable invasion of privacy and the concurrent right to privacy generally is beginning to take shape in Canada.

> **An unauthorized biography was published about the life and times of a successful folk singer, describing her personal and sexual relationships, her thoughts about a deceased fiancé, her health and diet, and her emotional vulnerability, among other matters. The book was authored by a former friend, who had worked and socialized with the performer and been privy to some of the events. Did the book breach the singer's privacy?**

---

9 S.N.W.T. 1994, c. 20.
10 S. 23(1).

Yes. This high-profile 2006 English case involving Canadian singer Loreena McKennitt may eventually have an impact in Canada on the right to privacy for public figures and others, if Canadian courts choose to adopt its reasoning.[11] Like Canada, England has no domestic tort for invasion of privacy. In protecting private information, English courts typically rely on Articles 8 and 10 of the European Convention on Human Rights, and the tort of breach of confidence. The lawsuit arose from the publication in 2005 of *"Travels with Loreena McKennitt: My Life as a Friend."* McKennitt alleged breaches of privacy or of obligations of confidence either by implication of law or express contractual provisions when the author was on contract to the singer. Courts at trial and on appeal found numerous grounds to support McKennitt's claim that she was entitled to keep the information private and that the author had breached her duty of confidentiality. For example, even though the author shared some of the experiences she wrote about, the courts determined they were McKennitt's experiences to share or not. In 2007, significantly, the British House of Lords declined leave to appeal the case.

THE RIGHT TO PRIVACY IN FEDERAL LAW

Personal Information Protection Act

While the federal government has had a Privacy Act in place for many years establishing the right of Canadian citizens to access their personal information in government records, very little existed in statutory law to protect personal information gathered or held by others. That changed in 2000 with the enactment of the Personal Information Protection and Electronic Documents Act (PIPEDA).[12]

Beginning in 2001, the Act applied to any organization governed by federal law that collects, uses or discloses personal information in the course of commercial activities, and personal information about employees of federal works, undertakings and businesses. It does not apply to non-commercial organizations or provincial governments, the latter of which have enacted similar legislation of their own for government activities.

By 2004, the law also applied to federally-regulated and provincially-regulated commercial organizations (unless a provincial law for the private sector has been enacted). A commercial activity includes any transaction or activity of an organization, including selling, bartering or leasing donor,

---

11 *McKennitt v. Ash* (2006), [2007] 3 W.L.R. 194 (C.A.).
12 S.C. 2000, c. 5.

membership or other fundraising lists. And, what is "personal information?" The federal Act says it is any information about an identifiable individual, with the exception of the name, title or business address or telephone number of an employee of an organization. For example, information about what car you drive, what you like to drink, your age and almost any other distinguishing personal element.

Fortunately for the news media and some others, there is a specific exemption that permits them to go about their business. Section 2 of the Act exempts any government institution that comes under the federal Privacy Act, anyone who collects information for personal use only (e.g., personal address book, holiday card list, etc.), and any organization that "collects, uses or discloses for journalistic, artistic or literary purposes and does not collect, use or disclose for any other purpose."

Other items commonly exempted from PIPEDA's reach include personal information in telephone directories made available to the public, professional or business directories, official registries, judicial or quasi-judicial records and documents, and information provided by an individual in a publication, such as a magazine, book or newspaper.

From that start, PIPEDA promised to have far-reaching effects and, slowly, it has changed the way business is done in both the private and public sector. In one of the first interpretations of the law by the federal Privacy Commissioner, a security business in Yellowknife (a jurisdiction in which businesses are governed by federal law) was told it could no longer engage in its unauthorized surveillance of city streets.[13] The Commissioner found the company's sole purpose for monitoring the citizens in public places was for commercial reasons — that is, in hopes of convincing local police to buy and install more cameras for crime control. Since then, there have been numerous rulings by the Privacy Commissioner that are beginning to develop into a body of precedents.

One of the unfortunate side effects of PIPEDA and other privacy protection laws has been the sometimes ridiculous and sweeping interpretations governments and commercial enterprises give the laws when faced with inquiries from news media. It is not unusual these days for a reporter to be refused the name, title or telephone number of a manager or executive because of "privacy laws" — details PIPEDA and other laws specifically do not protect. Perhaps the most outrageous example of the unintended effects of privacy legislation occurred in 2007 in New Brunswick, when prison authorities refused to release a photo of an escaped murderer because its privacy rules required the signed permission of the inmate. Despite

---

13   Finding was released in a letter of decision dated June 15th, 2001 by the Privacy Commissioner of Canada.

Corrections Canada's refusal, the RCMP issued the photo promptly after receiving a media request.

Intercepting Private Communications

A common area of confusion for many journalists is whether one can listen in on conversations or secretly record them. The answer is yes, but some conditions must be met first.

Sections 183 to 196 of the Criminal Code[14] deal with the interception of private communications and contain the only references in criminal law to invasion of privacy. In recent years, the federal government has made some amendments, but nothing that substantially alters the legal landscape. The unlawful interception of a private communication is a serious offence and is set out in s. 184(1):

> Every one who, by means of any electro-magnetic, acoustic, mechanical or other device, wilfully intercepts a private communication is guilty of an indictable offence and liable to imprisonment for a term not exceeding five years.

Aside from the jail term, anyone aggrieved by an unlawful interception can also be awarded punitive damages of up to $5,000.[15]

How to Stay Within the Law

A journalist or anyone else can lawfully intercept communications. But it's important first to understand some key definitions and elements of the offence.

To begin with, the communication in question must be private and the federal government now restricts the offence to interceptions of messages sent by someone in Canada or intentionally sent to someone in Canada. A private communication is defined in the Code as:[16]

> any oral communication, or any telecommunication, . . . that is made under circumstances in which it is reasonable for the originator to expect that it will not be intercepted by any person other than the person intended by the originator thereof to receive it, . . .

---

14 R.S.C. 1985, c. C-46.

15 S. 194.

16 S. 183.

Note that the law doesn't apply to situations where the "originator" of the communication cannot reasonably expect that it will be private.[17] For instance, if a camera crew is filming people talking during a break at a conference and people see the camera and microphone in front of them, they can't expect their conversations to be private. Similarly, people who use citizen band radios or send messages on telephone voice pagers can't expect their comments to be private.

The communication must also be oral or a telecommunication. The interception of a written note or other paper documents would not fall under this law.

The private communication must then be intercepted by an "electro-magnetic, acoustic, mechanical or other device," which is defined as:

> any device or apparatus that is used or is capable of being used to intercept a private communication, but does not include a hearing aid used to correct subnormal hearing of the user to not better than normal hearing.

This includes any device ranging from an electronic telephone bug to a tape recorder left in a room to (theoretically) a glass placed against a wall. Interestingly, this definition excludes interceptions of communications made solely by the unassisted human ear. The offence is clearly only concerned with man-made devices.[18]

Finally, it's useful to know what it means to intercept a communication:

> "intercept" includes listen to, record or acquire a communication or acquire the substance, meaning or purport thereof;

So, interception not only includes hearing or recording a message, it also includes finding out by any method the meaning, substance or purport of an unlawfully intercepted private communication. For example, if another person unlawfully heard or intercepted a communication and then told a journalist about it, the reporter could theoretically be found to have also unlawfully intercepted the communication.

---

17 In *R. v. Bengert* (1978), 47 C.C.C. (2d) 457 (B.C. S.C.), police investigating a narcotic offence told an airline to direct any call asking about a certain suitcase to a special police phone number. The police argued that this wasn't an unlawful interception because they were answering the phone and were therefore a consenting party to any recording of the conversation. But the court declared the evidence inadmissible because the caller thought he was speaking to the airline and didn't intend to be speaking with the police.

18 See *R. v. Watson* (1976), 31 C.C.C. (2d) 245 at 249 (Ont. Co. Ct.), where evidence of a conversation overheard by a police officer by ear was deemed to be admissible and not an unlawful interception as defined by the Code because a mechanical listening device wasn't used to intercept the communication.

The "Rule" for Lawful Interception

Understanding the limits of the offence, intercepting a private communication with some device is still permissible if it falls within one of four circumstances set out in s. 184(2). Three don't apply to journalists. (A person may intercept a communication if: (i) permission has been given by a judge (such as for police wiretaps); (ii) someone supplying a telephone, telegraph or other communication service must intercept communications to repair the system; or (iii) a person who is an officer or servant of the Crown intercepts a private communication during random monitoring for the management of the radio frequency spectrum.)

The "saving provision" or rule that can be used by journalists is s. 184(2)(a). It says the offence of unlawfully intercepting a private communication doesn't apply to:

> a person who has the consent to intercept, express or implied, of the originator of the private communication or of the person intended by the originator to receive it.

Translating that into plain language: a journalist can secretly record or listen to a private communication, using an electronic or acoustical device, if he or she has the consent of anyone who is the sender or intended receiver of the communication.

It's that simple (but, as we'll see further on, broadcasters are sometimes limited in how they make use of secret telephone recordings).

If a journalist is one of the parties to the communication, the only consent needed is his or her own. If a journalist isn't directly involved, then one of the conversation's participants must agree. For example, a journalist electronically and secretly eavesdropping on a telephone conversation would need permission of one of the other people on the line. If more than one person originates the message or is intended to receive it, the consent of any one of those people is enough.[19]

However, if a journalist isn't party to the communication, it's important that the right person gives permission for the interception. The law states that the private communication must be directed at a person intended to receive it. For example, on one occasion a television newsmagazine arranged for someone to take a small tape recorder into a meeting. The person later left the room for a few moments and the recorder continued to run in his absence. As it turned out, the newsmagazine wanted to use comments recorded during this short time period, but could not because no one left at the meeting had given consent to the interception or was aware of it.

---

19   R.S.C. 1985, c. C-46, s. 183.1, previously s. 184(3).

> **During a cocaine bust, the police find and seize a BlackBerry wireless device on the car seat of one accused's vehicle.** Lawyers for the accused challenge the admissibility of 164 email messages stored on the BlackBerry, arguing there was no warrant authorizing the interception of the messages and their use is contrary to s. 184 of the Criminal Code. Was this an illegal interception of private communications?
>
> **No.** In a British Columbia case with similar facts, the trial judge ruled the messages had been recovered from the device in the course of a lawful search that was incidental to the arrests. The judge also noted the messages had not been "intercepted" since they had safely arrived at their destination in the BlackBerry's email account.[20]

Other Dangers

As mentioned earlier, problems can also arise from the use of information gained by an unlawful interception. The Criminal Code makes it a separate offence to disclose any part of a private communication unless the person intercepting it has consent of one of the parties.[21] Disclosure includes divulging the substance, meaning and even the existence of a private communication or the wiretap.[22] This is an indictable offence punishable with a sentence of up to two years in prison. An exception is provided for the publication of such information if it's revealed in an open judicial or court proceeding.[23] Ottawa has also amended the legislation with s. 193.1, which makes it an offence to disclose information arising from the unlawful interception of cellular phone transmissions.

The Criminal Code also makes it an indictable offence to possess, sell or purchase:[24]

> any electro-magnetic, acoustic, mechanical or other device or any component thereof knowing that the design thereof renders it primarily useful for surreptitious interception of private communications.

Not all electronic devices are "primarily useful" for intercepting private communications. For example, this doesn't include radio receivers that

---

20 *R. v. Giles*, 2007 BCSC 1147 (S.C.).
21 S. 193(1).
22 *Ibid.*
23 S. 193(3).
24 S. 191(1).

intercept police communications.[25] It's also unlikely that it would include the sound recording equipment normally used by reporters during employment. But tape recorders and microphones are getting smaller and smaller and there may come a time when someone may suggest they are primarily designed for surreptitious interception, particularly if a reporter uses them as such.

An indication of that concern among law enforcers is a 1985 amendment (s. 191(2)(b.1)) allowing police operatives to use "body packs" without violating the Code and without having to apply for a licence for the device.

It might also be noted here that the Criminal Code sections pertaining to the illegal interception of communications and invasion of privacy don't apply to film or video recordings without sound.[26] Only the interception of the words in a private communication violates the Code privacy provisions, not pictures.

Finally, it is important to note that while the Criminal Code provisions may not apply, there are other circumstances where surreptitious electronic recordings may be a problem. For example, under federal and provincial laws governing the collection of personal information, organizations engaged in a commercial activity other than news gathering may be required to obtain the consent of individuals when telephone conversations are to be recorded (e.g., call centres). In provinces with statutes protecting against invasions of privacy, unauthorized recordings of conversations may be considered a breach of privacy unless there is a defence, such as news gathering.

Other Criminal Code Provisions

Trespassing at Night

Criminal Code s. 177 protects individuals against people trespassing at night around their home:[27]

> Every one who, without lawful excuse, the proof of which lies on him, loiters or prowls at night on the property of another person near a dwelling-house situated on that property is guilty of an offence punishable on summary conviction.

---

25 *R. v. Gasper*, [1976] W.W.D. 93 (Sask. Dist. Ct.).

26 *R. v. Biasi (No. 3)* (1981), 66 C.C.C. (2d) 566 (B.C. S.C.).

27 In *R. v. McLean* (1970), 75 W.W.R. 157 (Alta. Mag. Ct.), the court held it must be proven beyond a reasonable doubt that the accused was hunting in a stealthy manner for an opportunity to carry out an unlawful purpose. In other words, the simple act of trespass may not be enough to support a conviction under this section.

Note that the offence only involves prowling around a residence. This provision is sometimes called the "peeping-tom section."

Intimidation

The Criminal Code also has a provision involving the watching, hounding or "besetting" of a person or place. Section 423(1) states:

> Every one is guilty of an indictable offence. . . who, wrongfully and without lawful authority, for the purpose of compelling another person to abstain from doing anything that he or she has a lawful right to do, or to do anything that he has a lawful right to abstain from doing,
>
> . . .
>
> (c) persistently follows that person,
>
> . . .
>
> (f) besets or watches the place where that person resides, works, carries on business or happens to be . . .

But s. 423(2) offers this defence, which is particularly useful for journalists:

> A person who attends at or near or approaches a dwelling-house or place, for the purpose only of obtaining or communicating information, does not watch or beset within the meaning of this section.

Harassing Telephone Calls

The misuse of the telephone may constitute an invasion of privacy in certain circumstances set out in s. 372 of the Code:

> . . .
>
> (2) Every one who, with intent to alarm or annoy any person, makes any indecent telephone call to that person is guilty of an offence punishable on summary conviction.
> (3) Every one who, without lawful excuse and with intent to harass any person, makes or causes to be made repeated telephone calls to that person is guilty of an offence punishable on summary conviction.

Disrupting a Religious Service

Subsections 176(2) and (3) of the Code apply to the privacy of religious worship and certain "benevolent" gatherings:

> (2) Every one who wilfully disturbs or interrupts an assemblage of persons met for religious worship or for a moral, social or benevolent purpose is guilty of an offence punishable on summary conviction.
> (3) Every one who, at or near a meeting referred to in subsection (2), wilfully does anything that disturbs the order or solemnity of the meeting is guilty of an offence punishable on summary conviction.

Note that this section requires the disturbances to be of a wilful nature. An accidental or unintentional interruption would be unlikely to support a conviction.

Other Federal Privacy Restrictions

Radiocommunications

The Radiocommunication Act (formerly the Radio Act) makes it an offence to divulge or make use of the substance of a radio-based telephone communication or a "radiocommunication" without the consent of either the originator of the message or the intended receiver if either is in Canada.[28] In this case, a radiocommunication doesn't mean you can't make use of a commercial or public broadcast signal.[29] However, other radio transmissions (for example, police radio calls or cellular phone conversations) can't be broadcast or published without permission. Take note that even the information gathered from the radiocommunication supposedly cannot be used.

This section of the Act is overly restrictive. For example, news reporters often make use of the information gathered from scanners that pick up transmissions by police and other public officials. A violation can result in a summary conviction and a fine not exceeding $25,000 for an individual and/or 12 months in jail. A corporation is subject to a fine up to $75,000. There are no recorded convictions for journalists under this section. The best advice is to seek out legal counsel when dealing with such communications.

---

28 R.S.C. 1985, c. R-2, ss. 9(1.1) and (2), respectively.
29 S. 9(3).

Telephone Conversations

The Canadian Radio-television and Telecommunications Commission's Radio Regulations, 1986 state no licensee shall broadcast any telephone interview or telephone conversation, or any part thereof, with any person unless the person's oral or written consent to the interview or conversation is obtained before the broadcast.[30] The only exception is when the person telephoned the station for the purpose of participating in a broadcast.[31] Some would argue this restricts freedom of expression, however a 2005 attempt by a French language radio station to use the Charter's freedom guarantees to invalidate the CRTC's authority to govern the quality and content of broadcasts was unsuccessful.[32]

THE RIGHT TO PRIVACY IN PROVINCIAL LAW

As at the federal level, provincial legislation dealing specifically with invasion of privacy is spotty and inconsistent among jurisdictions. As will be discussed in more detail below, however, a few provinces do address the issue directly.

The protection of personal information collected and held by public and private bodies is a different matter. Every province and territory has privacy laws governing the collection, use and disclosure of personal information held by government and public agencies that provide a general right to individuals to access and correct their own personal information. The privacy of personal information held by organizations in the private sector is governed in most provinces and territories by PIPEDA, except in Alberta, British Columbia and Québec where laws are in force that are substantially similar to PIPEDA. Finally, personal health information is also specifically protected in Alberta, Saskatchewan, Manitoba and Ontario, where legislation deals with the collection, use and disclosure of this information by health care providers and other health care organizations.

As noted, five provinces do have laws that speak directly to an individual's right to be protected from unreasonable invasion of their privacy. The Privacy Acts in British Columbia, Saskatchewan, Manitoba and Newfoundland and Labrador create a civil remedy for such invasions of privacy.

---

30 SOR/86-982, s. 3(*e*)(i). A challenge of this section failed in *R. v. CKOY Ltd.* (1976), 70 D.L.R. (3d) 662 (Ont. C.A.). The appeal court held that a trial judge was wrong in declaring the section invalid and stated that the CRTC is empowered to make such regulations so as to ensure programming of high standards.

31 *Ibid.*

32 *Genex Communications Inc. v. Canada (Attorney General)* (2005), 260 D.L.R. (4th) 45 (F.C.A.).

Québec's Civil Code also can be applied to unreasonable violations of privacy. As with any civil matter, the law requires a plaintiff to initiate a court action and the laws don't create any criminal or provincial offences.

There have been a few cases involving alleged violations of these laws by the news media, but so far they have yet to seriously hamper journalists. One would expect the media to be frequent targets of civil suits with such laws; however, there have been few lawsuits because precisely what the laws cover is vague and there are broad exemptions for news gathering. The freedom of the press guarantee in the Charter of Rights also casts a different light on these laws. So far, no other provinces have indicated they will follow suit with their own invasion of privacy legislation.

The provincial invasion of privacy laws are based on similar legislation in the United States. South of the border, privacy laws have been used to protect individuals in a variety of circumstances. For example, some states protect people against publications of defamatory, yet true, statements, the unauthorized use of personal letters, harassing phone calls or photos that single out an individual in a public place for no valid reason. The news media have also had to watch how they use old or dated "file" pictures of people who were in accidents or were grief-stricken at some tragedy.

Although the U.S. legislation has been far-reaching in some states, actions for invasion of privacy are uncommon in Canada, perhaps because most people don't know about the Acts and because of the statutory defences for those involved in news gathering.

While Privacy Acts in four of the provinces are similar, there are subtle differences and each province will be dealt with separately.

British Columbia

The Privacy Act in this province states under s. 1(1):[33]

> It is a tort, actionable without proof of damage, for a person, wilfully and without a claim of right, to violate the privacy of another.

That would seem to be a fairly widesweeping prohibition against any violations of privacy. But to decide whether there has been an invasion of privacy, the statute directs courts to look at more than the simple fact that someone's privacy has been violated.

A court must examine the nature, incidence and occasion of the alleged invasion, and the relationship between the parties. For example, the rela-

---

33 R.S.B.C. 1996, c. 373.

tionship between a journalist and a public figure will be different from the relationship between a reporter and the average citizen.

The offended person doesn't have to prove that any damage was suffered by the invasion. But he or she does have to prove that the invasion of privacy was intentional and without a lawful right. For example, a police officer with a search warrant would have a lawful right to enter a specific property. According to the British Columbia Act, an invasion of privacy can occur with:

1. eavesdropping or surveillance, whether or not accomplished by trespass,

2. misappropriation of a person's name or portrait for the purpose of advertising or promoting the sale or trading of property or services, without consent, or

3. anything the court feels constitutes an invasion of privacy within the ambit of the Act.

Note that the first provision protects citizens against eavesdropping or surveillance even when there has been no act of trespass. For example, an invasion of privacy may occur if you take a photograph of someone while peering over the edge of his or her fence. There have been few cases to test these subsections and their potential is uncertain. For example, does eavesdropping include surreptitious recordings in which one of the participants to the private conversation consents to the taping? If so, someone may be able to sue for civil invasion of privacy even though such an invasion of privacy is lawful under the Criminal Code.

The second provision incorporates the general common law position on misappropriation of personality.

And the third provision gives the court a very wide latitude in deciding what's a violation of privacy.

The Defences

An act is not a violation of privacy, under s. 2(2), where:

    (a) it is consented to by some person entitled to consent;
    (b) the act or conduct was incidental to the exercise of a lawful right of defence of person or property;
    (c) the act or conduct was authorized or required by or under a law in force in the Province, by a court or by any process of a court; or

(d) the act or conduct was that of . . . a peace officer . . . or a public officer . . . in the course of his duty . . . [and the violation of privacy is not] disproportionate to . . . the matter [being investigated] nor committed in the course of a trespass.

One other defence, set out in s. 2(3), is particularly useful to reporters:

A publication of a matter is not a violation of privacy if

(a) the matter published was of public interest or was fair comment on a matter of public interest; or
(b) the publication was privileged in accordance with the rules of law relating to defamation;

but this subsection does not extend to any other act or conduct by which the matter published was obtained if that other act or conduct was itself a violation of privacy.

Deciding what is a matter of public interest will be up to the judge or jury. It would have to be a matter of public interest in the eyes of the "reasonable man" and it's irrelevant that the reporter felt it was a matter of public interest.

A reporter may also be able to prove that the matter published was in a situation of absolute or qualified privilege as defined in defamation law. For example, information brought out in court may be published without concern over a violation of privacy lawsuit under this Act. Note, however, that this defence only applies to invasions of privacy that fall within the ambit of the public interest or privilege subsections. For example, any other act by a reporter that amounts to an invasion of privacy, but doesn't fall under the two subsections, could be successfully pursued in court.

This section also does not allow the media to ignore court-ordered publication bans. In one recent B.C. case, a crime victim brought an action for negligence and invasion of privacy against a reporter and newspaper after her name was published despite a publication ban issued under s. 486(3) of the Criminal Code.[34] The newspaper believed the publication ban no longer applied because the sexual assault charge had been stayed in a plea bargain.

The victim said she suffered great stress, and had to sell her home and move away from the community. The jury awarded $3,000 in general damages, $15,000 in punitive damages for the privacy breach and $1,000 for the negligence. The trial judge intervened and ruled the reporter and newspaper had a defence under s. 2 of the Privacy Act and s. 3 of the B.C. Libel and Slander Act, finding the publication of the victim's name was

34 *F. (J.M.) v. Chappell* (1998), 158 D.L.R. (4th) 430 (B.C. C.A.).

privileged as a fair and accurate report of proceedings publicly heard before a court.

The victim appealed and the higher court agreed the trial judge made a mistake. The appeal judges said the defences in privacy and libel laws must always be interpreted in the context of the Criminal Code ban. An application for leave to appeal to the Supreme Court of Canada was dismissed.

For the most part, though, the B.C. Act doesn't appear to have interfered with the normal activities of the British Columbia news media. In 1985, the owner of a store involved in a bitter labour dispute sued a BCTV reporter and cameraman for invasion of privacy under the Act.[35] The journalists had approached the store owner for an interview and he told them to leave and stay off the store property, including the parking lot.

The cameraman and reporter went across the street and started filming. At one point, they moved back on to the parking lot for some shots and a fight broke out between the news crew, the owner and his security staff. The cameraman recorded the fight and it was later shown on television.

The court held there was not an invasion of privacy on either of two counts. First, the judge felt the act of filming the fight on the plaintiff's property was not a violation of privacy because it took place on a site that wasn't shielded from the public. While the property itself was private, anyone passing by could see what was happening there. Second, the broadcast of the fight also wasn't a violation of privacy because s. 2(3) of the Act permitted publication of any matter of public interest. In this case, the labour dispute was certainly within the public interest.

In 1993, another case of interest arose under this legislation involving the CBC.[36] The plaintiff, "John Doe," alleged he was defamed and his right to privacy violated during the course of two ambush interviews conducted by a TV reporter. Mr. Doe was allegedly involved with a company being investigated in the U.S. for environmental offences. The plaintiff had earlier refused a request for an interview when the CBC wouldn't agree to his conditions.

Mr. Doe said the reporter later confronted him in public, asking loud and provocative questions. In particular, the CBC reporter asked about whether the plaintiff had a U.S. drug conviction. Mr. Doe had indeed been convicted of a drug-related offence, but the conviction was later expunged under a U.S. statute. Mr. Doe told the reporter this and later had a lawyer demand that the conviction not be reported, asserting that it was private information. The CBC refused and the plaintiff got a court order barring the

---

35 *Silber v. B.C. Broadcasting System* (1985), 25 D.L.R. (4th) 345 (B.C. S.C.).
36 *John Doe v. Canadian Broadcasting Corp.* (1993), 86 B.C.L.R. (2d) 202 (S.C.).

TV network from using the information and the video from the ambush interviews.

The CBC asked a court to set aside the order and won. The judge said that the conviction was historical fact and in the public domain, as was the expungement. As well, the court said that just because the plaintiff was alleging defamation and an invasion of privacy under the B.C. law, it did not mean the press should automatically be barred from publishing the information.

A much more novel case involving the B.C. law arose in 1994.[37] A woman had witnessed a man being murdered in a parking lot of a rehabilitation centre where she was being treated. When reporters arrived later, she was interviewed and photographed. Later that day, she became concerned about the disclosure of her identity and tried to stop the news media from naming her in reports.

The media refused her request for anonymity and she later brought actions for psychological distress against Vancouver's two daily newspapers and the CBC under B.C.'s Privacy Act. She alleged the media published her identity knowing the murderers were still at large and they would have reason to silence anyone who had witnessed the crime.

At one point in pre-trial motions, the defendant news organizations asked a court to strike down the plaintiff's request for a jury trial. The province's Court of Appeal refused, noting that while there was no Canadian precedent for the case and that it involved important and controversial decisions on the law, it did not raise issues that were beyond a jury's capabilities.

Unfortunately for legal watchers, the case was settled out of court before the issues could be properly tried. Certainly, the plaintiff's arguments were novel and a court decision in her favour would have had a significant impact on the news media's rights. That said, it might have been argued that she willingly participated in the interviews and could not "take back" her consent after the fact. As well, there is ample room in the "public interest" defence of the Privacy Act to absolve the media and it's likely the Charter's guarantee of freedom of the press would also have made an appearance in the trial arguments.

---

37 *Pierre v. Pacific Press Ltd.* (1994), 113 D.L.R. (4th) 511 (B.C. C.A.).

Saskatchewan

As in British Columbia, the Privacy Act in Saskatchewan states:[38]

> It is a tort, actionable without proof of damage, for a person, wilfully and without claim of right, to violate the privacy of another person.

Again, the offended person doesn't have to prove that any damage was suffered by the invasion of privacy. But he or she does have to prove that the invasion of privacy was intentional and without a lawful right. The Saskatchewan Privacy Act is similar to the British Columbia Act because it directs the court to consider the circumstances of the alleged violation of privacy.

But the Saskatchewan law does appear to give a reporter more freedom to gather the news than is extended to journalists in other provinces, as will be discussed below.

However, s. 3 of the Saskatchewan law is more specific than the B.C. law as to what violates privacy:[39]

> Without limiting the generality of section 2, proof that there has been:
>
> (a)   auditory or visual surveillance of a person by any means including eavesdropping, watching, spying, besetting or following and whether or not accomplished by trespass;
>
> (b)   listening to or recording of a conversation in which a person participates, or listening to or recording of messages to or from that person passing by means of telecommunications, otherwise than as a lawful party thereto;
>
> (c)   use of the name or likeness or voice of a person for the purposes of advertising or promoting the sale of, or any other trading in, any property or services, or for any other purposes of gain to the user if, in the course of the use, the person is identified or identifiable and the user intended to exploit the name or likeness or voice of that person; or
>
> (d)   use of letters, diaries or other personal documents of a person; without the consent, expressed or implied, of the person or some other person who has the lawful authority to give the consent is *prima facie* evidence of a violation of the privacy of the person first mentioned.

As in British Columbia, the Act protects citizens against eavesdropping or surveillance even when there has been no act of trespass. For example, an invasion of privacy may occur if you take a photograph of someone

---

38   R.S.S. 1978, c. P-24, s. 2.
39   R.S.S. 1978, c. P-24, amended S.S. 1979, c. 69, s. 19.

while standing on the edge of their property. However, the Saskatchewan Act is more specific about other acts that constitute eavesdropping and surveillance (for example, following someone).

This Act also has a much more detailed definition of misappropriation of personality. A violation of privacy can occur not only with the unauthorized use of someone's name or likeness, but also their voice. The plaintiff must be identifiable and the defendant must have intended to exploit the name, likeness or voice of someone for either commercial purposes or "any other purposes of gain."[40]

The Defences

According to s. 4(1), an act or publication is not a violation of privacy in these cases where:

(a) it is consented to, either expressly or impliedly by some person entitled to consent thereto;

(b) it was incidental to the exercise of a lawful right of defence of person or property,

(c) it was authorized or required by or under a law in force in the province or by a court or any process of a court; or

(d) it was that of
    (i) a peace officer acting in the course and within the scope of his duty; or
    (ii) a public officer engaged in an investigation in the course and within the scope of his duty.

There are two other defences of importance to reporters, also stated in s. 4(1):

An act, conduct or publication is not a violation of privacy where:

(e) it was that of a person engaged in a news gathering:
    (i) for any newspaper or other paper containing public news; or
    (ii) for a broadcaster licensed by the Canadian Radio-Television Commission to carry on a broadcasting transmitting undertaking;

and such act, conduct or publication was reasonable in the circumstances and was necessary for or incidental to ordinary news gathering activities.

And, as set out in s. 4(2):

A publication of any matter is not a violation of privacy where:

---

40 R.S.S. 1978, c. P-24, s. 3(c).

(a) there were reasonable grounds for belief that any matter published was of public interest or was fair comment on a matter of public interest; or

(b) the publication was, in accordance with the rules of law relating to defamation, privileged;

but this subsection does not extend to any other act or conduct whereby the matter published was obtained if such other act or conduct was itself a violation of privacy.

As in B.C., deciding what is a matter of public interest will be up to the judge or jury. It must be a matter of public interest in the eyes of the "reasonable man" and it's irrelevant that the reporter felt it was a matter of public interest.

A reporter may also be able to prove that the matter published was in a situation of absolute or qualified privilege as defined in defamation law. For example, information brought out in court may be published without worry of a violation of privacy lawsuit under this Act.

But note that this defence only applies to invasions of privacy that fall within the ambit of the public interest or privilege subsections. For example, any other act by a reporter that amounts to an invasion of privacy, but doesn't fall under the two subsections, could be successfully pursued in court.

Manitoba

Manitoba's Privacy Act is somewhat different from the other two Western provinces.[41] It has this strongly-worded definition of invasion of privacy:

A person who substantially, unreasonably, and without claim of right, violates the privacy of another person, commits a tort against that other person.

As in the other provinces, the offended person doesn't have to prove that any damage was suffered by the invasion. But the plaintiff does have to prove that the invasion of privacy was substantial, unreasonable and without claim of right. The Manitoba law gives examples of violations of privacy in s. 3 that are similar to those set out in the Saskatchewan Act.

---

41 R.S.M. 1987, c. P125, s. 2(1).

The Defences

The defences to violations of privacy are also similar to those in the Saskatchewan law. But the provision about news gathering (as found in the Saskatchewan Act) isn't included. The only defence particular to journalists is set out in s. 5:

> In an action for violation of privacy of a person, it is a defence for the defendant to show
> (f) where the alleged violation was constituted by the publication of any matter
>   (i)   that there were reasonable grounds for the belief that the publication was in the public interest; or
>   (ii) that the publication was, in accordance with the rules of law in force in the province relating to defamation, privileged; or
>   (iii) that the matter was fair comment on a matter of public interest.

Newfoundland and Labrador

The Newfoundland and Labrador Privacy Act states:[42]

> It is a tort, actionable without proof of damage, for a person, wilfully and without a claim of right, to violate the privacy of an individual.

As in the other provinces, the offended person does not have to prove that any damage was suffered by the invasion. But he or she does have to prove that the invasion of privacy was intentional and without a lawful right. The Newfoundland and Labrador legislation gives detailed examples of violations of privacy similar to those set out in the Saskatchewan Act.

The Defences

The defences are similar to those in the Saskatchewan law. But the provision about news gathering (as found in the Saskatchewan Act) isn't included. The only defence available to reporters is set out in s. 5(2):

> A publication of any matter is not a violation of privacy where
>
>   (a) the matter published was of public interest or was fair comment on a matter of public interest; or

---

42 R.S.N. 1990, c. P-22, s. 3(1).

(b) the publication was, under the rules of law relating to defamation, privileged;

but this subsection does not extend to any other act or conduct where the matter published was obtained where the other act or conduct was itself a violation of privacy.

Québec

Article 35 of the Civil Code of Québec[43] outlines some of the key requirements for "Respect of Reputation and Privacy":

Every person has a right to the respect of his reputation and privacy. No one may invade the privacy of a person without the consent of the person unless authorized by law.

Article 36 of the Code goes on to identify a non-exhaustive list of acts that may be considered invasions of the privacy of a person:

*   entering or taking anything in his dwelling
*   intentionally intercepting or using his private communications
*   appropriating or using his image or voice while he is in private premises
*   keeping his private life under observation by any means
*   using his name, image, likeness or voice for a purpose other than the legitimate information of the public
*   using his correspondence, manuscripts or other personal documents

Art. 1457 of the Code is another rule often followed in cases involving injury to a person, including invasions of privacy:

Every person has a duty to abide by the rules of conduct which lie upon him, according to the circumstances, usage or law, so as not to cause injury to another. Where he is endowed with reason and fails in this duty, he is responsible for any injury he causes to another person and is liable to reparation for the injury, whether it be bodily, moral or material in nature. He is also liable in certain cases, to reparation for injury caused to another by the act or fault of another person or by the act of things in his custody.

Among the few "exemptions" or defences under the Civil Code is that "superior force" caused the "injury" through "an unforeseeable and irresistible event," such as an accidental invasion of provacy. That said, the Code also contemplates situations where information may have to be published

---

43 S.Q. 1991, c. 64.

in the interests of public safety. The Code will not permit exemptions if there is evidence of "gross fault," recklessness, carelessness or negligence.

Québec's Charter of Human Rights and Freedoms also speaks to privacy protections.[44] Section 5 promises every person "respect for his private life." Section 6 protects against trespass and ensures the "peaceful enjoyment . . . of . . . property." Section 9 states "Every person has a right to nondisclosure of confidential information."

To succeed in court under Québec's civil law system, the plaintiff must prove three elements. Each element must be proven on the balance of probabilities.[45]

The plaintiff must first prove the *fault* of the defendant.[46] Fault can be shown by negligence, incompetence or want of skill or the direct action of the defendant.[47]

The plaintiff must then prove he or she suffered damage. In Québec, even proof of hurt feelings or sensibilities can be enough.[48]

Then, the plaintiff must prove the causal link between the fault of the defendant and the damage suffered.[49] Therefore, ruthlessly intruding into the private life of an individual in pursuit of a story could be enough to sustain an action for invasion of privacy.

Fortunately, for journalists, the courts have used Québec's Charter of Human Rights and Freedoms, specifically s. 9.1, to assert that the public's right to information, supported by freedom of expression, places limits on the right to respect for one's private life in certain circumstances. The Supreme Court of Canada, for example, has stated that the balancing of the rights in question depends both on the nature of the information and on the situation of those concerned.[50]

In one invasion of privacy case brought under a predecessor of art. 1457, a broadcaster received a letter of complaint from a man. The broadcaster told his audience about the letter and then proceeded to read out the person's telephone number and address, and suggested everyone should call the complainant to give him their opinions.

The man received many phone calls, some threatening and harassing.[51] The lawsuit against the broadcaster was successful.

---

44   R.S.Q. 1977, c. C-12.
45   *Thibeault v. Porlier Transport*, [1971] C.A. 518.
46   See Nicholls, *Offences and Quasi-Offences in Québec* (Toronto: Carswell, 1938), at 38.
47   *Ibid.*
48   *Ibid.*
49   *Ibid.*, at 21.
50   Note 53, below.
51   *Robbins v. Canadian Broadcasting Corp.*, [1958] Qué. S.C. 152.

A very interesting privacy case arose in 1991.[52] A Québec newspaper had published a story about a teacher with Acquired Immune Deficiency Syndrome (AIDS) who was offered his full salary while on sick leave in exchange for not returning to work. The story did not identify the teacher by name; however, he was the only teacher at the school on sick leave. Before he died, the teacher sued the newspaper and reporter for violating his right to privacy by publicizing his illness and sexual orientation, both of which he had kept private.

The trial court agreed that the teacher's right to privacy had been violated, even though he was not named. Enough detail had been provided to identify him and the publicity had a detrimental effect on the teacher's emotional and physical state. The court also decided the newspaper was liable for additional damages because other media predictably picked up the story and spread it further.

This was a very unique case and it may only have been possible under Québec's civil law regime. That said, the fatal aspect of the newspaper's actions was likely in providing enough detail to allow readers to figure out which teacher had AIDS. If the story had been less specific, it is hard to imagine a similar court action succeeding.

GENERAL ISSUES IN PRIVACY

Visual Invasions of Privacy

Can you take someone's picture and use it as you wish? There are few laws dealing with visual invasions of privacy other than what's noted in the provincial Privacy Acts. Until recently, the common law in Canada was spotty in this area.

In 1998, the Supreme Court of Canada waded into this issue with an interesting case involving a photographer and an arts magazine that published a shot of a teenager sitting in a public place, enjoying a pleasant day.[53] The photo was taken and published without the teenager's permission. She launched a civil action under Québec's Charter of Human Rights and Freedoms, as noted above, which protects everyone's "right to respect for his private life" and the "right to the safeguard of his dignity, honour and reputation."

She alleged the publication of the photograph infringed her right to control her image and, thus, her privacy. She claimed damages, which arose from "teasing" by her friends and acquaintances when the photo appeared.

52 *Valiquette v. Gazette (The)* (1991), 8 C.C.L.T. (2d) 302 (Qué. S.C.).
53 *Aubry v. Editions Vice-Versa*, [1998] 1 S.C.R. 591.

The publication and photographer countered that this was an issue of freedom of artistic expression or, alternatively, the public's right to information.

The trial judge found that the unauthorized publication of the photograph constituted a "fault" under Québec law and ordered damages of $2,000. A majority of the province's appeal court agreed with the ruling. A majority of the Supreme Court of Canada also agreed and dismissed the appeal.

While most aspects of the Supreme Court ruling apply specifically to Québec's unique law, the majority did make some comments that should calm concerns about the media's right to use images without permission. The Supreme Court said the right to control one's image is indeed an element of the right to privacy under s. 5 of the Québec Charter. The ability to control the use of a person's image, reasoned the court, serves to protect an individual's "sphere of individual autonomy." That said, the right to privacy is also in direct conflict with the right to freedom of expression, which is protected by the Québec Charter in s. 3. To resolve the conflict, the court looked to s. 9.1 of the Québec law, which cites a need to balance fundamental freedoms and rights with "a proper regard for democratic values, public order and the general well-being of the citizens of Québec."

In this case, there was no evidence that the public's interest in seeing this photograph was predominant. The court also noted an artist's right to publish his or her work is not absolute and cannot include the right to infringe, without any justification, a fundamental right of someone whose image appears in the work. The judges ruled that the right to protection of the teenager's image was more important here than the publication's right to publish the photograph without getting her permission.

Does this mean that you now must have the permission of every individual who appears in images? No, and the Supreme Court very clearly set out the many circumstances in which permission would be unnecessary:

> It is generally recognized that certain aspects of the private life of a person who is engaged in a public activity or has acquired a certain notoriety can become matters of public interest. This is true of artists and politicians, but also, more generally, of all those whose professional success depends on public opinion. There are also cases where a previously unknown individual is called on to play a high-profile role in a matter within the public domain, such as an important trial, a major economic activity having an impact on the use of public funds, or an activity involving public safety. It is also recognized that a photographer is exempt from liability, as are those who publish the photograph, when an individual's own action, albeit unwitting, accidentally places him or her in the photograph in an incidental manner. The person is then in the limelight in a sense. One need only think of a photograph of a crowd at a sporting event or a demonstration.

Another situation where the public interest prevails is one where a person appears in an incidental manner in a photograph of a public place. An image taken in a public place can then be regarded as an anonymous element of the scenery, even if it is technically possible to identify individuals in the photograph. In such a case, since the unforeseen observer's attention will normally be directed elsewhere, the person "snapped without warning" cannot complain. The same is true of a person in a group photographed in a public place. Such a person cannot object to the publication of the photograph if he or she is not its principal subject. On the other hand, the public nature of the place where a photograph was taken is irrelevant if the place was simply used as background for one or more persons who constitute the true subject of the photograph.

Generally, you can take anybody's picture without their permission. The crucial question, though, is whether you need consent to publish it. As the Supreme Court notes, for day-to-day news reporting, where a person is photographed as part of an event or in a public place, consent isn't needed. And despite popular misconceptions, it's no different with children or minors and the consent of the parent is not needed.

As for crowd shots or the use of "file" photographs to illustrate or accompany a story, there's usually no need to worry about getting consent for news or feature stories. However, journalists should watch for potentially defamatory comments accompanying any pictures that might unintentionally suggest that an identifiable or particular person in the picture is the subject of the remark.

If someone isn't in a public place when photographed (for example, at home or on a private beach) and is not aware the picture has been taken, there's a chance they could sue for invasion of privacy in one of the provinces with privacy laws or maybe try a common law action in the other provinces. In this case, consent might be needed.

If a photograph is for commercial purposes (that is, for promotional or financial gain or profit), a signed consent from the subject of the photograph is usually required. In the *Aubry* case above, the Supreme Court noted that an arts magazine is still a commercial use despite its artistic quality. As well, using a person's image for a promotional or advertising campaign is basically stating that the person endorses the product. If he or she didn't authorize it, an action for *misappropriation of personality* can be pursued in the civil courts.

For extra protection, the subject of a commercial photo should also be told of the end use of a photo.[54] For example, a model who signs a general

<hr>

54 For an interesting take on this, see *Gould Estate v. Stoddart Publishing Co.* (1998), 161 D.L.R. (4th) 321 (Ont. C.A.). Glenn Gould, the famous Canadian pianist, was interviewed in 1956 for a magazine article by a journalist who took about 400 photographs and copious

release or consent may not expect her picture to end up on the cover of a book about hookers. The commercial use of a person's likeness can also be defamatory if their profession is one that requires members to steer away from commercialism (for example, an amateur athlete endorsing a product). News and current affairs programs are not generally considered commercial programs, but if the subject of an image appears to be promoting the program (such as in ad campaigns for news shows), permission may be needed.

Finally, it's worth remembering that the Criminal Code sections about interceptions of private communications don't apply to film or video recordings without sound.[55] This may seem unusual to point out, but it may someday be useful to know. An American network used this "twist" in the law to its advantage several years ago. While investigating a story in a state where privacy laws barred secret audio recordings, the journalists effectively used a hidden camera (without sound recording) to record the subject of the story completing a shady deal on a street corner. The pictures said it all and no law was violated.

Trespass to Land

Laws against trespass are forms of ensuring the privacy and enjoyment of a person's property.[56] Generally, a trespass is any invasion of another individual's property.[57]

Trespass to land can be an offence under provincial trespass laws or a distantly related Criminal Code offence. It may also be the subject of a private civil action even though the intrusion may have caused no damage at all. A person commits a trespass by simply going onto property without

---

notes, including tape recordings of their conversations. Almost 40 years later, the writer published a book on the late pianist that featured over 70 of the photos and excerpts from the conversations. The Gould estate claimed the author was not entitled, for his own exclusive benefit, to exploit commercially the photographs he had taken of the pianist. The appeal court dismissed the claim, ruling there was no evidence the pianist had placed limits on the use of the materials, had not commissioned or paid for the photos, and only the author as creator of the works in question was the sole copyright holder.

55 Note 26, above.

56 The oft-quoted phrase in the famous *Semayne's Case* (1604), 77 E.R. 194 at 195 (K.B.), is: "That the house of every one is to him as his castle and fortress. . . ."

57 *Entick v. Carrington* (1765), 95 E.R. 807.

express or implied permission,[58] causing something to go onto the property[59] or, after being allowed to enter, refusing to leave when asked.[60]

But there are limits to what is considered a trespass. For example, flying over property (for example, to take pictures) doesn't constitute trespass, unless it's so low that it interferes with the ordinary use of the land.[61]

Journalists often encounter situations in which someone orders them to leave a property or warns them not to enter. The law has recognized that anyone who is in lawful possession of the property can enforce his rights against an act of trespass. That person doesn't have to own the property. He or she only has to be in possession of it.[62] For example, someone leasing a property can protect it against trespass. In addition, any agent, representative or employee of that person can order you off the property.[63]

There's no general criminal offence of trespassing. But, as mentioned above, the s. 177 of the Criminal Code deals with the act of trespassing at night. The Criminal Code also gives a person in possession of property the right to defend it. Section 41(1) states:

> Every one who is in peaceable possession of a dwelling-house or real property, and every one lawfully assisting him or acting under his authority, is justified in using force to prevent any person from trespassing on the dwelling-house or real property, or to remove a trespasser therefrom, if he uses no more force than is necessary.

If the trespasser resists any attempt to prevent his entry or to remove him, he commits an assault "without justification or provocation."[64]

---

58 *Ashby v. White* (1703), 87 E.R. 810 at 816 (H.L.).

59 *Campbell v. Reid* (1857), 14 U.C.R. 305 (C.A.).

60 In *R. v. Peters* (1970), 16 D.L.R. (3d) 143 (Ont. C.A.), a boycott picket was ordered out of a shopping mall by management. The Supreme Court of Canada upheld the decision without comment in (1971), 17 D.L.R. (3d) 128 (S.C.C.).

61 See the English case of *Bernstein of Leigh (Baron) v. Skyview and General Ltd.*, [1977] 3 W.L.R. 136 (Q.B.). Here, an English nobleman was unsuccessful in proving a case of trespass after a plane flew over his land and took a picture of his estate.

Although flying over property may not be an act of trespass in England or Canada, it may be considered an invasion of privacy in provinces with Privacy Acts.

62 *Gidney v. Bates* (1862), 10 N.B.R. 395 (S.C.). In *Penney v. Gosse* (1974), 6 Nfld. & P.E.I.R. 344 at 346 (Nfld. S.C.), the court said anyone has "possession" who displays a clear and exclusive intention to possess the property.

63 *Ibid.*

64 Criminal Code, s. 41(2).

Provincial Trespass Laws

Most provinces have some form of legislation offering protection against trespass. The penalties range from fines to, in some provinces, the right to seize motor vehicles used in the trespass. Only Saskatchewan and the two territories have no Trespass Act. These jurisdictions rely on the common law.

Charges of trespass are usually prosecuted as summary conviction offences in provincial courts. However, an individual may also sue for trespass in the civil courts for damages suffered by the intrusion. As mentioned at the beginning of this section, the damage may be nominal or non-existent, but the action will still succeed.[65]

In addition, if the trespass is done in an arrogant or high-handed manner, the courts may award punitive damages to the plaintiff.[66] The motive of the trespasser is irrelevant at common law and it's no defence to say you made a mistake.[67]

As noted above, a person must have express permission to enter the property or there must be an implied invitation to enter (for example, a business which is open to the public). For instance, the pathway leading to a home's door is an implied invitation to walk up to the house (that is, unless signs state otherwise). But once the occupier, owner or agent of either says you must leave, you have no choice and can't stay. A "No Trespassing" sign, a fence or a natural boundary is clear evidence there is no implied invitation to enter a property.

The provincial laws vary from detailed prohibitions to short Acts setting out a basic offence and penalty. Some provinces provide a statutory defence that no trespass will have occurred where the accused has a fair and reasonable supposition that he or she can traverse the property or believed they had title to the land. Most provinces also spell out the requirements for notices prohibiting trespassing. Normally, signs must be prominently displayed at normal access points. Some provinces authorize the occupant of land to arrest the trespasser and immediately take the offender to a judge or justice of the peace.

---

65 *Demers v. Desrosier (No. 2)*, [1929] 2 W.W.R. 241 at 244 (Alta. S.C.).
66 *Townsview Properties Ltd. v. Sun Construction and Equipment Co.* (1974), 56 D.L.R. (3d) 330 at 334 (Ont. C.A.).
67 *Turner v. Thorne* (1959), 21 D.L.R. (2d) 29 at 31 (Ont. H.C.).

Public vs. Private Property

An oft-asked question is whether there are any special rights of access attached to public property or private property which is open to the general public, such as a shopping mall.

As a rule, private property which is open to the public may regularly allow or even invite public access. But at any time, a lawfully authorized person (for example, shopping mall manager) could exclude everyone or only one individual.[68] Even though members of the general public were invited onto the property, that invitation can be withdrawn at any time by a person with the proper authority.

The same applies to public property. Any lawfully authorized person can order a person out of a government building or even off a public street, if there's a lawful reason. For example, a peace officer or a public officer can require people to stay out of an area if he or she is administering or enforcing the law.

But the courts may start adopting the rationale of some American cases which give the public a broader right of access to public property. A 1986 Federal Court case ruled that Canadians have a constitutional right to engage in political activity or pass out pamphlets to passersby in airports. The judge said expelling the political activists was an infringement of their freedom of expression and said the public corridors of the airport were to be considered extensions of the streets.[69] This decision, however, was overturned on appeal.[70]

At least one other court has recognized that the media have a job to do, despite a clear trespass. In a 1984 case, seven members of the news media were each fined $200 under Ontario's provincial trespass law after they climbed over a fence at Toronto's international airport to investigate an air crash. A provincial court judge rejected a Crown request for the maximum $1000 fine, saying he was aware of the conflict between the news media trying to serve the public and airport officials maintaining security and safety. In the end, the judge imposed the smaller fine to stress the need to maintain airport security.

---

68 In *Harrison v. Carswell* (1975), [1976] 2 S.C.R. 200, the Supreme Court of Canada upheld the right of a shopping mall manager to order peaceful picketers off the property.

69 *Comité pour la République du Canada v. Canada* (1986), 25 D.L.R. (4th) 460 (Fed. T.D.).

70 (1987), 36 D.L.R. (4th) 501 (Fed. C.A.), affirmed [1991] 1 S.C.R. 139.

How to Handle Trespass Situations

Unless there's some sort of fence, boundary or warning sign, a journalist may wander into any area without immediate concern about trespass laws. However, once someone in authority says the journalist must leave, there is no sense resisting.

If a journalist is caught trespassing by the occupier of the property, it's important to note that he or she isn't required to hand over any of his or her belongings, notes or equipment.

The act of trespassing doesn't entitle the occupier to confiscate or destroy any tapes, notes or film. If you have film or video tape, even a policeman or other law enforcement officer cannot seize it, unless you're being arrested. If you are arrested, the film or tape may be seized to prove the trespass happened. But the police don't have the authority to destroy any belongings.

A PRIVACY CHECKLIST

1. In Canada, there is no general right to be protected against invasion of privacy. However, there are laws protecting privacy in select areas.

2. The Criminal Code prohibits the unlawful interception of private communications (such as by wiretap). However, a person can secretly record or listen to a private communication, using any electronic or acoustical device, if he or she has the consent of anyone who is the sender or intended receiver of the communication.

3. The Criminal Code indirectly protects privacy rights with sections concerning trespassing at night, intimidation, harassing telephone calls and disrupting a religious service.

4. Other federal laws affecting broadcasters guard against the unauthori zed use of radiocommunications and recordings of telephone conve sations.

5. British Columbia, Saskatchewan, Manitoba and Newfoundland enacted Privacy Acts which create a civil remedy for invasio privacy. Québec's Civil Code can also be used to assert privacy

6. Generally, photographs of people in public places or at publ can be used freely in news reports, particularly where there mate public interest in the subject matter. However, when u

or "generic" shots, journalists should guard against associating pictures of identifiable individuals with potentially defamatory remarks.

7.   Trespassing is a form of invasion of privacy and can be pursued in civil or criminal courts. A fence, boundary or sign can serve as sufficient warning to potential trespassers. Even without a warning sign, once a person is told to leave private property he or she must go. Even in public places, such as government offices or shopping malls, someone in authority can order individuals to leave the property.

r-

have
ns of
rights.

c events
s a legiti-
sing crowd

6

CONTEMPT

Any conduct which tends to undermine or bring into disrepute the authority and administration of justice or interferes with someone's right to a fair hearing before a court or other quasi-judicial body could be considered an act of contempt. Common examples of contempt are disobeying a court order, disrupting a hearing or publishing damaging information about someone involved in a trial.[1]

For journalists, committing a serious act of contempt can have staggering consequences. In theory, the penalty could be a jail term and/or a large fine. In practice, however, the courts are quite lenient and often ignore minor acts that don't pose a significant threat to a proceeding.[2]

Therein lies much of the difficulty with contempt. One judge may ignore a contemptuous act, while another may punish it. There are no hard and fast rules. Still, the "danger zones," particularly for journalists, are well defined. In recent years, there have been suggestions that contempt of court is an obsolete concept and should be done away with. Some argue, for instance, that scathing criticisms of judges or the justice system shouldn't

---

1 One case combining several of these examples is *R. v. Domm* (1996), 111 C.C.C. (3d) 449 (Ont. C.A.). Application for leave to appeal to the Supreme Court of Canada filed in 1997 (Court File No. 25803). While presiding over a trial, a judge issued an order postponing publication of certain evidence until after separate criminal proceedings against a third party were complete. Several parties contested the order, including the news media, but the order stood and eventually all appeals were exhausted. Domm, a citizen who didn't participate in the challenges, felt the order infringed his Charter right to freedom of expression. He purposely breached the order to force authorities to charge him. On appeal, the court upheld his contempt conviction saying "even orders that are constitutionally unsound must be complied with unless set aside in a proceeding taken for that purpose."

2 For example, see *R. v. Merz* (1999), 140 C.C.C. (3d) 259 (Ont. C.A.). In this murder case, the accused's lawyer applied to a judge for permission to exclude jurors exposed to pre-trial newspaper reports. An appellate court upheld the trial judge's refusal to grant the application, ruling that only one newspaper article cited referred to any potentially prejudicial material that was not admissible at trial. More important, that article was published almost two years before trial and, the court said, that eliminated any realistic possibility of prejudice.

be punishable acts of contempt.[3] However, contempt in all its forms has been around for hundreds of years for good reason. In many ways, it not only protects the individual, but also society.

Many of us rely on the news media for fair and objective reports of events, such as court proceedings. Writing a story and selecting facts or comments involves judgment calls on the part of the journalist. As a result, the courts are particularly mindful of the interpretation journalists give to happenings in the judicial system. But the power to punish for contempt shouldn't be seen to constitute a censor of the news or an instrument to stifle public discussion. The primary concern of any judge is that the trial he or she presides over is fair and recognized by all to be fair. It's this concern which often takes precedence over the rights of the news media and even the public, and invokes the use of contempt powers.

THE CATEGORIES OF CONTEMPT

Historically, a court's ability to punish contempt comes from an inherent power to preserve the sanctity of proceedings, to protect the reputation of the justice system and to ensure the public abides by the law. Over the years, statutes have even extended limited contempt powers to quasi-judicial bodies, such as public inquiries. However, not all bodies can punish all types of contempt.

At its simplest level, there are two basic categories of contempt. First, there is contempt *in facie curiae* (that is, "in the face of the court"). Such direct acts of contempt include witnesses refusing to testify, someone throwing an egg at the presiding official or creating a disturbance in the courtroom. For example, a reporter refusing to identify a confidential source's name during a trial may be charged with this type of contempt.[4]

---

3 In *R. v. Kopyto* (1987), 61 C.R. (3d) 209 (Ont. C.A.), where a lawyer was cited for contempt for saying the courts and police were stuck together "like Krazy Glue," a majority of the appeal judges held that the common law offence of contempt by "scandalizing the court" is an unjustified infringement of the guarantee of freedom of expression in s. 2(b) of the Canadian Charter of Rights and Freedoms [Part I of the Constitution Act, 1982, being Schedule B of the Canada Act 1982 (U.K.), 1982, c. 11 (hereinafter, Charter)]. However, the judges went on to say the problem lies in the loose definition of scandalizing the court and to suggest the offence would be valid if it were re-defined to require the Crown to prove there was an intention to bring justice into disrepute and to prove there was a serious or real risk to the administration of justice. The remaining appeal judge dissented, saying the offence is not an infringement of the Charter right.

4 See *St. Elizabeth Home Society (Hamilton, Ontario) v. Hamilton (City)*, 2004 CarswellOnt 9835, [2004] O.J. No. 5015 (S.C.), where a reporter for the *Hamilton Spectator* was called as a non-party witness in a civil case and asked to identify the confidential source of documents that were critical to the trial. The journalist refused to answer the question

A second type of contempt is the indirect act that happens outside the actual proceeding, or contempt *ex facie curiae* (that is, "away from the face of the court"). This is also called "constructive" contempt and journalists are most prone to this category. For example, it's constructive contempt when a journalist publishes stories that unfairly attack the court or adversely affect a hearing.

The second type of contempt is the indirect act which happens outside the actual proceeding, or contempt *ex facie curiae* (that is, "away from the face of the court"). This is also called "constructive" contempt and journalists are most prone to this category. For example, it's constructive contempt when a journalist publishes stories that unfairly attack the court or adversely affect a hearing.

Not all tribunals can punish both types of contempt. As a rule, most quasi-judicial tribunals and inquiries only have authority to deal with direct acts of contempt. Courts, as a rule, can punish both types. However, as will be discussed below, there are exceptions.

There are two other further categories of contempt. *Civil contempt* is the disobedience of a civil court judgment or civil court order. A common act of civil contempt is the failure of an ex-spouse to make child support payments. Technically speaking, a civil contempt is not considered to be an affront against the court, but rather an offence against the person to whom the dishonoured obligation or duty was owed under the civil judgment or order.

In one recent case, for example, a weekly Chinese newspaper in a Québec community was ordered by a court to stop publishing articles attacking practitioners of Falun Gong (a spiritual doctrine directed to improvement of mind, body and spirit) while a defamation lawsuit filed against was in process. The newspaper ignored the order and published critical articles. While a trial judge refused a motion for civil contempt because the safeguard order was too broad, an appeal court ordered the motion be heard. The court said the fact the order in question was worded to allow the newspaper to publish lawful information should not be confused with vagueness.[5]

The other category is *criminal contempt*, which is any behaviour which prejudices or unjustly insults the administration of justice in either civil or criminal proceedings. This is an offence against society and the justice

---

"Who is B?," stating he promised his source the identity would not be revealed. The court found the reporter in contempt of court and imposed an order for costs of $31,600. In 2008, the Ontario Court of Appeal overturned the judge's ruling as being "excessive." The appeal court said contempt powers should only be used as a "last resort" in these cases and that the trial court needed to consider the Charter rights of the media (*St. Elizabeth Home Society v. Hamilton (City) (in the matter of the citation of Ken Peters for contempt)*, 89 O.R. (3d) 81, 2008 ONCA 182).

5   *Zhang v. Chau* (2003), 58 W.C.B. (2d) 339 (Qué. C.A.).

system. For example, it's likely an act of criminal contempt for a news reporter to refer to an accused as a "mafia boss" before or during a trial.

In practice, the distinctions between criminal and civil contempt have become blurred. For example, the wilful and blatant disobedience of a civil court order, such as an injunction prohibiting broadcast of a defamatory news report, is considered just as much an act of criminal contempt as it is civil contempt.[6]

WHAT JOURNALISTIC BEHAVIOUR OFFENDS A COURT?

Within the class of criminal contempt are two sub-categories that often involve journalists:[7]

Scandalizing the Court

Scandalizing the court involves any accusation of bias, perverted justice or improper motives on the part of the court or the judge in the discharge of a judicial duty.[8] It's irrelevant there was no intention to scandalize the court.[9]

---

6 This was discussed in *Poje v. A.G. British Columbia*, [1953] 1 S.C.R. 516. In *R. v. Clement*, [1981] 6 W.W.R. 735 (S.C.C.), the Supreme Court of Canada affirmed that while an offence may constitute an act of civil contempt (such as disobeying a civil court order), it can still be prosecuted in a criminal proceeding under s. 127(1) of the Criminal Code.

7 Actually, courts have traditionally set out three categories of contempt: (i) scandalizing the court itself, (ii) abusing the parties to an action, and (iii) prejudicing mankind against persons in a trial. These divisions go back hundreds of years, as can be seen in the early English case of *Re Read and Huggonson* (1742), 2 Atk. 469. For the purposes of this chapter, though, the latter two categories will be dealt with under the heading of "prejudicing someone's right to a fair trial."

8 The case of *R. v. Murphy*, [1969] 4 C.C.C. 147 at 153 (N.B. C.A.), is a good example of why the offence of scandalizing the court will likely always be around. The accused, a writer for a student newspaper, testified at a trial and then wrote a story that lambasted the hearing. He called the court (at 148-149) "a mockery of justice," accused the judge of bias and stated that New Brunswick courts "are simply the instruments of the corporate elite."
    Some other examples: In *Re A.G. Canada and Alexander* (1976), 27 C.C.C. (2d) 387 (N.W.T. S.C.), a cartoon accused a judge of a double standard of justice, while the accompanying editorial alleged a cover-up by the judge in the trial of some public figures. In *Re Borowski* (1971), 3 C.C.C. (2d) 402 at 405 (Man. Q.B.), a Manitoba cabinet minister criticized a magistrate in an interview by saying "if that bastard hears the case I will see to it that he is defrocked and debarred." He also said the magistrate's court decision "is so blatant and so improperly judicially improper that I can only come to one conclusion, that it was based on political considerations, rather than on the facts. . . ." The court had no trouble finding this an obvious case of scandalizing the court.

9 See *R. v. Larose*, [1965] Qué. S.C. 318. However, in most cases, the motive or intention may be considered in sentencing.

This doesn't mean courts, judges or decisions can't be criticized. Still, any criticism of the administration of justice or judges must be within the limits of fair comment[10] or based on provable facts. A reporter can comment on a judgment or a judge's public actions, but shouldn't accuse a judge of improper motives or personally attack the judge without cause or proof.[11] Believe it or not, most judges would encourage reporters to point out errors in fact or law in their judgments.[12]

Generally, the courts have looked for some form of malice in the attack on the court. Evidence of malice can be found in an improper motive, ill will on the part of the journalist or carelessness or negligence in the publication of the statement.[13]

Prejudicing Someone's Right to a Fair Trial

In 1994, the Supreme Court of Canada issued a landmark ruling limiting the scope of publication bans, but it also set out some important new guidelines as to how courts should balance the individual's right to a fair trial against the Charter's guarantee of freedom of the press.[14] The Supreme Court said that while a fair trial is very important, the freedom of the press is of equal and sometimes greater importance. This was a major shift away from the traditional judicial view that a fair trial is paramount and the Supreme Court acknowledged that it was time for a new approach in this "post-Charter world." At the time, there was little doubt this case would reshape many areas of law affecting the news media, including contempt.

Unfortunately, many courts still see a distinction between publication bans and other discretionary court orders that limit future events involving the press and acts of contempt, which have already been committed and pose a "real and substantial risk" to a trial's fairness or the administration of justice.

---

10 See *Re Nicol*, [1954] 3 D.L.R. 690 at 699 (B.C. S.C.). In *R. v. Fotheringham*, [1970] 4 C.C.C. 126 (B.C. S.C.), the famed columnist criticized a coroner's inquest for its lack of sympathy toward the mother of a dead child. The coroner asked the court to punish Fotheringham for his comments. The court found that, although there were inaccuracies in the story, the comments were not made in bad faith or maliciously; all efforts had been made to ascertain the facts and that justice had not actually been impaired.

11 For example, in *R. v. Glanzer* (1963), 38 D.L.R. (2d) 402 (Ont. H.C.), judges were accused of perverting justice and breaching their oaths.

12 *R. v. Wilkinson; Re Brown* (1877), 41 U.C.Q.B. 47 (Ont. C.A.). The court said a judge's errors can be pointed out, but said it is improper to impute base motives to a judge, attack his honesty or say he is a liar. It might be added that the truth is a legitimate defence in circumstances such as this.

13 See *R. v. Murphy*, note 8, above.

14 The decision in *Dagenais v. Canadian Broadcasting Corp.*, [1994] 3 S.C.R. 835, is covered in detail in the chapter on publication bans.

To recap, in the *Dagenais* case, the Supreme Court said the new rule for courts is that a ban is only necessary: 1) to prevent a real and substantial risk to the fairness of the trial, and 2) when the need for the ban outweighs "the deleterious effects to the free expression of those affected by the ban." Since that decision, several courts have considered whether to apply this rationale in *Dagenais* to other areas involving limits on free expression by the news media, including pre-trial publicity.

One of the first significant rulings on contempt after *Dagenais* involved a B.C. TV station charged with contempt of court after its news report on a first-degree murder trial broadcast information that had not been placed before the jury.[15] There were three alleged violations. First, the report showed the accused being led away by a sheriff and noted he was spending the weekend at a correctional centre rather than a local jail. Second, the report discussed a witness' testimony about the back door of a nightclub where events had occurred and showed the door, which had not been seen by the jury. Third, the broadcast included an old Crime Stopper's public service video about the crime and then described the accused as the "prime suspect" in that crime.

At trial, the media argued that the *Dagenais* ruling should be taken into consideration in balancing any possible conflict between the rights of an accused to a fair trial and the rights of freedom of expression. The judge rejected that argument. "In my judgment, there is no conflict of rights in this case," the judge wrote. "The public is entitled to a fair reporting of the proceedings at trial. What is not allowed is publication that will tend to interfere with the course of justice as established by the authorities. To say otherwise or to rely upon the ability of a jury to separate that which is in evidence before it and that which is unfairly published could give rise to a situation where virtually no media conduct would be subject to sanction. . . . The result would either be a requirement for the sequestration of juries, or the taking of a calculated risk by the courts that "trial by newspaper" or "trial by television" (neither of which have any place in our system of criminal justice) might not adversely affect a jury verdict."

The trial judge held the broadcaster in contempt, specifically for showing the accused being taken to a correctional centre. While the other information broadcast might interfere with the trial, the judge noted the station sought legal advice before broadcasting the other two elements of the story and, in his view, this demonstrated due diligence and a lack of recklessness.

The B.C. Court of Appeal overturned the conviction, but skirted past any comment on whether *Dagenais* applied, saying there were no constitutional arguments made and no comment was needed. The appeal court ruled the key element in a contempt of this type is that a jury must get

---

15 *R. v. CHBC Television* (1999), 132 C.C.C. (3d) 390 (B.C. C.A.).

information it might improperly weigh, not just information it did not hear. "This must be a real risk, not a mere possibility of prejudice," the court said. In this case, the court found there was no real risk any juror who might have seen the program would be prejudicially affected. Even though publishing information heard in the absence of the jury was prohibited by s. 648 of the Criminal Code, "it did not necessarily follow that the report was in contempt of court." The key question, said this court, was whether the report created a real risk of prejudice to the fairness of the trial.

While the conviction was overturned, the appeal court also noted that if the publication had posed a real risk to the trial, the fact that legal advice was sought for some of the other information was irrelevant. The offence of contempt, the court said, speaks to the consequences of the acts in question rather than the lack of or presence of recklessness.

Another appeal court, however, has expressly rejected the use of *Dagenais* in assessing the impact of contempt.[16] In 2003, the *Edmonton Sun* published articles revealing a man who was charged with the murder of a 4-year-old child had also been convicted previously of assaulting the same child. The articles appeared shortly after the accused's arrest and months before a trial.

Charged with contempt, a trial judge convicted the newspaper after concluding the articles constituted a "real and substantial risk of prejudice to the integrity of the administration of justice." The trial judge rejected the media's argument that *Dagenais* can be applied to so-called publication contempt.

In an appeal of the conviction for contempt, the province's high court ruled the conviction should be set aside and acquitted the newspaper. The Alberta Court of Appeal, however, agreed with the trial judge that the *Dagenais* test was not the right one to apply to publication contempt. Unlike publications bans and other discretionary court orders limiting press freedoms for future circumstances or events, contempt of court "applies to events and circumstances which have occurred... While the [media's] suggested definition focuses on trial fairness, contempt addresses the creation of a real and substantial risk to the administration of justice and not trial fairness alone."

Also, the court said the Charter does not change the rules around common law contempt nor remove the press from under it. While noting the common law definition for contempt restricts both freedom of expression and freedom of the press, the appeal court held it is a reasonable limit demonstrably justified in a free and democratic society. Though *Dagenais* could not be applied in contempt cases, the appeal court used a "real and substantial risk" test in acquitting the newspaper. Here, the newspaper had

---

16   *R. v. Edmonton Sun* (2003), 170 C.C.C. (3d) 455 (Alta. C.A.).

a limited circulation in the area where the potential jury pool would be drawn, there was a lengthy delay between publication of the articles and the trial, and it was quite likely evidence of the prior assault against the child would be admissible in the trial.

All that said, since *Dagenais*, journalists in many news organizations have been reporting court cases differently. For example, some court reporters now closely scrutinize, assess and comment on the evidence against an accused rather than simply report what the jury heard. Without pre-judging guilt, some have openly mentioned an accused's prior criminal record or the background of the accused. Whether that is risky behaviour will often depend on the whims of the court or judge conducting the trial.

Still, no court or judge will allow "trial by newspaper" or "trial by press."[17] It is risky at this time for any journalist to assume every judge or court will fall in line with the thinking of *Dagenais*. The principle many judges follow is finely embodied in this quotation from an Ontario case:[18]

> ... no judge or juror should be embarrassed in arriving at his decision in a judicial proceeding by an expression of opinion on the case by any one unless he is before the Court as a party to the proceedings . . . . [N]either a judge nor a juror should be put in such a position that if he decides in accordance with the opinion expressed or the popular sentiment existing it can be said he has been influenced thereby, nor should he be put in a position where it can be said that he is antagonistic to any opinion or popular sentiment.

The court can also use its contempt powers to discourage the news media from "abusing the parties" involved in a court action. For example, if a journalist writes an editorial chastising someone for taking an issue to court such that it might discourage him or her from pursuing the issue or prejudices that person in the minds of prospective jurors, it could be considered an act of contempt. The court will look carefully at any comments that defame a party to an action. The key question is whether the abuse poses a serious and real threat to the trial.[19]

---

17 In *R. v. Vairo and CFCF Inc.* (1982), 4 C.C.C. (3d) 274 (Qué. S.C.), a man awaiting trial was referred to in a news report as a "mobster" and member of the "French Mafia." The court reiterated that a fair trial is paramount to the freedom of the press. In 1990, there was the case of *Alberta (Attorney General) v. Interwest Publications Ltd.* (1990), 73 D.L.R. (4th) 83 (Alta. Q.B.), in which the accused in a murder was the subject of a news story outlining his criminal past that ran after his arrest but before a preliminary hearing. In this case, the court felt the article represented a "real and substantial risk" to his fair trial and found the publication in contempt. The passage of time, however, between a prejudicial article and a trial can eliminate this risk, as shown recently in *R. v. Merz*, note 2, above.

18 *R. v. Thomas; Re Globe Printing Co.*, [1952] O.R. 22 at 24-25 (H.C.).

19 In *Staples v. Isaacs and Harris*, [1939] 2 W.W.R. 540 (B.C. S.C.), the court said every

WHEN DOES THE DANGER OF CONTEMPT ARISE?

The courts have a great reluctance to seriously impair the freedoms of the press and the power to punish for contempt of court is exercised very carefully.[20] Generally speaking, the danger of contempt for journalists begins from the time the courts become involved in a case and lasts until it ends. However, the degree of danger varies depending on what stage a proceeding is in and the circumstances involved.

Because judges have such broad and far-reaching powers to punish contempt, a judge will take many things into account when considering whether a hearing has been prejudiced by a news report. The judge will try to determine exactly what effect the report will tend to have on the hearing or the reputation of the court itself. The judge will also consider whether there is any sensationalism in the reporting, the story's prominence in the newspaper or broadcast, the story lead or headline, whether the trial has a jury and the timing of the article in relation to the trial.[21]

It's also no secret that the type of judicial proceeding involved has a bearing on whether an act of contempt is punished. Juries can be more easily swayed by public opinion than judges sitting alone[22] or hearings in the courts of appeal.[23] Although courts of appeal and judges sitting alone are less likely to be influenced by contemptuous publications, a journalist must still exercise care in discussing the merits of a case. If an editorial comment urges a court to reach a certain result, the "professional judge" will probably disregard the opinion. But the judge might be concerned that the public will think he has been influenced by the editorial comment.[24]

---

instance of defamation of a person about to be tried is not necessarily a contempt of court, but it could be found contemptuous if the accused can prove the trial has been prejudiced. In this case, an editorial was found not to be an act of contempt because the trial was still several months away.

20 In *Brown v. Murphy*, [1972] 6 W.W.R. 331 at 338 (B.C. S.C.), the court cautioned that the power to punish for contempt should be used sparingly and only in obvious cases that can be proven beyond reasonable doubt.

21 Some of these same points were mentioned in *Zehr v. McIsaac* (1982), 39 O.R. (2d) 237 at 246 (H.C.).

22 In *Re Depoe and Lamport* (1967), 66 D.L.R. (2d) 46 (Ont. H.C.), the court held a trial by judge alone was unlikely to be affected by a story urging a guilty verdict. But in *R. v. McInroy, Re Whiteside* (1915), 26 D.L.R. 615 at 619-620 (Alta. S.C.), the court held the mere fact a trial is by judge alone does not give a journalist the licence to publish any comment.

23 In *A.G. v. Times Newspapers Ltd.*, [1973] 3 All E.R. 54 at 65 (H.L.), the court said, "it is scarcely possible to imagine a case where comment could influence judges in the Court of Appeal."

24 In *R. v. Carocchia* (1973), 15 C.C.C. (2d) 175 at 184 (Qué. C.A.), the judge was concerned that the publication of a police press release could have been construed as influencing a non-jury criminal trial.

The moment a court becomes involved in a criminal or civil proceeding, the matter is said to be *sub judice*, or "in the course of trial," and reports about pending or current court cases must be carefully considered. That said, it may be difficult at times to tell when a court is "formally" involved. For example, in criminal proceedings, the court could be said to be formally involved in a case once it issues a search warrant during an investigation.

As a rule, however, the danger of contempt begins for journalists with any of the following: arrest without a warrant, issue of a warrant for arrest, issue of a summons to appear or service of an indictment or other document (for example, laying an information) specifying the charge. The danger of contempt in a criminal proceeding does not end until the appeal or appeal period has ended.

It's been held in some English cases that a matter can be *sub judice* even before criminal charges are laid and, particularly, when someone knows that a criminal charge is "imminent." For example, in England, the publication of the criminal record of a person who had barricaded himself in a house and was holding hostages was found to have prejudiced a later trial.[25] Canadian courts haven't taken a position on this issue to date.

However, even in Canada there are times when there could be a danger of prejudicing a trial before charges are laid. It's a wise and common practice when publishing a police photograph or sketch of a suspect to simply state the suspect is being sought for questioning about the crime, instead of declaring him or her as the villain or "prime suspect."[26] Quite apart from the contempt risk, there's a danger of being sued for defamation if an innocent person is shown.

For civil proceedings, the danger of contempt begins with the service of the writ or notice required by law to start an action and the danger doesn't end until the appeal or appeal period has passed.

The courts have held it is irrelevant that there was no intention to commit an act of contempt, but the judge can take the lack of motive into

25 This happened in *R. v. Beaverbrook Newspapers*, [1962] N.I. 15 (Q.B.D.). In another English case, *R. v. Savundranayagan*, [1968] 3 All E.R. 439 at 441 (C.A.), the court strenuously objected to a television interview with the accused that was conducted just before the accused's arrest with full knowledge that charges were imminent. But the court felt it was not necessary to punish the contempt because the interview was done well before the trial and there was such strong evidence against the accused that no jury could have reasonably found the accused not guilty.

26 In the English case of *R. v. Daily Mirror; Ex parte Smith*, [1927] 1 K.B. 845, a photograph of a suspect was published before charges were laid. The aggravating factor was that the identification of the perpetrator was in question. The court felt the publication of the photograph could influence witnesses in the trial.

consideration when sentencing.[27] It's also irrelevant that a journalist didn't make the contemptuous statement and only reported it. The court will punish the publisher of the statement as quickly as the author or originator.

A newspaper received a fax at 5:00 p.m. from the lawyer defending a man facing two murder trials for two high-profile killings that happened months apart. The fax was an advance notification to the news media that the defence would be requesting a wide-ranging publication ban for both cases the next day and the court would be willing to hear any news media submissions on the ban. With no ban in effect yet, the newspaper decided to publish the information in the fax as a news story for the next day's edition. Was this an actionable act of contempt?

Yes. It happened in 2001 to *The Province*, a Vancouver newspaper.[28] The news article resulted in a mistrial, the proceedings were moved to another venue, and the newspaper was charged with common law contempt. The editor-in-chief for the newspaper offered a detailed explanation of events that led to the article and an apology for the unintentional act of contempt. The court ruled it did not matter that the contempt was unintentional. All that mattered was that the publication "posed a real risk of prejudice to a fair trial." The newspaper was fined $8,000.

Since contempt of court can happen unintentionally, the courts are generally quite tolerant of comments in the news media. In fact, minor acts of contempt in our daily news media often go unpunished because judges feel no real harm has been done. In at least one very unique case, a print journalist who submitted an article to his employer for publication was able to avoid being held criminally responsible for the act of contempt caused by its publication because he was not aware of a ban in a sexual assault case and there was no evidence he intended to "aid or abet" in breaching the ban.[29] This unusual case involved a charge under s. 21 of the Criminal Code

---

27 See *A.G. Manitoba v. Winnipeg Free Press Co.*, [1965] 4 C.C.C. 260 at 263 (Man. Q.B.). In *R. v. Murphy*, note 8, above, the court held it must consider only the effect of the contemptuous act and not what was intended. The court in *R. v. Aster (No. 1)* (1980), 57 C.C.C. (2d) 450 (Qué. S.C.), held that intention is irrelevant and it considered an indifferent attitude or disregard of the consequences of a contemptuous act to be malicious. But in *Re Depoe*, note 22, above, the court decided the remarks in question did not actually interfere with the trial and, in dismissing the contempt charge, took into consideration that the accused clearly did not intend to influence the trial.

28 *R. v. Pacific Press*, 2001 CarswellBC 335, 50 W.C.B. (2d) 119 (S.C.).

29 *R. v. Helsdon*, 2007 CarswellOnt 336, [2007] O.J. No. 243 (C.A.).

— that is, purposely aiding and abetting another person in committing a crime.

The employer, *Tillsonburg News*, was convicted of contempt after it published a front page article on a sexual assault trial and named the complainant 10 times. A publication ban concerning the identity of the complainant was in force at the time but no one at the newspaper knew of it nor had the reporter asked. The newspaper itself was held responsible for the breach of the ban, but the trial court found "no evidence that the [reporter] was in a position to make decisions with respect to what did or did not get published." The Crown's attempt to use the aiding and abetting charge against the reporter failed on appeal since there was no evidence the journalist intentionally aided another in committing an offence.

This case had truly unique facts and involved the use of an unusual section of the Code to press the Crown's case for contempt. No journalist should rely on being excused from contempt charges simply because an employer has the ultimate decision to publish the story. In fact, other courts have held front-line reporters equally responsible with employers for breaches of publication bans.[30]

It's important to note that an act of contempt won't be ignored simply because the statement is made outside the court's physical jurisdiction. The courts know no boundaries, particularly when a contemptuous act or comment attacks the court itself. In one case, a federal minister in Ottawa made a contemptuous statement about a Québec court.[31] Although the Québec judge cited other grounds for his decision, he held that the court had the authority to go anywhere to punish contemptuous remarks attacking the court itself, regardless of the court's jurisdiction.

The courts have also punished contemptuous publications affecting a trial which, while not originating in the court's jurisdiction, are distributed in the area of the trial. The concern is that prospective jurors will hear or read details about the trial that are inadmissible or which prejudice the accused's right to a fair hearing. In these cases, the court will punish anyone they can find who is responsible for the contemptuous publication.[32]

---

30 See *R. v. Daly* (2003), 178 C.C.C. (3d) 31 (B.C. S.C.).

31 *Re Ouellet; R. v. Atlantic Sugar Refiners Co.* (1976), 34 C.R.N.S. 234 at 243-245 (Qué. S.C.).

32 In *R. v. Bryan*, [1954] O.R. 255 (H.C.), a U.S. magazine was distributed in a small Ontario town containing lurid details of a murder case about to be tried by a jury there. The court found the distribution of the magazine to be a serious contempt of court and issued a large fine against the local distributor of the magazine; the judge also warned he would fine the U.S. company and its editors if they ever came into his jurisdiction.

WHAT IS THE PUNISHMENT FOR CONTEMPT?

For now, no law or statute sets out a maximum penalty for the general offence of contempt of court.[33] In theory, the potential penalties are unlimited and at the complete discretion of the judge. The historical and inherent nature of the court's power to punish contempt is at the root of the reluctance to set limits. For example, even the Criminal Code pays homage to the court's common law power to punish contempt. Section 9 of the Code states that no one shall be convicted of a criminal offence under the common law, but specifically goes on to add that this isn't intended to interfere with a court's power to punish contempt.

Anyone, including a judge or a lawyer for one of the parties, can bring an act of contempt to the attention of the court and start proceedings. The method by which allegations of contempt are handled is unlike any normal court process. It's called a "summary process" and you won't find its procedure set out in the Code. The general aim of the summary process is to bring the offender before the court as quickly as possible to avoid further damage to the justice system. But some believe it borders on an infringement of our fundamental rights to a fair trial and due process.[34]

For serious contempt, for instance, a judge can immediately cite an offender for contempt and punish him on the spot. In most cases, however, a judge will issue a summons to the offender directing him or her to later appear in court to "show cause" as to why he or she shouldn't be punished. At the show cause hearing, the accused's lawyer can make out a case and call any evidence to support the accused's actions.

There have been several attempts in recent years to challenge the summary process and have it declared an unconstitutional infringement on our Charter rights. Courts have rejected the argument, noting that a person tried in a summary process does have a right to a lawyer, to offer an explanation and to call witnesses. However, the courts have also held that it doesn't include the right to a jury. Though there's no theoretical limit to

---

33 There are some sections of the Criminal Code which do set out penalties for certain direct acts of contempt such as the refusal of a witness in a preliminary hearing to testify (that is, s. 545). Also see s. 708 which makes it an offence for a witness required to attend a court hearing to fail to show up or remain at the hearing.

34 Recently, for example, in *R. v. Rudko* (1999), 178 D.L.R. (4th) 359 (Alta Q.B.), a lower court judge jailed a disruptive accused for two days and ordered him to appear later to show cause why he should not be found in contempt of court. A higher court released the accused and stayed the contempt proceeding because the trial judge had failed to address the issue of bail before sending the accused to jail. The court said, "A person who has been cited for *in facie* contempt is charged with an offence and has the right not to be denied reasonable bail without just cause pursuant to s. 11(e) of the Canadian Charter of Rights and Freedoms."

a contempt penalty and Charter s. 11(f) guarantees jury trials for offences involving jail terms of five years or more, courts have rejected the position that jury trials are a right. The courts have noted that an act of contempt rarely draws a penalty of more than a few months and therefore doesn't come under the Charter section.[35]

If convicted, the judge may simply want ample expressions of remorse and apologies in court. Jail sentences are usually only handed out to witnesses who refuse to testify. Journalists are rarely sentenced to jail for their contempt and more often are fined. In some cases, though, this can be expensive. Judges have ordered news media outlets to pay the costs of a mistrial caused by the contempt.

WHO CAN PUNISH FOR CONTEMPT?

As mentioned above, the ability to punish contempt is available to bodies other than courts. But not all official or government bodies that hold hearings have such a power. As a matter of public policy, the law has restricted the power to punish for contempt to bodies which act judicially, making decisions which affect an individual's rights.

The power is usually only found in judicial, quasi-judicial and legislative bodies. For example, Parliament, legislative assemblies and public tribunals (such as utilities boards and public inquiries) have a statutory and even inherent right to maintain the sanctity and order of their proceedings.[36]

---

35 In *R. v. Cohn* (1984), 15 C.C.C. (3d) 150 (Ont. C.A.), the Ontario Court of Appeal dealt with whether a witness who refused to testify has a right to a jury trial in a contempt proceeding under s. 11(f) of the Charter. The court held the actual penalties are never beyond two years and the Charter right cannot be invoked. See also *R. v. Kopyto*, note 3, above. Similar themes can be found in *A.G. Qué. v. Laurendeau* (1982), 3 C.C.C. (3d) 250 (Qué. S.C.) and *Re Layne and R.* (1984), 14 C.C.C. (3d) 149 (Alta. C.A.).

36 See, for example, *Hamilton v. Anderson* (1858), 6 W.R. 737 (H.L.). Also, see *Gauthier v. Canada (Speaker of the House of Commons)* (1994), 25 C.R.R. (2d) 286 (Ont. Gen. Div.), where the plaintiff had been banned from the precincts of the House of Commons by the Speaker. Gauthier argued his right to freedom of the press had been violated. The Speaker maintained the ban was necessary to ensure the House operated free from interference and, since he exercised Parliamentary privilege in denying access, the Charter did not apply. The court agreed with the Speaker and ruled it had no authority to review an exercise of Parliamentary privilege. The action was dismissed. More recently, see *Zundel v. Boudria* (1999), 46 O.R. (3d) 410 (Ont. C.A.); application for leave to appeal to the Supreme Court of Canada dismissed with costs (S.C.C. File No. 27655). The House of Commons unanimously passed a motion denying Ernst Zundel entry to the precincts of the Commons for the remainder of the session, preventing him from holding a planned press conference in the Parliament Buildings to discuss a case before the Human Rights Tribunal. Zundel asked a court to uphold his right to freedom of expression, but the trial and appeal judges held that parliamentary privilege is not subject to review in the courts.

But the scope of this power isn't the same for all bodies (including the courts). Although they all can deal with direct acts of contempt (such as expelling a raucous spectator), only a limited few can punish both direct and indirect acts of contempt, such as those committed by journalists.

From a jurisdictional standpoint, our judicial system is divided into federally-appointed superior courts and provincially-appointed inferior courts. Only the superior courts (for example, Supreme Courts, Courts of Queen's Bench, Appeal Courts and Federal Courts) have the broad common law power to punish direct and indirect acts of contempt. The inferior courts (for instance, Justices of the Peace, Magistrate's Courts and Provincial Courts) are limited to punishing acts of direct contempt.[37]

This doesn't mean a journalist is free to say what he or she wants about proceedings in inferior courts. As the common law has evolved, superior courts can punish acts of constructive contempt directed against inferior courts. All a judge in an inferior court has to do is ask a higher, superior court to punish the contempt on his or her behalf. So, all courts, one way or another, can punish a direct or constructive act of contempt.

Some public tribunals have the same powers as courts to punish acts of direct contempt, such as the refusal of a witness to testify. Often it's set out in the legislation that created the body. Examples are compensation boards, coroners' inquests, utilities boards, labour boards, police commissions, municipal boards and public inquiries. In most cases, the courts will look closely at the legislation creating the body to determine its contempt powers.[38]

But it's rare for legislation creating any administrative tribunal or inquiry, even a federally-appointed one, to allow for punishment of constructive contempt. However, there is precedent for tribunals, such as coroners' inquests, to also ask a superior court to punish someone who is

---

37 In *Canadian Broadcasting Corp. v. Cordeau*, [1979] 2 S.C.R. 618, a police commission inquiry into organized crime activity in Québec issued a direct order that the identity of a witness (that is, a police informer) not be published. The CBC published a picture of the witness and the commission tried to cite the network for contempt. The Supreme Court of Canada held that the statute that gave the commission the power to punish contempt applied only to acts of direct contempt, such as the refusal of a witness to testify. The court also made it clear the provinces have no constitutional power to grant a body the ability to punish acts of indirect contempt.

38 See *Pacific Press Ltd. v. British Columbia (Chief Coroner)* (1997), 147 D.L.R. (4th) 339 (B.C. S.C.). Two journalists refused to answer questions at a coroner's inquest and the coroner found they were in contempt. The court reviewing the contempt order held that while the Coroners Act includes the power to punish a witness who refuses to attend the hearing, it does not include a power to find a witness in contempt who attends, but refuses to answer questions.

seriously undermining the authority of the proceedings.[39] It is, however, very rarely done.

Although bodies other than courts may punish a contemptor, the vast majority of cases involve the courts. For that reason, much of this chapter will concern itself with court-related incidents. Keep in mind, though, the same rules can be applied to quasi-judicial tribunals.

THE DANGER ZONES

While any act of contempt is to be avoided if possible, the fact is the degree of danger for journalists varies depending on the stage of a judicial proceeding — that is, before, during and after a trial. The closer a civil or criminal action gets to trial, particularly when a jury is involved, the more cautious a journalist must be in his or her reports. When a case moves on to the appeal courts, the danger of contempt often lessens and freer comments can usually be published.

Many common problem areas in contempt fall within one of these three periods and being aware of the danger zones can help prevent a nasty encounter with a judge.

Before Trial

In the period preceding a trial, the standard of care required by a journalist will increase as the trial date gets closer. Conversely, the further away the trial is the less chance exists of influencing potential jurors. That said, there are still areas to be wary of.

Civil Pleadings

Pleadings are the statements of claim and defence from the parties to an action and include the affidavits, transcripts and other documents filed with the court before trial. Until recently, only Alberta imposed a partial restriction on the publication of pleadings, but that has now been repealed.[40]

---

39 See *Cordeau*, note 37 above, at 638. Also, see the case of *Levesque v. Rawley*, [1955] Qué. S.C. 36.

40 Under the repealed section of the Judicature Act, R.S.A. 1980, c. J-1, s. 30(2), a journalist could only publish the names and addresses of the parties and their solicitors and a concise statement of the "nature" of the claim (for example, "the party is seeking damages for personal injuries caused by negligent operation of a car"). The restriction was in effect until the end of the trial in Alberta or, if there is no trial, the proper determination of the proceedings.

Today, there's no statutory restriction in any province on publishing pleadings, although most news organizations are careful to state in stories that any allegations or statements in the pre-trial documents have yet to be proven in open court.[41]

The publication of the amount of damages sought in civil jury actions is another area that should be handled with care. Some courts are of the opinion that the judge and jury should be free to come to their own decision about how much should be awarded. Often the claims are over-estimated by each side and must be substantiated in court. It's generally accepted, however, that a journalist may publish the amount of damages sought when an action is first filed. But the current thought is that the amount shouldn't be published once the date of trial is set, so as to avoid influencing jurors.

Journalists should also be aware that courts are more likely to punish the litigants (that is, the lawyers or other participants) who reveal prejudicial information before it is submitted to open court. For example, a lawyer interviewed by the news media who reveals information gleaned from a civil discovery proceeding before a matter goes to trial may be found in contempt.[42]

Contemptuous Statements in Other Proceedings

Sometimes, a statement may be made in a court proceeding which could prejudice the outcome of a pending trial or one which is being heard in another court. While defamation legislation protects journalists giving fair and accurate reports of judicial proceedings, that protection extends only as far as the publication of defamatory matter. The publication of any contemptuous statements or information isn't protected by any privilege, even when the contemptuous remark is made in another court.[43]

---

41 At least one case has held that media reports of information in pleadings can be contemptuous. See *Bielek v. Ristimaki*, unreported, June 21, 1979 (Ont.). Judgment reprinted in Stuart Robertson, *Courts and The Media* (Toronto: Butterworths, 1981), at App. A, pp. 287-292. In that case, a newspaper published the amount of damages the plaintiff was seeking while the jury trial was going on. The court dismissed the jury and ordered a new trial. The judge said pleadings contain allegations that ought not to be known by a jury. He noted that pleadings are invariably wrong and, when they reach trial, are often greatly changed.

42 *N.M. Paterson & Sons Ltd. v. St. Lawrence Seaway Management Corp.*, 2004 CarswellNat 2878, 62 W.C.B. (2d) 54 (F.C.A.).

43 *Ibid.*, Robertson, at 22.

Describing Criminal Charges

Care must be taken in describing the charges the accused is facing.[44] It may be considered a contempt of court if an accused is reported as being charged with a more serious offence than the one actually laid. The proper title of the charge should be used where possible.

Evidence from Coroners' Inquests and Public Inquiries

An inquest or inquiry is not a formal "court" and can't determine criminal or civil guilt or innocence in most cases. The coroner and his jury or the inquiry board usually can only report on the facts or circumstances surrounding an event and make recommendations. The evidence garnered from the inquest (particularly admissions or confessions) shouldn't be re-published once criminal charges are laid or a civil jury trial begins. Evidence which was admissible at the inquest or inquiry could be inadmissible at trial.[45]

Hypothetical Cases

Sometimes, a journalist will want to discuss an issue that's before the courts and, hoping to avoid punishment for contempt, will pose the issue in the frame of a hypothetical case with no mention of the actual case trial. You should be very careful in discussing hypotheticals, particularly those relevant to high-profile cases. Any discussion favouring one side over the other or calling for a certain verdict, could be considered contemptuous

---

44 In practice, the courts are quite tolerant of innocent errors in describing charges. In *R. v. Hamilton Spectator; R. v. Globe and Mail*, [1966] 4 C.C.C. 375 (Ont. C.A.), the court took into consideration that an honest mistake was made in reporting a charge and that it was made without negligence by a journalist who was acting in good faith. In the case of *Westman v. Southam Inc.* (1984), 34 Alta. L.R. (2d) 189 (Q.B.), the use of the word "rape" in a news report instead of "sexual assault", was held not to be an act of contempt and did not endanger a fair trial. But in the English case of *R. v. Hutchison; Ex parte McMahon*, [1936] 2 All E.R. 1514, the court found that a newspaper photo of a man being arrested during a parade and captioned with the words "Attempt on the King's life" implied that the man would be charged with attempted murder. In actual fact, he was only charged with unlawful possession of a firearm, and the newspaper was found to be in contempt.

45 In *Re Editions MacLean and Fulford; R. v. Dion* (1965), 46 C.R. 185 (Qué. C.A.), an article was published three weeks before a trial that reviewed the accused's life and his own testimony at a coroner's inquest, along with confessions he had made. The court said, at 185, that this was contempt and it did not matter that the inquest's testimony had been well publicized.

depending on the timing and whether the discussion could incite public opinion one way or the other on issues involved in the case.

Interviewing Witnesses Prior to Trial

The courts frown on amateur investigations of crimes by reporters. But a factual presentation of the events can still be produced. In a contempt case where the court said it was done properly, the journalist had interviews with witnesses explaining what had happened without any expression of opinion by the reporter or any statement of facts other than those gleaned from the witnesses. At no point was the accused mentioned as actually being the perpetrator. The court said if the witnesses' statements were proved wrong in court, the accused could always sue for defamation.[46]

The danger in interviewing witnesses is that inadmissible evidence will be published and the fairness of the trial will be destroyed. The timing of this type of report is crucial. The closer it is to trial, the more dangerous it becomes to interview witnesses.

Other Court Proceedings Involving the Accused

When an accused is facing more than one criminal trial over a period of time or is involved in a concurrent civil proceeding, a journalist shouldn't link the proceedings together in a single story. It could prejudice either of the individuals' trials, particularly any proceeding with a jury.[47]

---

46 See *Fortin v. Moscarella* (1957), 11 D.L.R. (2d) 606 (B.C. S.C.). English courts have also condemned independent inquiries by the press. See *R. v. Evening Standard* (1924), 40 T.L.R. 833 (D.C.), where a newspaper systematically investigated a crime while the accused awaited trial and published play-by-play accounts of their investigation, including stories about the accused's troubled life and the suffering of his wife. The court held the newspaper would have no way of knowing what facts could become an issue at trial and was committing a serious contempt by conducting the amateur investigation.

47 In *R. v. Bochner and Ruby*, [1944] 3 D.L.R. 788 (Ont. H.C.), a newspaper published an account of concurrent divorce proceedings involving the accused just before his criminal trial. The article said he was a "notorious local underworld character" and brought up his criminal record. The court said it did not matter that the newspaper was unaware that the other trial was about to take place, since the paper knew charges were pending. In *Bédard v. Laviolette* (1981), 22 C.R. (3d) 230 (C.S. Qué.), the annual report of a professional society related that an action was being taken against one of its members and mentioned the result of another trial involving the member. Although technically an act of contempt, the court refused to punish the society because the offended party waited too long before bringing the complaint to court. In the English case of *R. v. Astor* (1913), 30 T.L.R. 10 (D.C.), a story reported the outcome of a case and then went on to tell of another upcoming case against the man, something the court felt might prejudice the second trial.

Police Comments

The police are no different from other individuals. Once charges have been laid, any comments from them suggesting guilt, admissions or confessions could endanger a fair trial, until presented as evidence at the trial in open court.[48]

Previous Criminal Record of Accused and Witnesses

As soon as criminal charges are laid (or perhaps even known to be imminent), a journalist should not make reference to the past criminal record of an accused or a potential witness until it is brought out in open court.[49]

One common scenario that troubles many newsrooms is what to do about someone who is arrested while on parole. Do you mention it? Generally, it's permissible to mention this fact at the time of the arrest. But as the trial date approaches, the person's record shouldn't be mentioned until it's brought out in court. In one recent B.C. case,[50] a journalist and his newspaper were convicted of contempt for revealing during the jury selection stage that an accused was on parole for a similar offence when arrested.

---

48 In *R. v. Carocchia* (1973), 15 C.C.C. (2d) 175 (Qué. C.A.), a police press release that announced an arrest implied the accused was guilty by listing other charges which police said were yet to come and which said the accused was linked to organized crime. The police were found to be in contempt. In *Steiner v. Toronto Star Ltd.* (1955), 1 D.L.R. (2d) 297 (Ont. H.C.), a journalist wrote a story before a trial in which a senior police officer was quoted as saying the accused had admitted his guilt. In the story, the reporter tried to cushion the impact of the police comment, by saying the accused had "allegedly" confessed. Still, the court cited the reporter and editors of the newspaper for contempt. It said the use of words like "alleged" are of no protection since the story would lead any reasonable person to assume the accused was guilty.

49 While publishing the criminal record of someone involved in a trial is usually a cut and dried case of contempt, in *Re Murphy and Southam Press Ltd.* (1972), 9 C.C.C. (2d) 330 at 335 (B.C. S.C.), the court held that the publication of the criminal record of a witness prior to his appearance was not contempt because the community knew of his record, the jury would have been told anyway and the trial was still some time off. But the court recognized that, generally, the criminal record of an accused or witness should not be brought out before it is tendered as evidence in the trial.

Also, see *R. v. CHEK TV Ltd.* (1987), 33 C.C.C. (3d) 24 (B.C. C.A.), where a broadcaster was found to have committed the offence of contempt after broadcasting information about the accused's criminal background during a trial. This case is notable because the court found it was contemptuous despite the fact the criminal record of the accused was placed before the jury. The appeal court felt that while there was no real risk of an unfair trial of the accused, the broadcast interfered with the justice process and created a perception of unfairness.

50 *R. v. Peebles* (2005), 205 C.C.C. (3d) 417 (B.C. S.C.).

The reporter, his editor and *The Prince George Citizen* were fined $1,000, $1,000 and $10,000, respectively.

A less problematic situation involves the prison inmate who murders a prison guard or commits some other crime while escaping custody. When he or she is brought to trial, it is certain the jury will be told the accused was in jail.

As an aside, consider whether it's really important to mention a criminal record. For example, is it fair to report that a person arrested for a petty theft is on parole from a murder charge? In civil cases, any references to the criminal record of an individual involved in the trial should also be avoided, particularly in jury trials, unless the record is brought out in open court.

Reporting Foreign Proceedings or Arrests

Sometimes, a person will be arrested in another country for a crime committed in Canada or there may be proceedings, such as an extradition hearing, to bring the person back to this country for trial. A reporter should be careful of sensational details reported in another country's media or from foreign authorities, particularly suggestions of confessions or admissions. Evidence that's admissible in another country may not be admissible here.

Re-Trials

A court may order a new trial of a matter or a mistrial could be declared which would require a re-trial. When a jury is involved in the second trial, a journalist must not make any reference to the fact that it is a re-trial or publish any details of the evidence, representations made or results of the original trial until after the second trial.[51]

Stories Relevant to a Case, Sidebars

The publication of features or related stories that are linked to a case being tried could theoretically be contemptuous. For instance, it could be considered an act of contempt to publish a story on the increasing use of illegal drugs by children alongside a court story about a jury trial of a major drug dealer. This doesn't mean to say that everyday news and features can't

---

51 For example, the June 24, 1982 edition of the *Whitehorse Star* reports that the staff was fined a total of $1000 for writing stories noting that a current trial was a re-trial and comparing evidence from the first trial with testimony in the second.

be published. A journalist should simply be careful in the line-up or placement of stories so that nobody could reasonably think the related story is a comment on the case before the courts.

Visuals

In some trials, the ability of witnesses to identify the accused is an important factor in proving the charge. A newspaper or broadcasting outlet could endanger a trial if it publishes a picture of the accused when identification is an issue.[52]

As mentioned above, police-supplied photographs for manhunts can also endanger a fair trial if the suspect is portrayed as the perpetrator. It's advisable to say the suspect is "sought for assistance" or "questioning" by the authorities in connection with a certain crime.

During Trial

The standard of care which a journalist must exercise before a trial begins is raised to a higher level as the court action goes to trial.[53] While the court may allow a contemptuous act or publication to go unpunished in the period leading to the trial, any contempt of court during the trial is less likely to escape judicial notice. Most of the "danger" areas listed above continue to apply during the trial. These problem areas can be added:

Audio and Visual Recording in Courts

Generally, all courts in Canada prohibit journalists from making visual or audio recordings of courtroom proceedings. In most jurisdictions, individual judges have the discretion to allow cameras or tape recorders into the courtroom, but it's rarely allowed. In some jurisdictions, journalists aren't even allowed to take pictures or record an interview with someone in the hallways of the court building. The policy regarding photographs can

---

52 See the English case of *R. v. Daily Mirror; Ex parte Smith*, [1927] 1 K.B. 845, where a newspaper published a photograph of a suspect arrested in a case where the identification of the culprit was in question. The photo appeared in the paper on the same morning as witnesses viewed a police line-up. Although the court was told no witnesses saw the picture and identification turned out not to be a crucial issue in the trial, the court still held it was an act of contempt because the newspaper knew at the time of publication that identification could have been an issue.

53 This was noted in *A.G. Manitoba v. Winnipeg Free Press Co.*, [1965] 4 C.C.C. 260 at 262 (Man. Q.B.).

usually be obtained through the court clerk. Any violations of the rule will be punished as acts of direct contempt of court.

In Ontario, a statute has established a formal offence for unauthorized audio and visual recordings in court buildings. Section 136 of Ontario's Courts of Justice Act prohibits the taking of photographs, motion pictures, audio recordings or other records capable of producing visual or aural representations by electronic means or otherwise:[54]

> (i)   at a court hearing,
>
> (ii) of any person entering or leaving the room in which a court hearing is to be or has been convened, or
>
> (iii) of any person in the building in which a court hearing is to be or has been convened where there is reasonable ground for believing that the person is there for the purpose of attending or leaving the hearing. . . .

Recently, the Ontario law was amended to permit reporters to use audio tape recorders to assist them in taking notes. The prohibition still exists on using the recordings in a broadcast.

The only other exceptions listed in the Ontario law are where the judge presiding at a court hearing authorizes the pictures or audio recording for the presentation of evidence or where solicitors use a tape recorder as a substitute for their notes or if the pictures or audio recordings are in connection with ceremonial proceedings with the permission of the judge or in connection with educational or instructive purposes with the permission of the judge, parties and witnesses.

The Ontario legislation also states that this law doesn't prohibit someone from "unobtrusively" making handwritten notes or sketches at a court hearing.[55]

There has been one case challenging this law as an infringement of the media's rights under the Charter.[56] A CBC journalist had instructed a camera operator to shoot pictures of a participant in a trial coming out of the courtroom. The CBC argued that the offence created by the statute was unconstitutional and violated the freedom of the press guarantee in the Charter. A provincial appeal court agreed that the law did infringe the media's Charter right, but ruled that it was a demonstrably justified and reasonable limit on the press. The court said the right to a fair trial was paramount and cameras in the courts could have a negative effect on witnesses and jurors. As a small consolation, the court did rule that the law's requirement for an educational component in granting access was unnec-

---

54 S.O. 1984, c. 11, now R.S.O. 1990, c. C.43, s. 136(1), (3).

55 *Ibid.*, s. 136(2).

56 *R. v. Squires* (1989), 69 C.R. (3d) 337 (Ont. Dist. Ct.), affirmed (1992), 18 C.R. (4th) 22 (Ont. C.A.).

essary and declared it to be of no force and effect. In 1993, the Supreme Court of Canada refused leave to appeal this decision.

More recently, a B.C. TV station was found guilty of criminal contempt and fined $2,000 for showing a video clip of a female undercover officer walking near the courthouse with a prosecutor in breach of a very specific ban on publication.[57] The order was issued during a high-profile murder trial and the judge had banned "the publication in print and the broadcasting on television, film, radio and the Internet of any information tending or serving to publicly identify the undercover police officers in the investigation of the accused in this matter, including but not limited to, any likeness of the officers, the appearance of their attire and their physical description, for a period of five years."

The news report did not clearly reveal the face of the officer, but did show "her clothing, build, gait and distinctive hair." The court noted that "pixellating" or electronically hiding the officer would not have altered the end result. The judge was clear that the ban prohibited any public identification of the officer, "including any likeness and their physical description." For example, someone who knew her might be able to recognize her gait or physical build.

End of the Trial

Determining when a proceeding has ended may seem obvious, but it has been a troublesome point sometimes. In criminal cases, the trial doesn't formally end until the judge passes sentence. Therefore, comments urging a particular punishment before the sentence is actually handed down could be viewed as attempts to influence the judge's decision.[58] In a civil court action the jury verdict usually signals the end of a trial, but a trial by judge alone will not be over until the decision is handed down.

Further to this, though, the courts have decided that a factual presentation of evidence brought out in court and published before the sentence is pronounced, with no comment on the jury verdict or what sentence should be rendered, would be unlikely to have any effect on a judge's final decision.[59]

---

57 *R. v. Black*, [2007] BCSC 74 (B.C. S.C.).

58 In *R. v. Panrucker* (1961), 34 W.W.R. 94 (B.C. Mag. Ct.), the accused pleaded guilty to his crime and a public outcry erupted prior to sentencing, prompting the judge to warn the public about comments urging a particular sentence.

59 Such was the case in *Bellitti v. CBC* (1973), 44 D.L.R. (3d) 407 (Ont. H.C.).

Evidence and Exhibits

Any document or evidence which is read into open court or filed as an exhibit can be included as a part of a report of judicial proceedings. Evidence which has been declared to be inadmissible or is not entered as evidence in open court has no place in a report of judicial proceedings and may be contemptuous.[60]

That said, when a case involves no jury and no publication ban has been ordered by the court, journalists may report on information entered in proceedings other than open court, such as *voir dire* hearings to consider the admissibility of evidence.[61] Remember, though, in a trial with a jury, *voir dire* evidence should not be published.[62]

Also remember information in any documents can be published after the trial and appeal period has passed, even those found inadmissible, but won't be privileged in a defamation action.

Headlines or Captions

A headline or caption is considered a part of the story and can be contemptuous, even if the main story itself is fair and accurate.[63] While this is a problem area that can crop up at any time, it most frequently happens when the news media report on an ongoing trial or proceeding. For example, headlines shouldn't state opinions as facts. A headline blaring "Jones is a thief" is more likely to influence a juror or the public than one saying "Jones is a thief, Crown tells court."

---

60 In *R. v. Dorion* (1953), 10 W.W.R. (N.S.) 379 (Man. Q.B.), a newspaper was found to be in contempt for publishing the contents of a document declared inadmissible during a *voir dire* conducted while the jury was excluded from the courtroom.

61 See *R. v. Yu*, 2006 CarswellBC 757, 2006 BCPC 0121 (Prov. Ct.), where Vancouver newspapers published accurate information from a *voir dire* in a trial by judge alone that later allegedly deterred a defence witness from appearing in the matter. The court denied an application for a stay of the proceedings and found no act of contempt by the newspapers. The judge ruled the publication of evidence presented in a *voir dire* before a judge alone, without a jury, is allowed where there is no publication ban or other statutory restriction on publication.

62 See *R. v. The Maple Ridge*, 2000 CarswellBC 2427, [2001] BCSC 1357 (S.C.), where a reporter did not know a ban had been issued on publishing the *voir dire* evidence, but the publisher, after becoming aware of it, insisted the newspapers be delivered after receiving legal advice. The newspaper was ordered to pay a $5,000 fine.

63 See *Hatfield v. Healy* (1911), 3 Alta. L.R. 327 (S.C.).

In-Camera Proceedings

Sometimes, a court will hold a hearing *in camera* or behind closed doors, perhaps to allow a nervous witness to testify. Occasionally, reporters are allowed to stay in the court while the general public is ordered out or transcripts of the *in camera* hearing may be made available after the trial. The common law rule is that a fair and accurate report in good faith and without malice, of proceedings held *in camera* isn't contemptuous, unless the court has ordered a ban on publication during the trial.[64] One province makes specific reference to this. In Ontario, the Courts of Justice Act expressly states that the publication of proceedings held *in camera* isn't a contempt of court, unless the judge has issued a ban on publication.[65]

However, a word of caution. Since the *in camera* proceedings aren't held in public, any news reports of the closed door hearings aren't privileged under defamation law.

Interviews with Lawyers

The professional conduct codes for lawyers caution them about speaking to the media and "touting" themselves.[66] However, the strict rules of the past are loosening and most law societies accept lawyers as media representatives. Still, many lawyers are careful not to appear unprofessional.

For example, the professional conduct code for New Brunswick lawyers is very detailed in outlining how to deal with the media. It says any comments by lawyers during a trial shall be of a non-confidential nature with factual information based on public records or evidence already given at a public hearing or in open court. The character or credibility of a party to the action or a witness shouldn't be commented upon. No statements should be made by lawyers as to the evidence yet to be offered or any other matter which could interfere with a fair trial.[67]

Despite the suggested guidelines for lawyers, it's important to note that law societies don't have a right to order lawyers not to contact the news

---

64 The seminal case is *Scott v. Scott*, [1913] A.C. 417 (H.L.), in which the House of Lords said a hearing can be held *in camera* under the common law only in proceedings involving wards, the mentally-disordered, trade secrets or where holding the trial in public would defeat the whole object of the proceeding. Statutes may set out some other exceptions to the "open court" rule.

65 S. 135(3).

66 For example, see the *Code of Professional Conduct*, Canadian Bar Association.

67 See the New Brunswick *Code of Professional Conduct*, Part F.

media,[68] and it's not contemptuous to ask a lawyer to repeat outside the courtroom what he or she said to the court.[69] Judges may, however, be disturbed by lawyers who first tell the news media what they plan to tell the court before the judge actually gets to hear it. But usually it's the lawyer who is cited for contempt, and not the journalist, in these cases.

Interviews with Judges

Judges aren't untouchables, but they do see their position in society as one which should remain impartial. One federal Department of Justice book gives judges the following advice. A judge shouldn't comment on current trials or actions that are before the courts or issues which have a potential to become court actions. The same goes for comments on new legislation or judicial decisions. If a judge feels there's a lack of public understanding of some part of the proceedings before him, he should make his comments in open court from the bench.[70]

Multiple Accused

A reporter should be careful when several people are charged in connection with the same incident and tried separately. After the first trial and sentencing, comment may have to be restricted if any of the accused are still awaiting trial or sentence. For example, the judge may think an editorial comment about the lax sentence given to one of the accused is urging him to impose a different sentence on the remaining accused.[71]

---

68 In *Re Klein and L.S.U.C.; Re Dvorak and L.S.U.C.* (1985), 50 O.R. (2d) 118 (H.C.), the court said a lawyer has a moral, civic and professional duty to speak out in the news media where he sees an injustice. A Law Society of Upper Canada rule restricting contact with the media infringed the Charter's guarantee of freedom of expression and impaired the right of the lawyer, client and public to disseminate information. The court said the public has a constitutional right to know about pending cases and the legal profession.

69 See *A.G. Ontario v. CBC* (1977), 39 C.C.C. (2d) 182 (Ont. H.C.). In this case, a motion was made to stay proceedings and during the subsequent break, a lawyer repeated the essence of the motion before a television camera. The court found no contempt because the lawyer was only repeating what was already said in court. A similar decision was made in *Residential Tenancy Commission v. Toronto Apartment Buildings Co.* (1983), 42 C.P.C. 314 (Ont. Div. Ct.).

70 The Hon. J.O. Wilson, *A Book for Judges* (Ottawa: Ministry of Supply and Services, Government of Canada, 1980), at 57-59.

71 This was the case in *R. v. Thomas; Re Globe Printing Co.*, [1952] O.R. 22 (H.C.).

During the Appeal Period or Appeal

The court's jurisdiction over a matter doesn't end with the completion of the trial. Each province has legislated the time period within which appeals must be launched (usually 30 to 45 days).

In theory, comments on trial decisions during the appeal period or appeal must be guarded and shouldn't be seen as an attempt to influence the court of appeal's decision. In practice, though, courts are quite generous in allowing fair comment upon cases during the appeal period and even during the hearing of appeals.

But what is fair comment is somewhat unpredictable. For example, in 1985, an Alberta judge issued an injunction banning the showing in that province of a CBC drama loosely based on the controversial case of James Keegstra, a school teacher accused of inciting racial hatred. The court felt the "thinly-guised characterization of . . . Keegstra"[72] would endanger an upcoming appeal of his conviction and a possible re-trial. However, on appeal, this injunction was ordered set aside.[73] The court noted that the appeal had yet to be held when the program was to air and that a re-trial would have been at least two years away. The court held there were no grounds for the injunction because the risk to the accused was neither real nor substantial.

Recently, one provincial appellate court has tackled the issue of whether news reports on any proceedings leading up to an appeal hearing could affect the appeal or a new trial.[74] Three accused were acquitted of first-degree murder in two shooting deaths. The Crown filed an appeal, alleging there was new evidence of a romantic connection between a juror and one of the accused. It was agreed that, before the appeal hearing was held, one judge would hear the new evidence and determine if it was admissible. The accused applied for a ban on the publication of the new evidence until the appeal hearing could be held.

The appeal court rejected the application for a ban. The hearing of fresh evidence in this pre-appeal proceeding, it said, should be conducted as it would normally be in any hearing. That is, openly and without any restraint on publicity.

The court went on to state the "fact that the public, including reporters, can view proceedings is not sufficient for achieving the goal of public scrutiny if publication is banned." The judges said it was not in the interests

---

72 Quoted in *Canadian Broadcasting Corp. v. Keegstra* (1986), 35 D.L.R. (4th) 76 at 77 (Alta. C.A.).

73 *Canadian Broadcasting Corp. v. Keegstra, ibid.*

74 *R. v. Budai* (2000), 185 D.L.R. (4th) 510 (B.C. C.A.).

of fostering public confidence to postpone their full scrutiny until the hearing of the appeal itself.

And, what if there was to be a new trial? Would the fresh evidence and appeal proceedings taint the minds of future jurors? No, said the court. A new trial was not going to be held soon and processes are in place to ensure a fair jury is chosen. Ultimately, said the court, "the need for full public scrutiny in any event vastly outweighed the risk that the accused might encounter if retried for murder."

There are really only two common areas of concern after a trial:

Criticism of Decisions

During the appeal period or before the appeal, a journalist may wish to comment upon a decision. As mentioned, in theory, the courts dislike any attempt to influence the decision-making process. But public interest usually demands discussion of the decision before the appeal is heard and appeal courts are unlikely to be influenced by such discussion.[75]

The courts seem to be very tolerant and an important question to the court in cases of serious contempt, is whether there's a real chance of a retrial of the matter which could be prejudiced by the report or comment.

Criticism of Juries

Any statements criticising jury members after the trial should be within the limits of fair comment. For instance, to brand jury members as "murderers," as one newspaper did, is beyond fair comment.[76] The personal virtues of the jury members shouldn't be attacked and a journalist may also run the risk of being sued for defamation. The court may be concerned that an unjustly critical comment on the jury could impede justice by making other people reluctant to serve on juries.

---

75 In *Re O'Brien; R. v. Howland* (1889), 16 S.C.R. 197, an article criticized a judgment on purely legal grounds. Despite inaccurate views on the law, it was not considered contemptuous because the comments were made in good faith and without malice. In *R. v. Thomas Sophonow* (1983), 2 C.R.D. 525.70-03 (Man. C.A.), the court held that a lawyer's request for a ban on the publication of "extra-judicial comment" until after the appeal is heard, is neither practical nor appropriate. The court said it would amount to censorship and a denial of a public hearing.

76 *Re Nicol*, note 10, above.

CONTEMPT AND LEGISLATIVE BODIES

As mentioned at the beginning of this chapter, provincial legislatures and Parliament are among the recognized bodies which can punish acts of contempt. Contempt proceedings involving a legislative body are rare, but do occur from time to time. Aside from the possibility of being accused of contempt by a legislature or Parliament, many journalists may not be aware that contempt proceedings can also arise from reporting contemptuous remarks made in a government proceeding.

Contempt of a Legislative Body

Legislative bodies have the power to punish both direct and indirect acts of contempt affecting their members or proceedings, and ultimately can send an offender to jail. The only legislative bodies which do not have a full power to punish for contempt are those in the Northwest Territories and the Yukon.[77] Worth noting is that the courts are very reluctant to interfere with the exercise of power by Legislative bodies.[78]

Any act which a court of law would find objectionable, a legislative body could too. Among the examples of punishable acts against legislative forums are false or perverted reports of debates, bribery of members of the legislative body, defamatory reflections on members or the body itself, and the wide-sweeping category of "disrespect to that which is entitled to legal regard."[79]

Parliament and the provincial legislatures rarely exercise this power against the news media. But it has happened, and recently legislative bodies have shown they are at least willing to consider punishing contemptuous acts. For instance, on April 1, 1985 several news outlets published the recommendations of a confidential House of Commons committee report the day before it was to be tabled. The committee had placed a ban on the publication of the report and a Member of Parliament accused the news outlets of contempt. The Speaker of the House agreed it was a serious issue and undertook to decide whether the news outlets should be made to appear before a special Commons committee. He decided the news outlets were not in contempt, despite the publication ban on the report, and cited three

---

77 See Joseph Maingot, *Parliamentary Privilege in Canada* (Toronto: Butterworths, 1982), at 175. Another excellent book on this topic is *Beauchesne's Parliamentary Rules and Forms*, 5th ed. (Toronto: Carswell, 1978).

78 Note 36, above.

79 *Ibid., Parliamentary Privilege*, note 77, above, at 196. For a list of examples of legislative contempt, see the Legislative Assembly Act of any province. For instance, in Alberta, see R.S.A. 2000, c. L-9.

Parliamentary precedents in support of the decision. The Speaker held that before an alleged act of contempt can be acted upon there must be some proof that the privileges of M.P.'s were violated. In this case, there was no such proof.

Although punishment for legislative contempt is rare, the power has been exercised on occasion. In most of the cases, the reporter or publisher of the contemptuous statement was called before the House to answer the charges and then made to apologize.

Reporting Contemptuous Remarks Made in the House

Members of our legislative bodies have always taken comfort in the fact that they can speak freely and even maliciously about any person or subject that concerns them without fear of a defamation action while they conduct their business in the House, Senate or legislative assemblies of the country. And journalists take comfort in the knowledge that they too enjoy a privilege for fair and accurate reports of even the most defamatory remarks made during these public debates.

The members debating in our legislative bodies enjoy this absolute privilege even when their remarks might constitute an act of contempt against the courts. But the court's respect of such privilege stops at the doors of the proceedings. While reports of defamatory matter arising from the proceedings of a legislative forum are privileged, a journalist is not protected from being punished for contempt for reporting a contemptuous remark made in the House, Senate or a legislative assembly.[80]

This includes statements in reports, papers, votes or proceedings of the legislature or Parliament. The "proceedings" include those in connection with the formal transaction of business or those necessarily incidental to a House or committee.[81] Therefore, if a Member of Parliament or of a legislature scandalizes the court or says something which could endanger the fair trial of an individual, the publication of the statement by reporters is not protected from contempt proceedings.

There has been a Supreme Court of Canada case on this point, though the attention of the court was not on the news media but the politician who made the remarks.[82] The accused was an RCMP officer, charged with breaking and entering and theft of computer tapes containing a list of Parti Québecois members. During the trial by jury, another RCMP officer testified about the police force's activities in hunting for separatists and terrorists in Québec. The testimony was reported and the leader of the Opposition asked

---

80 *Re Clark and A.G. Canada* (1977), 81 D.L.R. (3d) 33 at 56 (Ont. H.C.).
81 *Ibid.*, at 69-72.
82 *R. v. Vermette* (1988), 50 D.L.R. (4th) 385 (S.C.C.).

the Premier of Québec in the National Assembly to confirm or deny the RCMP allegations. The Premier attacked the integrity of the witness, accused, defence counsel and even the federal government. After the Premier's remarks were published, the trial judge declared a mistrial.

Before the new trial started, the accused successfully argued the charges should be dropped entirely because the Premier's remarks had been so widely publicized that a fair trial was impossible. The Supreme Court, however, disagreed, saying it is only at the stage when a jury is to be selected that a court can determine if an accused can be tried by an impartial jury. The court ordered a new trial.

POSSIBLE REVISIONS TO CONTEMPT LAW

There are very few references to contempt in statutory law. As noted, s. 9 of the Criminal Code preserves the common law right of courts to punish acts of contempt, but the Code sets out no maximum penalty and doesn't specify the procedure to be followed by a court to punish contempt.

This is seen by some people as too broad a power and in some cases not a specific enough power. In 1984, the Liberal government of the time proposed some major changes to the Criminal Code, including provisions dealing with contempt of court. The amendments would have done away with the common law power to punish acts of indirect contempt and replaced it with a formal offence of criminal contempt and an offence of scandalizing the court.

The proposed amendments would have preserved the common law power of the courts to punish acts of civil contempt (for example, disobedience of a civil court order), as well as the power to maintain order in the judicial proceedings (such as expelling a raucous spectator). Since the proposed amendments died on the order paper in 1984, little more has been said by the federal government. A new Criminal Code is in the works and chances are no further movement will be seen in the area of contempt until that work is completed.

It is interesting, however, to note what might have been changed. In 1984, the following criminal contempt offence would have been created:

131.11 (1) Every one who knowingly makes or causes to be made any publication that creates a substantial risk that the course of justice in any particular civil or criminal judicial proceeding pending at the time of the publication will be seriously impeded or prejudiced is guilty of

(a) an indictable offence and is liable for imprisonment for a term not exceeding two years; or

(b) an offence punishable on summary conviction.

If placed into law, the offence would have been prosecuted under the summary conviction process, thus enabling inferior courts to deal with the offence. This is a departure from the common law rule that only superior courts can punish indirect contempt. The phrase "knowingly makes or causes to be made" would require the Crown to prove that the contempt was intentional, which is another change from the common law which holds a person responsible for unintentional interferences with justice.

The proposed reforms also would have formally set out when the *sub judice* rule would be in effect. For criminal proceedings, the rule would begin upon arrest, issuance of a summons, warrant or appearance notice, or a preferred indictment. It would end after all appeals. For civil proceedings, it would be in effect from the time of setting down a trial date until the end of the appeal process. Note the change from the present approach for civil proceedings. Under the proposed law, the *sub judice* rule would not have begun until a date had been set down for trial. The proposed reforms also would have specified that when a new trial is ordered after an appeal, the *sub judice* rule would continue to apply up until the new trial was properly adjudicated and new appeals were over.

The reform also would have set out two defences:

(i)　the publication was a fair and accurate report of a legal proceeding held in public and was published contemporaneously and in good faith.

(ii)　the publication was made as or as a part of a discussion in good faith of public affairs or other matters of general public interest and the risk of impediment or prejudice was merely incidental to the discussion.

The defences would not have applied where a court order banned publication of evidence or information, nor would the defences apply to publications of the details of *in camera* proceedings.

The proposed amendments also would have created a specific offence for scandalizing the courts:

Every one who, without lawful justification or excuse, willfully makes or causes to be made any publication of a false, scandalous or scurrilous statement calculated to bring into disrepute a court or judge in his official capacity is guilty of

(a)　an indictable offence and is liable to imprisonment for a term not exceeding two years; or

(b)　an offence punishable on summary conviction.

The statutory defence would be that the publication was for the public benefit at the time of the publication and that the statement was true. There is no telling when these amendments or ones like them could be re-introduced. Journalists should keep an eye open for any new enactments concerning the Criminal Code and contempt.

SOME FINAL THOUGHTS

The law which has developed around "contempt of court" might be seen by some as judicial muzzling of the news media. But that is not the intention. The principles of contempt law seek to preserve the reputation of justice and guarantee a fair trial for the accused. On the other hand, the courts recognize the value of a free press and often quote this phrase from the 18th-century philosopher Jeremy Bentham:

> Where there is no publicity, there is no justice.

A CONTEMPT CHECKLIST

1. Any conduct which tends to undermine or bring into disrepute the authority and administration of justice or interfere with someone's right to a fair hearing before a court or other quasi-judicial body could be considered an act of contempt. Common examples of contempt are disobeying a court order, disrupting a hearing or publishing damaging information about someone involved in a trial.

2. Two types of contempt most often involve journalists: *scandalizing the court* and *prejudicing someone's right to a fair trial*. Scandalizing the court involves any accusation of bias, perverted justice or improper motives on the part of the court or the judge in the discharge of a judicial duty. The second type of contempt is concerned with what is usually called "trial by press."

3. Generally speaking, the danger of contempt for journalists begins from the time the courts become involved in a case and lasts until it ends. However, the degree of danger varies depending on what stage a proceeding is in and the circumstances involved.

4. Among the potentially contemptuous areas for journalists to watch are: civil pleadings, describing criminal charges, interviewing potential witnesses, reporting criminal records of accused or witnesses, police comments, multiple accused, foreign court proceedings and criticizing judges or juries.

5. Legislative bodies can also punish journalists for contemptuous stories.

However, it is rare. It should also be noted that journalists are not protected from being cited for contempt if they report contemptuous remarks made in a legislative proceeding.

7

PUBLICATION BANS
AND RESTRAINING ORDERS

The courts have always recognized and supported the news media's role in reporting what goes on in the halls of justice. There are times, however, when judges and others believe the ends of justice may be better served by restricting the flow of information to the public.

To do this the courts have at their disposal a variety of inherent common law and statutory powers to temporarily, and sometimes permanently, restrain the publication of certain information arising from hearings.

For example, the publication of evidence tendered in a preliminary hearing is usually banned until after a full trial can be held before an unbiased jury. Or a judge will ban the publication of a rape victim's name to lessen her trauma.

Publication bans have also been incorporated into some federal and provincial laws. For example, a provincial family law Act may prohibit the publication of the names of children and family members involved in a child abuse hearing.

That said, since the introduction of the Charter of Rights, the media have been successful in challenging many unreasonable restrictions on the public's "right to know." As several landmark Supreme Court of Canada rulings have recently emphasized, while publication bans often have a laudable goal in protecting an individual's right to a fair trial or preserving the proper administration of justice, the Charter's guarantees of freedom of the press and freedom of expression may deserve greater weight in deciding when to restrict the flow of information.

In practice, however, the news media do not always win the day because publication bans often involve discretionary decision-making by judges dealing with unique circumstances. Perhaps the most frustrating aspect of this area of law is the ignorance or even blatant refusal of some trial judges in following the various high-level precedents setting out the rights of the public and media. Too often, we still hear of a judge banning publication of a high-profile accused's name because it might be embarrassing or a judge unnecessarily restricting the reporting of evidence offered in open court. Unfortunately, the media must remain vigilant in asserting the rights of the public and it should never be assumed that a judge always has the authority to issue publication bans. If you have any doubts about the correctness of a ban, seek out knowledgeable legal counsel and challenge the order if possible.

We have entered a very interesting period for publication bans. As is explained below, the Supreme Court of Canada has issued guidelines in several recent cases for issuing publication bans. Also, not only is the Charter expanding the rights of the media, courts are discovering they can no longer control dissemination of information in some cases. New forms of communication, such as the Internet, allow individuals to publish anonymously details of trials around the world. Before and during the very high-profile 1995 murder trial of Paul Bernardo and Karla Homolka, for example, details and alleged details of their sex crimes were freely available to Canadians from Internet sites in other countries despite a publication ban.

Did having this information in the public domain negate the court-ordered ban? No, however, the Canadian news media were left in an awkward position of being unable to report information that anyone could find and, ironically, were unable to correct any wrong information that was being circulated. The Bernardo case also highlighted the problems that arise when two countries have different approaches to bans. Reporters in the U.S. told viewers details in their reports that Canadians could not hear, which then put the onus on cable TV companies to censor U.S. transmissions. Even U.S. broadcasters in some border stations were concerned that they might be charged with violating the ban.

What, then, is the future for publication bans? While bans are unlikely to disappear, the Internet, Charter and other developments may prompt courts and legislators to re-think their goals. For example, are potential jurors actually influenced or swayed by media reports of certain details? Some research suggests they are, while other studies say jurors decide on the evidence presented and largely ignore the news media. As noted, this is an interesting period for publication bans.

During the pre-trial stage of a civil matrimonial proceeding, the husband asked for a court order that he and his wife be identified only by their initials in court documents. The husband alleged the wife's allegations were malicious, false and involved embarrassing sexual matters. He claimed his wife and children from second and third marriages might also be hurt. Will the court grant his motion?

No.[1] The Ontario family court judge ruled it was "crucial to the rule of law that the courts were seen to function openly, and the public had a right to information pertaining to public institutions." In this case, the wife wanted an open trial and the judge said that "[h]umiliation of one

---

1 *T. v. T.* (2003), 2003 CarswellOnt 172, [2003] O.J. No. 132 (S.C.J.).

> party did not warrant the right to anonymity, and there was no pertinent legal protection for the members of the husband's second and third families."

THE SUPREME COURT RULINGS IN *DAGENAIS* AND *MENTUCK*

In 1994, the Supreme Court of Canada issued a landmark ruling attempting to limit the use of publication bans and outlining the factors courts must consider before issuing orders that infringe upon the freedom of the press. In a 6-3 decision, the Supreme Court ruled that while the constitutionally guaranteed right to a fair trial is important, freedom of the press is of equal and sometimes greater importance. This ruling and others since are having a significant impact on the news media's interaction with the justice system.

This case and another have become known as the *Dagenais/Mentuck* test. In these cases, the Supreme Court urges lower courts to always consider the Charter's guarantee of freedom of the press in issuing discretionary court orders (that is, where a judge's decision is not mandatory). In addition to stating that freedom of the press may take precedence over an accused's right to a fair trial at times, the Court also requires that court orders or bans in criminal proceedings be as limited as possible, if they are even necessary at all. Indeed, the Court urges judges to first consider all alternative measures to bans and orders that impede on the media's ability to cover the news.

Dagenais

The 1994 case of *Dagenais v. Canadian Broadcasting Corp.*[2] concerned a cross-Canada publication ban against the broadcast of a fictional drama, "The Boys of St-Vincent," which dealt with child sexual and physical abuse in a Catholic orphanage. The ban was issued by a lower court judge after hearing an application by lawyers for four members of a Catholic order who were charged with physical and sexual abuse of young boys in Catholic training schools.

Since they would soon be facing trial in Ontario, the judge agreed the television program might influence potential jurors and a ban was necessary to ensure the proceedings were fair. The judge prohibited broadcast until the end of the four trials and granted an order prohibiting publication of the fact of the application, or any material relating to it.

---

2 [1994] 3 S.C.R. 835.

The CBC appealed the injunction, but the Court of Appeal affirmed the decision. It did, however, limit the ban's scope to Ontario and Montreal. It also reversed the order banning publicity about the proposed broadcast and the very fact of the proceedings that gave rise to the ban.

Going to the Supreme Court, a number of issues had to be decided, including whether the television network had "standing" as a third party to challenge the order, whether the ban was within the common law or legislated authority of the judge, and whether the ban unreasonably infringed the Charter of Rights guarantee of freedom of the press.

The television program was obviously capitalizing on the spate of sexual abuse charges levied against various church and social agencies in recent years. The mini-series, however, was not about the four accused in Ontario and was set in Newfoundland.

First, the Supreme Court dealt with the proper procedure to apply for a ban and appeal it. To have a ban issued, the Court said the Crown and/or the accused should make a motion before the trial judge appointed for the case or before a judge in the court at the level where the case will be heard. At the very least, the motion should be made before a superior court judge. To challenge a ban on appeal, the Crown and the accused should follow the appeal routes set out in the Criminal Code.

The Court said a judge hearing a motion for a ban has discretion to give notice to third parties, such as the media, and to grant them standing. If third parties want to oppose the motion and don't receive notice, they should attend the hearing, argue for status, and if given it, make their case. The Supreme Court then laid out a road map for appeals of lower court decisions, potentially leading to the high court itself.

Moving on, the Supreme Court majority then looked at whether the judge exercised proper discretion in ordering the ban. The Supreme Court said discretion conferred by a common law rule must be exercised within the boundaries of the Charter. Traditionally, courts have issued a ban when there is "a real and substantial risk of interference with the right to a fair trial." This historical approach placed the right to a fair trial over the freedom of expression interests of anyone affected by the ban. The Supreme Court said the traditional common law rule can no longer be applied in "the context of post-Charter Canadian society" and "does not provide sufficient protection for freedom of expression." Which Charter right, however, should be given greater emphasis?

The Court then set out a new rule for judges. A publication ban should only be ordered when:

1.   such a ban is necessary in order to prevent a real and substantial risk to the fairness of the trial, because reasonably available alternative measures will not prevent the risk; and

2.   the salutary effects of the publication ban outweigh the deleterious effects to the free expression of those affected by the ban.

If the ban fails to meet this standard, then the judge ordering a ban committed an error of law. The Supreme Court said this isn't a clash of rights, but a question of which Charter guarantee is more important at the time. In some cases, there may be evidence of a real and substantial risk to a fair trial. In fact, the Court said the party wanting a publication ban, Crown or accused, bears the burden of justifying the limitation on freedom of expression. A judge hearing an application for a ban must consider other Charter rights, but also must keep the ban as limited as possible. In this particular case, the Supreme Court said the initial ban was too broad in prohibiting broadcast throughout Canada and even banning reporting on the ban itself.

Mentuck

By 2001, after some years of confusion in interpreting the *Dagenais* ruling, it was clear to the Supreme Court that it needed to offer lower courts more guidance. In *R. v. Mentuck*,[3] the accused was charged with second-degree murder, but had to be re-tried after key evidence was ruled inadmissible. The RCMP gathered better evidence in an undercover operation and a second trial began. The Crown asked for a publication ban to protect the identity of the officers and operational methods used in the investigation.

The accused and two newspapers opposed the motion. The trial judge granted a one-year ban as to the identity of undercover police officers, but refused a ban as to operational methods used. The Supreme Court eventually dismissed the media's appeal, allowing the one-year ban as to the identity of the undercover police officers.

In *Mentuck*, the Court reformulated its test for issuing court orders that restrict access and publication by requiring that judges consider the following factors:

1.   such an order is necessary in order to prevent a *serious risk to the proper*

---

3   [2001] 3 S.C.R. 442. As an aside, Mentuck's second trial ended with the declaration of a mistrial. At his third trial, he was acquitted.

administration of justice because reasonably alternative measures will not prevent the risk; and

2. the salutary effects of the publication ban outweigh the deleterious effects on the rights and interests of the parties and the public, including the effects on the right to free expression, the right of the accused to a fair and public trial, and the efficacy of the administration of justice.

The Court explained its modified test. In *Dagenais*, the test originally required a judge to, first, determine the necessity for the publication ban and, second, weigh the ban's good and bad effects on both the news media's freedoms and the fairness of the trial. In *Mentuck*, the Court sought to broaden the test to allow judges to not only consider the impact of a ban on the case itself, but also to consider other rights or outside factors — particularly, the overall administration of justice.

The first part of the test remains essentially the same. The risk to the fairness of the trial must be serious or, as originally stated, "real and substantial." Any risk must be based on reality and be well-grounded in evidence offered to the court considering the ban. The Court said it must also be a risk that poses a serious threat to the proper administration of justice.

Considering the impact on the justice system as a whole also comes into play in the second part of the test. In weighing the salutary and deleterious effects of a ban, judges were cautioned by the Supreme Court to use discretion in protecting the "administration of justice." For example, while police informers or witness protection programs are part of the administration of justice, "courts should not interpret that term so widely as to keep secret a vast amount of enforcement information the disclosure of which would be compatible with the public interest."

Again in *Mentuck*, the Court stressed judges should consider reasonable alternatives to a ban and, if a ban is still necessary, restrict its scope as much as possible to minimize its impact on the news media.

Since then, the Court continues to emphasize its thinking in *Dagenais/ Mentuck*. For example, in a 2005 case involving *The Toronto Star*,[4] the Supreme Court sent a strong message to lower courts and legislators by ruling the *Dagenais/Mentuck* test and its presumptions in favour of access apply to "all discretionary court orders that limit freedom of expression and freedom of the press in relation to legal proceedings." That is, not just publication bans, but discretionary orders concerning access to all court proceedings and records.

---

4 *Toronto Star Newspapers Ltd. v. Ontario*, [2005] 2 S.C.R. 188.

Notification Systems for Publication Bans

Apart from allowing more media freedom from publication bans, the Supreme Court's rulings have also prompted several courts across Canada to create a public notice and information system for pending and existing publication bans. As noted above, the Supreme Court suggested that judges have a discretionary authority to notify the news media when applications for bans are to be heard or have been granted. Some courts have seized upon the idea and created Internet-based systems to provide e-mail alerts for journalists or online databases for searching.

For example, Nova Scotia's courts offer a free e-mail subscription service to advise the news media of applications for publication bans and other similar court orders. Subscribers get an e-mail message explaining that an application has been made, as well as when and where it will be heard. Alberta courts, such as the Provincial Court of Alberta, also offer a service permitting the media to be notified of a publication ban via e-mail.

In British Columbia, "The Publication Ban Notification Pilot Project" provides a searchable and free online database of information on specific publication bans. The public can also subscribe to receive e-mail notification of applications to be made for discretionary publication bans. At the time of this publication, the pilot project is only in effect for criminal proceedings in the Vancouver and New Westminster registries. Note that this database only provides information on discretionary bans, not automatic or mandatory statutory bans.

In 2007, Ontario's government announced the Attorney General was in the process of conducting a cost and technology analysis, and would be consulting with the senior judiciary on an approach for implementing a similar electronic notification system for discretionary publication bans.

RESTRAINTS ON PUBLICATION IN CRIMINAL PROCEEDINGS

The Criminal Code is being amended on an ongoing basis to reflect the realities of modern society and change outdated ideas and laws, particularly in areas involving publication bans and the rights of participants in the court system such as the news media, crime victims and even the accused.[5] In some situations, Code sections applicable to journalists pre-date electronic media and only mention newspapers. Others that restrict activities of the news media are poorly-worded. For a few sections, no

---

5 R.S.C. 1985, c. C-46.

charges have been laid in recent memory and will likely be wiped off the books sometime soon.

Most of the Code's restraints on publication reflect the longstanding common law, however, lawmakers seem very keen lately to rapidly change sections of the Code that are struck down in court challenges using the Charter of Rights. It is also clear that judges are still using their inherent discretionary powers to issue bans or court orders "in the interests of justice," though many are realizing the news media is ever-watchful when its rights are trampled.

This section looks at the interaction of both Code provisions and the inherent powers of courts in the various stages of criminal proceedings.

Common Law Bans on Publishing Names of Accused

The common law indicates that a judge has the discretion to ban the publication of evidence, names of witnesses and crime victims, and even the fact that a court proceeding is happening. However, the common law also suggests there must be extenuating circumstances for such an order, such as concern over a threat to a witness's life or the possibility of compromising the fairness of another trial.

In the vast majority of cases, these are temporary bans. However, the courts do appear to also have a common law authority to permanently ban the publication of certain information, usually the names of witnesses, children or victims. In one prominent case, a permanent ban was upheld even though a public inquiry had been commissioned to investigate, among other things, whether a witness was partly responsible for wrongly convicting an individual.[6]

However, with very few exceptions, courts have agreed that a judge shouldn't ban the publication of the name of the accused.[7] This is in keeping

---

6 See *Re Ontario (Commission on Proceedings involving Guy Paul Morin)* (1997), 143 D.L.R. (4th) 54 (Ont. C.A.). After he was exonerated of a murder, Guy Paul Morin asked a court to set aside a permanent ban issued during his trial on the publication of a Crown witness's name. At the time, the judge ruled the publication of the inmate's name could jeopardize his safety and impede testimony from other inmates. A public inquiry that had been appointed into Morin's wrongful conviction supported setting aside the ban. The appeal court rejected the application, saying there had been no material change in the circumstances since the trial judge ordered the ban. "The acquittal of the individual seeking to set aside the ban was not a material change in the circumstances," they said, nor is the appointment of a public inquiry. The appeal judges noted the inquiry could perform its tasks without identifying any witnesses and was, in fact, precluded from making findings of criminal or civil liability regarding the inmate's conduct at the criminal trial.

7 In *R. v. Several Unnamed Persons (Orillia Opera House)* (1983), 44 O.R. (2d) 81 (H.C.), the court rejected a request to ban the publication of names of individuals charged with

with the principle of an open justice system. The only case where such a ban does tend to be ordered is in sexual assault trials where the accused is related to the victim or closely associated with the victim (such as a school teacher). The concern here would be identifying the victim by virtue of naming the accused.

---

gross indecency and tossed out the argument that pre-trial publicity about the accused would prejudice a fair trial and the presumption of innocence. In *R. v. Robinson* (1983), 5 C.C.C. (3d) 230 (Ont. H.C.), a man accused of murder asked for a court order banning the publication of his name prior to trial also on the basis that pre-trial publicity could prejudice his hearing. The court refused the order and rejected the argument that he was being denied the right to be presumed innocent. In *Re R. and Unnamed Person* (1985), 22 C.C.C. (3d) 284 (Ont. C.A.), a young woman charged with infanticide at the provincial court level applied to a superior court for an order to permanently ban the publication of her name to avoid embarrassment to herself and her family, and damage to her employment opportunities. The order was issued by the court, but the Ontario Court of Appeal later held there was no authority to make such an order. The court did note the inherent authority in a superior court to lend necessary assistance to an inferior court, such as a provincial court, but said there was no need for help in this case because there was no problem with the process of the court, only a problem of embarrassment for the accused.

But in *R. v. P.* (1978), 41 C.C.C. (2d) 377 (Ont. H.C.), a judge *did* grant a ban on the publication of the name of a man accused of soliciting. The accused feared for his ill wife and the embarrassment of his children. The court considered this and noted that because the soliciting charge against the man was a test case, his name wasn't important. It should be noted that when the soliciting charge was appealed, another judge who was asked to continue the ban on publication refused, because he felt that while he had the authority, mere embarrassment was not enough justification: *R. v. P.; R. v. DiPaola* (1978), 43 C.C.C. (2d) 197 (Ont. H.C.).

Another exception was made in *R. v. Southam Inc.* (1987), 40 C.C.C. (3d) 218 (Ont. H.C.), where the court held that a trial judge properly issued an order banning publication of the name of the accused. Here, the accused was a schoolteacher accused of gross indecency and sexual assault involving a pupil at the school. The order was issued under s. 486(3) (now s. 486.4(1)), the Code section dealing with sexual assault and violent crime charges.

Finally, an unusual twist was seen recently in *R. v. Roy* (1998), 165 D.L.R. (4th) 570 (Ont. Gen. Div.). The accused applied for a ban on the publication of any photograph of him. He had pleaded guilty and was awaiting sentencing when his defence lawyer learned a member of the media was requesting a picture of the accused. The lawyer argued the accused's life was in danger since he had previously made an attempt on his own life after the initial newspaper publication of his arrest. The court granted a temporary ban on publication of his photograph, ruling the sentencing process is part of the trial and the court needed to guard against anything that might impede its progress or fairness.

Bail Hearings

Section 517 of the Criminal Code gives a justice the authority during a bail hearing to ban the publication of evidence where a prosecutor or the accused intends to "show cause" as to whether the accused should be detained until further proceedings. If the request for the ban comes from the accused, the justice is obliged to grant the request. A request from the prosecutor may or may not be granted at the justice's discretion.

If the ban is ordered, a journalist can't report on the evidence taken, the information given, the representations made and the reasons given for the decision or conditions of bail. The ban is in effect until the accused is discharged after a preliminary hearing or the accused is committed to trial and the trial has ended. This doesn't mean a journalist can't report the accused's name, the charges, the fact that a bail hearing is being held and the actual decision as to whether bail is granted.[8]

A judge also cannot ban the publication of information obtained outside the bail hearing. In a 1987 Québec case, the police participated in media interviews after the arrest of several individuals. When the accused later appeared for their bail hearing, the judge issued an order that the media not publish the names of the accused or any of the information they had obtained from the police. Another court quashed the order, saying the judge exceeded his jurisdiction.[9] The court went on to state that the temporary ban in s. 517 is a reasonable limit on the press and if the publication of other information by police or the media endangers the fair trial of the accused, the court can always resort to its contempt power.

Be aware that the impact of s. 517 on the media will likely be examined by some appeal courts in the near future. For example, in 2007, portions of s. 517 were found to conflict with the media's Charter rights by one Alberta Queen's Bench judge.[10] The judge ruled the Code section should be amended such that it does not apply in cases that do not involve a jury and the ban should be issued at the discretion of a judge. The judge's interpretation was under appeal at the time of this publication.

---

8 In *Re Forget and R.* (1982), 65 C.C.C. (2d) 373 (Ont. C.A.), the appeal court said the actual decision as to whether to grant bail can be published and the restrictions set out in s. 517 apply only to those things listed (for example, representations made or reasons given).

9 *Re Southam Inc. and R.* (1987), 38 C.C.C. (3d) 74 (Qué. S.C.).

10 *R. v. White*, 2007 ABQB 359 (Alta. Q.B.).

A television news reporter covering a bail hearing involving two teens on a crime rampage was charged, along with his employer, with breaching the s. 517 ban on publishing the judge's reasons in the proceeding. The relevant excerpt from the news report was: "Judge Joel Groberman, noting carefully that the charges at this time remain unproven, said it's amazing to me that if the allegations are correct, these two young men are starting in crime at the highest level. He said the types of crimes described are breathtaking in their seriousness, and he said the accused are alleged to have been acting as land pirates. He noted the shock the parents must feel, but he said the charges are so serious that there is no bail. He said both teens must stay in jail to maintain the public's confidence in the justice system." Were these words enough to support a conviction?

Yes.[11] The court held the phrase "reasons, if any, given" in s. 517 must include any information that is prejudicial to the fair trial of the accused. The court also noted that it might be difficult at this stage in the proceedings for a reporter to even know what information is prejudicial or non-prejudicial. It also did not matter that the reporter had not intended to violate the Code's ban.

Preliminary Hearings

Bans on Publishing Evidence

Section 539 allows the accused to request a mandatory ban on the publication of evidence heard at the preliminary hearing.[12] The justice is obliged to grant the request and the evidence given cannot be published until the accused has been discharged after a preliminary hearing or the accused has been committed to trial and the trial has ended. If the prosecutor requests the ban, the justice has a discretionary power to order it.

The ban only applies to evidence, so a journalist can still report the non-evidentiary matters, such as that a preliminary hearing is being held and a publication ban has been ordered. It also appears the accused's right to a publication ban can be granted part of the way through the hearing and, moreover, can be withdrawn owing to the accused's own behaviour.[13]

---

11 *R. v. Daly* (2003), 178 C.C.C. (3d) 31 (B.C. S.C.), affirmed (2005), 256 D.L.R. (4th) 372 (B.C. C.A.).

12 In *R. v. Banville* (1983), 3 C.C.C. (3d) 312 (N.B. Q.B.), it was held on appeal from a provincial court's decision that s. 539 is constitutionally valid under the Charter of Rights.

13 In *R. v. Harrison* (1984), 14 C.C.C. (3d) 549 (C.S.P.), a ban imposed by the court in the middle of a preliminary hearing was revoked the day after because the accused had

Although the section clearly refers to preliminary hearings, some lawyers have tried unsuccessfully to apply it to collateral pre-trial proceedings, such as a motion to quash a subpoena ordering a witness to attend a preliminary hearing.[14]

> **Raymond Turmel was charged with producing and trafficking cannabis, but claimed he needed it for a medical condition. During pretrial proceedings, his brother, John, was charged with contempt of court for knowingly violating a temporary court order banning publication of evidence given in pre-trial motions. John published the information on Web sites, USENET boards and via e-mail. He claimed Health Canada was committing genocide by not allowing certain persons to use marijuana for medical purposes and asserted the defence of necessity. Will the defence succeed?**
>
> **No.**[15] The court ruled that John did not prove necessity – a defence that would have warranted publication of the information if it was done to prevent someone's death. The court said three elements were required for the necessity defence to succeed: i) an imminent peril or danger; ii) no reasonable legal alternative to the course of action the accused undertook; and iii) proportionality between the harm inflicted and the harm avoided. The wrongful acts must also be "committed under pressure which no reasonable person could withstand." Here, there was no imminent peril to the accused himself and his belief that others were dying because of Health Canada had "no air of reality."

Bans on Publishing Confessions

Section 542 absolutely prohibits the publication of any admission or confession that is "tendered" (that is, offered) in evidence at a preliminary hearing. For example, the Crown or a police witness at the preliminary hearing may tender evidence that the accused told them he committed the crime or did something that would suggest he committed the crime (for

---

conducted a news conference outside the court to discuss the evidence just after the ban was issued, leaving the impression that the court was being manipulated by the accused. The court felt any prejudice to the accused caused by the revocation was his own fault.

14 In *R. v. Stupp* (1982), 2 C.C.C. (3d) 111 at 118 (Ont. H.C.), a superior court judge held he had no statutory power under s. 539 to ban publication of the details of a hearing of a motion brought by a witness to quash a subpoena ordering him to testify to solicitor-client matters.

15 *R. v. Turmel* (2002), 2002 CarswellQue 1492 (S.C.).

example, showed the police where the body was). Section 542 applies even if there's no ban issued by the judge on the publication of evidence.

On rare occasions, the accused himself will testify at the preliminary hearing and testimony of this kind isn't considered to fall under this section. The prohibition on publishing evidence of confessions continues until the accused is discharged or has been committed to trial and the trial has ended, or the confession is admitted as evidence in an open trial.

In addition, there's a common law rule that once charges are laid, no information should be published which would amount to a confession or admission or directly confirm the guilt of the accused until the evidence is brought out in an open trial.[16]

Restrictions on Details of Search Warrants

In 1997, the federal government amended the Criminal Code to deal with issues of public access to executed search warrants, production orders and supporting information. The amendments also give judges wide discretion in banning publication:

> 487.3 (1) A judge or justice may, on application made at the time of issuing a warrant under this or any other Act of Parliament or a production order under section 487.012 or 487.013, or of granting an authorization to enter a dwelling-house under section 529 or an authorization under section 529.4 or at any time thereafter, make an order prohibiting access to and the disclosure of any information relating to the warrant, production order or authorization on the ground that
>> (a) the ends of justice would be subverted by the disclosure for one of the reasons referred to in subsection (2) or the information might be used for an improper purpose; and
>> (b) the ground referred to in paragraph (a) outweighs in importance the access to the information.
>
> (2) For the purposes of paragraph (1)(a), an order may be made under subsection (1) on the ground that the ends of justice would be subverted by the disclosure
>> (a) if disclosure of the information would
>>> (i) compromise the identity of a confidential informant,
>>> (ii) compromise the nature and extent of an ongoing investigation,

---

16 In *Steiner v. Toronto Star Ltd.* (1956), 1 D.L.R. (2d) 297 (Ont. H.C.), a newspaper was found to be in contempt after a reporter spoke with a policeman and then published the statement that a senior police officer "alleged" that the accused had admitted to committing the crime. The publication occurred before the trial began and the court felt the news report would lead any reasonable person to consider the accused guilty. The use of the word "alleged" was held to be of inconsequential value in clearing the contempt.

      (iii) endanger a person engaged in particular intelligence-gathering techniques and thereby prejudice future investigations in which similar techniques would be used, or

      (iv) prejudice the interests of an innocent person; and

  (b) for any other sufficient reason.

The words "any other sufficient reason" provided more than enough room for at least one appeal court to restrict media publication of the information supporting an application for a warrant.[17] In that case, a search warrant was used to search an accused's office before any charges had been laid. The warrant was based on very incriminating information from a police informer and accomplice. A provincial court judge granted a journalist's application to examine the warrant and supporting affidavit. The accused appealed, believing the publication of any information used to get the search warrant damaged the Charter right to a fair trial.

The appeal court agreed, saying the lower court judge had failed to consider the Criminal Code requirements in s. 487.3 that can be used to preserve the fairness of proceedings. Noting the information supporting the warrant was "obviously prejudicial" since it contained detailed descriptions of the accused's alleged role in offences, the appeal judges felt the lower court should have used discretion and issued a publication ban until after a trial was held. This discretion, they said, may be exercised without hearing evidence and on the judge's own initiative. The court said a judge may favour the rights of the accused over freedom of the press, particularly when the accused elects to be tried by a judge and jury.

While the appeal court said there was a distinct danger in allowing the information to be published, it went on to say the news media should generally be given access to these documents. "This would allow the press full scrutiny, in the public interest, of the search warrant documents notwithstanding the temporary ban on publication until after the accused's trial," said the ruling.

It should also be noted that an earlier amendment to the Criminal Code in 1985 made it an offence to publish certain information about search warrants where charges haven't been formally laid. Soon after this amendment was made, though, a court declared it unconstitutional, ruling it infringed on freedom of the press.[18]

---

17 *R. v. Flahiff* (1998), 157 D.L.R. (4th) 485 (Qué. C.A.). Application for leave to appeal to the Supreme Court of Canada dismissed without reasons, [1998] S.C.C.A. No. 87.

18 *Canadian Newspapers Co. v. A.G. Canada* (1986), 32 D.L.R. (4th) 292 (Ont. H.C.). The Québec Court of Appeal recently confirmed s. 487.2 is unconstitutional and of no force and effect in *Girard v. Ouellet* (2001), 198 D.L.R. (4th) 58 (Qué. C.A.), leave to appeal to the Supreme Court of Canada refused (September 20, 2001) Doc. No. 28590 (S.C.C.).

While the government didn't appeal the ruling, unfortunately the law is still on the books and hasn't been formally repealed or amended even though it is of no force or effect. However, the government has clearly indicated a desire to somehow limit the publication of details of search warrants, particularly where charges haven't been laid. It's possible the federal government will someday introduce an amendment to limit publication.

For interest's sake, at least, s. 487.2(1) states that anyone who publishes any information with respect to:

(a) the location of the place searched or to be searched, or

(b) the identity of any person who is or appears to occupy or be in possession or control of that place or who is suspected of being involved in any offence in relation to which the warrant was issued,

without the consent of every person referred to in paragraph (b) is, unless a charge has been laid in respect of any offence in relation to which the warrant was issued, guilty of an offence punishable on summary conviction.

The amendment reinforced a Supreme Court ruling that only details of executed search warrants which find something can be published, but it went on to require that a charge also be laid before the details regarding place and identity could be published. Also, the charge had to be related to the offence for which the warrant was issued. A journalist would have had to call in legal advice in most cases to determine if the charge laid is the same as the one outlined in the warrant. For example, say police found illicit drugs using a warrant allowing a search for gambling machines. If the drug charges were the only ones arising from the search, a reporter would need legal advice.

If no charges were laid, a journalist would then have needed the consent of all people named in the warrant and the requirements for consent were quite complicated. Consent was required from every person named in the warrant as being suspected of an offence and anyone who was in possession or control of the places searched.

It seems judges also have an inherent right in common law to prevent the publication of some information related to search warrants if it could affect the fairness of a trial or otherwise interfere with the administration of justice. In a 1992 British Columbia case,[19] a provincial court judge sealed from public view one paragraph of an information used to get a search warrant for a news station's videotape. The broadcaster had taped an interview with someone under police investigation. The court reviewing the

---

19 *Western International Communications Ltd. v. British Columbia (Provincial Court Judge)* (December 10, 1992), Doc. Vancouver XOA923237 (B.C. S.C.).

judge's sealing order said it was within his jurisdiction, but also said there must be public accessibility to judicial proceedings. The court said the judge should not have sealed the information from public view, but should simply have issued an order restraining the news media from publishing or broadcasting the paragraph until all trials and appeals had ended.

Other Pre-Trial Proceedings

The courts must resort to inherent discretionary powers to prohibit the publication of details of any other pre-trial proceedings. For example, one court issued a ban on the publication of evidence on the mental fitness of the accused submitted in a hearing held before the accused was actually arraigned (that is, charges read and plea taken). A newspaper was held in contempt when it disobeyed the order.[20]

In another case, a judge temporarily banned the publication of details of a change of venue proceeding and even that there had been an application for a change of venue, until after the trial was held. The court felt publishing the fact that an accused wanted a trial in another jurisdiction could taint the accused in the mind of prospective jurors.[21]

Trials

Bans on Publishing Names

The courts may use s. 486 of the Code to ban the publication of names of witnesses, crime victims or complainants in special circumstances.[22] Originally, this section was only supposed to be used to exclude the public from hearings "in the interests of justice," but various court decisions held

---

20 In *R. v. Southam Press (Ont.) Ltd.* (1976), 31 C.C.C. (2d) 205 (Ont. C.A.), the appeal court held the story containing a summary of evidence given by experts on the mental fitness of the accused while this ban was in effect, was indeed a contempt of court. The court felt the publication of the experts' statements could prejudice the accused in the minds of prospective jurors.

21 See *Re Southam Inc. and R. (No. 2)* (1982), 70 C.C.C. (2d) 264 (Ont. H.C.), where the court held on an appeal that this ban didn't violate the freedom of the press. The court distinguished this case from the situation in *Forget*, note 8, above, which held that a decision of a judge in a bail hearing can be reported despite a ban on representations made before the judge and the reasons for his decision. The court here held that reporting the fact that a bail decision had been made would not have any effect on the trial of the accused. But it said reporting the fact that a change of venue hearing was held could prejudice the minds of prospective jurors.

22 *R. v. McArthur* (1984), 13 C.C.C. (3d) 152 (Ont. H.C.). The special circumstances in this

it also allows judges to make special orders banning the publication of certain information where justice will be better served. Recently, the federal government has weighed in with several amendments to the Code specifically allowing publication bans for child witnesses, victims and complainants.

Whether in statute or common law, the special circumstances required to justify a publication ban on the news media must be substantial. In common law, the order may not be granted if the only concern of the witness is embarrassment, humiliation or even financial loss.[23] The order is likely to be granted where physical safety is at risk or a witness is likely to be put through extreme suffering because of the publicity.

However, it seems that the right of a judge to exclude the public under this Code section can't be used to create a select courtroom audience having no journalists present, and thus preventing the publication of witnesses' names. In 1979, the Manitoba Court of Appeal quashed a trial judge's order under s. 486(1), which allowed the general public to stay, but sent a reporter out of the courtroom so he couldn't publish the names of witnesses found in a bawdy-house.[24] The appeal court held this was an abuse of the Code section and was being used to censor the news. The court said the exclusion of any person must be on the basis that their presence is objectionable. In this case, the appeal court said the reporter was only doing his job and wasn't disrupting proceedings.

In proceedings that do not involve a sexual offence or violent crime cases, s. 486.5(1) of the Code allows a judge the discretion to order a ban on publishing the name or any other information that could identify a witness or a victim "if the judge or justice is satisfied that the order is necessary for the proper administration of justice." Similarly, s. 486.5(2) (introduced in Ottawa's 2001 anti-terrorism law) allows a judge to extend the ban on identifying victims or witnesses to a "justice system participant" (for example, a judge, jurors, informant or peace officer) in any proceedings involving criminal organization and terrorism offences, or other national security violations. In both instances, under s. 486.5(7), the factors to be considered by the judge for discretionary orders are:

---

case involved the risks of repercussions against prison inmates who were testifying in a murder trial against fellow inmates.

23 *Ibid.*, at 155. Also, see *R. v. D. (G.)* (1991), 2 O.R. (3d) 498 (C.A.), leave to appeal to S.C.C. refused (1991), 3 O.R. (3d) xiii (note) (S.C.C.). In that case, a Presbyterian minister had been charged with sexual assault. The judge banned publication of the minister's name until the end of the trial and forever if he was acquitted. He was acquitted, but the news media asked that the order be quashed. The provincial appeal court agreed and said the order violated the freedom of the press guarantee in the Charter.

24 *Re F.P. Publications (Western) Ltd. and R.* (1979), 51 C.C.C. (2d) 110 (Man. C.A.).

(a) the right to a fair and public hearing;
(b) whether there is a real and substantial risk that the victim, witness or justice system participant would suffer significant harm if their identity were disclosed;
(c) whether the victim, witness or justice system participant needs the order for their security or to protect them from intimidation or retaliation;
(d) society's interest in encouraging the reporting of offences and the participation of victims, witnesses and justice system participants;
(e) whether effective alternatives are available to protect the identity of the victim, witness or justice system participants;
(f) the salutary and deleterious effects of the proposed order;
(g) the impact of the proposed order on the freedom of expression of those affected by it; and
(h) any other factor that the judge or justice considers relevant.

Under s. 486.5(9), once the order is granted, no one may publish the contents of the application for the order, any evidence taken, information given, or submissions made at a hearing, or any other information that could identify the person in the proceedings.

Section 486.4 addresses publication restrictions in sexual and specific violent crime cases. A judge may issue an order banning publication of any information that could identify a complainant or a witness in these types of cases. The judge is required to inform any child witness under the age of 18 and a complainant of any age of the right to request the publication ban. The issuance of the order is mandatory if requested by the complainant, prosecutor or a child witness.

In cases involving child pornography, it is also mandatory for a judge to issue an order directing that information that could identify a witness who is under the age of 18 years, or any person who is the subject of a representation, written material or a recording that constitutes child pornography within the meaning of that section, not be published or broadcast.

Courts should require a reasonably high standard of proof from individuals seeking the discretionary order for a publication ban.[25] In a 2001 case, a judge dismissed a Crown application for a ban on the names of the accused, his victims and a small community where they lived. The accused had been charged with assault causing bodily harm by burning his teenage victims with a hot iron. The Crown argued the victims would suffer harm if they were publicly identified and might jeopardize the reporting of similar offences by others. A RCMP officer testified the victims thought they would "feel humiliated" if their identities were disclosed. No evidence was offered of how this might affect their ability to testify or actually harm them. Relying on several recent cases, including *Dagenais*, the judge denied the Crown

---

25 *R. v. Rhyno* (2001), 193 N.S.R. (2d) 250 (Prov. Ct.).

application on the basis it did not prove any of the conditions in now-s. 486.5(7) on a balance of probabilities.

It would also appear that superior courts (with federally-appointed judges) have an inherent power to issue a court order against the publication of names of witnesses or victims without resorting to s. 486(1). For example, one court permanently banned the publication of the names of patients who were sexually abused by a doctor who was under investigation by a medical body.[26] The former patient who applied for the ban argued that her professional reputation would be damaged by the publicity. The court held that nothing would be gained by allowing the media to publish names of former patients and noted that the patients had suffered enough.

Another B.C. court saw virtue in banning information identifying undercover police witnesses.[27] The police argued that evidence of their undercover techniques and the danger to officers from publication of names, identities, and likenesses outweighed the freedom of the press. The court said the danger to officers was not remote or speculative, citing an officer's affidavit alleging that publicity had previously led to undercover officers being murdered. Surprisingly, despite other court rulings to the contrary, this court said the fact that the proceedings were being conducted in open court was enough to provide public scrutiny. Two other cases involving bans on the publication of information involving undercover police officers were recently considered by the Supreme Court of Canada[28] and the high court said bans should only be granted when there is evidence (not speculation) of real risk.

Bans on Publishing Evidence

In addition to the Code sections, there is another statutory authority for banning the publication of evidence arising during trials. The Canada Evidence Act grants superior courts a discretionary power to ban the disclosure of information affecting national security or international relations, confidential cabinet records or anything that shouldn't be disclosed "on the

---

26 *Hirt v. College of Physicians & Surgeons of B.C.* (1985), 60 B.C.L.R. 273 (C.A.).

27 *R. v. Macki* (2001), 199 D.L.R. (4th) 178 (B.C. S.C.).

28 For example, in *Mentuck*, note 3 above, a limited publication ban involving information identifying undercover police officers and operational methods was first refused and then granted on appeal by Manitoba courts. The trial judge originally concluded the public interest in law enforcement methods was not a factor to be considered in determining whether to grant the ban nor was the security and well-being of the police officers involved. The Supreme Court of Canada ruled a ban was not justified where police methods or techniques are being discussed, but did agree the identities of officers should be protected for one year.

grounds of a specified public interest."[29] The court will consider issuing such a ban only if a specific objection to disclosure is made to the court.

The common law has also permitted courts to issue permanent bans on the publication of other confidential information, such as trade secrets. The rationale is that parties to the action would be discouraged from taking their dispute to court if the secret was publicized through the hearing.[30]

The Charter's guarantee of freedom of the press may further limit judges' inherent powers to ban publication during trials. In a 1988 Québec case, a Superior Court judge considered a defence counsel request to question a police officer who had worked with a police informant.[31] After a *voir dire*, the judge allowed the request on the condition that the defence not ask any questions that would disclose the informant's identity. While no such questions were asked, the judge also ordered a ban on the publication of the officer's testimony.

The news media asked another court to set the order aside on the basis that it was an unreasonable infringement on freedom of the press.[32] The appeal court judges said there was no justification for the ban since the trial judge had already decided that the identity of the informer wouldn't be disclosed. The court stated that the general rule as to openness of trials should prevail.

Bans Involving Multiple Accused

On occasion, the courts have resorted to their inherent powers to temporarily ban the publication of details of trials and even the verdicts in cases where more than one person is accused of crimes arising out of the same incident.[33] Increasingly, however, the courts are reluctant to issue such bans because of the Charter's guarantee of freedom of the press.[34]

---

29 Canada Evidence Act, R.S.C. 1985, c. C-5, ss. 37, 38 and 39.

30 *Scott v. Scott*, [1913] A.C. 417 (H.L.).

31 *R. v. Southam Inc.* (1987), Barrette-Joncas J. (Qué. S.C.).

32 *R. v. Southam Inc.* (1988), 42 C.C.C. (3d) 333 (Qué. C.A.).

33 In *R. v. Dolan* (1983), 2 C.R.D. 525.70-01 (Ont. Co. Ct.), the court placed a temporary ban of a few days on the publication of a guilty plea by a co-accused because it would have tainted the other accused's trial. The court said it was not a serious infringement to delay reporting the evidence, decision or plea until the other case on the same facts is heard. This happens rarely. One of the few cases like this goes back to 1821 (*R. v. Clement* (1821), 4 B. & Ald. 218).

In *Re Church of Scientology of Toronto v. R. (No. 6)* (1986), 27 C.C.C. (3d) 193 (Ont. H.C.), the court held that a provincial court judge has the power to issue a temporary publication ban on details and result of a proceeding when other co-accused are awaiting a trial or preliminary hearing. More recently, in *R. v. Muise (No. 3B)* (1993), 124 N.S.R. (2d) 98 (S.C.), an attempt by one accused to ban publication of evidence at a *voir dire* for the benefit of another accused awaiting trial was unsuccessful. The court said the accused's

In 1998, one court tried to strike a balance between the rights of the press and accused.[35] A stay of proceedings had been issued against one of four co-accused in a murder. With intense media interest, the Crown requested a ban on publication of all information relating to the prosecution of the accused and the stay until a jury retired to deliberate a verdict in the trial of all the co-accused. The court agreed the ban would be in the interests of a fair trial, but also took the unusual step of issuing a judicially-approved summary of the court proceedings held to date so that the public would be informed of at least some details. "If it is feasible to develop a judicial summary of information relating to the prosecution which, if released immediately, would not present a real and substantial risk to the fairness of the ongoing trial, it should be done," wrote the judge. "The public has a right to be aware of the course of the prosecution and to scrutinize and evaluate the administration of justice."

Restrictions in Sexual Assault Trials

As noted above, s. 486.4 gives a judge the discretion to place a restriction on the publication of the identity of a complainant or a witness, as well as any information that could disclose the identity of the complainant or witness. A 1985 Ontario Court of Appeal decision declared part of a predecessor of this section (which was similarly worded) to be in violation of the freedom of the press guarantee in the Charter.[36] The court held that a portion making it mandatory to ban the publication of the identity of the complainant on the application of the complainant or the prosecutor, is not a reasonable limit on the freedom of the press. However, in 1988, the Supreme Court of Canada overturned the lower appeal court decision and

---

"privacy was surrendered to the judicial process" and the reporting of the *voir dire* "was a price that he had to pay in the interest of ensuring public accountability of those involved in the administration of justice."

34 In *R. v. Wood* (1993), 124 N.S.R. (2d) 128 (S.C.), the court agreed it had the jurisdiction to ban publication of all evidence in the first of three separate trials involving related accused until all the trials were over. An open court, however, was deemed more important and the Charter's freedom of the press guarantee was paramount. Publication could only be restricted, it said, in the limited circumstances when evidence related specifically to the other two accused.

Pre-Charter, in the 1983 British Columbia case involving a group of alleged terrorists known as the Squamish Five, the trial judge considered the scanty case law on this subject and then refused to grant a temporary ban on the publication of details of all the accuseds' trials. The judge felt that an impartial jury could still be found for each trial despite the intense publicity surrounding the case. As it turned out, there was only one trial before the others pleaded guilty.

35 *R. v. Brown* (1998), 126 C.C.C. (3d) 187.

36 *Canadian Newspapers Co. v. A.G. Canada* (1985), 49 O.R. (2d) 557 (C.A.).

said that although the wording does infringe on freedom of the press, it does so justifiably.[37] Since then, Parliament has changed the wording of the section to state that a judge "may make an order" and exercise discretion.

That discretion, however, vanishes if the complainant or any witness under the age of 18 requests a ban on publication of his or her identity. This is mandatory and, under s. 486.4(2), the judge must inform a complainant or young witness of this right "at the first reasonable opportunity."

This section is also used on occasion to ban publication of the name of the accused, particularly when there is a family relationship that could identify the complainant. The same argument also arises in cases involving ministers, teachers and others with a known or professional link to a sexual assault victim. In some cases, the courts have been reluctant to ban the accused's name.[38]

During a sexual offence trial, a Saskatchewan court issued a mandatory ban on publishing any information identifying the complainant (known as AB). The accused was convicted and, on the day of the sentencing hearing, AB told a CBC reporter she had "thought about this for awhile" and wanted her identity revealed to "help others by coming forward." After the interview aired and the complainant's identity was revealed, CBC was charged with two counts of failure to comply with the court's publication ban. Since the complainant asked and agreed to be identified, should the charges against the media outlet succeed?

Yes.[39] Despite a lower court's finding that then-ss. 486(3) and (4) (now 486.4) of the Criminal Code unjustly violated the complainant's Charter right to free expression, a Saskatchewan appeal court disagreed and held the ban on publication was valid despite the complainant's desire to be identified. The appeal court held, among other points of law, that the news media can apply to a superior court judge for an order quashing the ban on the ground that neither the common law rule nor the Criminal Code authorize publication bans that limit Charter rights in an unjusti-

---

37 (1988), 43 C.C.C. (3d) 24 (S.C.C.).
38 See *R. v. D. (G.)*, note 23, above. In that case, a Presbyterian minister had been charged with sexual assault. The judge banned publication of the minister's name until the end of the trial and forever if he was acquitted. He was acquitted, but the news media asked that the order be quashed. The provincial appeal court agreed and said the order violated the freedom of the press guarantee in the Charter.
39 *R. v. Canadian Broadcasting Corp.*, [2005] 3 W.W.R. 77 (Sask. Q.B.), leave to appeal to the Supreme Court of Canada refused (without reasons) (2007), 2007 CarswellSask 318, 2007 CarswellSask 319, [2007] S.C.C.A. No. 110 (S.C.C.).

fiable manner. The CBC was fined $1,000 on each count. In 2007, the Supreme Court of Canada dismissed an application for leave to appeal.

While not naming an individual covered by the ban, a journalist must also be careful not to report any details of the case that could lead the "reasonable person" to figure out who it is. For example, after a sexual assault trial in 1994-95, some Halifax journalists found themselves charged with violating a publication ban. The Crown alleged the journalists had identified the victim by reporting she was the daughter of a police officer, identifying the school ground where the assault occurred and the fact she lived near the school. Charges were eventually dropped against the reporters. Still, journalists would be wise to be cautious in the details they report, especially in a small community.

Another interesting case arose recently when a TV news outlet and reporter were acquitted of breaching a publication ban ordered in a sexual assault trial after they ran a story two years later about a kidnapping with similar facts.[40] In this B.C. case, the alleged violation was in a news report about a young woman who had been kidnapped and was still missing — a case with striking similarities to another abduction case two years before. As background, the report showed video of the successful rescue of the complainant (clearly identifiable in the pictures) in the unrelated, but similar earlier case. The report made no mention of the legal proceedings that followed the earlier abduction or that sexual assault charges were involved. An appeal court acquitted the reporter and his TV station, noting the broadcast showing the complainant referred only to an incident of abduction or kidnapping. The earlier order, noted the court, only applied to identification of a sexual assault victim.

Journalists, however, would be wise to always check with legal counsel in situations where a news report involves an individual who is the subject of a publication ban. For example, in another B.C. case involving an alleged violation of a publication ban, the complainant was successful in a civil action under the province's Privacy Act.[41] A crime victim brought an action for negligence and invasion of privacy against a reporter and newspaper after her name was published despite a publication ban issued under the Criminal Code. The newspaper believed the publication ban no longer applied because the sexual assault charge had been stayed in a plea bargain.

The victim testified she suffered great stress, had to sell her home and move away from the community. The jury awarded $3,000 in general

---

40 *R. v. BCTV* (1999), 131 C.C.C. (3d) 414 (B.C. C.A.).
41 *F. (J.M.) v. Chappell* (1998), 158 D.L.R. (4th) 430 (B.C. C.A.). An application for leave
    to appeal to the Supreme Court of Canada was dismissed ([1998] S.C.C.A. No. 154).

damages, $15,000 in punitive damages for the privacy breach, and $1,000 for the negligence.

The trial judge intervened and ruled the reporter and newspaper had a defence under s. 2 of the Privacy Act and s. 3 of the Libel and Slander Act, finding the publication of the victim's name was privileged as a fair and accurate report of proceedings publicly heard before a court. The victim appealed and the province's appellate court agreed the judge made a mistake. The appeal judges said the defences in privacy and libel law must be interpreted in the context of the Criminal Code ban.

In a sexual assault trial, the introduction of evidence by the accused about the sexual activity of the complainant is limited by s. 276 and reporters are restricted in what they can publish when a court is determining whether to allow the evidence. To introduce such evidence, the accused's lawyer must apply to the court for permission to present it.

Under s. 276.3, the contents of an application (evidence) and the judge's decision cannot be published unless the judge decides the evidence is admissible or the judge orders that the decision and reasons may be published. To determine admissibility of such evidence, the justice will hold a hearing and the public and jury must be excluded from the hearing.

Section 278.9 also bans publication of the contents of an application by the accused seeking any records relating to a complainant or witness in a sexual offence proceeding, unless the judge orders that the decision on the application may be published.

Restrictions in Jury Trials

Bans on Evidence in a Voir Dire

Section 648 prohibits the publication of any evidence or information concerning any portion of the trial at which the jury was not present (that is, a *voir dire*). The section only applies to trials where juries are permitted by the court to "separate" (to go home during a long trial, for example). If a jury is sequestered during the trial, this prohibition doesn't apply. However, few juries today are sequestered for the length of a trial.

The prohibition continues only until the jury retires to consider its verdict and then the details of the *voir dire* can be published.

In a 1985 case, a judge tried to permanently ban publication of evidence in a *voir dire*. The *voir dire* had heard wiretap evidence that could be embarrassing to people not involved in the trial. The attempted ban arose when the accused decided to plead guilty and the judge ordered the jury to retire and return a verdict of guilty. The judge then told the news media they couldn't publish the details of the wiretap evidence since it had never been placed before a jury.

The Alberta Court of Appeal held that s. 648 doesn't extend past the point where the jury retires to consider its verdict. However, while the court allowed publication of the wiretap, it used its inherent powers to prohibit publication of the names and any facts identifying the people who were tapped in the wiretap.[42] In another Alberta case, a court ruled s. 648 cannot be used to ban publication of information from pre-trial proceedings.[43] While readying for a drug offences trial, the judge imposed a temporary publication ban on all evidence in an application involving courtroom security measures. The ban was later amended to apply only to evidence that was held inadmissible at the pre-trial hearing. In the course of a hearing on the merits of the publication ban, the accused applied for an order under s. 648 to prohibit publication of information arising from any proceedings before the jury selection, such as pre-trial motions.

The media intervened and argued s. 648 cannot be applied broadly and it only concerns information heard once the trial begins when the jury is absent. If it could be applied to information arising out of pre-trial proceedings, then the media asked the court to declare s. 648 unconstitutional. The accused's lawyer argued, among other things, that s. 648 was intended to be broadly interpreted and Parliament had once considered expanding the authority to issue a publication ban to all pre-trial proceedings.

The court, citing the *Dagenais* case, held the ban could not be extended to pre-trial proceedings and agreed with the news media that s. 648 applied only to information heard in court once a trial begins and when the jury is absent.

---

42 *Toronto Sun Publishing v. A.G. Alta.* (1985), 39 Alta. L.R. (2d) 97 (C.A.).

43 *Canada (Attorney General) v. Cheung*, [2000] A.J. No. 1463 (Alta Q.B.). Compare this with a contrary decision in *R. v. Regan* (1997), 159 D.L.R. (4th) 350 (N.S. S.C.). A former N.S. premier was charged with numerous sex-related offences. Preliminary defence motions were to be heard before jury selection, including applications for further Crown disclosure, a stay of proceedings and severance of the charges. Both the accused and the Crown asked for a publication ban on the proceedings, which was opposed by the media. The publication ban was granted under s. 648(1), with the judge ruling the proposed motions could be considered part of the accused's trial. The court held that s. 645 allows a trial judge to conduct *voir dires* before jury selection. The judge added that there was also a common law authority to grant such a ban in the circumstances of this case.

Bans on Jury Deliberations

Section 649 prohibits any member of a jury from ever disclosing information relating to the deliberations of the jury when it was absent from the courtroom. Only details about the jury's deliberations that are disclosed in open court can be published. If a reporter urges a juror to tell what went on in the jury room, the reporter could theoretically be charged with aiding in the commission of the offence.

The Supreme Court of Canada recently upheld the common law rule on jury secrecy and that the s. 649 prohibition on disclosure of jury deliberations is consistent with the Charter's principles of fundamental justice.[44] The common law rule and Criminal Code provision, it said, reflect a desire to preserve the secrecy of the jury deliberation process and shield the jury from outside influences. Any statements made, opinions expressed, arguments advanced and votes cast by members of a jury in their deliberations are inadmissible in legal proceedings (and most probably, it may be surmised, in news reports). The Supreme Court said jurors may not testify about the effect anything had on their or other jurors' minds, emotions or ultimate decision.

The common law rule, however, does not mean evidence of facts, statements or events outside the deliberation process that may have tainted the verdict are inadmissible in court. The Supreme Court said evidence indicating the jury was exposed to information or influence outside the jury is admissible to decide if there is a reasonable possibility it had an effect on the jury's verdict. Whether the information did in fact influence the jury, however, is not admissible — only that they had been exposed to it.

It's possible to interview a member of the jury if you carefully restrict the interview to matters that happened in open court and you don't try to get the juror's comments about what influenced their decision. For example, the CBC in 1984 interviewed one of the jurors in a case involving alleged illegal abortions by a well-known doctor. The trial was unique in many ways, but one interesting element was the use of jury selection experts from the United States. The interview with the juror confined itself to what the juror thought about the use of these experts. The interview stayed away from comments about jury deliberations and was consequently not in contravention of the Code section.

The Code also allows judges to protect the identity of jurors. Section 631(6) allows a Crown prosecutor or judge in a jury trial to make a discretionary order "directing that the identity of a juror or any information that could disclose their identity shall not be published in any document or broadcast in any way, if the court or judge is satisfied that such an order is

---

44 *R. v. Pan; R. v. Sawyer*, [2001] S.C.J. No. 44 (S.C.C.).

necessary for the proper administration of justice." This section not only prohibits naming jurors, but also would likely prohibit showing a likeness of a juror (for example, an identifying sketch or video).

Restrictions on Publishing Immoral Details

In 1994, the federal government repealed two outmoded sections of the Criminal Code restricting press freedoms. For historical reference, they are included here.

Indecent Matters

The now-repealed s. 166 prohibited anyone from printing or publishing any indecent matter or indecent medical, surgical or physiological details heard in judicial proceedings, which would tend to injure public morals. The Criminal Code offered no guidelines as to what indecent material would violate the section and it would be difficult to know where to draw the line in some of the more bizarre court cases heard today.

Divorces

Section 166, now repealed, also partly restricted the publication of details of judicial proceedings for dissolution of marriage, nullity of marriage, judicial separation or restitution of conjugal rights. Under the old law, only the following details could be published by the media:

(i)   the names, addresses and occupations of the parties and witnesses,
(ii) a concise statement of the charges, defences and countercharges in support of which evidence has been given,
(iii) submissions on a point of law arising in the course of the proceedings, and the decision of the court in connection therewith, and
(iv) the summing up of the judge, the finding of the jury, the judgment of the court and the observations that are made by the judge in giving judgment.

This section was intended to prevent the publication of embarrassing details of couples' love lives or their marital indiscretions. In practice, there were no recorded charges under this section in recent times. The ban on publishing indecent matters applied even when the same details were permitted for divorces.[45] Note that Alberta has also repealed a similar set of restrictions in its Judicature Act, which carried a maximum fine of $1000

---

45 S. 166.

for a person and up to a year in jail for default on the fine and a fine of up to $5000 for a corporation.[46]

A 1985 court challenge of this prohibition in Alberta, suggesting it was an infringement on the freedom of the press, was unsuccessful.[47]

Young Offenders

The Youth Criminal Justice Act, which came into force in April, 2003,[48] prohibits the publication of the identity of a young person who has committed a crime and other young persons involved either as a witness or a victim in a proceeding. This ban on publication not only includes the young person's name but also any other information that might tend to identify the youth, such as a relative's name.[49] The current law replaces the Young Offenders Act,[50] which replaced older Criminal Code provisions and the Juvenile Delinquents Act.

Under the current law, a *young person* is someone who is or, in the absence of evidence to the contrary, appears to be 12 years old or older, but less than 18 years old. It can also include any person who is charged under the Act with having committed an offence while he or she was a young person, or who is found guilty of an offence under this Act.[51]

While the identities of young persons involved in the criminal justice system are protected from publication, there are special circumstances in which names can be published. Previously, under the Young Offenders Act, youth court judges could only allow short-term publication of the name of

---

46 R.S.A. 1980, c. J-1, ss. 30(1) and 31(1), both now repealed, S.A. 1991, c. 21, s. 15.

47 The decision in *Edmonton Journal v. A.G. Alta.* (1985), 40 Alta. L.R. (2d) 326 (Q.B.), held that s. 30(1) of the Judicature Act was necessary to protect public morals. The court said the section protects the right of families to privacy in such intimate matters. The court held the section is not an infringement on the rights of the press because it allows the publication of some details and isn't a complete ban. The court also held it applies to the electronic media, as well as newspapers.

48 S.C. 2002, c. 1.

49 This protection existed in the now-repealed Juvenile Delinquents Act as well. In *Manitoba (Attorney General) v. Radio OB Ltd.* (1976), 70 D.L.R. (3d) 311 (Man. Q.B.), the court found an interviewer for an open-line radio program to have violated the Act after the mother of a juvenile delinquent appeared on the program to talk about inadequate facilities for mentally disturbed youths. The interviewer knew there was soon going to be an application to transfer the son to adult court. The court found that several comments in the interview suggested the woman's son was guilty of his crime and, despite the use of a false name by the mother, the well-publicized nature of the case allowed listeners to identify the youth being talked about as the same youth who was the subject of the application for transfer to adult court.

50 R.S.C. 1985, c. Y-1.

51 S. 2(1).

a young person who is at large and a danger to others. A young offender's identity could also be made known to school officials so as to protect staff or students.

Critics of the previous Act believed some young offenders were taking unfair advantage of this protection and that it did not help to deter crimes. The current law now addresses some of the public and media concerns by allowing the names of youths who receive adult sentences to be published, as well as those given youth court sentences for so-called "presumptive offences" — those where an adult-type sentence is presumed to be more appropriate, such as violent crimes committed by a young person of 14 to 16 years of age (depending on the province). Such offences include first or second degree murder, attempted murder, manslaughter, and aggravated sexual assault, as well as any serious violent offence for which an adult could be sentenced to jail for two or more years and there is a history of at least two prior serious violent offences. In cases involving presumptive offences, judges still have a statutory discretion to order that a young person's name not be made public, if requested by the Crown or accused.[52]

As noted, there are restrictions on publishing the identity or information that might identify the accused, as well as young persons who are the victim(s) or a witness in a proceeding. Section 110 deals with the restrictions on publishing the identity of the accused:

> 110. (1) Subject to this section, no person shall publish the name of a young person, or any other information related to a young person, if it would identify the young person as a young person dealt with under this Act.
>
> (2) Subsection (1) does not apply
>   (a) in a case where the information relates to a young person who has received an adult sentence;
>   (b) subject to sections 65 (young person not liable to adult sentence) and 75 (youth sentence imposed despite presumptive offence), in a case where the information relates to a young person who has received a youth sentence for an offence set out in paragraph (a) of the definition "presumptive offence" in subsection 2(1), or an offence set out in paragraph(b) of that definition for which the Attorney General has given notice under subsection 64(2)(intention to seek adult sentence); and
>   (c) in a case where the publication of information is made in the course of the administration of justice, if it is not the purpose of the publication to make the information known in the community.
>
> (3) A young person referred to in subsection (1) may, after he or she attains the age of eighteen years, publish or cause to be published information that

---

52   *Ibid.*, s. 65 and s. 75(3).

would identify him or her as having been dealt with under this Act or the Young Offenders Act, chapter Y-1 of the Revised Statutes of Canada, 1985, provided that he or she is not in custody pursuant to either Act at the time of the publication.

(4) A youth justice court judge shall, on the ex parte application of a peace officer, make an order permitting any person to publish information that identifies a young person as having committed or allegedly committed an indictable offence, if the judge is satisfied that

    (a) there is reason to believe that the young person is a danger to others; and

    (b) publication of the information is necessary to assist in apprehending the young person.

(5) An order made under subsection (4) ceases to have effect five days after it is made.

(6) The youth justice court may, on the application of a young person referred to in subsection (1), make an order permitting the young person to publish information that would identify him or her as having been dealt with under this Act or the Young Offenders Act, chapter Y-1 of the Revised Statutes of Canada, 1985, if the court is satisfied that the publication would not be contrary to the young person's best interests or the public interest.

In case it's not clear from this legalese, the current law allows media publication of an accused youth's identity when that youth:

(i)   Receives an adult sentence;

(ii) Receives a youth court sentence for murder, attempted murder, manslaughter, aggravated sexual assault or has a pattern of convictions for serious violent offences (unless the judge is persuaded to otherwise ban publication);

(iii) Is at large after having committed or alleged to have committed an indictable offence, and a judge determines that publication of the information is necessary to help apprehend the young person (note that permission to publish the identity ends after five days);

(iv) Authorizes publication after he or she becomes an adult and is not serving a sentence in custody; or

(v) Is not yet an adult but youth court judge is satisfied the publication is in the best interests of the youth.

The rights of victims and witnesses are protected in s. 111:

111. (1) Subject to this section, no person shall publish the name of a child or young person, or any other information related to a child or a young person, if it would identify the child or young person as having been a victim of, or

as having appeared as a witness in connection with, an offence committed or alleged to have been committed by a young person.

(2) Information that would serve to identify a child or young person referred to in subsection (1) as having been a victim or a witness may be published, or caused to be published, by

> (a) that child or young person after he or she attains the age of eighteen years or before that age with the consent of his or her parents; or
> (b) the parents of that child or young person if he or she is deceased.

(3) The youth justice court may, on the application of a child or a young person referred to in subsection (1), make an order permitting the child or young person to publish information that would identify him or her as having been a victim or a witness if the court is satisfied that the publication would not be contrary to his or her best interests or the public interest.

Under s. 118(1) of the Act, it is also an offence to access or possess a youth court or police record relating to an offence alleged to have been committed by a young person, unless access has been properly authorized or the record has been released under provisions of the Act. Under s. 129, it is an offence under this section for anyone who has been given permission to have access or a copy of such records, to also disclose their contents to anyone else unlawfully. Punishment for violating the restrictions on publication or access range from summary conviction to an indictable offence and imprisonment for a period up to two years.

The statutory prohibitions against publishing the identity of young people in the previous Young Offenders Act and the now-repealed Juvenile Delinquents Act have been challenged unsuccessfully on several occasions. The prohibition against identifying the young person is felt to be a reasonable limit on the press.[53]

In most situations, a reporter can mention the age and sex of the young offender unless otherwise ordered by the youth court judge. As with cases involving sexual assaults, as noted above, journalists must be careful not to provide any identifying details that might lead a "reasonable person" to figure out who is covered by the ban. For example, identifying an adult witness as a brother or sister or the accused would be a clear violation of the law's intent.

---

53 This section was unsuccessfully challenged in *Southam Inc. v. R.* (1984), 14 D.L.R. (4th) 683 (Ont. H.C.). After hearing extensive psychological testimony from the defence, the court held the prohibition against publishing the identity of the young offender was a reasonable limit on the press. The Ontario Court of Appeal later affirmed the trial judge's decision ((1986), 25 C.C.C. (3d) 119 (Ont. C.A.), leave to appeal to Supreme Court of Canada refused [1986] 1 S.C.R. xiv).

In those horrific cases where a young victim has died, one case under a previous version of the law determined that the ban on publishing the name of the young victim does not apply.[54] That said, each case must be considered on its own facts. For instance, you would still not identify a dead victim as a relative of the accused.

The current law only applies to Criminal Code and federal statute offences.[55] The bans on publication do not apply to federal commissions or inquiries involving young people. The federal law also does not apply to provincial or municipal offences, however most of the provinces and territories have enacted companion legislation similar to the Youth Criminal Justice Act to enforce provincially-created offences and the sections banning publication of evidence are usually included.

Mental Disorder

In those cases where there is a verdict of "not criminally responsible on account of mental disorder" or the accused is unfit to stand trial, a court may hold a so-called disposition hearing itself or refer the accused to a special Review Board. Under s. 672.5(6), the public may be excluded from either of these hearings if it is in the best interests of the accused and not contrary to the public interest.

Section 672.501 requires the Review Board to make an order in cases involving sexual offences or child pornography that bans publication of information identifying any victim or witness who is under the age of 18. This section also gives the Board a discretionary power to ban publication of information identifying a victim or witness of any age if it is satisfied the order is necessary for the proper administration of justice. Section 672.501(7) and (8) provide that a hearing may be held to determine whether the discretionary order is issued. The factors to be considered in issuing the order include:

- the right to a fair and public hearing;
- whether there is a real and substantial risk that the victim or witness would suffer significant harm if his or her identity were disclosed;

---

54 *R. c. Publications Photo-Police Inc.* (1986), 31 C.C.C. (3d) 93 (Que. C.A.). As the appeal court judge wrote: "The strongest argument in favour of acquittal, and the one relied upon by the trial judge, is the heading preceding s. 38 of the Act. As he pointed out, a dead young person has no life, private or otherwise to be protected. I agree that the main object of s. 38 is to protect young persons in their immaturity from the stigma that tends to mark anyone involved in penal offences, so their development and future success will not be jeopardized. Obviously a deceased person is not in contemplation."

55 See s. 2(1), "offence" of the Act.

- whether the victim or witness needs the order for his or her security or to protect him or her from intimidation or retaliation;
- society's interest in encouraging the reporting of offences and the participation of victims and witnesses in the criminal justice process;
- whether effective alternatives are available to protect the identity of the victim or witness;
- the salutary and deleterious effects of the proposed order;
- the impact of the proposed order on the freedom of expression of those affected by it; and
- any other factor that the Review Board considers relevant.

As for the disposition hearing itself, under s. 672.51(7), a Review Board may ban publication of certain evidence or "disposition information" that is withheld from the accused or any other party, or where the Board "is of the opinion that disclosure of the disposition information would be seriously prejudicial to the accused and that, in the circumstances, protection of the accused takes precedence over the public interest in disclosure." Disposition information can include psychiatric reports, case coordinator reports, exhibits and assessment reports. The actual prohibition on publication by the media is set out in s. 672.51(11) and includes any part of the record of the proceedings during which the accused was excluded.

Appeals and Eternity

Bans on publishing names of individuals or confidential information are generally intended to be for eternity.[56] While appeal courts rarely issue a ban on the publication of their own proceedings, it's within their inherent jurisdiction.[57]

---

56 In *R. v. T.R. (No. 1)* (1984), 10 C.C.C. (3d) 481 (Alta. Q.B.), the appeal court held that the statutory ban on publishing the identity of a juvenile delinquent (now referred to as a young offender) continued at the appeal level and is not an unreasonable infringement of the Charter's guarantee of freedom of the press.

57 See *R. v. Sophonow* (1983), 21 Man. R. (2d) 110 (C.A.), where the Manitoba Court of Appeal refused to issue a ban on the media's discussion of a murder case while it was being appealed to the court. While the judges said they had the authority to issue the ban, they felt it would amount to censorship of the news.

Still, as seen recently in *Smith v. Jones* (1999), 169 D.L.R. (4th) 385 (S.C.C.), rare circumstances may justify publication bans all the way to the Supreme Court of Canada. In this unusual case, an accused was charged with an aggravated sexual assault of a prostitute. During a pre-trial assessment, a psychiatrist learned the accused was dangerous and needed help. The accused later pleaded guilty to the assault and the psychiatrist learned the judge would not be advised of his concerns. The psychiatrist asked the court for a declaration he was entitled to disclose information he had received in the interests of public safety. From the trial level up to the Supreme Court, a rare publication ban was

One provincial appellate court has dealt with the issue of whether publication bans should be ordered in any post-trial proceedings that lead up to an appeal hearing — the concern being the post-trial information could affect the appeal or a new trial.[58] Three accused in the B.C. case were acquitted of first-degree murder in two shooting deaths. The Crown filed an appeal, alleging there was new evidence of a romantic connection between a juror and one of the accused that might have affected the trial's outcome. It was agreed that, before the appeal hearing was held, one judge would hear the new evidence and determine if it was admissible. The accused applied for a ban on the publication of the new evidence until the appeal hearing could be held.

The appeal court rejected the application for a ban. The hearing of fresh evidence in this pre-appeal proceeding, it said, should be conducted as it would normally be in any hearing. That is, openly and without any restraint on publicity.

The court went on to state the "fact that the public, including reporters, can view proceedings is not sufficient for achieving the goal of public scrutiny if publication is banned." The judges said it was not in the interests of fostering public confidence to postpone their full scrutiny until the hearing of the appeal itself.

Atomic Energy of Canada Ltd. went to court to stop Sierra Club of Canada, an environmental organization, from gaining access to documents it submitted to Ottawa asking for financial assistance in the construction and sale to China of two CANDU reactors. Is this Crown corporation entitled to a confidentiality order?

Yes.[59] After two lower courts rejected AECL's application, the Supreme Court of Canada granted the confidentiality order and set out guidelines for the proper analytical approach for exercising judicial discretion in such cases. The Court stated that, in light of the established link between open courts and freedom of expression, "the fundamental question for a court to consider in an application for a confidentiality order is whether the right to freedom of expression should be compromised" in the specific circumstances. The Court said a confidentiality order should only be granted when:

in effect during the appeal period and only pseudonyms were used for those involved. In the end, a majority of the Supreme Court agreed there was a real danger to the public and the doctor-patient privilege could be lifted in this case. The court noted that the sealing of the court file containing the psychiatrist's affidavit and the publication ban were justified during the appeal process.

58 *R. v. Budai* (2000), 185 D.L.R. (4th) 510 (B.C. C.A.).

59 *Sierra Club of Canada v. Canada (Minister of Finance)*, [2002] 2 S.C.R. 522.

- Such an order is necessary to prevent a serious risk to an important interest, including a commercial interest, in the context of litigation because reasonably alternative measures will not prevent the risk; and
- The salutary effects of the confidentiality order, including the effects on the right of civil litigants to a fair trial, outweigh its deleterious effects, including the effects on the right to free expression, which in this context includes the public interest in open and accessible court proceedings.

The risk, said the Court, must be real and substantial, and well-grounded in evidence. For example, it must pose a serious threat to the commercial interest. The important commercial interest must also be one that can be expressed in terms of a public interest in confidentiality, where there is a general principle at stake. Finally, a court is required to consider not only whether reasonable alternatives are available to such an order but also to restrict the order as much as is reasonably possible while preserving the commercial interest.

RESTRAINTS ON PUBLICATION IN CIVIL PROCEEDINGS

Publication bans in civil court trials are the same in certain respects as those in criminal trials. For instance, any evidence considered in a *voir dire* cannot be published to a civil jury during the trial.

Due to the structure of our court system, civil trial courts and criminal trial courts are often one and the same. As a result, civil courts have the same inherent powers to ban the publication of the names of witnesses or evidence in exceptional cases.

Statutory bans on publication are less common in the civil sphere (with the exception of family law matters discussed below). However, reporters should note that pleadings can be one-sided, inaccurate in fact and law, and defamatory. Besides the risk of defamation, the publication of pleadings can be contemptuous, particularly when a report close to the start of a trial mentions the amount of damages being sought.

Sometimes, a ban will be issued in a civil proceeding when a related criminal charge is involved. The courts, however, may be reluctant to issue bans in the civil action. For example, in an Alberta case,[60] the city of Edmonton had issued a statement of claim alleging that municipal money had been improperly used by the defendants. Since an arrest of one of the defendants was imminent, a court agreed to a request for a sealing order banning publication of the civil pleadings and other court records. Two

---

60 *Edmonton (City) v. Kara* (1995), 26 Alta. L.R. (3d) 28 (Q.B.).

media organizations asked that the order be set aside and another court agreed. The judge said the general rule was that court proceedings, both civil and criminal, must be open to the public. Citing the Charter's freedom of the press guarantee, the court said a publication ban was unnecessary in the civil proceedings since there were adequate measures available in the criminal process to ensure a fair trial.

One occasional concern for journalists arises when a presiding judge bans the parties involved in a case from any public discussion of the issues until the trial ends. Is a journalist also banned from reporting on the case? No. Sometimes, a judge issues an order like this to block tactical efforts by a side to use public opinion to force a settlement or to maintain an orderly trial. The media are still free to write about the case and may even use comments from the parties when they inadvertently or intentionally disregard the judge's order.[61]

A civil action was launched against the government of British Columbia, claiming damages for a sexual assault committed by a provincial jail employee. The Crown employee had been convicted of the offence in a criminal court, where a publication ban on identifying the complainant had been ordered under s. 486 of the Criminal Code. Does the ban always extend to the civil proceedings?

No.[62] The B.C. civil court was not willing to allow this plaintiff to "litigate anonymously" and held the ban on publication of the plaintiff's identity in the criminal proceedings did not extend to the civil proceedings in this case. The civil court did agree a publication ban ordered in a criminal proceeding does extend beyond the life of the criminal trial and typically does not expire when the trial ends or even on death of the complainant. The court even acknowledged that civil courts hearing matters involving sexual assaults can also issue a ban on publication. In this case, involving a plaintiff alleging a public jail was liable for his assault, the judge felt a ban conflicted with the open court principle. The courts "have an overriding obligation to protect the integrity of its process" and to ensure "what happens in a courtroom is beyond reproach or, when it is not, that the public is entitled to know." Here, a ban on publication of a plaintiff's identity was not necessary "to prevent serious risk to proper administration of justice."

---

61 *Richard v. Gauvin* (1991), 120 N.B.R. (2d) 193 (Q.B.).
62 *Loveridge v. British Columbia* (2005), 258 D.L.R. (4th) 131 (B.C. S.C.).

PUBLICATION BANS IN FEDERAL STATUTES

Most offences in federal statutes are prosecuted using Criminal Code procedures in criminal justice courts. Examples are the Food and Drugs Act,[63] the Controlled Drugs and Substances Act[64] and the Fisheries Act.[65] Unless a law specifically opts out of Code procedures, the same publication ban authority can be exercised, such as the ban on publishing evidence in a preliminary hearing.[66]

It should be noted that courts may also turn to the common law to ban publication. In a recent extradition hearing, a territorial court used the common law rather than statutory authority in an extradition hearing for an accused alleged to belong to a terrorist organization.[67] While there is a statutory power under the Extradition Act to order publication bans, it requires there be evidence of a risk to the fair trial of the accused in the extraditing country (not Canada). There was no such evidence in this case, but the accused requested the ban under common law because he was also facing charges in Canada under the Immigration Act and was to be tried by judge and jury.

The court agreed to use its common law authority to issue the publication ban because pre-trial publication of the allegations in the extradition hearing might taint his Canadian trial. The court noted that extradition hearings deal with allegations and not proven facts. "The extradition judge comes to no decision as to guilt or innocence or the truth of the allegations," noted the court.

---

63 R.S.C. 1985, c. F-27.

64 S.C. 1996, c. 19.

65 R.S.C. 1985, c. F-14.

66 In *Re Global Communications Ltd. and A.G. Can.* (1983), 5 C.C.C. (3d) 346 (Ont. H.C.), a county court judge conducting an extradition hearing under the Immigration Act, 1976 ordered a ban on the publication of evidence and representations at a bail hearing using s. 517(1) of the Criminal Code. On appeal, the Ontario High Court judge said the ban was within the rights of the extradition court, which used Criminal Code procedures, and it was a reasonable limit because it was temporary and protected the fair hearing of the accused.

67 *Germany (Federal Republic) v. Ebke* (2000), 150 C.C.C. (3d) 252 (N.W.T. S.C.).

PUBLICATION BANS IN PROVINCIAL STATUTES

Coroners

Some provinces have placed statutory restrictions on the publication of details heard in *in camera* coroners' hearings and at least one province has given coroners the authority to ban publication of evidence and the identities of people testifying at the inquiry. For example, in Alberta, no one may publish the details of oral testimony of documentary evidence heard *in camera* unless the evidence is contained in a public finding or official report of the proceeding.[68]

The legislation affecting coroners in Québec outlines several restrictions on the news media.[69] The legislation prohibits the publication of: a coroner's photograph of a dead body which is the subject of an inquest without the permission of the coroner; the name, address or any information identifying anyone under 18 years old who is implicated or is a witness in the proceedings; arrest warrants, bail decisions, transcripts of notes or recordings or a copy of the order issuing the publication ban; and photographs, sketches, or recordings of the inquest proceedings.

Where criminal proceedings are started in Québec against someone implicated in the same death as is the subject of the inquest, the law forbids the publication of evidence presented at the inquest until the end of the criminal trial and appeals. A Québec coroner also has the authority to issue a ban on the publication of any information where it is in the public's interest or to protect the right to privacy or the right to a fair hearing.[70] Any violation of the various prohibitions is considered a contempt of court.

In one Ontario case, a court said a coroner had exceeded his authority when he promised a witness that he could testify anonymously.[71] But the court refused to grant a media application to have the witness's name disclosed, primarily because the judges felt it would bring the administration

---

68   See the Fatality Inquiry Act, R.S.A. 2000, c. F-9, s. 46.

69   See An Act respecting the determination of causes and circumstances of death, S.Q. 1983, c. 41, ss. 141-148.

70   In *Re Suazo* (1996), 142 D.L.R. (4th) 313 (Qué. C.A.), leave to appeal to the Supreme Court of Canada dismissed with costs, the media was unsuccessful in challenging a coroner's decision. In an investigation of a shooting by police, the coroner ordered a publication ban on the identification of officers involved because of concern over threats to their lives. A newspaper applied to the court to quash the ban as an unjustified violation of freedom of expression. The provincial appellate court held the coroner's conclusions that the officers' lives were threatened is a factual matter and not subject to review by the court. The ban, it noted, was limited since it only prevented publication of the officers' names and photographs, not the content of the proceedings nor the right of the public to attend them.

71   *Re Canadian Newspaper Co. Ltd. and Isaac* (1988), 48 D.L.R. (4th) 751 (Ont. Div. Ct.).

of justice into disrepute to renege on the coroner's promise. One judge noted that freedom of the press was not denied since reporters were still permitted to publish the testimony itself.

Family Law Acts

All the provinces and territories have provisions imposing either automatic or discretionary bans on the publication of the name or identity of people involved in family law matters before the courts, such as child welfare and custody issues, adoptions, proceedings involving children of unmarried parents and family service matters.[72]

The restrictions are generally on the publication of the name or identity of any child witnesses, the child who is the subject of the proceedings, the parents, foster parents, guardian, any member of the family, or any person charged with an offence at the hearing.[73]

Similar restrictions on publication can be found in provinces that have enacted legislation dealing with domestic violence, stalking or the sexual exploitation of children.[74] Manitoba's Domestic Violence and Stalking Act,[75] for example, prohibits the identification in media reports of the name or information identifying parties or witnesses relating to an application for a protection order until the "latest" of the dismissal of the application or 20 days after service of the protection order upon the respondent.[76]

Alberta's Child, Youth and Family Enhancement Act[77] has drawn media attention recently for its ban on the publication of information iden-

---

72   In *R. v. M.C.* (1984), 4 C.R.D. 525.70-02 (Ont. Prov. Ct.), an Ontario court found the ban against identifying children and family in the Child Welfare Act to be an unreasonable limit on the press because it is absolute, instead of discretionary. However, the same provision continues in the Child and Family Services Act, S.O. 1984, c. 55, s. 41(8) and (9) [now R.S.O. 1990, c. C.11, s. 45(8) and (9)], which replaced the old Act. There have been no challenges of the absolute ban in the present Act and a 1988 decision on the rights of the media covering a wardship hearing did not question the validity of the relevant section. See *Re Children's Aid Society and L.* (1988), 49 D.L.R. (4th) 440 (Ont. U.F.C.).
      Some other provinces give a presiding judge a discretionary power to issue a ban. For example, see Nova Scotia's Children and Family Services Act, S.N.S. 1990, c. 5, s. 94(1), which prohibits any publication identifying a child, parent, foster parent, relative or guardian involved in any proceeding under the Act.
73   For example, see Ontario's Child and Family Services Act, R.S.O. 1990, c. C.11, s. 45, which automatically prohibits publication of such details.
74   For example, see Ontario's Rescuing Children from Sexual Exploitation Act, 2002, S.O. 2002, c. 5.
75   C.C.S.M., c. D93.
76   S. 13(1). Also see ss. 21(1) and 21(1.1) which permit a court to issue discretionary bans on the publication of information that might endanger a witness or a child.
77   R.S.A. 2000, c. C-12.

tifying a child (or a child's guardian) who is receiving or has received protection services under the Act. This includes placement in foster care, and other benefits provided by the Ministry of Children's Services. The Ministry itself suggests journalists can adopt one of two options when reporting on such children. First, a story can indicate a child has received services but leave out the child's name or identifying information. A second option is to name the child but not indicate he or she is receiving or has received services.

CBC aired a radio broadcast about a young murder victim, who had been the subject of investigations by Alberta's Ministry of Children's Services. Allegations included neglect and abuse of the girl and her siblings by the parents. The radio program identified the girl's name, and provided details about her involvement with the Ministry. While the radio program referred to her siblings and parents, it did not name them. CBC was charged with violating s. 126.2(1) of the Child, Youth and Family Enhancement Act by publishing information identifying the deceased child, her guardian(s) and siblings. Would the charge against CBC succeed?

No.[78] In a lengthy examination of the specifics of this case, the court dissected and debated the definitions of various key words in s. 126.2(1) before concluding the Crown had failed to prove its case. Under the law, it is an offence (subject to exceptions) to publish information identifying a child, or a guardian of a child, who has come to the Minister's or a Director's attention. The CBC argued several points, including that the term "child" cannot apply to a deceased child, that the law does not apply to siblings and that the child had not come to the "Director's attention." While agreeing in law that a dead child is no longer a "person" deserving of protection from publication, the judge concluded the offence set out in s. 126.2(1) is identifying someone "who has come to the attention of the Minister or a director." The court noted the child was alive at the time she came to the attention of the Ministry and the "subsequent death of child does not mean that information serving to identify child can be published," adding, the "ban is perpetual." In this case, CBC had named the child and provided enough information to identify two siblings who met the definition of child under the Act. The information also served to identify the parents or guardians of those children. However, the Crown failed to prove beyond a reasonable doubt that the deceased and her siblings had come to the attention of the Director before the broadcast.

---

78 *R. v. Canadian Broadcasting Corp. Radio One*, 2007 ABPC 168 (Alta. Prov. Ct.).

Venereal and Communicable Disease Prevention Acts

A very few provinces still have Acts on the books that aim to control the spread of venereal disease while most others have Public Health Acts that speak generally to controlling communicable diseases. Most public health statutes prohibit the unauthorized publication of the identity of anyone with a communicable disease or the fact that someone examined for a communicable disease is or was being treated.[79] Ontario's law, for example, states: "No person shall disclose to any other person the name of or any other information that will or is likely to identify a person in respect of whom an application, order, certificate or report is made in respect of a communicable disease, a reportable disease, a virulent disease or a reportable event following the administration of an immunizing agent."[80]

In some provinces, it's an offence to publish the details of any *in camera* hearings held under the Act.[81]

Provincial Offences

All the provinces have either adopted the Criminal Code procedure for their Summary Conviction Acts, which enforce provincially-created offences, or as a few provinces have done, they have their own procedure. In either case, a ban on the publication of evidence is usually within the provincial court's authority.

Provincial Young Offenders Acts

Most jurisdictions have adopted special legislation to handle young offenders who violate provincial laws. Most have also adopted provisions similar to the federal legislation in regard to prohibiting the publication of the identity of an offender or any other young person involved in the offence.[82]

---

79 See, for example, Alberta Public Health Act, R.S.A. 2000, c. P-37, s. 55 and Newfoundland and Labrador's Venereal Disease Prevention Act, R.S.N.L. 1990, c. V-2, ss. 13, 14.
80 Health Protection and Promotion Act, R.S.O. 1990, c. H.7, s. 39(1).
81 For example, see British Columbia, R.S.B.C. 1996, c. 475, s. 15; Saskatchewan s. 29; and Newfoundland and Labrador s. 13.
82 Such provisions can be found in Newfoundland and Labrador: R.S.N.L. 1990, c. Y-1, s. 20; Prince Edward Island: R.S.P.E.I. 1988, c. Y-3, s. 16(1); Alberta: S.A. 2000, c. Y-1, s. 24; Nova Scotia: S.N.S. 2001, c. 38, s. 30; Northwest Territories: S.N.W.T. 2003, c. 31, s. 61; Yukon: R.S.Y. 2002, c. 232, s. 33; and Nunavut: R.S.N.W.T. 1988, c. Y-1, s. 59.

Victim Compensation Boards

Most provinces and two territories allow victims of crime or their families to apply for compensation from a specially created provincial tribunal. The victim compensation boards may have either a discretionary or absolute authority to ban the publication of the name of a victim and evidence given at the hearing.[83]

A PUBLICATION BANS CHECKLIST

1. Courts have a variety of inherent common law and statutory powers to temporarily, and sometimes permanently, ban the publication of information arising from hearings, such as names of victims or witnesses, evidence and even the fact that a proceeding happened.

2. The Supreme Court of Canada ruled in 1994 and again in 2001 that judges must consider the Charter's guarantee of freedom of the press in deciding whether to issue a discretionary ban on publication. The onus is on the Crown and/or accused to establish the need for the ban and the ban must be as limited as possible, if it is necessary.

3. With very few exceptions, a court will not ban the publication of the name of a person accused of an offence.

4. The following Criminal Code sections may be used by a judge during criminal proceedings to issue publication bans:

    - Sections 276.3 and 278.9 (bans in sexual offence proceedings on details of applications to introduce evidence of a complainant's prior sexual activity or a record relating to a complainant or witness)
    - Section 517 (bail hearings)
    - Section 539 (preliminary hearings)
    - Section 542 (absolute ban on publishing confessions during preliminary hearings)
    - Section 487.3 (discretionary ban on disclosing information relating to the warrant, production order or authorization)
    - Section 486 (general authority to ban publication of names, as well as identities of crime victims, complainants and witnesses under the age of 18)

---

83 For instance, see Nova Scotia's Compensation for Victims of Crime Act, R.S.N.S. 1989, c. 83, s. 17, and Ontario's R.S.O. 1990, c. C.24, s. 13.

- Section 486.4 (ban on publishing names of victims and witnesses under 18 in a sexual assault trial)
- Section 486.5 (discretionary ban on identifying victims and witnesses in any trial at a judge's discretion, or a "justice system participant" (a judge, jurors, informant or peace officer) in an organized crime or terrorism matter)
- Section 631(6) (discretionary ban on information identifying a juror)
- Section 648 (mandatory ban on publishing *voir dire* evidence during jury trials)
- Section 649 (absolute ban on jurors disclosing jury deliberations)
- Sections 672.501 and 672.51 (mandatory and discretionary bans on disposition information heard after a verdict of "not criminally responsible on account of mental disorder" or unfit to stand trial)

5. Sections 110 and 111 of the Youth Criminal Justice Act ban publication of the identity of a young person who has committed or is alleged to have committed an offence, as well as the publication of the identity of a young person aggrieved by the offence or a young person who appeared as a witness in connection with the offence.

6. Provincial statutes may contain provisions banning the publication of certain information or names of individuals involved in proceedings. Such bans may be found in Acts dealing with coroners' inquests, family law matters, provincial offences, venereal disease and victim compensation boards.

8

GAINING ACCESS TO PUBLIC HEARINGS AND MEETINGS

The "open court principle"[1] is a general and oft-stated presumption in the common law that the public should have access to proceedings, meetings or hearings of official bodies that act on behalf of the public and deal with matters of public interest. As the case law initially evolved, it was clear that this principle was just a starting presumption, and there were often a variety of circumstances in which it was quite lawful for the public, and consequently the news media, to be excluded from hearings or meetings.

That changed with the introduction of the Charter of Rights and Freedoms. In recent years, the Charter has given the open court principle greater weight, and Supreme Court of Canada and provincial Court of Appeal decisions frequently emphasize the importance of openness. The Supreme Court, specifically, has issued a series of rulings that dictate guidelines that courts must apply when considering excluding the news media from proceedings. Throughout this chapter, there are references to this *Dagenais/Mentuck* test and its importance.

The Supreme Court's 1994 *Dagenais*[2] and 2001 *Mentuck*[3] decisions were important landmarks in media law. In those cases, the Court emphasized the importance of considering the Charter's guarantee of freedom of the press in issuing discretionary court orders. The majority in *Dagenais* stated freedom of the press may take precedence over an accused's right to a fair trial at times and judicial orders in criminal proceedings must be as limited as possible, if even necessary. In *Mentuck*, the court reformulated its test for issuing court orders that restrict access and publication by requiring judges to consider the following factors:

1)   such an order is necessary in order to prevent a serious risk to the proper administration of justice because reasonably alternative measures will not prevent the risk; and
2)   the salutary effects of the publication ban outweigh the deleterious

---

1   This rule that, subject to certain exceptions, courts must, as between parties, administer justice in public, was first set out in the House of Lords decision in *Scott v. Scott*, [1913] A.C. 417 (U.K. H.L.).
2   *Dagenais v. Canadian Broadcasting Corp.*, [1994] 3 S.C.R. 835.
3   *R. v. Mentuck*, [2001] 3 S.C.R. 442.

effects on the rights and interests of the parties and the public, including the effects on the right to free expression, the right of the accused to a fair and public trial, and the efficacy of the administration of justice.

In a 2005 case involving The Toronto Star,[4] the Supreme Court sent an even stronger message to lower courts and legislators by ruling the *Dagenais/Mentuck* test and its presumptions in favour of access apply to "all discretionary court orders that limit freedom of expression and freedom of the press in relation to legal proceedings." That is, not just publication bans, but discretionary orders concerning access to all court proceedings and records.

Clearly, the Charter of Rights has given the news media additional ammunition in its attempts to increase public access to hearings and meetings. In fact, courts and legislators both are increasingly throwing more and more doors open that once were shut to the public.[5]

WHEN DOES THE PUBLIC HAVE RIGHTS OF ACCESS?

The greatest chance of finding specific rules or laws generally ensuring public access is within the court system. The courts have long cultivated the idea of an open justice system, as in this comment from a Supreme Court of Canada judgment on the topic:[6]

---

4 *Toronto Star Newspapers Ltd. v. Ontario*, [2005] 2 S.C.R. 188.

5 It is interesting to note, however, that there is one public body which is seemingly exempt from the Charter's influence in this area — Parliament and the provincial legislatures. In 1993, the Supreme Court of Canada dealt with the issue of the Charter's application to legislatures in regard to news media access. In *New Brunswick Broadcasting Co. v. Nova Scotia (Speaker of the House of Assembly)*, [1993] 1 S.C.R. 319, the court ruled that the N.S. legislature was within its rights under parliamentary privilege to refuse to allow the news media to videotape the House proceedings. The Charter, the court said, would never apply to the legislatures or Parliament in the exercise of its own affairs. In *Gauthier v. Canada (Speaker of the House of Commons)* (1994), 25 C.R.R. (2d) 286 (Ont. Gen. Div.), the plaintiff had been banned from the precincts of the House of Commons by the Speaker. Gauthier argued his right to freedom of the press had been violated. The Speaker maintained the ban was necessary to ensure the House operated free from interference and, since he exercised Parliamentary privilege in denying access, the Charter did not apply. The court agreed with the Speaker and ruled it had no authority to review an exercise of Parliamentary privilege. The action was dismissed. More recently, see *Zundel v. Boudria* (1999), 46 O.R. (3d) 410 (Ont. C.A.). The House of Commons unanimously passed a motion denying Ernst Zundel entry to the precincts of the Commons for the remainder of the session, preventing him from holding a press conference in the Parliament Buildings. Zundel asked a court to uphold his right to freedom of expression, but the trial and appeal judges held that parliamentary privilege is not subject to review in the courts.

6 *MacIntyre v. A.G. N.S.*, [1982] 1 S.C.R. 175 at 186-187.

[C]urtailment of public accessibility can only be justified where there is present the need to protect social values of superordinate importance.

In some provinces, the procedural and administrative laws for the courts (found, for example, in Queen's Bench Acts or Rules of Court) expressly state that hearings shall be held in public, except in extreme circumstances.[7] In other provinces, courts operate on the general common law presumption that the justice system should be open.

While each province may or may not expressly state that its courts are open, it's clear that courts in all jurisdictions have inherent common law powers and certain statutory powers to limit public access in some situations.[8]

For administrative tribunals, quasi-judicial bodies and public forums (for example, public utilities boards, workers' compensation boards or municipal council meetings), the "right" of public access is less certain. If the statute that created the tribunal doesn't set out the public's right of access then it's usually up to the discretion of tribunal officials.[9] The general principle with such bodies is that the public should have access to public proceedings except when it's in the interests of the public and the administration of justice to have a closed hearing.

---

7 For example, Ontario's Courts of Justice Act, 1984, S.O. 1984, c. 11 [now R.S.O. 1990, c. C.43] states at s. 135, all court hearings shall be open to the public, except where there's a possibility of serious harm or injustice to any person.

8 Under the common law, the courts may only exclude the public in proceedings involving wards, the mentally disordered, trade secrets or where a public trial would defeat the whole object of the proceeding. Of course, statutes can add further exceptions. Also, see *Apotex Fermentation Inc. v. Novopharm Ltd.*, [1994] 7 W.W.R. 420 (Man. C.A.), in which a Manitoba court ruled that even though trade secrets or other confidential business information may be involved in a trial, the first presumption should be that the courts will be open to the public. The judge held that the onus was upon the parties requesting closure of the courtroom to explain why it is necessary. The court suggested there would almost always be ways to keep certain information confidential during the trial without closing the doors entirely.

9 Even when a statute does declare a right of public access, administrative officials can be less than co-operative. For example, see the case of *Southam Inc. v. Gauthier*, [1991] R.J.Q. 2377 (Qué. S.C.), reversed (1996), 135 D.L.R. (4th) 124 (Qué. C.A.). The public in Québec have a statutory right to attend lawyers' disciplinary hearings. The Bar, however, refused a newspaper's request for an advance list of the names of lawyers whose discipline cases would be heard. The newspaper argued that it could not afford to send a reporter to every hearing to find out who was involved. The court disagreed and said the Bar's only obligation was to allow public access to proceedings and that it did not infringe freedom of the press since reporters could attend the first few minutes of any hearing and quickly determine what it was about. This is a petty view of the right of public access. Not surprisingly, the Québec Court of Appeal overturned the lower court ruling. In some other provinces, the local Bar will provide reporters with a list of individuals charged in discipline matters, details of the alleged offence and the time of the hearing.

Another key factor for courts in deciding whether to allow public access is to look at the nature or character of the tribunal or body. If it has judicial or quasi-judicial qualities, then there is a higher likelihood that access will be required. A 1995 British Columbia case nicely illustrates this point.[10] The province's conflict of interest commissioner had received an allegation that a member of the legislature was in contravention of the Members' Conflict of Interest Act.

The commissioner conducted some informal interviews as he prepared his opinion on whether there was a conflict of interest. A magazine and its editor applied to the commissioner for copies of the opinion and were refused. Then, they launched a court action for an order requiring the commissioner to conduct his investigation in public. The court said four factors were to be considered in deciding whether an administrative decision was judicial or quasi-judicial.

First, does any relevant statute require a hearing before a decision or opinion can be handed over? Second, will the decision directly or indirectly affect the rights of a person? Third, is there an adversary process involved? And, finally, is there any obligation to apply substantive rules or law to the process? The court noted the Member's Conflict of Interest Act was silent on the issue of public access and the commissioner's activities were "merely information gathering." It also decided there was no adversarial process and the commissioner's opinion had no effect on the member's rights since it was the legislature that would decide his fate.

The following are many of the most frequently encountered statutory provisions and common law principles setting out guidelines for public access to the courts and other bodies.

FEDERAL LAWS

Dozens of federal laws permit various tribunals and quasi-judicial bodies to hold hearings or conduct investigations in private or *in camera*. Examples include the Canada Business Corporations Act, Canadian International Trade Tribunal Act, Employment Equity Act, Personal Information Protection and Electronic Documents Act, Petroleum and Gas Revenue Tax Act, Public Servants Disclosure Protection Act, Shipping Inquiries and Investigations Rules and the Telecommunications Act. Below are the Acts journalists are more likely to encounter that have provisions governing access to hearings and proceedings.

---

10 *Tafler v. British Columbia (Commissioner of Conflict of Interest)* (1995), 5 B.C.L.R. (3d) 285 (S.C.).

Criminal Code[11]

Generally

Section 486(1) sets out the court's general authority to exclude members of the public on certain occasions:

> Any proceedings against an accused shall be held in open court, but where the presiding judge, provincial court judge or justice, as the case may be, is of the opinion that it is in the interest of public morals, the maintenance of order or the proper administration of justice, or that it is necessary to prevent injury to international relations or national defence, or national security, to exclude all or any members of the public from the court room for all or part of the proceedings, he or she may so order.

The exclusion of the public "in the interest of public morals" is in reference to the evidence to be presented and not a reference to the charge against the accused.[12] The exclusion of a journalist from the courtroom must be for a valid reason. For example, to remove a journalist but not the general public, simply to prevent the names of witnesses found in a bawdy-house from being published, is not a valid reason.[13]

---

11 R.S.C. 1985, c. C-46.
12 In *R. v. Warawuk* (1978), 42 C.C.C. (2d) 121 at 126 (Alta. C.A.), the court said an exclusion order could not be issued simply because a sexual offence was involved. The court said the purpose of the exclusion order is to protect public morals and the question is whether the evidence could reasonably be expected to offend or have an adverse or corrupt effect on public morals. This line of thinking appears to have been broadened significantly by the Charter of Rights. In *French Estate v. Ontario (Attorney General)* (1998), 157 D.L.R. (4th) 144 (Ont. C.A.), the families of two girls brutally murdered by Paul Bernardo and Karla Homolka asked the courts to declare s. 486(1) of the Code and s. 135(2) of the Ontario Courts of Justice Act unconstitutional. Both provisions give judges discretion to exclude the public from a courtroom. The families also wanted a declaration of a proprietary interest in seized videotapes depicting the rape, torture and brutalization of their daughters. The Court of Appeal dismissed the case. The court said openness is the rule and exclusion of the public is the exception. The applicants' argument that child or coerced pornography are "antithetical to the notion of free expression" was given no credence by the court. The court also found no merit in the argument that public access to the videotapes offended the families' right to freedom of religion or conscience, or to be protected against cruel and unusual treatment or punishment.
13 *Re F.P. Publications (Western) Ltd. and R.* (1979), 51 C.C.C. (2d) 110 (Man. C.A.). It seems, however, judges may have an extremely broad discretion in their use of s. 486(1). In *Taylor v. Canada (Attorney General)* (2000), 184 D.L.R. (4th) 706 (Fed. C.A.), a judge in a criminal trial told spectators they would have to leave the courtroom unless they removed their religious headgear. A spectator attempted to bring a personal action against the judge, but both a human rights tribunal and a court ruled that judicial immunity protected the judge. At the Federal Court of Appeal, judges ruled the trial judge was

In 1996, the Supreme Court of Canada reaffirmed that the public and news media are only to be excluded in special cases.[14] Using s. 486, a provincial court judge accepted a motion by the Crown, with the accused's consent, excluding the public and media from parts of a sentencing hearing. The judge felt the publicity would cause harm to the victims and the accused, who had pleaded guilty to sexual assault and sexual interference with young girls.

The CBC challenged the court order and claimed s. 486(1) of the Code was an unjustified violation of the Charter of Rights. The provincial appeal court disagreed, saying the Code section was a reasonable limit and the judge had properly used his discretion.

The Supreme Court of Canada overturned the appeal court decision, in part. The high court ruled that s. 486(1) of the Code does infringe on Charter rights, but is justified since its objective is protecting the proper administration of justice. That said, the court said a judge must, based on sufficient evidence, conclude:

1.   There are no reasonable and effective alternatives to excluding the public;
2.   The order is as limited as possible; and
3.   Its salutary effects are proportionate to its deleterious effects.

The fact the case involves "sexual assaults on young females does not in itself warrant the order, but undue hardship to persons involved may be a legitimate reason to exclude the public in the interests of the administration of justice." As for the accused, the court said there will only be hardship to an accused who has pleaded guilty in exceptional cases.

As noted above, courts also have an inherent jurisdiction to exclude the public from trials. In one case, the accused had pleaded guilty and the lawyer for the accused asked the court if the submissions on sentencing could be heard *in camera*. The lawyer said the accused had something important to say and it could only be said in private. The judge ordered the public out, citing his inherent right to preserve the administration of justice. He held that the accused couldn't get a fair hearing, in this case, if the public was allowed to stay. The court felt the rights of the accused were more important than public access at that moment.[15]

---

acting within his jurisdiction to exclude some members of the public and it was not inconsistent with the basic values of the Charter of Rights. An application for leave to appeal to the Supreme Court of Canada was dismissed, [2000] S.C.C.A. No. 213.

14   *Canadian Broadcasting Corp. v. New Brunswick (Attorney General)* (1996), 139 D.L.R. (4th) 385 (S.C.C.).

15   *R. v. Parisian* (1985), 6 C.R.D. 525.70-03 (Alta. Q.B.).

In a trial of two individuals charged with terrorism offences relating to the 1998 explosion of Air India Flight 182, the Crown asked for a special investigative hearing under s. 83.28 of the Criminal Code to gather evidence from a potential Crown witness. In a closed-door application hearing, the judge agreed, requiring the investigative hearing also be held entirely *in camera* and that no notice be given to the accused, media or public. A Vancouver Sun reporter, who recognized lawyers from the trial later entering a closed-door court-room, was denied access and the newspaper's attempts to convince the trial judge to open the proceedings failed. While the judge later released a synopsis of the issues before her in the *in camera* hearing, should the special investigative hearing have been conducted in open court?

Yes.[16] In 2004, a majority of the Supreme Court of Canada ruled a large portion of such proceedings need not be held *in camera*. This was the first case at the Supreme Court involving the open court principle and judicial investigative hearings into terrorism. The Court said the open court principle should not be presumptively displaced in favour of an *in camera* process. The principle of openness extends to all judicial pro-ceedings, it noted, and the *Dagenais/Mentuck* test (requiring a balancing of media and other interests) should be applied to all discretionary judicial decisions that limit freedom of expression by the press. A 7-2 majority wrote that the openness principle is a "hallmark of democracy and a cornerstone of the common law" that guarantees the integrity of the judiciary and is inextricably linked to the freedom of expression guar-anteed by the Charter of Rights. Here, when considering whether it was necessary to go *in camera*, the court noted there were really two pro-ceedings at issue. First, the application for an investigative hearing and, second, the investigative hearing itself. The Court compared the appli-cation process to applying for a search warrant or a wiretap authorization. By their nature, these hearings must be *in camera*. The Court noted the Code, however, does not require the investigative hearing itself be held *in camera*. "[T]he proper balance between investigative imperatives and openness will best be achieved through the discretion granted to judges to impose terms and conditions on the conduct of a hearing under s. 83.28(5)(e)." In exercising that discretion, said the Court, "judges should reject the presumption of secret hearings." The existence of an order for such a hearing, and as much of its subject-matter as possible, should be made public unless, under the balancing exercise of the *Dagenais/Men-tuck* test, secrecy is deemed necessary.

16 *Vancouver Sun, Re*, [2004] 2 S.C.R. 332.

Applications for Search Warrants

In 1982, the Supreme Court of Canada held in *MacIntyre v. Attorney General of Nova Scotia* that the public has no right to attend a court proceeding where a search warrant is being issued.[17] Secrecy is crucial to the success of a warrant as an investigative tool and the court can't risk the chance that someone might destroy evidence if they knew a warrant was about to be executed.

Hearings for Issue of Summons or Arrest Warrants

In 1987, an Ontario judge considered whether the public has a right to attend hearings held under s. 507, where a justice receives sworn informations and issues summonses or arrest warrants.[18] Unless evidence was to be presented suggesting the accused may try to flee the jurisdiction, the judge held that conducting an *in camera* hearing under this section isn't a reasonable limit on the freedom of the press. The judge went on to note that the Charter's guarantee of freedom of expression and the press includes the right of free access to the courts.

In 1990, however, the Ontario Court of Appeal came to the opposite conclusion.[19] In this case, the appeal judges said an inquiry under s. 507(1) must be held *in camera*. It said that "protection of the innocent and the effective administration of justice justify exceptions to the principle of public access to judicial proceedings." The court noted that if no prosecution resulted from the s. 507 hearing, the reputation of the person named in the information may be harmed. Another concern was the publication of incriminating evidence against a person who was not entitled to be at the hearing. The appeal court acknowledged that this infringes the Charter's freedom of the press guarantee, but held it was a justified and reasonable limit.

Preliminary Hearings

Where an accused is charged with an indictable offence, s. 537(1)(h) states that a justice holding a preliminary hearing may:

> order that no person other than the prosecutor, the accused and their counsel
> shall have access to or remain in the room in which the inquiry is held, where
> it appears to him that the ends of justice will be best served by so doing.

---

17 [1982] 1 S.C.R. 175.
18 *Re Canadian Newspapers Co. v. R.* (1987), 38 C.C.C. (3d) 187 (Ont. H.C.).
19 *Southam Inc. v. Ontario* (1990), 75 O.R. (2d) 1 (C.A.).

The decision to bar the public from attending a preliminary hearing must be based on clear reasons.[20] In a 1982 case, a preliminary hearing involved an accused charged with manslaughter in a highly publicized killing. The judge was ready to begin proceedings when he was told that some American journalists who were present in the courtroom planned to publish the full details of the preliminary hearing contrary to s. 539 of the Code. Upon determining that the reporters did indeed plan to publish the evidence (in the United States there's no such ban), he used s. 537(1)(h) to bar the public from the hearing.[21] On a further application by Canadian journalists, the judge "reluctantly" refused to limit the exclusion order only to the American journalists. He held he didn't have the authority to make exceptions to the Code section and would have no way of knowing who in the court gallery might be acting for an American news outlet.[22]

Legal counsel for B.C. pig farmer Robert Pickton, the defendant in a high-profile mass murder case, requested a rare order under s. 537(1)(h) to exclude the public from the preliminary hearing. Citing "modern-day publication technology," such as Web blogs, and the lack of enforceable restrictions on foreign media outlets, the defendant argued an order merely banning publication of the proceedings is not sufficient to protect his right to a fair trial. In a high-profile case, should the court exclude the public from a preliminary hearing to protect an individual's right to fair trial?

No.[23] While the case against Pickton attracted considerable media attention, the court noted it was highly unusual and ultimately unnecessary to consider a request to have everyone excluded from the courtroom other than the prosecutor, accused and his counsel during a preliminary hearing. The judge stated: "I am not prepared to accept, at this stage of the proceeding, that the justice system is so fragile that appropriate corrective measures cannot be taken so as to ensure that an accused's right to a fair trial is not jeopardized." While the public was not excluded, the judge did order the usual ban on publication of evidence offered during the preliminary hearing.

---

20 *Re Vaudrin and R.* (1982), 2 C.C.C. (3d) 214 (B.C. S.C.).

21 *R. v. Sayegh (No. 1)* (1982), 66 C.C.C. (2d) 430 (Ont. Prov. Ct.).

22 *R. v. Sayegh (No. 2)* (1982), 66 C.C.C. (2d) 432 (Ont. Prov. Ct.).

23 *R. v. Pickton*, 2002 BCPC 526 (Prov. Ct.).

Proceedings Involving Sexual Offences

Under s. 276, the defence lawyer in a sexual assault trial must give notice to the court that he or she intends to enter evidence on the sexual activity of the victim. According to the Code, the judge, provincial court judge or justice must hold a *voir dire* (that is, trial within a trial) to determine if the evidence is admissible. Section 276.2 states that the *voir dire* can only be held after excluding the jury and other members of the general public from the courtroom. As well, under s. 276.1, the judge must exclude the public before hearing the initial application for the *voir dire* hearing. It should also be noted that journalists cannot report that a notice or application has been given by the defence counsel or the decision of the judge unless he or she rules the evidence is admissible. Regardless of the decision, a journalist also cannot report the evidence and representations made at the *voir dire* (s. 276.3).

Review Hearings for Mentally Disordered Criminals

Section 672.5 outlines the procedure to be followed by the review boards that must annually assess the state of incarcerated individuals who have been found not guilty of crimes by reason of insanity or other mental illness. Officials presiding over the "disposition hearing" may exclude the public or a specific person where it is considered by the board or a court to be "in the best interests of the accused and not contrary to the public interest."[24]

---

24 S. 672.5(6). In *Blackman v. British Columbia (Review Board)* (1993), 82 C.C.C. (3d) 5 (B.C. S.C.), affirmed (1995), 95 C.C.C. (3d) 412 (B.C. C.A.), the accused was found not guilty of murder by reason of insanity and argued at his disposition hearing that the public should be excluded because he was under a great deal of stress from unwanted media attention. The review board refused the request and the court agreed that s. 672.5(6) did not violate any of the accused's Charter rights. The court said the privacy interest of the accused did not "justify a complete abrogation of freedom of public access" and suggested that even if the section did violate the accused's Charter rights, the public's right to attend such judicial hearings overrode other constitutional rights.

Youth Criminal Justice Act[25]

On April 1, 2003, the Young Offenders Act was replaced by the new Youth Criminal Justice Act. Section 132 grants a judge this discretionary power:[26]

> 132. (1) Subject to subsection (2), a court or justice before whom proceedings are carried out under this Act may exclude any person from all or part of the proceedings if the court or justice considers that the person's presence is unnecessary to the conduct of the proceedings and the court or justice is of the opinion that
>
>> (a) any evidence or information presented to the court or justice would be seriously injurious or seriously prejudicial to
>>> (i)   the young person who is being dealt with in the proceedings,
>>> (ii) a child or young person who is a witness in the proceedings, or
>>> (iii) a child or young person who is aggrieved by or the victim of the offence charged in the proceedings; or
>> (b) it would be in the interest of public morals, the maintenance of order or the proper administration of justice to exclude any or all members of the public from the court room.
>
> (2) Subject to section 650 (accused to be present) of the Criminal Code and except if it is necessary for the purposes of subsection 34(9) (nondisclosure of medical or psychological report) of this Act, a court or justice may not, under subsection (1), exclude from proceedings under this Act
>
>> (a) the prosecutor;
>> (b) the young person who is being dealt with in the proceedings, the counsel or a parent of the young person or any adult assisting the young person under subsection 25(7);
>> (c) the provincial director or his or her agent; or
>> (d) the youth worker to whom the young person's case has been assigned.

---

25 S.C. 2002, c. 1.
26 A landmark decision involving the now-repealed Juvenile Delinquents Act, *Reference re s. 12(1) of the Juvenile Delinquents Act (Canada)* (1983), 41 O.R. (2d) 113 (C.A.), established that a provision requiring all juvenile trials to be held *in camera* was unconstitutional because it was an absolute ban on public access to the hearing and allowed for no judicial discretion. The court's discretionary power to exclude the public under the previous Young Offenders Act was also challenged. But in *Southam Inc. v. R.* (1986), 25 C.C.C. (3d) 119 (Ont. C.A.), the appeal court held that an order to exclude the public is a reasonable limit on the guarantee of freedom of expression. Leave to appeal to the Supreme Court of Canada was refused on May 22, 1986 ([1986] 1 S.C.R. xiv).

After a young person has been found guilty of an offence or during a review under this statute, a court may also exclude the general public, with specific exemptions, when it is being presented with information that may be seriously injurious or prejudicial to the young person.

A *young person* under this law is someone "who is or, in the absence of evidence to the contrary, appears to be twelve years of age or more, but less than eighteen years old and, if the context requires, includes any person who is charged under this Act with having committed an offence while he or she was a young person or who is found guilty of an offence under this Act."[27] Note that it can include someone who is no longer less than 18 years of age.

Canadian Human Rights Commission

Preliminary investigations of complaints by the commission may be conducted *in camera*.[28] But formal hearings or inquiries of the commission's tribunal must be held in public.[29] If there is an application by one of the parties for a hearing in private, the inquiry may only grant the exclusion order if one of four circumstances exists:

1. There is a real and substantial risk that matters involving public security will be disclosed;

2. There is a real and substantial risk to the fairness of the inquiry such that the need to prevent disclosure outweighs the societal interest that the inquiry be conducted in public;

3. There is a real and substantial risk that the disclosure of personal or other matters will cause undue hardship to the persons involved such that the need to prevent disclosure outweighs the societal interest that the inquiry be conducted in public; or

4. There is a serious possibility that the life, liberty or security of a person will be endangered.

---

27 S. 2(1).
28 This was confirmed in *McKenzie v. Canadian Human Rights Commission* (1985), 6 C.R.D. 525.70-04 (Fed. T.D.), where an M.P. wanted the public and reporters to be allowed into a commission meeting that was deciding whether to formally inquire into allegations made against the M.P.
29 Canadian Human Rights Act, R.S.C. 1985, c. H-6, s. 52.

Canadian Security Intelligence Service Act

The Review Committee (that is, public watchdog) established under this Act to examine complaints against the Service, is required to conduct its hearings in private.[30] A report on the complaints explored is filed annually with Parliament.

Competition Act

Section 10(3) states that all preliminary inquiries into alleged offences under this Act[31] shall be in private, unless the chairman of the Commission orders otherwise. Proceedings other than those in relation to a preliminary inquiry may be held in public.

Immigration and Refugee Protection Act

A judge in an immigration inquiry must conduct an inquiry in public, unless the judge believes there is: a) a real and substantial risk that matters involving public security will be disclosed; b) a real and substantial risk to the fairness of the inquiry such that the need to prevent disclosure outweighs the societal interest that the inquiry be conducted in public; or c) a serious possibility that the life, liberty or security of a person will be endangered. The Act also gives judges authority to issue orders where appropriate to ensure the confidentiality of such a closed-door hearing.[32] Appeals to the Immigration Appeal Board are also generally to be held in public, except where the tribunal receives a request or believes itself that the hearing be held *in camera*.[33] The Act also permits proceedings before the Refugee Protection Division and the Immigration Division concerning a claimant of refugee protection, proceedings concerning cessation and vacation appli-

---

30 R.S.C. 1985, c. C-23, s. 48.
31 R.S.C. 1985, c. C-34.
32 S.C. 2001, c. 27, s. 181. Until 1991, the Act said that public hearings should be the exception rather than the rule. That earlier provision was struck down as a restriction on freedom of the press in *Pacific Press Ltd. v. Canada (Minister of Employment & Immigration)* (1991), 127 N.R. 325 (Fed. C.A.). In *Blackwood v. Canada (Minister of Employment & Immigration)* (1991), 13 Imm. L.R. (2d) 246 (Imm. & Ref. Bd. (Ref. Div.)), it was ruled that the onus is upon a refugee claimant to prove that an *in camera* hearing is needed. The claimant said he intended to make revelations about the criminal connections of certain high-level Jamaican officials and public disclosure of this information would endanger his life or those of his family. The Refugee Division required the claimant to establish a serious possibility of harm and the board said the onus upon the claimant was greater than merely raising the possibility of harm.
33 *Ibid.*, s. 166.

cations, and proceedings before the Refugee Appeal Division to be held in private.

> **During an extradition hearing, the individual who was the subject of the proceeding informed the judge he was a confidential police informant and was acting on behalf of the state requesting his extradition. Before deciding whether the claim was true and if it was necessary to continue the entire hearing *in camera*, the judge considered the *Dagenais/Mentuck* test and determined the news media should be given an opportunity to challenge the *in camera* hearing. The judge sent a letter to legal counsel for several media organizations, advising them to attend and allowing access, subject to confidentiality undertakings, to information offered by the alleged informer. Did the judge err?**

Yes.[34] In a departure from recent cases favouring media access, a majority of the Supreme Court of Canada agreed in 2007 that "while open courts are undoubtedly a vital part of our legal system and of our society," openness cannot be allowed to compromise fundamental aspects of the criminal justice system, such as the absolute protection offered to informants. The Court confirmed the *Dagenais/Mentuck* line of cases still represents a "test" for the application of the open court principle in any discretionary actions by courts, but it did not apply here because a trial judge has no discretion in matters involving informants. One Supreme Court Justice offered a powerful dissenting opinion, arguing the "open court principle, which was accepted long before the adoption of the Canadian Charter of Rights and Freedoms, is now enshrined in it" and that the extradition judge was acting within his discretionary authority in involving the news media as public representatives. That said, the remainder of the Court agreed a judge "ought to make every effort to ensure that as much information as possible is made public, and that disclosure and publication are restricted only for that information which might tend to reveal the informer's identity." The majority did set out some guidelines for *in camera* determinations of the informer privilege. If there is such a privilege, the court is not required to conduct its entire proceeding *in camera* and must only hear evidence in private that identifies the informer. The majority suggested a court may, but not must, give notice to the media of such a proceeding and allow media or other submissions on how the open court principle can best be preserved or minimally infringed.

---

34 *Application to proceed in Camera, Re*, 2007 SCC 43.

Income Tax Act

A taxpayer has the right, upon request, to a hearing *in camera* when appealing assessments to the Federal Court and administrative bodies.[35] This right doesn't exist during prosecutions in criminal courts for income tax offences.

National Defence Act

The military start proceedings with a presumption of openness. Under s. 250.42, for example, the Complaints Commission dealing with military police must hold its hearings in public. Part or all of the hearing may be held in private if the commission believes information to be heard:

1. Could reasonably be expected to be injurious to the defence of Canada or any state allied or associated with Canada or the detection, prevention or suppression of subversive or hostile activities;

2. Could reasonably be expected to be injurious to the administration of justice, including law enforcement; and

3. Could affect a person's privacy or security interest, if that interest outweighs the public's interest in the information.

A court martial is to be held in public except where the evidence or information would endanger public safety, defence or public morals. The presiding official may exclude the public for all or part of the proceedings.[36] The Act also allows the Court Martial Court of Appeal the discretion to hold *in camera* hearings when new evidence is to be introduced.[37]

The controversy over the activities of some of Canada's peacekeeping troops in Somalia illustrated the fine line that sometimes is drawn in distinguishing among certain types of hearings. When a Board of Inquiry was established to review the principles, practices and policies of the Canadian Airborne Regiment Battle Group, the Chief of Defence Staff decided the proceedings would not be conducted in public. A court was asked to rule on whether this decision to bar public access infringed the Charter's guarantee of freedom of the press. The court ruled that this was not a violation of the Charter right because the Board of Inquiry was not a court and had

---

35 R.S.C. 1985, c. 1 (5th Supp.), s. 179.
36 R.S.C. 1985, c. N-5, s. 180, amended 1992, c. 16, s. 8.
37 *Ibid.*, s. 236(2).

no judicial or quasi-judicial function. It had no power to summon witnesses and could not issue any enforceable orders or obligations. It could only make recommendations and the fact that its mandate had been made public did not automatically trigger a right of access to its proceedings.[38]

Security of Information Act (formerly Official Secrets Act)

Until recently, the Official Secrets Act allowed an application to be made to exclude all or any part of the public from a trial or proceedings on appeal, where evidence or statements to be made would be prejudicial to the interests of the state. The new federal anti-terrorism law renames the Act and allows courts to use their general authority to exclude the public under s. 486(1) of the Criminal Code where matters of national or international security are at issue.[39]

Canada Evidence Act

Anyone may object to the disclosure of any information in a court (or any body with the power to compel witnesses or the production of documents) on the grounds of "a specified public interest."[40] A judge will determine the validity of this "public interest." For example, this can include information about the Queen's Privy Council, international relations, national defence or confidential government information. If the information involves international relations, national defence or security, the application for non-disclosure and any subsequent appeals must be held *in camera*.[41]

Access to Information and Privacy Acts

Each of these Acts provides for court appeals of requests for access to information held by the federal government. In each of these Acts, the Federal Court must, or may in some circumstances, hold the hearing *in camera*.[42] In addition, every investigation by the Information Commissioner must be conducted in private.[43]

---

38 *Travers v. Canada (Chief of Defence Staff)*, [1993] 3 F.C. 528 (T.D.), affirmed (1994), 24 C.R.R. (2d) 186 (Fed. C.A.).

39 R.S.C. 1985, c. O-5, as amended S.C. 2001, c. 41.

40 R.S.C. 1985, C-5, ss. 37-39.

41 S. 38(5)(a).

42 See ss. 47 and 52 of the Access to Information Act, R.S.C. 1985, c. A-1; ss. 46 and 51 of the Privacy Act, R.S.C. 1985, c. P-21.

43 See s. 35 of the Access to Information Act.

> **The federal Privacy Act requires a mandatory *in camera* hearing when the government seeks to deny an applicant's request for access to his or her personal information on the grounds that it may interfere with national security or the maintenance of foreign confidences. Is the mandatory *in camera* provision a violation of any Charter rights?**
>
> **Yes.**[44] The Supreme Court of Canada held in 2002 that the mandatory *in camera* requirement excluding both the applicant and public from such proceedings is a clear violation of the Charter's s. 2(b) right of freedom of expression. The Court held the provision is not a justifiable infringement since it requires the hearing of an application or appeal to be heard entirely *in camera*. This is "too stringent," the Court said, and its solution was to "read down" the section such that a reviewing court has the discretion to conduct the remainder of a hearing or any portion in public or *in camera*.

PROVINCIAL LAWS

Court Proceedings Generally

Some provinces have expressly established the authority in statutes or court rules for judges to exclude the public from proceedings.[45] Generally, the legislation says the courts shall be open, except:

1. where public morals are endangered;
2. for the maintenance of order;
3. for the "proper administration of justice;" or
4. in child and family matters.

---

44 *Ruby v. Canada (Solicitor General)*, [2002] 4 S.C.R. 3.

45 For example, see Québec's Code of Civil Procedure, R.S.Q. 1977, c. C-25 which allows judges in civil proceedings to exclude the public in the interests of good morals or public order. Also, see Québec's Charter of Rights and Freedoms, R.S.Q. 1977, c. C-12, s. 23, which speaks to the principle of an open court. In Ontario, see R.S.O. 1990, c. C.43, s. 135. In Nova Scotia, see the Judicature Act, R.S.N.S. 1989, c. 240, s. 37, which provides for open hearings except where public morals, maintenance of order or the proper administration of justice requires an *in camera* hearing. In New Brunswick, see Judicature Act, R.S.N.B. 1973, c. J-2. For example, s. 11.3(1) (as amended S.N.B. 1978, c. 32) allows family court judges to hold hearings *in camera* in the interests of public order or to prevent potential harm or embarrassment to any person.

For example, Ontario's Courts of Justice Act states that all court hearings shall be open to the public.[46] The only exception noted under the law is for hearings where the possibility of serious harm or injustice to any person justifies a departure from the general principle of an open court.[47]

However, the common law also gives courts an inherent power to exclude the public in certain circumstances, such as when trade secrets are involved.[48] But that same common law rule limits those circumstances. For example, an *in camera* hearing can't be held simply because both sides in a dispute want the hearing to be closed.[49]

Coroners

Ontario[50] and British Columbia[51] expressly allow coroners to exclude the public where evidence may endanger national security or where a witness is charged with an indictable offence under the Criminal Code. But the public can't be excluded where no criminal charges have been laid, even though the evidence given by a witness may be incriminating.

In Alberta,[52] all fatality inquiry hearings are public, except in matters of public security or where it's preferable to hear intimate or personal details in private. The Alberta statute says the public and private interests involved must be weighed against each other. The Act says the coroner's decision to bar the public cannot be reviewed by a court.

Québec legislation says all inquests shall be held in public, but a coroner can ban the publication of evidence or information arising out of the hearing in the name of the public's interest, to protect someone's right

---

46 R.S.O. 1990, c. C.43, s. 135(1).

47 *Ibid.*, s. 135(2).

48 See, note 8, above, in *Scott* at 436-438, where the court said judicial proceedings should always be open to the public except where it acts on behalf of wards or lunatics, where confidential information is concerned or where justice could not otherwise be done. Also, see *Apotex* in note 8, in which a Manitoba court said there would almost always be ways to keep certain information confidential during the trial without closing the doors entirely.

49 *Ibid.*

50 Coroners Act, R.S.O. 1990, c. C.37, s. 32.

51 Coroners Act, R.S.B.C. 1996, c. 72, s. 28.

52 See the Fatality Inquiries Act, R.S.A. 2000, c. F-9, ss. 41-44. In a decision prior to this Act being proclaimed, *Edmonton Journal v. A.G. Alta.* (1983), 28 Alta. L.R. (2d) 369 (Q.B.), the court held the decision to exclude the public from an Alberta fatality inquiry was not a violation of the Charter's guarantee of freedom of expression because the inquiry isn't a court. The court said full access by the public must be set out in statute and by prior practice. That requirement has now been fulfilled in the present legislation.

of privacy or preserve the right to a fair trial.[53] In New Brunswick[54] and Nova Scotia,[55] coroners have the discretion to hold hearings in private.

Family Law Acts

All the provinces and territories have legislation that gives judges a discretionary power to exclude the public in matters involving children and family disputes. This can involve laws dealing with child welfare, adoption, children of unmarried parents and family services matters. Generally, an exclusion order will be issued where there's a potential for harm or embarrassment to any person related to the proceeding or where it's in the public's interest or the interest of justice. But one province does make a special concession for news media. Ontario's Child and Family Services Act[56] states that two or more members of the media may be allowed by the presiding judge to attend hearings even if the public is excluded.[57]

Where a presiding judge does exclude the public, there must be a good reason for it. For example, one court held the news media can't be excluded simply because they are media. The court held there must be some proof offered to show that the presence of a particular person in the courtroom (for example, a journalist) is a hindrance to the proceedings.[58]

Human Rights Acts

Some provincial human rights laws or commissions may permit hearings to be conducted *in camera*. In one Ontario case, however, the Board of Inquiry refused such a request, citing the right of public access and the educational aspects of open hearings.[59] A complaint of sexual harassment was laid by an employee against several social workers at a Children's Aid Society. The society was worried that the hearing could damage its reputation and would also result in difficulties in raising money. The society

---

53 An Act respecting the determination of the causes and circumstances of death, S.Q. 1983, c. 41, ss. 140 and 146.
54 Coroners Act, R.S.N.B. 1973, c. C-23, s. 21.
55 Fatality Inquiries Act, R.S.N.S. 1989, c. 164, s. 12.
56 R.S.O. 1990, c. C.11, s. 45(5) and (6).
57 In *R. v. M.C.* (1984), 4 C.R.D. 525.70-02 (Ont. Prov. Ct.), a court held a similar provision in the now-repealed Child Welfare Act was constitutional because it was a reasonable limit on the press allowing a judge to exercise discretion.
58 In *Re S.D.A.* (1982), 28 R.F.L. (2d) 121 (B.C. Prov. Ct.), the court was considering an exclusion order requested under the Provincial Court Act, R.S.B.C. 1979, c. 341, s. 3, which empowers a judge to exclude members of the public during family law matters.
59 *Carere v. Family & Children's Services of Guelph & Wellington County* (1992), 18 C.H.R.R. D/240 (Ont. Bd. of Inquiry).

brought a motion that the hearing be held *in camera* and the venue be changed to a nearby town.

The board dismissed the motion, saying there was no reason why a fair hearing could not be conducted in the original venue. The board said an *in camera* hearing would only be ordered "where there was a possibility that matters involving public security or intimate personal or financial matters would be disclosed." That said, a publicity ban was ordered so "that parties would not be prejudiced in the presentation of their cases."

Police Commission Hearings

British Columbia is one province where meetings and hearings of the police commission must be open to the public except in specific cases, such as risk to public security. The police complaint commissioner is also required, except in minor cases, to grant requests by parties for open hearings in disciplinary proceedings involving officers accused of violating public trust. Other hearings of the police commission in that province may be held in private.[60] In Nova Scotia,[61] inquiries into police matters are to be held in public, but may be heard *in camera* in certain instances (that is, public interest or security). The Charter of Rights may give the news media greater opportunity to challenge *in camera* hearings involving police. In a P.E.I. case, the media successfully challenged a section of the Summerside Police Department Rules and Regulations that stated: "All [police] discipline hearings will be closed to the public." The court agreed it violated the Charter of Rights, saying a police officer holds a public position and the public has a strong interest in scrutinizing police discipline hearings. Since the rule was an absolute prohibition, it allowed for no discretion and the Charter cannot justify a blanket prohibition of public attendance.[62]

Provincial Offences Acts

Most of the provinces adopt the Criminal Code procedures in their Summary Conviction Act for enforcing provincially-created offences. Some Acts state that proceedings must be held in open court, while others don't say anything.

Some provinces, such as Ontario and Québec, have developed their own court procedure for provincial offences which allows the public to be

---

60 Police Act, R.S.B.C. 1996, c. 367, s. 60, 60.1 and 69.
61 Police Act, R.S.N.S. 1989, c. 348, s. 19(10).
62 *Canadian Broadcasting Corp. v. City of Summerside* (1999), 170 D.L.R. (4th) 731 (P.E.I. S.C., T.D.).

excluded in special circumstances.[63] In Ontario, the public may be excluded for the maintenance of order, to protect the reputation of a minor or to remove an "influence" on a witness.[64]

Public Inquiries Acts

Despite their name, inquiries struck by the provinces don't necessarily have to be in public. Ontario is the only province that requires inquiries to be public.[65] Even in that province, the public may be excluded for reasons of public security, intimate financial or personal matters or when the benefit of an *in camera* hearing outweighs the public need for access.

In 1990, a Northwest Territories Board of Inquiry ruling clearly stated that inquiries should be public as a general rule.[66]

Victim Compensation Board Hearings

Many provinces have established boards to compensate victims of crimes and other misfortunes. The compensation boards generally hold hearings in public, but some have the power to exclude the public. This may be done in circumstances where it's prejudicial to the trial of the person who caused the injury or death, in sexual offences where it is not in the interests of the victim or dependants or where it's in the public's interest.[67]

---

63 For example, in Québec, see Code of Penal Procedure, R.S.Q. c. C-25.1, s. 194.

64 Provincial Offences Act, R.S.O. 1990, c. P.33, s. 52(2).

65 Public Inquiries Act, R.S.O. 1990, c. P.41, s. 4. In *Starr v. Ontario (Commissioner of Inquiry)* (1990), 64 D.L.R. (4th) 285 (Ont. C.A.), reversed [1990] 1 S.C.R. 1366, this section of the Act was affirmed and the court ruled that *in camera* hearings are inappropriate except in special circumstances.

66 *Re Inquiry pursuant to s. 13(2) of Territorial Court Act*, [1990] N.W.T.R. 181 (Bd. of Inquiry). The inquiry was into comments made by a Territorial judge regarding the crime of sexual assault. The board ruled that its proceedings should be open since the subject-matter involved neither public security nor intimate personal or financial matters. The inquiry also ruled that cameras and radio coverage would not be appropriate.

67 For example, see the legislation in Manitoba: Criminal Injuries Compensation Act, R.S.M. 1987, c. C305, s. 8; Yukon: Compensation for the Victims of Crime Ordinance, R.S.Y. 1986, c. 27, s. 14; and Newfoundland: Criminal Injuries Compensation Act, R.S.N. 1990, c. C-38, ss. 19 and 20.

Provincial Youth Justice Acts

Most jurisdictions have enacted legislation setting out the procedure to be used when dealing with young offenders who violate provincial laws. Some have adopted the same provisions as the previous federal Young Offenders Act and the more recent Youth Criminal Justice Act, including the granting of a discretionary power to a judge to exclude the public.[68] In Québec, a notable exception to this rule can be found in its Youth Protection Act, where a tribunal "must at all times admit to its hearings. . . any journalist who requests admission, unless it believes the journalist's presence would cause prejudice to the child."[69]

ACCESS TO ADMINISTRATIVE TRIBUNAL HEARINGS

When legislation creates a formal tribunal (for example, a labour board), but does not state whether its hearings or meetings are to be held in public, the decision as to public access is usually at the discretion of the tribunal members. Administrative tribunals, such as public boards, usually have the right to determine their own rules of procedure.

But the public has some limited rights of access to tribunal hearings. One Ontario case set out guidelines for access to statutory tribunals.[70] The case involved an arbitration board hearing of an allegation of wrongful dismissal against a newspaper. The tribunal participants were asked if the press and public could attend. One of the parties to the hearing objected and, on the strength of that one objection, the tribunal felt it therefore had to reject the request for public access.

The court, in reviewing the tribunal's decision, stated that the public has a legitimate interest in any hearing of a statutory tribunal. The court said it was an error in law for the tribunal to exclude the public simply because one party to the hearing objected. The court pointed to the English case of *Scott v. Scott*, which stands for the principle that a hearing of a judicial body, which has the potential of greatly affecting a person's rights,

---

68 This exclusion power can be found in Prince Edward Island: Youth Justice Act, R.S.P.E.I. 1988, c. Y-3, s. 17; Newfoundland and Labrador: Young Persons Offences Act, R.S.N.L. 1990, c. Y-1, s. 21; Nova Scotia: Youth Justice Act, S.N.S. 2001, c. 38, s. 31; Alberta: Youth Justice Act, R.S.A. 2000, c. Y-1, s. 25; Northwest Territories: Youth Justice Act, S.N.W.T. 2003, c. 31, s. 77; Yukon: Young Persons Offences Act, R.S.Y. 2002, c. 232, s. 34; Nunavut: Young Offenders Act, R.S.N.W.T. 1988, c. Y-1, s. 61.

69 R.S.Q. c. P-34.1, s. 82.

70 *Toronto Star v. Toronto Newspaper Guild* (1976), 73 D.L.R. (3d) 370 (Ont. Div. Ct.).

cannot be held *in camera* simply because the parties in a dispute consent to it.[71]

In the case of quasi-judicial bodies, such as this tribunal, the court held that while the tribunal has a discretionary power to allow public access, it's not compelled to bar the public merely because one party objects to the media's presence. The court went on to suggest that for public bodies that are purely administrative and don't act judicially, they need not, and perhaps should not, be held in public. The court said the board made a mistake and asked it to reconsider its decision in this case.

ACCESS TO PUBLIC, PRIVATE AND MUNICIPAL MEETINGS

Public Meetings

There's no law speaking to a general right of the public to attend a "public meeting." Presumably, a public meeting by definition invites any member of the public to attend. At any time, however, someone can be ejected or asked to leave by the convenors of the meeting, particularly if it's held on property owned or controlled by the convenors. A journalist refusing to leave after being told to could be charged with trespassing under provincial law. Even public meetings in public places will have someone present (for example, a policeman) who can eject unwanted people.

Private Meetings

The news media has no legal right to demand access to a private meeting, even if its topic is one of intense public interest. If a journalist were to gain entry to such a meeting, the same rules apply as for public meetings and he or she would have to leave if asked.

Another type of private meeting that's sometimes of interest to journalists is corporate shareholders' meetings. Some journalists have been quite clever in their attempts to avoid getting tossed out of a meeting. On one occasion, a reporter who wanted to attend a shareholders' meeting for a company, bought some shares. But when the company officers discovered the reporter was present, he was kicked out. There was little the journalist could do, short of embarking on an expensive lawsuit alleging that minority shareholder rights were stomped on.

---

71 Note 8, above. Also, see notes 9 and 10, above, for similar rulings.

Municipal Meetings

A somewhat different set of rules apply to municipal council and committee meetings. Every province has a provision in their Municipalities Act that expressly states that regular municipal council meetings shall be held in public.

However, in many cases the law also permits a council to hold its other meetings or debates in private (such as committee of the whole meetings). What this can mean is that decisions from those closed-door meetings only have to be ratified in open council and the actual debate on the resolution may be in private. Only the final decision (that is, the vote) is required by law to be held in public and no province demands public debate.

Legislation in most provinces also allows committee meetings to be held in private. In Ontario, this right to *in camera* proceedings is extended to boards of commissioners of police and school boards (however, local bylaws may be passed to ensure public access).

In 1988, an economic development committee of Ontario's Hamilton-Wentworth Regional Council tried to get around a council bylaw that all council and committee meetings be held in public by calling an important meeting an *"in camera* workshop." The workshop was to review the committee's terms of reference and "directions for the future." The local newspaper felt it was really a full committee meeting and went to court. The Ontario Court of Appeal agreed with the newspaper and declared the meeting illegal.[72]

ELECTRONIC ACCESS TO HEARINGS AND CAMERAS IN THE COURTS

In recent decades, the debate over allowing the broadcast of tribunal hearings, court proceedings and even government inquiries has become quite fierce, and shows few signs of any final resolution. For many years, Canadian journalists have felt like disadvantaged cousins as they've seen their American counterparts seemingly given extensive access to courtrooms and government proceedings. The U.S. approach even spawned Court TV, a specialty cable network that broadcasted trials live and featured various legal shows.[73] Meanwhile, in Canada, journalists must be satisfied with broadcasting the still occasional "experimental" trial, the reading of a

---

72 *Southam v. Hamilton-Wentworth Regional Council* (1988), 12 A.C.W.S. (3d) 181 (Ont. C.A.).

73 In 2007, Court TV rebranded itself as truTV and now features non-legal reality-based programming along with legal shows. Since 2001, a separate entity, CourtTV Canada, has offered some domestic legal-based news shows and U.S. entertainment programming.

high-profile judgment or a provincial Court of Appeal or Supreme Court of Canada hearing.

Yet, all is not what it appears to be. In the U.S., jurists and others still vigorously debate the merits of cameras in the courts. The 1995-96 murder trial of celebrity O.J. Simpson brought to the surface the deep divisions of opinion that have always existed in that country. Indeed, after the O.J. trial, there was a backlash against cameras as individual judges in several states said they would no longer allow them in their courtrooms because of concerns over fairness to the parties, grandstanding by lawyers and the general reputation of the justice system.

In actual fact, though, courts in the U.S. have generally exercised a great deal of caution when allowing cameras in the courts.[74] Some levels of U.S. courts don't allow cameras at all and most states have strict guidelines for broadcasters. For example, journalists usually rely on a pooled camera and its movements may be limited, such as avoiding shots of jurors. Certain types of proceedings, such as family law or commercial cases involving trade secrets, cannot be broadcast in some states. Even the U.S. Supreme Court, which helped pave the way for cameras in the courts, does not allow them in its own proceedings. That said, most states do allow some level of courtroom access for electronic media.

There are some signs that the concern of courts and governments over cameras in the courts and their impact on public opinion is easing. In 2007, Ontario's Attorney General announced that the province's Court of Appeal was planning a pilot project allowing appeals to be broadcast from a pooled audio and video feed. At the time of this publication, those broadcasts had not yet begun. Other courts, such as the Federal Court of Canada and provincial courts in British Columbia, Nova Scotia, Manitoba and Newfoundland and Labrador, have allowed occasional access to the courts by broadcasters. The Federal Court of Appeal allows audio and video, and has a detailed set of media guidelines for broadcasting hearings, provided a request is submitted to the Chief Justice of the court with reasonable advance notice.

In 2002, the Canadian Judicial Council "modified its stand" on broadcasting court proceedings and stated that it is only concerned with the impact on trial proceedings, not courts of appeal. Some of the Council's members believe broadcasts of trials will still affect witnesses, jurors and other parties to proceedings.

In Canada, electronic access to court and other tribunal hearings is largely left in the hands of the presiding judge or official, and many do

---

74 For an excellent discussion of this issue, see Henry, "Electronic Public Access to Court: A Proposal for its Implementation Today," in *The Media, the Courts and the Charter*, Carswell, 1986.

refuse access. That will change over time. In recent years, some high-profile public inquiries have granted access to broadcasters and that experience often convinces more judges and tribunal officials to experiment. Still, there is considerable opposition among the judiciary to cameras in the courts and until there is a landmark court ruling or shift in legislative thinking, electronic journalists will have to bid for access one case at a time.

Some recent rulings illustrate the difficulties in convincing judges to allow the electronic media inside courtrooms. In 2000, many in the media believed there was major breakthrough in judicial thinking when a B.C. judge wrote "the time has now arrived to permit the introduction of equipment designed to more accurately depict public events."[75]

The media's application to record and broadcast proceedings came after the Crown had rested and the defence was ready to begin its case. The judge received a formal request for permission to videotape and take photographs during the trial. The Crown and defence opposed the application, concerned about fairness to defence witnesses who would have to face the cameras while Crown witnesses did not. The defence lawyer was also concerned for the safety of the accused, who did not want to be publicly displayed.

The court noted there is no statutory prohibition in B.C. against filming or photographing a trial. In the past, the court noted, it had been a common law matter and was left up to the judge's discretion. The judge went on, saying the concerns of the past had largely been settled. As long as the news media use modern equipment that is quiet and not disruptive, concerns are addressed about specific witnesses on a case-by-case basis, and no one objects, the court said cameras should be allowed in the courtroom. The court added it wasn't concerned that the use of cameras in the middle of a trial would result in partial coverage. Despite these views, however, the judge believed there were legitimate concerns about cameras capturing testimony in this specific case. That said, the court ruled video and still cameras could record lawyers' submissions to the jury and the instructions to the jury.

What one judge giveth, another takes away. A year later in another B.C. case, a court dismissed the application by the national and local media to televise the trial of former Premier Glen Clark.[76] The judge agreed the news media does have a right under the Charter to gather news, but there is no specific right to record proceedings for transmission to the public. The judge was also not swayed by the fact that B.C.'s chief justice had issued guidelines for the use of cameras in the courts. Finding that studies on the

75 *R. v. Cho* (2000), 189 D.L.R. (4th) 180 (B.C. S.C.).
76 *R. v. Pilarinos and Clark* (2001), BCSC 1332 (B.C. S.C.).

effects of cameras in courts are "inconclusive," the judge ruled that not knowing the effect is reason enough to keep cameras out.

A related issue to cameras "in the courts" is the quandary of what to do about cameras and the news media operating "around the courts." In some provinces, such as Manitoba, Nova Scotia, Québec and Ontario, there is legislation, rules of court or other guidelines for allowable media activity on court property, such as in the hallways or outside the doors of a court-house.

In Ontario, for example, there is a formal offence for unauthorized audio and visual recordings within court buildings. Section 136 of Ontario's Courts of Justice Act prohibits the taking of photographs, motion pictures, audio recordings or other records capable of producing visual or aural representations by electronic means or otherwise:[77]

(i)   at a court hearing,
(ii) of any person entering or leaving the room in which a court hearing is to be or has been convened, or
(iii) of any person in the building in which a court hearing is to be or has been convened where there is reasonable ground for believing that the person is there for the purpose of attending or leaving the hearing. . . .

The Ontario law does permit reporters to use audio tape recorders to assist them in taking notes, but the recordings cannot be used in a broadcast. An Ontario judge presiding at a court hearing may authorize pictures or audio recordings in connection with ceremonial proceedings or in connection with educational or instructive purposes with the permission of the judge, parties and witnesses. The Ontario legislation also states that this law doesn't prohibit someone from "unobtrusively" making handwritten notes or sketches at a court hearing.[78]

There has been one case challenging this law as an infringement of the media's rights under the Charter.[79] A CBC journalist had instructed a camera operator to shoot pictures of a participant in a trial coming out of the courtroom. The CBC argued that the offence created by the statute was unconstitutional and violated the freedom of the press guarantee in the Charter. A provincial appeal court agreed that the law did infringe the media's Charter right, but ruled that it was a demonstrably justified and reasonable limit on the press. The court said the right to a fair trial was paramount and cameras in the courts could have a negative effect on witnesses and jurors. As a small consolation, the court did rule that the law's

77 R.S.O. 1990, c. C.43, ss. 136(1), (3).
78 *Ibid.*, s. 136(2).
79 *R. v. Squires* (1989), 69 C.R. (3d) 337 (Ont. Dist. Ct.), affirmed (1992), 18 C.R. (4th) 22 (Ont. C.A.).

requirement for an educational component in granting access was unnecessary and declared it to be of no force and effect. In 1993, the Supreme Court of Canada refused leave to appeal this decision.

More recently, the issue of restricting media access in certain parts of courthouses and around the buildings has arisen in Québec. In a 2006 case, various media organizations challenged a series of changes to rules governing media activity on courthouse property.[80] Some of the key questions included:

- Should the media be permitted to solicit interviews and use cameras without restriction in the public areas of Québec courthouses?

- Does the court's authority stop at the door of the courtroom, regardless of what awaits individuals involved in court proceedings once they leave?

- Must the rights of those involved in court proceedings yield to the rights of the media in the courthouses?

In 2004 and 2005, new rules were put in place that restricted conducting interviews and the use of cameras to very specific marked areas in courthouses. Reporters could no longer "hinder or disturb the free circulation of users in public areas," "pursue persons with cameras or microphones inside the courthouses," or conduct interviews at courtroom exits or in areas adjacent to courtrooms. The media claimed the new rules violated their Charter rights, allowed parties in court proceedings to dodge them and forced electronic journalists to use areas that resulted in sub-standard video quality.

While somewhat sympathetic, the court hearing the media petition dismissed their complaints and held the impairment of freedom of expression and freedom of the press is "very minimal" and justifiable in the proper administration of justice.

As noted, administrative tribunals, such as public inquiries, have been more flexible and willing to consider electronic access. In Saskatchewan in 1994, the CBC asked for and got permission to record a human rights tribunal's proceedings for television.[81]

Sexual discrimination complainants had been brought against an employer and a union. The board ruled that while the presence of cameras had the potential to add to the stress, discomfort, and reluctance of witnesses,

---

80 *Société Radio-Canada c. Québec (Procureur général)* (2006), 2006 CarswellQue 14112, 2006 CarswellQue 9008 (S.C.).

81 *Andreen v. Dairy Producers Co-operative Ltd.* (1994), 22 C.H.R.R. D/80 (Sask. Bd. of Inquiry).

those factors should be balanced with the benefits of open proceedings that promoted the underlying policy objectives of the Human Rights Code. The board said the open process "had the potential to de-mystify the process in the eyes of the public." One camera was allowed in the room and a witness had the right to request the camera be turned off during that witness's testimony. The board also retained the overall right to order the camera turned off or to have it removed.

CAN YOU PUBLISH DETAILS OF CLOSED DOOR HEARINGS?

Sometimes, the general public is barred from a hearing to protect the interests of innocent parties or to allow a nervous witness to testify freely. Sometimes, journalists are allowed to stay, while the general public is shown out. Or a participant in a closed door hearing may decide to tell a journalist what went on.

The question that commonly arises then is, can you publish the details of a closed door hearing or meeting?

The answer is generally, yes — but with a caveat or two. In judicial proceedings, for example, the common law rule is that there's no contempt of court when publishing details of *in camera* hearings unless a ban on publication has been issued by the court. Under the common law, an order excluding the public or imposing a publication ban is typically issued in cases involving wards of the state, trade secrets, matters involving national security or where a public session would defeat the whole object of the proceeding.[82] Indeed, this has been incorporated into the legislation of at least one province. Ontario's Courts of Justice Act expressly states the disclosure of information relating to a proceeding heard in the absence of the public isn't a contempt of court, unless the court expressly prohibited the disclosure of the information.[83]

Of course, one shouldn't forget in judicial proceedings there may also be occasions in which a jury, but not the public, will be asked to leave the courtroom while lawyers debate points of law or admissibility of evidence. None of the details of these "closed" hearings may be reported until after the jury retires to consider a verdict (see s. 648 of the Criminal Code).

There are risks of another kind, however, in publishing details of *in camera* proceedings. The primary concern is defamation. For example, Québec's Press Act expressly states that reports of defamatory statements

---

82 Note 72, above.
83 Note 77, above, s. 135(3).

made in *in camera* hearings are not privileged.[84] The same rule is suggested in the common law provinces, where only reports of open court proceedings are protected from defamation actions. Similarly, publishing defamatory remarks uttered in *in camera* or private meetings is also not likely protected by an absolute or qualified privilege.

There may also be specific statutory restrictions on publishing the details of closed hearings of bodies other than courts, such as coroners' inquests or criminal injuries compensation boards.

AN ACCESS TO HEARINGS AND MEETINGS CHECKLIST

1. There is a general presumption in law that the public should have access to meetings or hearings of official bodies that act on behalf of the public and deal with matters of public interest.

2. The following Criminal Code sections may be used to exclude the public from court hearings:
    (i)   Section 486(1) affirms a court's general right to exclude members of the public on certain occasions;
    (ii) Section 537(1)(h) states that a justice holding a preliminary hearing may exclude everyone other than the prosecutor, the accused and their counsel;
    (iii) Section 276, which concerns sexual assault trials, contains a subsection stating that the public and jury must be excluded during a *voir dire* concerning the admissibility of evidence of the sexual activity of the victim; and
    (iv) Section 672.5 concerns disposition hearings for individuals incarcerated after being found not guilty of crimes by reason of insanity or other mental illness. Presiding officials may exclude the public or a specific person where it is considered by the review board or a court to be "in the best interests of the accused and not contrary to the public interest."

3. Section 132 of the new Youth Criminal Justice Act states that a judge may exclude the public from all or any part of proceedings in certain circumstances.

4. Most federal and provincial judicial or quasi-judicial tribunals have the authority to exclude the public from hearings.

---

84 R.S.Q. 1977, c. P-19, s. 10(*d*).

5. The public has limited rights of access to administrative tribunals. If legislation creating the tribunal does not state if its hearings or meetings are to be held in public, the decision as to public access is usually at the discretion of the tribunal members. A key factor may also be whether the tribunal has a judicial or quasi-judicial function.

6. As a rule, a public meeting may be attended by anyone. At any time, however, someone can be ejected or asked to leave by the convenors of the meeting.

7. Every province has a provision in municipal laws stating that regular municipal council meetings are to be held in public. However, in many cases, the law also permitted a council to hold its other meetings or debates in private (such as committee of the whole meetings).

8. The electronic news media have no right of access to many court hearings or tribunals. The decision to allow access is in the hands of the presiding judge or tribunal official.

9. The common law rule is that there is no contempt of court when publishing details of *in camera* or closed-door hearings unless a ban on publication has been issued by the court. Journalists should still be careful since publication of details of closed-door proceedings may not be protected under defamation laws.

9

GAINING ACCESS TO COURT DOCUMENTS

Should the news media have an unrestricted right to examine and publish any or all documents, exhibits, video or audio recordings, and other records submitted to a court once they are part of the public record? Should it matter if the request for access comes before a trial begins, during the proceeding or after its conclusion? Does it make a difference if it's a civil or criminal proceeding? And, what about the rights of "innocent persons" named in court documents, such as search warrants that result in nothing found?

These are difficult questions and the challenge for Canada's courts and lawmakers in recent years has been finding common ground to make these decisions. Of the many areas of media law affected by the Charter of Rights and Freedoms, this has been among those undergoing the most significant changes recently. As discussed here, "court documents" include exhibits, affidavits, transcripts of examinations for discovery, personal records or any documents submitted by the parties in a civil or criminal action.

The Supreme Court of Canada has stated in very clear terms that there is a presumption of "openness" in the news media's and public's right of access to courts and court documents. An important 2005 ruling allowing *The Toronto Star* and other news media access to pre-trial and investigatory information begins with this now much-quoted line: "In any constitutional climate, the administration of justice thrives on exposure to light — and withers under a cloud of secrecy."[1]

Thanks to the Supreme Court and pioneering efforts by enlightened courts in a handful of provinces, gone are the days when it had to be said that journalists have no common law right of access to court documents unless the privilege is set out in a statute or a court rule. At one time, not long ago, some courts even suggested the public itself had no right of access to court documents.[2]

Yet, despite the Supreme Court's clear messages in *Toronto Star* and other recent cases dealing with the media's right to court information, access requests continue to fuel heated debate. In too many cases, the media are being required to mount formal challenges of orders that seal files and other access denials by courts and their administrative managers.

Among the latest tactics used to argue against openness is the claim that the information sought would harm the interests of "innocent persons." As discussed below, some rulings have unfortunately expanded the definition of innocent persons beyond the traditional class of the vulnerable, such

---

1   *Toronto Star Newspapers Ltd. v. Ontario*, [2005] 2 S.C.R. 188.

2   In *R. v. Thomson Newspapers Ltd.* (1984), 4 C.R.D. 525.40-01 (Ont. S.C.J.), the court held the guarantee of freedom of the press in the Charter [Canadian Charter of Rights and Freedoms, Part I of the Constitution Act, 1982, being Schedule B of the Canada Act 1982 (U.K.), 1982, c. 11] gives the media and public no general constitutional right to compel the court to give access to any documents and no right to inspect, copy or photograph items before the court.

   This outdated, protectionist attitude stretches back through the centuries. In a note to the English case of *Caddy v. Barlow* (1827), 1 Man. & Ry. K.B. 275 at 279 (Eng. K.B.), it said only "interested parties" (that is, litigants) may have access to court records for their "necessary use and benefit."

   But, in recent times, some courts have said there is, at least, a limited presumption favouring a public right of access to court documents. In *Pacific Press Ltd. v. Vickers & Palmer* (1985), 60 B.C.L.R. 91 (S.C.), the court held the public's right to know and have access to court documents takes precedence over the privacy of the litigants, particularly when a case has formally ended (that is, the appeal period has passed). The court granted a newspaper access to the court files on a case in which an "infant" sued the Crown for damages after being placed in a foster home. However, the court used its inherent authority to ban the publication of names, locations and particulars of abuse mentioned in the files.

as children and adults in need of protection, to individuals under criminal investigation and, in one case, alleged members of the Hell's Angels.[3]

As will be shown below, rights of access to court documents can vary wildly from province to province, between courts in the same province and even on a county or city-by-city basis. Ease of access for news media is also highly dependent upon the stage of the court proceedings, nature of the proceedings, documents requested and, to some degree, the working relationship between the journalist and the court personnel. Strangely, rights of access can also differ depending on which form of media makes the request, with broadcast media having a particularly difficult time these days getting access to audio and visual court exhibits.

Generally, there are several variables that will determine whether a person who is not a party to an action can gain access to court records. At the heart of the restrictions is the court's concern about prejudicing a fair trial or interfering with the course of justice, which the Supreme Court says must now be balanced with the media's right to freedom of expression.

It is also important to remember that there is a difference between access and publication of court information. The court may permit full access to court records but, as explained in the chapter on publication bans, may temporarily or permanently prohibit dissemination of the information in the proceedings.[4]

---

3 In *R. v. Angel Acres Recreation & Festival Property Ltd.* (2004), 2004 CarswellBC 1575, [2004] B.C.J. No. 1428 (C.A.), two individuals who were allegedly members of a local Hell's Angels club were named in the Information to Obtain a Search Warrant but were not the subject of an investigation or criminal charges. The judge considering a media application to lift a sealing order and publication ban determined the two people named were innocent parties who should not be disclosed in published reports. The appeal court agreed and said, while stigmatization of innocent persons was important, the judge had also correctly noted the investigation focused on the Hell's Angels organization rather than individuals per se and the search warrant was executed on premises owned by the Hell's Angels rather than private dwellings.

4 See *Potash Corp. of Saskatchewan Inc. v. Barton* (2001), 207 Sask. R. 250 (C.A. [In Chambers]), in which court files remained open for public inspection while a publication ban was in place until the end of appeal proceedings.

THE SUPREME COURT'S EVOLVING POSITION

MacIntyre and *Vickery*

To understand the confusion surrounding the public's right to access court documents, it helps to know about a few Supreme Court of Canada decisions in the past three decades on the right to access court information.

First, the Supreme Court decided in a 1982 case, *MacIntyre v. Nova Scotia (Attorney General)*,[5] that once a search warrant was executed, the warrant and information upon which it was issued must be made available to the public and news media unless anyone seeking a sealing order can demonstrate public access would subvert the ends of justice.

At that time, the court said the public has no right to see an executed search warrant that finds nothing and no right to a warrant that is yet to be executed. Also, the *MacIntyre* case did not deal with other issues of the public's right to examine court documents, but the judges did say there is a strong presumption in favour of the public having access to court documents.

In the years that followed, lower courts and governments were all over the map in terms of whether the media should have access to court documents. Parliament, for example, tried unsuccessfully, with a 1985 amendment to the Criminal Code, to limit publication of and access to warrant information where charges have not been laid formally. Soon after the amendment, courts declared it unconstitutional, ruling it infringed on freedom of the press.[6]

Then, in 1991, the Supreme Court released a decision that has since become a thorn in the side of proponents of openness and media access to court information. In *Vickery v. Nova Scotia (Prothonotary, Supreme Court)*,[7] the court considered whether the public (news media, that is) should have access to audio cassettes containing an alleged confession and a videotape of an alleged re-enactment of a killing. While the accused was first convicted at trial of second-degree murder, a provincial appeal court later ruled the audio and video evidence was inadmissible, the confessions were forced and overturned the conviction.

The question then was, with the accused's trial and appeal at an end, should the media have the right to obtain a copy of the tapes? Should it

---

5   [1982] 1 S.C.R. 175.

6   *Canadian Newspapers Co. v. Canada (Attorney General)* (1986), 32 D.L.R. (4th) 292 (Ont. H.C.). The Québec Court of Appeal confirmed s. 487.2 is unconstitutional and of no force and effect in *Thibault c. Demers* (2001), 198 D.L.R. (4th) 58 (Que. C.A.), leave to appeal to the Supreme Court of Canada refused (2001), 2001 CarswellQue 2033, 2001 CarswellQue 2034 (S.C.C.).

7   [1991] 1 S.C.R. 671.

make any difference if the accused is acquitted?

The answer was "no" to the first question and "yes" to the second. Even though the tapes were admitted into evidence and reported on during the trial, a 6-3 majority of the Supreme Court ultimately held that the privacy interests of a person acquitted of a crime outweighed the public's right of access to exhibits found inadmissible. The open court principle, the majority reasoned, was fulfilled during the trial by allowing members of the public, including the media, to attend and hear the evidence at that time.

The majority also believed the accused and Crown had a proprietary interest in the tapes, since they created them jointly and the court was responsible as a "custodian" for their safekeeping. With the conviction overturned, reasoned the majority, "the subsequent release and publication of selected exhibits is fraught with the risk of unfairness."

The ruling went on to state that "curtailment of public accessibility is justified where there is a need to protect the innocent." That latter statement and the ruling as a whole would later prove to be a rallying point for anyone opposed to media access to court information. The majority also unfortunately declined to consider whether this restriction on inadmissible evidence infringed the freedom of the press right under the Charter, since it had not been "developed in the courts below."

Thus, the majority in *Vickery* determined that access to court records may be limited based on four factors:

1. Nature of the exhibits as part of the court record (another party may hold a proprietary interest in the exhibit);

2. The court has the jurisdiction to inquire into and regulate the use to be made of the exhibits;

3. The exhibits were already open to public scrutiny during the trial; and

4. The resulting value of public scrutiny or access if granted at a particular stage of proceedings (for instance, the value of public scrutiny may be reduced after hearings have ended).

In a powerful dissent, three justices of the Supreme Court made it clear that, in their view, "there can be no doubt that there exists in Canada a common law right of access to court documents." Those judges argued openness of the courts must prevail and that access should not be denied on the grounds the tapes were found to be inadmissible since "the public has a right to know what was excluded by the appellate court and the reason for its exclusion." To not allow access, they suggested, would permit the courts to operate in secret.

Many legal scholars and media lawyers now consider the majority's decision in *Vickery* to be bad law that has been refined by today's Supreme Court in subsequent rulings advocating more openness and media access. As a result of *Vickery*, however, some courts and governments, such as in Ontario, still hold on to an outdated notion the Supreme Court favours the rights of the accused and the "innocent" over those of the media and the public.

Dagenais, Mentuck and *Toronto Star*

Fast forward now to the Supreme Court's ruling in the 2005 case[8] involving *The Toronto Star* and other media seeking access to court-sealed search warrants and informations in an ongoing investigation of a meat packing company. The plant in Aylmer, Ontario, was suspected in 2003 of using dead cattle unsuitable for human consumption. The investigation was of great public concern, but the Crown brought an application for a time-limited court order to seal search documents until the investigation could be completed.

The media challenged the sealing order. The reviewing judge agreed to quash the order, but required documents be edited to avoid disclosing the identity of a confidential informant. The Ontario Court of Appeal upheld that decision and agreed editing was needed to protect the informant.

The Crown believed both Ontario courts were wrong and that the public should not have access to any information at all during the investigative phase of a criminal matter. The question put to the Supreme Court by the Crown was, what test should be used in deciding whether public access should be allowed to search warrant materials in pre-charge or investigative phases?

The Supreme Court ruled both of the lower courts were correct in applying the so-called *Dagenais/Mentuck* test to pre-charge or investigative matters. The 1994 *Dagenais*[9] ruling, later somewhat modified by the 2001 *Mentuck*[10] decision, was an important landmark in media law. In that case, the Supreme Court emphasized the importance of the Charter's guarantee of freedom of the press in deciding whether to ban publication of or access to court information. The majority in *Dagenais* stated freedom of the press may take precedence over an accused's right to a fair trial at times and judicial orders in criminal proceedings must be as limited as possible, if at all necessary.

---

8 Note 1, above.
9 *Dagenais v. Canadian Broadcasting Corp.*, [1994] 3 S.C.R. 835.
10 *R. v. Mentuck*, [2001] 3 S.C.R. 442.

In *Mentuck*, the court reformulated its test for issuing court orders that restrict access and publication by requiring judges to consider the following factors:

1. such an order is necessary in order to prevent a serious risk to the proper administration of justice because reasonably alternative measures will not prevent the risk; and

2. the salutary effects of the publication ban outweigh the deleterious effects on the rights and interests of the parties and the public, including the effects on the right to free expression, the right of the accused to a fair and public trial, and the efficacy of the administration of justice.

In *Toronto Star*, the Supreme Court sent an even stronger message to lower courts and legislators by ruling the *Dagenais/Mentuck* test and its presumptions in favour of access apply to "all discretionary court orders that limit freedom of expression and freedom of the press in relation to legal proceedings." That is, not just publication bans and sealing orders, but orders concerning access to any and all court records, including exhibits.

Contrary to the *Vickery* decision, the Supreme Court said there is, first and foremost, a presumption that all court proceedings are "open" in Canada and that public or media access should only be barred when a court, in its discretion, "concludes that disclosure would subvert the ends of justice or unduly impair its proper administration." If any party to a proceeding believes access should be limited, that party must prove to the court's satisfaction the order is necessary because there is a "serious risk" to the proper administration of justice with no reasonable alternatives available. That party also needs to demonstrate that the need for the restriction or ban outweighs the harmful effects it will have on the press, the accused and the justice system.

In this case, the court said, the Crown's evidence in support of the application to delay media access "amounted to a generalized assertion of possible disadvantage to an ongoing investigation." The court said anyone seeking to limit public access to legal proceedings must rely on more than a generalized assertion that publicity will harm the investigation. "The party must, at the very least, allege a serious and specific risk to the integrity of the criminal investigation. The Crown has not discharged its burden in this case."

It is important to note from *Toronto Star* that the Supreme Court is still not saying access by the public to all court information is guaranteed or absolute. Indeed, it stated: "Under certain conditions, public access to confidential or sensitive information related to court proceedings will endanger and not protect the integrity of our system of justice. A temporary shield will in some cases suffice; in others, permanent protection is warranted."

That said, the Supreme Court has made it clear that, subject to each court's well-founded discretion, there is a presumption of openness and access.

Protecting the "Innocent"

As noted, the Supreme Court has made strong statements on the common law and Charter-based presumptions of openness over the course of several recent decisions. The court made it clear pre-charge investigations and even the fairness of trials themselves may not be paramount to maintaining freedom of the press without sufficient proof of serious potential or actual risks to the justice system.

A common thread or exception, however, in many of the Supreme Court's rulings has been the desire to protect the innocent. Unfortunately, opponents of openness are increasingly seizing on this exception to defeat access applications. As a result, access requests are still refused in cases involving warrants that uncover nothing, individuals who are acquitted, and individuals charged but not convicted.[11]

The Ontario Court of Appeal recently set out some guidelines on protecting the "innocent" that, with hope, will evolve to be used by other courts.[12] In 2007, the court received an appeal from a public inquiry struck to look into the response of the justice system and other public institutions to allegations of historical abuse of young people in Cornwall, Ontario. The inquiry commissioner refused to impose a media ban on publishing the name of an Episcopal Corporation employee giving evidence at the inquiry. The employee was the subject of sexual abuse allegations and charges, but had been acquitted of the charges in 2001. Claiming to be an "innocent

11 In *Toronto Star v. R.* (2006), 2006 CarswellOnt 8787, [2006] O.J. No. 5448 (S.C.J.), the newspaper was investigating a large provider of methadone treatments funded, in large part, by Ontario taxpayer dollars. It sought access to sealed search warrant information. In ruling targets of the warrants were innocent persons, the court issued a partial ban allowing the press access to the sealed information but prohibiting publication of the names of the targets or information identifying them. The ban would only be in effect until and unless charges were laid against any target. In *Ottawa Citizen Group Inc. v. Ontario* (2005), 197 C.C.C. (3d) 514 (Ont. C.A.), the appeal court quashed a trial judge's sealing order and allowed access to search informations, but issued a publication ban prohibiting disclosure of the innocent persons named in the documents. The appeal court said this "alternative measure" was consistent with press freedom and open court concepts while also balancing fairness to the individuals affected.

12 *Episcopal Corp. of the Diocese of Alexandria-Cornwall v. Cornwall Public Inquiry Commissioner* (2007), 2007 CarswellOnt 112, [2007] O.J. No. 100 (C.A.).

person," the individual requested a publication ban on his name to protect his reputation and privacy. The commissioner applied the *Dagenais/Mentuck* test and found:

1. the individual's name was relevant to the mandate of the inquiry;

2. the individual had failed to provide medical evidence to substantiate the detrimental effect he claimed disclosure of his identity would have on his health; and

3. it was incorrect to presume the public would ignore his acquittal and make unfair or unfounded conclusions.

A reviewing judge and, later, the Court of Appeal, both upheld the publication ban refusal, dismissing the argument that it would protect the innocent. The appeal court, specifically, touched on several key points in determining when limits on openness are justified to protect the innocent:

1. Presumption of innocence and protection of the innocent are important interests that should be taken into consideration in the first branch of the *Dagenais/Mentuck* test (that is, requiring the order is necessary to prevent a serious risk to the proper administration of justice and reasonably alternative measures will not prevent the risk);

2. Presumption of innocence and protection of the innocent do not supercede the principle of open courts in all cases and depend on the circumstances of each case;

3. *Vickery* does not stand for the proposition that the protection of the innocent must inevitably prevail over openness and freedom of expression;

4. Here, the fact the individual has been acquitted will likely come out in testimony;

5. It cannot be assumed the public, knowing of the acquittal, will jump to unfair or unfounded allegations about the person;

6. The individual here has already been subject to a considerable amount of publicity;

7. The individual's name was relevant to the inquiry's mandate; and

8.   While there is an element of unfairness in permitting the publication of the identity of a person who is acquitted and a risk the employee's reputation may be damaged, the court believed the refusal was reasonable when weighed against the need for openness.

The appeal court's comments on *Vickery* and similar cases are particularly interesting. "One must always have regard to the particular context in which the request for a publication ban arises. In [*Vickery* and other cases], all proceedings had come to an end and the publication bans had no impact upon the openness or successful operation of an ongoing proceeding. In the present case we are dealing with a public inquiry called to clear the air of allegations of conspiracy and cover-up and to 'encourage community healing and reconciliation.' Openness is a factor relevant to the Commission's success in accomplishing that mandate, a factor not present in the cases upon which the appellant relies."

Ideally, in the near future, the Supreme Court will see fit to deal with an appropriate test for protecting the innocent and also put *Vickery* to rest.

A search warrant was issued and executed in a police station during the investigation of a police officer. Materials were seized in the search, but the accused was not charged with any offence. A newspaper applied for access to the search documents and disclosure of edited materials. Since the officer was not charged, will be the media application be successful?

Yes. In this recent British Columbia case,[13] the court of appeal allowed the media application, stating that while the fact that the accused was not charged was important, it was not the only consideration. Here, the failure of authorities to lay charges against a police officer in the performance of his duties was a matter of public interest and the individual's privacy rights were not a determining factor since the investigation focused only on his public duties.

MODEL POLICY FOR ACCESS TO COURT RECORDS

There is no question that more courts now recognize or pay some heed to a presumptive public right of access to exhibits and documents. An example of an enlightened approach by one court was the protocol accepted by the judge presiding over the grisly and high-profile 2007 trial of Robert

---

13   *Phillips v. Vancouver Sun* (2004), 238 D.L.R. (4th) 167 (B.C. C.A.).

Pickton, who was charged with murdering six Vancouver women and was facing a second trial on 20 counts of first-degree murder at the time of this publication.[14]

The judge agreed "it would be advantageous to both the Court and the media to set in place a system to facilitate the orderly access to exhibits without the necessity of bringing an application each time access was sought." While the media favoured a protocol that would categorize each exhibit as it was entered into the court record (unlimited access, view-only access or no access), concerns were raised about the voluminous nature of the exhibits, the need to edit the media's copies to protect the privacy interests of third parties, and financial cost of producing copies for each exhibit.

The court favoured a "request-driven" protocol. Members of accredited media at the trial could seek access to an exhibit by first indicating interest in writing using a simple court form. Court staff would then make copies of the form and provide it to the Crown and defence. The lawyers would then suggest one of the following categories for an exhibit:

1. unlimited access (accredited media may view, copy and publish the exhibit);

2. view-only access (accredited media may view but not copy or publish the exhibit);

3. conditional access (accredited media may view the exhibit but copying and publication of the exhibit may be subject to specified conditions); and

4. no access (the exhibit is not available for viewing, copying or publication).

Then, the lawyers' submissions would be returned to the judge, who would make a decision on access to the exhibit. If the Crown and defence lawyers disagree, the judge would hear submissions at a time when the jury was not present. Similarly, the media could apply to change the designation of any exhibit; as noted, this is a very progressive approach that says a lot about how far we have come.

Generally, many Canadian courts are interested in formulating a standard approach to dealing with media requests. The Canadian Judicial Council, which governs members of Canada's superior courts, has proposed a

---

14 The protocol ruling is set out in *R. v. Pickton* (2007), 2007 CarswellBC 1200, [2007] B.C.J. No. 1130 (S.C.).

model policy for access to court records. The policy was developed by its technology advisory committee and unveiled in 2005. While it has no force of law and is only a template for others to consider, this excerpted version is instructive for its statements about presumptions of openness and public access (the comments in "Discussion" are the Council's own):

Model Policy for Access to Court Records in Canada (Excerpted)

Access

4.1 Presumption of Access
Members of the public have presumptive right of access to all court records.

Discussion
The access policy should clearly state the principle of public access to court records. It is placed first in this section in order to emphasize the importance of the open courts principle.

4.2 Fees
Fees should not impede access under this policy.

Discussion
Tailored access to court information, remotely and in electronic format, might require the acquisition and operation of advanced information management systems, and in some jurisdictions the implementation of such systems might not be possible without asking users to contribute. However, case management systems may also reduce court administration costs, and overall may result in global savings. Those savings should serve the purpose of open courts and contribute to the reduction of access fees. The court should at the very least make sure that traditional access on the court premises will remain possible at no extra cost for members of the public.

4.3 Existence of a Case File
Members of the public are entitled to know that a case file exists, even when a case file is sealed or subject to a non-publication order.

Discussion
Public knowledge of the existence of a case file is a minimal requirement for openness, this being all the more important when the file is sealed. In such cases, the disclosure of the existence of a case file should be made in a manner that does not disclose its content. However, it must be stated that as provided for in Section 1.2.4 of this model policy, this section is subject to any applicable statutory provision prohibiting the disclosure of the existence of a file, such as any applicable provision related to national security.

4.4 Format of Records
Members of the public are entitled to access court records in the format in which they are maintained.

Discussion
This model policy allows for a progressive transition from traditional forms of access to more advanced technologies, namely from paper records to digital documents. However, each court may want to state more specifically which formats of access are actually provided to the public, e.g. paper, electronic, or both.

4.5 Search Functions
When accessing court records, members of the public shall be provided with appropriate search functions that allow for efficient research of court records but also limit the risk of improper use of personal information.

Discussion
Search functions should be made available to users who have access to court records. The availability of search tools should depend upon the type of court record accessed and the level of risk of misuse of information associated with the means of access provided. Search tools can be designed in a manner that limits the technical possibility of aggregation of information and secondary uses that are not related to the rationale for open access to court records, such as direct marketing solicitations. Such limitations include allowing searches only in certain fields of information and not allowing full text searches.

4.6 Type of Record and Means of Access
4.6.1 Judgments
Members of the public shall have on-site access and, where available, remote access to all judgments.

Discussion
The access policy should provide for broad public access to every judgment rendered by the court, subject to any applicable statutory or court-ordered publication ban. Online publication of judgments containing personal information about vulnerable persons involved in certain categories of cases, such as children and adults in need of protection, is a controversial issue. The evaluation of the level of risk associated with the publication of sensitive personal information about these innocent persons differs from one jurisdiction to another, as ascertained by variations in applicable restrictions on publication and disclosure of records throughout Canada. Many jurisdictions already provide for such protection by way of legislation. In jurisdictions where such restrictions are not put in place, judges are sometimes reluctant to post the full text of decisions on the internet.

4.6.2 Docket Information
Members of the public shall have both on-site and, where available, remote access to docket information, provided that personal data identifiers are not made remotely accessible.

Discussion

The access policy should provide for broad public access to docket information, which is essential for ensuring the openness of court proceedings. However, given the fact that the docket may contain personal data identifiers, it is important that relevant docket information be accessible in a way that does not disclose at the same time such personal data identifiers.

4.6.3 Case Files
Parties shall have both on-site and, where available, remote and registered access to their own case file. Members of the public shall only have on-site access to case files, unless otherwise provided in this access policy.

Discussion

Case files are the repositories of all documents pertaining to the court's cases. These documents include information such as personal data identifiers and other personally identifiable data, business proprietary information, details about financial situations and medical conditions of individuals, affidavits, exhibits, many of which are only partially relevant for the disposition of the case. The pleadings may also contain unsubstantiated and sometimes outrageous allegations, which may provide little assistance to the public's understanding of the judicial process or even be defamatory in nature.

Consequently, there are many risks to individual and public rights and interests associated with unrestricted remote access to materials contained in the case file, and often unclear benefit with regard to the open courts principle. The access policy should grant the parties with all available means of access to their own case file. However, as far as the public is concerned, access to such information should be limited to the court premises, except for those records that a specific court determines should be made remotely available to the public pursuant to Section 4.6.4, below, or for those persons who are granted extended access pursuant to Section 5, below.

Several jurisdictions have enacted statutory provisions that prohibit any public disclosure of certain sensitive materials found in case files such as financial statements or medical reports. For those jurisdictions where there is no such legal framework, it may be appropriate for courts to include similar restrictions in their access policy. Not all documents in the case file will raise the same level of concern regarding remote public access. If any court wants to only grant remote public access to part of their case files then they can use Section 4.6.4, below, to list the types of documents for which this type of access is available.

4.6.4 Other Court Records

In addition to the records already listed in this policy, members of the public shall have remote access, where available, to those court records, or portions thereof, listed in this subsection.

Discussion
This subsection of this model policy contemplates the possibility that specific courts may determine that some types of records can be made remotely available to the public without engaging serious risks to individual privacy, security, or to the proper administration of justice. If a specific court makes such distinctions between types of court records, then their policy should contain subsections listing those records. If a specific court does not make such distinctions, then this subsection is not needed.

Extended Access
5.1 Request for Extended Access

Any member of the public may make a request for access to a portion of the court record that is otherwise restricted pursuant to this policy. The request shall be made in the form prescribed by the court. In deciding whether or not access should be granted, and what specific terms and conditions should be imposed, including the possibility of registered access, the following criteria shall be taken into consideration:

- the connection between the purposes for which access is sought and the rationale for the constitutional right to open courts;
- the potential detrimental impact on the rights of individuals and on the proper administration of justice, if the request is granted; and
- the adequacy of existing legal or non-legal norms, and remedies for their breach, if improper use is made of the information contained in the court records to which access is granted. This includes, but is not restricted to, existing privacy laws and professional norms such as journalistic ethics.

Discussion
The access policy should be adaptable to the particular needs of certain members of the public. When a member of the public seeks access to court records by means that are not otherwise granted in Section 4, above, the court should be able to respond in a timely way to administrative requests for extended access. Such requests will typically be made by individuals who have a professional interest in accessing court record information with min-imal restrictions, such as journalists and researchers, but any member of the public should be able to make a request.

When granted, extended access will typically be governed by an "access agreement". Such an agreement may include terms and conditions primarily designed to minimize the risks that extended access will be used to undermine the privacy and security rights of individuals or the proper administration of justice. Such terms and conditions could provide for the rights and obligations

of the user regarding registered access, applicable fees, etc. If remote elec-
tronic access to case files is granted, a provision prohibiting massive down-
loading of files might be included.

Since it is foreseeable that certain categories of individuals will ask for
extended access, such as academics, law researchers or journalists, the court
may design boilerplate access agreements adapted to those categories of
users.

COURT RULES ON ACCESS TO RECORDS

Generally, it is up to each jurisdiction's courts and even judges individually to make rules for access to court records. In some provinces,
legislation establishing the various courts often speaks to the principle of
openness and public accessibility. Typically, on payment of a prescribed
fee, "a person is entitled to see any document filed in a civil proceeding in
a court, unless an Act or an order of the court provides otherwise."[15] The
legislation usually gives judges the discretion to seal selected information
so that it does not form part of the public record, such as personal financial
data.

It is also worth noting that courts are not subject to the privacy legislation found in most provinces and federally. Privacy laws exempt courts
from rules governing the possession and control of private information on
individuals. Courts are also unique in that they can and often will ask about
the use an individual will make of a court record and a reason for the access
request. This is in fulfillment of the court's role as a custodian of evidence
and records.

That said, court administrations in several provinces have taken significant steps to create clear and often progressive policies on access to
court records, including exhibits, transcripts and reports. At the time of this
publication, some leading jurisdictions in terms of providing guidelines for
media and public access are Manitoba, Nova Scotia, Prince Edward Island
and Saskatchewan.

Nova Scotia's media guidelines, which can be found on the Courts of
Nova Scotia Web site (www.courts.ns.ca), were developed by a media
liaison committee with ongoing input from working journalists and judges.[16]
Importantly, the court begins its guidelines with the statement: "As a general
rule, all court documents in all courts are a matter of public record unless a
legislative provision or court order restricts public access."

---

15 For example, s. 58(1) of the Supreme Court Act, R.S.P.E.I. 1988, c. S-10.
16 *Guidelines for Press, Media, and Public Access to the Courts of Nova Scotia Court*
    Records (Draft 02.22.06).

The 51-page document covers common questions and issues arising between court administrations and the media, explaining how to request access, restrictions on public access, search fees, proper courtroom behaviour and forms for making requests. It also provides guidance on its different access rules for various types of court records and documents, such as its child abuse registry, transcripts, dockets, Court of Appeal records, Family Court records, search warrants, etc.

As in most other provinces, Nova Scotia's courts do not provide unfettered access. Most records and documents must be viewed and read "in the presence of Court staff" and cannot be removed from the office for later return. During trials, for example, the guidelines suggest access may be more difficult since various parties may need the documents. The guidelines do allow for copies (photocopies, audio or video) to be made for a fee for most documents and even court exhibits, with the judge's permission. Where available in the province, audio tapes of proceedings can be copied or listened to in the court offices. Also, "media representatives may, as well, photograph or video tape court documentation in the Halifax Law Courts Administration office."

Saskatchewan's courts also have detailed guidelines for media and public access, which can be viewed on the Web (www.sasklawcourts.ca).[17] It has some similarities to the Nova Scotia guidelines, but also provides an interesting yet welcoming court-based perspective on public access. For example, it suggests a five-step process for court clerks to consider when considering an access request:

1. Does a court order exist in the case? If so, the terms of the order supersede these guidelines to the extent that the order and the guidelines conflict. What is the scope of the order? If there is any uncertainty, consult the judge who issued the order.

2. Is there any restriction in the Rules of Court or applicable legislation which relates to the access that is being requested? If so, what is the scope of the restriction?

3. Do the guidelines provide any specific direction . . . as to how to handle the situation?

4. Do any of the circumstances exist which would require an application to court to resolve the issue?

---

17 *Public Access to Court Records in Saskatchewan: Guidelines for Court Officials, the Media and the Public* (April 2007).

5. If access can be granted, what is the manner (phone, fax, personal pick-up) and time frame within which access can be provided, keeping in mind the other court responsibilities that must be carried out, the workload of the particular court office and the amount of material requested.

A very interesting initiative is British Columbia's Court Services Online (CSO) project (www.ag.gov.bc.ca/courts/cso/). A joint effort by the Court Services Branch of the Ministry of Attorney General and the British Columbia judiciary, CSO gives the public access to court files and documents via the Internet for a fee. For now, CSO offers access to Provincial and Supreme Court civil files, but not criminal matters, family law files, files subject to a judicial order restricting access or files before 1989 (or 2002 for the Victoria Supreme Court). Daily court lists are provided free of charge. At this time, the $6 service fee is only paid when viewing documents. Probing the database for a list of search results, for now, is free.

Manitoba, in addition to having a written policy on access to records on its Web site (www.manitobacourts.mb.ca), also offers online access to records of documents filed and hearings scheduled (www.jus.gov.mb.ca). And, the Supreme Court of Canada offers limited access to some documents through its "Media Portal" (www.scc-csc.gc.ca). Look for more courts across the country to join the electronic filing or e-filing movement.

Amidst these many advances in access to court records, at the time of this publication, one province is particularly notable for its backward position — Ontario. Since 1993, its Ministry of the Attorney General has reportedly had a policy in place that requires anyone who is not a party to a criminal proceeding to request a court application for access to exhibits in any criminal matter and to view even the criminal informations in cases involving sexual offences. As a result, court administrators in Ontario routinely refuse requests to view most items in a criminal file, including written arguments and documents that are not exhibits. Some court files can also only be viewed in the location where a trial has taken place, even though the records are stored in another jurisdiction.

Much of the Ontario position is rooted in the Supreme Court's outdated *Vickery* decision, which presumptively favours the protection of the innocent over the rights of a free press. The uneven, expensive and poorly-grounded rules of access were highlighted in a 2006 report to the Attorney General by a special committee on the role of the media in the province's courts.[18] While the committee recommended more access to court documents and affordable photocopying fees, little of substance has been done

---

18 *Panel on Justice and the Media: Report to the Attorney General for Ontario* (August 2006).

at the time of this publication other than lowering fees (from $32 to $10 for viewing files, and $2 to $1 per page for photocopying).

In the face of more progressive initiatives in other provinces, not to mention the recent Supreme Court rulings, expect court rules and policies in most of the remaining provinces to harmonize eventually.

CIVIL PROCEEDINGS

Pre-Trial Access

Most civil courts will allow anyone to see the "house-keeping" records that set out the names and addresses of parties involved in lawsuits, the remedy sought, the stage of proceedings and the coming date of trial or the result. Aside from these records, a court will keep a separate file for each case containing pleadings and other pre-trial documents, such as transcripts of examinations for discovery. However, not all documents may be examined by the public.

Some provinces have legislation setting out the public's rights of access to documents. Manitoba's Queen's Bench Act, for example, states in s. 77(2) that everyone has the right to inspect court records and entries. It further notes that a person doesn't have to ask for any one particular case to gain access.[19]

Ontario's Courts of Justice Act states that, on the payment of the prescribed fee, any person is entitled to see and copy any document filed in a civil proceeding, unless another statute or an order of the court provides otherwise.[20] The Ontario Act also states that any person can, on payment of the prescribed fee, see any list maintained by a civil court of proceedings started or judgments entered.

In one Ontario civil action by alleged victims of sexual assault, a judge ordered that all documents be kept confidential, sealed and not form part of the public record. However, another judge set that order aside and said the press and public have a right of access to documents under the Courts of Justice Act that shouldn't be interfered with except in the clearest of cases. In this case, the judge held there wasn't enough evidence to justify barring public access to the documents.[21] Even with statutory references to public

---

19 S.M. 1988-89, c. 4, ss. 76, 77.
20 R.S.O. 1990, c. C.43, s. 137.
21 *Smith v. Crampton* (1987), 7 A.C.W.S. (3d) 128 (Ont. S.C.). For a recent example, see *B. (A.) v. Stubbs* (1999), 175 D.L.R. (4th) 370 (Ont. Sup. Ct.). A patient who had a cosmetic surgical procedure to have his penis enlarged was unhappy with the results and sued the doctor. The patient sought an order banning publication of his identity and denying public access to documents filed in court, citing "acute embarrassment," the need to preserve

access like those above, the question may arise as to what is the definition of a "court record." In the eyes of some court officials, the definition may not go beyond the court books that register the names and addresses of parties to actions along with a short sentence on the remedy sought.[22]

There are other situations in which the court or its officers (such as a court clerk) may bar access to a court record or document. For example, documents containing intimate personal or financial information, transcripts of examinations for discovery or solicitor-client fee agreements may be sealed by the court and taken out of the file available for public perusal.[23] Most jurisdictions statutorily bar public access to documents for family matters, such as disputes over the custody of children.[24] When search warrants are issued and executed in civil matters, as in criminal investigations, the media can apply for access to the warrant and informations but details may be edited or blacked-out.[25]

---

doctor-patient confidentiality and to avoid discouraging other potential plaintiffs from coming forward. The court dismissed the motion, saying "embarrassment was an unavoidable consequence of an open justice system." The court also noted there is a clear danger in allowing plaintiffs' anonymity. Contrast these cases, however, with *National Bank of Canada v. Melnitzer* (1991), 5 O.R. (3d) 234. In this case, the bank was suing a lawyer accused of fraud involving large amounts of money. A receiver had been appointed to take control of the lawyer's assets and the minutes of a meeting between the lawyer and the receiver formed part of the civil court record. The lawyer agreed to the meeting on the basis that the receiver would support a court motion to have the minutes sealed. The lawyer's concern was that the news media would report the details of the meeting before criminal proceedings against him were completed. A newspaper asked that the order be set aside, but the court refused saying the Charter did not give the press the right to access all documents placed in the court record and the court order had been legitimately issued under the Courts of Justice Act, s. 137(2). The court did note, however, that the original order was excessive in suggesting the document would be sealed forever, when it actually was only intended to be sealed pending the outcome of the lawsuit and criminal proceedings.

22 In *Howes v. Accountant of the Supreme Court of Ontario* (1984), 49 O.R. (2d) 121 (H.C.), the court held the Ontario section permitting access to documents doesn't apply to records of moneys paid into court. The court said the right is restricted to records of writs issued and judgments entered. However, this may have been too restrictive an interpretation of the wording.

23 For example, see Alta. Rules of Court, rr. 199, 212(4) and 617, which contain some of these restrictions. In *Solomon and Southam Inc. v. McLaughlin* (1982), 37 A.R. 479 (Q.B.), the court said a clerk couldn't refuse access to documents without leave of the court. It was noted that while no Alberta statute compels public access, the public and news media do have a presumed right of access in most cases.

24 In *Bates v. Bates* (March 24, 1992), Doc. 91-FL-407 (Ont. Master), the court agreed to seal from the public any details of settlement negotiations and mediation efforts in a family law case. The judge reasoned that preserving confidentiality in mediation proceedings would further a public policy goal of encouraging family reconciliation.

25 *Canada (Attorney General) v. O'Neill* (2004), 2004 CarswellOnt 4801, [2004] O.J. No. 4649 (S.C.).

There's also a common law power in the courts to restrict access to documents to protect the rights of the innocent or in the interests of the administration of justice.[26] For example, in a British Columbia case dealing with complaints of unprofessional conduct against a doctor, the court agreed to order that the names of former patients be blacked-out from the transcripts kept in the file seen by the public. The court said the rights of the innocent were paramount, in this case, to the rights of the press.[27]

On one occasion, in Alberta in 1982, a man took a sheriff hostage as property foreclosure proceedings were being carried out. While the hostage-taking was going on, a journalist went to a court clerk to get a copy of the foreclosure documents, but was denied access. The Alberta Court of Queen's Bench held that the clerk's refusal to hand over the documents to the journalist was justified.[28] The protection of the sheriff's life was the primary concern and more important than the public's right to see the court document.

At one time, Alberta partly restricted the publication of civil pleadings until the end of the trial or, if there is no trial, until the proper determination of the proceedings. This restriction has been removed from the law books.[29] Only the names and addresses of the parties and the solicitors, and the general nature of the claim could be published under this obsolete law.[30] As a rule, the publication of details of civil pleadings and other court documents in all provinces should be carefully reported. Until recently, reports on pre-trial documents were not privileged under defamation law since pleadings or affidavits can have erroneous information and may even be contemptuous, as well as defamatory, if published before or during a trial.[31]

That rule on the status of pre-trial documents, however, was modified substantially by a 1995 Supreme Court of Canada ruling.[32] In that case, the court said publication of information in pleadings should be protected by a qualified privilege so long as a reporter has a right of access to the court

---

26 *Ibid., Solomon*, note 23, above, at 495-496.
27 *Hirt v. College of Physicians & Surgeons of B.C.* (1985), 60 B.C.L.R. 273 (C.A.).
28 *Solomon*, note 23, above.
29 R.S.A. 1980, c. J-1, s. 30(2). The now-repealed section partly restricted publication of statements of claim, statements of defence or other pleadings, transcripts of examinations for discovery, affidavits or any other pre-trial documents.
30 In practice, no Alberta journalists had recently been charged with an offence and it likely was a violation of the Charter's freedom of the press guarantee.
31 In *Bielek v. Ristimaki*, June 21, 1979 (unreported), an Ontario trial judge dismissed the jury and ordered a new trial after a journalist published the amount of damages being sought by the plaintiff during the trial. The court held the publication of the pleadings was an act of contempt because it could have released information to the jury which is not relevant or correct.
32 *Hill v. Church of Scientology of Toronto*, [1995] 2 S.C.R. 1130, affirming (1994), 114 D.L.R. (4th) 1 (Ont. C.A.).

documents under legislation or the Charter's freedom of the press guarantee, and there is no evidence of actual malice in the reporting.

Since that decision, however, some courts have made it clear that reporting on pre-trial documents must be very fair. In a recent B.C. case, the appeal court ruled that while reporters do now enjoy a qualified privilege when reporting on documents filed in court, this protection under defamation law can be easily lost.[33] A defamation action was launched after a news outlet broadcast five reports on court proceedings involving a charitable society in which individuals swore affidavits alleging misconduct and criminal wrongdoing by the plaintiffs. The plaintiffs and their supporters, in turn, had sworn opposing affidavits and filed them in court. One of the five news reports failed to state the plaintiffs had filed affidavits countering the allegations and gave the unfair impression the allegations were unopposed. The appeal court said the qualified privilege was lost and upheld a substantial defamation damages award against the news outlet and journalist.

Access During Trial

Whether the public may have access to exhibits and evidence presented in open court is a more difficult issue. There is no law that such evidence must be accessible to the public and a journalist must seek out the permission of the presiding judge to examine or photograph evidence. Some judges may allow public access immediately after the evidence is presented in open court, while most others maintain that the fair trial of the issues would be endangered by the possibility of sensationalized reporting.

Access After Trial

After the case is over, copies of most of the documents and exhibits entered as evidence will be kept in the court record, where they may be examined by the public. Some evidence, however, may not be kept in the court record and may be returned to its rightful owner. For example, personal or business records are usually returned to individuals after a court proceeding in accordance with s. 490 of the Criminal Code, which requires the return of evidence seized under a search warrant after the disposition of a matter or within three months if no charges are pressed. The Code also permits the Crown to make copies, however, which is why you may still find useful information in the public files.

That said, the courts may be sticklers for detail when it comes to giving permission to view evidence after a trial. In one criminal case, the news

---

33 *Taylor-Wright v. CHBC-TV* (2000), 194 D.L.R. (4th) 621 (B.C. C.A.).

media had been denied access during the trial to documents entered as evidence. After the trial was over, the CBC applied to the court for access to the documents and to determine if the court order was still in effect.

The court said the order was not in effect once the trial had ended and any appeal period had passed. However, the court noted that the documents in question were no longer the property of the court. It said they would normally be returned to the party that submitted them (the Crown, in this case) and permission to view the evidence would have to come from that party to the proceeding.[34]

CRIMINAL PROCEEDINGS

Pre-Trial Access

The documents of most interest to journalists before a criminal trial are search warrants, production orders and "informations" (that is, sworn documents outlining offences police allege have been committed, known as the Information to Obtain (ITO) a Search Warrant). Until recently, the seminal case in this area is *MacIntyre v. Attorney General of Nova Scotia*, decided in 1982 by the Supreme Court of Canada.[35] In that case, a television reporter was refused access to search warrants and informations held by a justice of the peace. The Supreme Court of Canada ruled that:

> [A]fter a search warrant has been executed, and objects found as a result of the search are brought before a justice pursuant to s. 446 [now s. 490] of the

---

34 *Re CBC and Clerk of the Supreme Court of Alta.* (1977), 77 D.L.R. (3d) 621 (Alta. T.D.). A similar, but more unusual situation arose in a 1992 case brought under the Nova Scotia Freedom of Information Act. In *Halifax Herald Ltd. v. Nova Scotia (Attorney General)* (1992), 7 Admin. L.R. (2d) 46 (N.S. T.D.), a person had been charged with and, ultimately, acquitted of charges of influence peddling. Three years later, a newspaper journalist sought access to four exhibits filed by the Crown at the hearing. The Deputy Attorney General, whose department had copies of the exhibits, refused access on the basis that they were "personal information" exempt from disclosure under s. 5(1) of the Act. Ironically, an attempt at the same time by the accused to get back all the copies of the documents seized from him three years ago was also refused. Both the newspaper and the accused asked a court for the copies. Both applications were dismissed. The court agreed the documents were private and personal information, and could not be compelled to be made public except under a search warrant. The court said the fact they had been introduced twice in criminal trials and were open to the public did not change the private nature of the information. The court said once the public had access in the context of the criminal trials, the requirements of open justice had been met. As for the accused's request, the court said the A.G. was permitted to make and preserve copies of all exhibits after a trial and did not have to return or destroy those copies.

35 [1982] 1 S.C.R. 175 at 190.

Criminal Code, a member of the public is entitled to inspect the warrant and the information upon which the warrant has been issued pursuant to s. 443 [now s. 487] of the Code.

More recently, the 2005 Supreme Court rulings in *Toronto Star* and other cases made it clear there is a presumption of openness and that all discretionary court orders limiting freedom of the press must be carefully weighed.

After the discovery of eight murdered bodies in rural Ontario, the execution of search warrants by police in Winnipeg and the laying of charges, a justice of the peace ordered the search warrants, information to obtain the warrants, and even the sealing order itself and evidence supporting it to be sealed indefinitely from the public and media. Was the justice correct?

No. In this recent Ontario case,[36] the reviewing judge determined the justice of the peace had no basis in law to seal the sealing order itself since it would not disclose other information sealed. As for sealing the warrants, the judge ruled the justice failed to consider whether there were reasonably alternative measures that would have prevented a serious risk to the proper administration of justice short of a complete and indefinite sealing order. The better course, said the court, would have been an order prohibiting access to and disclosure of edited portions of the Information to Obtain. In the end, the court ordered the search information be sealed only until the conclusion of the trials and final disposition of the charges.

Note that not all search warrants are accessible. The court in *MacIntyre* said the public has no right to see an executed search warrant that finds nothing and no right to a warrant that is yet to be executed. In 1997 and 2004, the federal government amended the Criminal Code to attempt to clarify the issue of access to executed search warrants, production orders and any supporting information. The amendments give a judge very wide discretion in banning publication and access:

---

36 *R. v. Canadian Broadcasting Corp.* (2007), 2007 CarswellOnt 417, [2007] O.J. No. 301 (S.C.J.), affirmed (2008), 2008 CarswellOnt 2877 (C.A.). Also see *Winnipeg Free Press, Re* (2006), 2006 CarswellMan 85, [2006] M.J. No. 93 (Q.B.), where a sealing order in a five-year old murder investigation was quashed but a new, narrower sealing order was re-issued because of the ongoing investigation. This court also held the original sealing order was too broad, the media had not received proper notice of it and that reasonable alternative measures were not considered (such as editing out portions of informations).

487.3 (1) A judge or justice may, on application made at the time of issuing a warrant under this or any other Act of Parliament or a production order under section 487.012 or 487.013, or of granting an authorization to enter a dwelling-house under section 529 or an authorization under section 529.4 or at any time thereafter, make an order prohibiting access to and the disclosure of any information relating to the warrant, production order or authorization on the ground that

(a) the ends of justice would be subverted by the disclosure for one of the reasons referred to in subsection (2) or the information might be used for an improper purpose; and

(b) the ground referred to in paragraph (a) outweighs in importance the access to the information.

(2) For the purposes of paragraph (1)(a), an order may be made under subsection (1) on the ground that the ends of justice would be subverted by the disclosure

(a) if disclosure of the information would

(i)   compromise the identity of a confidential informant,

(ii)   compromise the nature and extent of an ongoing investigation,

(iii) endanger a person engaged in particular intelligence-gathering techniques and thereby prejudice future investigations in which similar techniques would be used, or

(iv) prejudice the interests of an innocent person; and

(b) for any other sufficient reason.

The words "any other sufficient reason" provided more than enough room for at least one appeal court to restrict media publication of the information supporting a warrant.[37] In that case, a search warrant was used to search an accused's office before any charges had been laid. The warrant was based on very incriminating information from a police informer and accomplice. A provincial court judge granted a journalist's application to examine the warrant and supporting affidavit. The accused appealed, believing the publication of any information used to get the search warrant damaged his Charter right to a fair trial.

The appeal court agreed, saying the lower court judge had failed to consider the Criminal Code requirements in s. 487.3 that can be used to preserve the fairness of proceedings. Noting the information supporting the warrant was "obviously prejudicial" since it contained detailed descriptions of the accused's alleged role in offences, the appeal judges felt the lower court should have used discretion and issued a publication ban until after a trial was held. This discretion, they said, may be exercised without hearing evidence and on the judge's own initiative. The court said a judge may

---

37 *R. v. Flahiff* (1998), 157 D.L.R. (4th) 485 (Que. C.A.). Application for leave to appeal to the Supreme Court of Canada dismissed without reasons, [1998] S.C.C.A. No. 87.

favour the rights of the accused over freedom of the press, particularly when the accused elects to be tried by a judge and jury.

While the appeal court said there was a distinct danger in allowing the information to be published, it went on to say the news media should generally be given access to these documents. "This would allow the press full scrutiny, in the public interest, of the search warrant documents notwithstanding the temporary ban on publication until after the accused's trial," said the ruling.

The Criminal Code provisions do allow a judge some flexibility in deciding whether all or some supporting information is sealed from the public. As well, s. 487.3(4) specifically allows anyone to request a variation or termination of the order banning access or publication.

Courts may also take into consideration the time delay between the execution of warrants and the actual trial. In a recent Ontario case,[38] the Crown was unsuccessful in preventing media access to sealed production orders in a case involving a senior government official facing trial over a year away. The court said there was no substantive proof offered by the Crown that the publicity would endanger the trial or the proper administration of justice.

It should also be noted that an earlier amendment to the Criminal Code in 1985 makes it an offence to publish certain information about search warrants where charges haven't been formally laid. Soon after this amendment was made, though, a court declared it unconstitutional, ruling it infringed on freedom of the press.[39]

While the government didn't appeal the ruling, unfortunately the law is still on the books and hasn't been formally repealed or amended even though it is of no force or effect. However, the government has clearly indicated a desire to somehow limit the publication of details of search warrants, particularly where charges haven't been laid. It's possible the federal government will someday introduce an amendment to limit publication.

For interest's sake, at least, s. 487.2(1) states that anyone who publishes any information with respect to:

> (a) the location of the place searched or to be searched, or

---

38   *Globe & Mail (The) v. Canada* (2007), 2007 CarswellOnt 2490, [2007] O.J. No. 1561 (S.C.J.).

39   *Canadian Newspapers Co. v. A.G. Canada* (1986), 32 D.L.R. (4th) 292 (Ont. H.C.). The Québec Court of Appeal confirmed s. 487.2 is unconstitutional and of no force and effect in *Girard v. Ouellet* (2001), 198 D.L.R. (4th) 58 (Que. C.A.). Application for leave to appeal to the Supreme Court of Canada dismissed, [2001] C.S.C.R. No. 238.

(b) the identity of any person who is or appears to occupy or be in possession or control of that place or who is suspected of being involved in any offence in relation to which the warrant was issued,

without the consent of every person referred to in paragraph (b) is, unless a charge has been laid in respect of any offence in relation to which the warrant was issued, guilty of an offence punishable on summary conviction.

The amendment reinforced the Supreme Court's prior ruling that only details of executed search warrants which find something can be published. But it went on to require that a charge also be laid before the details regarding place and identity could be published. Also, the charge had to be related to the offence for which the warrant was issued. A journalist would have had to call in legal advice in most cases to determine if the charge laid is the same as the one outlined in the warrant. For example, say police found illicit drugs using a warrant allowing a search for gambling machines. If the drug charges were the only ones arising from the search, a reporter would need legal advice.

If no charges were laid, a journalist would then have needed the consent of all people named in the warrant and the requirements for consent were quite complicated. Consent was required from every person named in the warrant as being suspected of an offence and anyone who was in possession or control of the places searched.

There have been other court decisions pertaining to access to pre-trial criminal documents. The 1959 case of *Southam Publishing Co. v. Mack*, which is noted in the *MacIntyre* case, held that the public can have access to "all informations and complaints" laid before a provincial court judge (that is, the charges laid before the court).[40] That access didn't extend to "all documents," only the informations and complaints.

Another case, decided in 1978, confirmed that all documents relating to informations and warrants should be available to the public on demand without prior approval from the Attorney General or anyone else.[41] However, the court also recognized there would be cases where the administration of justice might be better served by not releasing a document.

Examples of such situations were noted in a 1982 Ontario case.[42] The court received a request from the Attorney General and the RCMP to restrict public access to eight sworn informations that were used to get search warrants. The judge said that to deny access to court documents it must be proven that access would be harmful to the ends of justice, such as in obstructing a police investigation, disclosing evidence of lawful electronic

40 (1959-60), 2 Crim. L.Q. 119.
41 *Realty Renovations Ltd. v. A.G. Alta.* (1978), 44 C.C.C. (2d) 249 (Alta. S.C.).
42 *Re Yanover; Re Hill* (1982), 26 C.R. (3d) 216 at 228-231 (Ont. Prov. Ct.).

surveillance,[43] disclosing the identity of a confidential informant or revealing police investigative techniques. In other words, the release of such documents could allow an individual to avoid arrest, destroy evidence and discourage informants from giving information.

The court agreed that the release of the informations might interfere with an on-going police investigation and noted they contained details of wiretap evidence that had not yet been tendered as evidence in any trial. The judge also referred to several American cases suggesting other situations in which access should be denied. For example, court documents could be used for an improper or immoral purpose (for example, publishing disgusting details of a divorce case).

A 1986 case added another ground for keeping sworn informations out of the public eye. After a search warrant was executed pursuant to the Competition Act, the company that owned the seized documents applied to a court for an order to have the sworn information for the warrant kept confidential unless formal charges were laid.[44] The sworn information contained business secrets. The court agreed, noting that while there was a public interest in access to court documents, no public interest would be served in allowing the secrets to be revealed unless charges were laid.

One Saskatchewan court allowed newspapers access to informations alleging fraud even though the accused had not made their first appearance in court. The court said the "issuance of process was a judicial act" and there is a presumption in favour of making the court process an open one. The court held that the Provincial Court had "supervisory and protective power over its records" and could decide using its own discretion whether justice would be endangered by disclosure of the informations. In this case, the court said disclosure would not subvert justice even though the accused had yet to appear to answer the criminal charges.[45]

Although the Criminal Code says little about access to warrants and informations, it does specifically limit access to one type of document. Section 187 of the Criminal Code states that a judge must seal applications for authorization for wiretaps in a "packet" and allow no public access.

---

43 In *National Post Co. v. Ontario* (2003), 58 W.C.B. (2d) 36 (Ont. S.C.), the Crown was allowed to edit out the contents of intercepted communications that were referred to in the Information to Obtain. The court did not want to encourage prejudicial pre-trial publicity, but also ruled it must balance the rights of a free press. Since a trial was years away, the media was entitled to publish the information disclosed.

44 *Re Dir. of Investigation & Research and Irving Equipment & Barrington Industrial Services Ltd.* (1986), 39 D.L.R. (4th) 341 (Fed. T.D.).

45 *Leader-Post (The) v. Neuls*, [1993] 3 W.W.R. 538 (Sask. Q.B.).

Access During Trial

Requests for access to exhibits during a criminal trial should be addressed to the court clerk or the judge presiding over the case. If the release of a document would prejudice the fair trial of the accused or harm the innocent, the court may restrict access. As with civil actions, the right of access to evidence presented in open court is a difficult issue. You can't just walk up during a court recess and examine exhibits or make a few notes on their contents. A journalist must seek the permission of the judge to examine or photograph evidence. Judges may allow public access immediately after the evidence is presented in open court, but some maintain that a fair trial of the issues would be endangered by the possibility of sensationalized reporting.

During the sentencing phase, some courts may permit media access to pre-sentencing reports and other evidence. In an interesting 2006 case,[46] a young offender found guilty of criminal negligence causing death and preparing to be sentenced as an adult failed to convince a provincial court that his name and pre-sentencing reports should continue to be subject to a publication ban issued under the Youth Criminal Justice Act. The accused argued his rehabilitation would be impaired. The court ruled the Act did not apply to young persons sentenced as an adult and the accused failed to prove the ends of justice would be subverted by the disclosure, or the records would be used for an improper purpose. The information in question was also in the public domain during the sentencing hearing and withholding the records from the public during sentencing would only cause uncertainty in the judicial process.

> During a murder trial in which the Crown tendered audio and video evidence of the accused's conversation with an undercover police officer, the television media applied for permission to broadcast the recordings. The accused opposed the application, saying it would violate his rights to privacy and could have deleterious effects on the administration of justice. Should the broadcast media be able to broadcast the recordings during the trial?

---

46 *R. v. B. (A.A.)* (2006), 2006 CarswelNS 229, [2006] N.S.J. No. 226 (Prov. Ct.). In *R. v. Quintal* (2003), 2003 CarswellAlta 566, [2003] A.J. No. 509 (Prov. Ct.), a judge rejected an application by the accused to have a pre-sentencing forensic assessment sealed. The psychiatric assessment revealed circumstances surrounding his offences, which involved sexual conduct toward animals. The accused provided no evidence to support his concerns about his safety in prison or any violation of his rights. The court ruled there was no doctor-patient privilege and the accused knew the report would be entered as evidence in open court.

Yes. In this recent Manitoba case,[47] the court held that the accused had not raised any evidence of personal privacy rights that would justify curtailing the media's right to report on the trial and had not proven any risk to the administration of justice. The court also stated: "Courts should be reluctant to restrict the media in the manner in which it reports on the processes before the courts. The jury has already viewed and listened to the audio and video tapes filed as evidence in this trial. Anyone present in court has also had the same opportunity. Without any compelling reason, the general public should not be restricted to the information available simply because they are unable to attend the court at the relevant times."

Access After Trial

After a case is over, some documents entered as evidence will be kept in the court record. But as mentioned in the above section on civil proceedings, access to some documents after a trial may no longer be within the control of the court. In the criminal case mentioned above, the court had denied a media request for access to exhibits during a trial. After it was over, the CBC again asked to see the documents. The court held the order wasn't in effect after the trial had ended and the appeal period had passed.[48] As noted above, the court said the documents would normally be returned to the party that submitted them (the Crown, in this case) and permission to view the evidence would have to come from the party that introduced it.

Again, though, in many cases, copies of the evidence remain with the court as a part of the court record and may still be accessible through normal channels. For example, in a recent high-profile Northwest Territories case,

---

47 *CTV Television Inc. c. R.* (2005), 2005 CarswellMan 232, [2005] M.J. No. 245 (Q.B.). Other courts, however, have discriminated against broadcast media. In *Canadian Broadcasting Corp. v. R.* (2007), 2007 CarswellOnt 3633, [2007] O.J. No. 2261 (S.C.J.), the court dismissed an application by the media for the release of audio and video tapes made by the accused on the killing of a victim. The court held the playing of the recordings in open court and availability of transcripts satisfied the requirements of open justice. In *R. v. Canadian Broadcasting Corp.* (2006), 2006 CarswellOnt 2584, [2006] O.J. No. 1685 (S.C.J.), a court dismissed the broadcast media's application for access to and broadcast of videotapes of the accused young persons, which were played during the trial. The court was of the opinion that the broadcast of videotapes that were edited in compliance with the court's own publication ban, during the ongoing trial, would not provide the public with an accurate record of trial proceedings. The judge was also not convinced all members of the media would take sufficient steps to safeguard the identities of the young accused. As custodian of the evidence, the court stated it had a duty to protect the accused's "proprietary interest" in the videotapes.

48 Note 34, above.

a judge took a much more enlightened view.[49] The accused was charged with nine counts of murder arising from a mine explosion. The police had entered audio tape, video tapes and photos as evidence at trial. The accused was convicted and before either the Crown or accused filed for an appeal, several media outlets asked for access to the exhibits.

The court allowed the media access based on the Charter's freedom of the press guarantee, but with some restrictions in the event of an appeal being launched. The court noted that it was within its discretion to deny access since there is no specific public right set out in local statutes or rules of court. That said, the court considered freedom of the press to be fundamentally important.

In some provinces, there may be rules of court or policy directives that specifically allow the public to apply for access to documents and evidence in appeals. In a 1999 B.C. case, a newspaper and journalist applied for access to evidence in a Charter appeal involving allegations of possession of child pornography.[50] The appeal books included photographs of nude children. The media's application was based on a written policy of the appeal court that permits the public to apply for access to documents or evidence and states: ". . . there is a presumption in favour of public access but that access must be supervised by the Court to ensure that no abuse or harm occurs to innocent parties."

The appeal court allowed the application, subject to certain conditions. While noting the court's practice directive did not have the force of law, the court said it "reflected high judicial pronouncements on the obligation to balance the presumption in favour of access, openness and judicial accountability against other important rights and interests, including the accused's right to a fair trial and the privacy interests of innocent persons."

The court allowed the journalist to examine the appeal books in a single, four-hour session at the courthouse. The reporter was permitted to take handwritten notes, but could not take photographs or photocopies. The journalist and newspaper were also prohibited from publishing information that would disclose the identity of any person in the photographic material.

Despite the restrictions, the appeal court made a point of noting that there was no basis to prohibit the journalist from expressing opinions as to what was seen and whether it was child pornography. "It was a reasonable expectation that access to information would conduce to accurate, informed and responsible comment, criticism and opinion," said the court ruling.

---

49 *R. v. Warren*, [1995] 3 W.W.R. 379 (N.W.T. S.C.).
50 *R. v. Sharpe* (1999), 181 D.L.R. (4th) 246 (B.C. C.A.).

A broadcaster filed an application for access to a videotaped statement that an accused had made to police. The tape was an exhibit at
the preliminary inquiry and the accused later pleaded guilty. After
the accused was sentenced, a judge dismissed the media application
because the courts were having problems convincing police to videotape statements of accused persons. The release of the tape to the
media would impair the proper administration of justice, reasoned
the court. Was the judge correct?

No. The appeal court[51] ruled the trial judge's conclusion that releasing
the videotape would have hampered the process of obtaining videotaped
statements generally had no underlying basis in fact. Even though the
trial judge based his conclusion on common sense and logic, there had
to be "real and substantial evidence" of prejudice to the administration
of justice.

OTHER PUBLIC PROCEEDINGS

Coroners' inquests, public inquiries and administrative tribunals allow
the public no general right to inspect exhibits or evidence in their proceedings. As in the court system, it's often up to the presiding officials. In
addition, if a journalist has been somehow able to gain access to documents
used in the inquiry or proceeding, he or she should be cautious in reporting
the contents of the documents if they aren't entered as evidence in open
proceedings. The primary concern would be that reports of such documents
wouldn't be protected under defamation legislation until they became a part
of the public record of the proceedings.

A COURT DOCUMENTS CHECKLIST

1.   The Supreme Court of Canada has handed down several rulings in
      recent years that presume a right of access for the news media to view,
      copy and publish court documents and exhibits, subject to evidence that
      a court order is: i) necessary in order to prevent a serious risk to the
      proper administration of justice because reasonably alternative meas-
      ures will not prevent the risk; and ii) the salutary effects of the publi-
      cation ban outweigh the deleterious effects on the rights and interests
      of the parties and the public, including the effects on the right to free

---

51 *CTV Television Inc. v. R.* (2006), 2006 CarswellMan 372, [2006] M.J. No. 403 (C.A.).

expression, the right of the accused to a fair and public trial, and the efficacy of the administration of justice.

2. Most courts will allow journalists to see "house-keeping" court records setting out the names and addresses of parties involved in lawsuits, the remedy sought, the stage of proceedings and the coming date of trial or the result. Courts keep a separate file for each case containing pleadings and other pre-trial documents, such as transcripts of examinations for discovery. However, not all these documents may be examined by the public.

3. Courts may bar access to a case file in accordance with statutes or where it contains intimate personal or financial information, solicitor-client fee agreements or family information in cases dealing with custody of children or abuse cases. There's also a common law power to restrict access to protect the rights of the innocent or in the interests of the administration of justice.

4. The public's access to exhibits and evidence presented in open court is determined by the presiding judge or official in each case, but the Supreme Court has directed judges to carefully weigh the news media's right to freedom of expression before issuing any discretionary orders limiting access.

5. Journalists have a general right of access to executed search warrants that find something, and to criminal informations and complaints laid before a judge. The Criminal Code states that applications for wiretap authorizations must remain confidential.

10

UNDERSTANDING POLICE
POWERS AND LIMITS

News reporting often involves encounters with law enforcement officials. The police, other peace officers and even public officers wield broad powers and it's to the journalist's advantage to know the scope of law enforcement authority.

WHO HAS LAW ENFORCEMENT POWERS?

What may surprise some people is the great number of officials who hold law enforcement authority and the fact that such authority is not restricted to police. Even the average citizen has the authority to call upon law enforcement powers in limited circumstances. Generally, though, law enforcement powers are limited to those defined in the Criminal Code as "peace officers" and "public officers."

The s. 2 definition of a "peace officer" illustrates the vast list of individuals with law enforcement powers:[1]

(a) a mayor, warden, reeve, sheriff, deputy sheriff, sheriff's officer and justice of the peace,

(b) a member of the Correctional Service of Canada who is designated as a peace officer pursuant to Part I of the Corrections and Conditional Release Act, and a warden, deputy warden, instructor, keeper, jailer, guard and any other officer or permanent employee of a prison other than a penitentiary as defined in Part I of the Corrections and Conditional Release Act,

(c) a police officer, police constable, bailiff, constable, or other person employed for the preservation and maintenance of the public peace or for the service or execution of civil process,

(d) an officer or a person having the powers of a customs or excise officer when performing any duty in the administration of the Customs Act or the Excise Act,

(e) a person designated as a fishery guardian under the Fisheries Act when performing any duties or functions under that Act and a person designated as a fishery officer under the Fisheries Act when performing any duties or functions under that Act or the Coastal Fisheries Protection Act,

(f) the pilot in command of an aircraft

(i) registered in Canada under regulations made under the Aeronautics Act, or

(ii) leased without crew and operated by a person who is qualified under regulations made under the Aeronautics Act to be registered as owner of an aircraft registered in Canada under those regulations,

while the aircraft is in flight, and

(g) officers and non-commissioned members of the Canadian Forces who are

(i) appointed for the purposes of section 156 of the National Defence Act, or

(ii) employed on duties that the Governor in Council, in regulations made under the National Defence Act for the purposes of this paragraph, has prescribed to be of such a kind as to necessitate that the officers and non-commissioned members performing them have the powers of peace officers.

---

1 R.S.C. 1985, c. C-46.

Section 2 also defines a "public officer" as:

(a) an officer of customs or excise,
(b) an officer of the Canadian Forces,
(c) an officer of the Royal Canadian Mounted Police, and
(d) any officer while the officer is engaged in enforcing the laws of Canada relating to revenue, customs, excise, trade or navigation.

These definitions of peace officer and public officer aren't exhaustive. For example, an animal control officer appointed under a municipal by-law pursuant to municipal legislation has been found by a court to be a "peace officer" within the definition of the Code and thereby entitled to exercise enforcement powers.[2] In another case, a court decided that an officer who reports to a provincial or municipal government, such as a municipal agriculture inspector, could be considered a "public officer."[3]

The territorial jurisdiction of peace officers is generally limited by the authority of the appointing body.[4] For example, a municipal police officer has no authority in another province. A peace officer's authority may also be limited by the "type" of individuals he or she meets. The best example is military police. In one case, it was held that a military police officer has no authority over a civilian who is not subject to the Code of Service Discipline unless it involves the maintenance of law and order, such as traffic regulation on an armed forces base.[5]

WHAT IS THE EXTENT OF LAW ENFORCEMENT POWERS?

Use of Force

The Criminal Code protects the people administering and enforcing the law and, in appropriate circumstances, allows authorities to use whatever force is necessary. This authority can even extend beyond peace and public officers to the average citizen. For example, s. 25(1) states:

---

2 *R. v. Jones* (1975), 30 C.R.N.S. 127 (Y.T. Mag. Ct.). The point in this case was that someone must be employed with the purpose of maintaining the public peace to be considered a peace officer.

3 *R. v. Cartier; R. v. Libert* (1978), 43 C.C.C. (2d) 553 (C.S. Qué.).

4 *R. v. Soucy* (1975), 23 C.C.C. (2d) 561 (N.B. C.A.).

5 *Nolan v. R.* (1987), 34 C.C.C. (3d) 289 (S.C.C.). Similarly, in *R. v. Parsons* (2001), 80 C.R.R. (2d) 355 (Alta. Q.B.), "special constables" hired to enforce provincial legislation were found to have no authority to enforce criminal law, but could make a citizen's arrest.

> Every one who is required or authorized by law to do anything in the administration or enforcement of the law
>
> (a)   as a private person,
> (b)   as a peace officer or public officer,
> (c)   in aid of a peace officer or public officer, or
> (d)   by virtue of his office,
>
> is, if he acts on reasonable grounds, justified in doing what he is required or authorized to do and in using as much force as is necessary for that purpose.

A person administering or enforcing the law isn't justified in using excessive force that is intended or is likely to cause death or grievous bodily harm unless he or she believes, on reasonable grounds, that it's necessary to use it for self-protection or to protect anyone else from serious harm or death.[6] An excessive use of force could be subject to criminal prosecution.[7]

Section 25(4) permits a peace officer to use as much force as is necessary to prevent a person who is about to be arrested from escaping, unless the escape could be prevented by reasonable means in a less violent manner.

The use of force isn't limited to peace officers. Section 27 permits any person to use as much force as necessary to prevent the commission of offences serious enough to allow arrest without a warrant or those that would be likely to cause immediate and serious injury to someone or their property.

Section 30 allows anyone who witnesses a breach of the peace to interfere with reasonable force so as to prevent the continuance of the breach. They may then detain the person involved in the breach of peace and must deliver the accused to a peace officer as soon as possible.

Section 32 allows a peace officer to use as much force as he or she believes, in good faith and on reasonable grounds, is necessary to suppress a riot. For example, an officer might order camera crews out of an area if the crowd is reacting to the presence of the media.

Power of Arrest

An arrest is a serious act and one might reasonably assume that only duly-appointed peace officers have that power. But the Criminal Code does permit any citizen to make an arrest without a warrant within limited circumstances.

Under s. 494(1), anyone may arrest without a warrant:

---

6 S. 25(3).
7 S. 26.

    (a)   a person whom he finds committing an indictable offence; or

    (b)   a person who, on reasonable grounds, he believes

        (i)   has committed a criminal offence, and

        (ii) is escaping from and freshly pursued by persons who have lawful authority to arrest that person.

It is important to note that a "citizen's arrest" can only be made under one of two conditions. First, the arrest may occur upon finding someone committing an indictable or "serious" offence. Note that summary conviction offences aren't included.

Second, a citizen may make an arrest after coming across someone whom he or she has "reasonable grounds" to believe has committed either a summary conviction or indictable offence and who is at the same time running away from the police (that is, "freshly pursued").

So, the average citizen only has a limited power of arrest and certainly doesn't have the broad powers of the police. Once a warrantless arrest has been made, the citizen is required to deliver the accused to the nearest police officer as soon as is practicably possible.

A citizen's arrest doesn't entitle the citizen to interrogate, search a person or seize belongings. If a citizen (for example, a store security guard) has been found to have made an improper arrest, the "accused" could sue in the civil courts for false arrest or false imprisonment.

There are other instances in which average citizens can make arrests. Under s. 494(2), anyone who is the owner of property or a person in lawful possession of property or a person authorized by the owner or person in lawful possession, can arrest someone without a warrant where he finds that person committing any criminal offence on, or in relation to, that property. Again, the accused must be found committing a criminal offence (in this case, either indictable or summary conviction). Merely having a suspicion that a crime has been committed is not good enough and could result in a civil action for false arrest. And again, the accused must be delivered to a peace officer immediately.

A peace officer can arrest anyone without a warrant whom he or she believes, on reasonable grounds, has committed an indictable offence in the past or present. A peace officer can even make an arrest if he or she believes an indictable offence is about to be committed.[8] More recently, post-9/11, the federal government enacted amendments to the Criminal Code via the Anti-terrorism Act[9] that strengthened police powers to arrest individuals without a warrant to prevent a terrorist act and compel witnesses to testify even before formal charges are laid. Under s. 83.3(4) of the Code, if a police

---

8 S. 495(1).

9 S.C. 2001, c. 41.

officer believes on reasonable grounds that a terrorist activity will be carried out, then a peace officer may arrest without a warrant but must bring the individual before a judge within 24 hours or as soon as possible thereafter. This sweeping power came with a "sunset" provision that expired in 2007; however, as of the time of this publication, the federal government was considering reinstating the relevant provisions.

What Constitutes an Arrest?

The Criminal Code does not set out exactly what constitutes an arrest. A person must be told that he or she is under arrest and the reason for the arrest unless it's obvious. Where possible, the peace officer must also go through the motion of seizing or simply touching a person with an intent to detain him or her.[10] The courts have also held that people are under "arrest" if they wilfully accompany a peace officer, even though there has been no physical contact, such that they acknowledge they are in custody.[11]

But voluntarily going with a police officer simply for questioning or investigative purposes is not considered a form of custody or arrest.[12] Indeed, this little-known fact is a valuable investigative tool for police. Under s. 10(b) of the Charter,[13] upon arrest or being detained you have a right to legal counsel and to be informed of that right by the police. But that right doesn't apply to situations where a person is merely accompanying an officer.

So, an investigator will often make a "request" that someone go with them to the police station to answer a few questions. Because most people don't know that they have a right to refuse to go along or are intimidated, they go along and may end up saying something incriminating without the advice of counsel.

This brings up another important question. When is a person actually in custody? In most cases, you'd know if you were arrested. But what if the police kept you in a room for 12 hours without telling you whether you're under arrest. Have you been "detained" such that you have a right to legal counsel?

A 1985 Supreme Court of Canada case discussed this very question.[14] The case involved a man's right to a lawyer upon being asked to go to the police station to take a breathalyzer test. The court held that the person was

---

10 *R. v. Whitfield* (1969), 9 C.R.N.S. 59 at 60 (S.C.C.).
11 *Ibid.*
12 *R. v. Acker* (1970), 9 C.R.N.S. 371 at 377-378 (N.S. C.A.).
13 Canadian Charter of Rights and Freedoms, Part I of the Constitution Act, 1982, being Schedule B of the Canada Act 1982 (U.K.), 1982, c. 11 (hereinafter, Charter).
14 *R. v. Therens*, [1985] 1 S.C.R. 613.

"detained" when he accompanied a police officer back to the police station for the test. It held that to be considered "detained" for the purposes of the Charter s. 10(b), there must be some form of compulsion or demand from the peace officer, which if refused, could have a legal consequence (for example, a criminal charge for refusing to take a breathalyzer test).

Power of Search and Seizure

A peace officer may only perform a search of a person or a place in certain circumstances. Authorization for a search can come in the form of a warrant or it can be based on the inherent warrantless search powers granted law enforcers in statutes or common law. The use of search warrants is discussed in the chapter on "Search Warrants." This section focuses on the use of warrantless powers.

There is no general power allowing the search of a place or a person without a warrant, unless the search is incidental to the arrest of someone or if there is consent. There is also no general power to seize something unless it's in connection with the commission of an offence or under a warrant.[15]

So, a peace officer has no right to seize a journalist's notes, tapes, films or other personal property unless it's in connection with an offence or a search warrant.

The Supreme Court of Canada has recognized that individuals rightly have a reasonable expectation of privacy and occasions of warrantless searches should thus be limited.[16] There are times, however, when unauthorized searches will be allowed. For example, a person going through

---

15 *R. v. Brezack* (1949), 9 C.R. 73 (Ont. C.A.).

16 *Dir. of Investigation and Research of the Combines Investigation Branch v. Southam Inc.*, [1984] 6 W.W.R. 577 (S.C.C.). An interesting view on the expectation of privacy can be found in the Supreme Court of Canada's *R. v. Belnavis*, [1997] 3 S.C.R. 341 (S.C.C.). The police stopped a car for speeding and, when no vehicle documents could be produced, the driver was asked to sit in the police cruiser. The officer went back to the driver's car to look for documents in the glove box and noticed several open garbage bags in the back seat with what would later be revealed to be stolen clothes with price tags still attached. The remaining passenger in the car claimed the bags belonged to her and the driver. The driver claimed to know nothing about the bags. Both were later charged, but the trial judge excluded the evidence after ruling the driver and passenger had an expectation of privacy and the search was unreasonable. The Supreme Court said the driver did indeed have a reasonable expectation of privacy since she was in charge of the vehicle. Her passenger, however, had no apparent control of the vehicle or the driver, did not lay claim to any specific bag and could have no expectation of privacy. The court noted it was not saying all passengers can be searched without a warrant, but that this was not an unreasonable search in the circumstances.

customs would not expect to be immune from questions or searches of their suitcases.

The Criminal Code also allows a search without a warrant in circumstances where a peace officer suspects violations of certain laws (for example, weapons or gambling offences).[17] At least a dozen federal laws ranging from dairy legislation to the Narcotic Control Act,[18] allow a peace officer to search a person or any place, other than in a dwelling-house, without a warrant.[19] But even in these statutes the use of the search power cannot be arbitrary and the search must be based on a reasonable belief that an offence has been committed.

A 911 caller tells police there are 10 "black guys" with guns outside of a club. The caller also describes the vehicles the men are driving. In minutes, police have a roadblock set up on both sides of the parking lot. One of the first cars to leave is stopped. While there are two black men inside, their car does not match the description given by the 911 caller. Are police within their authority to detain the men and search their vehicle?

Yes. Recently, the Supreme Court of Canada unanimously held no rights were violated when police set up a roadblock and searched two individuals leaving a parking lot.[20] The roadblock was erected after a 911 call said 10 "black guys," some with handguns, were outside a Toronto strip club. The car stopped was not among any described by the caller, but a search revealed the two black men in the vehicle had concealed and loaded prohibited weapons. The Supreme Court applied a two-part test. First, the Crown must show the police were acting in the exercise of a lawful duty when they engaged in the conduct at issue. Second, the Crown must show the impugned conduct amounted to a justifiable use of police powers associated with that duty. The latter point could only be determined after considering the nature of the situation, seriousness of the offence, information known to the police about the suspect or the crime, degree of detention that was reasonable, seriousness of the risk to public safety, and the liberty interests of members of the public. In this case, the court found the detention and roadblock to be constitutional. The caller had identified "black guys" and both men were black. The alleged

---

17   For example, see s. 101 which deals with weapons offences.
18   R.S.C. 1985, c. N-1.
19   For a discussion of this see Finkelstein, "Search and Seizure After Southam" (1985), 63 Can. Bar Rev. 193-199.
20   *R. v. Clayton* (2007), 2007 CarswellOnt 4268, 2007 CarswellOnt 4269, [2007] S.C.J. No. 32.

crime was serious enough to also warrant the violation of their liberty. As for the search that found the weapons, the court ruled it was justified based on the police assessment of the behaviour of the men.

OBSTRUCTION OF JUSTICE AND JOURNALISTS

Section 129 of the Criminal Code makes it an offence to resist or wilfully obstruct a public officer or a peace officer in the execution of his or her duty or any person lawfully acting in aid of such an officer.[21] It's this section that most commonly comes into play when journalists doing their jobs and police executing theirs, collide.

Generally, the courts have recognized that journalists have a job to do and have only punished serious acts of obstruction. In one case, a news photographer was taking pictures of a disturbed person who was being escorted away by a policeman under the authority of a Mental Health Act. The officer told the photographer to stop taking flash pictures because the patient was becoming hysterical. The photographer persisted and the charge of obstruction was laid. The court held that freedom of the press is not a right which is superior to the execution of a policeman's duty and found the photographer guilty.[22]

A Test for Obstruction

An important factor is that the obstruction must be wilful. In other words, the accused must know what he or she is doing and must intend to obstruct the officer. In one case, an experienced photographer was covering a spectacular car accident.[23] Crowds of 250 to 300 people gathered and the

---

21 This section also makes it an offence not to aid a public officer or peace officer, without a reasonable excuse, in the execution of his duty in arresting a person or in preserving the peace. You must be given a reasonable notice that you are required to help. It is also an offence under s. 129 to resist or obstruct any person in the lawful execution of a process against lands or goods, or in making a lawful distress or seizure.

22 *R. v. Kalnins* (1978), 41 C.C.C. (2d) 524 (Ont. Co. Ct.). Also see *Knowlton v. R.* (1973), 10 C.C.C. (2d) 377 (S.C.C.), where the Supreme Court of Canada said police were right to lay an obstruction charge against a press photographer who tried to push his way past a policeman guarding an area that had been cordoned off for a visiting dignitary. The court noted the dignitary had been assaulted several days earlier in another city and the photographer had inadequate identification.

23 *R. v. Sandford* (1980), 62 C.C.C. (2d) 89 (Ont. Prov. Ct.). This case and most obstruction cases are based on *R. v. Westlie* (1971), 2 C.C.C. (2d) 315 (B.C. C.A.), in which a man was charged with obstructing two plainclothes officers by pointing out to passersby that they were undercover cops. The court found the person guilty and said it was not necessary

police told everyone to stay on the sidewalk and keep off the street. The photographer was trying to get a good picture of the accident and stepped off the sidewalk. A charge of obstruction was laid. The court took a three step approach:

1.   Was there an obstruction of a peace officer?

2.   Was the obstruction affecting the peace officer in the execution of the duty he was then exercising?

3.   If there was an obstruction, was it wilful (that is, intentional) without lawful excuse?

The court found no wilful obstruction in the photographer's actions and found him not guilty. The judge defined "wilful" as being in the sense of having an "evil" intention to obstruct. He said the accused would have had to display an intention to actually obstruct the police in their duty.

YOUR RIGHTS WHEN DEALING WITH POLICE

The legal rights entrenched in the Charter are changing the shape of law enforcement powers and the methods of police investigation. Each right is important and can be expected to generate arguments and case law for generations to come. The following are some of your rights which pertain directly to the use of authority by the police:

1.   You have the right to be secure against unreasonable search and seizure (s. 8).

2.   You have the right not to be arbitrarily detained or imprisoned (s. 9).

3.   You have the right on arrest or detention,
      (i)   to be informed of the reasons,
      (ii) to retain and inform counsel without delay and to be informed of that right (s. 10).

---

for the peace officer to be executing a specific duty at the time of the obstruction. In *R. v. Anderson* (1996), 111 C.C.C. (3d) 540 (B.C. C.A.), the appeal court acquitted a citizen who blocked the path of a police vehicle that had entered onto his land. The court found reasonable doubt that the citizen was aware it was the police and that the officer was engaged in execution of his duty.

4.   You have the right on being charged with an offence,
     (i)   to be informed without unreasonable delay of the specific offence,
     (ii) to be tried within a reasonable time,
     (iii) to be presumed innocent, and
     (iv) not to be denied reasonable bail without just cause (s. 11).

5.   You have the right not to be subjected to cruel and unusual treatment
     or punishment (s. 12).

The Right to Silence

There is one important right which everyone has which isn't expressly
set out in the Charter or any other statute. In fact, there's nothing that
compels any law enforcer to even mention this right to you (arguably,
however, some officers do). It is the right to remain silent. Generally, there's
no legal obligation on a person to give police any information, particularly
during investigations. The only exceptions tend to be for identification
purposes.

One Ontario Court of Appeal case examined the authority of police
during an investigation.[24] The court noted that the police are entitled to ask
any question of a person on the street, whether they are suspected of a crime
or not. But the police have no lawful power to compel a person to answer.
As noted elsewhere in this chapter, the police also have no power to detain
someone against their will merely for questioning or investigation.

Still, there are some situations in which there could be a legal justification for police to ask for a person's identification. If a policeman is
investigating an offence and believes you may have had a role in it, he or
she may ask you to identify yourself. If you don't, the officer may take you
into custody to establish your identity. At this point, you could be charged
with obstructing justice.[25] But the officer must have reasonable grounds to
believe you committed an offence and you're not required to give out any
more than your identity. It should also be noted that a charge of obstructing
justice cannot be laid if there is no evidence of a person having committed
an offence.[26]

---

24 *R. v. Dedman* (1981), 32 O.R. (2d) 641 at 653 (C.A.).

25 In *Moore v. R.* (1978), 43 C.C.C. (2d) 83 (S.C.C.), the appellant committed a provincial
     offence while bicycling and refused to identify himself. While there was no provincial
     law requiring that a person identify himself, a court held that the bicyclist was obstructing
     the officer in the performance of his duties.

26 *R. v. Guthrie* (1982), 69 C.C.C. (2d) 216 (Alta. C.A.).

Some municipalities also have jaywalking by-laws which require citizens to identify themselves to a police officer when caught. In addition, a driver of a motor vehicle is required to supply identification when stopped under provincial motor vehicle laws. Under the Criminal Code s. 252, any driver involved in an accident must stop and give police his or her name and address.

The police have wide-sweeping powers, some real and some imagined in the mind of the average citizen. When a policeman asks someone to come to the station for "some questions," few citizens are likely to ignore the request. Obviously, it's best to cooperate with police. But remember the police have limits too and if you're not under arrest or being detained for some legal reason, you have a right to leave.

If you're arrested or detained, simply identifying yourself doesn't mean you have to answer any other questions and you should not say anything else before speaking to a lawyer.

A POLICE POWERS CHECKLIST

1. Law enforcement powers are held by "peace officers" and "public officers," as defined in the Criminal Code. However, all citizens may use some law enforcement powers in limited circumstances.

2. A person enforcing the law isn't justified in using excessive force that is intended or is likely to cause death or grievous bodily harm unless he or she believes, on reasonable and probable grounds, that it's necessary to use it for self protection or to protect anyone else from serious harm or death.

3. The Criminal Code does not set out exactly what constitutes an arrest. A person must be told that he or she is under arrest and the reason for the arrest. Where possible, the peace officer must go through the motion of seizing or touching a person with an intent to detain him or her.

4. There is no general power allowing the search of a place or a person without a warrant, unless the search is incidental to the arrest of someone or if there is consent. There is also no general power to seize something unless it's in connection with the commission of an offence or under a warrant.

5. Conflicts between police and journalists may bring a Criminal Code charge of obstructing justice. The court may examine whether there actually was an obstruction of a peace officer, whether it affected the peace officer in the execution of his or her duty and whether it was wilful. The accused must know what he or she is doing and must intend to obstruct the officer.

6. Aside from the protections in the Charter, a citizen's most important right in dealing with law enforcement authorities is the right to remain silent.

11

COURT ORDERS: SEARCH WARRANTS, INJUNCTIONS AND SUBPOENAS

At some time, a journalist or a news outlet may become the subject of a court order. It could be a search warrant demanding tapes, an injunction blocking the publication of a defamatory story or a subpoena demanding that a journalist testify at a hearing. The Charter of Rights is playing a very important role in determining how these orders affect journalists. In recent years, there have been numerous high-profile and important rulings supporting the principle that court orders targeting the news media directly must be weighed carefully to ensure disruption of the gathering and dissemination of news is as limited as possible. The news media as an entity is given special consideration in most cases now when authorities or others seek a search warrant, injunction or subpoena that names a journalist or media outlet.

The bottom line in dealing with court orders, though, remains the same. When you get one, the first step is to quickly call in legal counsel. There is nothing to be gained and much to be lost by resisting or ignoring a court order. With the Charter, a lawyer has more ammunition now then ever to strike down a search warrant, injunction or subpoena through legal channels. Meanwhile, court orders are an increasingly popular tactical weapon for civil litigants and law enforcers dealing with journalists. Thus, it's important to understand both the scope and limits of court orders that target the news media.

SEARCH WARRANTS AND PRODUCTION ORDERS

The legal authority for a search can come in two forms. It can be in the form of a warrant or it can be warrantless. The authority to search a person or place without a warrant is covered in the chapter on police powers and this chapter will only deal with court-ordered searches authorized by a warrant and directed at journalists or media outlets. The media's right of access to information in search warrants generally is covered in more detail in the chapter on publications bans.

The Canadian Charter of Rights and Freedoms guarantees in s. 8 the right "to be secure against unreasonable search or seizure."[1] The Supreme Court of Canada has made it clear that this fundamental guarantee isn't to be taken lightly. In one of its first Charter decisions, the Supreme Court set out the minimum acceptable standards needed before a warrant can be authorized by a judge or other public official.[2] These standards have been summarized as follows:

1. There must be a belief based on reasonable and probable grounds, established upon oath, that an offence has been committed;

2. There must be a belief based on reasonable grounds that the evidence of the offence is to be found at the place to be searched;

3. The area to be searched must be clearly described and the search must be limited to the probable area where the evidence is; and

---

1 Part I of the Constitution Act, 1982, being Schedule B of the Canada Act 1982 (U.K.), 1982, c. 11 (hereinafter, Charter).

2 *Dir. of Investigation and Research of the Combines Investigation Branch v. Southam Inc.*, [1984] 6 W.W.R. 577 (S.C.C.).

4.   The authorization for the search warrant must come from a neutral person who, if not a judge, is capable of acting judicially.[3]

In other words, the police or any other government agent can't go on a fishing mission and the issuance of the warrant must be based on reasonable grounds as determined by an independent third party. For example, a statute which gives the head of a government department the power to grant search warrants to his own employees would likely be found to be in violation of the Charter because of the lack of neutrality.

RCMP anti-terrorism investigators executed search warrants on the home of an *Ottawa Citizen* journalist and her newspaper office, seizing documents and computer information. The reporter was investigating the Canadian government's involvement in the case of Maher Arar, a Syrian-born Canadian citizen whom U.S. authorities arrested for alleged terrorism activities and deported to Syria for torture in 2002. The journalist was told she would be charged with criminal offences unless she co-operated with the RCMP investigation and revealed her confidential sources of information. Was the use of search warrants for this purpose an abuse of process?

Yes. In this landmark case,[4] RCMP officers obtained search warrants in 2003 by alleging the journalist had violated sections of the Security of Information Act (SOIA), dealing with official secrets and national security. In addition to declaring sections of the SOIA to be unconstitutional, the Ontario Superior Court judge also concluded the RCMP had engaged in abuse of process in obtaining the warrants. While the justice who issued the warrants had met the proper procedural standards, the police did not and the warrants were quashed and the items seized were returned. Based on evidence presented, the court found it was reasonable to infer the warrant and allegations of criminality against the journalist "were used to gain access to O'Neill for the purpose of intimidating her into compromising her constitutional right of freedom of the press, namely, to reveal her confidential source or sources of the prohibited information." The allegation of criminality amounted to "an intimidation of the press and an infringement of the constitutional right of freedom of the press. . . By its decision to allege criminal offences and obtain and

---

3 *Ibid.*, at 583-596.
4 *O'Neill v. Canada (Attorney General)* (2006), 2006 CarswellOnt 8672, 272 D.L.R. (4th) 193 (S.C.J.).

> execute the Warrants, the RCMP did treat O'Neill as one of its investigative arms to uncover the source of the leaks."

Since 2004, the Criminal Code has also provided for the issuance of "production orders" under s. 487.012. These orders are being used increasingly against the news media. A production order requires a person "other than a person under investigation" (for example, a journalist) to:

a)   produce documents or copies certified by affidavit to be true copies, or to produce data; or

b)   to prepare a document based on documents or data already in existence and produce it.

The production order requires documents or data to be produced within a set time period and to have them delivered to a peace officer or public officer named in the order. The judge issuing the order must be satisfied, on the basis of the *ex parte* application by authorities, that there are reasonable grounds to believe a criminal or other offence has been or is suspected to have been committed, the documents or data will provide evidence on commission of the offence, and the person named in the order has possession or control of the documents or data.

Recently, the CBC attempted to resist a production order for "all audio, video, digital recordings and verbatim transcriptions" of interviews with eight people involved in a documentary about the 1959 conviction of Steven Truscott for a first-degree murder.[5] Ontario's Minister of Justice had asked the province's Court of Appeal to determine the admissibility of fresh evidence and the Crown wanted the recordings and documents for its case.

The CBC initially refused and later advised the Crown it had only kept a few of the interview recordings. The appeal court ruled two of the three recordings may be of value to the court and ordered their production. The media's arguments that the order would have a "chilling effect" on news gathering and would turn the media into an "arm of the state" were rejected. "The witnesses who gave the interviews in question were aware that the respondents were producing a documentary that would be televised. There is nothing in the record to suggest that the respondents entered into confidentiality agreements with any of the witnesses," noted the court.

---

5   *R. v. Truscott* (2006), 2006 CarswellOnt 3594, 210 C.C.C. (3d) 91 (C.A.).

How is a Search Warrant or Production Order Issued?

Generally, a search warrant or production order is obtained from the courts. The Criminal Code sets out the general requirements for search warrants and production orders in ss. 487 to 490.[6] To get a search warrant under the Criminal Code, the informant swears under oath to a justice in an information, that there are reasonable grounds to believe there is, in a building, receptacle or place:[7]

(a) anything on or in respect of which any offence against this Act or any other Act of Parliament has been or is suspected to have been committed,

(b) anything that there are reasonable grounds to believe will afford evidence with respect to the commission of an offence, or will reveal the whereabouts of a person who is believed to have committed an offence, against this Act or any other Act of Parliament, or

(c) anything that there are reasonable grounds to believe is intended to be used for the purpose of committing any offence against the person for which a person may be arrested without warrant, or

(c.1) any offence-related property,

For the search warrant to be valid, courts have held that it must be filled out properly and completely:[8]

1. The warrant must disclose on its face the offence in relation to which the search is being conducted and the grounds of belief upon which the request for the warrant is made;

2. The place to be searched must be accurately described; and

3. The items to be searched for and seized must be reasonably described so they can be easily identified by the person at the premises and the officer executing the search.

Upon executing the search warrant the person conducting the search is required to meet certain standards:[9]

1. The warrant must be in his possession during the search;

---

6 R.S.C. 1985, c. C-46.

7 S. 487.

8 *Re McAvoy* (1970), 12 C.R.N.S. 56 at 65-66 (N.W.T. Terr. Ct.). The Criminal Code also now allows peace officers to request telewarrants, which are search warrants obtained over the telephone from a judge (s. 487.1) in circumstances where a personal appearance in a court is impractical.

9 *Wah Kie v. Cuddy (No. 2)* (1914), 23 C.C.C. 383 (Alta. C.A.).

2. The warrant must be exhibited for inspection upon request;

3. If the premises to be searched is a residence, there must be a demand
    to open before a forced entry is attempted (some exceptions allowed);
    and

4. The peace officer may only use the force which is necessary to enter
    the premises.

Without formal notice, the RCMP obtained and executed a general search warrant against the *National Post* newspaper seeking an envelope and a purported bank loan document sent anonymously to an investigative journalist looking into the Prime Minister's business dealings. The document suggested the Prime Minister had a conflict of interest in the bank loan. The police learned the original document and its envelope were hidden off-site. For the first time in a case involving the media, the police used an Assistance Order to require the editor-in-chief to get the document from the reporter and make it available to the police. The newspaper objected, arguing the warrant and Assistance Order made the editor-in-chief an agent of the state. Were the warrant and Assistance Order issued properly against the news media?

Yes. While an Ontario Superior Court judge originally quashed the warrant and Assistance Order as violations of the Charter right protecting freedom of the press,[10] the Ontario Court of Appeal overturned the lower court ruling in 2008.[11] Even though the newspaper had not received any advance notice of the application for a search warrant, the appeal court held the warrant was issued properly. During the appeal, the news media argued the Assistance Order violated their rights under s. 2(b) of the Charter because it "conscripts the editor-in-chief into becoming an agent of the police and compels him to breach his ethical obligations." The Assistance Order was also considered vague by the media because it did not define what steps the editor had to take if the reporter would not comply with the request to produce the items sought. The appeal court ruled the Assistance Order involving the editor was justified since the newspaper had made it clear the documents in question were under its

---

10 *R. v. National Post* (2004), 2004 CarswellOnt 173, 69 O.R. (3d) 427 (S.C.J.), reversed 2008 CarswellOnt 1104, 89 O.R. (3d) 1 (C.A.).
11 *R. v. National Post*, (2008), 2008 CarswellOnt 1104, [2008] ONCA 139 (C.A.).

control. For greater clarity, the court ruled, the reporter could also be added to the Assistance Order.

Search Warrants and the News Media

Quite often, the police and even those involved in private litigation try to use court orders, such as search warrants, to access the news media's work (interviews, video, audio, etc.) to supplement their investigation or support their cause. For example, police often want to seize video coverage of public demonstrations or crimes in progress to identify witnesses or perpetrators.

Until recently, there was some uncertainty about what degree of protection the Charter's freedom of the press guarantee offered in circumstances involving search warrants demanding the media's work product. Some believed, with a few supporting court rulings, that the news media should only be used as an investigative source of information as a last resort.[12] Unfortunately, that question has been clarified with only a partial victory for journalists.

In 1991, the Supreme Court of Canada issued rulings in two very similar cases (jointly, referred to as the *Lessard* decision) involving police search and seizure of journalists' videotape.[13] In both, TV cameras captured pictures of individuals damaging property during protests. The video had been aired and police later got warrants for the tapes. The news organization tried to argue that the police had failed to demonstrate they had exhausted all other avenues for the information. For example, in the New Brunswick

---

12 For example, in *Pacific Press Ltd. v. R.*, [1977] 5 W.W.R. 507 (B.C. S.C.), the Department of Consumer and Corporate Affairs had searched a news outlet for the notes of a journalist who covered a public demonstration. The Department wanted the names of picketers who had stopped an inquiry from being held and knew that reporters had spoken with some demonstrators. Although pre-Charter, the court considered the importance of the freedom of the press and the fact that people other than the news media were at the demonstration. The court quashed the warrant on the basis that the Department hadn't shown that it had tried to find the information through any other reasonable channels. The reasoning in this case was adopted by the Supreme Court of Canada in *Descôtteaux v. Mierzwinski* (1982), 1 C.R.R. 318.

13 *Société Radio-Canada c. Lessard*, [1991] 3 S.C.R. 421 and *Société Radio-Canada c. Nouveau-Brunswick (Procureur général)*, [1991] 3 S.C.R. 459. For an example following this precedent, see *Société Radio-Canada v. Québec (Procureur General)* (1999), 138 C.C.C. (3d) 567 (Que. C.A.). The appeal court supported a lower court justice's issuance of search warrants for video of a public disturbance. Although the police filmed the demonstration, their video was not of sufficient quality to identify individuals who committed criminal offences. The court was satisfied the police had exhausted all other investigative options.

case, it was shown that police officers were at the scene and could have supplied the necessary testimony.

The court took an interesting position. The judges ruled that the search warrants and seizures in both cases were valid and did not violate the Charter's freedom of the press provision. The court held that the failure of police to demonstrate that they had exhausted all other avenues or even that other sources existed could indeed be the basis for a justice of the peace to refuse a warrant application. However, the judges said there is no constitutional requirement to actually prove other sources exist when applying for a warrant and, unless the justice of the peace objects at the time, the warrants were properly granted. So, the news media may have a limited degree of immunity from search warrants, but it's at the discretion of officials issuing the warrants. When issuing a search warrant involving the premises of news media, the Supreme Court in *Lessard* outlined the nine factors to be considered in balancing the privacy interests of the media and the interests of the state in investigating and prosecuting crimes:

1. The requirements of s. 487(1)(b) of the Criminal Code must be met;

2. The justice of the peace should then consider all of the circumstances in determining whether to exercise his or her discretion to issue a warrant; and

3. Ensure that a delicate balance is struck between the competing interests of the state in the investigation and prosecution of crimes and the right to privacy of the media in the course of their news gathering and news dissemination. The press is truly an innocent third party; this factor is most important in attempting to strike an appropriate balance, including the consideration of imposing conditions on that warrant;

4. The affidavit in support of the application must contain sufficient detail to enable a proper exercise of discretion as to whether or not to issue a search warrant;

5. Although not constitutionally required, the affidavit material should ordinarily disclose whether there are alternative sources, and if reasonable and alternative sources exist, whether those sources have been investigated and all reasonable efforts to obtain the information have been exhausted;

6. Dissemination of the information by the media in whole or in part will be a factor favouring the issuance of the search warrant;

7. If a justice of the peace determines that a warrant should be issued for the search of media premises, consideration should then be given to the imposition of some conditions on its implementation;

8. The search warrant may be found to be invalid if, after its issuance, it is found that pertinent information was not disclosed; or

9. If the search is unreasonably conducted.

Despite the Supreme Court rulings, though, some courts are still insisting on high standards in police requests for search warrants involving the media. Subsequent decisions have underlined the importance of using the news media as a source for police information only as a last resort and not as the "starting point" for an investigation.[14]

A TV reporter arranged a 50-minute jailhouse interview with an accused sex offender while he was awaiting trial. The accused spoke willingly without his lawyer, telling how he committed a sexual assault, his survival in the wilderness while on the run and making other incriminating statements. An RCMP officer listened nearby to the interview but did not record it. A portion of the recorded interview that adhered to a pre-trial publication ban was broadcast over two days. The police and Crown later notified the TV station they would be getting a search warrant for a copy of the tape to present at trial. Was the warrant upheld as valid?

---

14 See *Canadian Broadcasting Corp. v. Newfoundland & Labrador*, 2005 CarswellNfld 351, [2005] N.J. No. 401 (N.L. T.D.), where the CBC applied successfully to quash a warrant seizing video recordings made during a 2004 public sector strike for a television documentary. The video captured a union member privately counselling others to commit an offence, contrary to s. 464 of the Criminal Code. The court quashed the warrant, agreeing it was issued without taking into account the special constitutional position of the news media, and failed to consider the balance between the administration of justice and the rights of the media. Also, see *Canadian Broadcasting Corp. v. Newfoundland* (1994), 119 Nfld. & P.E.I.R. 140 (Nfld. T.D.), where the trial judge said a search and seizure conducted against the news media, when there is proof that other information sources are available, is a violation of the Charter's guarantee of freedom of the press. Indeed, this judge held the police are "required" to seek out other sources first. Another factor in this case was that police had failed to disclose material evidence that other sources existed.

Yes. In a recent B.C. case,[15] offering a "best practices" example for authorities, a court upheld the validity of a search warrant executed at a CTV station in Vancouver. After the interview with the accused (Meigs) aired, the Crown notified CTV in advance that police planned to get a search warrant for a copy of the tape. CTV asked to appear at any warrant hearing to submit arguments. The Crown did not agree, but did tell the issuing judge of CTV's position opposing the warrant because of the media's role in society.

The warrant was granted with special conditions. CTV would keep the original footage, the seized copy was to be sealed by police and not opened for a period of seven days to allow CTV to apply to quash the warrant, and other steps were taken to ensure the search was reasonable and was "minimally intrusive for CTV." Later, applying to quash the warrant, CTV argued it was unreasonable since it made the media an "investigative arm of the state," and co-opted CTV and its reporter in "their constitutionally guaranteed function of gathering and reporting news without undue state interference." It also argued the police had overheard the entire interview and their own interviews with the accused would suffice.

The judge upheld the warrant based on several factors. There was advance notice of the warrant application, the issuing judge was made aware of the case law and arguments in warrants involving the media, and special conditions had been set to minimize disruption for CTV. Also acting against the media's application to quash was that a portion of the interview had been broadcast already over two days. "First, there is no risk that a confidential source will be identified because Mr. Meigs has already been identified in the public domain as the source of Ms. Brunoro's information. Second, CTV intends to broadcast the remaining portions of the videotaped interview when the trial is over," wrote the court, adding that CTV gave no assurance to Meigs the interview would be kept confidential.

---

15 *R. v. Meigs* (2003), 2003 CarswellBC 3283, 2003 BCSC 1816 (S.C.). On whether providing notice to the news media is required, see *R. v. Canadian Broadcasting Corp.* (2001), 2001 CarswellOnt 538, 42 C.R. (5th) 290 (C.A.), leave to appeal to the Supreme Court refused (2001), 2001 CarswellOnt 3075, 2001 CarswellOnt 3076 (S.C.C.), where it was ruled that applications for search warrants pursuant to s. 487 of the Criminal Code were generally *ex parte* hearings in which the issuing justice is required to determine, based upon information on oath, whether a warrant should issue. No notice of this hearing need be given, ruled the court, although the issuing justice retains a discretion to proceed on notice.

That said, courts may be swayed to accept a police request for searches of news media premises even when other sources may be available. One factor tipping the balance in favour of police is whether prospective evidence has already been published or broadcast. In fact, the 1991 Supreme Court decisions specifically noted that a factor in the rulings was that the tapes had been broadcast before the warrant was issued and the information had been passed into the public domain.

Other courts have picked up on this. In 1993, demonstrators gathered outside the British Columbia legislature to protest the government's environmental and forestry policies. Things got out of hand. Some people were charged with forcibly entering the legislature and committing a variety of offences. The police seized videotapes from local TV stations and offered them as evidence. In a rather novel twist, two non-media accused argued that accepting the tapes as evidence would violate the Charter's freedom of press guarantee since it would turn the media into "agents of the state" and bring the administration of justice into disrepute. The judge didn't agree, noting that once the news media publish information they gather, the information is in the public domain and that this is an important factor favouring a search warrant.[16]

Does this mean that information which is not broadcast or published is protected? At least one provincial appeal court has dealt with that issue since the 1991 Supreme Court rulings and rejected the idea.[17] In yet another case involving video, a TV station broadcast portions of a tape showing alleged crimes. It later argued the tape, at least what was not broadcast, was private property and it alone could decide what would be made public. The Québec Court of Appeal disagreed, validating the warrant and went on to state that reporters have a responsibility to report all the news and not just parts. Remarkably, the appeal court also said reporters have a duty, when required, to assist the justice system.

What Happens When a Search Warrant is Executed?

Usually, the execution of a search warrant in a newsroom is a low-key affair. The police often arrive quietly, will ask to speak with a manager or editor, explain why they are there and hand over a copy of the warrant. To avoid destruction of evidence, though, the police may move quickly to

---

16 *R. v. Lloyd* (October 21, 1994), Doc. Victoria 72458 (B.C. S.C.). Also see *Group VAT Inc. v. Lavoie* (2003), CanLII 33383 (Q.C. C.S.), in which a court upheld the police seizure of a video cassette capturing a farmers' demonstration, in part, because the video had been aired already and no confidential sources were being protected.

17 *Société Radio-Canada c. Gaudreault* (January 17, 1992), Québec 200-10-000164-876 (C.A. Qué.).

search the newsroom or a particular reporter's desk and files. Before that happens, however, an editor or manager might try asking for some time to look over the warrant and, perhaps, call a lawyer. There is no obligation on the police to agree to wait, but some will as a courtesy.

A recent case underlines the importance of actually reading the search warrant and getting legal advice, if possible.[18] After a public riot at Queen's Park in Toronto, the police got a search warrant to seize video tapes of the event in hopes of collecting evidence of law breaking. A police officer called a television station to alert the assignment editor to the warrant and make arrangements to come get the tape. The warrant contained a specific provision that, on the request of anyone at the news outlet, the tape could be sealed to preserve the privacy of its contents until a hearing could be held later. Before executing the warrant, a police officer gave the assignment editor a copy of the warrant and, pointing out the section with the written conditions, asked if the editor was providing the tape sealed or unsealed. The editor declined to read the conditions of the warrant and turned over the tape unsealed without seeking any legal advice. As a result, the police viewed the seized tape, made copies and notes from it, and used the information to make arrests. The TV station soon after applied for an order that the tape, the copies and notes be sealed pending a hearing of a motion to quash the search warrant.

The court dismissed the application, saying it was "too late now to turn back the clock." The court said the purpose of sealing the tape was to preserve a privacy interest in the thing seized until the matter could be dealt with in court. That privacy interest no longer existed since the police had viewed the film and used it in their investigations.

If you can, arrange for a lawyer to be on hand for the search and to review the validity of the warrant. Sometimes, simple typographical errors spotted by a lawyer can be enough to send the police out the door for another warrant. There's another important reason to have a lawyer on site or at least on the phone while the search is conducted. As noted above, the warrant must be specific about what can be searched for and seized, however, there is some flexibility in that. Criminal Code s. 489 allows a peace officer to seize anything, in addition to things mentioned in the warrant, that on reasonable grounds he believes has been obtained by, or has been used in, the commission of an offence.

The difficulty for news organizations comes when police decide it's better to be safe than sorry and take more than they should. For example, an officer may believe the hard drive on a computer could contain copies of a reporter's notes or information that would be useful in the investigation.

---

18 *R. v. CITY TV* (2000), 147 C.C.C. (3d) 128 (Ont. Sup. Ct.).

A lawyer or savvy editor may be able to convince the officer that removing the entire machine from the office is excessive.

If a search warrant is invalid, any person in control of the premises is entitled to eject the peace officer using as much force as is necessary.[19] But this would be risky without legal advice. Also, any active resistance or obstruction of a valid search could theoretically result in a charge under s. 129 of the Code (that is, obstructing a peace officer or public officer).

INJUNCTIONS

An injunction is a so-called "extraordinary remedy" and the power to issue one is exercised carefully. Where the news media is concerned, the Supreme Court of Canada has recently emphasized the importance of the Charter's guarantee of freedom of the press in deciding whether to ban publication of any information. The Supreme Court's 1994 *Dagenais* test for when to issue court orders affecting the news media[20] (later modified by the same court in 2001's *Mentuck* ruling[21]) is discussed in the chapter on publication bans; however, a majority of the court made it clear that freedom of the press can take precedence over the accused's right to a fair trial and orders in criminal proceedings must be as limited as possible, if at all necessary.

Further, in 2005, the Supreme Court went on to state in another case that the news media deserve special consideration care in the issuance of "all discretionary court orders that limit freedom of expression and freedom of the press in relation to legal proceedings."[22] Still, court orders, such as injunctions, will not go away. Among other things, an injunction can be used to prevent the release of confidential information or a defamatory or contemptuous publication. It can even be used after the publication of a defamatory news story to have the article removed from online databases.[23]

---

19 In *Colet v. R.*, [1981] 1 S.C.R. 2, the Supreme Court of Canada held that a warrant that was made out only "to search" a home didn't also include the authority to seize anything (in this case, firearms) unless it was specifically stated in the warrant. The court said Colet was justified in using force to eject the police.

20 [1994] 3 S.C.R. 835.

21 *R. v. Mentuck*, 2001 CarswellMan 535, 2001 CarswellMan 536, [2001] 3 S.C.R. 442.

22 *Toronto Star Newspapers Ltd. v. Ontario*, 2005 CarswellOnt 2613, 2005 CarswellOnt 2614, [2005] 2 S.C.R. 188.

23 See *Robbins v. Pacific Newspaper Group Inc.* (2005), 2005 CarswellBC 2809, 50 B.C.L.R. (4th) 306 (S.C.), where famed motivational guru Anthony Robbins successfully won damages in a defamation lawsuit and an injunction to remove relevant *Vancouver Sun*, *National Post* and *Victoria Times Colonist* articles from the Infomart news database.

Here are some common injunctions:

1. *interlocutory:* This injunction is issued after notice of an action has been served and restrains an act or maintains the status quo until a proper hearing on the matter can be held.

2. *quia timet:* This court order is issued in anticipation or in fear of an act which the applicant for the injunction wants to stop. It may be an illegal act or a lawful act which could cause injury, for which money would not provide an adequate remedy.

3. *ex parte:* This is an injunction issued without hearing from the party it affects. It's only issued when time is of the essence and the applicant for the injunction establishes he could suffer harm if it's not granted. Such an order can be used to prevent the broadcast or publication of a contemptuous or defamatory story.

4. *perpetual:* This injunction restrains an act forever after a proper hearing has been held on the merits of the case.

How is an Injunction Issued?

An injunction won't be granted unless there's a clear basis for a court action.[24] This is especially so in cases of alleged defamation. For instance, in one case the court held that an injunction shouldn't be issued for an allegedly defamatory story unless the words complained of are so manifestly defamatory that any jury verdict to the contrary would be considered perverse by a court of appeal.[25] The same court also said the injunction also shouldn't be issued if damages would constitute a sufficient remedy.

In another commonly cited case (which will be discussed more fully below), an injunction was issued to stop the broadcast of defamatory matter in a radio documentary on the CBC. On appeal, the injunction was dissolved and the appeal court said such an order should only be issued for an alleged libel in the clearest of cases.[26] The court said the story must be clearly defamatory, clearly untrue and clearly not fair comment. The court held that if the publisher of the defamatory matter is of the opinion that he can

24 In *Church of Scientology of B.C. v. Radio N.W. Ltd.*, [1974] 4 W.W.R. 173 (B.C. C.A.), an interim injunction was granted to the plaintiff because the defendant was unwilling to offer any evidence of the truth of the story's defamatory allegations and, furthermore, said it would broadcast them despite the lack of solid proof.

25 *Rapp v. McClelland and Stewart Ltd.* (1981), 34 O.R. (2d) 452 at 455 (H.C.).

26 *Can. Metal v. Canadian Broadcasting Corp.* (1974), 3 O.R. (2d) 1 at 16 (H.C.).

prove the truth of his statements or offer some other defence, then no injunction will be issued. The matter can then be resolved in a proper defamation action.

In other matters, such as cases alleging a breach of confidence, the law is less clear. A journalist may have to prove that there's a "public interest" at stake in allowing publication of confidential information. The court will try to balance the interests of all parties and find the least "harmful" decision. This is known as the "balance of convenience" test.

Injunctions have become a popular tactical tool to try to prevent journalists from publishing privileged or confidential information, such as proprietary research and solicitor-client documents. In an example of the latter, an application for a permanent injunction preventing the CBC from broadcasting details of correspondence to a lawyer was successful.[27] The court made a point of noting that freedom of the press is not "absolute" and the common law right of privilege and confidentiality for solicitor-client communications is not overridden by the media's freedom of the press guarantee.

Proving the confidential nature of information and just who is bound to keep it secret, however, is not always easy. In a 1996 appeal of an interim injunction, a Toronto consulting firm to the financial services industry argued unsuccessfully that the news media could not publish details of a survey it sold to clients because news editors had been forewarned in letters that the soon-to-be-released report was confidential. *The Globe and Mail* later received a copy of the survey from a third party and published aspects of it. The judge said the fact a letter had been sent to newspapers warning of the confidential nature of the information was immaterial and there was no breach of confidence since the report was not sent from the consulting firm. The court noted the company had failed to establish it would suffer irreparable harm from further publication. The judge also noted that while the report was "interesting" to the investing public, it was not "in the public interest" that it be published. That said, she said it was in the public interest that the news media not experience "unjustified restriction on freedom of the press."

An injunction may also be issued to stop the publication of a story or broadcast which could endanger the fair trial of an individual. In 1985, an Alberta court judge banned the showing in Alberta of a CBC drama which was loosely based on the controversial case of James Keegstra, a schoolteacher convicted of inciting racial hatred. The judge felt the one-hour

---

27 *Amherst (Town) v. Canadian Broadcasting Corp.* (1994), 128 N.S.R. (2d) 260 (S.C.), affirmed (1994), 133 N.S.R. (2d) 277 (C.A.).

program was "a thinly-guised characterization of . . . Keegstra" and would interfere with Keegstra's appeal of his conviction.[28]

However, the CBC later challenged the injunction and the order was set aside by the appeal court.[29] That court noted that the CBC drama was to be broadcast before Keegstra's appeal took place and in the event a new trial was ordered, it would not begin for at least two or three years. The appeal court held that there was no real or substantial risk of prejudice to any potential re-trial and hence no case for an injunction.

While the Keegstra case involved proceedings at the appeal stage, another case looked at whether any danger exists when a trial is closer at hand. In 1986, the last of seven people awaiting trial in the murder of Hanna Buxbaum applied for an injunction to delay publication of a book about the high-profile trial of co-accused Helmuth Buxbaum, husband of Hanna.[30]

The court noted that the author of the book was aware of the upcoming trial of the accused and had given an undertaking not to use the plaintiff's name in the book. Citing the freedom of the press and the need for public reporting of trials, the judge pointed out that the previous trial had been widely-reported and a fair and accurate report of it in book form should not be enjoined.

It is also becoming apparent that reporters must be careful of the promises they make to sources. Journalists may not realize an injunction can be issued in connection with an alleged breach of a contract or an agreement made with a journalist. In one case, a book publisher got an injunction which prevented the broadcast of an interview with a noted celebrity, Margaret Trudeau.[31] The publisher had an agreement with the CTV television network that the network would not broadcast the interview until just prior to the book's release. But disagreements arose after parts of the unreleased book were published elsewhere and the network maintained it no longer had an agreement and tried to broadcast the interview at an earlier date. The book publisher went to court and the result was that an injunction was issued until the matter of the breach of the alleged contract could be tried in court.

In 1985, a similar situation arose for the CBC's current affairs program, *The Fifth Estate*. The program was planning to broadcast a story involving a convicted serial killer. The accused was appealing some of his convictions at the time and applied for an injunction to stop the broadcast. The Alberta

---

28 Quoted in *Canadian Broadcasting Corp. v. Keegstra* (1986), 35 D.L.R. (4th) 76 at 77 (Alta. C.A.).
29 *Ibid.*
30 *Foshay v. Key Porter Books Ltd.* (1986), 36 D.L.R. (4th) 106 (Ont. H.C.).
31 *Paddington Press Ltd. v. Champ* (1979), 43 C.P.R. (2d) 175 (Ont. H.C.).

court judge was told by the accused that the CBC had agreed to let him see the finished product before it went to air.

In court, the CBC maintained that the agreement in question applied to an earlier interview and the story was using material from a later interview at which no such promise was made. The judge held that there was an agreement and that it had been breached. He issued a cross-country injunction against the airing of the television documentary based on the breach of the agreement.

In another case involving the CBC, an apparent agreement with a source again interfered with getting a story on the air.[32] The Canadian office of a large accounting firm had been hired by the Romanian government to help track down millions of dollars diverted by a deposed dictator. The accountants agreed to an interview on the condition that the information would not be used by the broadcaster without the firm's consent. When the firm learned a program was scheduled and no permissions had been sought, its lawyers asked for an interim injunction until the matter of the breach of confidence could be settled in court. The judge agreed the accounting firm had a legitimate issue to be settled at trial and that it would suffer greater damage in reputation if the broadcast was allowed than CBC would suffer in the delay. While agreeing there was a "public interest" at issue, the court noted the media had to be held accountable for protecting confidences.

What Happens After an Injunction is Delivered?

Obviously, anyone who is the subject of an injunction should call a lawyer. A lawyer may be able to have the injunction quashed and, at the very least, can advise a journalist on how to properly comply with the order.

Compliance can be a complex matter. It's important that the injunction be obeyed not only to the letter, but in spirit as well. This means one shouldn't try to "split hairs" when deciding how an injunction affects a story. A prominent example of this involved the CBC.[33]

---

32 *Peat Marwick Thorne v. Canadian Broadcasting Corp.* (1991), 84 D.L.R. (4th) 656 (Ont. Gen. Div.).

33 *Can. Metal v. Canadian Broadcasting Corp. (No. 2)* (1974), 19 C.C.C. (2d) 218 (Ont. H.C.). This decision holding the CBC and some of its employees in contempt of the injunction was upheld in the Ontario Court of Appeal at (1975), 65 D.L.R. (3d) 231. For a more recent example of the need to obey injunctions to the letter, see *Canada (Human Rights Commission) v. Canadian Liberty Net* (1998), 157 D.L.R. (4th) 385 (S.C.C.). A human rights tribunal got an injunction from the Federal Court of Canada to restrain an organization and individuals from making discriminatory telephone messages exposing people to hatred. After the order was issued, callers were told to phone a number in a foreign country where similar messages could still be heard. The Supreme Court held this action was indeed contempt of the court order.

In 1974, the CBC was preparing to broadcast a radio documentary on *As It Happens* involving two lead smelting companies. The documentary was entitled "Dying of Lead."

On the day of the broadcast, the smelting companies applied for an *ex parte* injunction to stop the CBC from making certain allegations about the safety of its smoke stacks. The action by the companies was prompted by a newspaper article outlining what the CBC story alleged.

The injunction was granted with this endorsement:[34]

> Ex parte injunction granted to plaintiffs restraining defendants, and each of them from alleging or implying by broadcasting on television or otherwise publicizing that the plaintiffs and/or either of them, have bought misleadingly favourable medical evidence and concealed material evidence from medical experts, and from misstating the amounts the plaintiffs are spending to install pollution control systems.

The CBC was notified by telephone of the injunction and shortly after, a copy of the injunction was personally delivered. By the time the notice of the injunction was delivered the program had already been heard in the Maritimes because of the earlier time zone.

The CBC producers and legal counsel sat down to edit the script for the Ontario and Western audiences to conform to the injunction. Some offending statements were removed and the program was broadcast in its revised form. But, the court was later to hold that substantial parts of the remaining story were also in contravention of the injunction. In addition, to explain the alterations to the story, the court order was read word-for-word at one point in the program. Later that same night, the CBC's national news program ran a story reporting the fact that the court injunction had been issued against the radio program. The television story also went on to quote the exact words of the injunction.

The judge felt that very little had been edited out of the story after the injunction was received. He said the airing of the story should have been postponed to allow for more careful examination of the script. The judge felt the people responsible for the story shouldn't have tried to edit it in such a short time. Besides the fact that errors in judgment were made in editing down the story, a major complaint of the judge was that the quotation of the injunction's endorsement published the exact allegations that the court was seeking to prevent from being broadcast.

As a result of the CBC broadcasts, other news agencies carried the story, quoting the wording of the injunction and also stating what was not intended to be published. The court found the publication of the wording of

---

34 (1974), 19 C.C.C. (2d) 218 at 221 (Ont. H.C.).

the injunction by the CBC and the other news outlets to be against the spirit of the court order. The court held that anyone who knows of the substance or nature of an injunction must obey it, even if they aren't named in the injunction. Therefore, the other news agencies were also in violation of the injunction and in fact several were cited for contempt along with the CBC.

SUBPOENAS

A *subpoena* is a judicial order requiring a person to appear in a court at a certain place and time to give evidence in a criminal or civil proceeding. The subpoena may require a person to personally take the stand and testify (that is, a *subpoena ad testificandum*) and/or it may require the person to present any documents in his possession or under his or her control relating to the subject-matter of the proceedings (that is, a *subpoena duces tecum*). In criminal cases, anyone who is "likely to give material evidence in a proceeding" may be the subject of a subpoena.[35] A similar standard is set in civil cases.[36]

The "likely to give material evidence" standard was put to the test in 2007 in a high-profile challenge of a subpoena issued to an Ontario journalist.[37] After Robert Baltovich was convicted in 1992 of murdering Elizabeth Bain, author Derek Finkle wrote a book in 1998, *No Claim to Mercy*, criticizing the police investigation and questioning Baltovich's guilt. In 2004, the Ontario Court of Appeal overturned Baltovich's conviction and ordered a re-trial. Before the new trial began, the Crown sought to make

---

35 Criminal Code, s. 698(1).
36 See *Fullowka v. Royal Oak Mines Inc.*, 2001 CarswellNWT 2, [2001] 5 W.W.R. 719 (S.C.), reconsideration refused 2002 CarswellNWT 16 (S.C.), affirmed 2002 CarswellNWT 88 (C.A.). In a civil lawsuit involving an explosion at a mine, an application by the plaintiffs sought pre-trial production of videotapes held by the Canadian Broadcasting Corporation, a non-party to the action. Citing the Charter's freedom of the press protections, the CBC resisted the application. In deciding on the application, the court noted "the Charter does not apply to the resolution of private disputes, but, the courts cannot ignore the values underlying the Charter in any decision they are called upon to make." Specifically, the court ruled that no material evidence would be contributed by the videotape and, "when I consider the special position of the press, I am of the opinion that the importance of the information sought must be much more evident than it is in this case." Contrast that case, however, with *R. v. Canadian Broadcasting Corp.*, 2006 CarswellOnt 1119, [2006] O.J. No. 722 (C.J.), in which both the Crown and defence lawyers in a criminal case before a Toronto court were successful in executing subpoenas for videotape of a demonstration by neo-Nazis. Here, the court believed the video was "material and relevant" and, since some of the video had already aired, it was in the public domain.
37 *R. v. Baltovich* (unreported ruling on motion to quash subpoena); *Finkle v. The Queen*, 2007 CarswellOnt 7365 June 28, 2007, Justice Watt (S.C.J.).

Finkle a "witness for the prosecution," as a judge later put it, and issued subpoenas for production of evidence, such as notes and printed material related to the case. The Crown also attempted to get access to audio or video interviews.

Citing freedom of the press and that he had no material evidence to offer, Finkle fought back in court. The judge reviewing the subpoena summarized the standoff: "One seeks everything. The other provides nothing."

The court ruled that the Crown blatantly failed to prove Finkle was "likely to give material evidence" at the re-trial — that is, proving there was a distinct probability that material evidence will be given, not merely a possibility. In other words, no fishing expeditions are allowed.

Citing the previous Supreme Court rulings on court orders involving the news media, the court here said: "Among the circumstances that fall to be considered where the premises to be searched or the person or organization ordered to produce documents is a media outlet or journalist are the availability of alternate sources from which the information may reasonably be obtained, and whether what is sought has already been disseminated by the media or journalist affected." In this case, alternate sources for the information were available and Finkle's information was already in the public domain.

A 2004 case, involving the infamous neo-Nazi Ernst Zündel, raised similar issues.[38] Zündel was facing deportation and sought enforcement of witness subpoenas issued to various members of the Jewish community and a journalist. The subpoenas were quashed on the basis that it was not proven that the witnesses would be likely to give material evidence.

The subpoena served on the journalist was extensive, requiring him to bring with him all materials, documents and statements in any way related to Zündel, the Canadian Security Intelligence Service and a book the author wrote on the spy agency. The court agreed the subpoena should be quashed because it would require the author to disclose confidential information and sources, contrary to rights recognized at common law and under the Charter of Rights and Freedoms. As well, information he might testify to was already in the public domain in his book.

How is a Subpoena Issued?

A subpoena may be issued by a superior court judge, a provincial court judge, justice of the peace or even a clerk of the court. Subpoenas issued by a superior court are effective throughout Canada, while those issued by a provincial court have authority only within that province. Clerks can issue

---

38 *Re Zündel*, [2004] F.C.J. No. 1089 (F.C.).

subpoenas for certain courts (for example, superior and appellate courts) and usually do so without questioning the lawyer who requested it.

But if a judge or justice of the peace issues a subpoena, he or she will have to be convinced that the person receiving it has "material evidence" to give at the trial. Material evidence is that which is necessary to the resolution of the dispute or has an important bearing on the issues in question.

Not all witnesses with material evidence can be subpoenaed. For example, a lawyer can't be called as a witness to testify to matters within solicitor-client privilege.[39] Although journalists may consider their relationship with sources to be similar to solicitor-client relationships, the courts have a different view in most cases and will usually require a journalist to reveal a source.[40]

As with search warrants, the courts may be reluctant to allow authorities to go on fishing missions with subpoenas. In a 1994 Saskatchewan case, two reporters were issued subpoenas ordering them to give evidence at a preliminary hearing into a murder charge. The journalists had conducted their own investigation and had also interviewed the accused. The subpoenas required them to bring "all notes, books, records, reports, videotapes and documents" related to the case. The judge quashed the subpoenas, saying they were too broad to ensure compliance and noting that care had to be taken to balance freedom of the press with the obligation of citizens to provide relevant evidence.[41]

What Happens After a Subpoena is Delivered?

The subpoena will usually be personally delivered to the witness. But if the witness can't be conveniently found, the subpoena can be left at his or her home with anyone who appears to be at least 16 years old.[42] Once a subpoena is received, the witness is required to attend the court as directed and cannot leave until excused by the judge.[43] If someone refuses to obey a subpoena and fails to show up, the court can issue a cross-country warrant for the arrest of the witness.[44] The witness may then be detained until the trial or released on recognizance.

The issuance of a subpoena may be challenged in a superior court. For example, a subpoenaed witness may not actually have "material evidence"

---

39 *R. v. Stupp* (1983), 32 C.R. (3d) 168 (Ont. H.C.).
40 See the chapter on "News Sources."
41 *Ehman v. Saskatchewan (Attorney General)* (1994), 121 Sask. R. 45 (Q.B.).
42 Criminal Code, s. 509(2).
43 *Ibid.*, s. 700.
44 *Ibid.*, ss. 698(2) and 705.

or the material evidence could be gathered easily through other channels. Journalists themselves may be called upon to appear in court to testify to any number of things. The journalist may have seen a crime committed, he or she may have to bring interview notes as evidence in a defamation action or an editor may be asked to bring copies of published stories to prove that they appeared (for example, as in a change of venue hearing based on prejudicial news reports).

Some witnesses may agree to show up in court, but will refuse to testify. The court has several options. If the refusal comes during the preliminary hearing in a criminal proceeding, the presiding judge may commit the witness to jail for a period of up to eight days.[45] If the witness refuses to answer questions after the end of the eight-day period, the judge may continue to issue eight-day internments — theoretically forever. In a criminal trial, the judge can cite the witness with contempt and under the Criminal Code the sentence is at the complete discretion of the judge, theoretically, with no limit as to the severity of the punishment.[46]

In one high-profile criminal proceeding, attempts by the media to use Charter and other arguments to quash subpoenas were unsuccessful.[47] Reporters had interviewed complainants in a sexual assault case involving a former Premier. A judge issued subpoenas on behalf of the defence for the journalists to testify at the preliminary inquiry. The reporters refused, citing a variety of reasons including freedom of the press, the right to privacy and the right to remain silent. The appeal court said the judge did not err in deciding their testimony was "material," even though it might only be "relevant" to the proceedings.

The argument that freedom of the press was infringed was rejected because no supporting evidence was offered. The claim of a right to privacy was also refused. The court noted the complainants claimed no privacy right in their communications with the journalists and there was no evidence of any expectation of privacy. Arguments the subpoenas betrayed both the principles of "fundamental justice" and the reporters' right to silence were also dismissed. If valid, the appeal court said, these concerns would apply to all subpoenaed witnesses, not just journalists. Also, any information revealed in the hearing was not to be used against the journalists themselves. Finally, the court held that the judge issuing the subpoenas did have the authority to order reporters to bring their notes and tapes and that any issue

---

45 *Ibid.*, s. 545.
46 See *R. v. Clement*, [1981] 2 S.C.R. 468, where the Supreme Court of Canada held that the power to punish for contempt under ss. 9 and 10 of the Code includes the right of the presiding judge to determine the proper punishment at his own discretion.
47 *R. v. Regan* (1997), 144 D.L.R. (4th) 456 (N.S. C.A.) Application for leave to appeal to the Supreme Court of Canada dismissed April 3, 1997 (Court File No. 25859).

of their admissibility would be within the domain of the preliminary inquiry judge.

A COURT ORDERS CHECKLIST

Search Warrants and Production Orders

1. The Charter guarantees in s. 8 "the right to be secure against unreasonable search or seizure." The minimum requirements for a warrant are that:

    • there must be a belief based on reasonable and probable grounds, established upon oath, that an offence has been committed;
    • there is a belief the evidence of the offence is to be found at the place to be searched;
    • the area to be searched must be clearly described and the search must be limited to that area;
    • the authorization for the search warrant must come from a neutral person who, if not a judge, is capable of acting judicially.

2. For a search warrant or production order to be valid:

    • the warrant must disclose the offence in relation to which the search is being conducted and the grounds of belief upon which the request for the warrant is made;
    • the place to be searched must be accurately described; and
    • the items to be searched for and seized must be described so they can be easily identified by the person at the premises and the officer executing the search.

3. The person conducting the search is required to meet the following conditions:

    • the warrant must be in his or her possession during the search;
    • the warrant must be exhibited for inspection upon request;
    • if the premises to be searched is a residence, there should first be a demand to open before a forced entry is attempted; and
    • a peace officer can only use the force which is necessary to enter the premises.

4. If a search warrant or production order is invalid, anyone in control of the premises is entitled to eject the peace officer with as much force as

necessary. But active resistance or obstruction of a valid search could result in a criminal charge of obstruction. Always contact legal counsel when presented with a search warrant.

Injunctions

1. Among other things, an injunction can be used to prevent a defamatory or contemptuous publication. It may restrain an act for a limited period or forever.

2. Generally, an injunction will not be granted unless there's a clear need for immediate action. In defamation matters, courts have held that an injunction shouldn't be issued except in cases of obvious defamation when damages would not constitute a sufficient remedy, and even then, shouldn't be granted if the news outlet indicates it's willing to defend any action. Where there is a risk of contempt of court and endangering a fair trial, the danger of prejudicing the trial must be real and substantial.

   In other matters, such as cases alleging a breach of confidence, the law is less clear. A journalist may have to prove there is a "public interest" at stake in not granting an injunction. The court will try to balance the interests of all parties and find the least "harmful" decision.

3. Anyone who knows of the substance or nature of an injunction must obey it, even if they aren't named in the injunction.

Subpoenas

1. A subpoena is a judicial order requiring a person to appear in a court at a certain place and time to give evidence in a criminal or civil proceeding. If someone refuses to obey a subpoena and fails to show up, the court can issue a warrant for the arrest of the witness. The witness may then be detained until the trial or released on recognizance.

2. A subpoena may be issued to anyone with "material evidence" in the dispute or issues in question. A lawyer may be able to challenge a subpoena. For example, a subpoenaed witness may not actually have "material evidence" or the material evidence could be gathered easily through other channels.

12

CONFIDENTIAL INFORMATION AND NATIONAL SECURITY

At some time in their career, many journalists come to know the excitement of receiving the famous "plain brown envelope" containing some confidential or secret document. Or perhaps a disgruntled company employee walks into the newsroom with a bundle of papers suggesting his employer has committed some illegal or immoral act.

Can a journalist publish these confidential documents? The answer is not an easy one and, as with many of the news media's legal problems, a lawyer must be called in to examine the circumstances of each case.

Recently, there have been at least two important court rulings involving attempts by investigating authorities to seize confidential information received by reporters and uncover sources of that information from news media outlets. In both cases, the media emerged victorious on certain points and one significant ruling has declared unconstitutional and invalid sections of the federal law governing wrongful communication and possession of official secrets. That said, journalists should be aware other court rulings have been critical of "whistle-blowers" (employees, public servants, police, etc.) who owe a duty of confidentiality to their employer or others.

What's certain is that any time a journalist receives secret or confidential information belonging to someone else, it must be handled carefully or the journalist could end up in civil or even criminal court.

JOURNALISTS AND THE "PLAIN BROWN ENVELOPE"

There can be many problems with publishing confidential documents received privately (as opposed to confidential information from a public proceeding, such as a court).[1] One of the first questions to be asked is, who is the source of the information?

If the source is known, a journalist must then consider whether that person is possibly breaching a confidence or trust. If so, the source and the journalist could be sued by the person or body to whom the confidence is owed. For example, a lawyer who hands a journalist incriminating documents belonging to a client may be breaching the solicitor-client privilege. The client could seek an injunction to prohibit publication and sue for damages.[2] A duty of confidentiality also binds other professionals, such as doctors and accountants, and even employer-employee relationships can prevent proprietary information from being divulged.

---

1 Generally, courts avoid preventing disclosure of documents filed in a proceeding. For example, in *Atomic Energy of Canada Ltd. v. Sierra Club of Canada* (2000), 187 D.L.R. (4th) 231 (Fed. C.A.), leave to appeal allowed, 2001 CarswellNat 20 (S.C.C.), the Crown corporation wanted a court order treating supplementary documents filed in court as confidential because they contained commercially sensitive material. The court ruled it was a public law case that involved wide public interest and such an order would harm the principle of open and accessible court proceedings.

2 See *Amherst (Town) v. Canadian Broadcasting Corp.* (1994), 128 N.S.R. (2d) 260 (S.C.), affirmed (1994), 133 N.S.R. (2d) 277 (C.A.). An application was granted for a permanent injunction preventing the CBC from broadcasting details of correspondence between the town and a lawyer. The court held that the Charter's freedom of the press guarantee did not override the common law solicitor-client privilege and the privilege had not been waived by the town allowing a third party to have access to the documents. More recently, in *Stewart v. Canadian Broadcasting Corp.* (1997), 150 D.L.R. (4th) 24 (Ont. Ct. (Gen. Div.), a famous defence lawyer participated in a television broadcast about an old criminal case involving his former client. The court ruled the lawyer's fiduciary duty to his client continued after the case had ended. The lawyer was found liable for damages for emotional harm and the profit derived from broadcast. The company producing the broadcast was not found liable since it did not know the lawyer had breached his duty and assumed the lawyer knew his legal obligations.

An RCMP investigator is ordered by his superiors not to discuss a high-profile criminal case with the news media. The officer believes national security is at stake and the gag order is unlawful. Not only does he discuss the case with the press, radio and television, he shares classified documents and information. With his grave concern for the public interest, is the officer protected from reprisals as a whistle-blower?

No. The Federal Court of Appeal (which has jurisdiction over the RCMP) rejected the whistle-blower defence in a similar case recently.[3] Corporal Robert Allan Read was accused of disobeying a lawful order not to discuss with the media an investigation into alleged criminal activity in the Immigration Section of the Canadian Mission in Hong Kong. Read believed the order was unlawful, and that criminals had infiltrated the computer system and were issuing false visas that might threaten national security. He claimed speaking to the media was a last resort and in the public interest. The court ruled Read owed a duty of loyalty to the RCMP. His "whistle-blowing" defence failed because there "simply was not enough evidence to lend credence to his allegations." The officer's "legitimate public concern" was no exception to his duty of loyalty. The restrictions on his right to speak out, said the court, were reasonable under the Charter since the need for an impartial and effective police force prevails.

If the source is unknown, other questions must then be answered. Is the information what it purports to be? For example, was that damning letter really written by the company president or is it a forgery using purloined letterhead? Without knowing the source, it's sometimes difficult to tell.

In either case, it's possible the documents may have been stolen or passed on without the owner's consent. If that's the case, publication could result in a civil lawsuit or even criminal charges.

This was amply illustrated in 1989 when a Global Television reporter was charged with possession of a stolen document after a "Deep Throat" handed him a copy of the federal government's budget brief on the day before the budget was to be brought down. While many people criticized, on a public policy basis, the RCMP's decision to charge the reporter, it's reasonable to assume such a document could have been stolen or the product

---

3 *Read v. Canada (Attorney General)* (2006), 2006 CarswellNat 5127, 2006 CarswellNat 2579, 272 D.L.R. (4th) 300 (F.C.A.), leave to appeal to the Supreme Court refused (2007), 2007 CarswellNat 1093, 2007 CarswellNat 1094 (S.C.C.).

of a government employee's breach of public trust. The police obviously felt that only a criminal trial could sort out the details.

Another question, best dealt with by a lawyer, is whether the information in question is truly "confidential." In a recent case, a company producing a "confidential report" distributed to brokerages applied for an injunction to prevent a newspaper from publishing some details in the document.[4] The judge ruled there was no issue to be tried since the newspaper had not received the information on a confidential basis (it came from an undisclosed third-party) and the information was "so widely disseminated it did not have the necessary quality of confidentiality." The court also cited the importance of freedom of the press in denying the request for an injunction. Again, a lawyer is the best individual to assess whether any documents received are truly confidential.

If a lawyer determines that a document was stolen or a breach of confidence, the journalist may be advised to return it to its owner or hand it to the authorities. However, this doesn't mean that you can't use the information in the documents to ask questions or look for another source to corroborate what is in the documents.

A "brown paper envelope" arrived anonymously at a newspaper, addressed to an investigative journalist working on a story about the Prime Minister's business dealings in his riding. The document purports to place the Prime Minister in a conflict of interest regarding a bank loan. When the newspaper tried to confirm its details, the bank and Prime Minister's Office denied the document's authenticity. At the same time, the bank claimed the document was confidential and should be returned. It asked the RCMP to investigate and the police got search warrants to seize the original document and envelope to check for fingerprints and DNA of its confidential source. Did the police have the right to seize the material from the news media?

Yes. In a landmark case involving the *National Post* newspaper, an Ontario Superior Court judge originally quashed the search warrant targeting the media in 2004, but the Ontario Court of Appeal overturned the lower court's ruling in 2008.[5] The appeal court ruled the warrant was issued properly even though the issuing justice had not given the *Post* notice of the warrant application. A mitigating factor may have been the

---

4   *B.W. International Inc. v. Thomson Canada Ltd.* (1996), 137 D.L.R. (4th) 398 (Ont. Gen. Div.).

5   *R. v. National Post* (2004), 2004 CarswellOnt 173, 69 O.R. (3d) 427 (S.C.J.), reversed 2008 CarswellOnt 1104, [2008] ONCA 139 (C.A.).

fact the issuing justice specifically stated in the warrant that, if requested by the *Post*, any items sought by police would be sealed and not disclosed to authorities until the validity of the warrant could be determined in a judicial review or court hearing. While the appeal judges accepted "the gathering and dissemination of news and information without undue state interference is an integral component of [journalists'] constitutional right of freedom of the press under s. 2(b) of the Charter. . . this does not mean that press organizations or journalists are immune from valid searches under s. 8 of the Charter. And s. 2(b) does not guarantee that journalists have an automatic right to protect the confidentiality of their sources." Importantly, the appeal court refused the Crown's argument that law enforcement's interest in requiring disclosure "will always trump the media's claim to a journalist-confidential source privilege." Issues of privilege and confidentiality, wrote the appeal justices, must always be decided on a case-by-case basis.

JOURNALISTS AND NATIONAL SECURITY

As one might suspect, concern over leaks of confidential government information can crop up when an agent for a foreign power is caught with military secrets or a journalist receives information involving national security. Until recently, the Official Secrets Act dealt with such issues and could even be used to stop publication of non-military government information. However, there were few prosecutions under the Act, largely because of its cumbersome and confusing language.[6]

The previous law was actually an adaptation of several English statutes dating back to the early part of the century and remained largely unchanged since then. One of its problems was that it didn't define an "official secret." It made several references to that which is "prejudicial to the safety or interests of the State" and information or documents that could be "directly or indirectly useful to a foreign power." The Act also made opaque references to "official documents" and "secret official code word[s]" or "password[s]." But this mixed bag of phrasing made a prosecution under the Act very difficult.

In late 2001, however, the Official Secrets Act was renamed as the Security of Information Act (SOIA) and several key aspects of the older law were repealed or replaced. As you will learn below, the SOIA was not in place for long before key sections relevant to the news media were deemed

---

6 R.S.C. 1985, c. O-5. See the *Mackenzie Royal Commission on Security*, June, 1969, where deficiencies in the Official Secrets Act are discussed.

by a court to be unconstitutional and invalid. At the time of this publication, the SOIA sections in question remain on the books but, with one major court ruling having declared them of no force, it will be up to Parliament to address the court's concerns in the near future. Since the SOIA has yet to be amended, we will review what the law currently says and then review the position that the court took in invalidating the relevant sections.

SOIA and the News Media

The sweeping nature of the current Security of Information Act and similar laws in many countries make this type of legislation a potentially dangerous instrument for censorship in the hands of a power-mad government. This was clearly illustrated in the 1980's, for example, when the British government tried unsuccessfully to use its own official secrets law to prevent publication of *Spycatcher*, a book examining the world of covert agents.

For journalists, a law of this type has to be balanced carefully with the Charter's guarantees of freedom of the press and expression. Unfortunately, the SOIA fails in this regard. For example, consider the broad scope of the Act's definition in s. 3(1) of actions that are prejudicial to the nation's safety and interests:

> 3. (1) For the purposes of this Act, a purpose is prejudicial to the safety or interests of the State if a person
>
> (a) commits, in Canada, an offence against the laws of Canada or a province that is punishable by a maximum term of imprisonment of two years or more in order to advance a political, religious or ideological purpose, objective or cause or to benefit a foreign entity or terrorist group;
>
> (b) commits, inside or outside Canada, a terrorist activity;
>
> (c) causes or aggravates an urgent and critical situation in Canada that
>   (i) endangers the lives, health or safety of Canadians, or
>   (ii) threatens the ability of the Government of Canada to preserve the sovereignty, security or territorial integrity of Canada;
>
> (d) interferes with a service, facility, system or computer program, whether public or private, or its operation, in a manner that has significant adverse impact on the health, safety, security or economic or financial well-being of the people of Canada or the functioning of any government in Canada;
>
> (e) endangers, outside Canada, any person by reason of that person's relationship with Canada or a province or the fact that the person is doing business with or on behalf of the Government of Canada or of a province;
>
> (f) damages property outside Canada because a person or entity with an interest in the property or occupying the property has a relationship with Canada or a province or is doing business with or on behalf of the Government of Canada or of a province;

(g) impairs or threatens the military capability of the Canadian Forces, or any part of the Canadian Forces;

(h) interferes with the design, development or production of any weapon or defence equipment of, or intended for, the Canadian Forces, including any hardware, software or system that is part of or associated with any such weapon or defence equipment;

(i) impairs or threatens the capabilities of the Government of Canada in relation to security and intelligence;

(j) adversely affects the stability of the Canadian economy, the financial system or any financial market in Canada without reasonable economic or financial justification;

(k) impairs or threatens the capability of a government in Canada, or of the Bank of Canada, to protect against, or respond to, economic or financial threats or instability;

(l) impairs or threatens the capability of the Government of Canada to conduct diplomatic or consular relations, or conduct and manage international negotiations;

(m) contrary to a treaty to which Canada is a party, develops or uses anything that is intended or has the capability to cause death or serious bodily injury to a significant number of people by means of
 (i) toxic or poisonous chemicals or their precursors,
 (ii) a microbial or other biological agent, or a toxin, including a disease organism,
 (iii) radiation or radioactivity, or
 (iv) an explosion; or

(n) does or omits to do anything that is directed towards or in preparation of the undertaking of an activity mentioned in any of paragraphs (a) to (m).

Most of these provisions are aimed at terrorists and other "foreign powers," but it is possible a muckraking journalist could also affect the security, economic or financial well-being of the nation. When the SOIA was introduced to Parliament initially, several lawyer and journalist groups fervently objected to its restrictions on freedom of expression. For instance, one submission said, the law could allow authorities to interpret a protest group's activities as intending to threaten public safety or prevent anyone from peacefully expressing unpopular opinions. The Canadian Bar Association (CBA) also believed the investigative powers could be used against journalists, forcing them to disclose information and reveal their sources without a proper hearing to determine the need to reveal the source. "The compulsory disclosure contemplated," said the CBA's submission to Parliament, "would have... a chilling effect on the media, and would likely result in people being less willing to come forward and give information to the media."

As in the previous official secrets law, the definition of secret or prejudicial information is very broad. It could be military (for example, information on the development of a new weapon or troop movements), political (for example, cabinet documents), administerial (for example, secret government discussion papers) or even economic (for example, a trade secret). The penalties for violating the Act can be up to 14 years in jail or even life imprisonment for terrorist-related offences. As noted below, there are several offences under the Act that could affect journalists. They involve spying near prohibited places, and the communication and possession of confidential information.

Wrongful Communication

Section 4 sets out some of the offences that journalists are likely to be in a position to worry about. This section deals with the wrongful communication of secrets and there are several offences set out in the subsections of s. 4.

Subsection 4(1) lists seven examples of confidential information coming under the ambit of the Act, namely any secret official code word or password or any sketch, plan, model, article, note, document or information:

1. relating to or used in a prohibited place or anything in such a place;

2. that has been made or obtained in contravention of this Act;

3. that has been entrusted in confidence to him by any person holding office under Her Majesty;

4. that he has obtained or to which he has had access while subject to the Code of Service Discipline within the meaning of the National Defence Act;

5. that he has obtained or to which he has had access owing to his position as a person who holds or has held office under Her Majesty;

6. that he has obtained or to which he has had access as a person who holds or held a contract made on behalf of Her Majesty or carried out in whole or in part at a prohibited place; or

7. that he has obtained or to which he has had access as a person working for someone who holds or held such a contract.

Subsection 4(1) then makes it an offence for any person who has possession or control of any secret official code word or password or any sketch, plan, model, article, note, document or information to:

1. communicate it to an unauthorized person;

2. use the information for the benefit of a foreign power;

3. use it in a manner prejudicial to the safety and interests of the state;

4. unlawfully retain it; or

5. fail to take reasonable care of the information or endanger its safety.

Subsection 4(2) makes it an offence to directly or indirectly communicate to a foreign power an official secret about munitions of war or communicate it in any other manner prejudicial to the safety and interests of the state.

Subsection 4(3) is also a potential problem for journalists. It says it's an offence to receive any official secret knowing, or having a reasonable ground to believe at the time it's received, that it's being communicated in contravention of the Security of Information Act. To be found innocent, a person placed in this position would have to prove that he or she received the secret "contrary to his desire."

Subsection 4(4) makes it an offence to keep, for purposes prejudicial to the safety and interests of the state, any "official document" which a person was once authorized to have or to allow an unauthorized person to have possession of that secret. It also is an offence under this subsection to unlawfully receive an official secret and then neglect or fail to return it to "the person or authority by whom or for whose use it was issued, or to a police constable."

It should also be noted that ss. 13 and 14 prohibit unauthorized communication of secret, confidential or special operational information by individuals permanently bound to secrecy (certain public officials, military, RCMP, etc.). While these provisions are obviously speaking directly to those pledged to secrecy, the SOIA does contemplate the possibility that the public interest may be served at times in revealing such information. Section 15 provides a defence for those bound to secrecy who can prove they acted in the public interest.

For example, a person bound to secrecy may act in the public interest in "disclosing an offence under an Act of Parliament that he or she reasonably believes has been, is being or is about to be committed by another person in the purported performance of that person's duties and functions for, or on behalf of, the Government of Canada." The Act also accepts the public interest may be served when a "disclosure outweighs the public interest in non-disclosure." The public interest defence, however, is not available for other provisions, such as s. 4 offences.

The *O'Neill* Case[7]

Journalist Juliet O'Neill, with the *Ottawa Citizen* newspaper, wrote an article on November 8, 2003 about the controversial events involving Maher Arar, a Syrian-born Canadian whom U.S. authorities arrested and deported to Syria in 2002. The story was based, in part, on information supplied by confidential sources.

On January 21, 2004, the RCMP executed two search warrants to search O'Neill's home and her *Ottawa Citizen* office. The warrants were issued to support a criminal investigation into alleged violations of ss. 4(1)(a), 4(3) and 4(4)(b) of the SOIA. That is, the wrongful communication of "secret official" information, and its subsequent receipt and retention. O'Neill was specifically named as having committed the receipt and retention offences under ss. 4(3) and 4(4)(b)). Documents and computer information were seized, but no charges have been laid to date. The news media challenged the validity of the searches and seizures, and asked for the return of the seized items.

Examining the specific sections of the SOIA, as opposed to the entire Act, the court found numerous "fatal defects." For example, there is no clear definition in the SOIA for "secret official," "official," "lawful authority" or "authorized," and no reference in any other Canadian statute as to how the terms are to be defined. "Therein lies the heart of the problem," said the court.

The judge determined the sections in question are "standardless, with the result that they are facially meaningless." The court ruled the sections give the state the unfettered ability to arbitrarily protect whatever information it chooses to classify as "secret official," "official" or unauthorized for disclosure, and to punish by way of a criminal offence any "speakers," "receivers" and "listeners" who come within that protected sphere.

The court found this a "difficult and dangerous" situation for those not bound by governmental policies or guidelines regarding the classification of government information. "There is no guidance for the public in the SOIA as to what amounts to the prohibited conduct prescribed by these sections and their arbitrariness and breadth allow for the possibility that the

---

7   *O'Neill v. Canada (Attorney General)* (2006), 2006 CarswellOnt 8672, 272 D.L.R. (4th) 193 (S.C.J.).

release and possession of government information that carries with it no harm to the national interest can be criminalized," wrote the judge.

In the end, the Ontario court ruled the three sections of the SOIA were overbroad, vague and unconstitutional. As a result, the court declared the sections should not be used by law enforcement and should immediately have no force and effect. The government of the day indicated it would not challenge the court ruling and planned to amend the law in Parliament at some point in the future.

The *Toronto Sun* Case

Until *O'Neill*, there had been only one other case of note involving journalists charged under the old Official Secrets Act. It is an interesting case to note, in light of its similarities to aspects of the *O'Neill* case.

In 1978, the *Toronto Sun* and two employees were charged with violating the Act by publishing information obtained from a classified RCMP document on KGB activities in Canada.[8] The document in question was entitled "Canadian Related Activities of the Russian Intelligence Services." It was stamped "Top Secret" and "For Canadian Eyes Only." The journalists and newspaper were charged with wrongfully communicating secrets (s. 4(1)) and knowingly receiving the information in contravention of the Act (s. 4(3)).

The case is an excellent example of why the Official Secrets Act was a confusing and cumbersome law. At a preliminary hearing, the Crown began by calling an expert witness to testify about the potential damage the newspaper article could have to the safety and interests of Canada. But at that point, the lawyers for the journalists objected that the testimony would only be hearsay since there was no documentary proof that Canada's safety or interests were actually damaged.

The Crown then decided it had enough evidence to support the charge without the expert's testimony and withdrew the witness. The result of this little bit of courtroom jostling was that the preliminary hearing judge then did not have to decide whether the publication of the information was actually prejudicial to Canada's security.

The sole issue then became whether the report was in fact "secret." The judge examined in detail what had been previously published. Most of the details in the *Sun*'s story by Peter Worthington had in fact been published previously. There was evidence that information from the document had been broadcast on television, had been mentioned in the House of Commons

---

8 *R. v. Toronto Sun Publishing Ltd.* (1979), 1979 CarswellOnt 1465, 98 D.L.R. (3d) 524 (Prov. Ct.).

and was even reported in Hansard. There were also 67 copies of the "official" document distributed throughout the government.

The court referred to two Canadian court judgments that held that information that has already been published is neither "official" nor "secret."[9] The judge said that even stamping the documents with the words "Top Secret" has no official meaning and, here, was mainly for administrative convenience. There was also no evidence from the Crown regarding how the information was obtained and whether it was obtained unlawfully.

The court discharged the accused at the preliminary hearing. The justice said the Crown had failed to prove that the document was secret and had not proven that the accused had reasonable grounds to believe at the time that the information was communicated to them in contravention of the Act.

Although the *Toronto Sun* escaped prosecution, a journalist who receives information that he or she believes is an "official secret" would be wise to contact legal counsel. The new Act is so broadly worded that journalists receiving confidential government information could theoretically be thrown into lengthy and expensive legal proceedings.

Prohibited Places

The *O'Neill* case only addressed s. 4. For now, all other sections of the SOIA stand unchallenged at this time. For example, ss. 6 and 7 of the Act state:

> 6. Every person commits an offence who, for any purpose prejudicial to the safety or interests of the State, approaches, inspects, passes over, is in the neighbourhood of or enters a prohibited place at the direction of, for the benefit of or in association with a foreign entity or a terrorist group.

> 7. Every person commits an offence who, in the vicinity of a prohibited place, obstructs, knowingly misleads or otherwise interferes with or impedes a peace officer or a member of Her Majesty's forces engaged on guard, sentry, patrol or other similar duty in relation to the prohibited place.

---

9   The court referred to the 1962 case of *R. v. Biernacki* (1962), 1962 CarswellQue 299, 37 C.R. 226 (Mun. Ct.), in which the accused collected information on social status, employment and the character of Polish immigrants, which appeared to be for the purposes of espionage. The court felt this information was neither secret nor official, even though it may have been for the purposes of espionage. The other case was *Boyer v. R.* (1948), 1948 CarswellQue 12, 94 C.C.C. 195 (C.A.), leave to appeal to the Supreme Court refused (1948), 1948 CarswellQue 13, 94 C.C.C. 259 (S.C.C.), in which the Court said the Official Secrets Act does not apply to material which has already been published or publicized or can be found in the public domain.

This section is concerned with people lurking about a "prohibited place," which is further defined in s. 2(1) as:

(a) any work of defence belonging to or occupied or used by or on behalf of Her Majesty, including arsenals, armed forces establishments or stations, factories, dockyards, mines, minefields, camps, ships, aircraft, telegraph, telephone, wireless or signal stations or offices, and places used for the purpose of building, repairing, making or storing any munitions of war or any sketches, plans, models or documents relating thereto, or for the purpose of getting any metals, oil or minerals of use in time of war,

(b) any place not belonging to Her Majesty where any munitions of war or any sketches, plans, models or documents relating thereto are being made, repaired, obtained or stored under contract with, or with any person on behalf of, Her Majesty, or otherwise on behalf of Her Majesty, and

(c) any place that is for the time being declared by order of the Governor in Council to be a prohibited place on the ground that information with respect thereto or damage thereto would be useful to a foreign power.

Communicating with Terrorists

Also unchallenged are ss. 16 and 17, which potentially pose grave dangers to journalists working on stories involving terrorist sources or foreign governments. These sections, warn some critics, could lead to the prosecution of any journalist or Canadian who receives and distributes information the government is "taking measures to safeguard," even if its publication is clearly in the public interest.

16. (1) Every person commits an offence who, without lawful authority, communicates to a foreign entity or to a terrorist group information that the Government of Canada or of a province is taking measures to safeguard if

(a) the person believes, or is reckless as to whether, the information is information that the Government of Canada or of a province is taking measures to safeguard; and

(b) the person intends, by communicating the information, to increase the capacity of a foreign entity or a terrorist group to harm Canadian interests or is reckless as to whether the communication of the information is likely to increase the capacity of a foreign entity or a terrorist group to harm Canadian interests.

(2) Every person commits an offence who, intentionally and without lawful authority, communicates to a foreign entity or to a terrorist group information

that the Government of Canada or of a province is taking measures to safeguard if

> (a) the person believes, or is reckless as to whether, the information is information that the Government of Canada or of a province is taking measures to safeguard; and
>
> (b) harm to Canadian interests results.

(3) Every person who commits an offence under subsection (1) or (2) is guilty of an indictable offence and is liable to imprisonment for life.

17. (1) Every person commits an offence who, intentionally and without lawful authority, communicates special operational information to a foreign entity or to a terrorist group if the person believes, or is reckless as to whether, the information is special operational information.

(2) Every person who commits an offence under subsection (1) is guilty of an indictable offence and is liable to imprisonment for life.

Criminal Code and National Security

The Criminal Code[10] also addresses the communication of official secrets under the offence of high treason. Among other offences, s. 46(2)(b) states that anyone commits high treason who:

> without lawful authority, communicates or makes available to an agent of a state other than Canada, military or scientific information or any sketch, plan, model, article, note or document of a military or scientific character that he knows or ought to know may be used by that state for a purpose prejudicial to the safety or defence of Canada.

Anti-terrorism amendments to the Code in 2001 expand the range of potential offences affecting national security to include financing of terrorism, attacks against diplomats, posting hate messages on the Internet and recruiting for terrorist organizations, to name a few.

The amendments have been criticized as violating Charter rights. For example, some offences may be committed even though a terrorist act may not be carried out or yet planned. Section 83.19(1) states anyone who "knowingly facilitates a terrorist activity" can go to jail for up to 14 years. Facilitation is defined in subsection (2):

---

10 R.S.C. 1985, c. C-46.

For the purposes of this Part, a terrorist activity is facilitated whether or not

(a) the facilitator knows that a particular terrorist activity is facilitated;
(b) any particular terrorist activity was foreseen or planned at the time it was facilitated; or
(c) any terrorist activity was actually carried out.

It is possible that a journalist might get in trouble under this section for telling citizens (and terrorists) about lax security points at a nuclear plant. It is difficult to say at this time how far this law could be pushed. Still, lawmakers have taken some steps to ensure the amendments won't interfere with peaceful dissent in s. 83.01(1.1):

For greater certainty, the expression of a political, religious or ideological thought, belief or opinion does not come within paragraph (b) of the definition "terrorist activity" in subsection (1) unless it constitutes an act or omission that satisfies the criteria of that paragraph.

The Canadian Bar Association (CBA) was particularly sharp in its criticism of the anti-terrorism amendments and their impact on journalists. For example, the anti-terrorism provisions give peace officers far-reaching powers to conduct "investigative hearings" under s. 83.28 of the Criminal Code that limit the traditional right to silence. While there are some safeguards in the investigative hearing provisions, the CBA believes there should be a special recognition of the relationship between journalists and their sources.

A CONFIDENTIAL INFORMATION AND NATIONAL SECURITY CHECKLIST

1. A journalist receiving confidential information should consult a lawyer. For example, the documents may have been stolen. If the source is known, a journalist must then consider whether that person is possibly breaching a confidence or trust. If the source is unknown, the documents themselves may be forgeries, incomplete or misleading.

2. While confidential documents may have to be returned, the information in them can still be used by a journalist to ask questions or to seek out a corroborating or alternative source.

3. Under the Security of Information Act, it appears that an official secret could involve military, political (such as, cabinet documents), administerial (for example, a secret policy paper) or even economic infor-

mation (for example, a business' trade secret). One court has found the lack of clear definitions to be a fatal defect making some sections invalid and of no force.

4.   Under the Security of Information Act, a person may be charged with "spying" for lurking about a government designated "prohibited place," making a sketch, plan, model or note that "might be or is intended to be directly or indirectly useful to a foreign power," or passing on any secret official code or password.

5.   Under the Security of Information Act, a person may be charged with "wrongful communication" of confidential government information or unauthorized possession of such information. It's also an offence for any person to have possession or control of an official secret and communicate it to an unauthorized person, use the information for the benefit of a foreign power, use it in a manner prejudicial to the safety and interests of the State, unlawfully retain it, or fail to take reasonable care of it or endanger its safety. One court has found aspects of these sections of the Act to be invalid and of no force.

6.   Court decisions have held that information which has already been published is neither "official" nor "secret." Stamping documents with the words "Top Secret" has no official meaning.

13

COPYRIGHT

When a radio journalist broadcasts a word-for-word version of a newspaper story, a blog journalist cuts-and-pastes another's story online or an article quotes a popular song at length, there may be an infringement of someone's copyright.

Simply put, a copyright is a legal right to make public, produce or reproduce any original written or artistic work, or a substantial part of it, in any material form.

Lately, Canada's copyright law has undergone much needed reforms and clarifications, but it is not quite state-of-the-art yet and the reforms continue as technology pushes legislators to act. Parts of the Copyright Act[1]

---

1   R.S.C. 1985, c. C-42.

have been around since the 1920's. For a long time, while the Internet, televisions, cable networks, computers and photocopiers were becoming a part of our lives, the Act remained frozen in its archaic state with no amendments or mention of such devices. The Act quickly became obsolete and only in recent years has it begun to receive a facelift.

In 1988, 1997 and 2004, amendments recognized computer programs and multimedia works, increased penalties and remedies for infringements and strengthened the rights of both creators of works and copyright holders (often separate individuals).[2] Amendments have also boosted the importance of moral rights. As will be discussed below, even when creators sell their copyright to others, they continue to enjoy a moral right in their works, affecting both journalist-creators and their editors. And, amendments have established numerous copyright "collectives," which license the use of copyrighted material and collect royalties on behalf of copyright holders, ranging from writers to musicians to performers.

Most recently, several important Supreme Court of Canada rulings were handed down, delivering a partial victory to freelance writers asserting copyright when works are used in multiple forms of media, clarifying moral rights and strengthening the Act's fair dealing rights.

GENERAL PRINCIPLES OF COPYRIGHT LAW

What Can be Copyrighted?

A copyright can be attached to any original writing, music, lyrics, choreography, sculpture, engravings, photographs, drawings, maps, charts, sound recordings, art or architectural works, such as buildings.[3] It also

---

2 S.C. 1988, c. 15 and S.C. 1997, c. 24. Amendments were also proposed in June 2008 that would bolster copyright protections for digital and online content, and limit statutory penalties to a maximum of $500 for certain infringements done for private use. The proposed amendments were not passed or enacted at the time of this publication.

3 Note the work must be original. What is "original"? In *Tele-Direct (Publications) Inc. v. American Business Information, Inc.* (1997), 154 D.L.R. (4th) 328 (Fed. C.A., appeal to S.C.C. dismissed without reasons, [1997] S.C.C.A. No. 660), a telephone directory company that arranged phone listings according to accepted commonplace standards or industry methods was not entitled to claim copyright. The federal appeal court held that for any compilation of data or work to be original, it must have been independently created by the author and display at least minimal degrees of skill, judgment and labour in its overall selection or arrangement. In this case, a formatted listing of non-copyrighted material was not enough to establish any new right. That said, publishers of directories containing information independently gathered and created, such as comparisons of retail car prices, have passed the threshold of originality.

applies to compilations of works, encyclopedias, dictionaries, and computer programs. It even applies to unpublished works.[4]

So, what is an original work? The Supreme Court of Canada recently considered the issue of originality.[5] Law book publishers had sued the Law Society of Upper Canada, which governs the practise of law in Ontario, for copyright infringement after the Law Society's Great Library began providing photocopies of published reports of court and other rulings to lawyers, judges and other authorized researchers. The publishers argued, among other things, they held copyright in the head notes, case summaries and other aspects of legal works copied. The Law Society countered, in part, that head notes and summaries were not original works and only mere summaries that did not reflect sufficient intellect or creativity were to be protected.

In deciding that head notes and summaries in general could be original works, the Supreme Court ruling offers comfort to those who summarize for a living. First, the court rejected a so-called "sweat of the brow" test, which would tie the effort required to create a work as proof of its originality. If adopted, that test would wrongly extend copyright to the mere facts assembled by an author, rather than protecting the expression of facts.

Instead, the court defined originality as the "non-trivial exercise of skill and judgment such that production of the work was not a purely mechanical exercise." With head notes, for example, a writer creating an abstract of a court ruling creates an original work if the author chose and arranged material rather than merely abridged or shortened the original work.

There are limits to the distance the law will go to protect the end-product of creativity. An interesting 1998 case tried unsuccessfully to stretch the boundaries of what can be considered copyright.[6] Glenn Gould, the famous Canadian pianist, was interviewed in 1956 for a magazine article by a journalist who took about 400 photographs and copious notes, including tape recordings of their conversations. Almost 40 years later, the writer published a book on the pianist that featured over 70 of the photos and excerpts from the conversations. The Gould estate claimed the author was not entitled, for his own exclusive benefit, to exploit commercially the photographs he had taken of the pianist and to use his notes and tapes of his interviews to write other articles on the pianist. The appeal court dismissed

---

4 In fact, unpublished works in Canada are given much broader protection than published works. While a published work is generally protected from infringement for 50 years after the death of the author and may be copied in small portions for review or criticism under the "fair dealing" defence, an unpublished work is protected in perpetuity and there are no defences, such as fair dealing, for infringement.

5 *CCH Canadian Ltd. v. Law Society of Upper Canada* (2004), 236 D.L.R. (4th) 395 (S.C.C.).

6 *Gould Estate v. Stoddart Publishing Co.* (1998), 161 D.L.R. (4th) 321 (Ont. C.A.).

the claim, ruling there was no evidence the pianist had placed limits on the use of the materials, had not commissioned or paid for the photos, and only the author as creator of the works in question was the sole copyright holder. The court noted the subject matter of a photograph or article has no bearing on determining copyright.

Generally, short combinations of words alone, such as titles, headlines or slogans, are not protected by copyright. Titles, however, may form part of the copyright of a more substantial work. Also not protected are fictional plot ideas or characters, short phrases, names and methods (for example, a particular dance step). And, as you will see below, creative works that become part of the public domain when their copyright term expires (for instance, Shakespeare's works) are not protected.

When Does a Copyright Take Effect?

What many people may not realize is that the actual act of creating an original work immediately establishes a copyright for the creator or, sometimes, his or her employer.[7] There is no requirement that a creator register his or her work with an official body or publish it to establish a copyright (though a copyright can be formally registered for a small fee with Ottawa's Copyright Office, if you wish).

This can have interesting consequences. For example, a book publisher wanting to publish personal letters written by a prominent person to a friend could theoretically find there are copyright problems. Neither the publisher possessing the letters nor the friend to whom they were written holds the copyright. The right to reproduce the letters rests with the creator.

Is Any Copying an Infringement?

There are numerous exemptions permitted under the Act that allow non-profit, religious, educational, government and, even, journalistic organizations to copy a work.[8] The news media frequently takes advantage of the exemptions for "fair dealing,"[9] which allow the reproduction of parts of

---

7 Note 1, above, s. 13(1) and (3).
8 The exemptions are not absolute and do not give these organizations complete freedom to copy all works. For example, in *Boudreau v. Lin* (1997), 150 D.L.R. (4th) 324 (Ont. Gen. Div.), a university that copied and sold a casebook containing an article plagiarized by one of its professors was deemed to know of the copyright infringement and was prevented from using the "fair dealing" defence. As well, recent amendments to the Act have established time limits, such as one year, preventing specific public institutions from using copyrighted materials forever without payment. For example, s. 29.6(1) allows an educational institution to make a copy of a news broadcast or program (except documen-

copyrighted material for the purposes of comment in reviews, criticisms or news publications.

The government revamped this section recently and journalists should be aware of some new requirements. When the copying is for the purposes of criticism, review or news reporting, the fair dealing provision now requires the report or commentary mention the source and the author's name (more on this below).

It should also be noted that the fair dealing section is not a licence to use freely all of someone else's work. Reproducing even a small part of an original work could still be an infringement of copyright if it could be considered a "substantial" part of the work.[10] This will also be discussed below.

Can Pure Information be Copyrighted?

Generally, there's no copyright in the ideas, facts or pure information in any works.[11] The law has clearly set out that copyright only protects the way in which an idea or information is expressed (that is, its format), not the idea or information itself.[12] For example, information in a copyrighted

---

taries) and show it to students for one year after the broadcast. After that year, the institution is required to destroy the copy or pay royalties.

9 Ss. 29.1 and 29.2.

10 Two recent cases offer interesting perspectives on what is substantial copying. In *Allen v. Toronto Star Newspapers Ltd.* (1997), 152 D.L.R. (4th) 518 (Ont. Ct. (Gen. Div.), the court ruled the owner of a copyrighted photo used for a magazine cover was not entitled to damages when the cover itself was copied. To illustrate a news story about a federal politician, the newspaper used a reduced image of the cover showing the politician on a motorcycle. The freelance photographer who took the photo sued for copyright infringement. At trial, the judge held the photographer's copyright was breached. On appeal, the court ruled that, while the photographer did own rights to the photo and it did comprise much of the cover image, he did not have copyright in the cover itself — a separate and distinct original work . The court also ruled the newspaper could rely on the "fair dealing" defence since the purpose of using the reduced image of the cover was simply to illustrate a current news event. Another perspective was set out in *Productions Avanti Ciné-Vidéo Inc. v. Favreau* (1999), 177 D.L.R. (4th) 568 (Que. C.A.). The defendant produced a pornographic film using characters clearly based on a popular Québec TV comedy that was a caricature of suburban life. The defendant maintained the characters were not protected by copyright and, even if they were, their use was a parody and allowed under the fair dealing defence. The court held the characters were subject to copyright since the plaintiff had used original talent, imagination and labour in creating them. Going on, the court said this was not a parody since there was no criticism involved. And, since the characters themselves represented a substantial part of the TV show, the court said a fair dealing defence could not be supported.

11 *Deeks v. Wells*, [1931] O.R. 818 at 834 (C.A.).

12 *Stevenson v. Crook*, [1938] 4 D.L.R. 294 at 303 (Ex. Ct.).

news story can still be re-published by competitors so long as subsequent stories don't copy the original story's wording or manner of expression. This will also be discussed further on.

While discussing potential topics for a dissertation, a Ph.D. student brought up an original idea for an analysis of German literature with his professor. Later, the supervising professor wrote an article on a similar topic. The student claimed the idea for the article was stolen from their conversations and he claimed copyright infringement. Is the student correct?

No. An Alberta court recently confirmed that only the expression of ideas, not the idea itself, is protected by copyright.[13] While confidentiality or fiduciary obligations can protect the disclosure of ideas to others, the student's musings were found to be "too vague and general to constitute more than an intention to explore the issues involved." The court cited the U.K. decision in *Baigent v. Random House Group Ltd.*, [2006] E.W.J. No. 10 (Ch. D.), in which "non-textual copyright infringement" was alleged in the writing of *The Da Vinci Code*. The court there confirmed the traditional principle that an author has no copyright in the facts or ideas, but only in the original expression of those facts or ideas.

THE COPYRIGHT ACT

Definitions

Parliament enacted the Copyright Act in 1921[14] and although steps have been taken to bring the Act up to date with amendments, it is still written in a cumbersome and awkward manner. The Act defines "copyright" itself as:[15]

> the sole right to produce or reproduce the work or any substantial part thereof in any material form whatever, to perform the work or any substantial part thereof in public or, if the work is unpublished, to publish the work or any substantial part thereof.

The Act goes on to state, in its obsolete terminology, that copyright also includes the sole right:

---

13 *Plews v. Pausch* (2006), 2006 CarswellAlta 1049, [2006] A.J. No. 998 (Q.B.).
14 S.C. 1921, c. 24.
15 S. 3(1).

(a) to produce, reproduce, perform or publish any translation of the work;

(b) in the case of a dramatic work, convert it into a novel or other non-dramatic work;

(c) in the case of a novel or other non-dramatic work, or of an artistic work, to convert it into a dramatic work, by way of performance in public or otherwise;

(d) in the case of a literary, dramatic or musical work, to make any sound recording, cinematograph film or other contrivance by means of which the work may be mechanically reproduced or performed;

(e) in the case of any literary, dramatic, musical or artistic work, to reproduce, adapt and publicly present the work as a cinematographic work;

(f) in the case of any literary, dramatic, musical or artistic work, to communicate the work to the public by telecommunication;

(g) to present at a public exhibition, for a purpose other than sale or hire, an artistic work created after June 7, 1988, other than a map, chart or plan;

(h) in the case of a computer program that can be reproduced in the ordinary course of its use, other than by a reproduction during its execution in conjunction with a machine, device or computer, to rent out the computer program; and

(i) in the case of a musical work, to rent out a sound recording in which the work is embodied;

and to authorize any such acts.

Who's Protected?

The Act automatically protects works of a:[16]

1. Canadian citizen or a person ordinarily resident in Canada (that is, a permanent resident);

2. citizen or subject of, or permanent resident in, a Berne Convention country, a Universal Copyright Convention country, a Rome Convention country (for sound recordings, performer's performance and communication signals only), or a country that is a member of the World Trade Organization (WTO); or

3. citizen or subject of, or a person ordinarily resident in any country to which the Minister has extended protection by regulations.

---

16 S. 5.

As noted above, Canadian citizens or permanent residents are protected in over 100 countries that have signed one of several international conventions or agreements on copyright, which have provisions similar to our Act.[17] Consequently, copyrighted material created in one of these member countries (for example, the United States) is entitled to the same protection in Canada as "home-grown" works.[18] But the international conventions themselves are not considered a part of the domestic law of Canada and our Copyright Act still has the final say on questions of copyright.[19]

How Long Does Copyright Last?

In Canada, the copyright for published works subsists for the life of the author, the remainder of the calendar year in which the author dies, and a period of 50 years following the end of that calendar year.[20] So, copyright protection for authors expires on December 31st of the 50th year after the year the creator dies. This is so even if the copyright has been sold to another individual. After that point in time, a work becomes part of the public domain for all to enjoy.

The Act has several provisions dealing with works published anonymously and under a pseudonym. An anonymous work is copyrighted for 50 years after the work is first published or 75 years after the work is initially created, whichever comes first. If the author becomes known, then the normal term of life plus 50 is applied. In cases where there is joint authorship and the authors are unknown, similar terms apply. If some or all of the identities become known, then the copyright subsists for the life term plus 50 years of the last author to die.[21]

---

17 Canada is a signatory of the *Berne Convention* (1885), *Berlin Convention* (1908), *Rome Convention* (1928) and the *Universal Copyright Convention* (Geneva, 1952), the latter of which was signed by Canada on May 10, 1962. Canada is also a signatory to the World Trade Organization's General Agreement on Tariffs and Trade (GATT) (1994), and the World Intellectual Property Organization (WIPO) Copyright Treaty (1996), and its Performances and Phonograms Treaty (1996).

18 The *Universal Copyright Convention, ibid.*, provides for international copyright protection without any formal registration of the copyright. But the convention does require placing a circled "c" on the work, along with the name of the copyright owner and the year it is published. This convention was spearheaded by the United States and reflected its copyright law at the time. However, in 1988, the U.S. acceded to the *Berne Convention*, prompting some copyright specialists to question the relevance of the *Universal Copyright Convention*.

19 See Fox, *The Canadian Law of Copyright and Industrial Designs*, 2nd ed. (Toronto, Carswell, 1967), at 548.

20 S. 6.

21 Ss. 6.1 and 6.2.

Works published after the death of the creator or unpublished works generally have copyright protection for 50 years after they are published.[22] However, if the posthumous work was created before July 25, 1997, then special rules set out in the Act apply.[23] Photos and movies are also protected for 50 years from the creation of the first negative. The same term applies to lectures and musical or dramatic performances.[24] Works produced for the Crown, such as government reports or information booklets, are under copyright protection for the remainder of the calendar year of the first publication of the work and for a period of 50 years following the end of that calendar year, unless some agreement has been struck with the author.[25]

Who Owns the Copyright?

The author, as first owner of the copyright, has a right to sell or assign his or her copyright to someone else.[26] But the assignment of copyright, other than in a will, can only be held (that is, owned) by a purchaser for 25 years after the creator's death, at which time the copyright reverts back to the creator's estate for the remaining 25 years.[27]

If the creator of a work was employed by another individual and the work was made in the course of employment, then the employer will be the first owner of the copyright.[28] But an author and an employer can also agree to another arrangement.[29] Freelance writers are not usually in an employment relationship (unless a contract states otherwise) and often sell only the first "serial" rights to a story. So, after the newspaper or magazine uses the story, the copyright reverts to the freelancer. Also, even when a creator is an employee, the Copyright Act allows creators to prevent contributions (such as, an article, photo or art) to periodicals from being used in other types of media. Section 13(3) states, in part, that "where a work is an article or other contribution to a newspaper, magazine or similar periodical, there shall, in the absence of any agreement to the contrary, be deemed to be reserved to the author a right to restrain the publication of the work, otherwise than as part of a newspaper, magazine or similar periodical." Thus,

---

22 S. 7.
23 *Ibid.*
24 Ss. 7, 10, and 11.1.
25 S. 12. An interesting application of Crown ownership arose in *Hawley v. Canada* (1990), 71 D.L.R. (4th) 632 (Fed. T.D.). An inmate in a penitentiary was permitted to do a large painting and charged the supplies to the institution. The painting was mainly done during work periods and the court agreed the painting was owned by the Crown.
26 S. 13.
27 S. 14.
28 S. 13(3).
29 *Ibid.*

whether freelance or employed, creators for periodicals can still exercise rights over works used for other types of publications, such as online databases or books.[30] Ideally, this situation should be covered in a contract between the two parties.

Similar rules for contracted employment apply to other works. When someone pays for an engraving, photograph or portrait, that person becomes the first owner of the copyright unless there's some other agreement.[31]

In 2001, U.S. freelance writers won a class action lawsuit establishing their right to prevent the publication of articles in other media, particularly on the Internet and in databases, without an agreement or additional payment.[32] In Canada, a class proceedings lawsuit similar to that launched in the U.S. was decided in 2006 at the Supreme Court of Canada.[33]

Canada's Supreme Court clarified the rights of authors and publishers in the area of collective works, finding that a newspaper publisher's electronic databases potentially infringed a freelance author's copyright in her articles, but that selling CD-ROMs with historical content from the newspaper was a valid exercise of the publisher's own copyright.

Freelance author Heather Robertson sued the publisher and owners of *The Globe and Mail* on behalf of thousands of freelance writers who had

---

30 That said, see the *Allen* case in note 10, above, where a photographer was unable to establish copyright in a magazine cover that used his photo.

31 S. 13(2). See the *Gould* case in note 6, above, for an example of the need for an agreement to alter the photographer's copyright. In June 2008, proposed amendments would change the presumption of ownership in favour of the photographer rather than the individual who commissions a photo. For all photographs taken after the proposed amendments come into force, copyright in photographs will be presumed to be owned by the photographer unless there is an agreement to the contrary. At the time of this publication, the amendments were not passed nor enacted.

32 See the U.S. Supreme Court decision in *New York Times Co., Inc. v. Tasini*, [2001] SCT-QL 139, No. 00201 (U.S. S.C., 2001). Tasini sued for copyright infringement on behalf of thousands of freelance writers who were independent contractors for the *Times* and other publications. They worked under freelance arrangements that said nothing about the placement of articles in an electronic database. The print publishers each licensed rights to copy and sell articles to LEXIS/NEXIS, owner and operator of an online database of articles, and to University Microfilms International, which reproduced articles on CD-ROM products. The U.S. Supreme Court agreed with the writers that "copyright in each separate contribution to a collective work is distinct from copyright in the collective work as a whole." In other words, a publication has copyright in its magazine or newspaper in that form, but a freelance writer included in that publication enjoys a separate copyright. Without an agreement providing an express transfer of rights, the U.S. copyright law does not allow publishers to distribute those articles standing alone, such as in a database. The court noted: "It would scarcely preserve the author's copyright in a contribution as contemplated by Congress if a print publisher, without the author's permission, could reproduce or distribute discrete copies of the contribution in isolation or within new collective works."

33 *Robertson v. Thomson Corp.*, [2006] 2 S.C.R. 363.

contributed to the newspaper (except those who died before 1944). At issue was the publisher's right to reproduce freelance works in other forms of media and collections, such as online databases and searchable CD-ROMs, without additional compensation. The Supreme Court split 5-4 in favour of Robertson.

In 1995, she had contributed two freelance articles for Thomson Corp. One was a book review for the national newspaper and the second was an excerpt from her book for its business magazine. There was only an oral agreement and nothing in writing on the use of the review and the publisher later took the position it had a right to distribute the newspaper's articles electronically, as well as in print. As for the book excerpt, there was an agreement with her book publisher that expressly referred to a "one time usage," but the newspaper publisher again believed it had a right to publish a version of its magazine in electronic form.

Robertson launched her action for copyright infringement after her works appeared in two databases, Info Globe Online and CPI.Q, and a CD-ROM. Importantly for the court, as will be explained below, the databases offered users the articles as standalone text alone while the CD-ROM mimicked the collective aspects of each edition of the daily newspaper.

The majority of judges held that "newspaper publishers are not entitled to republish freelance articles acquired for publication in their newspapers in Info Globe Online or CPI.Q without compensating the authors and obtaining their consent." While publishers have a right under the Copyright Act's s. 3(1) to "reproduce the work or any substantial part thereof in any material form whatever," the majority agreed a "substantial part" means the "essence of the newspaper is preserved."

Thus, reproducing the text of the individual articles in an online database without the original layout or appearance of a newspaper does not qualify as a proper reproduction. The CD-ROM, however, was "faithful to the essence of the original work" and kept much of the newspaper's appearance.

The majority made it clear that publishers, particularly the news media, do not have a "licence to override the rights of authors." The court, however, went on to state that a non-exclusive licence permitting a publisher to republish in either databases or CD-ROMs does not need to be in writing. In other words, the newspaper's right to use articles in a database without payment may be implied if it can be proven at trial that freelance authors knew this was a standard practice. Thus, this decision was a partial victory for freelance writers.

The ruling also only dealt with pre-trial motions and an actual trial of Robertson's claims has yet to be held. At the time of this publication, there was no public word on whether an agreement would be negotiated between the *Globe* and freelancers, or if the matter would go to trial. At the very least, the judgment underlines that it is vitally important for freelance journalists to address these copyright and extra payments for different forms of media in writing.

Helping creators collect the royalties owed by publishers is the role of the various copyright "collectives" established by 1988 amendments to the Act. Collectives can license the use of copyrighted material on behalf of all creators that join the organization and collect any royalties generated. Previously, only the music industry had such collectives and fees were collected from radio stations, theatres and other commercial operations on behalf of the copyright holders. Now, collectives can be formed for most any type of work.

Access Copyright (formerly known as CANCOPY), is the leading Canadian collective for freelance writers, authors and journalists. It pays out millions of dollars a year in royalties collected from libraries, schools and other consumers of works. To collect payments, journalists and other literary artists must first register with the collective (www.access copyright.ca).

What are Moral Rights?

Moral rights for creators are not new. The Copyright Act has always asserted that moral rights exist in a work and that they are separate from copyright.[34] Amendments to the Act in 1988 have raised moral rights to a new level of significance.

Section 14.1 (1) states:

> The author of a work has, subject to section 28.2, the right to the integrity of the work and, in connection with an act mentioned in section 3, the right, where reasonable in the circumstances, to be associated with the work as its author by name or under a pseudonym and the right to remain anonymous.

Note that s. 14.1 also ensures that a creator has the right to be associated with a work in whatever manner he or she wants, whether by pseudonym or real name. The moral rights section protects works against distortion, mutilation or major changes that are serious enough to damage or lessen

---

34 The now-repealed s. 14(4) of the Act previously stated that, "Independently of the author's copyright, and even after the assignment, either wholly or partially, of the copyright, the author has the right to claim authorship of the work, as well as the right to restrain any distortion, mutilation or other modification of the work that would be prejudicial to the honour or reputation of the author."

the reputation or honour of a creator.[35] Violations of moral rights carry the same remedies and penalties as for copyright infringements.

The bolstered moral rights section allows a creator to protect the integrity and original form of a work even when the copyright has been sold or assigned to another individual. In fact, the moral rights of a creator can't be sold or assigned to anyone else. They can only be expressly waived in writing by the creator.

The amendment was driven by a prominent court case in the early 1980's involving a well-known sculpture in The Eaton Centre in Toronto.[36] A flock of 60 Canadian geese had been fashioned by artist Michael Snow and sold to the shopping centre to be hung permanently from the ceiling. During one Christmas season, the mall's management decided to decorate festively the geese with red ribbons. Snow objected, saying it was an insult to his work and hurt his reputation. The dispute ended up in court where a judge sided with Snow and ordered the ribbons removed. Snow's moral rights came to his rescue, even though the copyright in the geese had been sold to the mall.

For most works, minor changes and modifications probably wouldn't be considered serious enough to harm the reputation or honour of a creator. However, for art works, any unauthorized change whatsoever to a work is deemed to be an infringement (such as cropping a picture or somehow altering it without permission).[37]

Using a sophisticated chemical process, an art gallery transferred authorized reproductions of a famous painter's works from paper-backed posters to canvas for resale. The transfer process leaves the poster blank. Is this an infringement of the painter's moral rights?

No. In a 2003 Supreme Court of Canada decision,[38] the court set out clear guidelines for determining whether moral rights are infringed. In this case, the transfer process left the posters blank and, thus, did not increase the total number of reproductions. A majority of the court agreed art galleries are within their rights to make the transfers since they are owners of the physical posters and there was no production or reproduction of an artistic work "or any substantial part thereof in any material form" within the meaning of the Copyright Act. As for the moral rights, the

35 S. 28.2.
36 *Snow v. The Eaton Centre Ltd.* (1982), 70 C.P.R. (2d) 105 (Ont. H.C.).
37 S. 28.2.
38 *Galerie d'art du Petit Champlain inc. c. Théberge*, [2002] 2 S.C.R. 336.

> majority said the integrity of a work is only infringed if it is modified to the "prejudice of the honour or reputation of the author."

The Act does try to avoid problems caused by overly-sensitive artists. Section 28.2(3) says a change in the location of a work, the physical means by which a work is exposed or the physical structure containing a work, and any steps taken in good faith to restore or preserve the work, shall not constitute a distortion, mutilation or other modification of the work.

What does this mean for journalists? It could be a double-edged sword when it comes to editing material. On the one hand, it allows journalists, whether employed or freelance, to assert a right over how their work is edited or re-written. If a journalist wished, a battle over editing a book or article could theoretically end up in court.

The other side of this is that it presents a potential hurdle for editors who know only too well that some journalists can be pig-headed about changes to stories. The solution to all this is an easy one. Any employment or freelance contract should state that the creator agrees to waive moral rights or, at least, that it is understood that final editing decisions rest with the editor.

It should be noted that under these sections, a moral right can also be infringed if a work is used in association with a product, service, cause or institution to the prejudice of the honour or reputation of the creator.[39] For example, using a piece of magazine art in a promotion campaign without the artist's approval could be considered an infringement, even if the copyright was purchased.

The moral rights in a work exist for the same period as the copyright and upon the creator's death, the rights pass on to the estate or to anyone to whom they are bequeathed.[40]

What are the Penalties for Copyright Infringement?

Copyrighted works, such as the ones mentioned above, can only be reproduced in their original form with the permission of the owner of the copyright and, possibly, the payment of a fee. If you infringe upon someone's copyright, you can be sued in civil court for damages and, under the copyright legislation, you may be subject to a hefty fine and/or a jail term. In most cases, the copyright holder will ask a civil court for an injunction to prevent publication of the copies and sue for damages suffered (such as lost profits).

---

39 S. 28.2(1)(b).
40 S. 14.2.

A summary conviction under the Copyright Act could bring a maximum fine of $25,000 and/or up to six months in jail, while a conviction on indictment could lead to a maximum fine of $1 million and/or up to five years in jail.[41] Since October 1, 1999, "statutory damages" have also been allowed, which permit copyright owners to recover $500 to $20,000 per work infringed without proving any actual losses suffered. Copyright owners also have better and less expensive remedies under the Act to quickly end infringements, such as the "wide injunction" to stop copying of any and all works of a creator rather than just one or two works involved in a particular claim of infringement.[42]

COPYRIGHT AND JOURNALISTS

Can News be Copyrighted?

Just as there's no copyright in ideas, there is no copyright in the "news."[43] As mentioned above, the copyright exists in the manner in which the news is expressed, not the news itself. Generally, a journalist who reprints a story from another news outlet will infringe the copyright only if the exact mode of expression, or a substantial part of it, is repeated. An exception is when the journalist's employer has a contract with the other news outlet allowing use of the stories (for example, wire services).

A complete or "substantial" re-write of the news story will not infringe a copyright. For example, an "exclusive" story in a newspaper can still be reported by other news outlets if the story is re-written in a different way. But this means changing more than just a few words or paragraphs around. The story should be completely re-written.

It's difficult to say what constitutes copying a substantial part of a work such as to amount to a copyright infringement. The courts have gen-

---

41 S. 42, amended S.C. 1988, c. 15, s. 10.

42 See ss. 38.1 for statutory damages and 39.1 for the wide injunction.

43 *Gribble v. Manitoba Free Press Co.*, [1931] 3 W.W.R. 570 (Man. C.A.). More recently, in *B.W. International Inc. v. Thomson Canada Ltd.* (1996), 137 D.L.R. (4th) 398 (Ont. Gen. Div.), an Ontario judge, in part, noted there is no copyright in the news itself. In this case, a company that published a confidential report on investments for stock market dealers alleged copyright infringement, among other things, when a newspaper published parts of the report. The judge was unable to definitively rule on the copyright infringement issue since the plaintiff failed to cite specific examples of report excerpts that were copied. Since the news or information in the report could not itself be subject to copyright, that claim went no further. That said, the judge did comment that, if there had been a breach of copyright, she might not have allowed a fair dealing defence by the newspaper because the report was not intended for publication and was only published because it had been leaked.

erally taken a quantitative approach to deciding whether a work has been "substantially" copied. Courts may try to determine if one-half, one-third or just one-sixteenth of a copyrighted work was used and then decide if it could be considered "substantial."

To determine what's "substantial," a court wouldn't have to look for any particular percentage of the original work to have been copied (for example, 50 percent or more). For instance, taking only a few paragraphs from some works can be an infringement of the copyright if the paragraphs are among the best and most detailed in the work. It depends on the length of the work and the degree of individual character involved in the manner of expression.

There's no requirement to give credit for a story to another news agency if the story is rewritten; however, note that the "fair dealing" provision of the Act requires mention of the source and author when parts of a copyrighted work are being directly quoted or used. That said, simply giving credit to the originator of the story isn't enough to escape liability for copyright infringement. If the story is to be used in its original form, a journalist must get written permission to use it.

Does the Copyright Act Say Anything about Journalists?

There are a few provisions of the Act that explicitly recognize the needs of journalists. These "fair dealing" sections provide the following rights:

29. Fair dealing for the purpose of research or private study does not infringe copyright.

29.1 Fair dealing for the purpose of criticism or review does not infringe copyright if the following are mentioned:

(a) the source; and
(b) if given in the source, the name of the

    (i)   author, in the case of a work,
    (ii) performer, in the case of a performer's performance,
    (iii) maker, in the case of a sound recording, or
    (iv) broadcaster, in the case of a communication signal.

29.2 Fair dealing for the purpose of news reporting does not infringe copyright if the following are mentioned:

(a) the source; and
(b) if given in the source, the name of the

    (i)   author, in the case of a work,

(ii)   performer, in the case of a performer's performance,

(iii) maker, in the case of a sound recording, or

(iv) broadcaster, in the case of a communication signal.

In 1997, the federal government also amended some obsolete wording referring to "newspaper summaries" in a section dealing with the reporting of speeches and public lectures:

32.2 (1) It is not an infringement of copyright

(c)   for any person to make or publish, for the purposes of news reporting or news summary, a report of a lecture given in public, unless the report is prohibited by conspicuous written or printed notice affixed before and maintained during the lecture at or about the main entrance of the building in which the lecture is given, and, except while the building is being used for public worship, in a position near the lecturer;

(d)   for any person to read or recite in public a reasonable extract from a published work; or

(e)   for any person to make or publish, for the purposes of news reporting or news summary, a report of an address of a political nature given at a public meeting.

News photographers and videographers will also be comforted by s. 32.2(b), which states it is not an infringement of copyright to reproduce "in a painting, drawing, engraving, photograph or cinematographic work" an architectural work or a sculpture or work of artistic craftsmanship "that is permanently situated in a public place or building."

Although there have been few cases of news media being accused of copyright infringement, the fair dealing provision is the one that most likely would come into play. Fair dealing is generally accepted to mean that copying of parts should be kept brief and for a clear purpose, such as to demonstrate the copied author's viewpoint. For example, in most cases, you could not quote large portions of an author's work to form the body of your news report. That said, recent case law has also made it clear the end purpose for which a work is copied under the fair dealing provision is a critical factor.

In a 2004 ruling involving legal publishers,[44] the Supreme Court of Canada greatly clarified the meaning and use of the fair dealing provision. The case concerned whether the Law Society of Upper Canada's photocopying for lawyers and other "authorized researchers" of published law reports (including head notes or summaries) was fair dealing.

First, the court stated the fair dealing exception is a right, not a defence, and should not be interpreted narrowly. Next, the court said it is important

---

44 Note 5, above.

in deciding whether fair dealing applies to define the purpose of the copying. Specifically, was it for research, private study, criticism, review or news reporting. In this case, the Law Society was copying material for authorized individuals (such as lawyers) to use in their research. Finally, the court identified other factors to consider, including the:

1.   character of the dealing (how the works were dealt with);

2.   amount of the dealing;

3.   alternatives available;

4.   nature of the creative work; and

5.   effect of the dealing on the work.

While there are obviously many variables to be considered in a fair dealing case, the Supreme Court has added considerable weight to the importance of this provision.

COPYRIGHT REFORM

In 2005, Bill C-60, An Act to Amend the Copyright Act, was tabled but died later on the Order Paper when a federal election was called. New copyright reforms have not been tabled at the time of this publication, but will likely take a similar form in the near future.

Bill C-60 would have given copyright holders the sole right to control the reproduction of their copyrighted material on the Internet. It would also have exempted Internet service providers (ISPs) from liability for copyright infringements on their systems when they act purely as intermediaries.

The Bill also proposed adding a new right — a "first sale" right over any tangible, material form of a work. The World Intellectual Property Organization (WIPO) Performances and Phonograms Treaty, to which Canada is a signatory, requires copyright holders have first right to the distribution of their material in a tangible form. The amendment would have served to reinforce the existing right of distribution and bring Canada into conformity with nations that have copyright systems in which the right to first distribution is equated with the right to sell the original copy in its tangible form.

Also, photographic works would no longer have been treated differently. Currently, ownership of copyright resides in the person commissioning the original photo, rather than the creator, even without a written assignment. The current term of protection is a fixed time from creation, rather than from the death of the author, for photographs owned by any corporation in which the author does not have voting control. The Bill would have eliminated those differences.

A COPYRIGHT CHECKLIST

1. Copyright applies to any published or unpublished original writing, music, lyrics, choreography, sculpture, engravings, photographs, drawings, maps, charts, sound recordings, art, architectural works, encyclopedias, dictionaries, and even computer programs.

2. Copyright does not apply to:
   - News, ideas or pure information
   - Quotations of short parts of original works for the purposes of comment or review
   - Complete or substantial rewrites of another's work
   - Copying for the purposes of private study or research
   - Speeches, lectures or public recitations of works
   - Photographs of sculpture or art that is permanently displayed in a public place or building, and photographs of architectural works of art

3. When done without permission, copyright infringement occurs with:
   - Substantial or wholesale reproduction of an original work
   - Copying of the form of expression of an idea or information
   - Translation and substantial reproduction of another's original work
   - Converting a non-dramatic work or novel into a dramatic work, or vice versa
   - Visual or audio recording of a literary, dramatic or musical work, except in small portions for the purposes of review or comment

4. Copyright subsists for the life of the creator plus 50 years. If a work is published after the creator's death, copyright generally subsists for 50 years after publication. Photographs and cinematographic works are protected for 50 years from the creation of the original negative.

5. Moral rights may be infringed by distortion, mutilation or major modifications to a work that are serious enough to damage or lessen the

reputation or honour of a creator (for example, substantial edits of writing or physical alteration of artwork). A moral right can also be infringed if a work is used in association with a product, service, cause or institution to the prejudice of the honour or reputation of the creator.

14

REPORTING ON ELECTIONS
AND POLITICAL BROADCASTS

Few things would appear to make politicians more nervous than the combination of elections and journalists. Despite the Charter of Rights and its guarantee of freedom of the press, electcd officials can't seem to resist tinkering with election laws to limit the impact of the news media and other real or imagined special interest groups. On an ongoing basis, it seems, governments try to limit what can be reported in elections and referenda.

Recently, there have been at least two significant Charter-based challenges of black-out periods and the limits on opinion poll reporting. Both were unsuccessful, from a media or reporting standpoint. As a result, the media must contend with an array of federal and provincial laws that impose some restrictions on reporting, and may even treat print, broadcast and Web-based media differently.

PUBLISHING ELECTION RESULTS

Broadcast, print and Web-based media must be conscious of the timing of the publication of any election results. The federal, as well as a few provincial and territorial, Elections Acts prohibit the premature publication of election results on the polling or election day.[1]

Publication of results or purported results cannot take place in any electoral district before the hour fixed by election officials for the closing of polls in that district. This applies to by-elections, as well as general elections.

This prohibition will be of particular concern to any media outlets or Web sites having the opportunity to publish results in two or more time zones. Although it applies to all news media, it's largely a point of interest to Internet publishers and broadcasters. For broadcasters, the Canadian Radio-television and Telecommunications Commission (CRTC) publishes guidelines shortly after any federal or provincial election writ is issued. As a general rule, polling stations for federal elections close between 7:00 p.m. and 9:30 p.m. (depending on which time zone or province you are in) and for broadcasters who may beam results into an earlier time zone, the CRTC advises that broadcasts of election results not happen before polls close in electoral districts within broadcast reach.[2]

Time zone	Federal Elections: Polls open and close in local time
Newfoundland Time	8:30 a.m. - 8:30 p.m.
Atlantic Time	8:30 a.m. - 8:30 p.m.
Eastern Time	9:30 a.m. - 9:30 p.m.
Central Time*	8:30 a.m. - 8:30 p.m.
Mountain Time*	7:30 a.m. - 7:30 p.m.
Pacific Time	7:00 a.m. - 7:00 p.m.

*In Saskatchewan, when daylight saving time is in effect for the rest of the country, voting hours are from 7:30 a.m. to 7:30 p.m. (local time). If the electoral district spans more than one time zone, the returning officer determines one local time for voting throughout the district.

---

1 For example, see Canada Elections Act, S.C. 2000, c. 9, s. 328 (transmission of results during the blackout period) and s. 329 (premature transmission of results).
2 See CRTC Circular no. 460, May 26, 2004.

Provincial and municipal elections are generally not subject to any blackout restrictions in regard to time zones since no province has more than two time zones. The Yukon, however, does prohibit the premature publication of results "by any medium whatsoever" (including the Internet) in any polling division or electoral district before the hour set by the law for closing of the polls.[3]

It should be noted that Elections Canada, the federal agency governing the electoral process, takes a strict view of what might interfere with the voting process or compromise the secrecy of the vote. For example, journalists filming or photographing candidates or electors without permission while they vote in a polling station or impeding the free movement of people can be charged under the federal Act with premature publication or interfering with the voting process. Under s. 135, only specific individuals (candidates, polling staff, etc.) are permitted in a polling station on election day. Elections Canada advises that media may obtain general footage by filming or photographing through an open doorway only with the permission of the returning officer.

Some jurisdictions, however, have gone a step further in ensuring via legislation that the news media can have access to polling stations under certain conditions. The New Brunswick legislation specifically states "representatives of a *bona fide* news broadcaster or news publication may be permitted by the returning officer to enter the room where the poll is held for the sole purpose of photographing or otherwise visually recording the casting of the ballot by a candidate of a recognized party provided: (a) the candidate agrees to the presence of the representatives; (b) previous arrangements to the satisfaction of the returning officer have been made; (c) no interviews shall be conducted in the room where the poll is held; and (d) the representatives immediately leave the room where the poll is held once the candidate's ballot has been cast."[4] Nunavut also allows the news media to "record images or sound in a polling station" before the polling station is open for voting with the approval of the Chief Electoral Officer.[5]

3 Elections Act, R.S.Y. 2002, c. 63, s. 347.
4 Elections Act, R.S.N.B. 1973, c. E-3, s. 72.1.
5 Nunavut Elections Act, S.Nu. 2002, c. 17, s. 254.1.

During a federal election, a citizen in British Columbia decides to post on his Web site the final voting results from Atlantic Canada during the same hours when polls are open in parts of Canada. Considering the Charter promises a right to free expression, is he within his rights to publish this information?

No. The Supreme Court of Canada recently decided the legislated restriction on reporting voting results before polling stations close on voting day is justified.[6] During the 2000 federal election, Paul Bryan posted results on his Web site for 32 ridings in Atlantic Canada while polls remained open in other provinces. He was charged with contravening s. 329 of the Canada Elections Act. Bryan argued the law was unconstitutional and a lower court appeal judge agreed. A majority of the Supreme Court overturned that decision and upheld his conviction, however, and found that while s. 329 did infringe freedom of expression, it was justified. The Court ruled the "true objective of the Canada Elections Act in the context of the provisions under scrutiny is to ensure informational equality" among voters. A minority of the Court found the law to be "an excessive response to an insufficiently proven harm."

PUBLISHING FALSE STATEMENTS

The federal and most provincial Elections Acts state that anyone who, before or during an election, knowingly makes or publishes a "false statement of fact" in relation to the personal character or conduct of a candidate or prospective candidate is guilty of an offence under the Act. You also cannot knowingly publish a false statement of the withdrawal of a candidate.[7] Note that it must be an intentional false publication designed to affect the results of the election. Penalties vary from fines to jail terms, depending on the particular Act.

Suffice it to say that care should be exercised, as always, when asserting "facts" about a candidate's personal life or actions. A malicious and false publication about a candidate not only can prompt a charge under elections laws, it can also trigger a defamation lawsuit.

Also, during the entire election period, it is an offence under federal law to use, aid, abet, counsel or procure the use of any radio or television

---

6 *R. v. Bryan* (2007), 2007 CarswellBC 533, 2007 CarswellBC 534, [2007] S.C.J. No. 12.
7 See ss. 91 and 92 of the federal Elections Act, note 1, above.

station outside Canada for broadcasting any matter with intent to influence people to vote or refrain from voting.[8]

ELECTION BLACK-OUT PERIODS FOR PARTISAN BROADCASTS

For many years, television and radio stations were prohibited from broadcasting "partisan" programming as voting day approached. A now-repealed section of the federal Broadcasting Act[9] created a two-day "black-out period" for partisan broadcasts on the day of and day before federal, provincial and municipal referenda, and provincial and municipal elections.

While the primary aim was to restrict commercials and paid political messages in the final days of an election, it also silenced editorialists. In 1973, a pre-Charter attempt to challenge the constitutionality of black-out periods failed.[10]

Today, the law has changed and black-out periods only apply to election advertising by political parties, candidates and third-parties. The concern about partisan news broadcasts or commentary, which strangely didn't apply to newspapers, no longer exists. In fact, the federal government and some provinces have taken steps to clarify what is considered election advertising:[11]

> "election advertising" means the transmission to the public by any means during an election period of an advertising message that promotes or opposes a registered party or the election of a candidate, including one that takes a position on an issue with which a registered party or candidate is associated. For greater certainty, it does not include

---

8 See s. 330 of the federal Act, note 1, above.

9 R.S.C. 1985, c. B-9.

10 *CFRB v. A.G. Canada* (1973), 38 D.L.R. (3d) 335 (Ont. C.A.). A Toronto radio station was charged under the now-repealed s. 19 of the Broadcasting Act after it broadcast an editorial that supported the incumbent Premier, within the black-out period of a provincial election. The court heard how veteran reporter Gordon Sinclair broadcast an editorial on the day before the provincial election advocating the re-election of then-Premier William Davis as a "man of decision" who had qualities which would be "an asset in any leader." Not only did the broadcaster express an opinion on the election, but the late Mr. Sinclair also spoke to the "stupid rule" which prevents the electronic media from making political comments during the black-out period. The Ontario Court of Appeal held that Parliament had a right not only to control the physical use of the airwaves, but also the intellectual content of programs. The court said this wasn't an unreasonable infringement on the freedom of the press.

11 See s. 319 of the federal Act, note 1, above.

(a) the transmission to the public of an editorial, a debate, a speech, an interview, a column, a letter, a commentary or news;

(b) the distribution of a book, or the promotion of the sale of a book, for no less than its commercial value, if the book was planned to be made available to the public regardless of whether there was to be an election;

(c) the transmission of a document directly by a person or a group to their members, employees or shareholders, as the case may be; or

(d) the transmission by an individual, on a non-commercial basis on what is commonly known as the Internet, of his or her personal political views.

A few Canadian jurisdictions have provisions dealing with black-outs of partisan activity on or before voting day, some of which might still be challenged in court by the news media since they only apply to broadcasters and Web sites. For example, the Elections Act in the Northwest Territories[12] states "every person who broadcasts a speech or any polling or entertainment or advertising program on polling day or on the day immediately before polling day in favour of or on behalf of a candidate or against a candidate at an election, is guilty of an offence and liable on summary conviction to a fine not exceeding $5,000."

New Brunswick has one of the most explicit black-out provisions, governing almost all forms of electronic and print communication. Partisan political broadcasts, publications and transmission are not permitted on polling day or the day preceding it. This includes broadcasts of speeches, entertainment or advertising in favour of, or on behalf of, a political party or any candidate. It also applies to any broadcasts emanating from outside of New Brunswick.[13] The N.B. provision, however, specifically exempts "a *bona fide* news broadcast or news publication referring to or commenting upon a speech or containing any excerpts from a speech."

In general, the intention of black-out periods is not to restrict the reporting of all political news. For example, it's not partisan to broadcast a review of the events of the election campaign, the details of the candidates' activities or any last-minute political announcements as long as the reporting is balanced.

---

12 R.S.N.W.T. 1988, c. E-2, s. 224.

13 R.S.N.B. 1973, c. E-3, s. 117(3) and (4). S. 117(3) states no one shall broadcast, print or publish a speech, entertainment or advertising in favour of or on behalf of any political party or any candidate. That includes transmissions via computers, fax machines or any device capable of receiving unsolicited communications.

ELECTION OPINION SURVEYS

The fear over the partisan impact of editorials and news articles has been replaced by a new political demon — the opinion poll. In recent years, some political parties have been frustrated by the publication of opinion survey results near election day which suggest they will lose. Right or wrong, politicians seem to believe media reports of last minute polls only serve to hasten their defeat or narrow their victory.

In 1993, the Canada Elections Act was amended to add a black-out on the reporting of opinion polls by all news media that would last for three days — from Friday at midnight to the closing of polls on Monday. In 1997, *The Globe & Mail* and other publications successfully challenged the lengthy black-out period.[14]

The Supreme Court of Canada said the three-day period violated the Charter's freedom of expression and was not a justifiable restriction, calling it a "crude instrument in serving the government's purpose."

In a strongly-worded ruling, a majority of the court said the publication of opinion survey results is part of the political process and "at the core of expression guaranteed by the Charter." The judges said there was no merit to the argument that it provided a period of rest and reflection for voters before going to the polls. In striking down the prohibition as then-written, the court also noted there was no evidence Canadian voters are a vulnerable group "in danger of manipulation or abuse by the pollsters or the media."

That said, the court recognized there is a need to guard against the possible influence of inaccurate polls late in the election campaign. Rather than a long black-out period, the judges suggested a better route for protecting the public from inaccurate results would be to require the media to publish the statistical methods and basis of the poll.

Subsequently, the federal law relating to the reporting of election surveys was amended to prohibit the publication or broadcast of an election survey (defined as a survey of how electors voted or will vote at an election, or on an issue that a registered party or candidate is associated) on the polling day only.[15] This prohibition applies only to an election survey that has not yet been transmitted to the public, so journalists are free to discuss previously-published polls on election day.

The amendments to the law added new requirements for everyone, including news organizations, revealing the results of a survey at anytime during a federal election, not just the black-out period. Under s. 326 of the law, the first person to transmit results (such as a survey's sponsor) and anyone else publicly transmitting results in the first 24 hours (such as a

---

14 *Thomson Newspapers Co. v. Canada (Attorney General)*, [1998] 1 S.C.R. 877.
15 See s. 328 of the federal Act, note 1, above.

broadcaster, newspaper publisher or other media outlet) must provide the following together with the poll's findings:

(a) the name of the sponsor of the survey;

(b) the name of the person or organization that conducted the survey;

(c) the date on which or the period during which the survey was conducted;

(d) the population from which the sample of respondents was drawn;

(e) the number of people who were contacted to participate in the survey; and

(f) if applicable, the margin of error in respect of the data obtained.

As well, anyone transmitting "to the public by means other than broadcasting" (such as a newspaper) must also provide:

(a) the wording of the survey questions in respect of which data is obtained; and

(b) the means by which [a written report by the survey's sponsor] may be obtained.

These new requirements might be subject to a challenge in court even though they reflect the Supreme Court's thinking. A court ruling in British Columbia struck down a similar law in 2000, finding that the provincial government could offer "no history of false or misleading election opinion surveys being published." There was also no evidence any individual had difficulty in getting methodological information and "very few individuals are in fact interested in obtaining further methodological information beyond the customary information routinely provided by the media."[16] Clearly, the federal government's lawyers might have similar difficulty proving their case for restrictions in an upcoming national election.

Interestingly, note that the federal requirements apply only to statistically-sound election surveys. Informal surveys, such as those conducted on radio call-in shows or in person-on-the-street interviews, can be reported at anytime in the election (even during the black-out period) as long as you declare the results are not based on scientific statistical methods. In fact, s. 327 of the federal law states:

The first person who transmits the results of an election survey that is not based on recognized statistical methods to the public during an election period and any person who transmits them within 24 hours after they are first

---

16 *Pacific Press v. British Columbia (Attorney General)* (2000), 94 A.C.W.S. (3d) 1122 (B.C. S.C.). In that case, the government was found to have no factual basis to conclude that election opinion surveys affected how British Columbia citizens voted.

transmitted to the public must indicate that the survey was not based on recognized statistical methods.

OTHER ELECTION REPORTING RESTRICTIONS

At the time of publication, there were no news media-specific restrictions (other than those mentioned above) in the provinces of Alberta, British Columbia, Manitoba, Newfoundland and Labrador, Nova Scotia, Ontario, PEI or Saskatchewan.

Québec's Referendum and Election Acts

Québec's Referendum Act,[17] working in concert with the province's Election Act,[18] is considered by some to be another attempt by a government to control free speech during public votes. Though the laws do not directly hinder the news media, aggressive attempts to play an active role in public debate may draw the attention of election officials on guard against unauthorized election spending.

The laws require that all paid political "publicity," announcements and advertising be approved and funnelled through two "national committees," which are in essence the two political parties of the province's National Assembly. They, in turn, are limited as to how much they can spend during an election or referendum campaign. The rationale in controlling spending is to prevent well-funded groups or individuals from dominating a referendum or election and unfairly swaying the minds of a susceptible public.

The law does not prevent any citizen or group from being quoted in the news media and espousing a point of view which is not "authorized" or part of the two national committee campaigns, so long as it is published or broadcast for free. Both Acts specifically state that election or referendum expenses do not include:[19]

(1) the cost of publishing articles, editorials, news, interviews, columns or letters to the editor in a newspaper, periodical or other publication, provided that they are published without payment, reward or promise of payment or reward, that the newspaper, periodical or other publication is not established for the purposes or in view of the election and that the circulation and frequency of publication are as what obtains outside the election period;

(2) the cost at fair market value of producing, promoting and distributing a

---

17 R.S.Q., c. C-64.1.
18 R.S.Q., c. E-3.3.
19 S. 404 of the Election Act.

book that was planned to be put on sale at the prevailing market price regardless of the election order;

(3) the cost of broadcasting by a radio or television station of a program of public affairs, news or commentary, provided that the program is broadcast without payment, reward or promise of payment or reward; . . .

So, how might freedom of the press be endangered by such a law? A problem arises when the news media takes on a public advocacy role. Broadcasters or publishers may spend money in a way that might be interpreted as a campaign contribution to one side. This happened during the 1995 referendum vote on Québec's possible secession.

During the campaign, the *Toronto Star* decided to send Québecers a message that other Canadians wanted the province to stay in Confederation. It published a special French-language supplement featuring letters written by readers on referendum issues. About 350,000 copies of the supplement were to be distributed by *La Presse*, but it didn't happen. The Montréal newspaper opted not to distribute the supplement, fearing it contravened Québec's referendum law against third-party advertising. The *Star*, with no other distribution options, decided to back off and simply asked its Ontario readers to send copies to relatives and friends in Québec. While the *Star* wasn't charged with any offence, it might have argued the Québec law was an unreasonable restriction on freedom of the press.

ALLOCATION OF POLITICAL BROADCAST TIME

As noted above, broadcasters must also be aware of regulations governing political broadcasts at all times during the period of their licence, not just during elections. While the average journalist won't have any need to be concerned about these regulations, they do apply to news broadcasts.

The federal Canada Elections Act deals with some aspects of the allocation of free broadcast time in ss. 332 to 348. The CRTC's regulations require each station or network operator which allocates time for the broadcast of partisan programs, advertisements or announcements to do so on "an equitable basis to all parties and rival candidates" during elections and throughout the licence period.[20]

The question of what is "an equitable basis" for allocating time is difficult to define, but it usually becomes an issue during election campaigns. The CRTC regulations say the political parties, candidates and broadcasters are all supposed to come to an agreement on what is an equi-

---

20 See Radio Regulations, 1986, SOR/86-982, s. 6 and Television Broadcasting Regulations, SOR/87-49, s. 8.

table distribution of time. If they can't agree, the matter may be referred to the commission.

In 1983, an independent candidate in the federal election was not invited to speak at a national free-time political broadcast and took his case to the Federal Court, saying the allocation of time wasn't "equitable."[21]

However, the court said "equitable" time doesn't mean equal time. It held that determining an equitable allocation isn't a purely mathematical equation devoid of discretion. With the wide variety and large number of candidates attracted to elections, the logistics of having them all speaking in a broadcast debate would be unconstructive. The Federal Court also said there was no duty on the CRTC to set out what an equitable allocation is, even though the commission has the authority to do so.

In another 1983 decision, the Ontario Supreme Court held that "equitable" referred not only to the political parties, but also to the viewing public.[22] The court said common sense must prevail and organizers of a debate are expected to use some discretion in deciding which parties should be represented. The court felt the tolerance level of the audience must be considered and a limited-time broadcast could not be expected to include every possible candidate.

In a 1993 Federal Court of Canada case, the Natural Law Party of Canada tried to force the CBC to include its party leader in any televised debate, even though all the networks had already decided which candidates would be invited in accordance with CRTC regulations. The party wanted to argue that, as an agent of the Crown, the CBC is theoretically bound by the Charter's equality guarantee. The court, however, surrendered jurisdiction to the CRTC, saying the Broadcasting Act left it up to that body to determine how broadcast time was used. The court added, as an aside, that it would have refused the party's request anyway since it was "not the function of the Court to dictate to the news media what they should report" and the networks did not make the decision as to who to include in the debate in an arbitrary, unfair or irrational manner.[23]

Although CRTC regulations speak primarily to the equitable use of airtime for political commercials and free-time political broadcasts between and during elections, they also apply to news editorials and any other program where a partisan opinion is expressed. For example, CRTC guidelines suggest the regulations apply to news stories which use partisan audio

---

21 *Turmel v. Canadian Radio-television and Telecommunications Commission* (1985), 16 C.R.R. 9 (Fed. T.D.).

22 *Gauvin v. Canadian Broadcasting Corp.* (1984), 5 C.R.R. 2-50.

23 *Natural Law Party of Canada v. Canadian Broadcasting Corp.* (1993), 52 C.P.R. (3d) 97 (Fed. T.D.).

and audio-visual material produced by a party (for example, using a sound or visual bite from a candidate's commercial).[24]

While broadcast journalists should be aware of the CRTC requirements regarding equitable use of broadcast time, particularly during elections, the regulations aren't meant to change the way news is reported and the regulations don't apply to objective news reports. A journalist shouldn't be concerned about whether one party has been "making the news" more often than another.

Journalists are also not compelled by the regulations to include comments from all the parties in every report that's done. Nor does each newscast have to have a story about all the parties in the running.

AN ELECTIONS CHECKLIST

1. According to federal and some provincial Elections Acts, the publication of election results or purported results cannot take place in any electoral district before the hour fixed by election officials for the closing of polls in that district. This applies to by-elections and referenda, as well as general elections.

2. The federal and many provincial Elections Acts state that anyone who, before or during an election, knowingly makes or publishes a "false statement of fact" in relation to the personal character or conduct of a candidate is guilty of an offence.

3. Federal law restricts the reporting of opinion polls during a legislated "black-out" period, typically on the day of referenda or elections. Journalists may still freely discuss surveys made public before the blackout period, conduct informal surveys on call-in shows or do street interviews as long as there are no claims of scientific statistical methods.

4. Prohibitions against partisan advertising or programming during blackout periods do not apply to objective news reports, including recaps of controversial issues, campaign events or last-minute political announcements.

---

24 For example, see CRTC Circular No. 249, s. 9.

15

ACCESS TO PUBLIC INFORMATION

Information is the stock and trade of a journalist and getting it calls for thorough research, asking the right questions and knowing "just where to look." Although the latter often involves leveraging private sources, a surprising amount of valuable information is available from public or government bodies.

That information has become even more accessible through the Internet, CD-ROMs (often available at local libraries), and various on-line subscriber services. In fact, Ottawa and many provincial governments are world leaders in making public information available electronically. Knowing how to gain access to all the records kept by governments and their agencies can yield fascinating stories on public spending, environmental or health studies, business trends, crime statistics and almost any topic imaginable.

By no means, however, does this suggest governments and their agencies will be any less secretive or difficult to deal with when the information is of a sensitive, embarrassing or complicated nature. Fortunately, Ottawa and every province and territory have laws permitting citizens to request public information, albeit not always with guaranteed results. This chapter outlines how to get access to a variety of sources of public information.

USING ACCESS TO INFORMATION LAWS

The federal government is arguably the largest storehouse of information in Canada. In many cases, the reports and studies it generates are readily available through its departments and agencies, such as Statistics Canada or Industry Canada. Provincial governments also churn out mountains of data of potential interest to the news media.

Sometimes, though, journalists and other individuals want information beyond what's available in canned reports and studies. For a long time, that wasn't possible and federal and provincial governments jealously guarded their information vaults. However, some enlightened politicians recognized that such secrecy often does a government more harm than good.

Starting in the early 1980's, Ottawa and every province and territory have enacted laws which recognize a general right of citizens to have access to public information in government files. Each of the laws sets out how requests for information are to be handled and identifies certain sensitive information that may or may not be released, depending on a number of exemptions set out in the laws. Numerous court cases have since established that accessibility is the rule and non-disclosure should be the exception, with the burden on the government to prove why a document cannot be released to the public.

It is important to note that the access laws were not meant to change the way the public normally gets information. For instance, it is not necessary to apply under access legislation for a government publication intended for public consumption. The purpose of the laws is to help individuals get unusual or unique information, even if it is ultimately embarrassing to the government.

The Pitfalls of Access Laws

Off the top, it should be said that many government officials charged with handling access requests are extremely helpful and efficient and some are notoriously not. Some are quite willing to help a journalist identify the proper government sources or routes for information. Sometimes, a telephone call to a department's access to information officer will be all that is needed to find a source or even secure the information. Of course, there are also plenty of horror stories about stonewalling in various departments or agencies.

As noted above, however, the legislation does not guarantee access to all information and the numerous exemptions are often loosely worded, giving government officials maximum freedom to deny access.

There are two main categories of exemptions within most access laws. One is the mandatory denial of access to specific information, such as personal records about a third person or information about police investigations. The other category allows a government minister or bureaucrat to exercise a discretionary power of release over the records, such as those dealing with intergovernmental affairs.

Journalists who frequently use the various provincial and federal access laws have noted certain delaying tactics by government officials looking to wriggle out of releasing information, such as inconsistent policies on access amongst departments, unfair extensions of time limits and exorbitant search and photocopy fees. Another tactic allowed by the legislation is to allow access to a document, but to "sever" or black-out sections (for example, names) which officials feel are exempt from the law. Some journalists have received documents with almost every word blacked-out by a marker or physically cut out from the document.

There have been an increasing number of court challenges of denials of access and exorbitant search fees. The court decisions have been mixed, with some supporting the government and others allowing access. For example, the court told a reporter seeking access to cabinet documents that it couldn't interfere with the government's decision to require deposits to cover search time since the fees were authorized by the Act.[1]

However, there have been some victories. In a decision involving the Immigration Appeal Board, a court held that a person's right of access to their own personal information overrides immigration legislation allowing the board to seal refugee records, even from the refugee himself.[2]

---

1 *Rubin and Minister of Finance, Re* (1987), 35 D.L.R. (4th) 517 (Fed. T.D.).
2 *Re Information Commissioner and Immigration Appeal Board* (1988), 51 D.L.R. (4th) 79 (Fed. T.D.). For cases in which the courts have supported a federal government decision to deny access, see: *Re Montana Band of Indians and Minister of Indian and Northern Affairs* (1988), 51 D.L.R. (4th) 306 (Fed. T.D.); *Re Robertson and Minister of Employment & Immigration* (1987), 42 D.L.R. (4th) 552 (Fed. T.D.); *Re Twinn and McKnight* (1987), 37 D.L.R. (4th) 270 (Fed. T.D.); *Re Rubin and President of CMHC* (1987), 36 D.L.R. (4th) 22 (Fed. T.D.); and *Minister of EMR v. Auditor General* (1987), 35 D.L.R. (4th) 693 (Fed. C.A.). For cases in which a court ordered disclosure or access, see: *Re Information Commissioner and Minister of Fisheries & Oceans* (1988), 50 D.L.R. (4th) 662 (Fed. T.D.); *Re Noel and Great Lakes Pilotage Authority; Dominion Marine Association* (1987), 45 D.L.R. (4th) 127 (Fed. T.D.); and *Davidson v. Solicitor General of Can.* (1987), 41 D.L.R. (4th) 533 (Fed. T.D.).

Health Canada maintains a detailed database of adverse drug reactions. After receiving an access to information request, it released much of the information in the database to the CBC, which used the data in two award-winning programs on dangerous drugs. Health Canada refused, however, to release any data on the provinces associated with each record and drug reaction, arguing the information was "personal information." Was Health Canada's decision upheld by the courts?

Yes.[3] The Federal Court of Canada ruled the information in the field of "province" was information about an identifiable individual since there is a chance a person could be identified by linking the data to other information that is public, such as death or obituary notices. Health Canada was able to demonstrate this, using obituaries published on the Internet. Also, the CBC itself, by also using obituaries, was able to track down the identity of an individual who had died of a drug reaction. The federal court judge agreed the database field should be withheld and ordered the CBC to pay Health Canada's legal costs.

Tips for Access Requests

1. Apply to more than one government department for access. Information is sometimes gathered on the same topic by several departments and if it is censored prior to release, it may not be censored the same way by each department.

2. Try to identify the exact nature and name of the document you are requesting. Government officials may tell you over the telephone what documents you should apply for.

3. Indicate a willingness to negotiate your request. Sometimes, the information you want may be too costly to gather or impossible to obtain in the detail you requested. By suggesting your request is negotiable, you may still end up with the information you want and perhaps more.

4. If appropriate, identify that you are a journalist and that the information is for public consumption. You don't have to explain why the information is needed, but requests sometimes receive less scrutiny when the end use of the data is explained.

---

3 *Gordon v. Canada (Minister of Health)*, 2008 CarswellNat 522, 2008 FC 258 (F.C.).

5. Always make a request in writing, even if the law allows a request for access orally. At the very least, it gives you a physical record of the initial request date and other particulars.

6. Ask for reviews of excessive fees, delays or refusals. For instance, if you are told you will have to pay for a search, ask for an estimate of costs and details on the qualifications of people serving you. In some cases, fees may be waived altogether for journalists who are gathering information for the "public benefit."

7. Make a point of requesting "records" rather than "information." A record is often defined as "any record of information however recorded." It is also useful to include the phrase "including but not limited to" when referring to specific records.

Charges in a high-profile 1997 murder case were stayed. The trial judge held the accused's rights had been violated because of "abusive conduct by state officials." The Ontario Provincial Police reviewed the conduct of police officers and Crown counsel in the case, and provided the Solicitor General with a 318-page report. The report was not made public despite a formal request by criminal defence lawyers under Ontario's Freedom of Information and Protection of Privacy Act. The Solicitor General refused the request, citing allowable exemptions for law enforcement records (s. 14), solicitor-client privilege (s. 19) and personal privacy (s. 21). Was the Solicitor General correct?

No. A leading 2007 Ontario Court of Appeal decision[4] ruled there was a compelling public interest in the disclosure of the record that clearly outweighed the intended purpose of the exemptions. The ability of the Criminal Lawyers' Association to express an opinion on the handling of the murder case "depended on access to the excluded material." A notable aspect of this ruling was that, while s. 23 of the province's freedom of information law allows disclosure of normally-exempted records where there is a "compelling public interest," it specifically excludes records involving law enforcement matters and solicitor-client privilege. Relying on the Charter's guarantee of freedom of expression, the appeal court ruled that is unconstitutional and "ss. 14 and 19 [should be] read into s. 23 of the Act." A majority of the court held the deleterious effects of not disclosing the report outweighed the salutary effects. Also, there was no

---

4 *Criminal Lawyers' Assn. v. Ontario (Ministry of Public Safety & Security)* (2007), 2007 CarswellOnt 3218, 280 D.L.R. (4th) 193 (C.A.).

> independent oversight of the Solicitor General's decision and "the lack of an independent means of determining whether the records should be disclosed left disclosure at the whim of the minister."

THE FEDERAL ACCESS TO INFORMATION LAW

Generally

The stated purpose of the Access to Information Act is to extend the present laws of Canada to provide a right of access to information held in records under the control of a government institution.[5] It also says any necessary exemptions to the right of access should be limited and specific.

Any person who is a Canadian citizen or a permanent resident (that is, a landed immigrant) has a right of access to records under the control of a government institution. It is a good practice to identify yourself as a citizen or landed immigrant in your application for access. It should be noted that corporations do not have a right of access, but their employees do as citizens. For instance, a request in the name of CXYZ Broadcasting might be rejected, while a request by CXYZ reporter Jane Doe will be handled normally.

There are some general definitions to note. A *government institution* is defined as any department, ministry of state, body or office of the Government of Canada listed in a schedule of the Act. The list includes over 140 government departments and institutions. A *record* includes "any correspondence, memorandum, book, plan, map, drawing, diagram, pictorial or graphic work, photograph, film, microform, sound recording, videotape, machine readable record, and any other documentary material, regardless of physical form or characteristics, and any copy thereof." An *Information Commissioner*, provided by the Act and situated in Ottawa, acts as an ombudsman between government departments and applicants.

There is a small administrative fee ($5) for each request to a department (check with the access to information officer for the latest amount) and the cost of any photocopies may have to be borne by the applicant. If a request involves substantial search time or research, the applicant may have to pay for the costs of the search, including wages of personnel. Note, however, that search and copy fees may be waived at the discretion of the access official or upon appeal to the Information Commissioner.

While the Information Commissioner can handle appeals of access refusals, the ultimate decision to release any information under this Act is with the Federal Court. A minister designated by the federal cabinet oversees

---

5 R.S.C. 1985, c. A-1, s. 2.

the administration of the Act (usually, the minister for the Treasury Board). But, heads of individual government institutions often deal with specific requests.

Not less than once a year, the minister who oversees the Act must publish a directory of federal information holdings, called Info Source (formerly, the *Access Register* and found online at www.infosource.gc.ca), containing descriptions of:

1. The organization and responsibilities of the government institutions;

2. The classes of records under the control of each institution;

3. The manuals of employees used to administer the programs and activities of each government institution; and

4. The title and address of the appropriate officer for each government institution to whom requests for access to records should be sent.

Unfortunately, the register is not as helpful as might be hoped. For instance, the discussion of classes of records available in each department generally involves only an identification number, a brief title, a brief idea as to the subject-matter and a list of key topics covered by the class. None of this may actually tell you what to expect or whether it is the information needed.

How to Make a Request

The request. The request must be made in writing by filling out a formal access to information request form (found on some government Web site or through government offices) or writing a detailed letter setting out the information needed. Send the request directly to the government institution that has control of the record along with the application fee. Some institutions may refuse requests that are not on official forms. The request must contain enough detail to allow an experienced employee to find the record with a reasonable effort.

The time limits. Once received, the head of the government institution (or access to information officer) must reply in writing to the request within 30 days. However, the 30-day limit may be extended in two circumstances.

First, if the head of the government institution feels another government institution has a *greater interest* in the record, he may transfer the request within 15 days of receiving it. (A greater interest occurs where the record was originally produced for the other institution, or the other institution was the first to receive the record). If this happens, the department that originally received the application must notify the applicant in writing of the transfer. The head of the other government institution must reply in writing within the remaining 15 days.

Second, the Act permits the head of a department to extend the time limit for a reply where the request is for a large number of records, where consultations are necessary to comply with the request or where it is necessary by law to give notice of the request to a third party (such as another government or a corporation). In the latter case, the notice of extension must be sent within the original 30-day limit. However, the extension itself can then be as long as 80 days. There is a right to appeal the extension.

Where a third party must be notified, such as a corporation that supplied confidential information to the government, it must be notified within the first 30 days of the application. Upon notice, the corporation or third party has 20 days to decide whether it will allow access to its information. Upon receiving the third party's reply, the government has 10 days to decide whether it agrees with the third party.

If the government decides to grant access to the information against the third party's wishes, the third party has another 20 days to decide whether to appeal to the Federal Court. If an appeal is launched, the applicant must then wait for the court process to run its course.

The appeal process. If an access request is not granted, the head of the institution must give written reasons and cite the provisions of the Act supporting the refusal. An appeal can be launched first to the Information Commissioner and then the Federal Court. An appeal to the commissioner can be made within one year of the request. Unfortunately, the commissioner has no time limit in dealing with the appeal and cannot be forced to hurry an investigation.

If the commissioner also rejects the access request or the government institution fails to comply with the commissioner's recommendation of disclosure, an appeal can be launched to the Federal Court within 45 days of receiving the commissioner's report.

Statutory Exemptions to the Right of Access

Under the Act, government officials may exercise discretion in granting access to certain records or may have a mandatory duty to refuse access to some records. However, there are exceptions within the exemptions and the loosely-defined parameters of the Act suggest journalists should still apply for records that may fall under the mandatory or discretionary categories.

The Eight Discretionary Categories

1. *Federal-provincial affairs*. Under s. 14, the government may use its discretion to refuse information that could reasonably be expected to be injurious to the conduct of the federal government in federal-provincial affairs, including information on federal-provincial consultations, deliberations, and information on federal strategy relating to the conduct of federal-provincial affairs.

2. *International affairs and defence*. Under s. 15, the government may use its discretion to refuse information which could reasonably be expected to be injurious to the conduct of international affairs, the defence of Canada or any state allied or associated with this country. The section also protects information dealing with the detection, prevention or suppression of subversive or hostile activities. This includes information:

(a) relating to military tactics or activities;
(b) relating to defence weapons;
(c) relating to defence forces;
(d) obtained or prepared for the purpose of intelligence for the defence of Canada, its allies and associates;
(e) obtained or prepared for the purpose of intelligence respecting foreign states, international organizations of states or citizens of foreign states used by the government in the process of deliberation and consultation or in the conduct of international affairs;
(f) on methods or scientific equipment involved in the information gathering process referred to in (d) and (e) or on sources of such information;
(g) on the positions of the government, foreign states or international organizations of states for the purpose of negotiations;
(h) that constitutes diplomatic correspondence;
(i) relating to the communications or cryptographic systems of Canada or foreign states used for the conduct of international affairs, the defence

of Canada, its allies and associated states or in relation to the detection, prevention or suppression of subversive or hostile activities.

3. *Law enforcement and investigations.* Under s. 16, the head of a government institution may use its discretion to refuse:

(a) information obtained or prepared by any government investigative body in the course of lawful investigations of crime or the enforcement of any law of Canada or a province if the record came into existence less than 20 years prior to the request;
(b) information relating to investigative techniques or plans for specific lawful investigations;
(c) information which could reasonably be expected to be injurious to the enforcement of any law in Canada or a province or the conduct of lawful investigations, including information relating to the existence or nature of a particular investigation, the identity of the confidential source of the information, or any record obtained or prepared in the course of an investigation;
(d) information which could reasonably be expected to be injurious to the security of penal institutions.

Several court decisions have made it clear that the exemption applies only to specific investigations that are ongoing or about to be undertaken. It does not apply to unspecified future investigations. Section 16 also allows the government to refuse access to a record that could reasonably be expected to facilitate the commission of a criminal offence (including information on criminal techniques, technical information relating to weapons or potential weapons or any record on the vulnerability of particular buildings, structures or systems, including computer or communication systems).

The section also protects information obtained or prepared by the RCMP while performing policing services for a province or a municipality, where the federal government has agreed not to disclose the information.

4. *Safety of individuals.* Section 17 allows an official the discretion to refuse any record which could reasonably be expected to threaten the safety of individuals.

5. *Economic interests of Canada.* The following information may be refused by the head of an institution under s. 18:

(a) valuable trade secrets or financial, commercial, scientific or technical information that belongs to the federal government or a government institution;

(b) information which could reasonably be expected to prejudice the competitive position of a government institution;

(c) scientific or technical information obtained through research by an officer or employee of a government institution;

(d) information which could reasonably be expected to be materially injurious to the financial interests of the federal government or the economy of the country. This includes information which could reasonably be expected to result in an undue benefit to any person in relation to:

   i) the currency of Canada;

   ii) contemplated changes in the rate of bank interest or in government borrowing;

   iii) a contemplated change in tariff rates, taxes, duties or any other revenue source;

   iv) a contemplated change in the conditions of operation of financial institutions;

   v) a contemplated sale or purchase of securities or of foreign or Canadian currency;

   vi) a contemplated sale or acquisition of land or property.

6. *Operations of government.* Section 21 states the head of an institution may refuse to disclose any record which came into existence less than 20 years prior to the request if it contains:

(a) advice or recommendations developed by or for the government;

(b) an account of consultations or deliberations involving government officials or employees;

(c) positions or plans developed for the purpose of government negotiations;

(d) plans relating to the management of personnel or the administration of a government institution that have not yet been put into operation.

This section does not apply to a record that contains an account of or a statement of reasons for a decision that is made in the exercise of a discretionary power or an adjudicative function and that affects the rights of a person. It also does not apply to a report prepared by a consultant or advisor who was not, at the time the report was prepared, an officer or employee of a government institution or a member of the staff of a minister of the Crown.

7. *Testing procedures.* Under s. 22, the government may refuse information relating to the testing, auditing procedures, techniques or details of specific tests to be conducted where such disclosure would prejudice the use or results of particular tests or audits.

8. *Solicitor-client privilege.* Under s. 23, any information which pertains to lawyer-client privilege may be refused.

The Three Mandatory Categories

1. *Personal information.* Section 19 states that the head of a government institution must refuse access to any *personal information* as defined in the federal Privacy Act, about an identifiable individual. Personal information includes:

(a) information relating to the race, national or ethnic origin, colour, religion, age or marital status of the individual;
(b) information relating to the education or the medical, criminal or employment history of the individual or information relating to financial transactions in which the individual has been involved;
(c) any identifying number, symbol or other particular assigned to the individual;
(d) the personal opinions or views of the individual except where they are about another individual or about a proposal for a grant, an award or a prize to be made to another individual by a government institution;
(e) correspondence sent to a government institution by the individual that is implicitly or explicitly of a private or confidential nature, and replies to such correspondence that would reveal the contents of the original correspondence;
(f) the views or opinions of another individual about the individual;
(g) the views or opinions of another individual about a proposal for a grant, an award or a prize to be made to the individual by an institution or a part of an institution or a part of an institution referred to in (e), but excluding the name of the other individual where it appears with the views or opinions of the other individual; and
(h) the name of the individual where it appears with other personal information relating to the individual or where the disclosure of the name itself would reveal information about the individual.

For the purposes of the Access to Information Act, personal information does not include:

(a) information about a past or present officer or employee of a government institution that relates to the position or functions of the individual, including the fact of employment, the title, business address and telephone number of the individual, the classification, salary range and responsibilities of the position held by the individual, the name of the individual on a document prepared by the individual in the course of employment, the personal opinions or views of the individual given in the course of employment;

(b) information about an individual who is or was performing services under contract for a government institution that relates to the services under contract, including the terms of the contract, the name of the individual and the opinions or views of the individual given in the course of the performance of such services;

(c) information relating to any discretionary benefit of a financial nature, including the granting of a licence or permit, conferred on an individual, including the name of the individual and the exact nature of the benefit, and

(d) information about an individual who has been dead for more than 20 years.

Personal information about an individual may be released where the individual consents to the disclosure, where the information is publicly available or in these instances:

(a) where the information was intended to be made publicly available;

(b) where federal law authorizes disclosure;

(c) where there is a subpoena or warrant;

(d) where the Attorney General of Canada wants it for legal proceedings involving the Crown or the federal government;

(e) where an investigative body specified in the Act's regulations requests it for the purpose of enforcing any law or carrying out a lawful investigation;

(f) under an agreement or arrangement between the federal government, a province, or foreign state for the purpose of enforcing any law or carrying out a lawful investigation;

(g) to a Member of Parliament for the purpose of assisting the individual to whom the information relates in resolving a problem;

(h) for internal audit purposes;

(i) for the Public Archives for archival purposes;

(j) to any person or body for research or statistical purposes if the head of the government institution is satisfied that the purpose for which the information is disclosed cannot reasonably be accomplished unless the information is provided in a form that would identify the individual to whom it relates, and the person or body gives a written undertaking that no subsequent disclosure of the information will be made in a form that could reasonably be expected to identify the individual to whom it relates;

(k) to any aboriginal group or government body for the purpose of researching or validating the claims, disputes or grievances of any of the aboriginal peoples of Canada;

(l) to any government institution for the purpose of locating an individual in order to collect a debt owed to the Crown or to make a payment to the individual, and

(m) for any purpose where, in the opinion of the head of the institution, the public interest in disclosure clearly outweighs any invasion of privacy or the individual in question would clearly benefit.

2. *Information obtained in confidence.* Section 13 states that the head of a government institution must refuse to disclose any record requested that contains information that was obtained in confidence from:

(a) a foreign government or one of its institutions;
(b) an international organization of states or one of its institutions;
(c) a provincial government or one of its institutions; or
(d) a municipal or regional government.

Subsection (2) states that the head of a government institution may use its discretion to disclose the record if he or she gets the consent of the affected body or the information is made public by that body.

3. *Third party information.* Section 20 states that a head of an institution must refuse access to a record that contains:

(a) trade secrets of a third party;
(b) financial, commercial, scientific or technical information that is confidential information supplied to a government institution by a third party and is treated consistently in a confidential manner by the third party;
(c) information which could reasonably be expected to result in material financial loss or gain to, or could reasonably be expected to prejudice the competitive position of, a third party, or
(d) information which could reasonably be expected to interfere with contractual or other negotiations of a third party.

In cases of product or environmental testing, the head of a government institution is not allowed to refuse to disclose the results of a test carried out by or on behalf of a government institution unless the testing was done as a service to a person, group or organization, other than a government institution, for a fee.

The head of a government institution also has a discretionary right to release any record that contains information described in this section where the third party consents to the disclosure or it would be in the public interest.

The public interest is defined as a situation relating to public health, public safety or the protection of the environment.

Some General Exemptions

The government may refuse to disclose information in a record where there is reasonable ground to believe the information will be published by the government within 90 days from receiving the request or within the period of time necessary for translation and printing.

The Act also does not apply to federal cabinet documents, memoranda of recommendations or proposals, discussion papers, agendas, minutes or records of cabinet decisions, briefs, draft legislation and policy documents. However, this exemption does not include cabinet documents in existence for more than 20 years.

In addition, where discussion papers have been prepared upon which decisions were made, a person may request immediate access to the discussion paper if the decisions have been made public. If the decision is not made public, access may still be requested, but not until four years after the time of the decision.

Note that other statutes also have provisions restricting public access to information. For example, there are privacy provisions in the Income Tax Act and the Bank Act protecting personal information.

Provincial Access to Information Laws

ALBERTA'S ACCESS TO INFORMATION LAW

Generally

Alberta's Freedom of Information and Protection of Privacy Act[6] sets out the goal of making public bodies more accountable to the public and, at the same time, to protect personal privacy. The government says the Act does not replace normal procedures for access to information nor does it limit access to information that is not personal information and is usually available to the public.

---

6 R.S.A. 2000, c. F-25.

How to Make a Request

The request. You must make a written request to the public body you believe has custody or control of a record. You may ask either for a copy of the record or to simply examine the record. While your right of access may be limited by one of the statutory exemptions, the Act suggests you may still have access to information if it can reasonably be severed or separated from the exempted portions of the record. A fee is charged for the initial review of a request.

The "head" of a public body and designated employees have a "duty" to assist applicants and respond without delay to each application. If the record only exists in machine readable form, then the public body must create a record for an applicant if it can be done using its normal computer hardware, software and technical expertise, and creating it would not unreasonably interfere with the operations of the public body.

The time limits. The public body must respond no later than 30 days after a request is received, unless it seeks the extension of another 30 days allowed under the Act, or the request has to be transferred to another public body. The public body may ask for a longer extension if there are many records requested, there isn't enough detail in the request, or a third party has to be consulted.

In responding, the public body must tell an applicant whether he or she is entitled access to the record or part of the record; if entitled, where, when and how access will be given; and, if refused, the reasons for the refusal, the section of the Act upon which a refusal is based, contact information for questions about the refusal; and information as to how an appeal can be made.

While reasons for refusal must normally be given, the Act does allow a public body to refuse to confirm or deny the existence of a record if the information would be harmful to law enforcement or the record contains personal information of a third party that, if its existence were disclosed, would be "an unreasonable invasion of that party's personal privacy."

The appeal process. You may initiate a review by the Act's commissioner of any public body's decision or failure to act by sending a written request within 30 days of the body's decision. A longer period may be allowed at the commissioner's discretion. A failure by a public body to respond within the time limits will be treated as a decision to refuse access to a record.

The commissioner may conduct investigations, audits or inquiries and may require any record to be produced or examine any information in a record, including personal information. The commissioner may authorize a mediator to investigate and try to settle a matter. If a mediator is not brought in, the commissioner must conduct an inquiry, which may be held in private. The person who asked for the review, the head of the public body concerned and any person given a copy of the request for a review must be given an opportunity to make representations during the inquiry.

If you are unhappy with the commissioner's decision or a failure to act, a written request must be sent to the minister administering the access to information Act within 30 days. The government may then appoint a judge or adjudicator to review the commissioner's decision or failure to act.

Statutory Exemptions to the Right of Access

The law outlines 14 specific categories, some of which trigger mandatory refusals, while others are discretionary.

The Eleven Discretionary Categories

1. *Disclosure harmful to individual or public safety.* A public body may refuse to disclose information, even about the applicant, if the disclosure could reasonably be expected to threaten anyone else's safety or mental or physical health, or interfere with public safety. A public body may also choose to refuse disclosure of your own personal information if the disclosure could reasonably be expected to result in immediate and grave harm to your safety or mental or physical health.

2. *Confidential evaluations.*

3. *Disclosure harmful to law enforcement.* A public body may refuse to disclose information to an applicant if the disclosure could harm a law enforcement matter; prejudice the defence of the country or any foreign state allied to or associated with Canada; or harm the detection, prevention or suppression of espionage, sabotage or terrorism. As in other jurisdictions, a body could refuse to give out information that may harm the effectiveness of investigative techniques; reveal the identity of a confidential source of law enforcement information; reveal criminal intelligence; endanger the life or physical safety of a law enforcement officer or any other person; reveal information relating to or used in the exercise of prosecutorial discretion; deprive a person of the right to a fair trial or impartial adjudication; facilitate the escape from custody of a person who is under lawful detention; or facilitate the commission of an offence under an enactment of Alberta or Canada.

4. *Disclosure harmful to intergovernmental relations or negotiations.* A public body may refuse to disclose information to an applicant if the disclosure could reasonably be expected to harm relations with other provincial, federal or foreign governments. This also includes harming relations with other government agencies, municipalities, aboriginal governments, and any international organizations of states.

If a public body does wish to release this information, the consent of the Attorney General is needed for records involving law enforcement information and the consent of cabinet is needed "for any other type of information." None of this, however, applies to records in existence for 15 or more years unless it is law enforcement information.

5. *Local public body confidences.* A local public body, such as a municipality, may refuse to disclose information concerning a draft of a resolution, by-law or other legal instrument of the local public body or a draft of a private Bill, or the substance of deliberations of a duly-held *in camera* meeting of its elected officials or of its governing body or a committee of its governing body. This exemption does not apply to drafts of resolutions, by-laws, legal instruments, or private Bills which have been considered in a meeting open to the public, or records in existence for 15 or more years.

6. *Advice from officials.* A public body may refuse to disclose information that would reveal advice or recommendations developed by or for a public body or a minister. The discretionary refusal does not apply to information in a record that has been in existence for 15 or more years.

7. *Disclosure harmful to economic and other interests of a public body.* A public body may refuse to disclose information which could reasonably be expected to harm the financial or economic interests of a public body or the provincial government, or the ability of that government to manage the economy, including trade secrets of a public body; valuable financial, commercial, scientific or technical information that belongs to a public body or government; plans that relate to the management of personnel of or the administration of a public body and that have not yet been implemented or made public; information which could be expected to result in the premature disclosure of a proposal or project or in undue financial loss or gain to a third party; and information about negotiations carried on by or for a public body or the government of Alberta.

The public body must not refuse to disclose records concerning the results of product or environmental testing carried out by or for that public body, unless the testing was done for a fee as a service to a person, a group of persons or an organization other than the public body, or for the purpose of developing methods of testing.

8. *Testing procedures, tests and audits.*

9. *Privileged information.* A public body may refuse to disclose to an applicant information that is subject to any special privilege, such as communications between solicitor and client.

10. *Disclosure harmful to the conservation of heritage sites, etc.* A public body may refuse to disclose information that could result in damage to, or interfere with the conservation of natural or historic sites, including endangered, threatened or vulnerable species.

11. *Information that is or will be available to the public.* A public body may refuse to disclose to an applicant information that is available for purchase by the public, or that is soon to be published or released to the public.

The Three Mandatory Categories

1. *Disclosure harmful to business interests of a third party.* A public body must refuse to disclose to an applicant information that would reveal trade secrets of a third party, or any commercial, financial, labour relations, scientific or technical information of a third party that was supplied, implicitly or explicitly, in confidence. Of particular concern is any information which could reasonably be expected to harm "significantly" the competitive position or interfere with the negotiating position of the third party. The law also is concerned if disclosure would result in similar information no longer being supplied when it is in the public interest that it continue to be given; or it would result in undue financial loss or gain to any person or organization; or it would reveal information given to an arbitrator or mediator in a labour relations dispute. Tax information about a third party also falls into this category.

The information, however, can be disclosed if the third party consents to the disclosure, an enactment of Alberta or Canada authorizes or requires the information to be disclosed, it relates to a non-arm's length transaction between the Government of Alberta and another party, or the information is in a record that is in the Alberta Archives or archives of a public body and has been in existence for 50 years or more.

2. *Disclosure harmful to personal privacy.* A public body must refuse to disclose personal information if the disclosure would be an unreasonable invasion of a third party's personal privacy. The law suggests the invasion of privacy is not unreasonable if it subjects the activities of the government or a public body to public scrutiny or promotes public health and safety.

The disclosure would likely be unreasonable if the third party is exposed unfairly to financial or other harm; the information has been supplied in confidence; the information is inaccurate or unreliable; or the disclosure may unfairly damage the reputation of any person referred to in the record. Also considered unreasonable is the disclosure of information relating to medical, psychiatric or psychological matters; law enforcement information; social benefits records; employment, occupational or educational history; tax and financial information; human rights information; character references or personnel evaluations; and mailing list details.

The disclosure is not an unreasonable invasion if the third party has, in writing, consented to or requested the disclosure; there are compelling health and safety circumstances; the law requires disclosure; or it is for a research or statistical purposes. The law also allows disclosure of information about a third party's position, functions or remuneration as an officer, employee or member of a public body or as a member of a minister's staff. This also applies to disclosure of financial and other details of a contract to supply goods or services to a public body, or concerning expenses incurred by the third party while travelling at the public's expense.

This exemption also does not apply if the individual has been dead for 25 or more years.

3. *Cabinet and Treasury Board confidences.* A public body must refuse to disclose information that would reveal the substance of deliberations of the Executive Council, Treasury Board or any of its committees, including any advice, recommendations, policy considerations or draft legislation or regulations submitted or prepared for these bodies.

This does not apply, however, to information in a record that is over 15 years old. Nor does it apply to information in a record of a decision made by cabinet or any of its committees on an appeal under an Act. Nor does it apply to background explanations or analysis presented to the Executive Council or any of its committees for its consideration in making a decision if the decision has been made public, the decision has been implemented, or five or more years have passed since the decision was made or considered.

BRITISH COLUMBIA'S ACCESS TO INFORMATION LAW

Generally

The British Columbia Freedom of Information and Protection of Privacy Act[7] begins by stating that the purposes of the Act include making public bodies more accountable to the public and to protect personal privacy. As in other jurisdictions, the government pledges that the Act does not replace other procedures for access to information nor should it limit access to information that is not personal information and is usually available to the public.

As in Ontario, whether a request for access is made or not, the head of a public body must, "without delay," disclose to the public, an affected group of people, or an applicant, any information about a risk of significant harm to the environment or to the health or safety of the public or a group of people. That said, the law also requires the public body to, if possible, notify third parties affected by the disclosure and the Act's commissioner.

How to Make a Request

The request. You must make a written request to the public body you believe has custody or control of a record. You may ask either for a copy of the record or to simply examine the record. While your right of access may be limited by one of the statutory exemptions, the Act suggests you may still have access to information if it can reasonably be severed or separated from the exempted portions of the record. A fee is charged for the initial review of a request.

The "head" of a public body must "make every reasonable effort to assist applicants and to respond without delay to each applicant openly, accurately and completely." If the record only exists in machine readable form, then the public body must create a record for an applicant if it can be done using its normal computer hardware, software and technical expertise, and creating it would not unreasonably interfere with the operations of the public body.

The time limits. The public body must respond no later than 30 days after a request is received, unless it seeks the extension of another 30 days allowed under the Act, or the request has to be transferred to another public body. The public body may ask for a longer extension if there are many

---

7 R.S.B.C. 1996, c. 165.

records requested, there isn't enough detail in the request, or a third party has to be consulted.

If a third party has to be notified, the public body must make a decision within 30 days of notice being given to that party but not before 21 days. A response from the third party before that time will, of course, require the public body to make a decision then.

In responding, the public body must tell an applicant whether he or she is entitled access to the record or part of the record; if entitled, where, when and how access will be given; and, if refused, the reasons for the refusal, the section of the Act upon which a refusal is based, contact information for questions about the refusal; and information as to how an appeal can be made.

While reasons for refusal must normally be given, the Act does allow a public body to refuse to confirm or deny the existence of a record if the information would be harmful to law enforcement or the record contains personal information of a third party that, if its existence were disclosed, would be "an unreasonable invasion of that party's personal privacy."

The appeal process. You may initiate a review by the Act's commissioner of any public body's decision or failure to act by sending a written request within 30 days of the body's decision. A longer period may be allowed at the commissioner's discretion. A failure by a public body to respond within the time limits will be treated as a decision to refuse access to a record.

The commissioner may conduct investigations, audits or inquiries and may require any record to be produced or examine any information in a record, including personal information. A public body must produce records for the commissioner within 10 days.

The commissioner may authorize a mediator to investigate and try to settle a matter. If a mediator is not brought in, the commissioner must conduct an inquiry, which may be held in private. The person who asked for the review, the head of the public body concerned and any person given a copy of the request for a review must be given an opportunity to make representations during the inquiry.

If you are unhappy with the commissioner's decision or a failure to act, a written request must be sent to the minister administering the access to information Act within 30 days. The government may then appoint a judge or adjudicator to review the commissioner's decision or failure to act.

Statutory Exemptions to the Right of Access

Before outlining the specific categories of exemptions, the B.C. law sets out a definition of applicable records which, in essence, exempt a variety of documents. The law states that it applies to all records in the custody or control of a public body, including court administration records, but it does not include:

(a) records in a court file or records of a judge, master, justice of the peace, or a record relating to support services provided to judges;
(b) a personal note, communication or draft decision of a person who is acting in a judicial or quasi-judicial capacity;
(c) a record that is created by or is in the custody of "an officer of the Legislature" and that relates to the exercise of that officer's functions under an Act;
(d) a record of a question that is to be used on an examination or test;
(e) a record containing teaching materials or research information of employees of a post-secondary educational body;
(f) material placed in the British Columbia Archives and Records Service by or for a person or agency other than a public body;
(g) material placed in the archives of a public body by or for a person or agency other than the public body;
(h) a record relating to a prosecution, if all proceedings in respect of the prosecution have not been completed;
(i) a record of an elected official of a local public body that is not in the custody or control of the local public body.

The law later outlines specific categories, some of which trigger mandatory refusals, while others are discretionary.

The Nine Discretionary Categories

1. *Local public body confidences.* A local public body, such as a municipality, may refuse to disclose information concerning a draft of a resolution, by-law or other legal instrument of the local public body or a draft of a private Bill, or the substance of deliberations of a duly-held *in camera* meeting of its elected officials or of its governing body or a committee of its governing body. This exemption does not apply to drafts of resolutions, by-laws, legal instruments, or private Bills which have been considered in a meeting open to the public, or records in existence for 15 or more years.

2. *Policy advice, recommendations or draft regulations.* A public body may refuse to disclose information that would reveal advice or recommendations developed by or for a public body or a minister. However, the public body must not refuse to disclose:

(a) any factual material;
(b) a public opinion poll;
(c) a statistical survey;
(d) an appraisal;
(e) an economic forecast;
(f) an environmental impact statement or similar information;
(g) a final report or final audit on the performance or efficiency of a public body or on any of its programs or policies;
(h) a consumer test report or a report of a test carried out on a product to test equipment of the public body;
(i) a feasibility or technical study, including a cost estimate, relating to a policy or project of the public body;
(j) a report on the results of field research undertaken before a policy proposal is formulated;
(k) a report of a task force, committee, council or similar body that has been established to consider any matter and make reports or recommendations to a public body;
(l) a plan or proposal to establish a new program or to change a program, if the plan or proposal has been approved or rejected by the head of the public body;
(m) information that the head of the public body has cited publicly as the basis for making a decision or formulating a policy; or
(n) a decision, including reasons, that is made in the exercise of a discretionary power or an adjudicative function and that affects the rights of the applicant.

The discretionary refusal does not apply to information in a record that has been in existence for 10 or more years.

3. *Legal advice.* A public body may refuse to disclose to an applicant information that is subject to solicitor-client privilege.

4. *Disclosure harmful to law enforcement.* A public body may refuse to disclose information to an applicant if the disclosure could:

(a) reasonably be expected to harm a law enforcement matter;
(b) prejudice the defence of Canada or of any foreign state allied to or

associated with Canada or harm the detection, prevention or suppression of espionage, sabotage or terrorism;

(c) harm the effectiveness of investigative techniques and procedures currently used, or likely to be used, in law enforcement;

(d) reveal the identity of a confidential source of law enforcement information;

(e) reveal criminal intelligence that has a reasonable connection with the detection, prevention or suppression of organized criminal activities or of serious and repetitive criminal activities;

(f) endanger the life or physical safety of a law enforcement officer or any other person;

(g) reveal any information relating to or used in the exercise of prosecutorial discretion;

(h) deprive a person of the right to a fair trial or impartial adjudication;

(i) reveal a record that has been confiscated from a person by a peace officer in accordance with an enactment;

(j) facilitate the escape from custody of a person who is under lawful detention;

(k) facilitate the commission of an offence under an enactment of British Columbia or Canada; or

(l) harm the security of any property or system, including a building, a vehicle, a computer system or a communications system.

A public body may also refuse to disclose information if it is in a law enforcement record and the disclosure would be an offence under an Act of Parliament; if the disclosure could reasonably be expected to expose to civil liability the author of the record or a person who has been quoted or paraphrased in the record; or if it is about the history, supervision or release of a person who is in custody or under supervision and the disclosure could reasonably be expected to harm the proper custody or supervision of that person.

Not included, however, are records or reports prepared in the course of routine inspections by an agency that is authorized to enforce compliance with an Act; a report, including statistical analysis, on the degree of success achieved in a law enforcement program unless disclosure of the report could reasonably be expected to interfere with law enforcement; or statistical information on decisions under the Crown Counsel Act to approve or not to approve prosecutions.

A public body must also not refuse, after a police investigation is completed, to disclose the reasons for a decision not to prosecute a person who knew of and was significantly interested in the investigation, including a victim or a relative or friend of a victim, or any other member of the public, if the fact of the investigation was made public.

5. *Disclosure harmful to intergovernmental relations or negotiations.* A public body may refuse to disclose information to an applicant if the disclosure could reasonably be expected to harm relations with other provincial, federal or foreign governments. This also includes harming relations with other government agencies, municipalities, aboriginal governments, and any international organizations of states.

If a public body does wish to release this information, the consent of the Attorney General is needed for records involving law enforcement information and the consent of cabinet is needed "for any other type of information." None of this, however, applies to records in existence for 15 or more years unless it is law enforcement information.

6. *Disclosure harmful to the financial or economic interests of a public body.* A public body may refuse to disclose information which could reasonably be expected to harm the financial or economic interests of a public body or the provincial government, or the ability of that government to manage the economy, including trade secrets of a public body; valuable financial, commercial, scientific or technical information that belongs to a public body or government; plans that relate to the management of personnel of or the administration of a public body and that have not yet been implemented or made public; information which could be expected to result in the premature disclosure of a proposal or project or in undue financial loss or gain to a third party; and information about negotiations carried on by or for a public body or the government of British Columbia.

The public body must not refuse to disclose records concerning the results of product or environmental testing carried out by or for that public body, unless the testing was done for a fee as a service to a person, a group of persons or an organization other than the public body, or for the purpose of developing methods of testing.

7. *Disclosure harmful to the conservation of heritage sites, etc.* A public body may refuse to disclose information that could result in damage to, or interfere with the conservation of natural or historic sites, including endangered, threatened or vulnerable species.

8. *Disclosure harmful to individual or public safety.* A public body may refuse to disclose information, even about the applicant, if the disclosure could reasonably be expected to threaten anyone else's safety or mental or physical health, or interfere with public safety. A public body may also choose to refuse disclosure of your own personal information if the disclosure could reasonably be expected to result in immediate and grave harm to your safety or mental or physical health.

9. *Information that will be published or released within 60 days.* A public body may refuse to disclose to an applicant information that is available for purchase by the public, or that, within 60 days, is to be published or released to the public.

The Three Mandatory Categories

1. *Cabinet confidences.* A public body must refuse to disclose information that would reveal the substance of deliberations of the Executive Council or any of its committees, including any advice, recommendations, policy considerations or draft legislation or regulations submitted or prepared for submission to the Executive Council or any of its committees.

This does not apply, however, to information in a record that is over 15 years old. Nor does it apply to information in a record of a decision made by cabinet or any of its committees on an appeal under an Act. Nor does it apply to background explanations or analysis presented to the Executive Council or any of its committees for its consideration in making a decision if the decision has been made public, the decision has been implemented, or five or more years have passed since the decision was made or considered.

2. *Disclosure harmful to business interests of a third party.* A public body must refuse to disclose to an applicant information that would reveal trade secrets of a third party, or any commercial, financial, labour relations, scientific or technical information of a third party that was supplied, implicitly or explicitly, in confidence. Of particular concern is any information which could reasonably be expected to harm "significantly" the competitive position or interfere with the negotiating position of the third party. The law also is concerned if disclosure would result in similar information no longer being supplied when it is in the public interest that it continue to be given; or it would result in undue financial loss or gain to any person or organization; or it would reveal information given to an arbitrator or mediator in a labour relations dispute. Tax information about a third party also falls into this category.

The information, however, may be disclosed if the third party consents to the disclosure, or the information is in a record that is in the British Columbia Archives and Records Service or archives of a public body and has been in existence for 50 or more years.

3. *Disclosure harmful to personal privacy.* A public body must refuse to disclose personal information if the disclosure would be an unreasonable invasion of a third party's personal privacy. The law suggests the invasion of privacy is not unreasonable if it subjects the activities of the government

or a public body to public scrutiny; promotes public health and safety; is relevant to a fair determination of the applicant's rights; or assists in researching or validating the claims, disputes or grievances of aboriginal people.

The disclosure would likely be unreasonable if the third party is exposed unfairly to financial or other harm; the information has been supplied in confidence; the information is inaccurate or unreliable; or the disclosure may unfairly damage the reputation of any person referred to in the record. Also considered unreasonable is the disclosure of information relating to medical, psychiatric or psychological matters; law enforcement information; social benefits records; employment, occupational or educational history; tax and financial information; human rights information; character references or personnel evaluations; and mailing list details.

The disclosure is not an unreasonable invasion if the third party has, in writing, consented to or requested the disclosure; there are compelling health and safety circumstances; the law requires disclosure; or it is for a research or statistical purposes. The law also allows disclosure of information about a third party's position, functions or remuneration as an officer, employee or member of a public body or as a member of a minister's staff. This also applies to disclosure of financial and other details of a contract to supply goods or services to a public body, or concerning expenses incurred by the third party while travelling at the public's expense.

MANITOBA'S ACCESS TO INFORMATION LAW

Generally

Manitoba's Act gives any person, including non-residents, the right to apply for access to examine or copy any record in the custody or control of the government.[8] It provides access to documents in the control of government departments and Crown agencies. A Crown agency includes boards, commissions and associations (whether incorporated or not) in which all directors are appointed by the government. It also includes corporations which have boards of directors controlled by the Crown or a government board, commission or association.

An *Access Guide* is published by the provincial government, outlining the types of documents held by the various departments. It must be updated every two years or less.

The Act has created several exemptions to the right to access. However, the head of a department must release any portions of a record which do not

---

8 Freedom of Information and Protection of Privacy Act, S.M. 1997, c. 50, s. 99.

qualify under the exemptions. The exempted material may be severed, where possible, from the record and the rest shall be released to the applicant.

In 2000, this legislation was extended to all local governments, school divisions, community colleges, universities, regional health authorities and hospitals.

How to Make a Request

The request. An application must be made in writing to the head of the government department (or an access to information officer) believed to possess the record. The request must supply sufficient detail to allow an experienced member of the department to locate the record. There is no fee charged to review a request.

The time limits. The head of the department must send a written notice of the decision on the application within 30 days. If the application should have been made to the head of another department, it must be forwarded to that department by the "original" department. An application may also be forwarded to another department if it has a "greater interest" in the record. A "greater interest" exists where a record was originally prepared for another department or where another department received the record first. Despite the transfer to another department, the 30-day limit continues to run from the day the original department received the application.

If an application requires a lengthy search or if the department has an unusually heavy workload, it may issue itself an extension of another 30 days. However, in addition to supplying written notice of the extension to the applicant, the applicant must be told of his or her right to appeal the extension.

The appeal process. If an application is unanswered within 30 days, it is deemed to have been refused and the applicant is free to appeal to the ombudsman. The ombudsman has the authority to hold a full investigation with no time limit. If an appeal to the ombudsman results in a further denial of access, the applicant may file an appeal with a court within 30 days after receiving notice of the ombudsman's denial. There is no appeal from the court's judgment.

Statutory Exemptions to the Right of Access

The Six Discretionary Categories

1. *Policy opinions, advice or recommendations.* Access may be refused to any record which discloses opinions, advice or a recommendation submitted by an officer or employee of the government or a minister, to the government or the minister. Records may also be denied which disclose the formulation of a policy, the making of a decision or development of a negotiating position of the government. This includes plans relating to the administration of a department and the contents of draft enactments.

However, the exemption does not apply to environmental impact statements, consumer test reports, government equipment test reports, scientific or technical research done in connection with policy formulation, instructions or guidelines to government officers or employees on programs affecting the public, reasons for a discretionary or adjudicative decision affecting the applicant or reports by consultants who are not employees or officers of the government or a minister.

Despite this category of exemption, access must be given to such records if they are more than 30 years old.

2. *Law enforcement and legal proceedings.* Access may be denied to records that would harm an investigation, facilitate the commission of a crime, threaten security of a prison or other building, threaten the security of a computer or communications system, violate solicitor-client privilege or harm an existing or anticipated legal proceeding.

This does not apply to records which disclose investigative or law enforcement techniques which are contrary to the law or discloses the structure or programs of a law enforcement agency or reports on the degree of success of a law enforcement program.

3. *Economic interests of Manitoba.* Access may be refused if the record discloses a trade secret of a department, innovative scientific or technical research done by a department, harms the government's competitive position, harms contractual negotiations or any government information which could result in an undue financial gain for a third party (for example, proposed tax changes).

4. *Federal-provincial relations.* Access may be denied if the record would harm the conduct of the government in federal-provincial relations.

5. *Testing or auditing procedures*. Information may be denied which could be used to prejudice the use or results of particular tests or audits.

6. *Materials to be made public*. If the head of a department believes on reasonable grounds that the information will be released in 90 days, access may be denied.

The Four Mandatory Categories

1. *Protection of personal privacy*. Access must be denied, in most cases, to a record which constitutes an unreasonable invasion of a third party's privacy. This can include details of education, health, criminal activities, employment or family history, personal details of tax matters, financial transactions or information which discloses the identity of a law enforcement informant.

This category does not apply to job-related information about government and ministerial officers or employees, details of personal-service contracts between third parties and the government or where a third party has received a licence, permit or other discretionary financial benefit (providing the third party represents 1 percent or more of the people in the province receiving the same benefit).

Access must also be allowed where the third party consents to the release of the information, the record is publicly available or the third party has been dead for more than 10 years. Access may also be granted for *bona fide* research or statistical purposes.

2. *Cabinet confidences*. An application for any record which discloses a confidence of cabinet (for example, an agenda of a cabinet meeting, policy analysis, proposals, and recommendations) must be denied. But the Act says access shall be allowed, subject to other exemptions, if the cabinet record is more than 30 years old or the cabinet which originally received the record consents.

3. *Information obtained in confidence*. Access must be denied, in most cases, if the record was obtained in confidence from the federal government, another province or a municipal or regional government. The information must be released if it is publicly available or the government affected consents.

4. *Commercial information belonging to a third party*. Access must be refused for records which disclose trade secrets of a third party, commercial information supplied to a department in confidence and treated consistently

as confidential or information which could reasonably be expected to result in significant financial loss or gain to a third party or interfere with the competitive position or contractual negotiations of a third party.

Access must be allowed where the record discloses the final result of a product or environmental test conducted for a government department, the third party consents or the record is publicly available.

Access may also be given if the public interest outweighs the private interest of the third party in areas of health, safety, environmental protection, or improved competition in government regulation of undesirable trade practices. A third party can go to court to object to such a release.

NEW BRUNSWICK'S ACCESS TO INFORMATION LAW

Generally

Any person, including non-residents, may request information by applying to the minister of the department where the information is most likely to be kept or filed.[9]

A *department* is defined in s. 1 as:

(a) any department of the Government of the Province;
(b) any Crown Agency or Crown Corporation;
(b.1) any community board, school board or hospital corporation;
(c) any other branch of the public service;
(d) any body or office, not being part of the public service, the operation of which is effected through money appropriated for the purpose and paid out of the Consolidated Fund.

The departments and agencies that fall under the Act are listed in the regulations (almost all are included).

Once a request is approved, a fee will be charged for inspection of the document and a charge may be levied for copies at the discretion of the minister.

This was among the first of the access to information laws in Canada, but it has a reputation for being cumbersome and erratically interpreted.

---

9 Right to Information Act, S.N.B. 1978, c. R-10.3.

How to Make a Request

The request. The request must be made in writing and specify the records believed to contain the information or specify the subject-matter of the information with sufficient particulars as to time, place and event so as to enable a person familiar with the subject-matter to identify the document. One court has ruled that the information requested must already exist in a recognizable form.[10] No fee is charged for the initial review of a request.

The time limits. The appropriate minister of the department or an access to information officer must answer the request within 30 days of the receipt of the application. If a document cannot be found, the minister must tell the applicant and allow the applicant to supply additional details on the request. If a document is likely to be found in another department, the minister must tell the applicant.

The appeal process. If an applicant is not satisfied with the decision of the minister or the minister has failed to reply, the matter can be referred to a Court of Queen's Bench judge or to the ombudsman. There are some important considerations in choosing between the two appeal routes. The ombudsman can only make a recommendation to the appropriate minister. The judge, however, can order the information to be released. But if a matter is referred to a judge and the request is denied, it cannot then be referred to the ombudsman. As well, if a matter is referred to the ombudsman, it can only be appealed to a judge if the minister ignored a recommendation from the ombudsman to disclose the record.

In an appeal to a judge, the onus is on the minister to show why the document must remain secret. There is no further appeal allowed, such as to the Court of Appeal.

The Twelve Statutory Exemptions to the Right of Access

The exceptions to the right to information are listed in s. 6 of the Act. It states that there is no right to information (mandatory) where its release:

    (a) would disclose information the confidentiality of which is protected by law;

---

10 In *Re Lahey and Minister of Finance of New Brunswick* (1984), 10 D.L.R. (4th) 758 (N.B. Q.B.), the applicant sought information from the Department of Finance which would require extensive searching of files and compilation of data. The minister refused the request and the court agreed that the information must already exist in some form.

  (b) would reveal personal information, given on a confidential basis, concerning another person;

(b.1) would reveal personal information concerning the applicant that

      (i)   was provided by another person in confidence, or is confidential in nature, or

      (ii)   could reasonably be expected to threaten the safety or mental or physical health of the applicant or another person;

  (c) would cause financial loss or gain to a person or department, or would jeopardize negotiations leading to an agreement or contract;

(c.1) would reveal financial, commercial, technical or scientific information:

      (i)   given by an individual or a corporation that is a going concern in connection with financial assistance applied for or given under the authority of a statute or regulation of the Province, or

      (ii)   given in or pursuant to an agreement entered into under the authority of a statute or regulation, if the information relates to the internal management or operation of a corporation that is a going concern;

  (d) would violate the confidentiality of information obtained from another government;

  (e) would be detrimental to the proper custody, control or supervision of persons under sentence;

  (f) would disclose legal opinions or advice provided to a person or department by a law officer of the Crown, or privileged communications as between solicitor and client in a matter of departmental business;

(f.1) would disclose information respecting the access to or security of particular buildings, other structures or systems, including computer or communication systems, or would disclose information respecting the access to or security of methods employed to protect such buildings, other structures or systems;

(f.2) would disclose the subject or substance

      (i)   of minutes of the meetings of a school board, of a community board, of the board of trustees of a hospital corporation or of a committee of any such board, that were not open to the public,

      (ii)   of briefings to members of such a board or committee respecting matters that were, are or are proposed to be brought before such a meeting, or

      (iii) of discussions, consultations or deliberations among members of such a board or committee respecting such a meeting;

(f.3) would disclose advice, opinions, proposals, recommendations, analyses or policy options provided, given or made to or for a school board, a community board, the board of trustees of a hospital corporation or a committee of any such board for the purposes of the board or committee in exercising its powers and performing its duties and functions;

(g) would disclose opinions or recommendations by public servants for a Minister or the Executive Council;

(h) would disclose the substance of proposed legislation or regulations, or

(h.1) would reveal information gathered by police, including the Royal Canadian Mounted Police, in the course of investigating any illegal activity or suspended illegal activity, or the source of such information;

(h.2) would disclose any information reported to the Attorney General or his agent with respect to any illegal activity or suspected illegal activity, or the source of such information; or

(i) would impede an investigation, inquiry or the administration of justice.

In this Act, *personal information* is defined as information respecting a person's identity, residence, dependants, marital status, employment, borrowing and repayment history, income, assets and liabilities, credit worthiness, education, character, reputation, health, physical or personal characteristics or mode of living.

NEWFOUNDLAND AND LABRADOR'S ACCESS TO INFORMATION LAW

Generally

Compared to the other provinces, Newfoundland and Labrador's Freedom of Information Act[11] is quite short and straight to the point. It pledges to give a right of access to information to any Canadian, Canadian corporation or permanent resident domiciled in the province. It also promises to retain the privacy of individuals while creating greater access to government information.

How to Make a Request

The request. An application for access is made by writing to the relevant government department where the information is kept. The request must identify the information as precisely as possible or so that the government can find it with reasonable accuracy. No initial fee is charged for reviewing a request, but a fee will be charged upon granting the request.

---

11 R.S.N. 1990, c. F-25.

The time limits. The application must be answered in writing within 30 days. If the request is granted, a fee will be assessed. Information which is exempted or restricted may be severed from a document. A request may be delayed if a department requires more time or if the request has to be transferred to another public body. The request may also be set aside if the information is to be published within the next 90 days.

The Appeal process. If access is not granted, an appeal must be launched to the trial division of the courts.

Statutory Exemptions to the Right of Access

The Six Discretionary Categories

1. *Information adversely affecting federal-provincial negotiations.*

2. *Law enforcement and investigations.*

3. *Information adversely affecting Newfoundland and Labrador's economic interests.*

4. *Solicitor-client or privileged information.*

5. *Proposed legislation or regulations.*

6. *Competitive third party information.* This includes financial, commercial, scientific or technical information, the disclosure of which might affect continued access to the information, would affect the competitive position of a person or result in undue financial loss or gain to a person.

The Eight Mandatory Categories

1. *Confidential intergovernmental information.* Any information obtained in confidence under an agreement or arrangement between the government of the province and the federal government or another province.

2. *Cabinet proposals or recommendations.*

3. *Cabinet agendas or minutes.*

4. *Advice to ministers.* These are records "used for or reflecting consultations among ministers of the Crown on matters relating to the making of government decisions or the formulation of government policy."

5. *Ministerial briefings.* This includes briefings to ministers of the Crown relating to matters which are before or proposed to be brought before the cabinet.

6. *Cabinet briefings.* This includes background explanations, analyses of problems or policy options for cabinet consideration in making decisions before those decisions are made.

7. *Confidential information under any legislation.*

8. *Personal information.* This includes information about an identifiable individual, including information about the person's race, national or ethnic origin, colour, religion, age or marital status; education, medical, criminal or employment histories; financial information; official numbers or "symbol" assigned to the person; address, fingerprints or blood type; personal opinions or views of the individual; private correspondence sent to a department; or the views or opinions of another person regarding the individual.

This does not include, however, information about an officer or employee of a department relating to his or her job function or position. Nor does it apply to details of contracts for personal services for the government, evaluations of the services or any discretionary benefits. It also doesn't include requests for such information about yourself.

THE NORTHWEST TERRITORIES AND NUNAVUT'S ACCESS TO INFORMATION LAW

Generally

The new territory of Nunavut has adopted the statutes of the Northwest Territories.[12] Under the law in both territories, any person has a right of access to records held by public bodies and a right to request correction of personal information, as well as preventing the unauthorized collection, use or disclosure of personal information by public bodies. The Act applies to all records in the custody or under the control of a public body, including court administration records. It does not apply to records arising from court files or judges' notes, personal communications of a person acting in a judicial or quasi-judicial capacity, prosecutions not yet completed, test questions, material placed in the Northwest Territories or Nunavut Archives by or for a person other than a public body, or a record in a registry where

---

12 Access to Information and Protection of Privacy Act, S.N.W.T. 1994, c. 20.

public access to the registry is normally permitted. As in other jurisdictions, the Act is not meant to replace existing procedures for access to government information or records.

How to Make a Request

The request. You must make a written request to the public body you believe has custody or control of a record. You may ask either for a copy of the record or to simply examine it. While your right of access may be limited by one of the statutory exemptions, the Act suggests you may still have access to information if it can reasonably be severed or separated from the exempted portions of the record.

The "head" of a public body and designated employees have a duty to assist applicants and respond without delay to each application. If the record only exists in machine readable form, then the public body must create a record for an applicant if it can be done using its normal computer hardware, software and technical expertise, and creating it would not unreasonably interfere with the operations of the public body. There will likely be fees to be paid for access and research, but you will receive an estimate first.

The time limits. The public body must respond no later than 30 days after a request is received, unless it seeks an unspecified, but "reasonable" extension or the request has to be transferred to another public body. The public body may seek a longer extension if there are many records requested, there isn't enough detail in the request, or a third party has to be consulted.

In responding, the public body must tell an applicant whether he or she is entitled to access to the record or part of the record; if entitled, where, when and how access will be given; and, if refused, the reasons for the refusal, the section of the Act upon which a refusal is based, contact information for questions about the refusal; and information as to how an appeal can be made.

While reasons for refusal must normally be given, the Act does allow a public body to refuse to confirm or deny the existence of a record if the information would be harmful to law enforcement or the record contains personal information of a third party that, if its existence were disclosed, would be "an unreasonable invasion of that party's personal privacy."

The appeal process. You may initiate a review by the Act's commissioner of any public body's decision or failure to act by sending a written request within 30 days of the body's decision. A failure by a public body to respond within the time limits will be treated as a decision to refuse access to a record.

The commissioner may conduct investigations, audits or inquiries and may require any record to be produced or examine any information in a record, including personal information. The review must be completed within 180 days after the receipt of the appeal. The commissioner may conduct an inquiry, which may be held in private. The person who asked for the review, the head of the public body concerned and any person given a copy of the request for a review must be given an opportunity to make representations during the inquiry.

The head of a public body must decide within 30 days to follow the commissioner's recommendation or not. Either way, everyone involved must be notified of the decision. If you or any other party is dissatisfied with the decision of the head, an appeal may be taken to the Supreme Court. The notice of appeal must be filed with the court and served on the head within 30 days after the day the appellant receives the written notice of the head's decision.

Statutory Exemptions to the Right of Access

The law outlines 14 specific categories, some of which trigger mandatory refusals, while others are discretionary.

The Ten Discretionary Categories

1. *Cabinet confidences.* The head of a public body may refuse to disclose information it could reasonably be expected to reveal, including any advice, proposals, recommendations, analyses or policy options developed by or for a public body or a member of the Executive Council. This does not apply to information that has been in existence in a record for more than 15 years or certain other exceptions, such as environmental reports.

2. *Privileged information.* The head of a public body may refuse to disclose information that is subject to any type of privilege, including solicitor-client privilege.

3. *Disclosure prejudicial to intergovernmental relations.* The head of a public body may refuse to disclose information that could reasonably be expected to impair relations between the government of the Northwest Territories or Nunavut and any other government, native band council or other government body. This section does not apply to information that has been in existence for more than 15 years unless the information relates to law enforcement.

4. *Economic and other interests of public bodies.* The head of a public body may refuse to disclose information that could reasonably be expected to harm the economic interest of the government of the Northwest Territories (or Nunavut) or a public body, or the ability of the government to manage the economy.

5. *Testing procedures, tests and audits.* The head of a public body may refuse to disclose information relating to testing, auditing procedures or techniques, or details of specific tests to be given or audits to be conducted where disclosure could reasonably be expected to prejudice the use or results of particular tests or audits.

6. *Disclosure harmful to the conservation of heritage sites.* The head of a public body may refuse to disclose information if it could result in damage to the conservation of fossil sites, natural sites, aboriginal sites, or any rare, endangered, threatened or vulnerable form of life.

7. *Disclosure prejudicial to law enforcement.* The head of a public body may refuse to disclose information where there is a reasonable possibility it could affect a law enforcement matter or the defence of Canada or of any foreign state allied to or associated with Canada. Information may also not be disclosed if it exposes the author of a record or individual who has been quoted or paraphrased to civil liability, or it would interfere with the control or supervision of an individual in a correctional facility. The head must refuse to disclose the information if it would be an offence under a federal Act.

8. *Disclosure harmful to another individual's safety.* The head of a public body may refuse to disclose information, including personal information about the applicant, where it could endanger the mental or physical health or safety of an individual other than the applicant.

9. *Confidential evaluations.* The head of a public body may refuse to disclose personal information that is evaluative or opinion material compiled solely for the purpose of determining the applicant's suitability, eligibility or qualifications for employment or for awarding of government contracts or other benefits when it has been in confidence.

10. *Information that is or will be available to the public.* The head of a public body may refuse to disclose information that is otherwise available to the public or will be in six months.

The Four Mandatory Categories

1. *Cabinet confidences.* The head of a public body must refuse to disclose information that would reveal a confidence of the Executive Council, such as advice, proposals, requests for directions, recommendations, analyses or policy options. It also includes briefings, agendas, minutes or records of decision of the Executive Council or the Financial Management Board or deliberations or decisions of the Executive Council or the Financial Management Board. This does not apply to information that has been in existence in a record for more than 15 years.

2. *Personal privacy of third party.* The head of a public body must refuse personal information where the disclosure would be an unreasonable invasion of a third party's personal privacy. Disclosure is allowed in certain circumstances, such as if you have the written consent of a third party.

3. *Business interests of third party.* The head of a public body must refuse to disclose information that would reveal trade secrets of a third party, or financial, commercial, scientific, technical or labour relations information obtained in confidence from the third party.

4. *Disclosure prohibited under another Act.* The head of a public body must refuse to disclose information if it is prohibited or restricted by another Act or a regulation under another Act.

NOVA SCOTIA'S ACCESS TO INFORMATION LAW

Generally

The Nova Scotia legislation begins with the statement that the government should operate openly and be accountable for its actions.[13] It states that these principles can be maintained by providing public access to all information, except that which would impede the operation of government

---

13 Freedom of Information and Protection of Privacy Act, S.N.S. 1993, c. 5. The courts have taken this quite literally. In *McLaughlin v. Halifax-Dartmouth Bridge Commission* (1993), 125 N.S.R. (2d) 288 (C.A.), the appeal court reversed a lower court ruling and found that the Halifax-Dartmouth Bridge Commission was a "Department" and the commissioners were "public officers" within the meaning of the Act. A journalist had applied under the Act for access to documents in the possession of the commission. The appeal court said that in light of the Act's purpose in s. 2, "it was appropriate that it be construed liberally." The commission was, it said, an arm of the government and was not a private corporation. It was a statutory body created by statute and given the power to act by statute. The

or disclose personal information pertaining to people or certain other matters.

Unlike other Acts, *access* is defined as the opportunity either to examine an original record or to be provided with a copy. Charges may be levied for requests and copies of documents. *Public body* is defined as any department, board, commission, foundation, agency, association, or other body of persons, whether incorporated or unincorporated, all the members of which, or all the members of the board of management or board of directors of which, are appointed by the government. If a member is not appointed by the government, the definition includes those who are public officers or servants of the Crown in the discharge of their duties and those who are directly or indirectly responsible to the Crown in the proper discharge of their duties.

Personal information means information respecting a person's identity, residence, marital status, employment, credit worthiness, education, character, reputation, health, physical or personal characteristics or mode of living. At least one court has added court exhibits to this category.[14]

Any person, including non-residents, may apply for access to information respecting:

(a) organization of a department;
(b) administrative staff manuals and instructions to staff that affect a member of the public;
(c) rules of procedure;
(d) descriptions of forms available or places at which forms may be obtained;
(e) statements of general policy or interpretations of general applicability formulated and adopted by a department;
(f) final decisions of administrative tribunals;

---

commissioners' positions were created and defined by statute and they performed public duties.

14 In *Halifax Herald Ltd. v. Nova Scotia (Attorney General)* (1992), 115 N.S.R. (2d) 65 (T.D.), a trial court ruled that exhibits in criminal proceedings were personal information and exempt from disclosure. The accused was charged with and ultimately acquitted of charges of influence peddling. A journalist working for a local newspaper sought access three years later to four exhibits filed by the Crown. The Deputy Attorney General, whose department had copies of the exhibits, refused access to them on the basis that they constituted "personal information," exempt from disclosure under s. 5(1) of the Freedom of Information Act. The court ruled that the fact they had been introduced twice in criminal trials and had been accessible to the public did not change the personal nature of the information. The use of the information in the context of a criminal trial was a justifiable invasion of the accused's privacy rights. Once the public had had access to the information in the context of the criminal trials, the court said, the requirements of open justice had been met.

(g) personal information contained in files pertaining to the person making the request;
(h) the annual report and regulations of a department;
(i) programs and policies of a department; and
(j) each amendment, revision or repeal of the foregoing.

If a department record contains some information which cannot be released, that portion will be deleted or severed and the remainder will be released.

The Nova Scotia access law is awkwardly constructed, limited in scope and easily lends itself to abuse in interpretation.

How to Make a Request

The request. An application for access is made by contacting the department where the information is kept, either by telephone or in writing. The request must identify the information precisely. No initial fee is charged for reviewing a request.

The time limits. The application must be answered within 15 working days. If no answer is received within 15 working days, the request is deemed to be denied.

The appeal process. If access is not granted, a written application must then be made to the deputy head of the department where the information is kept. Within 15 days after that request is denied, the applicant may appeal in writing to the minister of the department. The minister has 30 days in which to affirm, vary or overrule the decision.

The final and only stage of the appeal process is before the Nova Scotia House of Assembly. The appeal must be presented by a member in the form of a motion.

Statutory Exemptions to the Right of Access

Access must be denied (mandatory) for information which:

(a) might reveal personal information concerning another person;
(b) might result in financial gain or loss to a person or a department, or which might influence negotiations in progress leading to an agreement or contract;
(c) would jeopardize the ability of a department to function on a competitive commercial basis;

(d) might be injurious to relations with another government;
(e) would be likely to disclose information obtained or prepared during the conduct of an investigation concerning alleged violations of any enactment or the administration of justice;
(f) would be detrimental to the proper custody, control or supervision of persons under sentence;
(g) would be likely to disclose legal opinions or advice provided to a department by a law officer of the Crown, or privileged communications between barrister and client in a matter of department business;
(h) would be likely to disclose opinions or recommendations by public servants in matters for decision by a minister or the Executive Council;
(i) would be likely to disclose draft legislation or regulations;
(j) would be likely to disclose information the confidentiality of which is protected by an enactment.

ONTARIO'S ACCESS TO INFORMATION LAW

Generally

The stated purpose of the Ontario legislation is to provide a right of access to information under the control of a provincial government ministry, agency, board, commission, corporation or other designated body.[15] One of the principles of the Act is that decisions on the disclosure of government information should be reviewed independently of government through an ombudsman, as in the federal law. Every person, including non-residents, has a right of access to records, unless the information falls within one of the exemptions. An attempt to challenge the Ontario exemptions as a violation of the Charter's freedom of the press guarantee failed in 1994,[16] but a 2007 Ontario Court of Appeal ruling promises to open up new possibilities for accessing government records and information where there is a "compelling public interest."[17]

Under s. 23 of the province's freedom of information law, "an exemption from disclosure of a record under sections 13, 15, 17, 18, 20, 21 and 21.1 does not apply where a compelling public interest in the disclosure of the record clearly outweighs the purpose of the exemption." Citing the Charter's guarantee of freedom of expression, the appeal court ruled s. 23's "compelling public interest" exception may also apply to law enforcement records (s. 14) and records involving solicitor-client privilege (s. 19).

---

15 Freedom of Information and Protection of Privacy Act, 1987, R.S.O. 1990, c. F.31.
16 See *Ontario (Attorney-General) v. Ontario (Inquiry Officer, Information and Privacy Commission)* (1994), 116 D.L.R. (4th) 498 (Ont. Gen. Div.).
17 Note 4, above.

This decision has been duly noted by other Ontario courts and tribunals. For example, a 2007 decision of the Ontario Information and Privacy Commissioner took notice of the ruling and considered what requirements must be met to trigger the use of s. 23.[18] "First, there must be a compelling public interest in disclosure of the records," stated the ruling. "Second, this interest must clearly outweigh the purpose of the exemption."

In determining if there is a "compelling public interest" in disclosure, the Commissioner suggests there must be a relationship between the record and the freedom of information law's central purpose of "shedding light on the operations of government." The information in the record must also serve the purpose of informing "the citizenry about the activities of their government, adding in some way to the information the public has to make effective use of the means of expressing public opinion or to make political choices." A public interest does not, however, exist where the interests advanced are private in nature or simply because the requester is a member of the news media. The public interest in non-disclosure of sensitive information also must be considered. The Commission listed some examples of situations where a compelling public interest has been found to exist:

- records relating to the economic impact of Québec separation
- records calling into question the integrity of the criminal justice system
- public safety records relating to the operation of nuclear facilities
- disclosure of records shedding light on the safe operation of petrochemical facilities
- records containing information about contributions to municipal election campaigns

On the other hand, a compelling public interest has been found not to exist where:

- another public process or forum has been established to address public interest considerations
- significant amounts of information have already been disclosed, which are adequate to address public interest considerations
- court processes provide an alternative disclosure mechanism, and the reason for the request is to obtain records for a civil or criminal proceeding
- there has already been wide public coverage or debate of the issue, and the records would not shed further light on the matter

---

18 *Ontario (Attorney General) (Re)*, (2007) PO-2630, PA-050262-1 (Ont. I.P.C.).

It will be interesting to follow the impact of this decision in Ontario and other provinces in the coming years. For journalists and public advocacy groups in Ontario, the recent decisions on matters of "public interest" should provide fuel for more access to information requests.

An access guide, listing all of the institutions and general details on their records, is published annually. In addition, each institution must make available any documents produced to aid employees in handling access requests. The Act allows an institution to demand fees for searches lasting longer than two hours, the cost of preparing the record, computer and other costs of retrieving, processing and copying a record and shipping costs. The head of the department in question must give the applicant a reasonable estimate of the costs if they total more than $25. The Act gives the head discretion to waive the fees in certain circumstances, such as financial hardship, or public health or safety. The applicant may also ask Ontario's information commissioner to review the decision regarding fees.

One unique aspect of the Act is the requirement that the head of a government institution or ministry must disclose, as soon as possible, to the public or any people affected, any record which the head has reasonable and probable grounds to believe is in the public interest and reveals a grave environmental, health or safety hazard to the public.

How to Make a Request

The request. An application for access must be made in writing to the institution which is believed to have custody or control of the record. The letter must provide "sufficient detail to enable an experienced employee of the institution, upon a reasonable effort, to identify the record." If the request does not give sufficient detail, the institution must notify the applicant and must offer assistance to allow the request to conform to the requirements. There is a $5 fee to review requests.

If the request should have been made to another institution, the head of the institution that received the request must make "all necessary inquiries" to find the appropriate institution. An application may also be transferred to another institution if it has a "greater interest." A greater interest exists where the record was originally produced for another institution or the other institution was the first to receive the record.

The time limits. If a request is re-directed, the head of the "original" institution must forward the application to the other institution and notify the applicant within 15 days after the request was received.

Upon the appropriate institution receiving the request, a decision must be made within 30 days after the request was first made. The time limit may be extended for a time that is "reasonable in the circumstances" if the request is for a large number of records or if consultations on whether to grant the request will not be completed within the 30-day limit or to notify a party affected by the disclosure of the government's intention to release the information.

The applicant must be notified of the length of the extension, the reason for the extension and told that the Act's Information Commissioner may be asked by the applicant to review the extension.

If notice is given to a third party, that party has 20 days upon receiving the notice to reply. The head of an institution must make a decision within 30 days of notifying the third party, but not before either the day the third party replies to the notice or 21 days after notice is given, whichever is earliest.

The appeal process. If the request is refused, the head of an institution must state whether the record exists and the reason under the Act for the refusal. The applicant must also be told that he or she may appeal to the Information Commissioner. Under certain provisions of the Act, the head may refuse to confirm or deny the existence of the record, but must notify the applicant that he or she can appeal to the Information Commissioner.

The appeal process is then distinctly different from any other jurisdiction. An appeal may be made to the Information Commissioner on any decision, with the exception of those decisions involving the exercise of discretion in all of the exempt categories. Of course, apart from appealing a mandatory denial, it is hard to imagine what one has left to appeal from. The only exception to that rule is if the request involves a question of personal privacy.

A written notice of appeal must be made within 30 days of receiving notice of the decision. The commissioner will appoint a mediator to investigate the request, and if that fails to resolve the issue, an inquiry may be conducted in public or in private.

Statutory Exemptions to the Right of Access

The Eight Discretionary Categories

1. *Advice to government.* Access may be denied to the records of advice or recommendations of public servants or any other person employed by an institution (including consultants).

But, access cannot be refused to advice or recommendations which disclose factual material, statistics, environmental impact statements, product tests, reports by valuators, efficiency studies of government institutions, feasibility studies of government policies or projects, results of field research performed for formulating a policy proposal, details or reorganization plans for institutions or programs, reports of interdepartmental committees or task forces, reports of committees, councils or bodies making inquiries or recommendations for institutions and final decisions by officers of institutions involving an exercise of discretionary power.

Access must also be given to records more than 20 years old.

2. *Law enforcement.* Access may be denied if the record could be reasonably expected to interfere with law enforcement matters or investigations; reveal investigative techniques or procedures; disclose the identity of informants; endanger a life; interfere with judicial proceedings; interfere with intelligence operations; endanger security; facilitate the escape of someone from custody; or help in the commission of an offence. It also includes investigative reports and certain law enforcement records.

Under this category, the head of an institution may even refuse to confirm or deny the existence of a record.

3. *Relations with other governments.* Access may be denied to records that could prejudice the conduct of intergovernmental relations, information received in confidence from another government or its agency or information received in confidence from an international organization of states. In addition, the provincial cabinet must approve the disclosure.

4. *Defence.* Access may be refused where the record could reasonably be expected to prejudice the defence of Canada or its allies or information which would be injurious to efforts against espionage, sabotage or terrorism. In addition, the provincial cabinet must approve the disclosure.

5. *Third party information.* Access may be denied if the record discloses a trade, scientific, technical, commercial or financial secret supplied in confidence. The release of the information must be reasonably expected to prejudice the competitive or contractual position of the third party; result in a loss of future information to the institution which is supplied in confidence and necessary in the public interest; or result in an undue loss or gain to anyone.

The record must be disclosed if the public interest outweighs the private interest.

6. *Economic and other interests of Ontario.* Access may be refused if the record discloses a trade secret of a department, discloses innovative scientific or technical research done by a department, harms the government's competitive position, harms contractual negotiations or any govern-

ment information which could result in an undue financial gain for a third party (for example, proposed tax changes).

This does not include results of product or environmental tests carried out by an institution unless someone paid for the tests or the tests were conducted to help develop testing methods. The record must be disclosed if the public interest outweighs the government interest.

7. *Solicitor-client privilege.* These are documents such as correspondence between a lawyer and his client.

8. *Danger to safety or health.* Access may be denied where it is reasonably expected the information could seriously threaten the safety or health of an individual.

The Two Mandatory Categories

1. *Personal privacy.* Access to personal information must be refused except where the individual consents in writing to disclosure of a record to which the person has access, compelling circumstances of health or safety dictate disclosure, for the purpose of creating a public record, or where an Act of Ontario or Canada authorizes the disclosure and for research purposes.

2. *Cabinet records.* Access to cabinet records must be refused if the information would reveal the substance of deliberations of the Executive Council. This can include agendas, minutes of meetings, recommendations and briefs.

But, a head of an institution cannot refuse to disclose a record which is more than 20 years old or to which the cabinet it was originally prepared for, consents to its disclosure.

PRINCE EDWARD ISLAND'S ACCESS TO INFORMATION LAW

Generally

Compared with other jurisdictions, Prince Edward Island was late to the game in creating access to information legislation and enacted its current law in 2002.[19] The law's objective is "to make government more open and accountable" and also ensure personal information held by government is

---

19 Freedom of Information and Protection of Privacy Act, R.S.P.E.I. 1988, c. F-15.01.

protected. The legislation applies to all government departments, agencies, boards (including school boards), commission and Crown corporations of the provincial government. Any person has a right to request access to records.

How to Make a Request

The request. An application for access can be made by completing a two-page form, which can be found on the government's Web site (www.gov.pe.ca/foipp), and submitting the form and a $5 fee to the relevant government body where the information is kept. There is no fee for viewing your own personal information. The form guides an applicant through most of the requirements. The request must identify the information as precisely as possible so that the government can find it with reasonable accuracy.

The time limits. The application must be answered in writing within 30 days. If the request is granted, other fees may be assessed. Information which is exempted or restricted may be severed from a document. A request may be delayed if a department requires more time or if the request has to be transferred to another public body or a third party must be notified. The request may also be set aside if the information is to be published within the next 60 days. If no answer or decision is received, the Act states a failure to respond is a refusal of the request.

The Appeal process. If access is not granted, a request for an independent review of the decision may be made to the province's Information and Privacy Commissioner within 60 days (20 days for a third party requesting review). There is no fee for this step. An applicant may also request a judicial review.

Statutory Exemptions to the Right of Access

The Fourteen Discretionary Categories

1. *Disclosure harmful to individual or public safety.*

2. *Disclosure harmful to applicant's health or safety.*

3. *Disclosure revealing the identity of an individual who has provided information to a public body in confidence about a threat to an individual's safety or mental or physical health.*

4. *Confidential evaluations or opinions compiled for the purpose of determining the applicant's suitability, eligibility or qualifications for employment or for the awarding of contracts or other benefits by a public body when the information is provided, explicitly or implicitly, in confidence.*

5. *Disclosure harmful to law enforcement.*

6. *Disclosure harmful to civil liability and prisoner custody interests.*

7. *Disclosure harmful to intergovernmental relations.*

8. *Public body confidences, such as draft legislation.*

9. *Advice from officials.*

10. *Disclosure harmful to economic and other interests of a public body.*

11. *Testing procedures, tests and audits if disclosure could reasonably be expected to prejudice the use or results particular tests or audits.*

12. *Privileged information pertaining to a public body.*

13. *Disclosure harmful to the conservation of historic sites.*

14. *Information that is or will be available to the public within 60 days.*

The Seven Mandatory Categories

1. *Prohibited or restricted disclosure under an existing law.*

2. *Disclosure harmful to business interests of a third party.*

3. *Taxation information on a third party.*

4. *Disclosure harmful to personal privacy, particularly information that would be an unreasonable invasion of an individual's privacy.*

5. *Law enforcement record where the disclosure would be an offence under an Act of Canada.*

6. *Cabinet confidences including any advice, recommendations, pol-*
    icy considerations or draft legislation or regulations submitted or
    prepared for submission to the Executive Council or any of its
    committees.

7. *Privileged information pertaining to a person other than a public*
    body.

QUÉBEC'S ACCESS TO INFORMATION LAW

Generally

The Québec Act recognizes that every person, including corporations and other artificial "people," has a right of access to the documents held by public bodies, subject to certain restrictions.[20] Non-residents may also apply.

The public bodies encompassed by the Act are the Conseil exécutif, the Conseil du trésor, the Lieutenant-Governor, the National Assembly, government departments, government agencies, municipal bodies, school bodies, governing bodies of professional groups, and health and social services establishments (including universities and other public institutions).[21]

Under the legislation, a *document* can be recorded in writing or print, on sound tape or film, in computerized form or otherwise. The Act does not apply to acts and registers of civil status, documents registered in a registry office, the register respecting the legal publicity of sole proprietorships, partnerships and legal persons, or certain private archives. It also does not apply to sketches, drafts, outlines, preliminary notes or similar documents.

The person with the highest authority in a public body is in charge of access to documents. But, that power can be delegated to any other member of the organization. The Ministry of Communications publishes a list each year of the names, addresses and telephone numbers of the people responsible for access to documents.

---

20 Act Respecting Access to Documents Held by Public Bodies and the Protection of Personal Information, R.S.Q., c. A-2.1.

21 It also includes the province's judicial council. In *Quebec (Conseil de la magistrature) v. Quebec (Commission d'acces a l'information)*, [1994] R.J.Q. 2666 (C.S.), the judicial council had refused a request for a document in the file of a judge who had been the subject of a complaint. The access to information commission determined it had the jurisdiction to review the refusal. The council objected, saying it threatened the independence of the judiciary. The court disagreed, saying the council was not a court and its duty was to investigate complaints against judges and ensure public confidence in the judiciary. Thus, it had no immunity from the Act.

This Act has a good reputation for fulfilling access requests.

How to Make a Request

The request. The request can be made orally or in a written form to the appropriate person. It must provide enough detail to allow the appropriate official to find it. No initial fee is charged to review a request.

The time limits. The person in charge of access has 20 days to reply to a request. If access to a document is granted, there will be no charge if the document is viewed on the spot where it is kept. If that is not possible, there may be charges for transcription, reproduction or transmission of the document.

The appeal process. Any refusals must be accompanied by reasons. If a written request is refused, a person may then appeal to the Commission d'accès à l'information. Any decisions based on points of law or competence can be further appealed to the Provincial Court.

Statutory Exemptions to the Right of Access

The Five Discretionary Categories

1. *Information affecting intergovernmental relations.* There is a discretionary power to refuse any information received from another government, agency of another government or international organization.

2. *Information affecting negotiations between public bodies.* A public body may use its discretion to refuse to disclose information which would likely hamper negotiations in progress with another public body.

3. *Information affecting the economy.* There is a discretionary power to refuse economic information which could:

(a) unduly benefit or seriously harm a person;
(b) have a serious adverse effect on the economic interests of the public body or group of persons under its jurisdiction;
(c) constitute an industrial secret owned by a public body;
(d) hamper negotiations for a contract, or result in a loss for the public body or a considerable profit for another person.

In addition, the industrial secrets of a third party or confidential industrial, financial, commercial, scientific, technical or union information which is supplied by a third party, and considered confidential by that party, cannot be released without consent.

Consent is also needed to release information supplied by a third party which might hamper negotiations in a contract, result in losses for the third party or considerable profit for another person or substantially reduce the third party's competitive margin. Also any information which would reveal the strategy concerning the negotiation of a collective agreement or a contract, may be refused for a period of eight years from the opening of negotiations. A study prepared for the purposes of taxation, tariffing or the imposition of dues may be refused for a period of 10 years from its date.

No public body can refuse to disclose industrial, financial, commercial, scientific, technical or union information which reveals or confirms the existence of an immediate hazard to the health or safety of persons, or a serious or irreparable impediment to their right to a healthy environment.

4. *Information affecting administrative or political decisions.* The Conseil exécutif may refuse to disclose or confirm the existence of a decision resulting from its deliberations or orders. The same applies to the Conseil du trésor.

A public body may refuse to disclose a legal opinion concerning the application of the law to a particular case, or the constitutionality or validity of legislative or regulatory provisions, or a preliminary or final draft of a bill or regulations. Information may also be refused if it would affect the outcome of judicial proceedings.

5. *Information affecting auditing.* The Auditor General or a person carrying out an auditing function in or for a public body may refuse to release or confirm information which would hamper an audit, reveal an auditing program or operation plan, reveal a confidential source of information regarding an audit, or seriously impair the power of appraisal granted to the Auditor General.

The Three Mandatory Categories

1. *Information affecting the administration of justice and public security.* A public body must refuse to release or confirm the existence of information received by a person responsible under the law for the prevention, detection or repression of crime or statutory offences, if its disclosure would likely:

(a) impede the progress of proceedings before a person or body carrying on judicial or quasi-judicial proceedings;
(b) hamper an investigation;
(c) reveal a method of investigation, a confidential source of information, or a program or plan of action designed to prevent, detect or repress crime or statutory offences;
(d) endanger the safety of a person;
(e) cause prejudice to the person who is the source or the subject of the information;
(f) reveal the components of a communications system intended for the use of a person responsible for law enforcement;
(g) reveal information transmitted in confidence by a police force having jurisdiction outside Québec;
(h) facilitate the escape of a prisoner; or
(i) prejudice the fair hearing of a person's case.

A public body must refuse information concerning a method or a weapon likely to be used to commit a crime or statutory offence, or the efficiency of a security system. A public body must also refuse to release or confirm the existence of information if disclosure would jeopardize state security.

2. *Information affecting administrative or political decisions.* The preliminary draft of a bill or regulation must remain secret for 10 years following its date. A communication between the Conseil exécutif and certain other bodies or persons must remain secret for 25 years. For example, this includes recommendations to the conseil, unless the author or the person receiving them decides otherwise. The same rule applies to an executive committee of a municipal body, to the recommendations made to it by its members, and to communications among its members.

Access to a document of a member of the National Assembly of Québec, or a document produced for that member by the Assembly's services must be refused unless the member deems it expedient. The same applies to documents from the office of the President of the Assembly or documents from staff of a member of a municipal or school body.

A public body must refuse to disclose the records of a meeting of its board of directors, or of its members in the performance of their duties until 15 years from its date. Recommendations to a public body must remain undisclosed for up to 10 years. Certain studies of recommendations have a five-year restriction.

3. *Personal information.* Any information which allows a person to be identified is "personal information" under this Act and must be refused to

everyone other than the person the information is about. This does not apply to information about a person which is public. Public information includes:

(a) names, addresses, duties, and other job-related facts of public body officials and employees (not including those involved in the prevention, detection or repression of crime);
(b) information about a person as a party of a service contract entered into with a public body (including the terms and conditions of the contract); and
(c) the name of a person who is getting an economic benefit from a public body by virtue of a discretionary power and any information on the nature of the benefit.

The information may be released if the person concerned consents. Certain government agencies and officials can have access to the personal information.

SASKATCHEWAN'S ACCESS TO INFORMATION LAW

Generally

As in most other jurisdictions, Saskatchewan's Freedom of Information and Protection of Privacy Act[22] preserves existing rights of access to information. Any person has the right to apply for access to examine or copy any record in the custody or control of the government. The Act has created several exemptions to the right to access. Exempted material may be severed, where possible, from the record and the rest shall be released to the applicant. An interesting feature of this province's Act is that if it conflicts with any other provincial legislation that prohibits access to information, then the access prevails.

How to Make a Request

The request. An application must be made in writing to the head of the government department (or an access to information officer) believed to possess the record. The request must supply sufficient detail to allow an experienced member of the department to locate the record. There is no fee charged to review a request.

---

22 S.S. 1990-91, c. F-22.01.

The time limits. The head of the department must send a written notice of the decision on the application within 30 days. If the application should have been made to the head of another department, it must be forwarded to that department by the "original" department. An application may also be forwarded to another department if it has a "greater interest" in the record. A "greater interest" exists where a record was originally prepared for another department or where another department received the record first. Despite the transfer to another department, the 30-day limit continues to run from the day the original department received the application.

If an application requires a lengthy search or if the department has an unusually heavy workload, it may issue itself an extension of another 30 days. However, in addition to supplying written notice of the extension to the applicant, the applicant must be told of his or her right to appeal the extension.

The appeal process. If an application is unanswered within 30 days, it is deemed to have been refused and the applicant is free to appeal to the ombudsman. The ombudsman has the authority to hold a full investigation with no time limit. If an appeal to the ombudsman results in a further denial of access, the applicant may file an appeal with a court within 30 days after receiving notice of the ombudsman's denial. There is no appeal from the court's judgment.

Statutory Exemptions to the Right of Access

The Six Discretionary Categories

1. *Information injurious to inter-governmental relations or national defence.* Access may be denied if the record would harm the conduct of the government in federal-provincial relations or harm national defence.

2. *Law enforcement and investigations.* Access may be denied to records that would harm an investigation, facilitate the commission of a crime, threaten security of a prison or other building, threaten the security of a computer or communications system, or harm an existing or anticipated legal proceeding.

This does not apply to records which discloses general outlines of law enforcement topics, discloses the structure or programs of a law enforcement agency or reports and statistics on the degree of success of a law enforcement program.

3. *Advice from officials.* Access may be refused to any record which discloses opinions, advice or a recommendation submitted by an officer or employee of the government or a minister, to the government or the minister. Records may also be denied which disclose the formulation of a policy, the making of a decision or development of a negotiating position of the government.

However, the exemption does not apply to environmental impact statements, consumer test reports, government equipment test reports, scientific or technical research done in connection with policy formulation, instructions or guidelines to government officers or employees on programs affecting the public, reasons for a discretionary or adjudicative decision affecting the applicant or reports by consultants who are not employees or officers of the government or a minister.

Despite this category of exemption, access must be given to such records if they are more than 25 years old.

4. *Economic and other interests.* Access may be refused if the record discloses a trade secret of a department, innovative scientific or technical research done by a department, harms the government's competitive position, harms contractual negotiations or any government information which could result in an undue financial gain for a third party (for example, proposed tax changes).

5. *Testing procedures, tests or audits.* Information may be denied which could be used to prejudice the use or results of particular tests or audits.

6. *Danger to health and safety.*

The Five Mandatory Categories

1. *Protection of personal privacy.* Access must be denied, in most cases, to a record which constitutes an unreasonable invasion of a third party's privacy. This can include details of education, health, criminal activities, employment or family history, personal details of tax matters, financial transactions or information which discloses the identity of a law enforcement informant.

2. *Records from other governments.* Access must be denied, in most cases, if the record was obtained in confidence from the federal government, another province or a municipal or regional government. The information

must be released if it is publicly available or the government affected consents.

3. *Cabinet confidences*. An application for any record which discloses a confidence of cabinet (for example, an agenda of a cabinet meeting, policy analysis, proposals, recommendations) must be denied. But the Act says access shall be allowed, subject to other exemptions, if the cabinet record is more than 25 years old or the cabinet which originally received the record consents.

4. *Third party information*. Access must be refused for records which disclose trade secrets of a third party, commercial information supplied to a department in confidence and treated consistently as confidential or information which could reasonably be expected to result in significant financial loss or gain to a third party or interfere with the competitive position or contractual negotiations of a third party.

Access must be allowed where the record discloses the final result of a product or environmental test conducted for a government department, the third party consents or the record is publicly available.

Access may also be given if the public interest outweighs the private interest of the third party. A third party can go to court to object to such a release.

5. *Solicitor-client privilege*.

THE YUKON'S ACCESS TO INFORMATION LAW

Generally

Any person has a right of "reasonable access" to information in records of departments, subject only to specific and limited exceptions.[23] Yukon departments include any branch or unit of the public service of the Yukon government, and any board, commission, foundation, corporation or other agency established as an agent of the territorial government.

---

23 Access to Information and Protection of Privacy Act, S.Y. 1995, c. 1.

How to Make a Request

The request. Anyone can make a written or oral request during normal working hours for information in a record of a department by applying to the archivist — a designated individual in each department. If the request is made orally, the person who receives it must make a written record of the particulars of the request. You must describe the record or subject matter with enough detail about time, place, person or event to enable a person familiar with the information to identify the right record. If the record cannot be identified or easily found, the archivist must, in writing, tell you and ask for more details that might help find it or tell you when it will be available. You may ask either for a copy of the record or simply examine it. A fee will be charged to make the records available or provide copies. While your right of access may be limited by one of the statutory exemptions, the Act suggests you may still have access to information if it can reasonably be severed or separated from the exempted portions of the record.

The time limits. A request for information must be granted or denied within 30 days after the request is made or after more details are supplied. A request not granted within 30 days is deemed to have been denied and the reasons for the denial must be provided.

The appeal process. If a request is denied, you may appeal the denial by delivering to the archivist a written notice of appeal within 15 days after the day your request was denied. In the Yukon, the appeal must be considered by the Executive Council Member for the department. The Act says this is an informal review and not a judicial proceeding. The Executive Council Member has 30 days to uphold, vary or overrule the denial and must give reasons for the decision. If a request is denied by the Executive Council Member, you may appeal by petition to a judge of the Supreme Court. There is no time limit for launching an appeal to the courts.

Statutory Exemptions to the Right of Access

The law outlines 11 specific categories, some of which trigger mandatory refusals, while others are discretionary.

The Eleven Statutory Exemptions to the Right of Access

Sections 15–25 list the mandatory and discretionary exemptions to access:

1. *Cabinet confidences.* A public body must refuse to disclose the substance of deliberations of the Executive Council or any of its committees, including any advice, recommendations, policy considerations, or draft legislation or regulations submitted or prepared. This does not apply to information in a record that has been in existence for 15 or more years, Executive Council decisions, background information, or public decisions made public, implemented or more than five years old.

2. *Policy advice, recommendations, or draft regulations.* A public body may refuse to disclose information that would reveal advice, recommendations, or draft Acts or regulations developed by or for a public body or a Minister. It must disclose certain information, such as any factual material, public opinion polls, appraisals of property, economic forecasts, environmental impact statements and technical studies or reports, to name a few of the many exceptions listed.

3. *Disclosure harmful to the financial or economic interests of a public body.* A public body may refuse to disclose information which could reasonably be expected to harm the financial or economic interests of a public body or the Government of the Yukon, or its ability to manage the economy (such as its personnel management, trade secrets, financial, commercial, scientific or technical information).

4. *Legal advice.* A public body may refuse to disclose information subject to solicitor client privilege or prepared for a public body in contemplation of legal proceedings.

5. *Disclosure harmful to law enforcement.* A public body may refuse to disclose information that could reasonably be expected to interfere with law enforcement, an investigation, reveal investigative techniques or a confidential source, endanger lives or public safety, to cite a few examples.

6. *Disclosure harmful to intergovernmental relations or negotiations.* A public body may refuse to disclose information relating to Yukon that might harm relations with the federal government, other provinces or territories, municipalities, a foreign state or government organization, or a First Nation government.

7. *Disclosure harmful to the conservation of heritage sites.* A public body may refuse to disclose information interfering with fossil, natural or historical sites or even endangered plants, animals and resources.

8. *Disclosure harmful to individual or public safety.* A public body may refuse to disclose to an applicant information, including personal information about the applicant, if it might threaten anyone else's health or safety, or interfere with public safety.

9. *Information that will be published or released within 90 days.*

10. *Disclosure harmful to the business interests of a third party.* A public body must refuse to disclose information involving trade secrets of a third party, or commercial, financial, labour relations, scientific, or technical information of a third party that is given in confidence and harms its competitive position.

11. *Disclosure harmful to personal privacy.* A public body must refuse to disclose personal information about a third party if it would be an unreasonable invasion of the third party's personal privacy.

UNITED STATES' ACCESS TO INFORMATION LAW

Generally

The benefits of the United States' Freedom of Information Act are available to non-citizens, as well as to the American public.[24] It applies only to documents held by the administrative agencies of the "executive" branch of the U.S. federal government (most states, counties and municipalities have their own but similar legislation). This includes access to records of the military, government corporations and independent regulatory agencies, but it does not include agencies in the legislative and judicial branches. The *United States Government Manual* and *The Congressional Directory* list all of the federal agencies and bodies that come under the Act and their functions. It is also available from the U.S. Government Printing Office or at some Canadian libraries, as well as the Internet (www.gpoaccess.gov).

In addition, the Act grants public access to manuals, handbooks and policy statements of any of the particular agencies. A person can gain access to records in any form (for example, computer records, paper or tape). The request can be made to the agency headquarters in Washington or to branch

---

24   5 U.S.C.A. (1970).

offices in the state that is believed to have the information. A request can also be addressed to the Freedom of Information Act officer with most agencies.

Each agency is required to publish a schedule of fees and the fee cannot exceed the actual cost of the search and obtaining copies. Rather than asking for copies, a person may request to simply inspect records. It is possible to have the fee waived or reduced if the information will benefit the public. Journalists frequently have their fees waived.

For more information, an excellent source is *A Citizen's Guide on How to Use the Freedom of Information Act and the Privacy Act in Requesting Documents*, available on the Internet.

How to Make a Request

The request. A request must be made in writing to the agency's Freedom of Information Act officer, the head of the agency or a person directly responsible for the documents. The envelope containing the written request should be marked "Freedom of Information Act Request" in the lower left-hand corner. The letter should state that the request is being made under the provisions of the Act. The request must "reasonably describe" the documents, which allows "a professional employee of the agency who was familiar with the subject area of the request to locate the record with a reasonable amount of effort." There is no requirement to express a reason for making the request. But, it is suggested that where an agency head has discretion in releasing the information, an explanation may facilitate disclosure. Optional information you may include in a request include: your telephone number or email address; a request to be notified of the fee or a stated limit on the maximum fee you will pay; a request for a waiver or reduction in fees; the format desired for the records (electronic vs. paper); and, if you have a "compelling need," a request for expedited processing.

The time limits. The targeted federal agency is required to reply to a request within 10 working days. In certain cases, an agency may be unable to respond within the time limit and must then notify the person making the request that an extension is needed. However, the extension cannot be for more than 10 working days.

If a request is denied (that is, it falls within one of the exemptions), the person making the request must be notified in writing with reasons for the refusal.

The appeal process. Once a request has been refused, an appeal should be made to the head of the agency involved stating a case for being allowed access to the information. In most cases, appeals must be made within 30 days. A reply to the appeal must be made within 20 working days or 30 working days if the initial request was answered within the 10-day limit. If there is no answer after 20 working days from when the agency received the appeal, a court action may be launched. The burden will be on the agency in question to justify its decision to withhold the information.

The Nine Statutory Exemptions to the Right of Access

The U.S. federal government allows agency heads to reject requests for the following information on a discretionary basis:

1. *Classified documents concerning national defence and foreign policy.* Documents which are classified as "Top Secret" may still be requested. The Act requires the agency head to review whether a document should continue to be classified. On appeal of a rejected request, a judge is given authority to review the documents and the agency decision.

2. *Internal personnel rules and practices of an agency.* This applies to information such as rules on internal employment practices and policies and use of agency facilities, such as parking spaces.

3. *Information exempt under other laws.* The statute barring public access must leave no room for discretion or provide a set of criteria to be met before information is released. This can include income tax returns and records on nuclear testing.

4. *Confidential business information.* This includes trade secrets and commercial or financial information obtained from a person confidentially. Confidential information is that which could harm the government or the competitive position of the company.

5. *Internal communications.* This includes memos and letters within and between agencies which would not normally be available unless a party needed it for litigation. This exemption does not apply to documents written after a policy or decision has been made. It only applies to documents involved in free-for-all discussions before a policy being developed.

6. *Protection of privacy.* This includes medical and personnel files, the disclosure of which would constitute a clear invasion of privacy.

7. *Investigatory files.* This refers to files prepared for law enforcement purposes, but applies only to records that would interfere with enforcement proceedings, deprive someone of a fair trial, constitute an unwarranted invasion of personal privacy, disclose the identity of a confidential source of information, disclose investigative techniques or endanger the lives of law enforcement personnel.

8. *Information concerning financial institutions.* This includes documents or reports concerning banks, stock companies or similar institutions.

9. *Information concerning wells.* This includes geological wells and geophysical information, including maps.

ACCESS TO MUNICIPAL RECORDS AND INFORMATION

Municipalities are only bound to provide public access to certain documents as set out in provincial legislation. Beyond that, the inspection of any other municipal documents is entirely at the discretion of the local municipal authorities.[25]

Most provinces specifically allow public inspection of minutes of open council meetings, council agendas, minutes of open committee meetings, audit statements, voting lists, assessment rolls, consultants' reports submitted to open council, contracts, budgets, and by-laws.[26] Some provinces may only allow some of the above to be inspected. In some cases, only residents of the municipality or ratepayers enjoy the right of public inspection.[27] Usually, confidential, internal or "in-house" reports are not required to be produced.[28] For example, legal opinions submitted to municipal councils are usually considered privileged or confidential.

While municipal records are noted in many provincial access to information laws, Ontario has enacted a Municipal Freedom of Information and

---

25 *Journal Printing Co. v. McVeity* (1915), 33 O.L.R. 166 (C.A.).

26 Only Alberta and Prince Edward Island have no mention of the public's right to municipal documents. Some of the provinces and territories (for example, Manitoba, Nova Scotia, Saskatchewan and Newfoundland and Labrador, and the Yukon) are very explicit in what documents may be examined and copied. Other provinces may only refer to the public's right of access to "records" of a municipality, which is a vague term subject to the discretion of municipal officials. For example, see Municipal Government Act, R.S.A. 2000, c. M-26 (Manitoba), Municipal Government Act, S.N.S. 1998, c. 18 (Nova Scotia), and Municipal Act, R.S.Y. 2002, c. 154 (Yukon).

27 This is the case in New Brunswick, Newfoundland and Québec.

28 *Charbonneau v. London and Reynolds* (1958), 15 D.L.R. (2d) 74 (Ont. H.C.).

Protection of Privacy Act (MFIPPA),[29] which provides individuals with the right to access records of information, including your own personal information, that is under the custody and control of a local government institution. These institutions include the municipality itself, school boards, public utilities (except electrical distribution), transit and police commissions, fire departments, conservation authorities, boards of health and other local boards.

Requests for information of municipalities can begin with a simple telephone call or visit to City Hall. In theory, appropriate departmental staff will determine if your request should be submitted formally under the MFIPPA or if records can be provided as a "routine disclosure," such as general records and records containing your own personal information. The legislation states an institution must provide a requester with information or a decision within 30 calendar days from the date a request is received. An "institution" may ask for an extension, if the request is for an extensive number of records or an outside third party needs to be notified.

ACCESS TO CORPORATE INFORMATION

Corporate bodies operating in Canada are required by legislation to publicly disclose certain information, some of which could be useful to a reporter. There is one cautionary note about using such information. While corporations may be required by law to disclose information, it may not be up-to-date. In many cases, information must only be filed once a year and some corporations may not even bother to file on time or for several years. This affects the accuracy of information about company directors, officers, share allocations or financial information.

Corporations Returns Act

Under this legislation, corporations are required to file specific information with the government each year.[30] The Act applies to public, private and holding corporations with gross annual revenues of over $15 million or assets of over $10 million, with the exception of Crown corporations. The corporation must file the following information with the chief statistician of Canada:

---

29 R.S.O. 1990, c. M.56. Saskatchewan also has a specific access to information law for local authorities, such as municipalities and boards. See Local Authority Freedom of Information and Protection of Privacy Act, S.S. 1990-91, c. L-27.1.
30 R.S., 1985, c. C-43, s. 1; 1998, c. 26, s. 63.

1.   The corporate name of the corporation;

2.   The address of the head office of the corporation, and in the case of a corporation not resident in Canada, the address of its principal place of business in Canada or place to which communications may be directed;

3.   The manner in which the corporation was incorporated, and the date and place of its incorporation;

4.   The amount of authorized share capital, the number of shares of each class, and a description of the voting rights;

5.   The number of issued shares of each class, and the numbers of shares owned by residents and non-residents of Canada;

6.   The number of shares held by other corporations (where the shareholding is 10 percent or more);

7.   The name and address of each person, other than a body corporate, holding 10 percent or more of the issued shares;

8.   The details of any body corporate holding 10 percent or more of the issued shares;

9.   The total face value of issued and outstanding debentures of the corporation;

10. For public corporations, the total number of shares and debentures offered in Canada during the past five years;

11. The name, address, nationality, and citizenship of each corporate director;

12. The name, address, nationality, and citizenship of each officer of the corporation; and

13. The number of shares of each class owned by each director and officer and a description of the voting rights attached to such shares.

A *holding corporation* is entitled to file the above information on behalf of its subsidiaries. The Act states the above information must be made available for inspection to any person for a nominal fee. The information on corporations is to be made available by the Minister of Industry for no more than $1 per corporation.

Canada Business Corporations Act

This Act applies to every federally incorporated company.[31] It does not apply to banks, insurance companies, trust companies or loan companies or companies incorporated only under provincial statutes (provincial or federal incorporation is often a matter of choice). The public rights of access are very limited in regard to the records of private companies (those that do not sell shares to the public). But the public does have a right of access to certain corporate records of *distributing corporations* under s. 21(1). A distributing corporation is generally defined in the regulations as meaning:

> a corporation, any of the issued securities of which are or were part of a distribution to the public and remain outstanding and are held by more than one person.

The corporate records of distributing corporations which can be examined for a fee at the corporation's registered office are:

(a) the articles and the by-laws, and all amendments thereto, and a copy of any unanimous shareholder agreement;
(b) minutes of meetings and resolutions of shareholders;
(c) copies of all notices of directors or changes of directors;
(d) a securities register of all securities issued and the names and addresses of the security holders.

Private corporations are also required to keep these records in their registered office, but only shareholders, creditors and their legal representatives can demand access.

Under s. 160, financial statements for publicly-traded (that is, distributing) corporations must be filed with the director (administrator) of the Act and according to s. 266, these and most other documents required to be submitted to the director are available to anyone through the director upon payment of the prescribed fee. Financial statements must include comparative financial statements from the first year to the present, the report of the auditor and any other information respecting the financial position of the corporation.

Non-distributing corporations falling under this Act are generally not required to disclose corporate records to the public. In certain cases, a

---

31 R.S.C. 1985, c. C-44.

corporation may apply to the director for an exemption from the requirement of financial disclosure. The exemption will generally be granted where the disclosure would be detrimental to a corporation's financial well-being.

Section 129 requires the director to regularly publish a periodical, available to the public, consisting of information about any insider trading of shares in a distributing corporation. Regulatory exemptions which are granted under the take-over provisions of the Act are also to be included in this periodical.

Provincial Corporations Acts

All provincial and territorial jurisdictions have Companies Acts or Business Corporations Acts which require private and publicly-traded corporations to file basic declarations with a provincial government department overseeing corporations, such as a ministry of consumer and corporate affairs. Once deposited with the government, the documents can be viewed by anyone, usually for a small fee. In some provinces, the government department may give out general information about a company over the phone.

Even private companies are required to file information such as the address of the corporation, names and addresses of company directors and notices of changes in directors or corporate structure. Publicly-traded corporations (also called distributing corporations, in some provinces) file the same documents and may also have to file the names and addresses of shareholders, the number of shares held by each shareholder and names and addresses of individuals holding options to purchase shares.

Depending on the province, the information supplied to the government and available for public scrutiny may be scanty. Alberta, the Northwest Territories, Manitoba and Saskatchewan have fairly detailed filing requirements.[32] But most other jurisdictions only require information such as the latest address of the corporation and changes in its directors.[33]

Public and private corporations may also be required to make minutes of shareholder or director meetings and financial records available at their registered office or head office of the corporation. But access is restricted according to the type of company. In most provinces and both territories, such information is available on publicly-traded corporations to anyone during normal business hours, sometimes for a small fee. Private corporations, however, do not have to make this information available in their offices to anyone other than shareholders and directors. In the latter case, a

---

32 For example, see Alberta, Business Corporations Act, R.S.A. 2000, c. B-9, s. 23(4) and (5).

33 For example, see British Columbia, Company Act, R.S.B.C. 1996, c. 62, s. 336.

journalist must rely on information available through government corporate records offices or a corporate registry. In New Brunswick, Prince Edward Island and Québec, both private and public companies are required to allow access to records to shareholders, creditors and their legal representatives and directors of the corporation.

Business Organizations Other than Corporations

Sole Proprietorships

There is no general requirement for a sole proprietor (unincorporated) to make information about his or her business available to the public. But, if a sole proprietor plans to operate under a name other than his or her own, the law in all jurisdictions requires that that name be registered with the provincial corporate affairs department. The registration process usually requires a declaration setting out the name and address of the sole proprietor and this then is available to the public.

Partnerships

If a partnership is required by provincial law to be registered, the public may gain acccss to a declaration consisting of the names of the partners, addresses, the name of the partnership and other general details.

Non-Profit Corporations

A non-profit corporation may also by required by provincial law to register its address, directors and other general information and this information is also available to the public.

Securities Legislation

Journalists may want to keep provincial securities bodies in mind when researching information about a particular company. Any public offering of securities (such as shares, debentures, bonds, private placements) requires disclosure of financial information such as earnings, income projections, expenses and other important information for prospective shareholders. Securities bodies also compile regular bulletins noting insider trades by directors, company executives and shareholders. The information and reports are filed with the provincial securities commission and are generally available to the public.

USING STATISTICAL INFORMATION

The Statistics Act[34] gives Statistics Canada the authority to demand and gather information on many aspects of Canadian life: social and cultural, economic, manufacturing, trade and commerce, agricultural, education and employment. The information is published on a regular basis, sometimes even weekly or monthly. Since Statistics Canada is an agency of the government, most of the information collected is for public consumption. In fact, "Stats Can" actively encourages people to use their services and a great deal of information is available on the Internet at www.statcan.ca.

Statistics Canada publishes an annual catalogue containing an index of the publications available through the department. The catalogue also contains a brief abstract or summary of each publication along with the date of publication and the price. A copy of this catalogue is available to anyone, free of charge, from any Statistics Canada User Advisory Service. There are also over 45 libraries throughout the country which are "depositories" for Statistics Canada material. Compiled information may be found in university libraries, public libraries and legislative libraries.

Statistics Canada also provides toll free numbers to allow researchers to quickly find facts and figures (contact local directory assistance or 1-800-555-1212 for the 800 number nearest you). This service is free of charge where the information is readily accessible. If the request requires extensive research, you may be charged on a cost-recovery basis. The staff can quickly, often within a day, find figures on almost anything or offer advice on other potential sources of information.

Interpreting Statistical Information

Be sure that you check the introduction, footnotes, explanatory notes and definitions published with statistical reports. In accordance with the Statistics Act, certain information gathered by the department may have to be kept secret. Some tables, for instance, may contain an "x" in place of a statistic. This is because the Statistics Act forbids the publication of statistics which might identify a company or individual.

For example, when dealing with industrial statistics the *rule of three* is followed. That is, no figure made up of data from fewer than three industries can be published. If only two companies were in one industry, one company would obviously know about the figures from the other.

Another method of protecting the information obtained by Statistics Canada is random rounding. The final digit in every number in a table is

---

34 R.S.C. 1985, c. S-19.

rounded up or down to a 0 or a 5. This technique is used in the Census of Population tables where there is a danger of an individual being identified. Statistics Canada points out that its survey areas sometimes cover only a few city blocks and identifying a source of information is possible.

CANSIM

CANSIM is a Statistics Canada database which provides time series and cross-classified data on Canadian social and economic issues, sometimes daily. The time series data shows changes over a certain period (for example, consumer price index) and cross-classified data shows the relationship between different social and/or economic issues at a given point in time (for example, how and if unemployment rates affect vacancy rates).

This database is an excellent source for custom-made statistics. Stats Can also makes CANSIM available via the Internet. It is operated on a cost-recovery basis for the public. Quotes are available online in most cases or CANSIM staff members can offer you help in determining what the database has to offer. CANSIM can be accessed via the Internet (cansim2.statcan.ca) or through any of the User Advisory Regional Reference Centres located in cities such as St. John's, Halifax, Montreal, Ottawa, Toronto, Winnipeg, Regina, Edmonton and Vancouver.

16

MISCELLANEOUS LAWS

The Criminal Code[1] and other statutes contain various sections which journalists should note. While the provisions may not always be directed at the news media, it's best to be forewarned.

---

1 R.S.C. 1985, c. C-46.

PUBLISHING OBSCENE MATERIAL

The publication of obscene pictures and words is the subject of both the Criminal Code and broadcasting regulations. Determining what is obscene is difficult because the level of tolerance in a community changes over time. The laws we have enacted don't provide any clear guidelines regarding what's obscene so each case must be judged individually.

For example, obscene material presented as a form of art may be allowed on a television broadcast, but the same material presented in an exploitative manner in a magazine may be obscene. These inequities, often based on a judge's assessment of community standards, result in an uncertain legal climate for the news media.

In recent years, pressure has been building on the federal government to come up with a more comprehensive definition of obscene matter. The following are the relevant provisions in current law.

Criminal Code

Section 163(1)(a) of the Criminal Code makes it an offence to make, print, publish, distribute, circulate, or have in your possession for the purpose of publication, distribution or circulation any

> obscene written matter, picture, model, phonograph record or other thing whatever.

A complex issue of interest to journalists is precisely what is a "publication" of obscene matter. A 1985 Supreme Court of Canada decision held that even the display of objects only seen by patrons entering a sex store can be a publication. A Montréal store selling sex aids (that is, vibrators and inflatable dolls) was charged and convicted under the Code's obscenity section. The court dismissed an appeal by the store and the majority ruling was that the window signs declaring the adult nature of the shop and the "undue exploitation of sex" in the printed descriptions on cards beside the sex aids all combined to create a "publication." The court said a publication is "an article, the character of which is made public."[2]

The motive for publishing the obscene material is irrelevant.[3] The Code also offers this general definition of what is "obscene":[4]

---

2 *Germain v. R.*, [1985] 2 S.C.R. 241.
3 S. 163(5).
4 S. 163(8).

any publication a dominant characteristic of which is the undue exploitation of sex, or of sex and any one or more of the following subjects, namely, crime, horror, cruelty and violence, shall be deemed to be obscene.

Generally, in deciding whether a publication is obscene, the courts will look to see what is the "dominant characteristic" of the publication.[5] If the dominant characteristic is one of "undue exploitation of sex," or of sex combined with acts of violence, then the publication will probably be held to be obscene.[6]

To decide whether the use of sex in a publication is "undue exploitation," the courts will look to the overall standards of tolerance in Canadian society. An undue exploitation of sex is one which has no redeeming purpose in the eyes of the community and is in bad taste.[7]

However, just because a publication has objectionable or sex-related material doesn't make it obscene. The courts will look at why the author published the material.[8] The material may be included for "a frank and sincere depiction of a non-sexual subject."[9] The objectionable material may also be part of the "internal necessities of the work" in question. For example, an expert may be able to testify about the artistic or literary merit of the work.[10]

As mentioned above, deciding whether something is obscene involves a court's interpretation of the standards of acceptance in a community. This is how one judge viewed his task:[11]

> Those standards are not set by those of lowest taste or interest. Nor are they set exclusively by those of rigid, austere, conservative or puritan taste and habit of mind. Something approaching a general average of community thinking and feeling has to be discovered.

Determining the community's standards can involve evidence of public opinion polls and testimony from experts. But the courts are likely to give little weight to these "opinions" and, in the end, a judge will decide whether the publication is obscene.[12] The courts have maintained that they must consider contemporary community standards of all of Canada and that all

---

5 *R. v. Brodie* (1962), 132 C.C.C. 161 (S.C.C.).

6 *R. v. Ariadne Devs. Ltd.* (1974), 19 C.C.C. (2d) 49 (N.S. C.A.).

7 *R. v. Standard News Distributors Inc.* (1960), 34 C.R. 54 (Que. Mun. Ct.).

8 Note 5, above.

9 Note 6, above.

10 *Ibid.*

11 See, *Dominion News and Gifts v. R.*, [1964] S.C.R. 251, which adopted this statement from the dissenting judgment in the lower court ruling (that is, (1963), 42 W.W.R. 65 at 80).

12 *R. v. Pink Triangle Press* (1980), 51 C.C.C. (2d) 485 at 496 (Ont. Co. Ct.).

segments of the community must be considered, not just one faction (for example, a college campus or a church group).[13]

This was stressed by the Supreme Court of Canada in 1978 when considering whether a restricted movie was obscene if consenting adults were the only ones viewing it.[14] The court said the standards of tolerance are not what Canadians think is right for themselves to see, but what Canadians would not tolerate or "abide" others to see.

This line of thinking was followed in a 1996 Ontario Court of Appeal case in which a woman was charged with committing an indecent act after a complaint to police about her walking bare-breasted along several city streets. The community standard of tolerance test was applied to decide if her acts were indecent. The appeal court overturned a lower court decision that incorrectly considered how women normally behave in public. The higher court said the test involves asking, first, what a community would tolerate, not what is typically practised. Second, was there harm resulting from the public's exposure to the act? The appeal court said there was no evidence of harm other than that some people didn't agree with the accused's choice of clothing. The act also was not degrading, dehumanizing or commercial, and no one who was offended was forced to continue looking at her.[15]

Courts also don't judge all publications in the same way. For example, newspapers are handled differently from magazines. In a case involving a gay newspaper, the court looked at the entire newspaper to determine if the publication of some of the articles was obscene. There were only three articles judged to be obscene and the charge was dismissed.[16]

But, in a case involving a men's magazine, the court felt it could look at the publication page-by-page because there was no overriding theme.[17]

Finally, the Code recognizes that a publication of obscene material may be in the public interest and this defence is set out in s. 163(3):

> No person shall be convicted of an offence under this section if the public good was served by the acts that are alleged to constitute the offence and if the acts alleged did not extend beyond what served the public good.

The Criminal Code was amended in recent years to add the specific offence of "child pornography." Section 163.1 defines the offence as

13 *Towne Cinema Theatres Ltd. v. R.*, [1985] 1 S.C.R. 494.
14 *R. v. Sudbury News Serv. Ltd.* (1978), 39 C.C.C. (2d) 1 (Ont. C.A.).
15 *R. v. Jacob* (1996), 142 D.L.R. (4th) 411 (Ont. C.A.).
16 *R. v. McLeod* (1970), 10 C.R.N.S. 229 (B.C. Co. Ct.).
17 *R. v. Penthouse International Ltd.* (1979), 23 O.R. (2d) 786 (C.A.), leave to appeal to S.C.C. refused (1979), 23 O.R. (2d) 786n (S.C.C.).

(a) a photographic, film, video or other visual representation, whether or not it was made by electronic or mechanical means:

  (i) that shows a person who is or is depicted as being under the age of eighteen years and is engaged in or is depicted as engaged in explicit sexual activity, or

  (ii) the dominant characteristic of which is the depiction, for a sexual purpose, of a sexual organ or the anal region of a person under the age of eighteen years; or

(b) any written material, visual representation or audio recording that advocates or counsels sexual activity with a person under the age of eighteen years that would be an offence under this Act;

(c) any written material whose dominant characteristic is the description, for a sexual purpose, of sexual activity with a person under the age of eighteen years that would be an offence under this Act; or

(d) any audio recording that has as its dominant characteristic the description, presentation or representation, for a sexual purpose, of sexual activity with a person under the age of eighteen years that would be an offence under this Act.

Under s. 163.1(4), it is an offence to even possess child pornography. It is not a defence for an accused to say he believed the child was 18 or more unless he proves he took "all reasonable steps" to determine the child's age and ensure the depiction did not suggest the individual was a child. Another valid defence is when the representation or written material has artistic merit or an educational, scientific or medical purpose, and the offensive act does not pose an undue risk of harm to persons under the age of eighteen years.

The editor of your celebrity news section receives a sensational videotape from a "secret admirer" of an actress showing her sunbathing nude and having sex poolside at her home. The video appears to have been recorded by lifting the camera over a high fence. Could you be charged with a Criminal Code offence for publishing these images?

Yes. Section 162(1) of the Criminal Code outlines the new offence of voyeurism, which involves surreptitiously making a visual recording or observing, including by mechanical or electronic means, a person who is in circumstances that give rise to a reasonable expectation of privacy and is nude or engaged in explicit sexual activity. The observation or recording must also be done for a sexual purpose (here, a "secret admirer"). News organizations need to be aware of s. 162(4), which prohibits anyone knowing that a recording was obtained by the commission of an offence under subsection (1) from possessing, printing, copying,

publishing, distributing, circulating, selling, advertising or making available the recording. A successful defence, under s. 162(6), would have to
show the acts that are alleged to constitute the offence "serve the public
good and do not extend beyond what serves the public good." Whether
a charge against a news organization under this section of the Code
would hold up would involve a case-by-case determination by a court.

Broadcasting Regulations

The Canadian Radio-television and Telecommunications Commission
(CRTC) has regulations on the broadcasting of obscene, indecent or profane
matter via radio or television.[18] For example, the television regulations
(which mirror the radio regulations except for the words "or pictorial representation") say:

5. (1) A licensee shall not broadcast

    (a)   anything in contravention of the law;

    (b)   any abusive comment or abusive pictorial representation that, when
taken in context, tends to or is likely to expose an individual or a
group or class of individuals to hatred or contempt on the basis of
race, national or ethnic origin, colour, religion, sex, sexual orientation, age or mental or physical disability;

    (c)   any obscene or profane language or pictorial representation; or

    (d)   any false or misleading news.

These regulations are meant to prevent a broadcaster from using obscene material for shock value or without an appropriate or artistic reason.
Many broadcasters make it a point to warn their audience of potentially
objectionable material.

---

18 See *Radio Regulations, 1986*, SOR/86-982, s. 3 and *Television Broadcasting Regulations,
1987*, SOR/87-49, s. 5(1).

Proposed Changes to the Criminal Code

In 1984, the federal government considered this change to the "definition" section of the Criminal Code. Section 163(8) would be replaced with the following:[19]

> For the purposes of this Act, any matter or thing is obscene where a dominant characteristic of the matter or thing is the undue exploitation of any one or more of the following subjects, namely, sex, violence, crime, horror or cruelty, through degrading representations of a male or female person or in any other manner.

This amendment would have removed the necessity for a link between sex and crime, horror, cruelty or violence in order to constitute "obscenity." It also includes "degrading representations" as a means of undue exploitation. In addition, this amendment would have made it clear that the test for obscenity applies to any "matter or thing" and isn't limited to publications. The amendments weren't enacted and soon after, the Fraser Committee Report[20] outlined more extensive proposals for the revision of obscenity law.

The Fraser Committee recommended first that the term "obscene" be done away with in the Criminal Code because it doesn't adequately describe all the material which the committee felt should be controlled. The report suggests a three-tiered system for dealing with pornographic material.

The committee recommends the repeal of s. 163 of the Code and suggests three major offences which would make it a crime to make, print, publish, distribute or possess for the purposes of publication or distribution the following:[21]

1. The first tier is reserved for the most serious offences, such as those showing a person under 18 years old participating in explicit sexual conduct. *Sexual conduct* is "any conduct in which vaginal, oral or anal intercourse, masturbation, sexually violent behaviour, bestiality, incest, necrophilia, lewd touching of the breasts or the genital parts of the body, or the lewd exhibition of the genitals is depicted." The first tier also includes material which advocates, encourages, condones, or presents

---

19 Set out in s. 36 of Bill C-19, introduced by the Liberal government in the 1983-84 session of Parliament. First reading given in February, 1984, but it did not reach second and third reading.
20 "Pornography and Prostitution in Canada," Report of the Special Committee on Pornography and Prostitution, Minister of Supply and Services (Ottawa), 1985 (2 vol.).
21 Recommendations 5 and 7 of the Fraser Report.

as normal the abuse of children or material which actually involved physical harm to a person in its making.

This is an indictable offence with a maximum sentence of five years in jail. Anyone who sells or rents these materials can be charged with an indictable offence with a maximum sentence of up to two years or a summary conviction offence liable to up to six months in jail, a fine between $500 and $2000 or both.

2. The second tier is less onerous and involves any material which depicts or describes sexually violent behaviour, bestiality, incest or necrophilia. *Sexually violent behaviour* involves sexual assault and any physical harm depicted for the purpose of causing sexual gratification or stimulation to the viewer.

    This is an indictable offence punishable with a maximum sentence of five years. Anyone who sells, rents or displays these materials can be charged with an indictable offence with a maximum sentence of up to two years or a summary conviction offence liable to up to six months in jail, a fine between $500 and $1000 or both.

3. The third tier of offences involves the display of visual pornographic materials in public. *Visual pornographic material* "includes any matter or thing in or on which is depicted vaginal, oral or anal intercourse, masturbation, lewd touching of the breasts or the genital parts of the body, or the lewd exhibition of the genitals," but does not involve a depicted person under 18 years of age or sexually violent behaviour. This offence is punishable on summary conviction.

Among the recommended defences is that the pornographic material is a part of a work of artistic merit. The recommended provisions would require a court to look at the impugned material in the whole context of the work when it's presented in a book, film, video recording or "broadcast which presents a discrete story." It says "in the case of a magazine or any other composite or segmented work" the court should look at the material in the context of "the specific feature of which it is a part."

Other defences involve the use of these materials for a genuine educational or scientific purpose. The display of pornographic materials can be excused where the public would encounter a "prominent warning notice advising of the nature of the display therein." There is also a "due diligence" defence for anybody who sells or rents the material who can prove that they did everything which could reasonably be expected to be done to ensure the pornographic material wasn't in violation of the Code.

Another attempt by Ottawa in 1988 to introduce a new obscenity law was also unsuccessful and, at the time of this publication, there was no pressing public demand for reform.

HATE PROPAGANDA

Criminal Code

Sections 318 and 319 establish indictable and summary conviction offences involving the promotion of genocide and hatred. A provincial or federal Attorney General must give permission to prosecute these offences. There have been an increasing number of prosecutions or convictions under these sections. One of the most notable cases was the conviction of Alberta school teacher James Keegstra, who taught his students that the Jewish Holocaust may not have happened.[22]

Section 318(1) states:

> Every one who advocates or promotes genocide is guilty of an indictable offence and is liable to imprisonment for a term not exceeding five years.

The offending statements can be spoken or in a written form. According to s. 318(2), "genocide" means:

> any of the following acts committed with intent to destroy in whole or in part any identifiable group, namely,
> (a) killing members of the group; or
> (b) deliberately inflicting on the group conditions of life calculated to bring about its physical destruction.

The Code defines an "identifiable group" as any section of the public distinguished by colour, race, religion, ethnic origin or sexual orientation. The reference to sexual orientation was added by Parliament in 2004.

Also prohibited is the incitement of hatred in any public place. A "public place" is defined as including any place to which the public has

---

22 Other recent prosecutions under these sections include *R. v. Ahenakew* (2005), 31 C.R. (6th) 354 (Sask. Prov. Ct.), in which the chair of the Federation of Saskatchewan Indian Nations Senate was convicted of making public comments that wilfully promoted hatred against people of the Jewish faith (on appeal, the conviction was quashed and a new trial ordered; see (2008), 53 C.R. (6th) 314 (Sask. C.A.)), and *Mugesera c. Canada (Ministre de la Citoyenneté & de l'Immigration)*, [2005] 2 S.C.R. 100, in which a permanent resident was alleged to have incited murder, genocide and hatred in a speech made in Rwanda before he obtained residency in Canada. The court agreed the resident should be deported.

access as of right or by invitation, express or implied. The actual offences are outlined in the following sections.

Section 319(1):

Every one who, by communicating statements in any public place, incites hatred against any identifiable group where such incitement is likely to lead to a breach of peace, is guilty of
- (a) an indictable offence and is liable to imprisonment for a term not exceeding two years; or
- (b) an offence punishable on summary conviction.

Section 319(2):

Every one who, by communicating statements, other than in private conversation, wilfully promotes hatred against any identifiable group is guilty of
- (a) an indictable offence and is liable to imprisonment for a term not exceeding two years; or
- (b) an offence punishable on summary conviction.

The defence to a charge under s. 319(2) is set out in s. 319(3):

No person shall be convicted of an offence under subsection (2)
- (a) if he establishes that the statements communicated were true;
- (b) if, in good faith, he expressed or attempted to establish by argument an opinion upon a religious subject or an opinion based on a belief in a religious text;
- (c) if the statements were relevant to any subject of public interest, the discussion of which was for the public benefit, and if on reasonable grounds he believed them to be true; or
- (d) if, in good faith, he intended to point out, for the purpose of removal, matters producing or tending to produce feelings of hatred towards an identifiable group in Canada.

The Fraser Committee Report, mentioned above, recommends that the definition of "identifiable group" in s. 318(4) be broadened to include sex, age and mental or physical disability. The report also recommends the word "wilful" be removed to do away with the requirement that there must be a specific intent to promote hatred against an identifiable group. The word "statement" was also considered to be too narrow by the committee and it was suggested that it should be expanded to include graphic images of pornography. Finally, the report suggests that the section calling for the Attorney General's consent for a prosecution be repealed.[23]

---

23 See recommendations 38 to 41 of the Fraser Committee Report.

Section 320.1 allows courts to order the deletion of any publicly available online hate propaganda from computer systems when it is stored on a server that is within the jurisdiction of the court — regardless of where the owner of the material is located. Anyone who posts such material has the opportunity to be heard by a judge before the material is deleted.

Recently, Parliament added s. 430(4.1) to the Code to create an offence of mischief motivated by bias, prejudice or hate based on religion, race, colour or national or ethnic origin, that is committed in relation to property used as a place of religious worship. It also protects an object associated with religious worship located in or on the grounds of such a building or structure, including cemeteries.

Broadcasting Regulations

The CRTC also seeks to prevent the spread of hate propaganda. For example, the television regulations (which mirror the radio regulations except for the words "pictorial representation"), in part, say:[24]

5. (1) A licensee shall not broadcast
  (a) anything in contravention of the law;
  (b) any abusive comment or abusive pictorial representation that, when taken in context, tends to or is likely to expose an individual or a group or class of individuals to hatred or contempt on the basis of race, national or ethnic origin, colour, religion, sex, sexual orientation, age or mental or physical disability.

Canadian Human Rights Act

Federal human rights legislation makes it a discriminatory practice to communicate hate messages based on race or religion by all telecommunications technologies, including the Internet, telephone message machines and "hot lines." In 1990, the Supreme Court of Canada agreed that s. 13(1) of the Canadian Human Rights Act was an infringement on the Charter's freedom of expression guarantee, but it was also a reasonable and justified limit.[25]

---

24 Note 18, above.
25 *Canada (Canadian Human Rights Commission) v. Taylor* (1990), 75 D.L.R. (4th) 577 (S.C.C.). More recently, in *McAleer v. Canada (Human Rights Commission)* (1999), 175 D.L.R. (4th) 766 (Fed. C.A.), the federal appeal court agreed s. 13(1) does violate the Charter, but the infringement of freedom of expression is justified as a rational and proportionate means of promoting equal opportunity. In this case, the court ruled the Canadian Human Rights Tribunal was correct in ordering operators of a telephone service to stop posting messages that exposed homosexuals to hatred and ridicule.

MISCELLANEOUS CRIMINAL CODE SECTIONS

Advertising Rewards

Section 143 prohibits any public advertisement of a reward for the return of any stolen or lost item, in which words are used to indicate that no questions will be asked if it is returned. The offence also extends to anyone who prints or publishes such an advertisement.

Counselling Offences

Section 22 forbids anyone from counselling or getting another person to be a party to an offence, such that a crime is committed. It doesn't matter that the offence may have been committed in a different way from what was counselled. The Code will hold the counsellor responsible for any foreseeable consequence of the counselling. In addition, s. 464 will hold you responsible for counselling or procuring another person to be a party to an offence, even though an offence may not be committed as a result. In one case involving a British Columbia newspaper, readers were told how to grow marijuana and the newspaper was charged under this section.[26] The newspaper tried to argue that the person who complained about the "advice" to the authorities did not even try to grow the illicit plant. The paper was convicted and the court held the recipient of the counselling doesn't have to be influenced by it to sustain a conviction.

Ignorance of the Law

You can't get away from a conviction by simply saying you didn't know you were committing a crime. Section 19 states that ignorance of the law is not an excuse for committing an offence.

Counselling Mutiny or Desertion

Section 62 prohibits the publication of anything which counsels or urges insubordination, disloyalty, mutiny or refusal of duty by a member of a military force (Canadian or any other military force lawfully in the country).

---

26 *R. v. McLeod* (1970), 1 C.C.C. (2d) 5 (B.C. C.A.).

Disturbing an Assemblage

Section 176(2) creates a summary conviction offence for anyone who wilfully disturbs an assemblage of persons meeting for religious worship or for a moral, social or benevolent purpose.

False News and Public Mischief

Section 372(1) makes it an indictable offence for anyone, with provable intent to injure or alarm any person, to convey or cause to be conveyed by letter, telegram, telephone, cable, radio or other method any information known to be false. Section 181 also makes it an offence to knowingly publish a false statement, tale or news that causes or was likely to cause injury or mischief to a public interest. In 1992, the Supreme Court of Canada ruled that section 181 was an unreasonable infringement on the guarantee of freedom of expression in the Charter of Rights and struck the law down. The section is still on the books, of no force and effect.[27] It should be noted that broadcasting regulations make it an offence under the Broadcasting Act to spread false or misleading news.[28]

Note that s. 140 creates the offence of public mischief for anyone who, with intent to mislead, causes a peace officer (such as the police) to investigate a false statement that accuses some other person of having committed an offence, that causes some other person to be suspected of having committed an offence that the other person has not committed or to divert suspicion from himself, reports an offence has been committed when it has not, or falsely reports that he or some other person has died. Note that there must be a clear intention to mislead justice.

Harassment

Journalists shouldn't become pests while chasing down a story such that a person feels he or she is relentlessly being hounded. Section 372(3) prohibits intentionally making harassing or threatening telephone calls. A newer "criminal harassment" offence is section 264(1), which makes it illegal to knowingly or recklessly engage in behaviour that causes another person reasonably, in the circumstances, to fear for his safety or the safety of anyone known to them. The specific behaviour is:

---

27 *R. v. Zundel* (1992), 95 D.L.R. (4th) 202 (S.C.C.). Ernst Zundel was charged under the
     section with spreading false news about the Holocaust.
28 Note 18, above.

(a) repeatedly following someone from place to place;
(b) repeatedly communicating with, either directly or indirectly, that person or anyone known to them;
(c) besetting or watching the dwelling-house, or place where that person, or anyone known to them, resides, works, carries on business or happens to be; or
(d) threatening conduct directed at that person or any member of their family.

This offence is aimed primarily at stalkers or those bound by restraining orders, but overeager journalists might theoretically also find themselves in trouble if a person reasonably feels threatened. The offence is punishable by a jail term up to five years and the federal government is proposing increasing this to 10 years.

Intimidation of a Journalist

The Criminal Code has been amended to include an unprecedented new offence — the intimidation of a journalist reporting on the activities of criminal organizations. This offence was created after a Québec journalist who regularly reported on crime organizations was ambushed and seriously injured. Section 423 prohibits anyone who, wrongfully and without lawful authority, compels "another person to abstain from doing anything that he or she has a lawful right to do, or to do anything that he or she has a lawful right to abstain from doing." Section 423.1(1)(c) specifically makes it an offence for anyone, without lawful authority, to "provoke a state of fear in . . . a journalist in order to impede him or her in the transmission to the public of information in relation to a criminal organization."

Prohibited conduct includes using violence or threats of violence against the individual or family members, damaging property, threatening relatives in other countries, persistently following a person, hiding their personal property, following a person in a disorderly manner on a highway, besetting or watching the place where that person resides, works or happens to be, or blocking or obstructing a highway.

Reproducing Likeness of Money

Section 457 makes it a summary conviction offence to print or publish (including with electronic or computer-assisted means) anything *in the likeness of* a current bank note, paper money or government or bank security or obligation. But, no conviction will result if:

the length or width of the likeness of the bank-note is less than three-fourths or greater than one-and-one-half times the length or width, as the case may be, of the bank-note and

(a) the likeness is in black-and-white only; or

(b) the likeness of the bank-note appears on only one side of the likeness.

PROVINCIAL HUMAN RIGHTS CODES

Most provinces and territories have human rights laws that bar the publication or broadcast of any "notice, sign, symbol, emblem or other representation" discriminating against any person or class of persons for any purpose because of race, religion, religious creed, political opinion, colour or ethnic, national or social origin, sex, marital status, physical disability or mental disability of that person or class of persons.[29] But, the legislation also states nothing in this provision interferes with the free expression of opinions upon a subject by speech or in writing.[30]

A Manitoba case held that a newspaper report doesn't fit into this category of a "notice, sign, symbol, emblem or other representation."[31] The article in question made allegedly racist remarks about Indians while discussing the topic of native leaders attending an Ottawa conference. In turning down the appeal, the Court of Appeal turned to one of the principles of statutory interpretation which states that the meaning of a word in a statute is "coloured" by the words surrounding it. The court said a notice or a sign isn't the same as a complicated newspaper article and found the newspaper not guilty of violating the human rights legislation.

In 1989, a Saskatchewan appeal court also found that newspaper articles in an engineering students' publication were not "notices, signs, symbols, emblems or other representations."[32] Since those court decisions, both provinces have changed their legislation to add a reference to "statements" or "articles." Other provinces, such as Ontario, have done away with this prohibition.

In 1993, British Columbia also introduced a change to its human rights legislation[33] that extends the scope of its Act to include articles and statements in publications. Journalists in B.C. publicly called the amendment an infringement of the Charter's guarantee of freedom of the press and hope

---

29 For example, see Newfoundland Human Rights Code, R.S.N. 1990, c. H-14, s. 14(1).

30 *Ibid.*, s. 14(2).

31 *Warren v. Chapman* (1985), 31 Man. R. (2d) 231 (C.A.).

32 *Saskatchewan (Human Rights Commission) v. Engineering Students' Society* (1989), 56 D.L.R. (4th) 604 (Sask. C.A.).

33 Human Rights Code, R.S.B.C. 1996, c. 210.

to see it challenged. In B.C., with the addition of "publication" and "statement," s. 7(1) of the law now says:

> A person must not publish, issue or display or cause to be published, issued or displayed any statement, publication, notice, sign, symbol, emblem or other representation that
>
> (a) indicates discrimination or an intention to discriminate against a person or a group or class of persons, or
>
> (b) is likely to expose a person or a group or class of persons to hatred or contempt
>
> because of the race, colour, ancestry, place of origin, religion, marital status, family status, physical or mental disability, sex, sexual orientation or age of that person or that group or class of persons.

The B.C. prohibition does not apply to private communications. Since the changes were enacted, one high-profile B.C. columnist and his newspaper were found to have violated the law. They were ordered to pay $2,000 compensation to the complainant and publish a summary of the tribunal decision in the newspaper.[34]

Alberta has similar legislation regarding publications and investigative powers, though the law states it shall not "be deemed to interfere with the free expression of opinion on any subject."[35]

EMERGENCIES ACT

In the event of an international, national or provincial emergency, mass disaster, war, invasion or insurrection, the Emergencies Act (previously, in a more draconian form, called the War Measures Act) empowers the federal government (that is, the cabinet) to do whatever may be reasonably necessary to maintain public order and safety.[36]

---

34 In *Collins v. Abrams* (2001), 196 D.L.R. (4th) 570 (B.C. C.A.), controversial newspaper columnist Doug Collins launched a constitutional challenge against a human rights tribunal finding that he and the North Shore News violated s. 7(1) by publishing a series of articles alleged to expose Jewish persons to hatred and contempt. The appeal court ruled it was premature for it to hear the columnist's challenge because the human rights tribunal had not yet had an opportunity to address the issues. Subsequently, Collins died before the human rights tribunal could hear the constitutional arguments, but his estate carried on the challenge because his widow wanted to publish his writings. In *Abrams v. Collins (No. 5)*, 2001 BCHRT 43, the tribunal ruled the issues at hand were not moot and heard the case. It held that Collins' right to freedom of expression was *prima facie* infringed, but it was demonstrably justified in a free and democratic society under s. 1 of the Charter.

35 R.S.A. 1980, c. H-11.7, s. 2(2).

36 R.S.C. 1985, c. 22 (4th Supp.).

This is a much kinder and gentler piece of legislation than the War Measures Act, however. The Act specifically notes the importance of the Charter of Rights and various international conventions. It bars the arbitrary imprisonment or detention of people based on race, ethnic origin or other protected areas of human rights. It also has eliminated the government's right under the old law to censor writings and photographs.

Section 30(2) of the Act states that any sweeping powers granted to government, such as the right to temporarily seize control of an industry or service, shall not be used to censor, suppress or control publications or communication of information regardless of its form or characteristics.

17

INTERNET LAW AND JOURNALISM

The Internet continues to be the proverbial double-edged sword for journalists. On the one side, electronic publishing offers reporters and their audiences unparalleled access to information worldwide. On the other side are uncharted legal "danger zones" where there are few borders, few police and even fewer hard-and-fast rules. Blogs, wikis, podcasts, RSS feeds, spam, and moderated and unmoderated Web forums, to name a few evolving forms of media, each present different challenges for journalists, publishers and lawmakers.

Issues of defamation, contempt of court and copyright, can take on new meaning when transported over the Internet. The sheer size of potential Internet audiences, conflicting laws in other jurisdictions and questions about cross-border enforcement are just some of the problems to be tackled in settling electronic-based disputes or alleged infringements of others' rights.

The Internet itself has spawned situations for which there was little or no law before. Can a commercial Web site use hypertext links to a page in an unrelated site without permission? (Courts are split on the issue.)[1] Should

---

1 In *Ticketmaster v. Tickets.com*, pre-trial motions from the U.S. District Court, Central District of California (August 10, 2000 and March 27, 2000), ruled the practice of "deep

you knowingly provide links to content that infringes the law? (Courts in most countries are likely to disapprove).[2] Is it legal to forward e-mail to others without permission? (Technically, no. The copyright resides with the author, but others argue there may be a reasonable expectation that e-mail will be forwarded or copied.) Is a Web site operator or news media outlet responsible for what visitors say on discussion boards? (Yes, if it is a moderated forum or discussion board, say some courts.)[3]

Some once thought no country or court could ever create or enforce rules to govern how the Internet was used. The ability to browse Web sites anywhere or make our thoughts available to anyone gave people the idea the Internet was about freedom. The freedom to view, use or copy the work

---

linking" or bypassing a competitor's home page with links to an inside page is not a copyright infringement. This case, however, involved a very specific use of technology to cull information from the competing site and present it in a new format. Tickets.com was not just copying Ticketmaster pages and offering them to users. In a somewhat related but contradictory case, *eBay, Inc. v. Bidder's Edge, Inc.*, 100 F.Supp.2d 1058 (U.S. N.D. Cal., 2000), a judge granted an injunction preventing Web "crawler" software from extracting information through links to eBay's auction site. The judge resorted to the law of trespass because the crawler was using the resources of eBay's server and degrading performance. The issue of linking first arose in a 1999 case involving Ticketmaster and Microsoft. The software company settled out of court before it got to trial and agreed to redirect users to the ticket site's home page rather than specific event pages. In Canada, see *Imax Corp. v. Showmax Inc.*, [2000] F.C.J. No. 69, 2000 CarswellNat 135 (T.D.), where a judge issued an injunction that, among other things, prevents the use of links to a competitor's Web site because of potential user confusion over whether the businesses are affiliated. More recently, courts in some jurisdictions, such as Europe, have wrestled with the question of whether a link is just a citation or reference, or an actual copy of a Web page that infringes copyright (a Dutch high court eventually ruled in 2003 that linking was not copyright infringement). In 2006, in a case dealing with the right of search engines to crawl and catalogue sites, a Danish Maritime and Commercial Court ruled anyone publishing information on the Internet must assume search engines will deep link to individual pages.

2 Some U.S. courts have held a hyperlink to content that infringes laws, such as copyrighted material or child pornography, is itself an illegal act or "contributory infringement." U.S. courts have, however, excused Web sites such as Google that have a purpose other than to provide links to the copyrighted content of others, provide links in "good faith" that other sites operate within the law, and that respond to "takedown notices" from rights holders.

3 Early U.S. decisions in Internet defamation lawsuits tried to classify defendants with discussion boards as either distributors or publishers, each with different liability. In *Cubby, Inc. v. CompuServe, Inc.*, 776 F.Supp. 135 (U.S. S.D. N.Y., 1991), a New York court ruled CompuServe had, by contract, given up any control of messages posted by users. In this case, CompuServe was a distributor, not a publisher. A later case, *Stratton Oakmount Inc. v. Prodigy*, 23 Media L. Rep. 1794 (U.S. N.Y. Sup., 1995), arose out of an allegedly defamatory posting on a Prodigy Online Service bulletin board. In a pre-trial motion, the judge ruled Prodigy was a "publisher" because it exercised editorial control over the content of its boards, posted "content guidelines" to users, used software to watch for offensive language, hired "board leaders" to enforce the guidelines, and deleted postings that violated guidelines.

of others. The freedom to say what we think. The freedom to like or hate whomever we want and declare so.

We now know the Internet cannot operate without rules. Copyrights and trade-marks have to be protected, reputations can be damaged over the Internet as elsewhere, and society still needs to guard against evils such as child pornography and hate literature. The question often asked in court is, how do we apply the laws built up over hundreds of years to this relatively new medium and its various tools? Here is a sampling of issues and guidelines developing in a variety of areas:

Blogs and RSS Feeds: Web logs or blogs are the online equivalent of a diary or journal with opinions, visual content and other information offered in a chronological order. With over 100 million blogs on the Internet at the time of this publication, blogs are a convenient tool for news junkies. A major difference, however, between most blogs and conventional news vehicles is the lack of an editor. As many well-intentioned journalists know, an editor is a valuable sounding board and objective reader who can help screen out potential problems.

Therefore, bloggers must be mindful of the law's application to journalists and act as their own editor to weed out sensationalism, untruths, baseless opinions and other common hazards. As with defamation in print and broadcasting, bloggers should be very cautious when alleging criminal, unethical or immoral conduct by others. Businesses, such as restaurants and theatre companies, can also be particularly sensitive to unfounded critical comments and have the financial resources to pursue legal action.

Bloggers also need to be on guard against copyright and trade-mark infringement. A blogger should know the legal limits of the "fair dealing" defence in Canada's Copyright Act (for example, not excerpting too much content and rewriting as much as possible). Bloggers should also consider seeking permission for hyperlinks to commercial sites and excerpts of copyrighted material, or at least give proper attribution or credits to copyright and trade-mark owners.

It should come as no surprise that blogs are held to the same legal standards as other forms of news media when it comes to allegations of defamation, contempt of court or copyright infringement. Blogs have already been a factor in numerous court rulings, including labour and employment matters where employees break rules of confidentiality.[4]

RSS or Really Simple Syndication feeds are an integral element for promoting many blogs and Web sites, since they allow subscribers to receive

---

4 See *Chatham-Kent (Municipality) v. CAW-Canada, Local 127* (2007), 159 L.A.C. (4th) 321 (Ont. Arb. Bd.), where a caregiver was fired for disclosing personal information in breach of a confidentiality agreement about residents of a home for the aged on a blog that was accessible to the public.

alerts when new editorial content is uploaded by their favourite blogger or site. A potentially interesting risk for RSS feeds lies in the summation of information. As in traditional defamation cases, a defamatory headline alone can support a successful lawsuit even though the full online story itself explains away any innuendo or mistaken meanings. When creating RSS feeds, content providers should be alert to any defamatory statements or meanings in headlines and story summations.

It has been observed that bloggers tend to be a free-spirited group who feel they are carrying the flag for freedom of expression and may not back down when warned of legal action. This is, of course, a potentially expensive position to take and bloggers would be wise to remove offensive material when warned it may be defamatory or otherwise in violation of the law. A retraction or apology is also a powerful way to mitigate damages or eliminate the threat of a lawsuit.

Forums, Discussion Boards, Chat Rooms and Mail Lists: A body of Canadian case law is beginning to form that underlines the importance of monitoring and quickly removing defamatory public postings and discussion threads when warned. For example, the B.C. Court of Appeal recently held one Web site publisher liable for failing to remove defamatory material in its discussion forums in a timely fashion.[5]

So far, however, Canadian courts have not required Web site operators to pro-actively monitor and remove objectionable content that is believed to be posted in good faith and voiced as honestly-held opinion. Unless a Web site operator, such as a news media outlet, intentionally or knowingly permits or encourages defamatory content on its discussion boards, the courts have so far been satisfied to know that swift action was taken once a warning was received. Users of forums and discussion boards also should be put on notice via online disclaimers of their responsibility to post information within the confines of the law. As for whether a Web site must reveal posters' identities, courts will typically compel a Web site owner to reveal them, if it is important to a lawsuit.

E-mail and Spam: There should be no doubt that e-mails, whether directed at specific individuals or broadcast to thousands as spam, are on the same footing as any other publication in lawsuits alleging defamation, contempt, copyright infringement, or even criminal harassment (cyberstalking). One of the first Internet-based defamation cases in Canada involved a $40,000 award in 1995 against a self-described "Internet god," Dr. Joe Baptista, who used e-mail to send defamatory messages about London, Ontario's then-Police Chief, Julian Fantino. Since then, several defamation cases have involved e-mails as a vehicle for defamatory statements.

---

5 *Carter v. B.C. Federation of Foster Parents Assn.* (2005), BCCA 398 (B.C. C.A.).

While Canada does not have anti-spam legislation, anyone sending "commercial" e-mail to individuals or businesses in the United States must be aware of its CAN-Spam law. The *Non-Solicited Pornography and Marketing Act of 2003* provides a national standard for regulating commercial e-mail, including news information. Commercial e-mail is defined as any e-mail message "the primary purpose of which is the commercial advertisement or promotion of a commercial product or service." Since most news organizations carry advertising on their Web site or within e-mails, this likely fits within the definition. The Act requires those sending or initiating commercial e-mail to:

- Avoid misleading subject headings
- Include a valid return e-mail address or Internet-based reply mechanism
- Include a physical postal address in the body of each message
- Include a conspicuous notice identifying each message as an advertisement or solicitation (unless it is sent with the "affirmative consent" of the recipient)
- Indicate how recipients can prevent the transmission of future messages
- Honour "opt-out" requests within 10 business days of receipt
- Refrain from selling, exchanging or otherwise transferring the e-mail address of any recipient who has made an "opt-out" request

A budding entrepreneur in Alberta sends out teaser e-mails to almost 500 people for his Web site, offering to sell "Top Secret" information on topics ranging from generating valid credit card numbers electronically to how to make bombs to how to commit burglaries. The police charge the spammer under s. 464 of the Criminal Code — counselling the commission of indictable offences that were not committed. Was the spammer convicted?

No. In a case that went all the way to the Supreme Court of Canada, the accused, René Luther Hamilton, was acquitted after he testified he did not read the contents of the files he was selling in compressed (i.e., zipped) format and had not even used the information himself to generate credit card numbers. Despite the accused's lack of a "guilty mind" or evil intention, the Crown argued his recklessness in offering the information was proof he intended to cause commission of the crimes. The courts at every level, including a majority of the Supreme Court, rejected that argument and said the Crown must prove beyond a reasonable doubt there was "deliberate encouragement or active inducement of the commission of a criminal offence. . . while aware of the unjustified risk that the offence counselled was in fact likely to be committed as a result of the accused's conduct." Notably, the Supreme Court was not willing to see the use of the Internet as a factor in deciding the case. "The Internet provides fertile ground for sowing the seeds of unlawful conduct on a borderless scale," commented the Court, but went on to add that "courts cannot contain the inherent dangers of cyberspace crime by expanding or transforming offences, such as counselling, that were conceived to meet a different and unrelated need."

Podcasts, Screencasts and Videocasts: Many of the legal rules that apply to journalists in broadcasting will apply to online video and audio. Defamatory uses of stock footage or graphics, juxtaposition of identifiable individuals and libellous words, and sensationalized editing of visual or audio tracks can be danger zones.

Wikis: A shortened version of wiki wiki, a Hawaiian phrase for quick or fast, this is a Web site or Web page that is written and modified collaboratively with others. The best example is Wikipedia.org, an online encyclopaedia allowing anyone to add and edit information on thousands of topics. With legal actions over incorrect and defamatory information, Wikipedia itself has now become wise to the potential legal dangers in a collaborative writing tool that is accessible to the public. While wikis are usually self-policing, anyone hosting a wiki should take care to ensure changes can be attributed to specific contributors and that moderators monitor changes to popular wikis that may fall victim to vandalism or "trolling" (posting of controversial messages online).

General Guidelines: Fortunately, amidst all of these new forms of electronic media, courts and lawmakers in Canada and abroad are starting to develop a consistent line of thinking to address online defamation, contempt, intellectual property and Internet-specific matters affecting journalists and others. Not all courts and lawmakers agree and inconsistencies exist between various jurisdictions, but there are some general rules that many are following, such as:

- If you create or exercise physical control over Internet content (such as words, pictures, designs, etc.), you will likely be responsible for damage you cause, just as in any other medium;

- If it is within your power to exercise control over content and you learn it is infringing another's rights or a law, you will likely be liable if you do nothing about it;

- If you directly or knowingly infringe the rights of another (such as copyright), you will be liable for damages caused;

- If you unintentionally or indirectly infringe the rights of another after exercising due diligence, you may still be liable but there may be a reduction in damages awarded;

- If you use the Internet to commit an act elsewhere that is illegal in Canada, you can still be held responsible here; and

- If there is not a "real and substantial connection" between a Canadian defendant and the damages suffered by another in a foreign jurisdiction, courts here are unlikely to hear a claim or enforce a judgment.

These are general rules gleaned from recent cases and laws, but there are grey zones and individual jurisdictions may take different approaches. The U.S., for example, has aggressive legislation in place that exempts Internet service providers (ISPs) who meet specific requirements from any liability for customers who infringe copyright on their Web site.[6] ISPs in Canada, however, must rely on the old common law defence of "innocent dissemination" to be absolved of liability.[7] Unlike the U.S., Canada has been slow to pass similar legislation and the public consultation process is still on-going.

As you may have noticed, this is one area of law that pays particular attention to how courts and legislators in other jurisdictions are dealing with the issues. In the coming years, journalists would be wise to keep an eye on international legal developments and efforts to harmonize Internet-related law. In the meantime, here is how Canadian and other jurisdictions are dealing so far with areas of interest to journalists.

---

6 See the Digital Millennium Copyright Act, U.S. Public Law 105-304. The Act exempts ISPs from monitoring what subscribers do and limits liability for copyright infringement by customers if the ISP meets these conditions: the ISP doesn't actually know the material is infringing; the ISP isn't aware of information from which the infringing nature of the material is apparent; if the ISP acquires such knowledge or awareness, the ISP expeditiously removes or blocks access to the material; the ISP doesn't get a financial benefit from the infringing material; and the ISP complies with the "notice and take down" provisions of the Act.

7 Innocent dissemination is explained in the English case *Vizetelly v. Mudie's Select Library*, [1900] 2 Q.B. 170 (Eng. C.A.), which has been cited by Canadian courts. To use this defence, a defendant must show he was innocent of any knowledge of the libel contained in the work disseminated by him, there was nothing in the work or circumstances that ought to have led him to suppose it contained a libel, and it was not through any negligence on his part that he was not aware of the libel. In 2005, the federal government proposed Bill C-60, which would have exempted ISPs from liability for copyrighted material circulating on their networks for which they act purely as intermediaries. Liability would have remained with ISPs that posted or transmitted copyrighted material without authorization. Bill C-60, however, died on the order paper when the government of the day lost a non-confidence motion and had to call an election.

THE INTERNET AND DEFAMATION

The basic elements of defamation law remain unchanged on the Internet. Individuals or entities are still responsible for defamatory statements they publish, just as they are in print or broadcast media, and the same defences apply. Courts have also demonstrated they are not willing to allow Internet defamers to claim anonymity.[8]

However, with so many players involved in creating and disseminating content — from the Internet service provider to the Web site designer to the writer — the responsibility for publishing defamation is often an issue. Fortunately, the courts have dealt with this before. In the formative years of defamation law, courts were asked to decide if everyone in the chain of publication — the printer, the news stand operator and even the paperboy — was responsible. Then, as now, courts tied liability to the degree of control exercised over the content. If you have physical control or authority over the publication and know or should know it is defamatory, you will likely have a duty to make reasonable inquiries into its accuracy. If you are just passing on the publication without any knowledge or authority to control content, you will likely not be liable.

While there have been very few cases of "cyberlibel" in Canada, the courts have shown they are quite willing to hold responsible anyone who uses the Internet to defame others, even if the defamer is outside the country.[9] One of the most striking examples of Internet-based defamation in Canada concerned a foreign journalist for an Internet investment newsletter.[10] George Chelekis, a Florida-based journalist writing for investment newsletters published over the Internet, interviewed David Baines, a well-

---

8 See *Irwin Toy Ltd. v. Joe Doe*, [2000] O.J. No. 3318, 2000 CarswellOnt 3164 (S.C.J.). A toy company and its president launched an action against an anonymous plaintiff identified only as John Doe. They claimed damages for defamation after the unidentified defendant sent an e-mail with confidential information to about 75 people. Using an Internet consulting firm's services, the plaintiffs identified an Internet e-mail address alleged to be involved in sending the message and also identified the ISP. The ISP would not voluntarily disclose the identity of the sender, but said it would not oppose an application to the court for an order obliging it to disclose the identity. The court noted there is no duty or obligation on the ISP to voluntarily disclose the identity of an Internet protocol address. That said, the court agreed the ISP has material knowledge in the defamation action and the plaintiffs had established merit for a case.

9 Actually, Canadian courts have always been willing to deal with cross-border cases so long as the defamation occurred in Canada. In *Jenner v. Sun Oil Co.*, [1952] O.R. 240 (H.C.) at 251, leave to appeal allowed [1952] O.W.N. 370 (H.C.), the court held the essential element of the defamation was not the statement itself and where it originated, but its publication and where it is received by the public. In this case, a radio broadcast originated in a foreign country, but was heard in Ontario.

10 *Southam Inc. v. Chelekis*, [1998] B.C.J. No. 848, 1998 CarswellBC 837 (S.C.), leave to appeal refused, [2000] S.C.C.A. No. 177, 2000 CarswellBC 2162.

known B.C. business reporter and newspaper columnist. After a telephone interview that left the columnist unsettled, he decided he did not want his name published or any quotes used and sent a fax saying so to Chelekis.

Chelekis went ahead and wrote an article saying the columnist threatened him and was the subject of a criminal investigation. The article attacked the reputation of Baines and another person, characterizing them as "muckrakers, snitches and pipelines of information." A second article in the Internet newsletter, which had a circulation of 30,000 copies, implied the two individuals were being investigated for criminal offences involving a conspiracy to receive illegal payments.

Mainstream publishers picked up the story, but a major newspaper eventually reported the allegations were false. Undaunted, Chelekis issued a news release repeating what he wrote and again saying the columnist received illicit payments. That release was sent to all media through an electronic news service, which later issued an apology. Chelekis also falsely told a group of business people and journalists that the columnist was HIV positive.

To no one's surprise, Chelekis was sued successfully. The court ruled the first set of allegations were untrue, he knew they were false and "his publisher was indifferent to their truth." The subsequent statements were even more damaging and malicious. The fact that Chelekis was outside Canada and made no appearance at trial was of no matter.

Damages were awarded against the defendant and his publisher for $75,000 for the first article and $200,000 for the second article. Further damages of $250,000 were awarded against Chelekis and a publisher who republished the story. Chelekis was also liable for $100,000 for the press release and $50,000 for the slander. Aggravated damages of $100,000 were awarded against Chelekis for his conduct, which the court called arrogant, vindictive and continuous. Punitive damages were also ordered for $150,000 because Chelekis' intention was to inflict maximum damage. An attempt was made by Chelekis and the publisher to appeal to the Supreme Court of Canada, questioning whether the traditional rules of defamation could be applied to information found on the Internet and the size of the damages. The high court dismissed the application without giving any reasons.

The flip side of Canadian courts' willingness to hear cases involving defamation originating outside the country is that there is a fear the Internet makes it even easier for plaintiffs to go "forum shopping." At one time it was thought that differences in defamation laws and damages awarded in Canada, U.S., U.K. and Europe may give allegedly defamed individuals (particularly high-profile plaintiffs) pause to consider where to sue.[11] That

---

11 Not all jurisdictions are willing to entertain foreign claims or judgments. In the U.S., see

has, so far, not been the case and having only a "tenuous connection" to a Canadian jurisdiction will likely not work for plaintiffs shopping the world's courts.[12]

In a leading case that was the first judicial consideration of the "real and substantial connection" test, the Ontario Court of Appeal recently held it was not appropriate for courts to assume jurisdiction to hear the case simply because a plaintiff resides in the province or the publication was available in the jurisdiction via the Internet.[13]

The plaintiff, Bangoura, had launched a defamation action against *The Washington Post* and three of its reporters over two newspaper articles published in January 1997 and available on the Internet. At that time, Bangoura was working for the United Nations in Kenya and the articles concerned his activities while working in the Ivory Coast. When the stories were published, the *Post* had just seven subscribers in Ontario and Bangoura was not a resident of the province. It was only when the action was launched six years later that Bangoura was an Ontario resident. In putting an end to what some refer to as "libel tourism" or shopping for favourable legal forums for defamation actions, the appeal court found there was no connection with Ontario three years after the publication of the articles and no evidence Bangoura had suffered significant damages in Ontario. Also, there was no evidence of a significant connection between the *Post* and Ontario.

In most defamation lawsuits, the issue of jurisdiction will be decided on a case-by-case basis. For example, in a 2007 case, an Ontario court held it did have jurisdiction to hear a claim against a newspaper and Web site in India about events in that country.[14] The plaintiffs, who were from the Punjab but lived in Canada since 1992, proved to the court that the publication's Web site was accessed by 8,000 readers per day in Canada. Also, three other newspapers distributed in Ontario and read by the Punjabi-speaking population had published the same article or a similar version. Canadian courts have also held they have jurisdiction even though a Web

---

Matusevitch v. Telnikoff, 702 A.2d 230 (U.S. Md., 1997), where a court refused to enforce an English defamation award because of differences in their law.

12 See *Olde v. Capital Publishing Ltd. Partnership* (1996), 5 C.P.C. (4th) 95 (Ont. Gen. Div.), (affirmed [1998] O.J. No. 237, 1998 CarswellOnt 179 (Ont. C.A.)), where a judge refused to hear a libel case in which the plaintiff and his company were U.S.-based but the plaintiff lived in Canada for only two months of the year.

13 *Bangoura v. Washington Post* (2005), 2005 CarswellOnt 4343, [2005] O.J. No. 3849 (C.A.), leave to appeal to the Supreme Court of Canada refused (2006), 2006 CarswellOnt 933 (S.C.C.).

14 *Bains v. Sadhu Singh Hamdard Trust* (2007), 2007 CarswellOnt 1773, [2007] O.J. No. 1129 (S.C.J.), affirmed (2008), 2008 CarswellOnt 260 (C.A.).

site's server may be located in another jurisdiction[15] or another related action is already underway in a neighbouring jurisdiction.[16]

A columnist for the *New York Post* allegedly implied in print and on its Web site that a hockey player set out to "get" or injure another player during a game between the Vancouver Canucks and Colorado Avalanche that was played in Vancouver. When sued, the *Post* pointed out that its Web site was directed primarily at New York readers, it did not have offices in B.C., derives little or no advertising or other income from B.C. persons or entities, and less than 250 copies of its paper that day were available in Canada and none in B.C. So, did the B.C. court have jurisdiction to hear the matter?

Yes.[17] First, the hockey player in question was a Vancouver resident at the time of the alleged defamation. Second, even though the newspaper was not distributed in B.C., the court ruled by "publishing on its website a matter which was of interest to people in British Columbia . . .it was foreseeable that the Column would be picked up by the media in British Columbia given the [prior] publicity." The court cited other cases that held "the tort of defamation occurs where the words are heard or read." In settling the issue of jurisdiction, the court also considered these eight factors:

- The connection between the forum and the plaintiff's claim
- The connection between the forum and the defendant
- Any unfairness to the defendant in assuming jurisdiction
- Any unfairness to the plaintiff in not assuming jurisdiction
- The involvement of other parties in the suit
- The court's willingness to recognize and enforce a foreign judgment rendered on the same jurisdictional basis
- Whether the case is interprovincial or international in nature
- Comity and the standards of jurisdiction, recognition and enforcement prevailing elsewhere

---

15 See *Investors Group Inc. v. Hudson* (1998), 1998 CarswellQue 4282, [1998] Q.J. No. 4543 (S.C.), where the court ruled the defendant had prepared the Web site in Québec, lived in Québec, and the plaintiff's potential and actual customers resided in Québec and Canada.

16 See *Direct Energy Marketing Ltd. v. Hillson* (1999), 34 C.P.C. (4th) 200 (Alta. Q.B.), where a defamation action involving a Web site was permitted to proceed in Alberta, where the plaintiff lived and worked, even though a parallel action was underway by a related party in Saskatchewan, where the defamation originated.

17 *Burke v. NYP Holdings Inc.*, 2005 BCSC 1287 (B.C. S.C. [In Chambers]).

Another concern for news organizations, heightened by the Internet's broad reach, is the quantum of damages. Should a defamatory statement available on the Internet prompt a stratospheric damage award because of the huge, worldwide audience? While Canadian courts have not been shy in awarding large damages to successful plaintiffs for Internet-based defamation,[18] they have shown they are not willing to tie damages to the Internet's potentially huge audience without proper proof of a defamatory statement's large-scale impact.

In one B.C. case, the plaintiff was a technology company incorporated in Nevada, domiciled in British Columbia, and doing business in various U.S. jurisdictions.[19] It sued in Texas against a resident of B.C. alleging the defendant put defamatory information on an Internet bulletin board. The defendant had no other connection with Texas other than that Internet users there could read his comments.

The Texas Civil Practice and Remedies Code deems a non-resident to be doing business in the jurisdiction if it commits a tort or wrong there. The plaintiff company got a default judgment in Texas and tried to have it enforced in B.C. The province's appeal court overturned the Texas court's judgment, ruling that a wrongdoer must have a "real and substantial connection" to a foreign jurisdiction. In this case, the defendant's only connection to Texas was a "passive posting on an Internet bulletin board." Since there was no proof that anyone in Texas saw the alleged defamatory material, the court said it could not simply presume damages occurred in jurisdictions where the defamatory statements are accessible and likely to have been read.

THE INTERNET AND COURT ORDERS

Courts orders, such as publication bans and media-related injunctions, frequently include references to the Internet these days. When enforcing court orders, judges view the Internet in the same light as any publication in print or broadcasting. A common question is whether an individual can

---

18 Examples include: $676,000 to 11 plaintiffs defamed by over 60 statements in chat rooms, a Web site and e-mails (*Newman v. Halstead*, 2006 BCSC 65); $400,000 for defamatory statements published on at least seven Web sites (*Reichmann v. Berlin* (2002), 2002 CarswellOnt 2278, [2002] O.J. No. 2732 (S.C.J.)); $257,500 to two companies offering kayaking tours (*WeGo Kayaking Ltd. v. Sewid*, 2007 BCSC 49); $220,000 for over 30 Web postings defaming doctors (*Assoc. des médecins traitant l'obésitée c. Breton* (2007), 2003 CarswellQue 1309, [2003] J.Q. No. 6601 (S.C.)); and $200,000 for articles in a Web-based publication (*Ager v. Canjex Publishing Ltd.* (2003), 16 C.C.L.T. (3d) 188 (B.C. S.C.) and varied from $300,000 in 2005 BCCA 467).

19 *Braintech Inc. v. Kostiuk* (1999), 171 D.L.R. (4th) 46 (B.C. C.A.), leave to appeal refused (2000), [1999] S.C.C.A. No. 236, 2000 CarswellBC 546, 2000 CarswellBC 537.

circumvent a court order by using a Web site, server or other technology located outside Canada to publish banned information or engage in some other prohibited conduct. The Federal Court of Canada dealt with this issue and ruled that such tactics will not work.[20]

Ernst Zündel, living in Canada, caused text and graphic hate messages to be posted on the Internet from a server located outside the country. A holocaust survivor complained to the Canadian Human Rights Commission and it struck a tribunal to investigate a violation of s. 13 of the Canadian Human Rights Act.

Section 13 prohibits the communication "telephonically" of any matter that is likely to expose a person to hatred or contempt on the basis of a prohibited ground of discrimination. There was evidence that Zündel effectively controlled what material was posted on the foreign Web site. Zündel argued, among other things, the Commission lacked jurisdiction and violated his right to freedom of expression because the materials were not communicated "telephonically," and the server for the Web site and the person who managed it were outside Canada.

The court dismissed Zündel's arguments, saying the Commission's decision was correct. The court agreed a person in Canada causes material to be communicated for the purpose of s. 13 if that person effectively controls the content of material posted on a Web site maintained from outside Canada.

Other jurisdictions also agree. In the U.S., a court ruled its injunction prohibiting publication of copyrighted material was breached when a Web site placed hypertext links pointing to other sites that had posted the same information.[21] The bottom line for anyone in Canada is that you cannot circumvent or breach a Canadian court order by using a foreign jurisdiction via the Internet.

THE INTERNET AND INTELLECTUAL PROPERTY

As someone once said, the Internet "is the world's largest copying machine." With so much information freely available online and the ease with which one can copy it, it's no surprise there is confusion (or complacency) about intellectual property rights.

It is not unusual for Internet users to assume that any material on Web sites is in the public domain. That's just not so. A work enters the public

---

20 *Zündel v. Canada (Attorney General)* (1999), 175 D.L.R. (4th) 512 (Fed. T.D.), additional reasons at 1999 CarswellNat 1355 (Fed. T.D.), affirmed (2000), 195 D.L.R. (4th) 394 (Fed. C.A.).

21 See *Intellectual Reserve*, note 23, below.

domain when its copyright expires (such as 50 years after the death of the author in Canada and longer in other countries).

There should be no doubt, however, that copyrights, trade-marks and other aspects of intellectual property law apply to the Internet in the same way as other media. For example, you cannot post the works of others on your Web site without permission (adding a line identifying the source is not good enough). Similarly, you cannot copy a substantial amount of another's work from the Web and claim it as your own.

Thanks to the Internet, even some obscure aspects of copyright law may come to the forefront. For example, the copyright in an e-mail, as with any personal letter or other work, resides with the author. Again, in theory, permission is needed to publish an e-mail or a substantial portion of it. Some even make the case that forwarding e-mail infringes copyright by republishing (though no lawsuits have been heard on that issue yet). And, what about messages posted on a discussion board (another form of e-mail, one might say)? Here, some argue a posting carries implicit grants of permission for copying, but others disagree or contend that publication in other forms (such as in print) requires permission since U.S. and Canadian Copyright Acts specifically protect anonymous and pseudonymous works from unauthorized copying. For now, these are unsettled issues.[22]

As noted above, the Internet has created questions in areas where no law existed before. For example, as noted at the beginning of this chapter, several copyright cases have come before courts, mostly in the U.S., over the issue of linking to unrelated Web sites. In one U.S. case, a Web site was found to have infringed copyright and breached a court-ordered injunction by placing hypertext links on its site to material it was specifically prohibited from displaying.

In that case,[23] the defendant, Utah Lighthouse Ministry, was critical of the Mormon Church and posted 17 pages from a 160-page Church Handbook of Instructions without permission. The plaintiff, owner of the Church's intellectual property assets, got a temporary restraining order forcing ULM to remove the material. Later, ULM posted an e-mail message from a user noting the Handbook could be found at three other Web sites. The court agreed this was an attempt to circumvent the order and constituted "contributory infringement" since it encouraged users to wilfully infringe copyright. This case notwithstanding, some commentators believe the news media should still be able to cite such links as valid news information, and

---

22 There is even a suggestion in some legal circles that Web browsers may infringe copyright by storing copies of documents in their cache or memory. (If such a case ever landed in court, the fact that the storage of material from browsing is temporary would no doubt be a major hurdle for a plaintiff.)

23 *Intellectual Reserve, Inc. v. Utah Lighthouse Ministry, Inc.*, 75 F. Supp. 2d 1290 (D. Utah, 1999).

claim the "fair dealing" or "fair use" defence allowed under copyright law for news reporting.

Another copyright issue of interest to journalists, particularly free-lancers, is whether print publishers have the right to post an article on the Internet without negotiating a separate copyright agreement or fee. In 2001, U.S. freelance writers won a class action lawsuit establishing their right to prevent the publication of articles in other media, particularly on the Internet and in databases, without an agreement or additional payment.[24] In Canada, a class proceedings lawsuit similar to that launched in the U.S. was decided in 2006 at the Supreme Court of Canada.[25]

Canada's Supreme Court clarified the rights of authors and publishers in the area of collective works, finding that a newspaper publisher's elec-tronic databases potentially infringed a freelance author's copyright in her articles, but that selling CD-ROMs with historical content from the news-paper was a valid exercise of the publisher's own copyright. Freelance author Heather Robertson had sued the publisher and owners of *The Globe and Mail* over the right to reproduce freelance works in other forms of media and collections, such as online databases and searchable CD-ROMs, without additional compensation. The Supreme Court split 5-4 in favour of Robert-son.

The majority of judges held that "newspaper publishers are not entitled to republish freelance articles acquired for publication in their newspapers in Info Globe Online or CPI.Q without compensating the authors and ob-taining their consent." While publishers have a right under the Copyright Act's s. 3(1) to "reproduce the work or any substantial part thereof in any material form whatever," the majority agreed a "substantial part" means the "essence of the newspaper is preserved." Thus, reproducing the text of the

---

24 See the U.S. Supreme Court decision in *New York Times Co., Inc. v. Tasini*, [2001] SCT-QL 139, No. 00201 (U.S. S.C., 2001). Tasini sued for copyright infringement on behalf of thousands of freelance writers who were independent contractors for the *Times* and other publications. They worked under freelance arrangements that said nothing about the placement of articles in an electronic database. The print publishers each licensed rights to copy and sell articles to LEXIS/NEXIS, owner and operator of an online database of articles, and to University Microfilms International, which reproduced articles on CD-ROM products. The U.S. Supreme Court agreed with the writers that "copyright in each separate contribution to a collective work is distinct from copyright in the collective work as a whole." In other words, a publication has copyright in its magazine or newspaper in that form, but a freelance writer included in that publication enjoys a separate copyright. Without an agreement providing an express transfer of rights, the U.S. copyright law does not allow publishers to distribute those articles standing alone, such as in a database. The court noted: "It would scarcely preserve the author's copyright in a contribution as contemplated by Congress if a print publisher, without the author's permission, could reproduce or distribute discrete copies of the contribution in isolation or within new collective works."

25 *Robertson v. Thomson Corp.*, [2006] 2 S.C.R. 363.

individual articles in an online database without the original layout or appearance of a newspaper does not qualify as a proper reproduction. The CD-ROM, however, was "faithful to the essence of the original work" and kept much of the newspaper's appearance. The majority made it clear that publishers, particularly the news media, do not have a "licence to override the rights of authors."

In the future, expect to see even more developments and complications in the application of intellectual property law to the Internet. For example, there have already been cases alleging that the use of frames or windows on Web sites showing pages from other sites infringe copyright.[26]

Another issue yet to be navigated are the moral rights granted under the Copyright Act, which protect the "integrity" of a work and the author's reputation. In the past, moral rights have stopped others from distorting or modifying works in a way that prejudices a creator's reputation (such as works of art). Moral rights can't be assigned to others and must be specifically waived by the creator, even when other rights have been purchased. Moral rights may become an issue because Internet technology allows information to be filtered or reassembled, such that the meaning of a work may be changed. For example, some "blocking" software placed on children's computers deletes selected words and inserts "safer" words that may change the "integrity" of an author's work.

THE INTERNET AND LEGISLATION

For now, the 200 or so references to the Internet in federal or provincial laws refer largely to the terms of online sales contracts, required postings to government sites of certain information and other administrative matters. There are very few legislative provisions speaking to Web-based dissemination of news or restricting journalists in their activities.

One example is the federal elections law, which specifically protects "the transmission by an individual, on a non-commercial basis on what is commonly known as the Internet, of his or her personal political views" in the section prohibiting election advertising during black-out periods.[27] (Web site operators, however, still have to be as mindful as any other citizen of section 328, which prohibits the premature publication of election results or results of unpublished opinion polls on election day.) Another example is the prohibition against using the Internet or any group of computers to

---

26 "Framing" is the practice of displaying the content of another site within a Web page. One of the first lawsuits to deal with framing was filed in 1997 in the U.S. Southern District of New York, but *Washington Post v. TotalNEWS* settled out of court before a judge could hear the issues.

27 Canada Elections Act, S.C. 2000, c. 9, s. 319.

expose a person or persons to hatred or contempt by reason of the fact that that person or those persons are identifiable on the basis of a prohibited ground of discrimination.[28]

That said, legislation dealing with privacy rights, personal information, intellectual property, broadcasting and other areas is being applied to Internet issues. Governments are also broadening the scope of various laws, from those governing corporations to the regulation of firearms, to allow for technological changes, such as electronic meetings, form filing, access to records and even legal authority for digital signatures in e-mailed documents.

In time, legislators in Canada will no doubt increase the number of legislative provisions mentioning the Internet, however, lawmakers will likely strive hard to ensure that today's rules are applied equally to tomorrow's technology.

AN INTERNET LAW CHECKLIST

1. Generally, the laws governing defamation, contempt of court, court orders, intellectual property (copyright) and other areas of interest to journalists are the same whether the issue involves the Internet or not.

2. If you exercise physical control over Internet content (words, pictures, designs, etc.), you will likely be responsible for damage you cause, such as in defamation.

3. If it is within your power to exercise control over content and you learn it is infringing another's rights or a law (such as copyright), you will likely be liable if you do nothing about it.

4. If you directly or knowingly infringe the rights of another, you will be liable for damages caused.

5. If you unintentionally or indirectly infringe the rights of another after exercising due diligence, you may still be liable but there may be a reduction in damages awarded.

6. If you use the Internet to commit an act elsewhere that is illegal in Canada, you can still be held responsible here.

7. If there is not a "real and substantial connection" between a Canadian defendant and the damages suffered by another in a foreign jurisdiction, courts here are unlikely to hear a claim or enforce a judgment.

8. Canadian courts are quite willing to hold responsible anyone who uses

---

28 Canadian Human Rights Act, R.S.C. 1985, c. H-6, s. 13.

the Internet to defame or damage the rights of others, even if the wrongdoer is outside the country.

9. You cannot circumvent a Canadian court order by using a Web site, server or other technology located outside Canada to publish banned information or engage in some other prohibited conduct.

10. Most material available on the Web is not in the public domain and permission is likely needed to reproduce it or a substantial portion of the work, including articles, e-mails, promotional literature, and possibly even message board postings. Even posting hypertext links to another Web site may require permission, though this is unsettled law and likely does not apply to news media that cite links as part of a story.

11. Early court decisions suggest explicit or separate copyright agreements are needed between freelancers and print publishers who make an online or archival database of articles available.

18

THE JOURNALIST AS EMPLOYEE AND FREELANCER

It is not uncommon for many freelance and employed journalists, editors and even executives to be uncertain about their legal rights and obligations in the news workplace. Questions about personal liability for defamation, the law affecting copyright in electronic media and what's fair in standard freelance agreements are among the common concerns this chapter addresses.

THE JOURNALIST AS EMPLOYEE

Employees, whether journalists or not, have a variety of common law and legislative rights and responsibilities in the workplace. So, too, do employers. Before going much further, though, it is important to confirm that a journalist is in an employment relationship and is not, for example, an independent contractor.

An "employer-employee relationship" can arise from either an oral or written agreement. From a contractual standpoint, the employee agrees to work on a full-time or part-time basis for an employer for either a set or indeterminate period. So, for instance, a reporter who has a 6-month contract to work part-time for a newsroom is, generally, considered an employee for that period. In return, the employer agrees to pay a specific salary or hourly wages. Unionized workers are part of a "collective agreement," which also establishes an employer-employee relationship. The distinguishing factor in these relationships is that the employer has the right to decide where, when, and how the employee's work will be done.

An independent contractor or self-employed individual, however, is in a "business relationship." It also can be based on an oral or written agreement to perform specific work in return for payment. One difference from the employee is that the independent contractor has the freedom to decide where, when, and how that work will be done. In fact, the independent contractor does not even have to carry out all of the work and may be able to subcontract it (subject to an agreement, in some cases). In most cases, the independent contractor works for a variety of clients or businesses at one time.[1]

The law applying to employees is substantially different from that used for business relationships with independent contractors or freelancers.[2] The freelancer's rights and obligations are covered later in this chapter.

In common law, the employee's responsibilities include showing up on time for work, putting in the required hours, behaving honestly, following the employer's instructions, keeping trade secrets and, generally, doing the job to the best of his or her ability. In the absence of a written contract or legislation, though, both employees and employers may find there are grey areas that erupt into disputes later. Employed journalists, for example, often wonder whether they can write freelance articles or even take on a part-time job. Moonlighting is generally permitted at common law unless there is an employment contract saying otherwise. So long as it does not interfere with

---

1 In *Société Radio-Canada v. Syndicat des communications de Radio-Canada* (2005), 2005 CarswellNat 5960, 2005 CarswellNat 5961 (C.I.R.B.), an arbitrator agreed with a union grievance that a daily reporter for radio and TV, who was hired on contract as a freelancer six years before, had eventually become a permanent employee upon assuming the same duties and schedule of a full-time journalist for the corporation.

2 In *Lamontagne v. Canada* (July 5, 1976), Doc. T-3153-75, [1976] F.C.J. No. 600 (T.D.) a journalist who ran various businesses had a contract to supply news and information daily to a CBC radio station in Québec. After successive one-year contracts for 10 years, the CBC severed the relationship. The court said the CBC had the right to end the association, it was clear this was not an employer-employee relationship and it fell strictly under contract law.

a journalist's work or involve a competitor, an employer would have a difficult time establishing this was a breach of the employment relationship.

Once individuals are in an employment relationship, they are protected by a variety of federal and provincial laws. Each province, for example, legislates basic working conditions, such as minimum wages, hours of work, rest periods, eating periods, overtime pay, paid public holidays, vacation with pay, pregnancy or parental leave, and termination or severance notice and pay. Many of these are minimums, it should be noted, and an employee may be entitled to additional protection.

Other laws affecting the workplace govern health and safety, human rights, retirement, benefits, workers' compensation and unemployment insurance, to name a few. With variations in the law across Canada, as always, specific employment situations should be referred to a lawyer. This section will focus generally on the areas of unique interest to journalists.

A reporter fired from his job claims he is owed an estimated 700 hours of overtime by his former employer, citing the section of the Employment Standards Act requiring payment for overtime beyond 40 hours worked per week. The employer responds it is "industry practice" in the journalism business for reporters to simply get the job done without regard to hours worked. Is the employer correct?

No.[3] In an Alberta case, the employer was unsuccessful in arguing that "industry practice" was that reporters are to complete their work within specified periods but are not paid by the hour nor do they record their time. The court found the employer had no idea what others in the industry actually did about overtime. Despite that, the reporter had no agreement with the employer speaking to overtime rates or time off in lieu, had never pressed his case for overtime when he was employed, and his rough estimate of 700 hours failed to meet the evidentiary needs of the employment standards law.

Liability of Employed Journalists

When a defamation lawsuit is launched against a news organization or a reporter gets hauled into court for breaching a judge's order, a common question is whether the individual journalist is solely responsible for his or her actions.

---

3 *Diotte v. Interwest Publications Ltd.* (1987), 1987 CarswellAlta 480, [1987] A.J. No. 401 (Master).

It is a long-established legal principle, known as "vicarious liability," that an employer is jointly responsible for the actions of an employee as long as the employee is acting within the scope of his or her employment. Wrongful conduct is said to be within the scope of employment if it involves acts authorized by an employer or even unauthorized or improperly performed acts that are connected with what the employer assigned.[4]

A reporter covering a court case involving a violent sexual assault wrote a story revealing the name of the crime victim, contrary to an earlier publication ban. The reporter had failed to inquire about any publication restrictions. Is the journalist's employer responsible for negligent actions that fall below the standard of a prudent reporter?

Yes. An Ontario civil case involved a claim of damages arising from the breach of a court order banning publication of a crime victim's identity.[5] The plaintiff, a police officer, was sexually assaulted while working undercover. The defendant publisher printed an article written by a reporter that named the officer. The court awarded general damages of $12,000 and punitive damages of $5,000. "The publisher was responsible for the negligence of its employees," stated the judge, even though "the reporter fell below the standard of a reasonably prudent reporter who would have asked some questions and exercised caution before publishing the explicit details of the assault."

Does this mean a journalist who is an employee is not responsible in any way for his or her actions? No. A court will often hold both employee and employer responsible, especially if there was negligence or willful disregard for the law or another's rights. Even if the employer is the only entity held responsible, an employee may later be terminated for "just cause" if there was an unauthorized act or negligence.

Wrongful or Constructive Dismissal

Journalists often work in environments where workplace changes come quickly and emotions run high. In many respects, though, journalists facing dismissal, layoffs or major changes in working conditions are no different than other types of employees.

---

4 For a recent Supreme Court of Canada discussion of vicarious liability, see *B. (P.A.) v. Curry*, [1999] 2 S.C.R. 534, where an employer operating residential facilities for children was held responsible for the unauthorized acts of an employee who was a pedophile.

5 *R. (L.) v. Nyp* (1995), 1995 CarswellOnt 397, [1995] O.J. No. 2017 (Gen. Div.).

In every jurisdiction, legislation dictates the minimum requirements and compensation that employers must give employees who are facing dismissal or layoff. For some employees, an independent legal advisor may suggest they be entitled to more than the legislated minimums.

Employers have a right to fire any employee as long as they adhere to statutory and other legal requirements. An employer does not even have to give reasons for terminating your employment. In many cases, an important question is whether the employee was given sufficient notice or advance warning, based on his or her position, length of service, contractual requirements or other factors. With sufficient notice, an employer can also make almost any changes to your working conditions or position.

In very specific circumstances, employees can be dismissed without any additional compensation or notice where there is "just cause." Generally, just cause can arise where there are repeated or significant instances of incompetence, insubordination, absenteeism, dishonesty, sexual harassment or conflict of interest. Courts often require that employers citing just cause show there is a history of warnings that dismissal may be imminent and opportunities were available for an employee to improve.

Wrongful dismissal is the claim employees make in court when an employer terminates without just cause and without reasonable notice or pay in lieu of notice. Courts take wrongful dismissal cases very seriously, meaning they are not just trying to settle an outstanding debt but will award damages for both direct and even indirect losses, such as mental suffering. Similarly, the dismissed employee is under an obligation to reduce or mitigate his or her losses by trying to find another job.

One 1992 case involving a high-profile journalist is typical of wrongful dismissal cases.[6] Geoffrey Stevens was the managing editor of *The Globe and Mail* and had worked for the paper since 1962, except for a few years. He had risen through the ranks to a point where he served on the management committee, entitling him to annual bonuses. He supervised about 300 employees and a budget of $25 million. The court heard that, shortly before leaving on a business trip in 1989, Stevens asked for and got assurances from the CEO about his job. The editor-in-chief had recently left the paper and Stevens was concerned that a new chief would change his role.

When he got back from his trip, despite assurances, Stevens found he had been removed from his position by the new editor-in-chief. Though he was told about another position as the newspaper's Washington analyst, there were no details offered. Stevens went on a four-week vacation almost immediately and the newspaper said nothing more until a termination letter

---

6 *Stevens v. Globe & Mail (The)* (1992), 7 O.R. (3d) 520 (Gen. Div.), additional reasons at 1993 CarswellOnt 928 (Gen. Div.), varied (1996), 28 O.R. (3d) 481 (C.A.).

was delivered two months later. He was fired as of that day and his salary and benefits were extended only for two months more.

The court agreed Stevens had been wrongfully dismissed. The fact he did not pursue the Washington opportunity, said the judge, did not mean he failed to mitigate his loss. "He had lost confidence in the newspaper as an employer, and could not fairly evaluate the Washington position, because sufficient details had never been supplied," ruled the judge. Stevens was not entitled to any aggravated or exemplary damages because of the false assurances before his business trip since they "were not made knowing that the statements were false, or recklessly, without belief in their truth."

That said, as a long-term employee and a senior manager, the period of reasonable notice should have been much longer than a few months. In fact, the court awarded Stevens 21 months — one of the longest notice periods in Canadian employment law history. The court ruled he was also entitled to benefits and management committee bonuses that would have been paid during the notice period.

Another very common employment law claim these days is for constructive dismissal. In these cases, the employer is accused of trying to make working conditions so intolerable that employees quit. This may involve drastically reducing salaries, changing job duties, relocating people to smaller offices or diminishing a person's prestige in the organization with a different job. To prove constructive dismissal, an employee must show a court that the employer's actions are so inconsistent with the previously agreed-upon employment contract that they are, in fact, a repudiation of the contract. Cutting your salary in half, for example, is a clear repudiation of the employment relationship but courts have allowed employers to cut salaries by as much as one-quarter, if circumstances justify it.[7]

---

7 Many of the constructive dismissal claims in journalism involve changes in job responsibilities. In *Kidd v. Southam Press Ltd.* (1981), 1 C.C.E.L. 167 (Ont. H.C.), a journalist was employed in various newspaper and news service positions for 19 years. He reported directly to the managing editor, but the employer proposed that his responsibilities be changed and that he report to the city editor. The journalist saw the reassignment as a demotion and refused to accept it. He was dismissed with four weeks' pay in lieu of notice. The court ruled the proposed change in his position was "so fundamental to the contract of employment as to constitute a repudiation of that contract." In *Cosgrove v. T.M. Publications Ltd.* (March 28, 1985), Doc. Vancouver C835951, [1985] B.C.J. No. 1152 (S.C.), the court dismissed a claim of constructive dismissal from a news editor in a small weekly newspaper who believed a newly-hired managing editor was given some of his responsibilities. The judge found the publisher had merely delegated his own powers and duties to the new managing editor and did not take away or interfere with any powers or duties of the plaintiff. In *Mullin v. Thomson Newspapers Co.*, [1995] M.J. No. 260, 1995 CarswellMan 552 (Q.B.), a court dismissed a wrongful dismissal action by a newspaper's ombudsman against the publisher personally. The plaintiff alleged the publisher forced him to resign by introducing measures to monitor the ombudsman's column after he wrote

One aspect of wrongful dismissal cases that may be particularly relevant to claims by terminated journalists is evidence of industry practice. For example, "insubordination" is a daily occurrence in some newsrooms and a journalist plaintiff may be able to show that a minor outburst or sharp words are common practice in a high-pressure workplace. Industry practices, in fact, can help a court see a wrongful dismissal in entirely different light. In one case, for example, a court ruled that an employer who terminates a journalist for failing to reveal sources cannot claim "just cause" unless the potential for such disclosure was made a condition of employment when hired.[8]

The journalist, an editor for two local newspapers, sued her employer for wrongful dismissal after she became involved in a defamation lawsuit against the publication. In its defence, the employer claimed just cause; specifically that the editor failed to disclose to a duly authorized company representative the source of information in a disputed article and she had failed to fully co-operate with the insurers in the defence of the defamation action.

The editor told the court she had indeed refused to reveal her sources to anyone. The publisher did not actually ask her to reveal her source but wanted a commitment that she would if ordered by the court, saying the newspaper was not about to embark on a costly crusade for reporter's privilege.

Finding in favour of the editor in this case, the judge ruled that: "Before a newspaper publisher is entitled to require a reporter to reveal a confidential source to anyone, including the insurer's solicitor, and to consider a refusal to do so a "cause" for dismissal, the publisher must make it clear at the time of employing the reporter that [she] should refuse to give an informant an undertaking that the reporter will not reveal their identity if ordered to do so by a court, or, by a publisher, as the case may be."

Otherwise, said the court, the reporter is entitled to assume she is not in breach of the contract of employment in refusing to violate an undertaking that is common in journalism.

---

an article critical of the paper. The court ruled the publisher acted within his authority and there was no evidence of any personal malice.

8   *Fitzgibbons v. Westpres Publications Ltd.*, [1983] B.C.J. No. 164, 1983 CarswellBC 403 (S.C.).

Conflict of Interest and Abuse of Position

What happens when a journalist uses his or her position for personal benefit or in a way that reflects poorly on a media employer? At what point does a conflict of interest or poor judgment become just cause for termination or discipline?

One common example of risky behaviour is when a journalist opts to mention his or her high-profile position to a person in authority for personal gain. In one recent case,[9] a journalist covering the real estate beat was fired after a member of the public told his employer the reporter had used his position to secretly extract a personal benefit from a property developer. The journalist had problems with a townhome purchase and mentioned his position at the newspaper in a series of abusive letters to the developer. Eventually, his problems were resolved by the developer and he received a reduced purchase price. When confronted by newspaper management, he denied the conflict of interest and that he had verbally abused a party on his beat. Then later, he changed his story again and claimed a release he had signed with the developer prevented him from revealing more details.

Even though the journalist was 56-years-old, had a clean disciplinary record, was a long-time employee and there was no evidence of bias in his reporting, the arbitrator found the misconduct struck "at the fabric of the employment relationship. The Grievor broke a cardinal rule of journalism. He placed his objectivity and impartiality at risk. He compromised his own integrity, that of his Employer and has harmed the reputation of the Employer." The arbitrator ruled the employer was justified in dismissing him and that employment relationship was irreparable.

Potential conflicts of interest can also arise when a reporter engages in "activist" journalism and becomes part of the story. A key question adjudicators in these cases often consider is whether the journalist's activism will reflect poorly on the integrity of the employer or the reporter, and whether editorial management sanctions the activity.[10]

---

9 *Pacific Newspaper Group Inc. v. C.E.P., Local 2000* (2005), 137 L.A.C. (4th) 12 (B.C. Arb. Bd.).

10 In *Toronto Star Newspapers Ltd. v. Southern Ontario Newspaper Guild, Local 87* (1993), 33 L.A.C. (4th) 353 (Ont. Arb. Bd.), a newspaper reporter was discharged after he took it upon himself to write a lengthy brief for public submission to a provincial inquiry on policing. After his editors became aware of it, the brief was not submitted (after his termination, however, he did release the document). The employer claimed the journalist breached the news organization's conflict of interest provisions by attempting to be both "actor and critic." The dismissal was grieved by the union and the arbitrator found the reporter had intended to act in the public interest and did not intend to harm the newspaper. In this case, dismissal was judged as too severe a penalty. Also see *Windsor Star v. Windsor Newspaper Guild* (1992), 26 L.A.C. (4th) 129 (Ont. Arb. Bd.), where unionized newspaper reporters were disciplined for joining a picket line at a TV station under a

Journalists also must be mindful of outside engagements they accept that arise from their position. In one case,[11] an investigative news reporter was suspended for three weeks without pay for controversial comments he made at an outside speaking engagement on journalism and his actions during a subsequent management inquiry. The CBC claimed he had violated its policies on conflict of interest, outside work and journalistic standards. It also said he "obstructed, interfered with and misled the Corporation during our investigation."

Speaking at a local university, the journalist had expounded on the foibles and biases of the press, as well as offering advice on influencing the news media. A subsequent news report on the speech suggested he felt the media could not be trusted and his managers believed the article could damage CBC's journalistic reputation.

In hearing a union grievance, the arbitrator ruled that, while the journalist had good intentions in being so candid, he was essentially speaking as a CBC reporter and showed a "serious lack of judgment" in his comments. Further, he lied during the investigation of the matter. The discipline was deemed just.

The head of a political activist group was publicly critical of a CBC reporter — among other things, accusing him of being a "government toady." The comments ate away at the journalist personally and he decided to send a box of chocolates rubbed in dirt and raw chicken to his perceived nemesis. Within hours, he realized his mistake in judgment, reporting his behaviour to his intended victim, CBC management and consulting a psychologist. Should the journalist's employment be terminated?

No, according to the latest ruling in this contentious case,[12] which has gone from an arbitration hearing up to a provincial court of appeal, and was recently refused leave to appeal to the Supreme Court of Canada. Initially, the CBC fired the journalist and the union challenged the dismissal. The arbitrator held the dismissal was excessive and accepted an expert report from a psychologist stating the reporter had learned from the events. The arbitrator substituted a three-month suspension and an

---

strike. Under the newspaper's collective agreement, a conflict of interest included situations where "the reporter's degree of involvement is so fervent that the reporter actually has a personal stake or interest in the portrayal of the news."

11 *Canadian Broadcasting Corp. v. Canadian Media Guild*, [1995] C.L.A.D. No. 1179 (Can. Arb. Bd.).

12 *Canadian Broadcasting Corp. v. Canadian Media Guild* (2007), 156 A.C.W.S. (3d) 614 (B.C. C.A.)

order to attend an anger management course, after concluding the CBC's reputation would not suffer significant injury if the reporter kept his employment. The arbitrator also ruled the behaviour was aberrant and disciplinable, but not journalistic misconduct. In a judicial review, a chambers judge found the arbitrator's decision to be "patently unreasonable." The B.C. Court of Appeal, however, upheld the arbitrator's ruling and use of the psychologist's report.

The Unionized Environment

Journalists working in a unionized environment must, in most cases, rely on their collective agreement to govern the employment relationship. In fact, the courts are reluctant to use common law remedies, such as wrongful dismissal, to override a collective agreement.[13] That said, a journalist under a collective agreement can still be terminated for common reasons, such as poor work performance, insubordinate behaviour, etc.[14]

Most collective agreements attempt to shield workers from sudden dismissals by providing for "progressive discipline" (several warnings or lesser penalties before termination), seniority provisions, and an opportunity to grieve or challenge management's decisions. In a recent example of the discipline process in a union environment, a cameraman was suspended by his media employer after a verbal altercation with a member of the public while covering a story.[15] The cameraman escalated the situation by calling the police, following a woman in the TV station's van and taunting her. When the union challenged the punishment, an arbitrator ruled the two-day suspension was justified. While this was a long-time employee with a relatively clear record, he had difficulty controlling his emotions and had not acknowledged the inappropriateness of his actions. His behaviour and

---

13 For example, see *Hussey v. Chum Ltd.*, [1987] N.S.J. No. 356, 1987 CarswellNS 193 (T.D.), where a member of NABET brought an action for wrongful dismissal against his employer, a radio station. The court said it did not have jurisdiction to hear the wrongful dismissal action because of the existence of the collective agreement providing for a settlement of disputes by arbitration. The court cited a "leading authority," the decision of the Supreme Court of Canada in *St. Anne-Nackawic Pulp & Paper Co. C.P.V.U., Local 219* (1986), 28 D.L.R. (4th) 1 (S.C.C.).

14 In *CJOH-TV v. Ottawa Newspaper Guild, Local 30205*, [2003] C.L.A.S.J. 20195 (Can. Arb. Bd.), a journalist was terminated for poor work performance within the probationary term of her employment. The union protested her firing, claiming the collective agreement promised "job security" even during a probation period. The arbitrator sided with the employer, finding it did not act in bad faith or arbitrarily, provided the reporter with training and was reasonable in dismissing her when she failed to achieve performance standards.

15 *CHBC-TV Kelowna v. C.E.P., Local 823-M*, [2006] C.L.A.S.J. 23 (Can. Arb. Bd.).

poor judgment, the arbitrator noted, crossed the line "between aggressively pursuing a story and pursuing a person."

It appears courts can be supportive of union activity in a news environment, even when questions of journalistic ethics are raised. In a 1995 case involving the CBC, the Supreme Court of Canada upheld the right of a journalist to voice strong political views in his role as union president — contrary to the CBC's ethics guidelines requiring journalists to be impartial.[16]

The CBC ordered the journalist to resign his position as union president after he took a public position in a union publication opposing a major federal government policy during an election campaign. The CBC, relying on its written policy requiring journalistic impartiality, rejected a suggested compromise whereby the journalist would continue to act as president of the union, but not as its spokesperson.

The Canada Labour Relations Board upheld a complaint from the union alleging unfair labour practice. Section 94(1)(a) of the Canada Labour Code[17] prohibits an employer from participating in or interfering with the formation or administration of a trade union. The Supreme Court agreed, saying the union membership has a right to choose its president.

THE JOURNALIST AS FREELANCER

Many journalists operate successful businesses as freelancers. This section outlines some of the common issues that arise between freelance journalists and media organizations.

Liability of Freelancers

Being in a business and not an employment relationship, the freelancer is not protected by the legal doctrine of vicarious liability that makes an employer jointly liable for the authorized and even unauthorized acts of employees acting within the scope of their duties.

Like any supplier, a freelancer is responsible for the quality of the "product" delivered. For freelance journalists, this might include an implied guarantee that the work will not infringe any copyright, violates no laws, does not intentionally defame anyone and was not negligently or recklessly created.

---

16 *Canadian Broadcasting Corp. v. Canada (Labour Relations Board)* (1995), 121 D.L.R. (4th) 385 (S.C.C.).

17 R.S.C. 1985, c. L-2.

In reality, almost no freelancer can comfortably offer such a guarantee. Freelancers are typically underpaid, one-person businesses with no support staff or legal counsel to fact-check or vet every aspect of their research or final work. Certainly, few freelancers can afford to indemnify a publisher in the event of a legal action (though, some media organizations have been known to put such clauses in their freelance contracts).

Knowing that most freelancers are not capable of fully vetting their work, it could easily be argued that the "reasonable publisher" must share the responsibility for ensuring a freelance work meets proper standards. The freelancer, however, is not devoid of responsibility in the process.

To help reduce personal liability, the freelancer should make every effort to document the research and interviews that go into creating the final product. If there are any questionable aspects that might result in a legal action, the freelancer should make every effort to point them out in writing to the publisher or editor. Freelancers should also insist on seeing the final version of a work to ensure changes have not been made that create liability. If a freelancer does not agree with the changes, he or she should ask that the by-line be removed, for both professional and liability reasons. These proactive measures can help establish that the freelancer exercised due diligence and may reduce potential personal liability.

In defamation cases and other litigation involving freelancers, it's not uncommon for all potential defendants to be named in the action. If the freelancer is sued along with the publication, editor and publisher, there is no obligation on the publication to provide legal counsel to the freelancer. That said, if the publication wants to present a common front and doesn't want any unpleasant surprises in the freelancer's testimony, it is in its best interests to provide legal counsel to all involved.

It should be noted that there could be a risk in a freelancer and publication sharing legal counsel. Many media outlets carry litigation insurance and the insurer may decide early on in the legal process to settle out of court. This may involve issuing an apology, declaring that errors or negligence occurred, and paying a settlement. If the freelancer doesn't agree with the insurer's decision, he or she may not be able to afford to do anything about it.

In any contract a freelancer signs, he or she should not agree to a clause that indemnifies the publisher for a claim or legal action based on an alleged breach. Such clauses typically state the freelancer "will indemnify and hold harmless the publisher against any and all claims or actions based on a breach or alleged breach." While a freelancer may be held personally liable for a proven breach, it should only be after a court or other tribunal declares so. Legal counsel for writers frequently advise they should not agree to pay any defence costs initially if they are not to blame and are simply caught up in an action that may be dropped or otherwise settled. The publisher is the one who traditionally assumes the risks of publishing.

Contracts and Freelancers

In the past, freelancers only rarely did business under a contract, particularly for one-off or occasional writing assignments. That has changed in recent years as both publishers and freelancers face increased liability and battles have broken out over the extent of copyright, especially electronic rights.

As will be discussed below, U.S. and Canadian freelancers have made significant progress in asserting copyright over the use of their work in print, electronic databases and on the Web. In many cases, confusion over the rights of freelancers and publishers has come about because contracts were so rare and often very basic and poorly written. Today, both freelancers and publishers are realizing why comprehensive agreements are necessary.

Unfortunately for freelancers, the publishers often have the upper hand and some of the agreements that media organizations are asking journalists to sign can be one-sided and unfair. This section focuses on elements that should be in any freelance contract, as well as typical clauses to avoid. The issues surrounding copyright will be discussed later in this section.

First off, a formal contract may not be needed for every assignment. A brief letter or e-mail may be enough to confirm the details of the assignment and rights being licensed. The informal agreement should conclude by asking the editor or writer to confirm the details by either signing a copy back or acknowledging it in e-mail. This can be proof, if needed, of the parameters of the agreement. That said, many writers' associations in Canada and the U.S. offer sample contracts for downloading free on their Web sites allowing writers and publishers to simply fill in the blanks of a formal agreement.

What should a formal agreement or informal letter include? Aside from the important issues of the copyright to be licensed (discussed below), here is a checklist of other common details that may be in standard agreements:

- Approximate length of article or broadcast item;
- Editorial credit or by-line;
- Description of work or assignment to be performed;
- Deadline and method of delivery (courier, e-mail, etc.);
- Tentative publication or broadcast date;
- Fee amount (flat-rate or hourly, plus applicable taxes);
- Number of rewrites or reediting included in the fee;
- Allowance for disbursements (photocopying, data inputting, long-distance calls, travel, couriers, etc.);

- Payment period expected upon acceptance (for example, within 10 or 30 days of acceptance of work);
- Written notice required for termination of assignment by either the writer or publication, specifying that any work to date will be compensated;
- "Kill fee" if the work is deemed unacceptable and beyond reworking. If the work is not published for any other reason, the entire fee is payable;
- Notification period for acceptance or revisions (for example, within 10 days of delivery of work), otherwise the work shall be considered accepted;
- Final edited version of the work to be sent to the writer, with any changes made, before publication;
- If the work is not published within (for example, 3, 6 or 12 months) of delivery, the copyright licensed reverts to the author without penalty;
- The work may be privately stored in a database or computer for legal and historical reasons only, but not for republication in any other way unless specifically licensed;
- In some cases, publishers or freelancers may want to indicate the law of a specific province will be used to settle disputes or that an arbitrator must be used to settle disputes before engaging the court process; and
- Some agreements address liability. A freelancer, for example, may request indemnification or legal counsel to be provided in the event of a legal action where "questionable material" was brought to the attention of the publisher before publication.

While these are the common elements set out in agreements, both publishers and freelancers can try to negotiate other contract provisions. For example, some major publications ask writers to agree that all notes or interviews with individuals are the property of the publication.

Formal agreements may also set out the conduct or obligations expected of freelancers and publishers. The Professional Writers Association of Canada (PWAC) at www.pwac.ca, for instance, promotes a standard downloadable contract that states writers will, among other things, "not deliberately write a dishonest, plagiarized or inaccurate statement into the manuscript," will assist the publication in verifying sources and information, and will alert a publication to potential defamation problems.

In return, publishers signing the PWAC agreement will "respect" promises of confidentiality given to sources, hire a lawyer to review the manuscript when needed, pay extra fees for revisions that are significant departures from the original assignment, and withdraw the writer's by-line if the final edited version is not satisfactory.

Apart from establishing the extent of copyright, another advantage in having a contract is setting out mutually acceptable terms and definitions. The standard agreement proposed by the Editors' Association of Canada, for example, includes an appendix that clearly defines what is involved in different types of editing and proofreading.

The "kill fee" is the best example of an event where confusion reigns over terms. In the past, kill fees were used only when a work was beyond repair. If a publisher decided not to use it because of a lack of space or change in editorial direction, the freelancer was still paid the full fee. Sadly, there is not always agreement on what triggers a kill fee and a contract can help sort that out. As an example, this is the current "kill fee" section of the PWAC standard contract:

> If the Writer delivers a manuscript that fails to meet the originally agreed upon requirements of the assignment and if the Editor considers that the manuscript cannot be made acceptable through rewriting, the Editor may terminate the assignment by providing the Writer with written notice and paying the Writer not less than one half of the agreed fee, plus the Writer's expenses to date.

> If, in the course of research or during the writing of a manuscript, the Writer concludes that the information available will not result in a satisfactory article, the Writer will inform the Editor and give reasons to discontinue the assignment. If the Editor agrees, the assignment is terminated. The Publisher/Client will pay a reasonable fee, to be negotiated, to compensate the Writer for work done prior to termination, on presentation of the Writer's research documentation.

> If the Editor wishes to cancel this agreement after work has begun, the Publication will pay a reasonable fee, to be negotiated, to compensate the Writer for work done prior to termination.

For those working as freelance broadcasters, here is the "kill fee" clause in the CBC's standard contract for 2000.

> The following fees may apply only in cases where full payment is to be made upon completion of the Freelance Contributor's work

> If, during any time of the production of the work, the Corporation determines that the idea is not feasible or possible, the Corporation agrees to pay the Freelance Contributor a minimum of twenty per cent (20%) of the full contract amount. Nothing in this article shall preclude the parties from negotiating a greater percentage of the full contract amount.

> In the event the Corporation decides not to use a contribution after the Freelance Contributor has completed it according to the specifications agreed to by the parties, the CBC shall pay 100% of the contracted fee. However, no pyramiding of payments or double payments are allowed under this clause.

> *Sometimes, through no fault of the freelancer, a project doesn't pan out. This clause entitles you to a minimum payment of 20% of the full contract amount.*

Depending on what stage you were at, you may wish to negotiate a higher payment.

If you have completed all of the work and the Corporation decides for whatever reason not to use it, you must be paid 100% of the fee.

Pyramiding means you can't "double dip." You can't receive payment for the item and the applicable kill fee.

The CBC and other visual media outlets also negotiate standard agreements with the Writers Guild of Canada (www.wgc.ca), which is the national association representing writers working in film, television, radio and multimedia production. Its Web site offers a selection of information on legal rights, such as whether to sign screenplay releases and finding experienced legal advisors.

Obviously, while trying to strike a balance between the needs of freelancers and media organizations, these standard agreements may not be acceptable to everyone. In fact, almost every major media organization in the U.S. and Canada has created their own version of a "standard agreement."

So, what can you do if you don't agree with the terms of a proposed contract? It is a business relationship and you must negotiate the best deal you can. Some freelancers, for example, accept the all-encompassing terms but demand a higher payment. Others refuse the terms and make a principled stand against one-sided deals.

Copyright and Freelancers

With the popularity of the Internet and more publishers using content to generate extra revenue through news databases, Web sites and mobile devices, the freelance community has become quite militant lately about the copyrights they hold in their work.

Before electronic rights became an issue, freelance journalists typically sold "first rights" to a work. After a newspaper, magazine or broadcaster used it, the copyright reverted to the freelancer and he or she was free to license the work to others. Disputes arose when news database services and Web sites became viable sources of income and most publishers took the position that the first rights included electronic rights because they were simply making the same "collective work" available via the Internet or through databases.

It took over a decade of court decisions, but freelance writers in the U.S. and Canada have scored major victories in asserting their electronic rights. First, in the U.S., freelance writers succeeded in a landmark class action suit at the U.S. Supreme Court which established their right to prevent the republication of articles, particularly on the Internet and in databases, without an agreement or additional payment.[18]

In the 2001 *Tasini* case, a freelance writer sued for copyright infringement on behalf of thousands of freelance writers who were independent contractors for the New York Times and other publications. They worked under freelance arrangements that said nothing about the placement of articles in an electronic database. The major publishers each licensed rights to copy and sell articles to LEXIS/NEXIS, owner and operator of an online database of articles, and to University Microfilms International, which reproduced articles on CD-ROM products.

The U.S. Supreme Court agreed with the writers that "copyright in each separate contribution to a collective work is distinct from copyright in the collective work as a whole." In other words, a publication has copyright in its magazine or newspaper in that form, but a freelance writer included in that publication enjoys a separate copyright. Without an agreement providing an express transfer of such rights, the U.S. copyright law does not allow publishers to distribute articles in any other form, such as a database. The court noted: "It would scarcely preserve the author's copyright in a contribution as contemplated by Congress if a print publisher, without the author's permission, could reproduce or distribute discrete copies of the contribution in isolation or within new collective works."

In Canada, a class proceedings lawsuit similar to that launched in the U.S. was finally decided in 2006 at the Supreme Court of Canada.[19] Freelance author Heather Robertson sued the publisher and owners of *The Globe and Mail* on behalf of thousands of freelance writers who had contributed to the newspaper (except those who died before 1944). At issue was the publisher's right to reproduce freelance works in other forms of media, such as online databases and CD-ROMs, without additional compensation. The Supreme Court split 5-4 in favour of Robertson.

In 1995, she had contributed two freelance articles for Thomson Corp. One was a book review for the national newspaper and the second was an excerpt from her book for its business magazine. There was only an oral agreement and nothing in writing on the use of the review and the publisher later took the position it had a right to distribute the newspaper's articles electronically, as well as in print. As for the book excerpt, there was an agreement with her book publisher that expressly referred to a "one time usage," but the newspaper publisher again believed it had a right to publish a version of its magazine in electronic form.

Robertson launched her action for copyright infringement after her works appeared in two databases, Info Globe Online and CPI.Q, and a CD-

---

18 *New York Times Co., Inc. v. Tasini*, [2001] SCT-QL 139, No. 00201 (U.S. S.C.).
19 *Robertson v. Thomson Corp.*, [2006] 2 S.C.R. 363.

ROM. Importantly for the court, as will be explained below, the databases offered users the articles as standalone text while the CD-ROM mimicked the collective aspects of each edition of the daily newspaper.

The majority of judges held that "newspaper publishers are not entitled to republish freelance articles acquired for publication in their newspapers in Info Globe Online or CPI.Q without compensating the authors and obtaining their consent." While publishers have a right under the Copyright Act's s. 3(1) to "reproduce the work or any substantial part thereof in any material form whatever," the majority agreed a "substantial part" means the "essence of the newspaper is preserved."

In other words, reproducing the text of the individual articles in an online database without the original layout or appearance of a newspaper does not qualify as a proper reproduction. The CD-ROM, however, was "faithful to the essence of the original work" and kept much of the newspaper's appearance.

The majority made it clear that publishers, particularly the news media, do not have a "licence to override the rights of authors." The court, however, went on to state that a non-exclusive licence permitting a publisher to republish in databases or CD-ROMs does not need to be in writing. In other words, the newspaper's right to use articles in a database without payment may be implied if it can be proven at trial that freelance authors knew this was a standard practice.

In many respects, this decision was a major victory for writers. The ruling, however, only dealt with pre-trial motions and an actual trial of Robertson's claims has yet to be held. At the time of this publication, there was no public word on whether an agreement would be negotiated between the *Globe* and freelancers, or if the matter would go to trial. At the very least, the judgment underlines that it is vitally important for freelance journalists to address these copyright and extra payments for different forms of media in writing.

As this case illustrated, it is important for all freelancers to understand copyright law and how it is interpreted. For example, the licensing of "first serial rights" or "first Canadian rights" does not include both print and electronic uses unless an agreement says otherwise. The electronic rights should always be licensed separately. Why? Because print publications have a limited life span while electronic publications or databases can generate income forever. Some publishers do try to claim that first serial rights include electronic copyright, but freelancers should dispute it. In fact, one major Canadian magazine publisher even tries to assert that it owns not just electronic rights, but also rights "for any means of transmission yet to be invented."

Here are some common terms in copyright licensing:

- **All rights:** No freelancer should accept this clause. It is what it says and prevents a freelancer from reselling or licensing rights to anyone.

- **Canadian, North American or territorial rights:** Defines the geographic area of rights.

- **Electronic rights:** Broadly applied to databases, computer disks, CD-ROMs and Web sites.

- **English, French or other language rights:** Permits translations of a work into named languages.

- **Exclusive:** As it says, no one else may have this right. For example, "exclusive North American rights."

- **First rights:** A right to be the first publisher of a work.

- **Non-exclusive:** Common in Web-based licensing, this allows the copyright holder to license the work to anyone else.

- **One-time first rights:** One-time use of the right to be the first publisher of a work.

- **One-time rights:** Newspapers, which often don't worry about who else is publishing the work, buy the right to publish the piece once.

- **Reprographic rights:** A right to make duplicates of a work, such as photocopies. Common in situations where a corporation or conference group seeks permission to copy an article for a defined audience (such as, delegates or employees).

- **Second rights:** A right to the subsequent publication of a work.

- **Serial rights:** A reference to "serial publications," such as a magazine or newspaper.

- **Work-for-hire:** This puts the freelancer on the same footing as an employee and means you surrender all your claims to the work forever. This is a bad deal for any freelancer.

It is important for a freelancer to be specific about all aspects of rights being licensed, including the timeframe. For example, electronic rights for a Web site may be for a specific number of days, weeks or months. Typically these days, rights for Web content must be renewed annually. It's also a good idea to be specific about what happens after the timeframe expires. If a writer is receiving payment for first rights, for instance, it is wise to state in a letter or contract that "if you do not publish the article within [6 or 12] months of delivery, all rights granted revert back to the author."

Many of the freelance writers associations in Canada and the U.S. do an excellent job of monitoring the latest standard contracts being proposed by publishers and can offer up-to-date advice on whether others are accepting the terms. For example, the American Society of Journalists and Authors suggests freelancers should watch carefully for clauses such as:

- **"For educational or research purposes only..."**: Content sales by publishers to educational buyers or databases can represent sizeable income.

- **"Publisher may revise, edit, augment, condense or otherwise alter the work..."**: Any editorial changes should be made with the freelancer's approval or, at least, the opportunity to withdraw his or her by-line.

- **"The work is not libelous, obscene or otherwise in contravention of law and does not violate the proprietary right, privacy or any other right of any third party..."**: This indemnification clause establishes a very onerous situation for the freelancer, who may not be able to guarantee the work to this extent.

- **"The right to publish, distribute and license others to publish and distribute the article in all its forms [or in any media]..."**: This is, essentially, the transfer of both electronic and print rights.

- **"Use the article and your name, biography and likeness for promotion and advertising of the publication..."**: An advertisement or promotional material should be treated as a separate publication and involve an additional fee.

- **"You will indemnify and hold harmless the publisher against any and all claims or actions based on a breach or alleged breach of the above warranties..."**: Again, an impossible standard for a freelancer to meet on a limited budget.

As noted earlier, understanding copyright law can help avoid uncertainty about a freelancer's rights and open potential opportunities for more revenue. It's not uncommon for freelancers to discover others infringing on their copyright, sometimes unknowingly. For example, freelance magazine articles are often reprinted in corporate employee newsletters, included in press kits or placed on corporate Web sites under the guise of publicity. Correcting these problems usually means sending an e-mail, letter or calling to alert the offender to the infringement and requesting a reprint fee (usually 25%-50% of your normal fee to produce a work).

Collectives and Freelancers

In Canada, the Copyright Act allows "collectives" (government authorized organizations or industry groups) to collect license fees from broadcasters, libraries, corporations, schools, governments and others who may use copyrighted works. The collectives then distribute royalties, often annually, to Canada's writers, musicians, performers and other copyright holders.

For organizations such as libraries, which may allow the public to photocopy from books and magazines, the collectives have no way of knowing who should be compensated so the license fees collected are pooled and distributed among the copyright holders on record. Any Canadian citizen who has published works in Canada can benefit from one of the collectives. No fees are charged for "affiliates" to join and the copyright licensing agreement with a collective is non-exclusive.

Access Copyright (formerly known as CANCOPY), one of the leading Canadian collectives, pays out $15-$20 million a year in royalties, so there is good potential for extra income for freelancers. To collect payments, journalists and other literary artists must first register with a relevant collective, such as:

- **Canadian Copyright Licensing Agency:** Canadian Copyright Licensing Agency has a Web site at www.accesscopyright.ca. It represents most writers, publishers and other creators in all provinces, except Québec.

- **Canadian Screenwriters Collection Society (CSCS):** The Canadian Screenwriters Collection Society has a Web site at www.writersguildofcanada.com/cscs. It was created by the Writers Guild of Canada to claim, collect, administer and distribute royalties and levies that film and television writers are entitled to under Canadian and foreign copyright legislation.

- **Playwrights Guild of Canada:** Found at www.playwrightsguild.ca, the Playwrights Guild of Canada is the national collective for professional playwrights. Its equivalent in Québec is Association québécoise des auteurs dramatiques, which has a Web site at www.aqad.qc.ca.

- **Société des auteurs et compositeurs dramatiques:** With a Web site at www.sacd.ca, this group represents authors, composers and choreographers of dramatic works.

- **Société québécoise de gestion collective des droits de reproduction:** Found at www.copibec.qc.ca, this is the Québec equivalent of Access Copyright.

EMPLOYER AND FREELANCER CHECKLIST

1. The law applying to journalists working as employees is substantially different from that used for business relationships with independent contractors or freelancers.

2. The legal principle of "vicarious liability" makes an employer jointly responsible for the actions of an employee as long as the employee is acting within the scope of his or her employment. That said, a court may hold both a journalist and employer responsible, especially if there was negligence or willful disregard for the law or another's rights.

3. Wrongful dismissal is a court action journalists may undertake when an employer terminates them without just cause and without reasonable notice or pay in lieu of notice.

4. Another common claim is for constructive dismissal, which arises when an employer changes a journalist's working conditions to such an extent that a court rules it is a fundamental repudiation of the employment contract.

5. Journalists working in a unionized environment must, in most cases, rely on their collective agreement to govern the employment relationship.

6. Being in a business and not an employment relationship, the freelancer is not protected by the legal principle of vicarious liability that makes an employer jointly liable.

7. In civil litigation, it's not uncommon for all potential defendants (including a freelancer writer) to be named in the action. If the freelancer is sued along with the publication, editor and publisher, there is no obligation on the publication to provide legal counsel to the freelancer.

8. The risks of increased liability and battles over the extent of copyright licensed to a media organization, especially electronic rights, have made formal contracts (or informal letters setting out terms of the assignment) more common.

9. Electronic rights (CD-ROMs, databases, Internet) to freelance works should always be licensed separately from typical print rights.

10. Freelancers should consider joining one or more of Canada's copyright collectives, which collect and distribute millions of dollars in license fees each year.

19

JOURNALISTIC ETHICS AND THE LAW

It is increasingly popular in journalism studies these days to pair discussions about the law with debates on the ethical dilemmas and decisions that reporters often face on a daily basis. And, rightly so. There are many points where legal and ethical considerations intersect in the business or process of good reporting.

In many ways, the rule of law and other fundamental principles that have developed in jurisprudence reflect the ethical objectives and standards of our society. Similar to our laws, ethics speak to a code of behaviour, principles of conduct or moral values expected of an individual, group, organization or profession. Ethics can also be considered a form of "best practices" or industry standards for a profession or vocation.

One might even argue that ethical standards often demand better conduct from us than legal standards. It is not hard to think of situations where the law requires or does not require a minimum standard of behaviour that falls short of what ethical or moral standards demand. In journalism, for example, there is no law requiring reporters to refuse payments in exchange for favourable stories, show compassion for victims of tragedy when choosing photos or video, or separate news from opinion or advertising from editorial. In most cases, these are moral decisions — doing what's right, not just what's minimally required.

This chapter does not attempt to explain the wide-ranging and rich history of ethical studies, nor the various theories and models of behaviour that have developed in contemporary journalism. This chapter also offers fewer hard and fast rules than other sections of this book. By its nature, ethics is a discipline that tackles a labyrinth of situations where there is often more than one defensible choice.

Take, for example, the case of a journalist who witnesses a crime being committed, such as a violent sexual assault. Would the ethical journalist intervene and attempt to stop the crime or call the police? Or, should the ethical journalist remain detached and report the crime objectively on the assumption that the story will help police catch the criminal?

Similarly, should a reporter working on a story about the homeless give money to a panhandler on the street? Or, is it more useful to tell his story to raise public awareness and promote change at the government level? These are dilemmas in every sense of the word.

That said, it is worth noting the areas where the law and ethics do cross paths. While the law may not offer a complete answer to an ethical dilemma, it can often help nudge you in the right direction. Just as understanding the law affecting the news media can help make your stories better, the same can be said for vetting your own stories from an ethical standpoint. For example, asking whether you have provided a full right of reply to individuals criticized in your story, whether you have clearly declared what is opinion and fact, and identified what is unverifiable or unproven.

WHERE LAW AND ETHICS INTERSECT

Codes of conduct abound in almost every vocation and profession, including journalism. Many of journalism's associations, guilds and societies provide ethical guidelines or codes, and some are available on the Internet, such as the Canadian Broadcasting Corporation's *Journalistic Standards and Practices.*[1] The guidelines of the CBC and other media organizations speak to a wide variety of situations and journalistic issues, including reporting on public opinion surveys, protecting sources, avoiding indirect commercial advertisements in stories, covering public demonstrations and terrorist incidents, and conducting interviews.

As these codes of ethics often illustrate, there are usually legal considerations in many ethical questions. While not an exhaustive list, the following are some common situations where ethics and law intersect.

---

1 The CBC's guidelines can be found on the Web at cbc.radio-canada.ca/accountability/ journalistic/. Other Canadian codes of ethics can be viewed online at the Web site for the International Center for Journalists (www.ijnet.org), including those of the Alberta Press Council, Canadian Association of Broadcasters, Canadian Association of Journalists, Daily Newspaper Association, Québec Professional Federation of Journalists and the Radio-Television News Directors Association of Canada.

Accuracy, Impartiality and Objectivity in Reporting: Ethically, a journalist is expected to report a story's facts, opinions and other information in an impartial yet objectively critical manner. While a reporter does not have to be unquestioning or refrain from expressing opinions, particularly in this era of "first-person" or activism journalism, both ethics and the law demand that reporters clearly distinguish among facts, opinions and mere conjecture. Accuracy demands that reporters apply due diligence in researching stories and speak to as many sources as possible to corroborate information. As the old reporter's saying goes: "If your mother says she loves you, check it out." From a legal standpoint, the same standard of care is expected of journalists when reporting on matters involving the justice system or potentially defamatory subjects. For example, a journalist reporting on the courts should adhere to the presumption of innocence until the court makes its decision. Also, recent developments in defamation law's defence of qualified privilege suggest the standard of care and due diligence of a responsible or "reasonable reporter" in researching and reporting a story will become very important in future case law. In 2007, the Ontario Court of Appeal adopted a new "public interest responsible journalism" defence broadening a reporter's ability to claim qualified privilege in a defamation cases. Following the lead of courts in the U.K. and U.S., the defence protects properly researched stories on matters "the public has a legitimate interest in hearing," and that journalists have "every reason to believe" are true and meet the standards of responsible journalism.[2]

Statements of Fact vs. Opinion: It is a long-standing rule of journalism that it should be clear to the reader or audience when an opinion is being expressed and when facts are being asserted. Ethically, opinions should be presented honestly and fairly, without distortion of the supporting facts. This standard is reflected in law as well and can be found in the defamation defence of fair comment. The essence of this defence is that commentaries on matters of public interest should be a fair and honest expression of opinion without malice, and be based on known and provable facts. As noted in Chapter 2, it is essential that a comment or opinion not be dressed up as an assertion of fact. It is not even necessary for the opinion to be one that everyone would hold or a reasonable perspective on the facts.[3]

Use and Protection of Sources: The ethical use and protection of sources can prompt great debate in journalism and law. The two often clash when it

---

2 *Cusson v. Quan* (2007), 2007 CarswellOnt 7310, 2007 CarswellOnt 7311, 2007 ONCA 771 (C.A.), leave to appeal to the Supreme Court of Canada allowed (2008), 2008 CarswellOnt 1862 (S.C.C.).
3 In *Vander Zalm v. Times Publishers*, 1980 CarswellBC 6, [1980] 4 W.W.R. 259 (C.A.), a political cartoon showed the plaintiff pulling the wings off a fly in apparent glee. The court said at 265 it was fair comment so long as the author has an honest belief in what he says and it is unnecessary for the comment to be a reasonable perspective on the facts. The court said the opinion may even be exaggerated or prejudiced, as long as it is an honest view that could be held by someone.

comes to the issue of disclosing the identity of confidential sources during criminal or civil matters, as explained in Chapter 3. Some lawyers and judges believe the name of a source can be material evidence at some point in a legal proceeding, while most journalists believe the promise of confidentiality should be kept at all costs (even if it means going to jail for contempt). This is one area where there will likely never be agreement. Law and journalism generally do agree, however, in another area — that sources should, where possible, be attributed. Attribution of information (whether facts or opinion) is important to a story's credibility. The inability to attribute a fact or comment to a source can have dire consequences if there is a defamation or other legal action. Most journalists and lawyers would also agree reporting on controversial matters calls for multiple corroborating sources. Another interesting area of debate involves off-the-record interviews. While some media outlets do not permit the publication of off-the-record information, most reporters understand it can be used to develop new leads or facts in a story. Ethically, journalists should also be clear with sources about the meaning of an off-the-record interview. For example, the source and reporter should decide in advance if the information may not be used at all (truly off-the-record), used but not attributed ("unattributable"), quoted but attributed generally to an "official" or "insider" ("not for attribution"), or with no direct quoting and for information purposes only ("background").

The Right of Reply: Most codes of ethics urge journalists to offer a criticized individual or organization the opportunity to respond to other's comments, or to justify and explain their perspective — ideally, in the same story. When it is not possible for a spokesperson or an individual to respond in time or the opportunity is refused, this should be explained to the audience or reader in as objective a fashion as possible. In such cases, a follow-up story may be merited as soon as possible to give an individual another opportunity to offer his or her side of the story. While some might suggest there is no legal "right" of reply, that is not entirely correct. In defamation law, for example, the statutory defence of absolute privilege in many provinces requires that media defendants in actions involving "fair and accurate" reports of judicial and government proceedings and official reports must prove they offered a plaintiff the opportunity for a "reasonable letter or statement of explanation or contradiction" for the defence to succeed.[4] In other cases where a right of reply is not offered and other defences are unsuccessful, a court may view the media's actions as an aggravating factor in assessing damages or malice.[5]

---

4 The opportunity for the right of reply, for example, is found in Ontario's Libel and Slander Act, R.S.O. 1990, c. L.12, ss. 3(7) and 4(1).
5 For example, in *Vogel v. Canadian Broadcasting Corp.*, 1982 CarswellBC 44, [1982] 3 W.W.R. 97 at 122 (S.C.), the court noted that a defamatory story gave the impression, on at least two occasions, that key people who could have offered the "other side" refused to speak with the CBC. The truth was that a public relations representative was contacted by a journalist about a possible interview and was told only that the interview would involve allegations about three court cases. The PR representative wasn't told what the allegations

In at least one province, offering a right of reply paired with a retraction can negate damages. In Québec's Press Act, which governs only newspapers, a newspaper may escape "prosecution" by publishing a full retraction in good faith in the next issue after the notice of the defamation lawsuit was received, and allowing the plaintiff to publish in the newspaper a reasonable reply to the defamatory statements. If the retraction and reply are published without comment, the plaintiff will not be able to sue at all. If a newspaper only publishes the retraction and the plaintiff does not exercise his right to reply, the court will only award actual (special) damages.

Sensationalism: Ethically, journalists should refrain from unduly sensationalizing a story. As explained in Chapter 4's discussion of investigative reporting techniques, reporters must exhibit honesty, integrity, thoroughness and fairness in reporting and editing stories, headlines and even in the use of graphics and images. The *Vogel* case[6] illustrated the dangers of sensationalizing a story. For example, the CBC reporter in that matter stated: "While no cabinet ministers have been implicated in the allegations so far, the whole business is obviously embarrassing to the Social Credit government." The court found the story implied that cabinet ministers might be involved in the alleged scandal, however, no proof was offered to justify the statement. The court concluded it was puffery designed to give the story a more serious tone. The judge offered this comment: "It is an accepted tenet of our democratic society that the press serves the public interest by exposing corruption and misconduct by those in public life, and that it is essential that it perform that role. It is, however, sometimes hard to see that any public interest is served other than the interest in being entertained. In this case, that was the interest intended to be served. The program was conceived and executed as a form of entertainment presented in the guise of news... ."

Admitting Errors and Issuing Retractions: From a professionalism standpoint, as well as ethically, a journalist or media organization often stands to benefit from a reasonably rapid admission of harmful inaccuracies or errors. Issuing corrections or even apologies can avert lawsuits and, at the very least, reduce damages in the eyes of many courts. This ethical standard is also reflected in our laws, particularly in defamation statutes. Legislation in all provinces and territories state that a "full and fair" retraction precludes the awarding of general or non-specific damages. If the conditions set out in the law for placement and prominence of the retraction are met, the courts will usually confine the award to what are called "special damages." These are damages that are a foreseeable result of the defamation, such as the loss of financial credit. Note, however, that corrections or retractions in some cases should be crafted with the advice of knowledgeable legal counsel to avoid creating unnecessary or additional liability.

---

were about and he saw no urgency in arranging an interview. The court said the request was, at best, a deceptive half-truth.

6 Note 5, above.

Respect for Diversity and Human Rights: Many codes of conduct urge journalists to avoid mentioning a person's age, race, colour, nationality, religious convictions, disability, marital status, sex or sexual orientation unless it is relevant to the story. Journalists should also avoid the promotion of hatred, discrimination or ridicule of individuals or groups on any similar basis. The law reflects this ethical standard as well in our federal and provincial human rights laws against discrimination, and even the Criminal Code provisions prohibiting hate crimes. While human rights codes in many jurisdictions provide exceptions for free expressions of opinions, several provinces specifically prohibit a publication in articles or statements that discriminates "against a person or a group or class of persons. . ." or "is likely to expose a person or a group or class of persons to hatred or contempt." See Chapter 16 for more information.

Internet and Online Considerations: While many of the same ethical and legal considerations apply to the Internet (Web sites, blogs, forums, etc.), there are some interesting ethical issues in cyberspace. For example, online journalists must consider the ethical consequences of hypertext links that lead to sites beyond their control. Most media outlets do not permit editorial copy to feature links to outside commercial content or paid links, without advance notice to the reader. Media outlets must also consider whether to allow editorial articles or links to be used on an advertiser's site (most require a copyright notice be inserted and the phrase "Reprinted with permission"). Bloggers, particularly, wrestle these days with issues of copyright and plagiarism. Many blogs are built on the content of others and their authors should be careful to properly attribute sources of information and seek permission to reprint, if possible. As in the print world, media Web sites must ensure that quotations, headlines, subheads, video and images do not misrepresent or distort stories. Online reports also must be careful to display corrections or retractions prominently, and clearly date and time-stamp material to avoid confusion over the currency of information. These factors and others not only have a bearing on the ethics of reporting online, but also could have an impact on any resulting legal proceedings.

OTHER COMMON ETHICAL CONCERNS

There is no shortage of ethical dilemmas that arise in journalism for which the law has no or few answers. They range from tall to small, in significance. For example, is it ethical for a journalist to arrange an interview with a known fugitive in a murder case without alerting the police? Should a writer provide an editor with her list of news contacts so the advertising team can chase potential ads? Should you accept lavish gift bags handed out at a news conference? What about the free lunch provided at a keynote speaker's event? In some media organizations, there are rules on such issues; in others, these questions might provoke derisive laughter.

Nonetheless, here are some other common areas where journalists must come to terms with what's right.

Conflicts of Interest: Being impartial and objective witnesses to history, journalists are generally expected to avoid conflicts or the appearance of conflicts of interest. For example, codes of ethics advise reporters to not accept bribes or payments in return for favourable stories. Journalists are also advised to shun commercial endorsements or advertisements for products or services. Business reporters, particularly, must avoid using insider information to take advantage of news that is not yet public. Some organizations, for example, do not allow their reporters to invest in companies or industries they cover. Reporters, in most cases, must also be careful not to become the focus of the story. In a 1993 case, a newspaper reporter was accused by his employer of attempting to be both an "actor and critic" after preparing a brief for submission to a provincial inquiry on an issue he had covered.[7] In this case, the reporter was found not to be in conflict because he decided not to submit the brief in the end.

Separation of Advertising and Editorial: These days, this is a sore subject in some newsrooms. Financial survival often depends on co-ordination of editorial and advertising opportunities. That said, most codes of conduct suggest journalist should never distort or suppress information based on advertising or other considerations. Ideally, there should also be a clear separation from a viewer or reader's perspective between editorial copy and advertising. Similarly, editorial topics, issues and decisions should not be influenced by advertisers, and most media organizations never allow advertisers to review stories before publication. Typically, any advertising that has the appearance of editorial copy must be clearly distinguished for the reader or viewer. For instance, most publications print the word(s) "special advertising supplement" or "advertorial" along the edge of the copy. Generally, the design and fonts used in special advertising sections are different from those used by the publication.

Decency and Good Taste: What is in good taste or decent by your community's standards? Most media organizations generally strive to reflect the accepted values in society on matters such as profanity, morality or sexual behaviour. Broadcasters are governed by rules issued by the Canadian Radio-Television and Telecommunications Commission. In many cases, print and online publishers have much greater latitude in deciding what is in good taste. Ethically, even broadcast journalists may come upon situations where profanity or nudity, for example, are integral elements of the story. A related issue concerns occasions of extreme violence, grief or personal distress. Most media organizations recognize that images or video showing violent or distressing scenes, or moments of personal suffering can be alarming to audiences. Many codes of conduct recommend that these occasions not be ex-

7 *Toronto Star Newspapers Ltd. v. Southern Ontario Newspaper Guild, Local 87* (1993), 1993 CarswellOnt 1237, 33 L.A.C. (4th) 353 (Arb. Bd.).

ploited unduly. At the very least, for example, common decency in broadcasting requires journalists to warn viewers of potentially upsetting images.

Privacy: What are the limits of privacy in pursuing journalistic ends? There is no simple answer and many fine lines to debate. For example, we expect journalists to report on the names of individuals accused but not yet convicted of crimes. Playing devil's advocate, one might ask why we do not always identify the victims of crimes, particularly in cases of sexual assault? Most people understand the public policy reasons behind this restriction, but it is clear that one rule cannot govern all situations. Another example is the ethical practice of most media to not report suicides or attempts to commit suicide, unless there is a public interest component (for example, where the story involves a politician or celebrity). Privacy interests also enter the picture where medical information is involved or children. The CBC's guidelines offer an interesting scenario to consider. It is very common these days for community members or the police to publicize the release of a sex offender who has served his or her prison term. Since Canadian law allows the justice system to declare a person who has committed repeated offences a dangerous offender and to be jailed indefinitely, is it fair to violate the right to privacy of an individual who has been released into the community? The CBC urges its journalists to make "an informed and independent assessment of the potential dangerousness of the released offender, in light of all available information." It suggests "revenge, extra-judicial punishment or frustration with the law and the courts" may be at the root of the public outrage and the fact that other news media are running with the story is not justification enough.

Gifts, Favours and Payments: Most media organizations accept that journalists will receive occasional meals and beverages from those they report on and interview. However, some media outlets believe it is unethical to accept gifts or favours, beyond those of nominal value, from individuals, businesses or groups they cover. For example, payments for travel and hotel expenses are often carefully considered when offered. Similarly, journalists are generally discouraged by their employers from accepting freelance work from individuals or organizations they must cover. Not all payments are forbidden in most media organizations, though. Reporters who appear as expert guests on television or radio shows are often paid a stipend. Travel and other reasonable expenses incurred in making speeches are also likely to be accepted.

Demonstrations and Violent Acts: What is the ethical obligation of a journalist who is covering a riot, demonstration or other potentially disruptive event who discovers that he or she is influencing its outcome? It is not unusual these days to see the impact that cameras can have on a crowd or group of protestors who discover their message is being broadcast to the masses. The CBC and other media organizations typically recommend that the presence of cameras and microphones not be allowed to provoke or encourage violence. If it appears clear a dangerous situation is developing because of media presence, the CBC recommends its reporters stop using or conceal their equipment. The CBC also asks its journalists and crews to avoid communicating to others outside the newsroom that it plans to attend protests, to maintain some distance from organizers and demonstrators, and to avoid allowing individuals to perform for cameras or microphones.

IN SUMMARY

It is said that one of the first goals in any journalism education is to create sceptics. In other words, to question and verify as much as possible before publishing a story. When considering the intersection of ethics and law, particularly, developing skills in questioning, verifying, debating and defending what is "right" to do will serve you well. Ultimately, whether dilemmas are ethical or legal, it is important to remember that both ethics and law are dynamic in nature and are constantly adapting to the community's principles and values. For that reason, each story can bring a new opportunity to shape the boundaries of law and ethics in journalism.

Appendix 1

THE LEGAL SYSTEM

Simply speaking, Parliament and the provincial legislatures make the laws and the courts interpret and enforce them. But that is "simply speaking." In fact, our courts sometimes end up making the law by virtue of the way legislation is interpreted. This chapter is a primer on the court system, leaving the explanation of the legislative process to political scientists.

Generally, there are two main bodies of law administered by the courts. The *civil law* is concerned with private rights and remedies, such as in contracts or defamation. The *criminal law* punishes behaviour which is an offence against the state or society.

SOURCES OF THE LAW

Much of our legal system is founded on the "rule of law." This umbrella of principles dating back to the earliest legal systems holds that the law should be accessible to everyone, that we should all be able to know what the law requires, that the law should apply equally to all, that no one is above the law, and that the law must be enforced with fairness for everyone. The courts look to many sources to interpret the rule of law and decide issues: Constitution Acts, statutes, previous cases and even the writings of learned authors. In some instances, Canadian courts will consider the court decisions of other countries, particularly those in the United Kingdom and the United States.

The Constitution

The documents and unwritten conventions (that is, traditions or customs) that form our Constitution date from early English history to Confederation to the present. Because of our parliamentary system of government, we share many of the constitutional traditions of England and the courts often reach back to early times to help interpret a point of constitutional law. There are also numerous constitutional documents, the most important of which are the Constitution Acts (including the former British North America Act and the Canadian Charter of Rights and Freedoms). The Constitution is sometimes referred to as the "Supreme Law of the Land" because it forms the basis upon which the courts determine the individual powers and limits of the federal and provincial legislatures.

Statutes and Regulations

Statutes are the tools of governments. They may create completely new laws to govern behaviour or they may just codify existing practices. Statutes are passed by the federal Parliament or provincial legislatures according to the powers and limits set out by the constitutional law. For example, the Constitution Act, 1867 (that is, British North America Act) states that the federal Parliament has exclusive jurisdiction to create criminal offences, but the provincial governments have the right to administer the operations of the criminal courts. Sometimes, a legislature will over-step its boundaries and the courts will declare a statute *ultra vires* or beyond the legislature's power and thus having no effect. Regulations are, in theory, subordinate to their corresponding statutes and authority to draft regulations is often granted by a statute to the government of the day and its bureaucrats.

Regulations are supposed to be used for setting amounts for fines, official forms to be used and other administrative matters. Increasingly, however, legal scholars have noticed a trend toward using regulations as a way of seemingly bypassing public debate over controversial changes to the law. In reviewing changes to the law, it is wise these days to pay close attention to both regulations and statutes.

Case Law

All of the provinces, with the exception of Québec, have a system of law which gives great authority to previously-decided cases on various topics of law. The legal system which relies heavily on case precedents is known as *common law*. Although no two cases are ever the same, certain general principles can be extracted from similar cases. The legal principle of *stare decisis* gives precedents great authority and, in most cases, case precedents are binding on lower courts.

All of the provinces and territories use case precedents in the criminal law. Precedents are also used in civil cases, except in Québec, where there is a European-based *civil law* system as opposed to the English-based *common law* system followed in the rest of Canada. In Québec, a precedent is authoritative in civil law only because of the soundness of its reasoning, rather than the fact other judges have followed it. Québec courts are not bound to follow the previous decisions of other judges and theoretically decide cases according to civil law principles codified in a text known as the Civil Code. These basic statements or principles attempt to fit every possible legal problem. If the Code does not speak directly to the problem, then the judge may use the general provisions of the Code to come to a decision. However, in practice, Québec judges generally do follow precedents.

OUR COURT SYSTEM

As stated earlier, the purpose of the courts is to interpret the law, not to make the law. But as times change, so do the attitudes of the courts and new principles can evolve to interpret the law. When a court makes a decision which is unique, it is important to consider the court's decision in the context of the judicial hierarchy or pecking order. This basic point is made because some members of the news media overreact when a lower court makes an unusual ruling. It should be remembered that such a decision could be quickly overturned by an appeal court if it is appealed.

The Court Hierarchy

The Supreme Court of Canada is the ultimate court of appeal and has the final word on the interpretation of the law of the country. For example, if a Supreme Court of Canada decision states that a certain statute is invalid, only an Act of Parliament or a legislature can change the resulting effect of the interpretation. Until that happens, the decision of the Supreme Court of Canada is binding on all other courts.

The next level down is the Court of Appeal of each province. The decisions of the Court of Appeal are binding on all of the lower courts in that province. Other courts of appeal will note decisions of the appeal court in other provinces, but, while the other court's decision is persuasive, there is no express requirement to follow the decision.

Lower courts in other provinces are also obliged to take note of the decisions of other courts of appeal, but the decisions are not expressly binding, as is the case when their own court of appeal makes a decision.

Below the appeal courts are the trial courts and, below the trial courts, are specialized courts which deal with minor criminal offences and/or small civil actions. Throughout the hierarchy, the principle is that a lower court must follow the precedents set by higher courts in that province. Decisions by courts of equal or higher ranking in other provinces must be noted and may be persuasive, but are not binding.

Canadian courts also consider decisions in other common law countries such as Australia, England or the United States. Often where there is no precedent in a certain area of the law, the courts will look to other jurisdictions for guidance.

Court Jurisdictions

The structure of our courts is rooted in the Constitution Act, 1867. Under the Constitution, the individual provinces establish the actual framework of their court system. There are two major categories of courts which are found in each province's judicial system: superior courts and inferior courts.

Superior courts are the high level trial and appeal courts. The judges to these courts are appointed by the federal government (even though the province enacts legislation establishing the particular levels of superior courts). Below the superior courts are the so-called inferior courts or provincial courts with judges appointed by the province.

The actual names and jurisdictional scope of the court levels vary from province to province. Some have special courts to handle wills and estates or family law matters. Most trial and appeal courts in each province and territory have authority to deal with matters in both criminal and civil law, but some, particularly low level provincial courts, may be restricted to either criminal or civil law. The following charts set out the general structure of our criminal and civil courts:

The Civil Court System

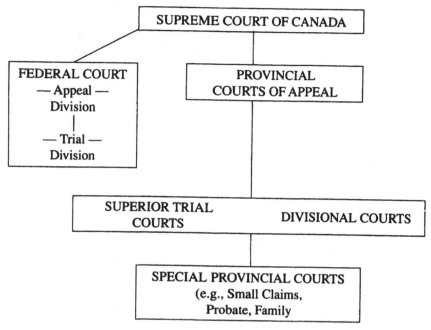

Supreme Court of Canada. The ultimate court of appeal. Only cases of national, constitutional or legal importance are given permission to be heard in this court. The court can confirm or overturn a decision or order a new trial.

Federal Court. Formerly known as the Exchequer Court, the two divisions of this body have exclusive jurisdiction over patents, copyrights, trademarks, disputes over shipping and navigation, inter-governmental disputes and certain actions against the federal government.

Provincial Courts of Appeal. The highest court in each province. It can confirm or overturn a decision or order a new trial.

Superior Trial Courts. These courts are generally the first level for a civil law case. They are known variously in the provinces as the Court of Queen's Bench, Superior Court, Supreme Court, and Supreme Court, Trial Division.

Divisional Courts. Divisional courts, such as those that existed in counties and districts, have been merged with the superior courts in almost every province. In Québec, so-called Québec Courts fulfil similar duties to the old county courts and hear small civil matters. These courts usually have jurisdiction over civil actions involving claims with a ceiling of small to medium amounts (for example, $30,000).

Special Courts. These courts have limited jurisdiction over such matters as small claims, wills, estates and family law matters.

The Criminal Court System

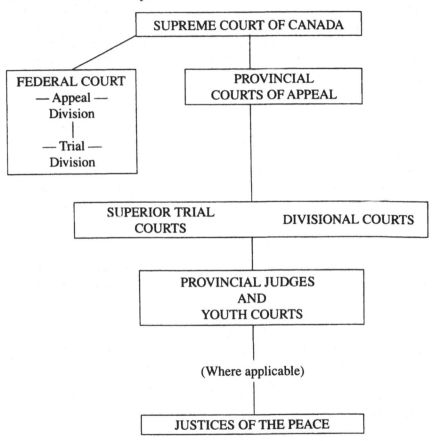

Supreme Court of Canada. This is the ultimate court of appeal. Only cases of national, constitutional or legal importance are given permission to be heard in this court. The court can confirm or overturn a decision or order a new trial.

Federal Court. Formerly known as the Exchequer Court, the two divisions of this body hear some criminal matters (for example, income tax prosecutions).

Provincial Courts of Appeal. The highest court in each province. The court can confirm or overturn a decision, or order a new trial. For criminal cases, these courts are defined as "superior courts of criminal jurisdiction."

Superior Trial Courts. These courts handle any offences that are not within the jurisdiction of a provincial court judge or when an accused has elected this trial level. These courts are known variously in the provinces as the Court of Queen's Bench, Superior Court, Supreme Court, and Supreme Court, Trial Division. These courts are also considered "superior courts of criminal jurisdiction" for the purposes of jurisdiction in the criminal justice system. In Québec, the Superior Court is both a court of appeal and court of original jurisdiction for criminal matters.

Divisional Courts. Divisional courts, such as those that existed in counties and districts, have been merged with the superior courts in almost every province. In Québec, the Court of the Sessions of the Peace hears criminal cases without a jury. This level of the court system has jurisdiction over most criminal matters, except those within the jurisdiction of the "superior courts" (for example, murder). This level of the court system is known simply as a "court of criminal jurisdiction."

Provincial and Youth Courts. These are often the courts of first appearance in a criminal case. The power of the Youth Court may be vested in provincial court or family court judges depending on the province.

Justices of the Peace. The justice of the peace is the court of first appearance in a few provinces, such as Ontario and Québec. Justices adjudicate a few minor criminal offences or violations of provincial and municipal laws. But for serious offences they have no jurisdiction other than to process the accused for a higher court (for example, justices of the peace cannot take an accused's plea for offences which they have no authority to adjudicate).

ADMINISTRATIVE TRIBUNALS

There is another decision-making process within the legal system which can affect the rights of individuals and can involve the courts. Although most official bodies in government exercise purely administrative or "rubber-stamping" powers, statutes can create tribunals or bodies which exercise a quasi-judicial or judicial function. Many of these tribunals are not courts *per se*, but do make decisions in a judicial or quasi-judicial manner after considering presentations or evidence (for example, public utility boards, public inquiries, municipal boards and disciplinary committees). Some administrative tribunals even have the same authority as superior courts to enforce their rulings.

Many of these bodies, such as labour boards, have exclusive jurisdiction to make decisions under the legislation. For example, a dispute over whether a company has used unfair bargaining practices will be settled by a labour board and not by the courts. However, in most cases, the courts have the power to review the decisions for procedural defects (rather than the correctness of the decision) which are not in accordance with the principles of natural justice or fairness. If the tribunal is found to have made its decision improperly, the court may be able to order a new hearing or other suitable remedy.

UNDERSTANDING COURT JUDGMENTS

To understand the legal system, it is helpful to understand how court decisions are structured. As formidable as court judgments may sometimes seem, they are generally understandable to the layman who takes the time to follow them. Some are poorly written and thought out, and even a lawyer may not be able to fully understand the judge's points.

But there is a pattern to look for when reading a court judgment. The decisions usually begin with a recital of the facts presented at trial. The judge will outline the events leading up to trial and what each party wants. The judge will then discuss the arguments presented at trial. This will include a review of the case law and the statutes which the lawyers feel supports an argument. This is often the most difficult part of a judgment to follow. But it is among the most important because the judge will begin to indicate which argument is best supported and why.

Eventually, the judge will select one or several points which he or she feels will win the case for one of the parties. The winning point or points of the case are known as the *ratio decidendi*. This is the "bottom line" which determines the final decision. During the discussion of the case law or arguments, the judge may also offer an opinion which is not directly concerned with the matter at hand or crucial to the *ratio decidendi*. This opinion is known as *obiter dictum*. It is an opinion which is unnecessary for the resolution of the case. The comments do not form a binding precedent to be followed by other courts. Sometimes, it is difficult for lawyers to figure out if a comment is the *ratio* of a case, or merely *obiter*.

As the judgment nears the end, many judges will summarize the reasons for the decision in the last few paragraphs.

Just as important as understanding a judgment is knowing whether the court's decision is considered authoritative and binding by others. In reading case law, particularly older rulings, it is important to investigate whether a judgment has been overturned on appeal or reversed in some part by another court. For example, other judges may "distinguish" a case before them from an earlier court decision and not apply it by finding the relevant facts in the two cases are different. Lawyers and law students refer to this as "noting-up" a case or determining its history. Many of the electronic databases and reporting series for case law assist in the noting-up process.

CITATIONS

Cases

When the courts first started issuing judgments with reasons, a system was designed to note and catalogue significant judgments. Lawyers refer to this unique series of numbers and words as *citations* (for example, *Smith v. Smith* (2007), 266 D.L.R. (4th) 257 (S.C.C.)). Citations are used to identify cases and statutes throughout this book, in legal texts and in the court judgments you may read.

If you want to know more about a particular case or law, the citations will help you find it in local law libraries. The structure of the citation for cases is very simple:

Name of Case	Year	Volume	Reporting Series	Page	Court
A. v. B et al.,	[1971]	3	O.R.	222	(C.A.)
C v. D	(1985)	5	O.R. (2d)	123	(C.A.)

The first thing to notice is the name of the case (style of cause). The plaintiffs or initiators of the action are the first name or names encountered and the defendants are the name or names after the *v.* (*versus*). Sometimes, an "et al." will be in the case name. This is Latin for "and others" and is used as an abbreviation for listing other parties.

Next is the year. The year of the judgment is always included, in "()" (round brackets), except where a particular reporting series uses the year of publication to identify a volume, in "[]" (square brackets). In that case, if the judgment year and publication year are the same, only the publication (square bracketed) year is included; if the judgment year and publication year are different, then the judgment (round bracketed) year is included first, followed by the publication year.

The next number, if there is one, is the volume of the reporting series. "Reporting series" are publications containing full texts of the decisions rendered by the court. By knowing the reporting series, it is easy to identify the province. In the above examples, the case will be found in the Ontario Reports. Sometimes, in old cases or cases from other countries, the letters of the reporting series will not indicate the jurisdiction (for example, (1883), B. & R. 234). In a case such as this, a law librarian will help you find the case.

The letters of the reporting series will sometimes be followed with a "(2d)" or "(3d)," to denote the second or third series. A new series of reports is started when the number of volumes of cases becomes unwieldy. The page at which the case can be found is next. Finally, the level of the court is indicated in brackets (and is usually abbreviated) after the citation (for example, Court of Appeal would be abbreviated as (C.A.)).

Statutes

For statutes, the citations are somewhat different:

Statute Name	Statute Series	Year	Chapter
X Act	R.S.C.	1985	c. X-100
Y Act	S.C.	1989	c. 100

The system of cataloguing statutes is simpler than for cases. The name of the Act comes first, followed by the statute series. In the above example, R.S.C. stands for Revised Statutes of Canada. In 1985 (the year indicated), the government revised and reassembled its legislation. This placed all of the statutes in one series for one year. All of the provinces have revised their statutes at one time or another. In the second example, only the letters S.C. are used, meaning Statutes of Canada for 1989 (the year indicated). Since laws are amended and new ones have been passed in the years since 1985, the citation is making reference to a law passed in 1989. The same practice is followed in the provinces. Finally, the chapter of the relevant legislation is indicated and, in some cases, the section number at issue.

Figuring out which province the citation for a statute series is referring to is fairly easy (for example, R.S.A. is Revised Statutes of Alberta). Here is a guide to some of the abbreviations used for case reporting series, which can be more difficult to decode:

REPORTING SERIES

A.C.W.S.	— All Canada Weekly Summaries
A.P.R.	— Atlantic Provinces Reports
All E.R.	— All England Reports
Alta. L.R.	— Alberta Law Reports
A.R.	— Alberta Reports
B.C.L.R.	— British Columbia Law Reports
C.A.	— Recuils de jurisprudence de Québec, Cour d'appel
C.C.C.	— Canadian Criminal Cases
C.P.R.	— Canadian Patent Reporter
C.R.	— Criminal Reports
C.R.D.	— Charter of Rights Decisions
C.S.	— Recuils de jurisprudence de Québec, Cour supérieure
D.L.R.	— Dominion Law Reports
M.P.R.	— Maritime Provinces Reports
Man. R.	— Manitoba Law Reports
N.B.R.	— New Brunswick Reports
N.S.R.	— Nova Scotia Reports
Nfld. & P.E.I.R.	— Newfoundland and P.E.I. Reports
Nfld. R.	— Newfoundland Reports
O.A.R.	— Ontario Appeal Reports
O.L.R.	— Ontario Law Reports
O.R.	— Ontario Reports
O.W.N.	— Ontario Weekly Notes
Qué. C.A.	— Quebéc Official Reports, Court of Appeal
R.F.L.	— Reports of Family Law
S.C.R.	— Supreme Court of Canada Reports
Sask. L.R.	— Saskatchewan Law Reports
W.W.R.	— Western Weekly Reports

FINDING CASES AND LEGISLATION VIA THE INTERNET

Reading up on an area of case law or researching the statutes and regulations enacted by governments has become much easier in recent years. In addition to the legal books and reporting series available at law and public libraries, many now have this information available on CD-ROM's and the Internet (for example, the Supreme Court of Canada and many provincial superior courts make their judgments available online.

WWW Resources

A useful and free Web site for reading the full-text decisions of many courts is hosted by the Canadian Legal Information Institute at **www.canlii.org**. In seconds, you can find full-text and condensed versions of relatively new and old court decisions or statutes with little regard to the proper citation, names of parties, jurisdiction or other past essentials. Other good starting points to find both current legislation and court judgments are the Web sites of the federal and provincial Attorneys General or Justice ministries. Other online sources of law include:

Supreme Court of Canada	**www.scc-csc.gc.ca**
Federal Court of Appeal	**decisions.fca-caf.gc.ca**
Federal Court of Canada	**decisions.fct-cf.gc.ca**
Tax Court of Canada	**decision.tcc-cci.gc.ca**

Parliament of Canada (Members' Bills and progress of new legislation)   **www.parl.gc.ca**

Federal Department of Justice (Canada's Acts and Regulations)   **laws.justice.gc.ca**

Canada Gazette (new or amended federal legislation and regulations)   **canadagazette.gc.ca**

CANADIAN CHARTER OF RIGHTS AND FREEDOMS*

Whereas Canada is founded upon principles that recognize the supremacy of God and the rule of law:

Rights and freedoms in Canada

Guarantee of Rights and Freedoms

1. The *Canadian Charter of Rights and Freedoms* guarantees the rights and freedoms set out in it subject only to such reasonable limits prescribed by law as can be demonstrably justified in a free and democratic society.

Fundamental freedoms

Fundamental Freedoms

2. Everyone has the following fundamental freedoms:
   a) freedom of conscience and religion;
   b) freedom of thought, belief, opinion and expression, including freedom of the press and other media of communication;
   c) freedom of peaceful assembly; and
   d) freedom of association. . . .

Life, liberty and security of person

Legal Rights

7. Everyone has the right to life, liberty and security of the person and the right not to be deprived thereof except in accordance with the principles of fundamental justice.

Search or seizure

8. Everyone has the right to be secure against unreasonable search or seizure.

Detention or imprisonment

9. Everyone has the right not to be arbitrarily detained or imprisoned.

Arrest or detention

10. Everyone has the right on arrest or detention
    a) to be informed promptly of the reasons therefor;
    b) to retain and instruct counsel without delay and to be informed of that right; and
    c) to have the validity of the detention determined by way of *habeas corpus* and to be released if the detention is not lawful.

Proceedings in criminal and penal matters

11. Any person charged with an offence has the right

a) to be informed without unreasonable delay of the specific offence;

b) to be tried within a reasonable time;

c) not to be compelled to be a witness in proceedings against that person in respect of the offence;

d) to be presumed innocent until proven guilty according to law in a fair and public hearing by an independent and impartial tribunal;

e) not to be denied reasonable bail without just cause;

f) except in the case of an offence under military law tried before a military tribunal, to the benefit of trial by jury where the maximum punishment for the offence is imprisonment for five years or a more severe punishment;

g) not to be found guilty on account of any act or omission unless, at the time of the act or omission, it constituted an offence under Canadian or international law or was criminal according to the general principles of law recognized by the community of nations;

h) if finally acquitted of the offence, not to be tried for it again and, if finally found guilty and punished for the offence, not to be tried or punished for it again; and

i) if found guilty of the offence and if the punishment for the offence has been varied between the time of commission and the time of sentencing, to the benefit of the lesser punishment.

Treatment or punishment

12. Everyone has the right not to be subjected to any cruel and unusual treatment or punishment.

Self-crimination

13. A witness who testifies in any proceedings has the right not to have any incriminating evidence so given used to incriminate that witness in any other proceedings, except in a prosecution for perjury or for the giving of contradictory evidence. . . .

Equality before and under law and equal protection and benefit of law

Equality Rights

15. (1) Every individual is equal before and under the law and has the right to the equal protection and equal benefit of the law without discrimination and, in particular, without discrimination based on race, national or ethnic origin, colour, religion, sex, age or mental or physical disability.

Affirmative action programs

(2) Subsection (1) does not preclude any law, program or activity that has as its object the amelioration of conditions of disadvantaged individuals or groups including those that are disadvantaged because of race, national or ethnic origin, colour, religion, sex, age or mental or physical disability. . . .

Enforcement of guaranteed rights and freedoms

Enforcement

24. (1) Anyone whose rights or freedoms, as guaranteed by this Charter, have been infringed or denied may apply to a court of competent jurisdiction to obtain such remedy as the court considers appropriate and just in the circumstances.

Exclusion of evidence bringing administration of justice into disrepute

(2) Where, in proceedings under subsection (1), a court concludes that evidence was obtained in a manner that infringed or denied any rights or freedoms guaranteed by this Charter, the evidence shall be excluded if it is established that, having regard to all the circumstances, the admission of it in the proceedings would bring the administration of justice into disrepute.
. . .

Multicultural heritage

General

27. This Charter shall be interpreted in a manner consistent with the preservation and enhancement of the multicultural heritage of Canadians.

Rights guaranteed equally to both sexes

28. Notwithstanding anything in this Charter, the rights and freedoms referred to in it are guaranteed equally to male and female persons. . . .

Legislative powers not extended

31. Nothing in this Charter extends the legislative powers of any body or authority.

Application of Charter

Application of Charter

32. (1) This Charter applies

a) to the Parliament and government of Canada in respect of all matters within the authority of Parliament including all matters relating to the Yukon Territory and Northwest Territories; and

b) to the legislature and government of each province in respect of all matters within the authority of the legislature of each province.

* Excerpted from *Constitution Act, 1982*. The Canadian Charter of Rights and Freedoms was enacted as Schedule B to the Canada Act 1982 (U.K.) 1982, c. 11, which came into force on April 17, 1982.

Appendix 2

COURT PROCEDURE

As mentioned in Appendix 1, the two bodies of law administered by the courts are civil law and criminal law. Journalists should have a general understanding of the different procedures involved with each body of law, as well as the stages at which the law places restrictions on what can be reported about the court proceeding.

Once a case is within the formal jurisdiction of the courts, or *sub judice*, comments concerning the merits of the case or the law involved must be carefully considered. Further detail on the *sub judice* rule is given in the chapter on contempt.

CIVIL COURT PROCEDURES

A civil legal action may involve people, corporations or other legally recognized groups. The party starting the lawsuit is known as the *plaintiff*. The plaintiff is seeking a remedy, such as money or the enforcement of a civil right. The *defendant* is the party denying the plaintiff's claim. An important point to remember in a civil case is that, even though illegal acts may be alleged by one side or the other, no one is formally charged with anything or subject to criminal penalty. The parties usually go to court because they cannot agree on a matter which has arisen between them. A civil lawsuit does not involve any crimes against society and the defendant will not be found "guilty" or "not guilty" in the end. The court will instead find for or against the defendant or plaintiff. These are the steps in a civil action:

Notice of Intention to Sue

In many cases, this is the first step in the civil process. The government and certain Crown corporations may have to be given notice by the plaintiff within a set time period of a potential lawsuit. A failure to give such notice may mean a plaintiff cannot include the government as a party in an action. This type of notice may also be required for parties in certain other actions. For example, defamation legislation often requires the plaintiff to serve notice on print or broadcasting outlets within set time limits of an intention to sue (for example, within as little as six weeks of an alleged defamatory broadcast or article in Ontario to within three months in other provinces).

Notice of Action

In all provinces a special document is used to signal the formal start of a lawsuit. It may be called a writ or notice of action. Once the plaintiff is prepared to sue, this formal notice is filed with the court and all of the parties named in the action.

Filing of Pleadings

At the same time the notice of action is filed, or within a specified time afterwards, a statement of allegations and claims is filed with the court and the other parties by the plaintiff. The defendant replies to the claims of the plaintiff by filing a statement of his defences with the court and other parties, within another specified time period. These *pleadings* are the allegations and defences which may be presented during the trial. The idea is to make all of the parties aware of the issues.

A journalist should be aware that pleadings are one-sided and can distort claims, facts and allegations. A 1995 Supreme Court of Canada decision ruled that publication of information in pleadings is protected by a qualified privilege in defamation law.[1]

Examination for Discovery

Prior to a trial, one side in a dispute will usually want to question the other side and examine their documents prior to trial. This allows the parties to *discover* the various facets of the case. The discovery process, involving witnesses or parties, can be by oral or written questions which are answered under oath.

Reporters are not allowed to attend discoveries and they are not open to any other members of the public. The publication of transcripts from the discovery, before being entered into evidence in open court, could be defamatory or contemptuous. The evidence or statements at discoveries may ultimately be inadmissible or inaccurate.

Pre-Trial Conference

Many jurisdictions allow a judge to call a pre-trial conference to settle points about the trial procedure and the dispute itself. Usually, the judge will attempt to find out if the parties can come to an out-of-court settlement before starting the expensive trial process. The pre-trial conference is usually held in chambers and is not open to the public.

The Trial

The trial is the forum for the arguments and evidence. The trial may be by judge alone or judge and jury. The plaintiff must prove his case *on a balance of probabilities* which means that the allegations are in all likelihood true. The plaintiff does not have to meet the high standard of proof set for criminal cases in which the Crown must prove the allegations *beyond a reasonable doubt*. The public is permitted to attend, except in exceptional circumstances.

The reporting of open judicial proceedings is privileged in most provinces. But, there are conditions on this privilege, such as the requirement

---

1 *Hill v. Church of Scientology of Toronto*, [1995] 2 S.C.R. 1130.

that the report be fair and accurate, that there is no comment by the journalist in his or her story, that the report is contemporaneous with the proceedings and there is no publication of any seditious, blasphemous or indecent matter.

The Appeal

After the trial of an issue and the decision of the court is handed down, an appeal may be taken to a higher court. An appeal must be launched within a specified time period (usually 30 days in most provinces). Depending on a province's rules of court, an appeal may be based on a question of pure law, a disputed fact or both. In most civil cases, the losing party has the right to appeal, but it may be necessary in some provinces to apply for permission, or *leave*, to appeal depending on whether the appeal is based on disputed points of law or simply disputed facts. The party appealing the case is called the *appellant* and the opposing party is called the *respondent*. In Canada, the courts of appeal have the power to reverse or uphold the decision or order a new trial.

The news media should not attempt to influence the decision of the appeal judges through editorial comments. In practice, the courts have been relatively tolerant of comments during the appeal process. If a new trial is ordered by the appeal court, any reports comparing aspects of the original trial with the new hearing while it is in progress, could be contemptuous.

CRIMINAL COURT PROCEDURES

The criminal court system is very complex because of the potential severity of its results. The criminal system is used to prosecute offences under a number of Federal and provincial statutes and can be of a criminal or non-criminal nature.[2]

The provinces cannot constitutionally create criminal offences. But, a province can still punish violations of laws within provincial jurisdiction[3]

---

2 An offence does not have to be "criminal" in nature to be prosecuted in the criminal courts. S. 34(2) of the Interpretation Act, R.S.C. 1985, c. I-21, says that federal statutes creating offences are to use the procedure set out in the Criminal Code.

There is no exhaustive definition of what is a "criminal" offence. The Supreme Court of Canada said in *Canadian Federation of Agriculture v. A.G. Saskatchewan* (*sub nom. Reference as to the Validity of Section 5(a) of the Dairy Industry Act*), [1949] S.C.R. 1 at 49, that a crime is an act which the law forbids with penal sanctions. At p. 50, the Court went on to say a criminal law serves "a public purpose," such as in the protection of public peace, morality, health, order and security. Parliament can create a non-criminal or regulatory offence, which has as its object economic or trade control.

3 The provincial power is derived from s. 92(15) of the Constitution Act, 1867 (U.K.), 30 & 31 Vict., c. 3.

and all provinces use the summary conviction jurisdiction of the criminal courts for enforcing these laws.[4] Some provinces, such as Ontario, have comprehensive statutes which outline their own procedure to be followed by the criminal courts when handling provincial offences.[5]

There are three classifications of offences in the criminal court system:

1. *Indictable:* These are serious offences which are punishable by jail terms of two, five, ten or fourteen years or a life sentence (for example, murder).

2. *Summary conviction:* These offences are punishable by a maximum of a $2000 fine and/or six months in jail, unless otherwise provided by statute (for example, trespassing at night).

3. *Dual procedure:* Also known as hybrid or mixed offences, these offences can be prosecuted either as indictable or summary conviction offences at the discretion of the Crown. With this type of offence, the accused is presumed to be charged with an indictable offence until the Crown indicates to the court that it plans to proceed under summary conviction procedures (for example, common assault).

There also are some important definitions to note regarding the judiciary in the criminal court process. The Criminal Code[6] makes reference to justices, provincial court judges and superior court judges. Essentially, a superior court judge is more powerful than a justice or a provincial court judge, and has the jurisdiction to deal with all offences. A judge serves in a "superior court of criminal jurisdiction."

A justice is defined by section 2 as "a justice of the peace or a provincial court judge." Justices of the peace have limited powers and deal only with minor offences, such as violations of provincial or municipal laws. In some provinces, the justice of the peace is the first person an accused is brought before. He or she begins the process of determining the proper court to deal with the charges. In other provinces, provincial court judges are the first people the accused appears before. Provincial court judges have more authority than justices of the peace and can try certain indictable offences.

To confuse matters, judges at the Superior Court level are referred to as "Madam Justice" or "Mr. Justice" when they are addressed. This is not to be confused with the Criminal Code's definition of a justice. To add to the confusion, justices are often referred to as judges when they are addressed.

---

4 Part XXVII of the Criminal Code.
5 For example, see Provincial Offences Act, R.S.O. 1990, c. P.33.
6 R.S.C. 1985, c. C-46.

Below are the steps involved in a criminal proceeding:

The Investigation

The court may become involved in the investigative process (that is, issuing search warrants or authorizing wiretaps). At this stage, no formal charges have been laid.

A journalist's access to court orders issued during the investigative process is usually restricted. But, some documents, such as executed search warrants, may be available for public inspection.

The Arrest or Charge

There are three ways in which an accused can be brought before a court:

1. A person may be arrested without a warrant having been issued (usually after being found committing an offence).[7] A number of events will then occur:[8]

    (a) the accused may be detained until a first appearance before the courts, or

    (b) may be released after the peace officer or officer-in-charge issues an appearance notice which sets out a time and place for the accused to appear.

    As soon as possible after an appearance notice is issued or the person is detained, the peace officer must lay an *information* before a justice.[9] An information is a document sworn under oath, which outlines one or more allegations against a person or persons. The justice of the peace or a provincial court judge will then decide whether the officer has a case and confirm or quash the appearance notice or the detention of the accused.[10]

2. Anyone, who on reasonable and probable grounds believes that a person has committed an offence, may *lay an information* before a justice of the peace or a provincial court judge.[11] The justice will decide whether

---

7   S. 494.
8   See ss. 496, 497 and 498.
9   Ss. 503 and 505.
10 Ss. 507 and 508.
11 See s. 504 for indictable offences and s. 788 for summary conviction offences.

a case has been made out and may then issue a summons or a warrant for the arrest of the accused.[12]

3.   An appearance notice or document requiring the accused to show up at court at a certain time and place, may be issued by a peace officer without actually arresting the accused.[13] As set out in section 495(2), a person will not be arrested for summary conviction offences, dual procedure offences or section 553 offences in any case:

(i)   where the officer is able to identify the accused,
(ii) where there is no chance of evidence being destroyed,
(iii) where there is no chance of a repetition or continuation of the offence or another offence, and
(iv) the officer has reasonable and probable grounds to believe that the person will attend court.

As soon as possible after the appearance notice is issued, an information must be laid before a justice, who will decide if a case has been made out.

The First Appearance

The accused's first appearance in court usually determines the type of procedure which will be followed (that is, summary conviction or indictment procedures) and the appropriate level of court to adjudicate the matter (that is, justice of the peace, provincial court, superior court). Section 503 states that if someone has been arrested and detained, he or she must be brought before a justice within 24 hours, or if a justice is not available, as soon as possible. If a person is arrested and released, the accused must show up in court in accordance with the appearance notice ordering him or her to appear.

In some cases, the court of first appearance may not be a court which has the jurisdiction to conduct a trial of the charge.[14] For example, a justice of the peace may not have the authority to deal with an offence which is under the absolute jurisdiction of a provincial court judge.[15] In this case, the accused will not be asked to plead guilty or not guilty until an appropriate court can deal with the charges. But, some offences do allow the accused at the court of first appearance (including a justice of the peace) to *elect*, or

---

12 See ss. 507 and 508 for indictable offences and s. 788(2) for summary conviction offences. S. 507.1 requires a justice to refer a private prosecution to a provincial court judge for further consideration before a summons or warrant is issued.

13 S. 496.

14 For example, a justice of the peace would have no jurisdiction to try a case of murder. But, he or she may be able to deal with a minor provincial traffic offence.

15 S. 536.

choose, a mode of trial.[16] The accused will be asked to elect to be tried by a provincial court judge without a jury, a judge without a jury or a judge with a jury. It should be remembered that the election of the mode of trial still does not constitute a plea of guilty or not guilty. It merely establishes which court the accused wants to appear before to adjudicate the matter.[17]

The Bail Hearing

At the court of first appearance, the justice is obligated in most circumstances to grant the accused temporary release, unless the offence is one which is outlined in section 469 (for example, murder) or the accused pleaded guilty or the Crown wishes to *show cause* as to why the accused should not be released or released without conditions.[18]

If a show cause hearing is held, the court may grant the Crown or the accused a *remand* of three days in custody before proceeding with the interim release hearing.[19] The justice will eventually decide if the accused can be released and he may place restrictions or conditions on the release.[20] Only Superior Courts can decide on interim release for the offences listed in section 469.

At some point, the justice or judge may make an order banning the publication of evidence taken during the bail hearing, the information given, the representations made and the reasons, if any, given by the justice. You may still report the outcome of the bail hearing and any conditions imposed on the accused. The ban on the other details is in effect until the trial ends or until the accused is discharged after a preliminary hearing.[21]

Subsequent Appearances and Mode of Trial

After the first appearance or the election of the mode of trial, the procedure to be followed will depend on the type of offence involved:

Summary conviction offences:

In most provinces, the first appearance will be before a provincial court judge with the jurisdiction to deal with a summary conviction offence. Part XXVII of the Code (that is, the Summary Convictions Part) refers

---

16 Ss. 536 and 554 establish the offences offering election.
17 See s. 536(3).
18 S. 515.
19 S. 516.
20 S. 515(2) and (4).
21 S. 517.

to the person charged as the *defendant* rather than the accused. After the charge is read to the defendant, he will be asked to plead guilty or not guilty, providing the court has the power to handle summary conviction offences.[22] If the defendant does not plead guilty, the trial is conducted using the same procedure followed for preliminary hearings of indictable offences outlined in Part XVIII of the Code.

Indictable offences:

There are three categories of indictable offences, two of which allow the accused to select the mode of trial:

1.   Section 553 offences are within the exclusive jurisdiction of a provincial court judge. These offences include theft, fraud and keeping a common bawdy house.
2.   Section 469 offences may be tried only by a superior court of criminal jurisdiction (that is, a Supreme Court, a Superior Court or a Court of Queen's Bench). These offences include high treason, inciting mutiny, sedition and murder).
3.   Section 554 governs all other indictable offences. The accused has a right to elect to be tried by a provincial court judge without a jury, a judge without a jury, or a judge and a jury.

If a justice of the peace is presented with an information outlining an indictable offence, the accused will be remanded to later appear before a court which is empowered to deal with the matter.[23] A guilty or not guilty plea will not be requested until the accused is before a court with the jurisdiction to handle the information, despite the fact the justice may ask the accused to elect a mode of trial.

The Preliminary Hearing

A preliminary hearing is held in cases involving indictable offences to determine if there is sufficient evidence to hold a trial. The deciding factor as to whether an accused will be committed for trial is whether there is sufficient evidence which, if it were believed, would result in a conviction.[24] The preliminary hearing can be held by a justice of the peace or a provincial court judge.

At the end of the preliminary hearing, the accused will either be *discharged* or ordered to stand trial. It should be noted that a discharge does

---

22   S. 801.
23   S. 536.
24   *United States of America v. Shephard* (1976), [1977] 2 S.C.R. 1067 at 1080.

not mean the accused is innocent. It means there was not enough evidence to proceed to trial.

The preliminary inquiry can be by-passed in two ways:[25]

1. The accused may waive his right to a preliminary hearing.
2. The Crown may bring an accused back to court after he has been discharged after a preliminary hearing by *preferring a direct-line indictment*. This permits the Crown to try the accused before a superior court judge without another preliminary hearing.

During the preliminary hearing, the court may impose a ban on the publication of evidence.[26] The ban is in effect until after the trial or until the accused is discharged. There is also a Criminal Code provision prohibiting the publication of admissions or confessions of the accused tendered in evidence during the preliminary hearing until it is brought out in an open trial or the accused is discharged.[27] This prohibition exists even when there is no ban on the publication of other evidence. For more information, see the chapter on publication bans and restraining orders.

The Trial

If the accused is committed for trial or an indictment has been preferred,[28] a trial date will be set. It may be before a provincial court judge, a judge and jury or a judge alone. The trial will begin with the Crown presenting evidence which must eventually prove the guilt of the accused *beyond a reasonable doubt*. The defence will usually respond to the Crown's evidence, but there is no requirement for the accused to testify or even present a defence.

After the two sides have presented their evidence and given their final arguments, the judge or provincial court judge will prepare for the verdict. If there is a jury, the judge will give his *charge* to the jury in which he states the law as he interprets it. The judge will also outline the responsibilities of the jury members. The jury will then retire to consider its verdict.

At some point during the trial, it may be necessary for the judge to determine if certain evidence is admissible or acceptable. If it is a jury trial, the judge will send the jury out and hold a trial within a trial, known as a *voir dire*. The Criminal Code prohibits the publication of details of any of the court proceedings conducted while the jury is out of the courtroom, until

---

25 Respectively, s. 549 and Part XX.
26 S. 539.
27 S. 542(2).
28 The indictment is essentially the *information* rewritten and presented as a "new" document to the higher court. See Part XX of the Code.

after the jury retires to consider its verdict.[29] For more details, see the chapter on contempt.

The Appeal

Both summary conviction and indictable decisions can be appealed. An appeal may be on a question of pure law, a question of fact or both. The nature of the appeal (question of fact or law) will determine whether the appellant (party seeking the appeal) must apply for permission or *leave* to go to the higher court.[30] Generally, formal notice of an appeal must be given within 30 days of the decision or the sentence.

In theory, comments by reporters during the appeal process which could be interpreted as attempting to influence the court of appeal are contemptuous. But, in practice, the courts have been tolerant of comments during the appeal period. For more information, see the chapter on contempt.

ADMINISTRATIVE TRIBUNAL PROCEDURES

The administration of government regulations, statutes and rules sometimes falls on the shoulders of administrative tribunals (that is, boards and commissions). These public bodies handle formal applications or investigate complaints and infractions of statutes or regulations. Each of the bodies may develop their own rules of procedure, but certain degrees of procedural standards are expected from certain administrative tribunals. These tribunals can be categorized as administrative, quasi-judicial or judicial, depending on the importance of the body's function or purpose. The minimum requirement for all tribunals in administrative law is *fairness* in the procedures. For example, a higher standard of procedural fairness is expected of public utilities boards than taxi licensing commissions.

A tribunal which handles purely administrative tasks, or "rubber-stamps" matters without any exercise of discretion, only has a duty to act fairly. There is no compulsion on these bodies to follow any judicial procedures (for example, hear evidence or allow cross-examination). A quasi-judicial or judicial tribunal has a greater duty to make its procedure follow the *principles of natural justice*. These principles can include the right to a fair hearing, the right to be represented by counsel, the right to call witnesses, the right to cross-examine witnesses or the right to examine all evidence. The civil courts can become involved with an administrative tribunal when an aggrieved individual feels there has been a defect in the procedural

29 S. 648.
30 Ss. 675, 676, 813 and 839.

fairness of the body or where the decision-making process is contrary to the basic principles of natural justice. The court is usually restricted to examining the procedure followed and cannot change the decision, other than to order a new hearing. In some statutes, the courts are expressly prohibited from reviewing the decisions of certain bodies.

Appendix 3

MINI-LAW COURSES

The purpose of this chapter is to acquaint you with some of the major branches of law. The law is constantly changing and these summaries are very general and are not meant to implant "instant legal knowledge" into a journalist. In most cases, as some real-life case examples below show, there are exceptions to the general rule.

ADMINISTRATIVE LAW

Government functions on rules and regulations which are often enforced and administered by administrative bodies or tribunals (for example, a labour relations board).

Administrative law deals with the principles of fairness and natural justice which should be followed by tribunals. In most cases, courts can review tribunal decisions to ensure the procedure is, at the very least, fair. A tribunal may exercise an administrative, quasi-judicial or judicial function. The type of function determines the level or standard of procedural fairness which is expected or required.

Tribunals that perform strictly administrative functions are required to be "fair," but don't usually have to abide by the principles of natural justice expected in a court (for example, the right to a hearing).

A quasi-judicial or judicial function is more easily reviewed and monitored by the courts. A judge usually can't change the decision of a tribunal, but he or she can review the procedures of the tribunal for fairness and adherence to the principles of "natural justice." These principles could include the right to a hearing, the right to be represented by counsel, or other basic requirements of our legal system. If an administrative tribunal is found to be in the wrong, procedurally, the court may order a re-hearing of the matter or some other remedy.

A planning committee in your municipality wants to widen your street and has told you it will be shortening your front lawn by two feet to do it. Can the government just take your land without your consent?

Yes. The government, however, does have to buy your piece of property for a fair market price and may have to pay additional costs for loss of use or enjoyment. Expropriation or seizing private property for public use is legal, but may also be subject to a public hearing process.

CONFLICT OF LAWS

This is a complex area dealing with the interaction of laws in different countries or jurisdictions. For example, a court action in a province involving a car accident in another country involves the law of several jurisdictions. The study of "conflicts" aims to determine which jurisdiction's laws should be applied to a particular case, which jurisdiction is the best forum for a case and the enforceability of laws and judgments from other jurisdictions.

CONSUMER AND COMMERCIAL LAW

This branch of law deals with the purchase and sale of goods. A "good" is generally any chattel. All provinces have laws which deal with the sale of commercial goods. Some provinces have laws that specifically protect consumers.

Under the common law, the rule was usually "buyer beware." All Acts now spell out the ground rules for selling or buying goods. For commercial transactions, the Acts determine when and how the title to goods is transferred from the seller to the buyer and what remedies are available when disputes arise. The consumer legislation seeks to protect the unsuspecting consumer who buys a good for personal use. The Acts also protect the seller in many cases.

This is really another type of contract law. Where the statutes don't help, the rights of individuals hinge on the "conditions" (that is, essential terms) of the contract. A condition should be distinguished from a "warranty" which is a promise or representation (for example, about the quality of a product). A breach of a condition is a serious infringement of a contract and may result in it being declared null or void by the courts. A breach of a warranty must be remedied, but does not necessarily destroy the contract.

You bought a vase, but decided you didn't like the design when you got it home. Is the store obliged legally to accept its return?

No. If goods you purchased do not work as advertised, are defective in a way that you did not know about at the time of purchase or what you ordered was not delivered, you likely do have a right to a refund or, at least, a replacement. If, however, you simply don't want the product anymore, don't like the colour or you saw it for a better price elsewhere, you will have to rely on the business' refund and return policy.

CONTRACTS

This is known as private law. It involves an agreement between individuals promising to do or not do something. It can be written or oral.

A legally binding promise or contract has several elements. There must be an offer by one party and an acceptance communicated back by the other party. It is important that each party have the capacity to form the contract (for example, an insane person could not sign a contract).

Along with the offer and acceptance, the parties must have an intention to form a contract. There must also be something of value exchanged for the contract, known as the "consideration." The consideration is an inducement to enter into the contract. It can be money or even an act.

The courts will only enforce a contract with a legal purpose or object. There are also various grounds which destroy or breach a contract. A misrepresentation, a mistake, the presence of duress or undue influence, and the failure to perform that which is required by the contract, can all be grounds for a lawsuit.

Shortly after Jerry proposed, Alice decided not to marry him and broke off their engagement. Will Alice have to give back the engagement ring if Jerry asks for it?

Yes. An engagement is one form of contract. As in any breach of contract, the generally accepted rule is that whomever broke the deal (in this case, the engagement) forfeits any unearned benefits (in this case, the ring). If the ring's giver breaks it off, the receiver gets to keep the ring. If the recipient, however, breaks the deal, the ring has to be returned.

CORPORATE LAW

This complex body of law deals with the legislation and common law that has evolved in the business world. There are basically three types of business entities.

A "sole proprietorship" is a one-person operation (for example, a corner store) in which all profits and liabilities flow directly and personally to one individual. There is no obligation to register a proprietorship (with some exceptions where licences are needed). If someone sues a proprietorship and wins, they are entitled to both business and personal assets of the owner.

The "partnership" is an entity with two or more individuals carrying on a business "with a view to profit." It also doesn't have to be registered in most cases. Partners generally share in profits and losses, at both the business and personal level.

The "corporation" is a legally-registered entity with most of the same rights of a person. This is the most complex form of business operation. The corporation is owned by "shareholders" who elect "directors." Company "officers" (for instance, the president) run the day-to-day operations and "directors" determine policy and long-range plans. One of the chief advantages of a corporation is that generally none of the people involved or investing in a corporation are personally liable for its losses. The corporation survives apart from its owners. It can sue and be sued. But, there may be some occasions in which directors, officers or shareholders could be found by the courts to be liable for their actions (for example, a director approving of toxic wastes being dumped in a river).

A "public" corporation is one which "distributes" or sells shares in the company to the public in a stock market. A "private" corporation is held by one or more individuals who do not trade shares publicly. Other aspects of corporate law involve financial transactions and the legal responsibilities of those who run and own businesses.

> **A media outlet publishes a scathing story about a company's environmental misdeeds and ends the article with the dramatic statement that the business "is committing murder." Can the company sue for defamation over the murder allegation?**
>
> **No.** Courts have held a defamation action will fail if a corporation is not physically capable of an alleged act. Corporations themselves cannot commit murder or rape. This said, allegations of illegal or improper actions by anyone running a corporation (such as a CEO or owner) can still be the subject of a successful defamation lawsuit.

CRIMINAL LAW

This is public law. It aims to punish behaviour that is an offence against the state or society, even though only one person may have suffered.

There are usually two elements to a criminal offence. There must be a *mens rea* or a "guilty mind" or intention. There must also be an *actus reus* or "guilty act." Together, the two form the elements of a criminal offence. In a few circumstances, the law provides for "strict liability" offences in which the Crown must only prove that an illegal act has been committed.

The Criminal Code and other federal statutes spell out what constitutes the various criminal offences. Only the federal government can constitutionally enact criminal offences. The provincial governments must establish non-penal laws to enforce provincial statutes.

> **During a routine traffic stop, a police officer asks you to open the trunk of your car. Do you have to do it?**
>
> **No.** Unless the police officer has a search or arrest warrant, perceives there is some imminent danger to the public, or you have been placed under arrest and the search is within the bounds of the reason for your arrest, you do not have to comply.

INSURANCE LAW

This is an offshoot of contract law. An insurance policy is a contract where one party agrees to compensate another party for any losses suffered in certain circumstances, in return for a price (that is, the insurance policy premium). The basic principle is that the risk of loss is passed on to another party (that is, the insurance company) which, in turn, shares the loss among other customers who have paid premiums.

The "insured" is the person who takes out the insurance policy. The "insurer" is the party who must pay for any loss and underwrites the policy. (The only exception is in life insurance, where the person whose life is covered by the policy is called the insurer). The party buying the insurance must have an "insurable interest." This can only occur when the party derives a benefit of some sort from the continued existence of the subject-matter of the insurance or would suffer a loss if the subject-matter were destroyed. This is why individuals cannot insure the life or belongings of a complete stranger.

INTELLECTUAL PROPERTY

As we gravitate more towards an information-based society, this area of law will take on increasing importance. Intellectual property (IP) is the end product of human creativity and expression. Music, writing, paintings, computer software, inventions, industrial processes and many other original creative endeavours can be intellectual property. Among the most common types of IP are patents, trade-marks, copyright and industrial designs. Other types include trade secrets, integrated circuit topography registrations, industrial designs, plant breeders' rights and personality rights. Like owners of any private property, IP owners and creators (not always the same) have enforceable legal rights preventing others from using or profiting from their IP without permission and allowing owners to sell, license or transfer rights.

A business accidentally published on its Web site a secret recipe for its award-winning cooking sauce. Can it sue competitors successfully if they use the trade secret?

No. The mere fact of publishing details of a trade secret immediately affects the owner's ability to protect it. Once the secret is out, the owner has no rights of exclusive ownership. That means anyone can then use the trade secret.

INTERNATIONAL LAW

This is the law between nations. Just as individuals make contracts or follow rules of behaviour, so do countries. Treaties are a common form of international agreement. This body of law also deals with the accepted customs followed by nations in times of peace and war. For example, it is generally accepted in international law that an independent nation does not send its troops into another nation without permission or declaring war. This is an area of the law that relies on co-operation. An offending state cannot be punished as readily as an individual and violations of international law often go unpunished.

LABOUR AND EMPLOYMENT LAW

This branch of the law is relatively new. Prior to unions and minimum employment standards laws, the workplace functioned with a "master-servant" relationship. An employee could be fired at any time for any reason and there were practically no limits on the conditions or terms of employment.

The principle of "collective bargaining" and unionized labour has changed the workplace significantly. All provinces have laws which regulate the relationship between unions and employers. A union must be "certified" as the official agent of the employees in a bargaining unit (usually after a vote by the employees).

The union and employer then negotiate a collective agreement within time limits established by the law. If an agreement isn't reached, the union or management may apply for government mediation or conciliation to help settle disputed issues. In some cases, the parties may agree to submit the issues to binding arbitration by an impartial third party.

The ultimate tactics are strikes (a union action) or lock-outs (a management action). In each case, all other avenues of settling the dispute must have been attempted. A strike can continue forever or until there is a voluntary or compulsory (that is, back-to-work legislation) settlement.

The contract provides the ground rules for the workplace. It tells the employer what the employees can and cannot do, and tells the employees what to expect of the employer. Any strikes or lock-outs during the period of a collective agreement are illegal and subject to punishment by law. Disputes involving the agreement are usually settled through a grievance process administered by the government or union-management committees.

There is also an area of case law dealing with those who are not governed by a collective agreement. Most of these cases involve "wrongful dismissal" actions. An employer must have "just cause" or proper reason to fire someone. If the employer cannot prove there is just cause, then the employer must have given the employee sufficient notice of dismissal. Depending on the age, position, experience and other factors concerning the employee, proper notice may range from as little as a week to a year.

Your employer fired you today with no advance warning and ordered you out of the building immediately, without citing any reason. Is your boss acting within the law?

Yes. Contrary to what many employees think, an employer can end a non-union employee's job at any time and for any reason. However, the employer is required by law to give the employee a minimum amount of notice or pay instead of notice, unless the employee was fired for wilful misconduct or neglect of duty.

PROPERTY

There are two types of property. Real property is land, including everything attached, below and above (within normal use). Personal property is any tangible or intangible thing other than land, which has a right of ownership attached to it.

Real property law involves the rights and obligations attached to land. A person can own land outright (a freehold estate) or may lease or rent (a leasehold estate). A person may hold almost limitless rights to deal with land or his or her rights may be restricted by the terms of the conveyance (that is, sale or transfer) that brought the property into his or her possession. Ultimately, the Crown owns all land and local laws often add further restrictions to conveyance terms (for example, public zoning requirements).

Personal property law involves the ownership of anything from a car to stocks and bonds. An item of personal property is called a "chattel" in law and this area deals with the rights of ownership and possession. This branch of the law also concerns itself with who is responsible for the safety of chattels when the owner delivers them to another individual for safe-keeping. This is known as bailment.

REMEDIES

This is the study of the remedies which a court can offer to a party in a civil court action. A remedy can be in the form of a court award of money or an order to do or not do something. Damages are generally compensatory and/or punitive awards of money. Depending on the dispute, the way in which damages will be awarded can vary significantly. In contract law, the court compensates a person for the loss of any benefits which were expected under the agreement. In tort law, the court will only return the victim to the point where he was before the damage occurred and does not try to compensate the victim for anything extra. Punitive damages are awarded where the judge wants to show the displeasure of the court in the behaviour of the offending party. A court can also issue an order restraining behaviour or requiring an act to be done (for example, an injunction).

TORTS

A "tort" is a civil wrong by one individual against another (apart from criminal offences or contractual breaches). Tort law provides a remedy for someone who has been harmed through the fault of another (for example, defamation, personal injury and negligence). It is essentially, a violation of a duty which is imposed by statute or common law.

There are several elements to a tort action. The plaintiff must prove that the defendant owed him a duty. Then the plaintiff must prove that the duty was violated. And finally, the plaintiff must prove that the defendant was at fault for the injury.

In negligence actions, the plaintiff must prove that the damage was foreseeable by the defendant. The court will also consider the standard of care expected of the "reasonable man" in the circumstances. A tort can range from simple trespass of property to medical negligence, with each "wrong" having its own complexities.

TRUSTS

A trust is a right to real or personal property which is held by one person for the benefit of another individual. The creator of the trust (that is, the settlor) transfers the property to the trustee to hold for a beneficiary (*cestui que trust*). The trustee has the legal title to the property, but the beneficiary has an equitable (moral) right to it. The intention to create a trust must be clear. Sometimes, the courts will recognize a trust which is implied by law or circumstance (for example, in a divorce, business assets owned by one spouse may be split if the other spouse contributed to the firm). A trust can be invalid if the court cannot determine the subject-matter of the trust (that is, the property in question) or the object of the trust (that is, the beneficiary). A trust with an illegal purpose will also not be enforced.

GLOSSARY

This glossary of legal terms is intended to give a journalist a general definition of some words and phrases commonly used by the courts and lawyers. As with any "point-form" glossary, the definitions are approximate and, in many cases, there are other definitions for a word.

abet: To encourage someone to do a wrongful act, usually without actually participating in the crime itself.

ab initio: Latin meaning "from the beginning" (for example, an invalid contract may be void *ab initio*).

abstract of title: A history of the chain of ownership of land with details on all restrictions and rights associated with the property.

action in personam: A civil court action against a person or involving the rights of a person.

action in rem: A civil court action directly against a "thing" without regard to ownership of it (for example, the arrest of a ship).

actus reus: Latin meaning "the wrongful act." To commit a crime, in most cases, there must be an *actus reus* along with a *mens rea* (that is, guilty mind).

affidavit: A written statement of facts sworn under oath. The "deponent" (that is, person stating the facts) must have personal knowledge of the facts and cannot base remarks on hearsay.

agent: One who acts on behalf of an employer or any other person who expressly or impliedly consents to be represented.

aid: To participate in the commission of a crime.

amicus curiae: Latin meaning "a friend of the court." This refers to a situation in which the court allows an outside party with an interest in the subject-matter of a case to present their views on the issue.

animus: Latin meaning "an intention."

appellant: The party appealing a decision. The other party is the "respondent."

arbitration: A method of settling a dispute using an impartial third party. By their own agreement, the decision of the arbitrator is usually binding on the parties.

assault: A threat or attempt to harm an individual is an assault. The victim does not have to be touched, but there must be a reasonable fear the accused was capable of causing the harm.

assign: To transfer or shift ownership of something to another individual (for example, assigning the remainder of a lease to another individual).

assumpsit: A reference to an undertaking to do something.

attempt: In criminal law, there is an "attempt" when a series of acts are performed which fall short of committing an actual crime, yet, are beyond mere preparation.

audi alteram partem: Latin meaning "hear the other side." One of the basic principles of natural justice.

automatism: A defence in criminal law referring to an uncontrollable act by the accused.

autrefois plea: Where an accused has previously been found guilty or acquitted on the same charge and circumstances, he will enter an autrefois plea.

bailment: To give something to a person, other than the owner, for delivery or safekeeping. The bailor is the one who hands the goods over and the bailee receives them (for example, giving your car keys to a parking attendant).

balance of probabilities: A standard of proof in civil cases requiring evidence that the claim is, in all probability, true. The probability must be more than fifty percent, but the standard is not as stringent as requiring proof "beyond a reasonable doubt" as in criminal cases.

battery: The use of physical force against a person.

beyond a reasonable doubt: A standard of proof in criminal cases requiring evidence that the guilt of the accused be clear and beyond any reasonable doubt.

bona fide: Latin meaning "in good faith."

capacity: A legal term referring to the ability or legal power of an individual to perform an act. For example, an insane person lacks the mental capacity to understand the significance of signing a contract.

caveat: Latin meaning "beware."

certiorari: Latin meaning "to be informed of." A writ of certiorari is used by Superior Courts to review the decisions of an inferior body (for example, a lower court or administrative tribunal).

cestui que trust: A reference to the beneficiary in a trust arrangement.

chain of title: A chronological history of the successive owners of a piece of land.

chattel: Belongings other than land (for example, a car) including intangible property (for example, shares in corporations).

circumstantial evidence: A consistent series of facts which will not directly prove the facts in dispute, but by deduction, lead one to come to the conclusion that the alleged crime or act is true.

codicil: A supplementary document to a will, usually offering further details or updating bequests.

collateral contract: A supplementary contract made along with the main contract.

collusion: An arrangement between individuals to commit a fraud or bring harm to another individual.

comity: A term used to describe the courtesy and respect offered by one legal jurisdiction in giving effect to the laws and court decisions of another jurisdiction.

consanguinity: The blood relationship of people descending from the same ancestor.

consideration: In law, something of value (for example, payment of money or property in return for an agreement).

constructive knowledge: Knowledge which is presumed to be known or ought to be known.

constructive trust: A trust created by the courts based on the circumstances of a case such as when a party has no legal right to the benefits of property, yet deserves a share in it because of a valuable contribution (for example, a farmer's wife may receive a share of the farm's assets in a divorce action because she helped support the business).

contribution: The principle of sharing the loss or blame. Contributory negligence by the careless victim of an accident can reduce the court award.

conversion: The unauthorized use or disposition of someone else's property. For example, borrowing someone's car and then selling it without permission.

conveyance: The transfer of ownership in property.

corroboration: Additional evidence backing up a fact or assertion.

costs: In law, usually a reference to the expense of the court action.

count: In criminal cases, a reference to each individual charge.

covenant: A promise.

creditor: The individual who is owed money. The debtor is the individual owing the money.

cross-claim: Claim between co-parties (for example, a claim by one defendant against the other defendant).

culpable: Guilty of or responsible for a criminal act or wrong.

cy-prés doctrine: This rule allows the court to alter a will or trust arrangement and to carry out, as best it can, the wishes of the deceased (for example, to give annual donations to a certain charity) when for some reason the original purpose cannot be achieved (for example, the charity may no longer exist).

cyberlaw: The law as it involves the Internet, in information technology and electronic commerce.

cyberSLAPP: An Internet variation on a SLAPP (Strategic Lawsuits Against Public Participation) legal action. Often launched with the aim of determining the identity of an anonymous or unknown online user of an email address or Web site account.

damage: A loss.

damages: The compensation claimed or awarded in court for damage. There are two common types of damages. Compensatory damages replace the actual loss suffered. Punitive damages punish the wrongdoer and can be awarded in addition to compensatory damages in special circumstances.

debtor: One who owes money. The debtor pays his debt to the creditor.

declaratory judgment: A court decision which settles a disputed fact between parties but orders no remedy.

de facto: Latin meaning "in fact."

de jure: Latin meaning "in law."

delict: A wrong or offence.

de minimis non curat lex: This doctrine stands for the principle that the law does not bother with small matters or trifling offences.

demise: To convey property.

demonstrative evidence: Tangible evidence as opposed to testimony (for example, a photograph or map).

demur: An objection by one party to the facts or law as outlined by the other party.

deposition: Written testimony of a witness under oath, usually in the form of an affidavit. The witness, in this case, is referred to as the "deponent."

desuetude: In reference to laws which have become obsolete.

detinue: An old civil action to recover personal property which has been unlawfully kept by another individual.

devise: The conveyance of land by a will.

dicta: Statements by the court which are not directly related to the issue at hand. Dicta are not vital to the final resolution of the case and are not expressly binding on other courts.

discharge: To excuse or dismiss.

donatio inter vivos: A gift from a living donor.

donatio mortis causa: A gift made in contemplation of death.

due process of law: The course of justice. A reference to fair and equitable procedures.

duress: Unlawful coercion of an individual by threat or actual force to do an act contrary to his will.

duty: A legal or moral responsibility to do or not to do something.

encumbrance: An interest held by an individual, other than the owner, in property.

equity: A body of law which seeks to find the fairest solution to a court action. The rules of equity will be applied where the solution offered by the common law is too harsh or unfair.

escheat: The forfeiting of property to the State. It frequently occurs when there are no heirs to an estate.

estate: In reference to wills, this is the sum total of the real and personal property of the deceased.

et al.: Latin meaning "and others."

executory: Of a contract or obligation which hasn't been fulfilled yet.

ex facie: Latin meaning "from the face."

ex parte: Latin meaning "from one side." A court will sometimes grant an *ex parte* injunction to stop an act where time is of importance, even though only one side has been heard.

expressio unius est exclusio alterius: A principle of statutory interpretation which basically means that anything expressly stated is all-inclusive. For example, a statute which allows only one exception to a rule cannot be interpreted as allowing other unexpressed exceptions.

ex turpi causa non oritur actio: A maxim meaning that a court action cannot be based on an illegal or immoral act (for example, you cannot sue on an illegal contract).

face of the record: A reference to the entire record of a court's proceedings.

factum: A lawyer's brief stating the facts in a case and his or her arguments.

fee simple: A right held in land. The "fee simple absolute" grants an individual and his heirs limitless power to hold and deal with the land.

fee tail: A right held in land. The fee tail limits the rights of heirs to deal with the land.

fiduciary: One who agrees to act for the benefit of another individual (for example, a trustee acts for the good of the beneficiaries of the trust).

fieri facias: A court order requiring a sheriff or other official to sell off a debtor's property.

foreclosure: The legal process brought by a mortgagor which ends the rights of a mortgagee (for example, the person who borrowed the money) to property.

fraud: An intentional misrepresentation.

freehold: A right to own a piece of land for an indefinite time or life.

gaol: A term for "jail."

goods: Merchandise or personal property.

guardian ad litem: A court appointed representative for a handicapped or infant party in an action.

habeas corpus: Latin meaning "you must have the body." This ancient writ is used to demand the delivery of a person in custody to a court in order to review the lawfulness of the detention.

headnote: A summation of the issues, arguments, and points of law before the court in a particular case, and the reasons for the decision. The headnote is usually found at the beginning of a case in a legal reporting series (that is, published cases).

hearsay: Evidence based on the word of a person who is not at the hearing to testify as to its veracity (for example, "X" told me that he saw "Y" commit the crime). It is admitted as evidence on rare occasions.

holograph: A handwritten will which is not witnessed.

immovables: Property which cannot be moved, such as land or things attached to land.

impute: To accuse or suggest.

in camera: Latin meaning "in chambers."

indemnify: To compensate.

indictable offence: A serious offence under the Criminal Code, subject to higher penalties such as prison or large fines.

indictment: A written charge against a person presented to a criminal court. In Canada, an indictment is presented at superior trial court levels, but an "information" is the first document presented at lower court levels. The indictment is usually the "information" re-written for the higher court.

information: A sworn statement charging a person with the commission of an offence. Anyone may "lay" an information. The information is the first document presented to a justice.

infra: Latin meaning "below."

injunction: A court order which commands someone to do or not do a particular act.

innuendo: An implication or suggestion.

in pari delicto: Latin meaning "in equal fault."

insurable interest: In insurance law, this is the legitimate interest that a person has in insuring something or someone. The person with the insurable interest must derive a benefit of some sort from the continued existence of the thing or person.

inter alia: Latin meaning "among other things."

interlocutory: Temporary.

intestate: To die without a valid will.

intra vires: Latin meaning "within the power."

jurisprudence: The philosophy of law and legal systems.

just cause: Reasonable and fair grounds for an act.

laches: This is the principle that someone who does not assert his rights over a long period of time, loses any chance of special treatment by the courts in reclaiming the rights (for example, neglecting to stop trespassers who have used a path over many years).

legacy: A gift in a will.

lessee: One who rents from another.

lessor: One who rents to another.

lien: A claim against personal or real property (for example, a contractor can have a lien against a project if he is not paid).

lis alibi pendens: Latin term meaning "a suit pending elsewhere."

maintenance: In divorce law, it refers to support payments paid by one ex-spouse to the other.

mala fides: Latin meaning "bad faith."

malfeasance: A wrongful act, as opposed to nonfeasance which is a wrongful omission.

mandamus: A writ, issued by a superior court, which commands an inferior body or person to do something. It is sometimes used against inferior court judges who have misused their powers.

material: That which is important and relevant to a matter (for example, a material witness).

may: In law, this word denotes that discretion may be used. "Shall" is an imperative which commands action.

mens rea: Latin meaning "the guilty mind." An important factor in criminal cases which shows an evil intention to commit the offence. A guilty mind must be accompanied by an "actus reus" or wrongful act.

misfeasance: The improper performance of a lawful act.

mitigation: The reduction of loss (for example, in contract law, the innocent party in a breached contract is under a duty to reasonably try to reduce his losses).

moot: That which is undecided (for example, law students sharpen court-room skills in moot courts arguing hypothetical cases).

movables: In reference to movable property (for example, a car).

necessaries: The essentials of survival or life.

negligence: The failure to use reasonable care or fulfill a legal duty owed in the circumstances.

nisi decree: A temporary order which will eventually become final. In a divorce, the court will issue such a decree for a short period before making the final decree, in case the couple should have a change of heart.

nolo contendere: Latin meaning "I will not contest (it)."

nonfeasance: The omission of an act one has a duty to perform.

non-suit: A court declaration ending an action before it can be decided on its merits (for example, the plaintiff may have failed to present the bare elements of a case).

noscitur a sociis: A Latin maxim stating that the meaning of a word can be taken from the words which surround it. It is a tool of statutory interpretation.

oath: A promise by an individual.

obiter dictum: An opinion by a judge on an issue which is not important to the resolution of the case and not binding on other courts.

paralegal: An individual with legal skills who is not trained to be a lawyer.

parens patriae: A reference to the role of the State as "parent" to us all (for example, it is sometimes used to make children a ward of the province).

parol evidence rule: A reference to oral evidence which changes the meaning or terms of a written contract. The rule prohibits the use of such oral evidence in most situations.

particulars: The details of an issue or the precise act in dispute.

parties: Those who are directly affected by a court matter (for example, plaintiff and defendant).

pecuniary: In reference to money (for example, pecuniary loss).

penal: That which involves a penalty.

per curiam: Latin meaning "by the court."

peremptory challenge: The right of a party to reject a potential juror during jury selection without giving any reason. Each party has a set number of such challenges in criminal or civil jury trials.

perjury: Lying under sworn oath.

personal property: Property other than land (for example, a car).

pleadings: Allegations, claims and defences of the parties to a court action which are formally filed with the court. The pleadings form the basis for the trial arguments.

prerogative writs: Extraordinary Superior Court orders which can be used against inferior courts or public bodies to prevent them from exceeding their jurisdiction. Commonly used for judicial review of administrative tribunal decisions.

prima facie: Latin meaning "on first appearance."

private law: Law that applies between individuals (for example, a contract) as opposed to public law which involves the State.

probate: Pertaining to wills.

probative evidence: Evidence which establishes a fact is true.

promissory: An obligation or a promise.

proviso: A provision of a contract or statute which expands or explains other terms.

public law: That which involves the State and society (for example, criminal law) as opposed to private law which applies between individual citizens only.

quantum meruit: A principle of equity or fairness which states that a person should be compensated for the value of the work performed.

quare: Latin meaning "wherefore."

quasi: Latin meaning "as if."

quo warranto: A prerogative writ which is issued to prevent the unlawful use of authority by someone.

ratio decidendi: The primary reasons for a court decision.

real property: Land.

reasonable man: A fictitious person who provides the standard for behaviour which the courts expect of people. The reasonable man is fair, rational and can foresee damage which might be caused by his own negligence.

recognizance: A bail document stating terms and conditions for an accused to be released.

regina: Latin referring to the "Queen" or Crown.

remand: In a criminal proceeding, when a matter is put over to another date.

replevin: An old civil action which allows the owner of goods to re-claim them from someone who unlawfully takes them.

res judicata: A reference to that which has already been decided by the courts on its merits.

rescind: To withdraw or revoke.

respondent: The party responding to the claims of a party appealing a lower court decision.

restitution: The principle that someone who suffers a loss should be restored to their original position.

retroactive law: A new law which changes rights or obligations created under previous laws.

retrospective law: A new law which changes the effect of an act or omission which occurred under a previous law.

rex: Latin for the "King" or Crown.

riparian: Pertaining to shore or river bank.

semble: Latin meaning "it appears." The word is used when an opinion is offered.

service: A term used in the court system in relation to the delivery of an official court document to a party or witness (for example, a subpoena).

severable: That which can be divided or "cut out." For example, some contracts are severable (that is, having portions which are unrelated to each other).

shall: In law, this is an imperative word which makes an action or obligation mandatory. "May" denotes a discretion.

sine die: Latin for "without day." A court proceeding may be adjourned "sine die" or with no specific date set for the proceeding to continue.

SLAPP: Strategic Lawsuits Against Public Participation. Legal actions, usually in defamation, designed to silence public criticism.

specific performance: In contract law, the court will sometimes grant this remedy, which compels the parties to fulfill the contract obligations.

standard of care: The degree of care which the law expects of the reasonable man in similar circumstances.

standard of proof: In criminal cases, the case must be proven beyond a reasonable doubt. In civil cases, the case must be proven on a balance of probabilities based upon a preponderance of the evidence.

standing: In law, a term used to denote an individual's interest in a case which allows him to intervene in court.

stare decisis: Latin meaning "to abide by the decision."

stay: To halt. In criminal law, the Crown may "stay" a charge and the subsequent trial, leaving it in limbo for a set period or forever.

subpoena: A court document requiring an individual or thing to be presented at a certain time and place.

summary conviction offence: A lesser or minor criminal offence as opposed to the more serious indictable offences. Maximum penalty for a summary conviction offence under the Criminal Code is a fine of $2,000 and/or imprisonment for six months.

talesman: Someone who is chosen from the by-standers in a courtroom or off the street to act as a juror.

testamentary: Referring to a will or document that takes effect after death.

third party: An individual who is not a party to an agreement or event, but has an interest in it.

tort: A civil wrong (for example, defamation) involving a violation of a duty imposed by law.

trover: An old term used to describe a civil court action against an individual who has wrongfully sold goods he or she found.

trust: A right to property which one person holds for the benefit of another.

unconscionable: In contract law, an unconscionable agreement is one which unfairly takes advantage of another party.

unjust enrichment: A principle of equity which states that no person should benefit unjustly at the expense of another person.

venue: A place for trial. When there has been prejudicial publicity in a criminal case, a defence lawyer may ask for a change of venue.

vested: A right or interest becomes "vested" when it is triggered by an event and comes into force.

viva voce: Latin meaning "with the living voice." Usually a reference to oral testimony.

void: Null or having no legal effect.

voidable: That which may be void.

volenti non fit injuria: A Latin maxim stating that one who voluntarily assumes a risk cannot then seek a remedy for any injury or loss.

waiver: The abandonment of a right.

wanton: Reckless.
warranty: A promise.
writ: A court document authorizing an act or making an order.

INDEX